Modeling Aboveground Forest Biomass: New Developments

Modeling Aboveground Forest Biomass: New Developments

Guest Editors

Ana Cristina Gonçalves
Teresa Fidalgo Fonseca

MDPI

Basel • Beijing • Wuhan • Barcelona • Belgrade • Novi Sad • Cluj • Manchester

Guest Editors

Ana Cristina Gonçalves
Departamento de Engenharia
Rural, Tecnologia
University of Évora
Évora
Portugal

Teresa Fidalgo Fonseca
Departamento de Ciências
Florestais e Arquitectura
Paisagista
University of Trás-os-Montes
and Alto Douro
Vila Real
Portugal

Editorial Office
MDPI AG
Grosspeteranlage 5
4052 Basel, Switzerland

This is a reprint of the Special Issue, published open access by the journal *Forests* (ISSN 1999-4907), freely accessible at: https://www.mdpi.com/journal/forests/special_issues/76I91IB6BE.

For citation purposes, cite each article independently as indicated on the article page online and as indicated below:

Lastname, A.A.; Lastname, B.B. Article Title. *Journal Name* **Year**, *Volume Number*, Page Range.

ISBN 978-3-7258-6137-8 (Hbk)
ISBN 978-3-7258-6138-5 (PDF)
https://doi.org/10.3390/books978-3-7258-6138-5

Contents

About the Editors . . . . **vii**

Preface . . . . **ix**

Patrick Osei Darko, Samy Metari, J. Pablo Arroyo-Mora, Matthew E. Fagan and Margaret Kalacska
Application of Machine Learning for Aboveground Biomass Modeling in Tropical and Temperate Forests from Airborne Hyperspectral Imagery
Reprinted from: *Forests* **2025**, *16*, 477, https://doi.org/10.3390/f16030477 . . . . **1**

Guohui Zhang, Donghua Chen, Hu Li, Minmin Pei, Qihang Zhen, Jian Zheng, et al.
Estimation of Aboveground Biomass of *Picea schrenkiana* Forests Considering Vertical Zonality and Stand Age
Reprinted from: *Forests* **2025**, *16*, 445, https://doi.org/10.3390/f16030445 . . . . **27**

Muhammad Imran, Guanhua Zhou, Guifei Jing, Chongbin Xu, Yumin Tan, Rana Ahmad Faraz Ishaq, et al.
Assessing Above-Ground Biomass Dynamics and Carbon Sequestration Potential Using Machine Learning and Spaceborne LiDAR in Hilly Conifer Forests of Mansehra District, Pakistan
Reprinted from: *Forests* **2025**, *16*, 330, https://doi.org/10.3390/f16020330 . . . . **51**

Robertas Damaševičius and Rytis Maskeliūnas
Modeling Forest Regeneration Dynamics: Estimating Regeneration, Growth, and Mortality Rates in Lithuanian Forests
Reprinted from: *Forests* **2025**, *16*, 192, https://doi.org/10.3390/f16020192 . . . . **83**

Bo Qiu, Sha Li, Jun Cao, Jialong Zhang, Kun Yang, Kai Luo, et al.
Uncertainty Analysis of Forest Aboveground Carbon Stock Estimation Combining Sentinel-1 and Sentinel-2 Images
Reprinted from: *Forests* **2024**, *15*, 2134, https://doi.org/10.3390/f15122134 . . . . **112**

Luana Duarte de Faria, Eraldo Aparecido Trondoli Matricardi, Beatriz Schwantes Marimon, Eder Pereira Miguel, Ben Hur Marimon Junior, Edmar Almeida de Oliveira, et al.
Biomass Prediction Using Sentinel-2 Imagery and an Artificial Neural Network in the Amazon/Cerrado Transition Region
Reprinted from: *Forests* **2024**, *15*, 1599, https://doi.org/10.3390/f15091599 . . . . **133**

Feng Liu, Xiaolin Liu, Mengyuan Zeng, Jianjun Li and Chang Tan
Thinning Effects on Aboveground Biomass Increments in Both the Overstory and Understory of Masson Pine Forests
Reprinted from: *Forests* **2024**, *15*, 1080, https://doi.org/10.3390/f15071080 . . . . **153**

Shan Wang, Zhongke Feng, Zhichao Wang, Lili Hu, Tiantian Ma, Xuanhan Yang, et al.
Construction of Additive Allometric Biomass Models for Young Trees of Two Dominate Species in Beijing, China
Reprinted from: *Forests* **2024**, *15*, 991, https://doi.org/10.3390/f15060991 . . . . **175**

Yam Bahadur KC, Qijing Liu, Pradip Saud, Chang Xu, Damodar Gaire and Hari Adhikari
Driving Factors and Spatial Distribution of Aboveground Biomass in the Managed Forest in the Terai Region of Nepal
Reprinted from: *Forests* **2024**, *15*, 663, https://doi.org/10.3390/f15040663 . . . . **192**

Şerife Kalkanlı Genç, Maria J. Diamantopoulou and Ramazan Özçelik
Tree Biomass Modeling Based on the Exploration of Regression and Artificial Neural Networks Approaches
Reprinted from: *Forests* **2023**, *14*, 2429, https://doi.org/10.3390/f14122429 . . . . **212**

Sushil Nepal, Bianca N. I. Eskelson, Martin W. Ritchie and Sarah E. Gergel
Thinning Combined with Prescribed Burn Created Spatially Heterogeneous Overstory Structures in Contemporary Dry Forests: A Comparison Using LiDAR (2016) and Field Inventory (1934) Data
Reprinted from: *Forests* **2023**, *14*, 2096, https://doi.org/10.3390/f14102096 . . . . **230**

Khwanchai Duangsathaporn, Narapong Sangram, Yenemurwon Omule, Patsi Prasomsin, Kritsadapan Palakit and Pichit Lumyai
Formulating Equations for Estimating Forest Stand Carbon Stock for Various Tree Species Groups in Northern Thailand
Reprinted from: *Forests* **2023**, *14*, 1584, https://doi.org/10.3390/f14081584 . . . . **260**

About the Editors

Ana Cristina Gonçalves

Ana Cristina Gonçalves is an Assistant Professor of Habilitation at the University of Évora, in the Department of Rural Engineering, Portugal, and is a researcher at the Mediterranean Institute for Agriculture, Environment and Development (MED). She represents the University of Évora and Portugal at the International Union of Forest Research Organizations (IUFRO), and is the coordinator of the IUFRO research group 1.04.00—Agroforestry. She holds a PhD in Forest Engineering, has authored more than 100 publications, and has participated in 20 research projects. Her research is focused on silviculture and modelling in pure, mixed, even-aged, and uneven-aged stands; forest management; planning integrated in a GIS environment; and forest biomass modelling.

Teresa Fidalgo Fonseca

Teresa Fidalgo Fonseca is an Associate Professor of Habilitation at the University of Trás-os-Montes e Alto Douro (UTAD), Portugal, and a researcher at the Centre for the Research and Technology of Agroenvironmental and Biological Sciences (CITAB). Her research focuses on silviculture, forest management, biometrics, forest resource modelling, and data science applied to forest ecosystems. She is a member of the CAPSIS community (INRAE, France) as a modeller, and is currently Co-Coordinator of Division 1—Silviculture of IUFRO. Throughout her career, she has led and participated in numerous national and international research projects, funded by national and European programmes. Her work has been published in high-impact scientific journals, with over 100 scientific publications.

Preface

A fundamental aspect of contemporary forest science is the assessment and prediction of forest biomass. This provides a basis for understanding, monitoring, and managing carbon stocks, forest productivity, and ecosystem resilience. As biomass varies significantly depending on species, stand structure, ecological gradient, and site conditions, robust models are essential for accurately capturing this natural diversity.

Biomass modelling relies on an integrated framework supported by field measurements (including destructive sampling), forest inventory data, remote sensing technologies, vegetation indices, and complementary environmental datasets. The rapid advancement of data science and artificial intelligence has transformed the field of biomass modelling. Machine learning, deep learning, and artificial neural networks are increasingly being used to develop biomass models and improve predictive performance at different spatial and temporal scales.

This reprint brings together a collection of scientific contributions that provide a comprehensive overview of biomass estimation methods and their practical applications. Topics covered include tree-level and stand-level modelling, methodological advances, integration with remote sensing data, and decision-support applications in forest and environmental management. The aim is to provide readers with a consolidated reference and an up-to-date set of relevant contributions for those interested in advancing their knowledge of biomass models. These advancements are essential for evaluating forest management strategies, estimating carbon sequestration potential, and supporting broader assessments of ecosystem services.

Ana Cristina Gonçalves and Teresa Fidalgo Fonseca
Guest Editors

forests

MDPI

Article

Application of Machine Learning for Aboveground Biomass Modeling in Tropical and Temperate Forests from Airborne Hyperspectral Imagery

Patrick Osei Darko [1], Samy Metari [2], J. Pablo Arroyo-Mora [3], Matthew E. Fagan [4] and Margaret Kalacska [1,*]

1 Applied Remote Sensing Laboratory, Department of Geography, McGill University, Montréal, QC H3A 0B9, Canada; patrick.oseidarko@mail.mcgill.ca
2 Automotive and Surface Transportation, National Research Council of Canada, Ottawa, ON K1A 0R6, Canada; samy.metari@nrc-cnrc.gc.ca
3 Flight Research Laboratory, National Research Council of Canada, Ottawa, ON K1A 0R6, Canada; juanpablo.arroyo-mora@nrc-cnrc.gc.ca
4 Department of Geography and Environmental Systems, University of Maryland Baltimore County, Baltimore, MD 21250, USA; mfagan@umbc.edu
* Correspondence: margaret.kalacska@mcgill.ca

Abstract: Accurate operational methods used to measure, verify, and report changes in biomass at large spatial scales are required to support conservation initiatives. In this study, we demonstrate that machine learning can be used to model aboveground biomass (AGB) in both tropical and temperate forest ecosystems when provided with a sufficiently large training dataset. Using wavelet-transformed airborne hyperspectral imagery, we trained a shallow neural network (SNN) to model AGB. An existing global AGB map developed as part of the European Space Agency's DUE GlobBiomass project served as the training data for all study sites. At the temperate site, we also trained the model on airborne-LiDAR-derived AGB. In comparison, for all study sites, we also trained a separate deep convolutional neural network (3D-CNN) with the hyperspectral imagery. Our results show that extracting both spatial and spectral features with the 3D-CNN produced the lowest RMSE across all study sites. For example, at the tropical forest site the Tortuguero conservation area, with the 3D-CNN, an RMSE of 21.12 Mg/ha (R^2 of 0.94) was reached in comparison to the SNN model, which had an RMSE of 43.47 Mg/ha (R^2 0.72), accounting for a ~50% reduction in prediction uncertainty. The 3D-CNN models developed for the other tropical and temperate sites produced similar results, with a range in RMSE of 13.5 Mg/ha–31.18 Mg/ha. In the future, as sufficiently large field-based datasets become available (e.g., the national forest inventory), a 3D-CNN approach could help to reduce the uncertainty between hyperspectral reflectance and forest biomass estimates across tropical and temperate bioclimatic domains.

Keywords: convolutional neural network; REDD+; wavelet scattering; continuous wavelet transform; deep learning; spectra-spatial feature extraction

1. Introduction

Forests are globally important ecosystems that play critical roles in maintaining the carbon balance of our planet through a dynamic cycle (e.g., growth, decay, disturbance, and succession), storing and releasing carbon, and mitigating climate change [1,2]. In recent years, international efforts in environmental conservation, like the United Nations' initiative REDD+ program (Reducing Emissions from Deforestation and Forest Degradation) [3,4], have focused on initiatives in developing countries. The REDD+ program serves as a global forest governance system to help mitigate anthropogenic disturbance of forests at multiple spatial scales. Since its inception, the REDD+ initiative has sparked global discussions on necessary actions to help minimize the impacts of deforestation in tropical forests [4]. Thus, periodic mapping and monitoring of aboveground biomass (AGB) have become increasingly important and have been viewed as key initiatives to support REDD+ and broader forest conservation goals [5]. Similarly, in Canada, the government has a responsibility to maintain national forest inventory and to help meet international and countrywide reporting requirements on the state of forest resources [6]. The Canadian government has committed to forest carbon accounting and modeling at the national level to monitor the periodic changes in forests and their impact on climate change. This commitment is evidenced in the implementation of initiatives such as Canada's National Forest Carbon Monitoring, Accounting and Reporting System (NFCMARS) [7].

A major challenge in implementing the REDD+, NFCMARS, and similar conservation initiatives is the reliable quantification of AGB at a large spatial scale (e.g., ecosystem or country levels). The traditional methods for quantifying AGB involve direct (destructive) and indirect (non-destructive) sampling approaches. While direct sampling involves felling trees and weighing them to determine their mass, indirect sampling relies on in situ measurements of the physical and structural parameters of tree stands to estimate AGB using previously determined allometric equations [8–10]. However, relying solely on field methods is limited and laborious, especially when capturing multitemporal changes in biodiversity across large landscapes [11]. Operational methods that can be used to measure, verify, and report changes at the landscape scale are still required to support conservation initiatives (such as REDD+) and mitigate global forest loss accurately and reliably [12].

Empirical models (e.g., parametric and nonparametric regression) that combine in situ measurements with spectral and other information from active and passive remote sensing systems have shown promising results in estimating AGB [13–16]. Remote sensing techniques are used to map landscape-scale variability in forest AGB across environmental gradients, thereby serving as a cost- and time-saving alternative [17–19]. Due to the absence of a standardized remote-sensing-based method for estimating AGB, researchers have prioritized efforts towards reducing uncertainties in AGB prediction [10]. It has been reported that, during AGB modeling, the size of the training sample does not necessarily correlate with the prediction accuracy. Instead, the modeling approach and sensor type employed play significant roles in reducing uncertainties of AGB prediction [20]. Additionally, the sample size effect on AGB modeling accuracy is mainly dependent on the method adopted [21] and possible sources of spatial variability of the dependent variable [22]. In recent years, the use of different remote sensing data from multispectral and hyperspectral sensors, coupled with machine learning methods, has gained popularity in AGB modeling in support of carbon budget accounting [13,23,24]. Unlike multispectral data, hyperspectral sensors collect hundreds of narrow contiguous bands, which can be related to biophysical parameters such as leaf area index, crown volume, AGB, and foliar chemistry [25–27]. With this amount of information, it is possible to conduct predictive modeling of AGB across various spatiotemporal scales and bioclimatic conditions [23,28,29].

Considering the recent advancements in remote sensing technologies, it has become possible to integrate optical imagery with other sensor types, such as LiDAR and synthetic aperture radar (SAR), to improve the accuracy of AGB estimation [15]. For instance, studies conducted by [30,31] demonstrate that combining optical and SAR data improves AGB estimation accuracy compared to using either data source alone. References [32,33] reinforced this idea by showing that data integration combining optical, LiDAR, and SAR data achieved the best performance in AGB estimation. Moreover, different predictive modeling approaches have been applied to hyperspectral imagery (HSI) to harness the wealth of information for AGB estimation [15,29,34]. Parametric methods, such as linear regression relating spectral data with AGB, have been utilized extensively in the literature. Machine-learning-based methods (non-parametric), such as random forest, support vector machines, and artificial neural networks, as well as parametric methods, such as partial least square regression and allometric equations, have been applied to extract features from both LiDAR and optical imagery across tropical and temperate forests, as well as other ecosystems [19,35–40]. The results from these studies suggest that the use of spectral features alone results in less robust estimates of AGB than the use of approaches complemented by datasets from other sensors (e.g., LiDAR) [35,38]. However, in the absence of LiDAR, a combination of spectral and spatial features can help to improve the accuracy of AGB prediction, especially in structurally simple systems such as pine forests [16], but requires more study with more advanced methods if it is to be applied to a variety of structurally complex forests such as tropical and temperate forests [41].

Advanced analytical methods, such as wavelet decompositions and deep convolutional neural networks (3D-CNN), have shown promise in extracting spectral and spatial features for AGB prediction [42]. The use of advanced analytical methods such as SNN and 3D-CNN to extract spectral and spectral–spatial features, respectively, from HSI for AGB modeling has been less explored in the literature. While the use of CNN for hyperspectral image classification and target detection applications have gained popularity [43–47], new innovative modeling approaches are needed to reduce uncertainties in AGB estimates across multiple spatial scales, supporting conservation initiatives such as REDD+ and NFCMARS. However, very few studies have explored the utility of these approaches for AGB modeling using HSI in tropical and temperate forest ecosystems. Our study thus provides valuable insights into large-scale AGB modeling, demonstrating the potential of HSI and machine learning, specifically wavelet-based shallow neural networks and deep convolutional neural networks, for AGB estimation.

Moreover, the acquisition of very large training sets needed for deep learning applications to improve model performance and generalizability and to prevent overfitting is generally infeasible by field inventories [48–50]. The primary objective of this study is to investigate the utility of airborne HSI together with sufficiently large training datasets for modeling AGB using the shallow neural network (SNN) and 3D-CNN across different tropical and temperate forests in Costa Rica and Canada. Additionally, this study aims to assess and compare the effectiveness of wavelet decomposition, SNN, and 3D-CNN in predicting AGB from airborne HSI. Consequently, we demonstrate the utility of these methods as novel approaches to reduce the uncertainty between reflectance and forest AGB estimates across tropical and temperate bioclimatic domains. When a large training set is available, the methodology and findings from this study are expected to offer a robust foundation for future advancements in machine-learning-based approaches to AGB modeling in both tropical and temperate forest ecosystems.

2. Materials and Methods

2.1. Study Areas

Our study was carried out in four conservation areas in Costa Rica and one in Canada, with a combined spatial area of approximately 176,332 ha (Table 1). The conservation areas in Costa Rica can be classified as tropical wet or moist forests, according to Holdridge Life Zones [51,52]. The forest in Mont Saint Bruno (MSB) National Park is classified as a predominantly deciduous, northern temperate forest [53].

Table 1. Characteristics of the tropical and temperate forest ecosystems where hyperspectral imaging data were acquired for this study in Costa Rica and Canada. The elevation presented is the mean with one standard deviation.

Region of Interest	Conservation Area	Forest Type	Precipitation (mm/Year)/Elevation (m)	Total Area (ha)	Total Flight Lines
ACCVC	Area de Conservacion Cordillera Volcanica Central	Tropical wet	4000–8000/206 ± 182	50,251	32
ACHAN	Area de Conservacion Huetar Norte	Premontane wet	4000–8000/117 ± 44	11,989	5
ACOSA	Area de Conservacion Osa	Tropical wet	4000–8000/100 ± 119	67,959	16
ACTO	Area de Conservacion Tortuguero	Tropical wet	4000–8000/41 ± 39	45,177	15
MSB	Mont Saint Bruno National Park	Temperate	50–1300/12 ± 9	990	2
			Total	176,336	74

2.2. Hyperspectral Imagery

Airborne HSI was acquired in Costa Rica for the Mission Airborne Carbon 2013 (MAC13) project in April 2013 with two pushbroom systems, the Compact Airborne Spectrographic Imager (CASI-1500), hereafter referred to as CASI, and the Shortwave Airborne Spectrographic Imager (SASI-644), hereafter referred to as SASI [28]. Table 2, Tables S1 and S2 describe the sensor characteristics and acquisition parameters of each area. While the CASI sensor records data in the visible and near-infrared portions of the reflective electromagnetic spectrum (375 nm–1050 nm) in up to 288 bands, the SASI records the shortwave infrared (SWIR) region of the electromagnetic spectrum from 883 nm to the 2523 nm in 160 bands. For the flight lines used here, the CASI data were summed spectrally on-chip, resulting in 199 bands.

Table 2. Characteristics of the CASI and SASI sensors employed for the MAC13 and CABO projects' data acquisition. The SASI-644 was used for MAC13 which the SASI-640 was used for CABO.

Sensor Characteristics	CASI-1500	SASI-644	SASI-600
Field of view (°)	39.9	39.7	39.7
No. of across-track pixels	1493	640	600
No. of spectral channels	288 (max) (programmable)	160 (non-programmable)	100 (non-programmable)
Spectral range (nm)	375–1050	883–2523	957–2442
Spectral resolution (nm)	3.2 nm	16 nm at 883 nm and 12 nm at 2523	15 nm

Through the Canadian Airborne Biodiversity Observatory (CABO) in July 2022, the same CASI, along with a newer SASI-600 SWIR system (Figure 1, Tables S1 and S2), were deployed. This newer SASI has two distinct detectors covering the right and left halves of the flight line, recording spectral information over 100 spectral channels (957–2442 nm).

Both the MAC13 and CABO datasets underwent standard preprocessing routines (Figure S1), including spectroradiometric calibration and geocorrection, using software from the sensor manufacturer, as described in [54–57]. Atmospheric compensation and topographic and BRDF correction were conducted using the Atmospheric/Topographic Correction for Airborne Imagery (ATCOR 4) program (version 7.3.0 2020) (ReSe Applications GmbH, Wil, Switzerland) following the steps described by [55,56,58]. During geocorrection, the final reflectance product was resampled to 2.5 m pixel size for the MAC13 data and 1 m pixel size for the CABO dataset.

Following the fusion workflow outlined in [59], full range (VINIR–SWIR) reflectance products were generated for all of the study areas. Next, the HSI was spatially resampled to 30 m in ENVI v.5.6.1 (NV5 Geospatial, Broomfield, CO, USA). Subsequently, as described by [56], for the fused imagery, wavelength ranges < 400 nm in the visible spectrum, as well as atmospheric water absorption (i.e., wavelength ranges of 1367–1492 nm and 1800–2200 nm) in the SWIR, were excluded from the analysis.

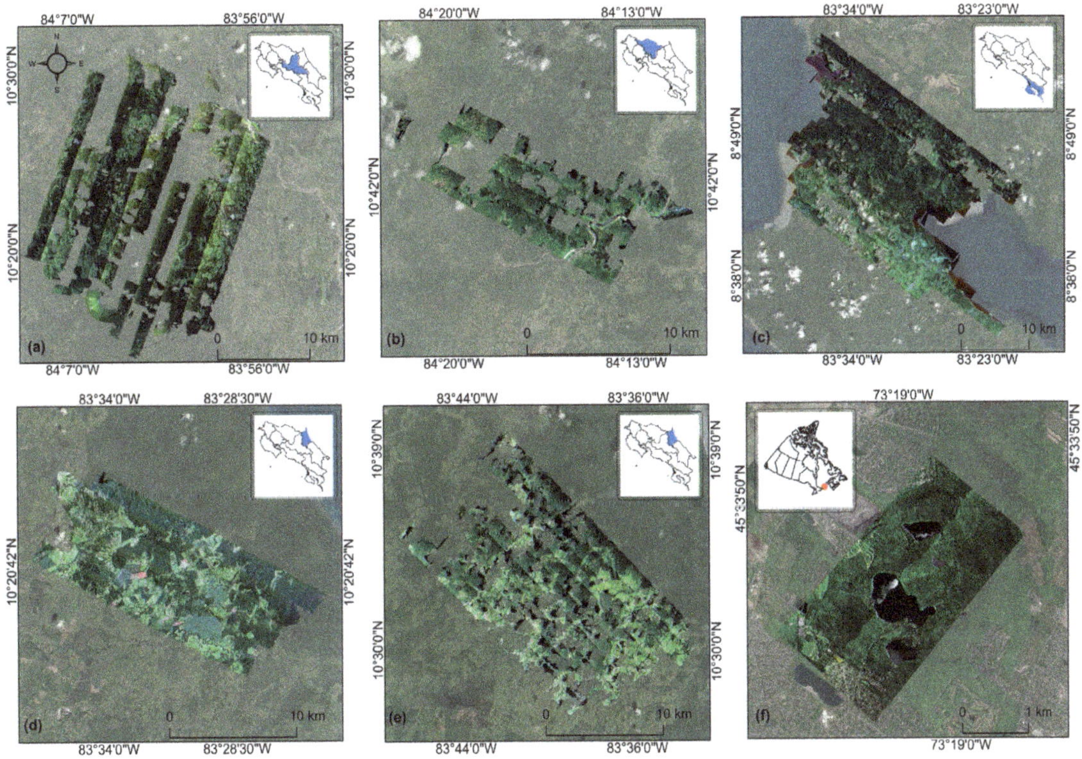

Figure 1. RGB composite showing the areas selected for the study in Costa Rica, (**a**) ACCVC, (**b**) ACHAN, (**c**) ACOSA, (**d**)ACTO-1, (**e**) ACTO-2, and (**f**) MSB in Canada. The map produced is a composite of red (650 nm), green (550 nm), and blue (450 nm) wavelengths. The holes in the imagery correspond to clouds that have been masked out.

2.3. Training and Field Data

Considering the large training data requirements for machine learning models, in this study, we used an existing AGB dataset as the predominant source of training data for all sites (Section 2.3.1). This training data requirement, more than what is currently available from field data, is necessary for deep learning approaches such as CNNs to avoid overfitting and poor model generalization [49]. Separately, for MSB, we also used airborne LiDAR data for training. Due to their relatively small sample size, field data (Section 2.3.3) were used as a separate validation dataset for our results. Consequently, 2000 virtual plots, each measuring 100 m × 100 m and collectively representing approximately 12% of the total image area, were randomly selected from across the boundary of the ACTO-1 experimental site for training, validation, and testing (Figure S2). The size of these polygons matched the spatial resolution of the global AGB dataset.

2.3.1. Global Above Ground Biomass Map (Tropical and Temperate)

The Global Aboveground Biomass (GAGB) map [60] was used as the primary source of AGB training data for both the tropical and temperate forest sites. This global AGB map was produced for the year 2010 using a combination of C-band synthetic aperture radar data from Sentinel-1 and L-band ALOS-2 in conjunction with some multispectral datasets. It has a spatial resolution of 100 m [60,61]. The GAGB accuracy was assessed to be 58.6 Mg/ha and 44.4 Mg/ha overall RMSE for tropical and temperate forests, respectively [62].

2.3.2. Airborne LiDAR (Temperate Forest)

This study employed discrete multi-return airborne LiDAR previously acquired for the Montérégie region of Quebec, Canada, for the provincial government [63]. The LiDAR data have a point density of approximately 2 points per square meter. The LiDAR point cloud underwent an initial segmentation process to distinguish ground and non-ground points in MATLAB v2023b (Mathworks, Nattick, MA, USA). Subsequently, normalization of the non-ground points was conducted, employing the ground points as a reference before calculating LiDAR metrics such as the 7th decile. To relate the LiDAR metrics to AGB and generate a second independent training dataset, we selected the northern hardwood-mixed wood/deciduous forest model described by [64]. This model relates 7th decile LiDAR height to biomass derived from ground inventory plots to estimate AGB with a reported R^2 of 0.73 (RMSE of 20.6 Mg/ha).

2.3.3. Field Data

As verification of the applicability of the GAGB dataset, a comparison with independent field data was made for the ACTO-1 conservation area (the least cloudy area from the Costa Rican HSI—Figure 1), and the MSB site in Canada. For ACTO-1, an existing geographic information system (GIS) geodatabase with forest inventory information from Costa Rica's Natural Forest Management Plans (NFMP) [65] was used. To account for total AGB within a plot, census and tree inventory data from private land holdings were extracted from this database. The census includes trees with a diameter at breast height (DBH) greater than or equal to 60 cm, while the tree inventory data includes all trees in 0.3 ha plots greater than or equal to 30 cm (see [52,65] for details). The polygons of the parcel boundaries were cleaned to avoid duplications, overlaps, and to correct the topology. Parcels with forest loss between the date of the inventory and April 2013 (i.e., acquisition of the HSI data) were also removed. A total of 34 parcels ranging in area from 5 ha to 312 ha remained after data cleaning and quality assurance checks. For these, tree-level AGB was calculated with Equation (1) for the census data using the Brown Equation for tropical wet forests [66]. The estimated biomass for the inventory was then extrapolated to the farm level and added to the census biomass.

$$Y = 21.297 - 6.953\,(D) + 0.740\,(D^2) \tag{1}$$

where D is the DBH.

For MSB, field inventory data from the CABO repository [67] were used for the estimation of AGB. Fifteen field plots (30 m × 30 m) with a minimum of 30 individual trees were inventoried in 2019. For each plot, measurements of every tree within a 15 m radius from a precisely georeferenced and permanently marked plot center were conducted. Every tree with a DBH of <9 cm, whose canopy is visible from above, and all trees with a DBH of ≥9 cm were measured, including the inventory of their height and canopy dimensions using a T3 Transponder and LaserGeo (Haglöf, Sweden AB, Långsele, Sweden) instruments. Each tree was identified to the species level, and a canopy dominance value (dominant, codominant, intermediate, or suppressed) was assigned. To estimate AGB, the trees marked as dominant and codominant were selected, since they are the trees whose canopies are readily mapped by remote sensing. The methods outlined in [68,69] were used to calculate the AGB for each tree stand, and the results were aggregated to the plot level.

2.4. Machine Learning Model Development and Evaluation

To compare the output of different machine learning approaches and wavelet transformations, the ACTO-1 conservation area was selected as a proof-of-concept test site. The model type with the lowest RMSE was then independently developed for the remaining tropical forest sites and MSB. As summarized in Figure 2, three types of wavelet transformations (i.e., continuous wavelet transform—CWT, discrete wavelet transform—DWT, and wavelet scattering transform—WST) were tested along with two neural networks (i.e., shallow neural networks—SNN and 3D deep convolutional neural networks—3D-CNN). The objective is to compare the performance of these two distinct methods—wavelet transforms combined with SNN and 3D-CNN. As described below, the first method utilizes wavelet coefficients at different scales as features, which are then used to train the SNN. This approach leverages the multiresolution capabilities of wavelets and the simplicity of shallow networks, ensuring computational efficiency for smaller datasets. The second method directly inputs spectral images into a 3D-CNN model, treating each pixel as a 3D data cube with multiple spectral bands. The 3D-CNN extracts spatial and spectral features by analyzing data across three dimensions, making it highly effective for complex datasets. A brief description of these methods is presented below.

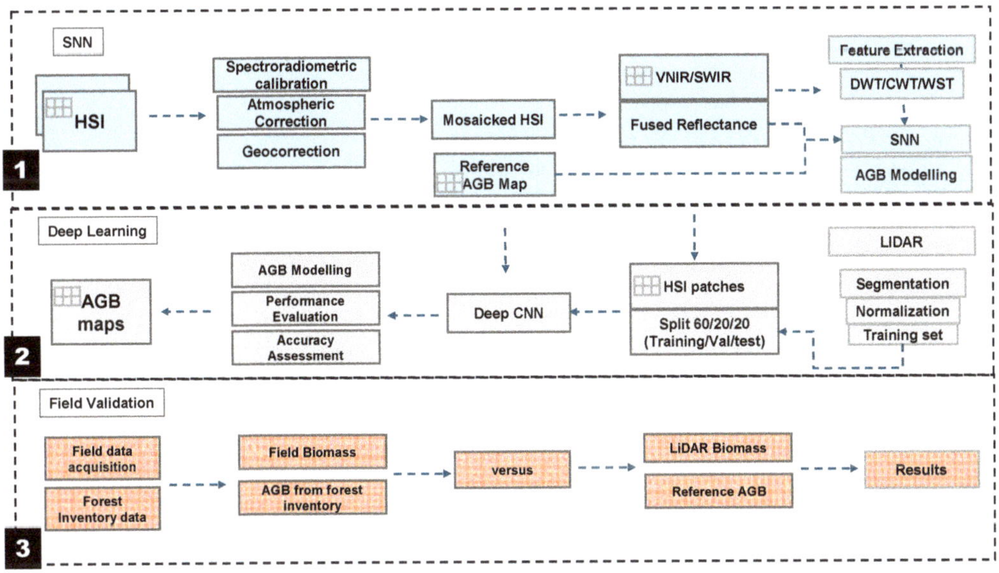

Figure 2. A flow chart summarizing the proposed methods adopted for AGB modeling from HSI. In this figure, HSI patches refer to the plots extracted from the HSI. The numbers 1–3 break the workflow into three main parts with 1. SNN, 2. Deep Learning and 3. Field Validation.

2.4.1. Wavelet Decomposition

A wavelet is a waveform of limited duration used to decompose a signal (e.g., spectrum) into shifted and scaled representations of the original waveform (i.e., the mother wavelet), which is equivalent to increasing levels of spectral details or radiant frequencies [70]. Wavelet decomposition permits the simultaneous analysis of the reflectance spectra in the time and frequency domains [71,72]. The two main types of wavelet transforms explored in this study are continuous (CWT) and discrete (DWT). These two wavelet types differ in how they both discretize the scale and translational (or shifting) parameters of the mother wavelet. While the DWT uses a finite set of scales (subset of scales and positions) known as discrete dyadic scales, where scales are on the order of the power of 2 [73], the CWT can operate at every scale and includes the scale as determined from the input signal to a scale specified by the user.

The set of wavelet basis functions is computed for the input signal by shifting and scaling $\psi(\lambda)$, which is known as the mother wavelet, across the signal (Equation (2)), as follows:

$$\psi_{a,b}(\lambda) = \frac{1}{\sqrt{a}}\psi\left(\frac{\lambda - b}{a}\right) \; a > 0, \; b \in \mathbb{R} \tag{2}$$

where a is the scaling factor and b is the shifting factor.

The calculated coefficients for the shifting and scaling factors constitute the sum of the multiplication of the reflectance spectrum across all wavelengths by the scaled and shifted representations of the mother wavelet. For the CWT, Morse, bump, and Morlet mother wavelets were chosen for comparison, while, for the DWT, two mother wavelets from the Daubechies family (db6 and db5) and a symlet wavelet (sym7) were chosen based on [74].

In addition to DWT and CWT, we also tested a wavelet scattering transform (WST) to extract spectral features for AGB modeling. The WST extracts informative spectral features with low variance and stable representation of the reflectance data. The method applies wavelets and scaling functions to reflectance data to extract features that can be packaged as inputs for deep learning and other machine learning applications. The steps in WSTs include convolution applied to the input spectrum using wavelets (i.e., Gabor and Morlet wavelets were tested), followed by non-linearization and averaging (pooling) using scaling functions. Three scattering networks (WST-N1, WST-N2, and WST-N3) were tested to determine the appropriate sampling frequency that would maximize the information content. Sampling frequencies of 20, 30, and 50 were used to produce scattering coefficients with lengths of 60, 30, and 15, respectively.

2.4.2. Spectral Feature Selection

After transforming each spectrum using the DWT, CWT, and WST, as demonstrated by [75], the correlation coefficient between AGB and the coefficients at various levels of decomposition was calculated per wavelet transform to select robust spectral features. Considering the variability of the number of coefficients at various levels of decomposition for each wavelet type, we selected a different threshold for each wavelet type that would produce features not exceeding 250 for the modeling. Several runs were conducted to identify the optimal thresholds for determining robust spectral features for AGB modeling. This involved including preliminary models with varying thresholds and evaluating their performance based on criteria such as model accuracy and computational efficiency. For instance, for the DWT and CWT, thresholds of 0.45 and 0.6 were selected, respectively. For the WST, except for WST-3, where a threshold of 0.2 was applied, no threshold was applied for WST-1 and WST-2 since the produced features were within the set feature limit.

Additionally, mutual information feature selection was used to rank the spectral features. This method captures linear and non-linear relationships in datasets [76]. The spectral features within the set limit, as mentioned above, were subsequently used for AGB modeling, and their modeling performance was compared with the threshold-based feature selection described above.

2.4.3. Shallow Neural Network (SNN)

A typical artificial neural network (ANN) architecture comprises the following three main components: an input layer, hidden layer, and output layer (Figure S3) [77]. For the ACTO-1 conservation area, the selected spectral features from the wavelet coefficients were used to train a two-layer feed-forward SNN with ten sigmoid hidden neurons in the first layer and an output linear neuron with MATLAB 2021b. The network was trained using the Levenberg–Marquardt back-propagation training algorithm. A total of 60% of the training data was randomly assigned for training, with 20% used for validation and the remaining 20% for testing. The weights and biases of the SNN were adjusted using the selected training data to help to predict the dependent variable (AGB) from the selected spectral features. The generalization ability of the model was then evaluated based on its performance on the validation and test sets. For instance, during training, overfitting of the model was avoided by stopping the learning process early using the outcome from the validation data (i.e., if no improvement in the validation error was observed in successive epochs). Meanwhile, the test set served as an independent validation of the generalization abilities of the model.

2.4.4. Deep Transfer Convolutional Neural Network Framework (3D-CNN)

A three-dimensional convolutional neural network (3D-CNN) is a type of neural network designed to analyze a three-dimensional dataset like HSI. Hyperspectral data cubes comprise two spatial dimensions (i.e., X and Y) and a spectral dimension. The high dimensionality of HSI results in high computational complexity when a 3D-CNN model is employed to extract spectral–spatial features for regression or classification. Therefore, to improve the efficiency of 3D-CNN implementation and reduce spectral correlation and noise while preserving the spectral information content, a Principal Component Analysis (PCA), Maximum Noise Fraction Transform (MNF), and t-Distributed Stochastic Neighbor Embedding (t-SNE) were implemented on the HSI before employing the 3D-CNN to extract spectral–spatial features for modeling AGB [47], and their results were compared. Figure S4 shows a subset of the HSI from ACTO-1 with dimensions of 190 columns × 163 rows × 238 bands. After implementing a PCA or MNF, the spectral bands are reduced to the first 15 components. For the t-SNE, three components remained. Next, each pixel vector was assigned a corresponding AGB value extracted from the GAGB reference map or LiDAR. Blocks of pixels representing a 3D patch from the HSI and centering on each pixel were created from adjacent pixels with a stride of 1 to produce a patch with dimensions of m × m × P. Here, m × m is the window size used for splitting the imagery into 3D patches, and P is the number of bands following PCA, MNF, or t-SNE. The output of the spectral–spatial feature extraction using the 3D-CNN is produced by applying a 3D convolution three times, each followed by a Rectified linear Unit (ReLU), an activation function that introduces non-linearity in the output of the network, with the last one followed by max-pooling and a flattened layer. These flattened layers are also followed by a dropout layer (i.e., a regularization technique). Figure S5 shows the model architecture. The model is based on the architecture shown in [78]. Multiple splits were tested through several runs and analyses, and data splits of 60% for training, 20% for validation, and 20% for testing were found to be sufficient to ensure model generalization. To mitigate overfitting, regularization methods such as dropout layers, weight decay, and early stopping based on the performance of the 20% unseen validation data were employed. In summary, the inclusion of max-pooling in the deep learning architecture, a reduced training time for the model (i.e., 40 epochs), the utilization of 30% and 20% dropout rates, a window size of 15 for extracting spatial and spectral features, and a split ratio of 60:20:20 for training, validation, and testing were key measures implemented to help avoid overfitting and improve model generalization.

2.4.5. Hyperparameter Tuning

The process of optimizing or tuning parameters such as batch size, number of epochs, number of hidden layers, learning rate, and the dropout parameter is known as hyperparameter tuning, which was performed using MATLAB 2023b for the SNN and 3D-CNN models (Table 3). We employed a learning rate of 0.1, which is frequently used for the Levenberg–Marquardt algorithm, and 0.001, which is also commonly employed for the Adam optimizer.

Table 3. Hyperparameters employed in the SNR and 3D-CNN models. The hyperparameters were selected by running several tests and analyzing the results.

	Epochs	Minibatch Size	Optimizer	Learning Rate	Loss Function
SNN	1000	-	Levenberg M	0.1	MSE
CNN-3D	40	256	Adam	0.001	RMSE

2.4.6. Performance Metrics for Model Evaluation

The models' performances were evaluated per network architecture (SNN and 3D-CNN), as well as the input data/wavelet type. We selected three main metrics frequently used in the literature to assess the performance of the models. These metrics were the mean square error (MSE), root mean square error (RMSE), and mean absolute error (MAE). To compare the differences between the GAGB map pixels (and LiDAR-based AGB at MSB) and the predicted AGB map, an AGB bin of 40 Mg/ha was selected, and the predicted values were tabulated and graphed based on this bin versus the corresponding GAGB (or LiDAR-based) values. Two main accuracy metrics, namely the root mean square difference (RMSD) and mean difference (MD), which can be referred to as the bias, were used to assess the accuracy of each model. The RMSD was calculated according to Equation (3), as follows [79]:

$$RMSD = \sqrt{\sum_{j=1}^{n} \frac{\left(AGB_{Pm}(i) - AGB_{Refm}(i)\right)^2}{n}} \quad (3)$$

where AGB_{Pm} is the predicted aboveground biomass, AGB_{Refm} is the reference aboveground biomass (i.e., GAGB- or LiDAR-based AGB), and n is total number of observations.

The mean difference was calculated according to Equation (4) as follows:

$$MD = (\mu AGB_{Pm} - \mu AGB_{GAGBm}) \quad (4)$$

where μAGB represents the mean aboveground biomass.

2.5. Proof-of-Concept Model Development

As mentioned in Section 2.4, to compare the output of the SNN (with different wavelet transformations) and the 3D-CNN, the ACTO-1 conservation area was selected as a proof-of-concept test site. To set up the input data, firstly, 2000 virtual plots (100 m × 100 m) were randomly distributed across ACTO-1. The area of these plots is equivalent to the pixel size of the GAGB dataset, and the GAGB values for each plot were assigned to the polygons. For both the SNN and the 3D-CNN, pixels were extracted from the HSI for the 2000 plots and used as training samples, which constituted approximately 22,000 pixels. The samples were split into 60% for training (n = 13,200), 20% for validation (n = 4400), and 20% for testing (n = 4400). The range of the GAGB-based AGB values was 0–300 Mg/ha (μ = 150.1 ± 86.5 Mg/ha).

2.6. Aboveground Biomass Modeling in Different Forest Types

Development of AGB models based on forest type is recommended to account for the variability of the forest types and spectral characteristics [80], therefore, a separate 3D-CNN model following the architecture described in Section 2.4.4 was developed for each of the other Costa Rican sites (i.e., ACHAN, ACOSA, and ACCVC) and for MSB in

Canada. At MSB, a 3D-CNN model was also developed using the LiDAR-based input data (see Section 2.3.2). Summary statistics of the reference GAGB (and LiDAR-based AGB for MSB) data are shown in Figure 3.

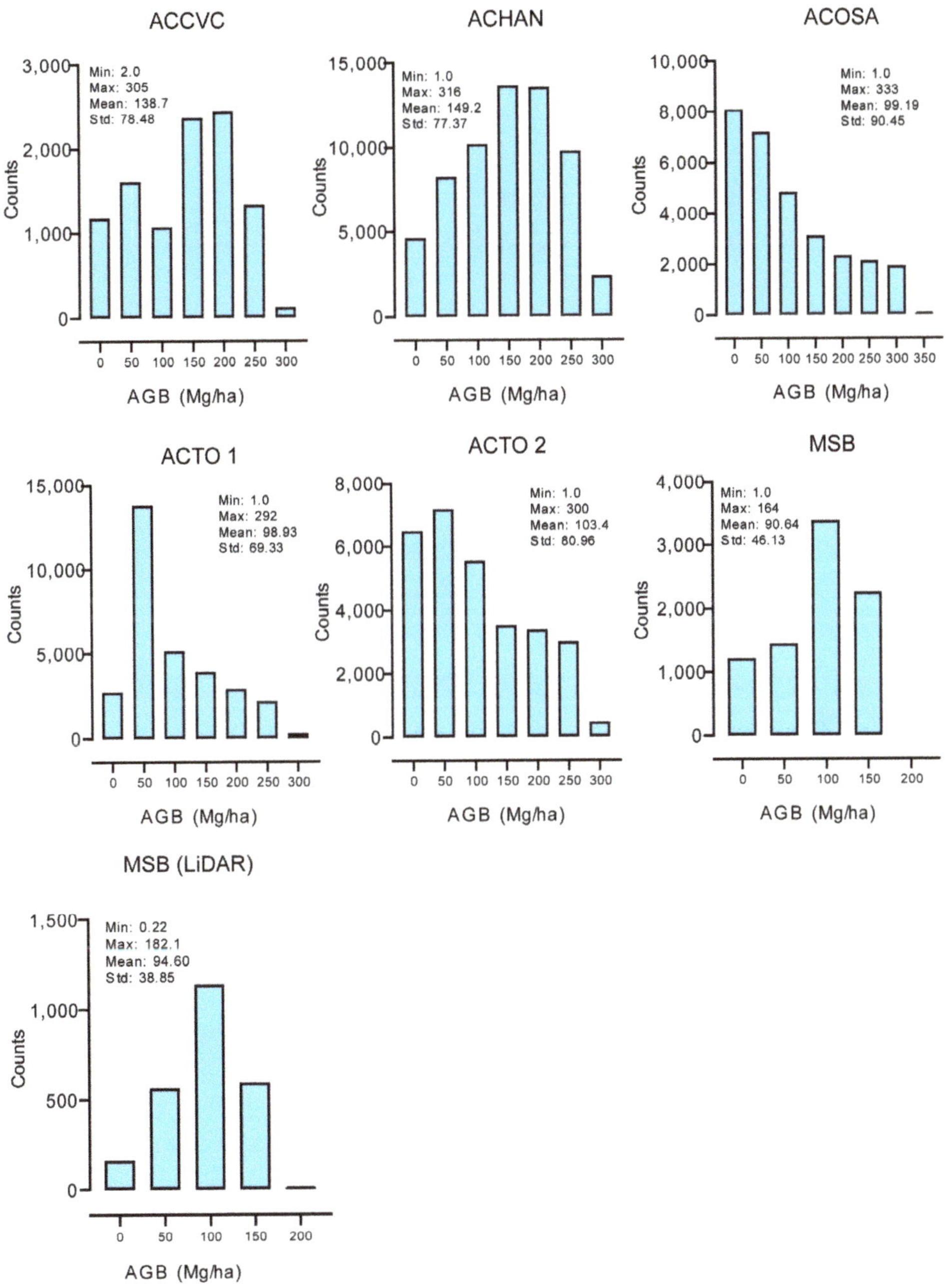

Figure 3. Distribution of extracted AGB values used for prediction as part of the training process for the site-specific models.

3. Results

3.1. Comparison of Training Data with Field-Based AGB

The results comparing forest inventory estimates of AGB and the reference GAGB data used for training are shown in Figure 4. For both tropical and temperate forests, a moderate relationship can be seen. For ACTO-1, an RMSE and R^2 of 36.68 Mg/ha and 0.45, respectively, were found, while, for the temperate forest (MSB), an RMSE of 26.1 Mg/ha and an R^2 of 0.40 were found (Figure 4). The comparison between the estimated field AGB and the LiDAR-based AGB estimates for MSB resulted in an RMSE of 19.54 Mg/ha and an R^2 of 0.42 (Figure 4).

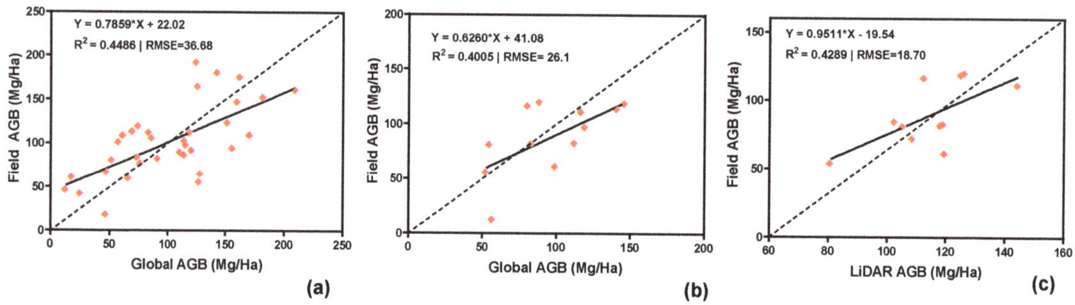

Figure 4. (**a**) Reference GAGB versus field-based estimate of AGB for ACTO-1; (**b**) Reference GAGB versus field-based estimate of AGB for MSB; (**c**) LiDAR-derived AGB versus field-based estimate of AGB for MSB.

3.2. Proof-of-Concept Model Comparison

3.2.1. SNN Model Comparisons

For the ACTO-1 conservation area proof-of-concept model development, the results of 20 iterations of the SNN model for each type of wavelet transform are presented in Table 4. Across the wavelet decomposition types, the CWT resulted in the highest RMSE, ranging from 57.52 Mg/ha to 79.23 Mg/ha for the threshold-based feature selection and 49.66 Mg/ha to 57.63 Mg/ha for the mutual-information-based feature selection. The best CWT model was found to be with the bump wavelet, which resulted in an RMSE of 49.66 Mg/ha. In contrast, the results for the DWT and WST are similar in the range of RMSE across all combinations and produced lower RMSE values than the CWT, ranging from 43.478 Mg/ha to 52.02 Mg/ha. For instance, the model derived from DWT-db6 features improved the AGB prediction by approximately 6.2 Mg/ ha compared to the best CWT model. Similarly, all three WST models showed an improvement of model performance by 6 Mg/ha compared to the best CWT model with the best WST models, achieving an RMSE of ~44 Mg/ha (Table 4 and Table S4).

3.2.2. Spectral–Spatial Features (3D-CNN)

Extracting spatial information along with spectral information for AGB modeling using the PCA-based 3D-CNN resulted in a low RMSE of 21.12 Mg/ha and an R^2 of 0.94 compared to an R^2 range of 0.8–0.92 and RMSE values of 24.15–35.92 Mg/ha for the MNF- and t-SNE-based 3D-CNN (Figure 5 and Table 5). The results for the 3D-CNN models represent the lowest RMSE values compared to the SNN approach, which relies on spectral features alone (Tables 4 and 5). Figure 6 presents the 3D-CNN learning curve, showing the training and validation RMSE and loss for PCA-based 3D-CNN AGB modeling. From Figure 6, it can be deduced that convergence was reached after approximately the 10th epoch, where the training RMSE and loss tends to become stable (Figure 6a,b).

Table 4. Shallow neural network model comparisons across wavelet decomposition inputs with results ordered by RMSE (best to worse). Units for RMSE, MSE, and MAE are in Mg/ha. The average is based on 20 iterations.

Input Variable	# Extracted Features	Performance	MSE	MAE	R	R^2	RMSE
DWT-db6	225	Best Model	2032.36	34.97	0.85	0.72	45.08
		Average	2132.71	35.88	0.85	0.72	46.17
WST-N3	199	Best Model	2039.68	34.66	0.85	0.72	45.16
		Average	2159.49	35.92	0.84	0.71	46.46
WST-N2	210	Best Model	2050.8	35.09	0.85	0.72	45.29
		Average	2241.14	36.73	0.84	0.71	47.33
WST-N1	135	Best Model	2071.35	35.06	0.85	0.72	45.51
		Average	2266.27	36.9	0.84	0.71	47.6
DWT–sym7	203	Best Model	2123.02	35.55	0.85	0.72	46.08
		Average	2266.12	36.86	0.83	0.69	47.58
DWT–db5	213	Best Model	2158.07	36.01	0.84	0.71	46.46
		Average	2274.16	37.04	0.83	0.69	47.68
CWT bump	35	Best Model	3308.62	44.35	0.75	0.56	57.52
		Average	3503.86	45.7	0.73	0.53	59.19
CWT–amor	119	Best Model	3530.41	45.95	0.73	0.53	59.42
		Average	3688.4	47	0.71	0.5	60.73
CWT–morse	79	Best Model	3531.01	46.07	0.73	0.53	59.42
		Average	3823.43	47.04	0.70	0.49	61.7

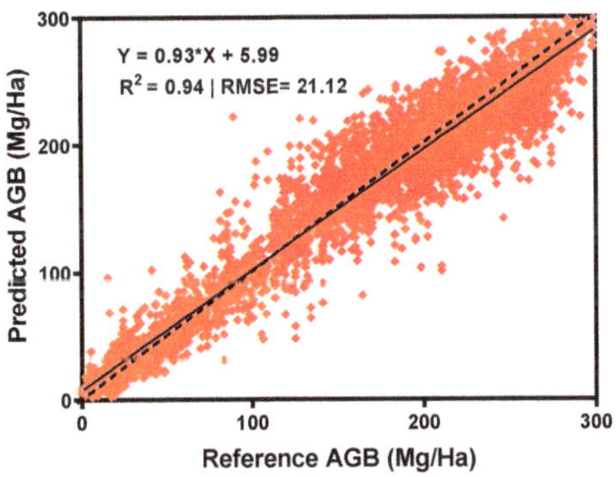

Figure 5. A scatter plot comparing the predicted AGB and reference GAGB data, including a 1:1 reference line (dashed) and a regression fit line (solid), demonstrating the model's performance and deviation from ideal predictions for the experimental site (ACTO-1). This plot shows the results of the 3D-CNN implemented on the ACTO-1 mosaic at landscape scale. Only the testing pixels not included in the model development are shown here.

Table 5. A comparison of 3D-CNN-based AGB modeling performances for different HSI dimensionality reduction approaches.

	PCA	MNF	t-SNE
R square	0.94	0.92	0.83
RMSE (Mg/ha)	21.1	24.15	35.92

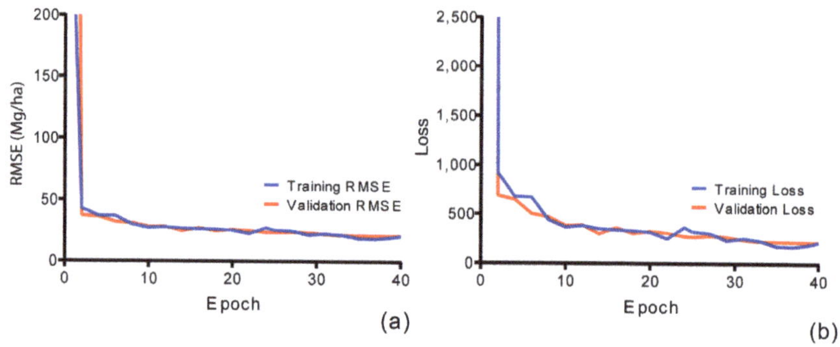

Figure 6. Model performance assessment for the experimental site (ACTO-1). This plot represents the results of the 3D-CNN implemented on the ACTO mosaic at landscape scale, where (**a**) is a plot of training and validation RMSE at each epoch and (**b**) is training and validation loss at each epoch.

Additionally, Figure 7 shows a predicted AGB map derived from the best SNN-WST-N3 model developed at the ACTO-1 experimental site and the PCA-based 3D-CNN model at the landscape scale for the same site. In comparison to the reference GAGB map, the landscape-scale SNN-WST-N3 model resulted in an R^2 of 0.72, while the 3D-CNN model based on PCA performed better, resulting in an R^2 of 0.94. Given the split ratio of 60:20:20 for training, validation (seen), and testing (unseen) data in the AGB modeling, a comparison between the results of the validation and testing sets revealed no significant performance drop. For instance, the final validation RMSE achieved was 20.83 with an R^2 of 0.941 for the validation set (Figure 6a). Meanwhile, using the test set (unseen data), the final validation RMSE resulted in 21.12 Mg/ha with an R^2 of 0.939 (Table 5 and Figure 5). A summary of a comparison of the results with or without PCA methods is presented in Table 5 and Figures S7 and S8.

3.3. Benchmark Dataset Comparison

When the 3D-CNN model developed for the ACTO-1 site (experimental site) is applied to imagery of the same forest type in a nearby location (ACTO-2) and compared to the reference GAGB, the results show an R^2 of 0.62 (Figure S6a). A drop of approximately 0.3 in the R-squared values between the results for the ACTO-1 experimental site model (R^2~0.9) and that of the ACTO-2 benchmark site (R^2~0.6) was recorded, indicating a correlation of 0.77 between the reference and the prediction (Figure S6). Similarly, a drop of 0.3 in R^2 was observed when the SNN model for ACTO-1 was applied to the ACTO-2 site, recording an R^2 of 0.40 (Figure S6b).

3.4. Model Performance Across Forest Types (Hyperspectral Imagery)

The summary results of the development of a PCA-based 3D-CNN (best performing model type at the test site) for each forest type are presented in Figure 8. While the lowest RMSE can be seen for MSB (16.69 Mg/ha), all forest types have similar results with RMSE, ranging from 24.70 Mg/ha (ACCVC) to 30.1 Mg/ha (ACAHN). Applications of the 3D-CNN models at the landscape scale for each forest type are shown in Figure 9. The figure shows that, apart from ACHAN, the tropical wet forests ACCVC, ACOSA, and ACTO produced the best model performance, with an RMSE in the range between 19 and 28 Mg/ha. Compared to the tropical forests, the predicted AGB range was the lowest at MSB (temperate forest), with a minimum and maximum of 0 and 176 Mg/ha, respectively.

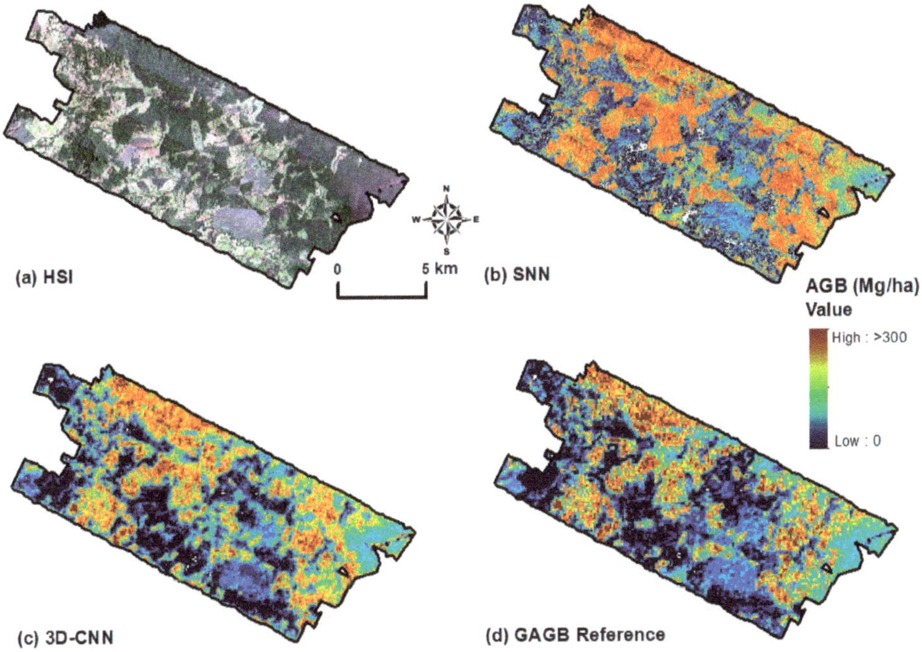

Figure 7. Application of the best AGB prediction models to the ACTO-1 imagery. (**a**) An RGB composite (R: 660 nm, G: 550 nm, and B: 480 nm) of the hyperspectral imaging data for the ACTO-1 experimental site; (**b**) SNN-WST (N3) model applied to the HSI; (**c**) A 3D-CNN model applied to the ACTO-1 image to produce an AGB map; (**d**) Reference GAGB map used for training the SNN and 3D-CNN models.

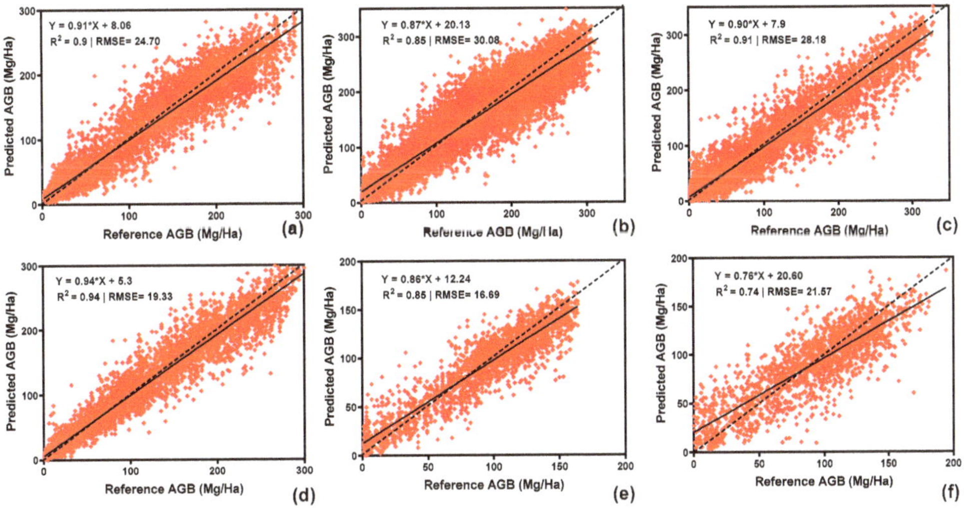

Figure 8. PCA-based 3D-CNN model performance evaluation for all forest types. Each plot shows a scatter plot of predicted AGB and reference AGB, including a 1:1 reference line (dashed) and the regression fit line (solid), demonstrating the model's performance and deviation from ideal predictions for (**a**) ACCVC, (**b**) ACHAN, (**c**) ACOSA, (**d**) ACTO-2, (**e**) MSB GAGB, and (**f**) MSB LiDAR. Only the testing data not used in the model development are shown in the scatter plot.

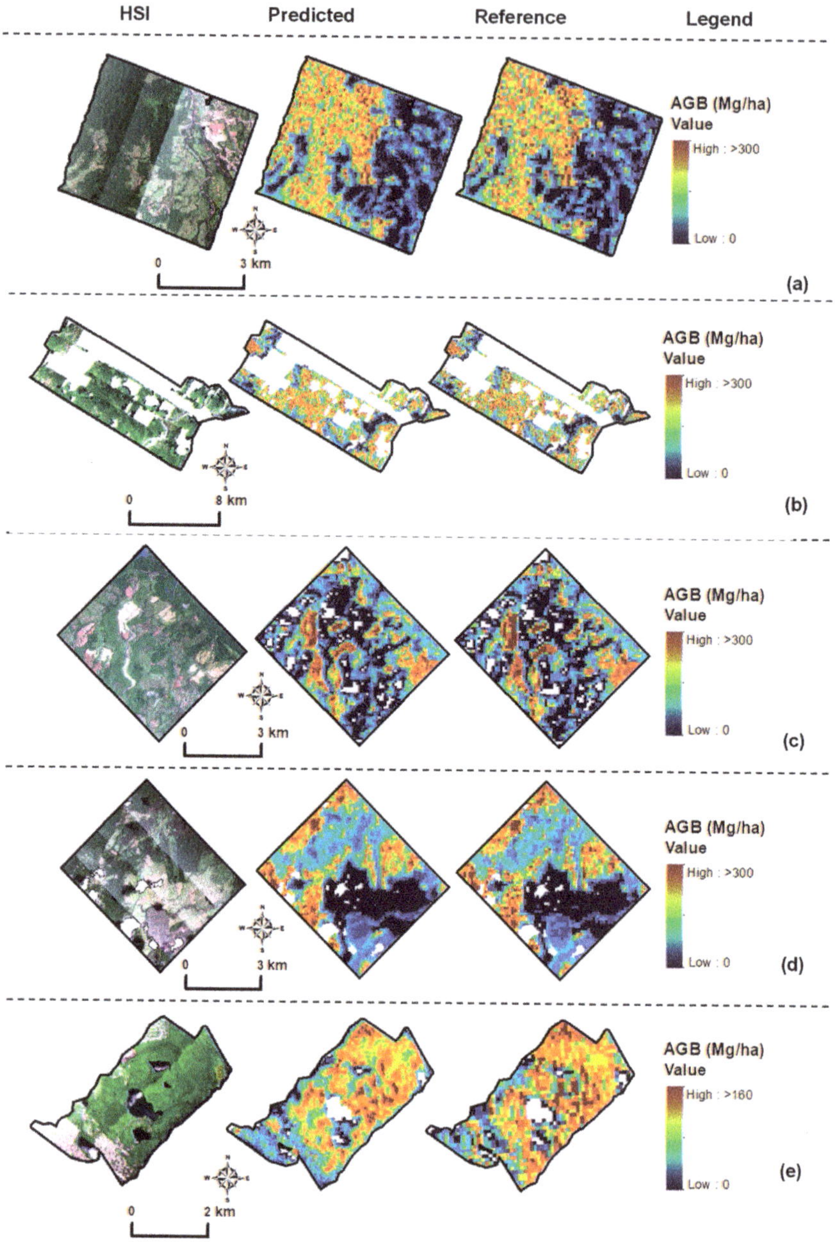

Figure 9. Example application of the PCA-based 3D-CNN models based on the reference GAGB map to HSI acquired for each forest type. (**a**) ACCVC, (**b**) ACHAN, (**c**) ACOSA, (**d**) ACTO-2, and (**e**) MSB. From the left is an RGB (R: 660 nm, G: 550 nm, and B: 480 nm) composite of the individual conservation sites, followed by the predicted map showing the spatial variability of AGB for each site and the reference GAGB map for each site.

A plot of the biases of selected AGB bins showing which range of AGB was under- or overpredicted is shown in Figure 10, and a tabulation of the results for the selected accuracy metrics (RMSD and MD) are also presented in Table S3. Overall, it can be deduced that the predicted AGB values were closely related to those of the reference map. For instance, Figure 10 shows that, for all of the tropical forests, apart from ACOSA, AGB values within the range of 0–280 were underpredicted up to 5 Mg/ha, while the AGB greater than 280 Mg/ha were overestimated up to about 20 Mg/ha. At ACOSA, AGB was underpredicted up to about 10 Mg/ha and overpredicted up to approximately 5 Mg/ha. However, MSB recorded the lowest underprediction of the AGB values within the range of 0–160 Mg/ha (4 Mg/ha) but overpredicted up to 6 Mg/ha for the AGB values above 160 Mg/ha. Moreover, Table S3 shows that the highest RMSD values (19.0 Mg/ha–25.4 Mg/ha) for all of the tropical forests were found to be for the AGB range of 160–200 Mg/ha, and the lowest RMSD was recorded for the 0–40 Mg/ha range. Similarly, for MSB, the lowest RMSD (~15 Mg/ha) was recorded for the AGB range of 0–40 and the highest (16–21 Mg/ha) was recorded for the AGB range of above 40 Mg/ha.

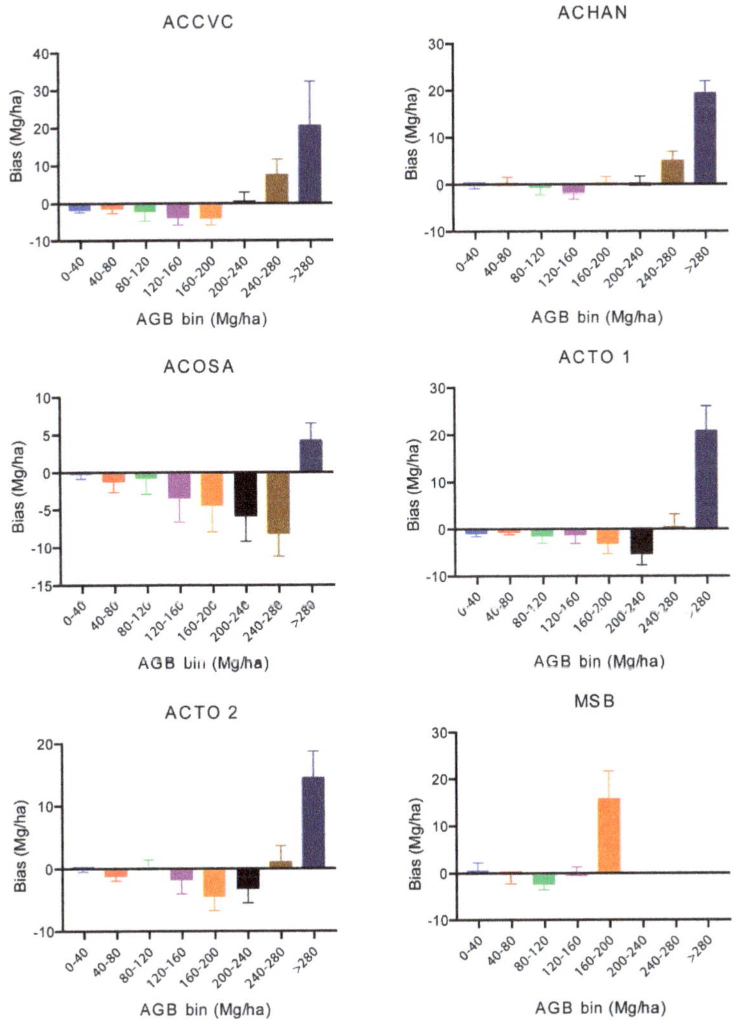

Figure 10. Distribution of bias for each forest type's AGB models for the tropical forests in Costa Rica and the temperate forest in Canada (MSB).

3.5. Model Performance—Airborne LiDAR

The results of a 3D-CNN model based on the airborne LiDAR data as an input for the MSB site showed an RMSE of 21.57 Mg/ha (R^2 = 0.74). Figure 11 shows the spatial variability in AGB values for both the reference and predicted AGB of the MSB site. In comparison to the model using the GAGB data, there was a drop in model performance from an R^2 of 0.85 to 0.74, representing an approximately 13% drop in model performance.

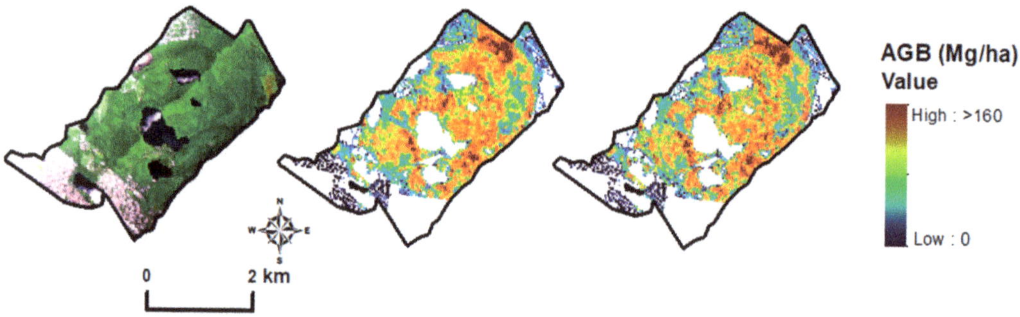

Figure 11. Comparison of predicted AGB and reference LiDAR data from MSB. From the left, the reference LiDAR map and the predicted AGB map (3D-CNN based on the LiDAR input).

4. Discussion

Large training datasets are crucial in AGB modeling, as they capture heterogeneity, help improve accuracy, enhance generalization, and increase model robustness [48–50]. In this study, we demonstrate that, when sufficient training datasets are available for deep learning, 3D-CNN can be used to extract spectral and spatial features simultaneously from HSI to model AGB for improved modeling performance in tropical and temperate forest ecosystems. While other studies have demonstrated the use of 3D-CNN for classification and related tasks (e.g., [47]), our study is the first to show that, with large datasets (i.e., those that are comprehensive and diverse enough), 3D-CNN can achieve a low RMSE in modeling AGB in these ecosystems.

As shown in Figure 4, field-based AGB estimates and the GAGB data (and LiDAR for MSB) have moderate relationships of R^2 of 0.4–0.44 and RMSE of 18.7–36.7. While they indicate that the GAGB is reasonable in our study areas, those results should be interpreted with caution, as the sample size is small (n = 13–34). The need for, but also the challenges in, establishing large numbers of field plots for forest characteristics such as AGB have been reiterated by many studies, e.g., [81–84]. There is a large training data requirement for ML approaches to ensure that overfitting is avoided and that the model can generalize well to unseen pixels in the imagery [48,49]. Moreover, as stated earlier, the RMSE of the GAGB dataset is 58.6 Mg/ha and 44.4 Mg/ha for tropical and temperate forests, respectively. While our results show lower RMSE in comparison to the GAGB dataset, it remains a proxy for field data. Therefore, it is important that the overall uncertainty in comparison to ground-based estimates needs to consider not only the uncertainty from our model results, but those from within the GAGB dataset as well. Nonetheless, the 3D-CNN employed in this study has shown promise. As larger field-based datasets become available (i.e., those large enough for the methods employed in this study), the 3D-CNN approach is expected to offer a robust modeling alternative, advancing machine-learning-based approaches to AGB modeling using HSI.

Previous studies (e.g., [85–87]) have shown improved model predictive power of vegetation characteristics and classification from wavelet decomposition of HSI over other approaches, including vegetation indices and PCA. Our proof-of-concept model comparison from the ACTO-1 study area compared SNNs with different wavelet decompositions as inputs with a deep learning 3D-CNN. We found that the best wavelet decomposition SNN model was the DWT (db6), with an RMSE of 43.47 Mg/ha. However, our results ultimately showed that the best performing model was the PCA-based 3D-CNN, with an RMSE of 21.12 Mg/ha (Figure 5). This was an improvement in RMSE of 22.35 Mg/ha over the best SNN model, which relies only on spectral features. While the R^2 values are not comparable between studies, our RMSE range of 21.12 Mg/ha to 30.1 Mg/ha across the forest types is lower than those reported by others, such as [88] (~68.11 Mg/ha), [89] (~91.2 Mg/ha), and [19] (~64.4 Mg/ha), employing individual hyperspectral bands or vegetation indices calculated from HSI. In terms of R-squared values, the use of spectral features from optical imagery and other datasets has shown promising results in estimating AGB, with R^2 values ranging from 0.84 to 0.92, compared to an R^2 of 0.5 to 0.68 when hyperspectral features are used alone [29,35,38]. For instance, ref. [90] reported that when temporal features extracted from multiple satellite imagery are used for AGB modeling, an R^2 of 0.58 can be attained. Spectral metrics, such as vegetation indices extracted from HSI for AGB prediction, also produced an R^2 of 0.55 in a study conducted by [38]. It has also been reported that the use vegetation indices alone from HSI for AGB prediction in the Brazilian Amazon resulted in an R^2 of 0.58 [88]. Similarly, [35] reported a moderate relationship (R^2 ranging between 0.56 and 0.65) for tree- and plot-level AGB estimates. Even in the absence of LiDAR, the results obtained in this study were promising (R^2 of 0.94 and an RMSE of 21.12 Mg/ha) and comparable to the results obtained in previous studies that employed both optical imagery and LiDAR (e.g., [88]).

By extracting both spectral and spatial information for AGB modeling, our results showed a reduction in AGB prediction uncertainties of the model that relies only on spectral features by ~50% (Figure 5 and Table S4 and Table 4). Using a random forest model to predict tropical forest carbon from LiDAR, ref. [91] also found that a model considering the spatial context performed best. However, the inclusion of the spatial context is not without challenges. The extraction of spatial features simultaneously with spectral features requires a neighborhood of pixels (in this case, 15 × 15 equivalent to ~20 ha). For such a window size (or larger), where high AGB pixels are found among low AGB pixels, less accurate prediction is expected. This also applies to edge pixels and areas transitioning into low-AGB areas (Figure 7c,d). From a flight planning perspective, future studies that employ a 3D-CNN model with airborne HSI should consider the issue of edge pixels to ensure that a sufficient area is covered outside of the area of interest to account for the planned neighborhood window size. Future studies may explore using different kernel sizes to better align with the spatial and spectral characteristics of the imaging data. Misaligned kernel sizes could lead to inefficient feature extraction, causing important patterns to be overlooked. Experimenting with kernel sizes tailored to the spatial and spectral resolutions of the data is usually recommended. In other words, future studies can employ separate kernel sizes for spatial dimensions (height and width) and the spectral dimension (depth) to capture relevant features more effectively. When resizing the spatial dimensions, proportional scaling must be ensured to preserve the original aspect ratio (e.g., resizing to 18 × 15 instead of 15 × 15).

The spatial autocorrelation unaccounted for during the training and validation of a model can result in an overly optimistic modeling performance [92]. In the benchmark data comparison, where the ACTO-1 model was applied to the ACTO-2 imagery, the best performing model had a decrease of 0.3 in the R-square values and an increase in RMSE of 35.83 Mg/ha (Section 3.3 and Figure S6). This drop can potentially be attributed to spatial autocorrelation affecting the model's generalization. Spatial autocorrelation is known to cause an overestimation of CNN model performance, owing to the potential proximity of the test set pixels to the training data [92]. Although our study relied on unseen datasets (test set) for accuracy assessment, the spatial proximity of some of these pixels may have caused spatial autocorrelation. Another factor that can lead to overestimation of the model performance in spatial–spectral hyperspectral feature extraction is information leakage in the testing sets [93–95]. Extraction of the patches and random splitting for training, validation, or testing can cause information leakage in the testing set [93,94]. Recent studies, such as [94], have proposed a novel, non-overlapping approach for sampling training and testing sets for hyperspectral classification problems. Future modeling studies should also explore this approach to improve model generalization.

The distribution of bias for each forest type's AGB model (Figure 10) illustrates that the greatest uncertainty in the model results is found in areas with the highest AGB (>280 mg/ha for the tropical forests and >160 mg/ha for the temperate forest). These are also the AGB classes with the fewest training samples (Figure 3). This illustrates the importance of large training datasets across the entire range of expected values [81,96]. Similar biases are also reported in the GAGB training dataset, where retrieval of high-carbon-stock forests with AGB > 250 Mg /ha have high uncertainty [60]. In addition, while not directly investigated here, canopy reflectance biomass saturation has been shown for densely vegetated regions [97], including in tropical forests, e.g., [98–100], and at higher latitudes [101–103].

As stated by [60], the GAGB data show similar trends in AGB to other datasets; however, they note large spatial divergences between datasets and, therefore, reiterate the ongoing uncertainty in global AGB and forest carbon. For example, within the latitude range of our tropical forest sites, GAGB was found to be similar to that reported by [104] but was up to 50% lower than that reported by [105]. It is for such reasons that our current study does not claim to model actual AGB as measured in the field, rather, we show the potential of ML algorithms, particularly the 3D-CNN, to exploit HSI in order to generate models with low RMSE if the training dataset is large. Also, temporal discrepancies between the AGB map (2010) and the HSI data (2013 for Costa Rica, 2022 for Canada) could introduce potential errors, due to forest dynamics (e.g., growth, disturbances, or deforestation). However, the low growth rates characteristic of mature forests suggest that biomass accumulation likely has a negligible impact over short timescales, reducing the potential for significant errors from growth [106]. For instance, as summarized in this study, the growth rates in mature forests like ACCVC is notably slow, with a mean difference between the reference and the predicted AGB equal to ~5 Mg/ha between 2010 and 2013 (i.e., average annual biomass accumulation rates in ACCVC range from 1 to 3 Mg ha^{-1} $year^{-1}$) (see Figure 10 and Table S3). This is because biomass accumulation is more influenced by existing tree diameter and height increases than by recruitment or turnover [106]. This suggests that discrepancies in timing are less likely to introduce substantial inaccuracies from growth-related changes in mature forests. Nonetheless, using a 2010 AGB map to train models with imagery from 2013 and 2022 remains a limitation. Future research could address this by incorporating temporally aligned calibration data, such as field measurements or more recent AGB maps, to improve model accuracy and account for any dynamics that do occur.

As stated by [53], additional work is necessary to determine whether the spectral expression of differences in forest carbon (of which AGB is a proxy) is driven by composition, diversity, or other characteristics, such as canopy structure. From the same HSI of MSB, [53] (2023a) found that forest composition was related to the spectral signatures of plots, however, the spectral diversity of the plot was not found to be significant. Importantly, the average reflectance spectrum of a plot was a stronger predictor of carbon. Our work follows up on this finding through an application of ML to spectra rather than metrics such as diversity.

5. Conclusions

Our study highlights the effectiveness of two novel approaches, as follows: (1) combining HSI and deep learning (3D-CNN) and (2) artificial neural networks and wavelet analysis for predicting AGB in both tropical and temperate forests. Specifically, our findings demonstrate that the 3D-CNN model outperforms approaches that rely on spectral features alone for AGB modeling, yielding the lowest RMSE in AGB estimation. This improvement is consistent across various tropical forest types and a temperate forest ecosystem, suggesting the potential of the 3D-CNN approach to reduce uncertainties in AGB estimates across different climate zones. These findings are very promising, showing the future prospect of using HSI to map forest AGB on a large spatial scale. Thus, the availability of large enough plot level training data will allow the development of 3D-CNN models that will generalize well for other forest types.

Supplementary Materials: The following supporting information can be downloaded at: https://www.mdpi.com/article/10.3390/f16030477/s1, Table S1: Sensor characteristics for the tropical forests (ACTO-1, ACTO-2, ACCVC, ACHAN, and ACOSA) and temperate forest (MSB) region of interest. The VNIR region was acquired with the CASI-1500 and the SWIR with the SASI-644 at the tropical sites and SASI-640 for the temperate forest. Table S2: Flight planning considerations for the tropical forests (ACTO-1, ACTO-2, ACCVC, ACHAN, and ACOSA) and temperate forest (MSB) region of interest. The VNIR region was acquired with the CASI-1500 and the SWIR with the SASI-644 at the tropical sites and SASI-640 for the temperate forest. Table S3: Tabulated results of the computed accuracy metrics for each conservation area in Costa Rica and MSB. AGB (reference) and AGB (predicted) values represent the average for the bin. Other than MSB (LiDAR), all reference data are from the GAGB map. Table S4: SNN model based on the mutual information feature selection (non-linear) technique, with comparisons across wavelet decomposition inputs and results ordered by RMSE (best to worst). Units for RMSE, MSE, and MAE are in Mg/ha. The average is based on 20 iterations. Figure S1: Processing workflow to generate atmospherically and geometrically corrected imagery (L2G). Intermediate processing levels include L1A (non-geocorrected radiance), L2A (non-geocorrected reflectance), and L1G (geocorrected radiance). Modules in steps 1 and 3 project the sensor manufacturer, whereas, in step 2, ATCOR-4 is commercial software. Figure S2: A map showing the distribution of the randomly selected polygons in red (100 m $\times$ 100 m plots) across the experimental site (ACTO-1). Figure S3: SNN architecture used for modeling AGB from the wavelet-transformed spectra. Figure S4: An RGB composite of the HSI showing portions of the ACTO-1 study site. The red boxes represent sample plots, with plot sizes equivalent to an area of 1 ha (100 m $\times$ 100 m) to be used as the input to the 3D-CNN. Figure S5. Architecture of the 3D-CNN used for AGB modeling, including the PCA preprocessing step (MNF and t-SNE were substituted for PCA in the model development). The red box represents a 15 $\times$ 15 patch extracted from the original image with dimensions of 190 pixels in height and 163 pixels in width. These patches represent localized regions of the image and are used for analysis without altering or shrinking the original image. For the t-SNE-based 3D-CNN, this architecture was modified, e.g., only one 3D convolution (3 $\times$ 3 $\times$ 1) was applied to the HSI, since, after dimensionality reduction with t-SNE, the output was 3 bands. Figure S6: Independent testing of (a) 3D-CNN and (b) SNN models using ~12,000 pixels from the ACTO-2 site with the models developed for ACTO-1. Reference values are from the GAGB map. The plot shows a 1:1 reference line (dashed) and a regression fit line (solid), demonstrating the model's performance and deviation from ideal predictions. Figure S7: Implementation of a 3D-CNN model based on MNF dimensionality reduction at the ACTO-1 site, using the corresponding AGB values from the reference GAGB map. The plot shows a 1:1 reference line (dashed) and a regression fit line (solid), demonstrating the model's performance and deviation from ideal predictions. Figure S8: Implementation of a 3D-CNN model based on t-SNE dimensionality reduction at the ACTO-1 site, using the corresponding AGB values from the reference GAGB map. The plot shows a 1:1 reference line (dashed) and a regression fit line (solid), demonstrating the model's performance and deviation from ideal predictions.

Author Contributions: Conceptualization, P.O.D., M.K. and J.P.A.-M.; methodology, P.O.D., M.K., S.M. and M.E.F.; validation, P.O.D. and S.M.; formal analysis, P.O.D.; resources, M.K. and J.P.A.-M.; data curation, P.O.D.; writing—original draft preparation, P.O.D.; writing—review and editing, P.O.D., M.K., S.M., M.E.F. and J.P.A.-M.; funding acquisition, M.K. and J.P.A.-M. All authors have read and agreed to the published version of the manuscript.

Funding: This research was funded by the Canadian Airborne Biodiversity Observatory (CABO), which was funded by a Discovery Frontiers grant from the Natural Sciences and Engineering Research Council of Canada (NSERC; grant number 509190-2017); the Mission Airborne Carbon-13 (MAC-13) project, which was funded by the Canadian Space Agency (FAST-AO; grant number 11STFAMG16); and the Department of Geography Rathlyn GIS Award. The APC was funded by the NSERC Discovery Grant (RGPIN-2022-05288).

Data Availability Statement: Data available upon request.

Acknowledgments: We thank Mark Vellend, Anna Leigh Crofts, and Sabine St-Jean from the Université de Sherbrooke, and Etienne Laliberté from Université de Montréal for their assistance with the Mont Saint Bruno field data acquisition and feedback on earlier versions of the manuscript. We further thank Nicolas Cadieux for assistance with the LiDAR data and Oliver Lucanus and Gary Elson for their assistance in manuscript edits.

Conflicts of Interest: The authors declare no conflict of interest.

References

1. Dar, J.A.; Subashree, K.; Bhat, N.A.; Sundarapandian, S.; Xu, M.; Saikia, P.; Kumar, A.; Kumar, A.; Khare, P.K.; Khan, M.L. Role of major forest biomes in climate change mitigation: An eco-biological perspective. In *Socio-Economic and Eco-Biological Dimensions in Resource Use and Conservation*; Springer International Publishing: New York, NY, USA, 2020; pp. 483–526. [CrossRef]
2. Sedjo, R.A. The carbon cycle and global forest ecosystem. *Water Air Soil Pollut.* **1993**, *70*, 295–307. [CrossRef]
3. Birdsey, R.; Angeles-Perez, G.; Kurz, W.A.; Lister, A.; Olguin, M.; Pan, Y.; Wayson, C.; Wilson, B.; Johnson, K. Approaches to monitoring changes in carbon stocks for REDD+. *Carbon Manag.* **2013**, *4*, 519–537. [CrossRef]
4. Danon, S.; Bettiati, D. Reducing Emissions from Deforestaton and Forest Degradation (REDD+)–what is behind the idea and what is the role of UN-REDD and Forest Carbon Partnership Facility (FCPF)? *South-East Eur. For.* **2012**, *2*, 95–99. [CrossRef]
5. Gizachew, B.; Solberg, S.; Næsset, E.; Gobakken, T.; Bollandsås, O.M.; Breidenbach, J.; Zahabu, E.; Mauya, E.W. Mapping and estimating the total living biomass and carbon in low-biomass woodlands using Landsat 8 CDR data. *Carbon Balance Manag.* **2016**, *11*, 13. [CrossRef] [PubMed]
6. Wulder, M.A.; Hermosilla, T.; White, J.C.; Bater, C.W.; Hobart, G.; Bronson, S.C. Development and implementation of a stand-level satellite-based forest inventory for Canada. *For. Int. J. For. Res.* **2024**, *97*, 546–563. [CrossRef]
7. Kurz, W.A.; Apps, M.J. Developing Canada's national forest carbon monitoring, accounting and reporting system to meet the reporting requirements of the kyoto protocol. *Mitig. Adapt. Strateg. Glob. Chang.* **2006**, *11*, 33–43. [CrossRef]
8. Chave Jr Andalo, C.; Brown, S.; Cairns, M.A.; Chambers, J.; Eamus, D.; Fölster, H.; Fromard, F.; Higuchi, N.; Kira, T. Tree allometry and improved estimation of carbon stocks and balance in tropical forests. *Oecologia* **2005**, *145*, 87–99. [CrossRef]
9. Ketterings, Q.M.; Coe, R.; van Noordwijk, M.; Palm, C.A. Reducing uncertainty in the use of allometric biomass equations for predicting above-ground tree biomass in mixed secondary forests. *For. Ecol. Manag.* **2001**, *146*, 199–209. [CrossRef]
10. Mohd Zaki, N.A.; Abd Latif, Z. Carbon sinks and tropical forest biomass estimation: A review on role of remote sensing in aboveground-biomass modelling. *Geocarto Int.* **2017**, *32*, 701–716. [CrossRef]
11. Torre, L. Biomass estimation using LiDAR data. *Int. J. Sustain. Energy Plan. Manag.* **2018**, *17*, 79–90. [CrossRef]
12. UNFCCC. Methodological guidance for activities relating to reducing emissions from deforestation and forest degradation and the role of conservation, sustainable management of forests and enhancement of forest carbon stocks in developing countries. In *Proceedings of the Conference of the Parties, Copenhagen, Denmark, 7–19 December 2009; Decision 4/CP.15.*; United Nations Framework Convention on Climate Change: Bonn, Germany, 2009. Available online: https://unfccc.int/resource/docs/2009/cop15/eng/11a01.pdf (accessed on 20 February 2023).
13. Li, Y.; Li, M.; Li, C.; Liu, Z. Forest aboveground biomass estimation using Landsat 8 and Sentinel-1A data with machine learning algorithms. *Sci. Rep.* **2020**, *10*, 9952. [CrossRef] [PubMed]

14. Pizaña, J.M.G.; Hernández, J.M.N.; Romero, N.C. Remote sensing-based biomass estimation. *Environ. Appl. Remote Sens.* **2016**, *10*, 9952. [CrossRef]
15. Tian, L.; Wu, X.; Tao, Y.; Li, M.; Qian, C.; Liao, L.; Fu, W. Review of remote sensing-based methods for forest aboveground biomass estimation: Progress, challenges, and prospects. *Forests* **2023**, *14*, 1086. [CrossRef]
16. Zhang, X.; Li, L.; Liu, Y.; Wu, Y.; Tang, J.; Xu, W.; Wang, L.; Ou, G. Improving the accuracy of forest aboveground biomass using Landsat 8 OLI images by quantile regression neural network for Pinus densata forests in southwestern China. *Front. For. Glob. Chang.* **2023**, *6*, 1162291. [CrossRef]
17. Bauer, L.; Huth, A.; Bogdanowski, A.; Müller, M.; Fischer, R. Edge effects in amazon forests: Integrating remote sensing and modeling to assess changes in biomass and productivity. *Remote Sens.* **2024**, *16*, 501. [CrossRef]
18. Cao, L.D.; Pan, J.J.; Li, R.J.; Li, J.L.; Li, Z.F. Integrating airborne LiDAR and optical data to estimate forest aboveground biomass in arid and semi-arid regions of China. *Remote Sens.* **2018**, *10*, 532. [CrossRef]
19. Clark, M.L.; Roberts, D.A.; Ewel, J.J.; Clark, D.B. Estimation of tropical rain forest aboveground biomass with small-footprint LiDAR and hyperspectral sensors. *Remote Sens. Environ.* **2011**, *115*, 2931–2942. [CrossRef]
20. Fassnacht, F.E.; Hartig, F.; Latifi, H.; Berger, C.; Hernandez, J.; Corvalan, P.; Koch, B. Importance of sample size, data type and prediction method for remote sensing-based estimations of aboveground forest biomass. *Remote Sens. Environ.* **2014**, *154*, 102–114. [CrossRef]
21. Shu, Q.; Xi, L.; Wang, K.; Xie, F.; Pang, Y.; Song, H. Optimization of samples for remote sensing estimation of forest aboveground biomass at the regional scale. *Remote Sens.* **2022**, *14*, 4187. [CrossRef]
22. Chinembiri, T.S.; Mutanga, O.; Dube, T. A multi-source data approach to carbon stock prediction using bayesian hierarchical geostatistical models in plantation forest ecosystems. *GIScience Remote Sens.* **2024**, *61*, 2303868. [CrossRef]
23. Jacon, A.D.; Galvao, L.S.; Dalagnol, R.; dos Santos, J.R. Aboveground biomass estimates over Brazilian savannas using hyperspectral metrics and machine learning models: Experiences with Hyperion/EO-1. *GIScience Remote Sens.* **2021**, *58*, 1112–1129. [CrossRef]
24. Naik, P.; Dalponte, M.; Bruzzone, L. Automated machine learning driven stacked ensemble modeling for forest aboveground biomass prediction using multitemporal sentinel-2 data. *IEEE J. Sel. Top. Appl. Earth Obs. Remote Sens.* **2022**, *16*, 3442–3454. [CrossRef]
25. Arroyo-Mora, J.P.; Kalacska, M.; Inamdar, D.; Soffer, R.; Lucanus, O.; Gorman, J.; Naprstek, T.; Schaaf, E.S.; Ifimov, G.; Elmer, K. Implementation of a UAV–hyperspectral pushbroom imager for ecological monitoring. *Drones* **2019**, *3*, 12. [CrossRef]
26. Huber, S.; Kneubühler, M.; Psomas, A.; Itten, K.; Zimmermann, N.E. Estimating foliar biochemistry from hyperspectral data in mixed forest canopy. *For. Ecol. Manag.* **2008**, *256*, 491–501. [CrossRef]
27. Schlerf, M.; Atzberger, C.; Hill, J. Remote sensing of forest biophysical variables using HyMap imaging spectrometer data. *Remote Sens. Environ.* **2005**, *95*, 177–194. [CrossRef]
28. Kalacska, M.; Arroyo-Mora, J.P.; Soffer, R.; Leblanc, G. Quality control assessment of the mission airborne carbon 13 (mac-13) hyperspectral imagery from Costa Rica. *Can. J. Remote Sens.* **2016**, *42*, 85–105. [CrossRef]
29. Shen, X.; Cao, L.; Liu, K.; She, G.; Ruan, H. Aboveground biomass estimation in a subtropical forest using airborne hyperspectral data. In Proceedings of the 2016 4th International Workshop on Earth Observation and Remote Sensing Applications (EORSA), Guangzhou, China, 4–6 July 2016; IEEE: New York, NY, USA; pp. 391–394. [CrossRef]
30. Shao, Z.; Zhang, L.; Wang, L. Stacked Sparse Autoencoder Modeling Using the Synergy of Airborne LiDAR and Satellite Optical and SAR Data to Map Forest Above-Ground Biomass. *IEEE J. Sel. Top. Appl. Earth Obs. Remote Sens.* **2017**, *10*, 5569–5582. [CrossRef]
31. Tamiminia, H.; Salehi, B.; Mahdianpari, M.; Beier, C.M.; Johnson, L.; Phoenix, D.B.; Mahoney, M. Decision tree-based machine learning models for above-ground biomass estimation using multi-source remote sensing data and object-based image analysis. *Geocarto Int.* **2022**, *37*, 12763–12791. [CrossRef]
32. Migolet, P.; Goïta, K.; Pambo, A.F.K.; Mambimba, A.N. Estimation of the total dry aboveground biomass in the tropical forests of Congo Basin using optical, LiDAR, and radar data. *GISci. Remote Sens.* **2022**, *59*, 431–460. [CrossRef]
33. Wang, L.; Ju, Y.; Ji, Y.; Marino, A.; Zhang, W.; Jing, Q. Estimation of Forest Above-Ground Biomass in the Study Area of Greater Khingan Ecological Station with Integration of Airborne LiDAR, Landsat 8 OLI, and Hyperspectral Remote Sensing Data. *Forests* **2024**, *15*, 1861. [CrossRef]
34. Gao, L.; Chai, G.; Zhang, X. Above-ground biomass estimation of plantation with different tree species using airborne LiDAR and hyperspectral data. *Remote Sens.* **2022**, *14*, 2568. [CrossRef]
35. Brovkina, O.; Novotny, J.; Cienciala, E.; Zemek, F.; Russ, R. Mapping forest aboveground biomass using airborne hyperspectral and LiDAR data in the mountainous conditions of Central Europe. *Ecol. Eng.* **2017**, *100*, 219–230. [CrossRef]
36. Güner, Ş.T.; Diamantopoulou, M.J.; Poudel, K.P.; Çömez, A.; Özçelik, R. Employing artificial neural network for effective biomass prediction: An alternative approach. *Comput. Electron. Agric.* **2022**, *192*, 106596. [CrossRef]

37. Kumari, K.; Kumar, S. Machine learning based modeling for forest aboveground biomass retrieval. In Proceedings of the 2023 International Conference on Machine Intelligence for GeoAnalytics and Remote Sensing (MIGARS), Hyderabad, India, 27–29 January 2023; pp. 1–4. [CrossRef]
38. Luo, S.; Wang, C.; Xi, X.; Pan, F.; Peng, D.; Zou, J.; Nie, S.; Qin, H. Fusion of airborne LiDAR data and hyperspectral imagery for aboveground and belowground forest biomass estimation. *Ecol. Indic.* **2017**, *73*, 378–387. [CrossRef]
39. Singh, B.; Verma, A.K.; Tiwari, K.; Joshi, R. Above ground tree biomass modeling using machine learning algorithms in western Terai Sal Forest of Nepal. *Heliyon* **2023**, *9*, e21485. [CrossRef] [PubMed]
40. Thapa, B.; Lovell, S.; Wilson, J. Remote sensing and machine learning applications for aboveground biomass estimation in agroforestry systems: A review. *Agroforest. Syst.* **2023**, *97*, 1097–1111. [CrossRef]
41. Naik, P.; Dalponte, M.; Bruzzone, L. Prediction of Forest Aboveground Biomass Using Multitemporal Multispectral Remote Sensing Data. *Remote Sens.* **2021**, *13*, 1282. [CrossRef]
42. Ghasemi, N.; Sahebi, M.R.; Mohammadzadeh, A. Biomass estimation of a temperate deciduous forest using wavelet analysis. *IEEE Trans. Geosci. Remote Sens.* **2012**, *51*, 765–776. [CrossRef]
43. Jia, S.; Jiang, S.; Lin, Z.; Li, N.; Xu, M.; Yu, S. A survey: Deep learning for hyperspectral image classification with few labeled samples. *Neurocomputing* **2021**, *448*, 179–204. [CrossRef]
44. Paoletti, M.E.; Haut, J.M.; Plaza, J.; Plaza, A. Deep learning classifiers for hyperspectral imaging: A review. *ISPRS J. Photogramm. Remote Sens.* **2019**, *158*, 279–317. [CrossRef]
45. Ranjan, P.; Girdhar, A. A comprehensive systematic review of deep learning methods for hyperspectral images classification. *Int. J. Remote Sens.* **2022**, *43*, 6221–6306. [CrossRef]
46. Li, Q.; Wen, Y.; Zheng, J.; Zhang, Y.; Fu, H. HyUniDA: Breaking Label Set Constraints for Universal Domain Adaptation in Cross-Scene Hyperspectral Image Classification. *IEEE Trans. Geosci. Remote Sens.* **2024**, *62*, 5518415. [CrossRef]
47. Yin, J.; Qi, C.; Chen, Q.; Qu, J. Spatial-spectral network for hyperspectral image classification: A 3-D CNN and Bi-LSTM framework. *Remote Sens.* **2021**, *13*, 2353. [CrossRef]
48. Krizhevsky, A.; Sutskever, I.; Hinton, G.E. Imagenet classification with deep convolutional neural networks. In *Advances in Neural Information Processing Systems*; MIT Press: Cambridge, MA, USA, 2012; Volume 25, Available online: https://proceedings.neurips.cc/paper_files/paper/2012/file/c399862d3b9d6b76c8436e924a68c45b-Paper.pdf (accessed on 11 February 2023).
49. Krizhevsky, A.; Sutskever, I.; Hinton, G.E. ImageNet classification with deep convolutional neural networks. *Commun. ACM* **2017**, *60*, 84–90. [CrossRef]
50. Tappayuthpijarn, K.; Vindevogel, B.S. High-accuracy machine learning models to estimate above ground biomass over tropical closed evergreen forest areas from satellite data. *IOP Conf. Ser. Earth Environ. Sci.* **2022**, *1006*, 012001. [CrossRef]
51. Holdridge, L.R. *Life Zone Ecology*; Tropical Science Center: San Jose, Costa Rica, 1967.
52. Svob, S.; Arroyo-Mora, J.P.; Kalacska, M. A wood density and aboveground biomass variability assessment using pre-felling inventory data in Costa Rica. *Carbon Balance Manag.* **2014**, *9*, 9. [CrossRef]
53. Wallis, C.I.B.; Crofts, A.L.; Inamdar, D.; Arroyo-Mora, J.P.; Kalacska, M.; Laliberte, E.; Vellend, M. Remotely sensed carbon content: The role of tree composition and tree diversity. *Remote Sens. Environ.* **2023**, *284*, 113333. [CrossRef]
54. Inamdar, D.; Kalacska, M.; Arroyo-Mora, J.P.; Leblanc, G. The directly-georeferenced hyperspectral point cloud: Preserving the integrity of hyperspectral imaging data. *Front. Remote Sens.* **2021**, *2*, 675323. [CrossRef]
55. Soffer, R.J.; Ifimov, G.; Arroyo-Mora, J.P.; Kalacska, M. Validation of airborne hyperspectral imagery from laboratory panel characterization to image quality assessment: Implications for an arctic peatland surrogate simulation site. *Can. J. Remote Sens.* **2019**, *45*, 476–508. [CrossRef]
56. Osei Darko, P.; Kalacska, M.; Arroyo-Mora, J.P.; Fagan, M.E. Spectral complexity of hyperspectral images: A new approach for mangrove classification. *Remote Sens.* **2021**, *13*, 2604. [CrossRef]
57. Schläpfer, D.; Richter, R.; Feingersh, T. Operational BRDF effects correction for wide-field-of-view optical scanners (BREFCOR). *IEEE Trans. Geosci. Remote Sens.* **2014**, *53*, 1855–1864. [CrossRef]
58. Schläpfer, D.; Richter, R. Evaluation of brefcor BRDF effects correction for HYSPEX, CASI, and APEX imaging spectroscopy data. In Proceedings of the 2014 6th Workshop on Hyperspectral Image and Signal Processing: Evolution in Remote Sensing (WHISPERS), Lausanne, Switzerland, 24–27 June 2014; IEEE: New York, NY, USA, 2014.
59. Inamdar, D.; Kalacska, M.; Darko, P.O.; Arroyo-Mora, J.P.; Leblanc, G. Spatial response resampling (SR2): Accounting for the spatial point spread function in hyperspectral image resampling. *MethodsX* **2023**, *10*, 101998. [CrossRef]
60. Santoro, M.; Cartus, O.; Carvalhais, N.; Rozendaal, D.; Avitabile, V.; Araza, A.; De Bruin, S.; Herold, M.; Quegan, S.; Rodríguez-Veiga, P. The global forest above-ground biomass pool for 2010 estimated from high-resolution satellite observations. *Earth Syst. Sci. Data* **2021**, *13*, 3927–3950. [CrossRef]
61. Quegan, S.; Rauste, Y.; Bouvet, A.; Carreiras, J.; Cartus, O.; Carvalhais, N.; LeToan, T.; Mermoz, S.; Santoro, M. D6–Global Biomass Map: Algorithm Theoretical Basis Document. 2017. Available online: https://globbiomass.org/wp-content/uploads/DOC/Deliverables/D6_D7/GlobBiomass_D6_7_Global_ATBD_v3.pdf (accessed on 1 February 2023).

62. Rozendaal, D.M.A.; Santoro, M.; Schepaschenko, D.; Avitabile, V.; Herold, M. DUE GlobBiomass (D17) Validation Report. In D17 Validation Report. 2017. Available online: https://www.dropbox.com/home?checklist=close&preview=GlobBiomass_D_17_Validation_Report_V06.pdf (accessed on 1 February 2023).
63. GéoMont Acquisition of the 2008 MTQ LiDAR Survey in Montérégie. 2008. Available online: https://www.geomont.qc.ca/projets/fiche/?id_projet=70 (accessed on 1 January 2024).
64. Boudreau, J.; Nelson, R.F.; Margolis, H.A.; Beaudoin, A.; Guindon, L.; Kimes, D.S. Regional aboveground forest biomass using airborne and spaceborne LiDAR in Québec. *Remote Sens. Environ.* **2008**, *112*, 3876–3890. [CrossRef]
65. Svob, S.; Arroyo-Mora, J.P.; Kalacska, M. The development of a forestry geodatabase for natural forest management plans in Costa Rica. *For. Ecol. Manag.* **2014**, *327*, 240–250. [CrossRef]
66. Brown, S.; Estimating Biomass and Biomass Change of Tropical Forests: A Primer. Food Agriculture Org. 1997. Available online: https://www.fao.org/docrep/w4095e/w4095e00.HTM (accessed on 1 February 2023).
67. Crofts, A.L.; St-Jean, S.; Vellend, M. Canadian Airborne Biodiversity Observatory's Forest Inventory Field Survey Protocol v.2. Protocols.io. 2022. Available online: https://doi.org/10.17504/protocols.io.q26g7rn23vwz/v2 (accessed on 10 February 2023).
68. Ung, C.-H.; Bernier, P.; Guo, X.-J. Canadian national biomass equations: New parameter estimates that include British Columbia data. *Can. J. For. Res.* **2008**, *38*, 1123–1132. [CrossRef]
69. Paré, D.; Bernier, P.; Lafleur, B.; Titus, B.D.; Thiffault, E.; Maynard, D.G.; Guo, X. Estimating stand-scale biomass, nutrient contents, and associated uncertainties for tree species of Canadian forests. *Can. J. For. Res.* **2013**, *43*, 599–608. [CrossRef]
70. Rioul, O.; Vetterli, M. Wavelets and signal processing. *IEEE Signal Process. Mag.* **1991**, *8*, 14–38. [CrossRef]
71. Hubbard, B.B. *The World According to Wavelets: The Story of a Mathematical Technique in the Making, Second Edition*, 2nd ed.; A K Peters/CRC Press: New York, NY, USA, 1998. [CrossRef]
72. Mallat, S.G. A theory for multiresolution signal decomposition: The wavelet representation. *IEEE Trans. Pattern Anal. Mach. Intell.* **1989**, *11*, 674–693. [CrossRef]
73. Bruce, L.M.; Koger, C.H.; Jiang, L. Dimensionality reduction of hyperspectral data using discrete wavelet transform feature extraction. *IEEE Trans. Geosci. Remote Sens.* **2002**, *40*, 2331–2338. [CrossRef]
74. Zhou, X.; Zhao, C.; Sun, J.; Cao, Y.; Yao, K.; Xu, M. A deep learning method for predicting lead content in oilseed rape leaves using fluorescence hyperspectral imaging. *Food Chem.* **2022**, *409*, 135251. [CrossRef] [PubMed]
75. Cheng, T.; Rivard, B.; Sánchez-Azofeifa, A.G.; Féret, J.-B.; Jacquemoud, S.; Ustin, S.L. Deriving Leaf Mass per Area (LMA) from foliar reflectance across a variety of plant species using continuous wavelet analysis. *ISPRS J. Photogramm. Remote Sens.* **2014**, *87*, 28–38. [CrossRef]
76. Fu, Y.; Jia, X.; Huang, W.; Wang, J. A comparative analysis of mutual information-based feature selection for hyperspectral image classification. In Proceedings of the IEEE China Summit & International Conference on Signal and Information Processing (ChinaSIP), Xi'an, China, 9–13 July 2014; pp. 148–152. [CrossRef]
77. Schreiber, L.V.; Atkinson Amorim, J.G.; Guimarães, L.; Motta Matos, D.; Maciel da Costa, C.; Parraga, A. Above-ground biomass wheat estimation: Deep learning with UAV-based RGB images. *Appl. Artif. Intell.* **2022**, *36*, 2055392. [CrossRef]
78. MATLAB. Classify Hyperspectral Images Using Deep Learning. 2023. Available online: https://www.mathworks.com/help/images/hyperspectral-image-classification-using-deep-learning.html (accessed on 10 February 2023).
79. Araza, A.; De Bruin, S.; Herold, M.; Quegan, S.; Labriere, N.; Rodriguez-Veiga, P.; Avitabile, V.; Santoro, M.; Mitchard, E.T.; Ryan, C.M. A comprehensive framework for assessing the accuracy and uncertainty of global above-ground biomass maps. *Remote Sens. Environ.* **2022**, *272*, 112917. [CrossRef]
80. Li, Y.; Li, C.; Li, M.; Liu, Z. Influence of variable selection and forest type on forest aboveground biomass estimation using machine learning algorithms. *Forests* **2019**, *10*, 1073. [CrossRef]
81. Dong, J.; Kaufmann, R.K.; Myneni, R.B.; Tucker, C.J.; Kauppi, P.E.; Liski, J.; Buermann, W.; Alexeyev, V.; Hughes, M.K. Remote sensing estimates of boreal and temperate forest woody biomass: Carbon pools, sources, and sinks. *Remote Sens. Environ.* **2003**, *84*, 393–410. [CrossRef]
82. Lu, D. The potential and challenge of remote sensing-based biomass estimation. *Int. J. Remote Sens.* **2006**, *27*, 1297–1328. [CrossRef]
83. Mauya, E.W.; Hansen, E.H.; Gobakken, T.; Bollandsås, O.M.; Malimbwi, R.E.; Næsset, E. Effects of field plot size on prediction accuracy of aboveground biomass in airborne laser scanning-assisted inventories in tropical rain forests of Tanzania. *Carbon Balance Manag.* **2015**, *10*, 10. [CrossRef]
84. Wheeler, C.E.; Mitchard, E.T.A.; Nalasco Reyes, H.E.; Iñiguez Herrera, G.; Marquez Rubio, J.I.; Carstairs, H.; Williams, M. A new field protocol for monitoring forest degradation. *Front. For. Glob. Chang.* **2021**, *4*, 655280. [CrossRef]
85. Anand, R.; Veni, S.; Aravinth, J. Robust classification technique for hyperspectral images based on 3d-discrete wavelet transform. *Remote Sens.* **2021**, *13*, 1255. [CrossRef]
86. Pu, R.; Gong, P. Wavelet transform applied to EO-1 hyperspectral data for forest LAI and crown closure mapping. *Remote Sens. Environ.* **2004**, *91*, 212–224. [CrossRef]

87. Yao, X.; Si, H.; Cheng, T.; Jia, M.; Chen, Q.; Tian, Y.; Zhu, Y.; Cao, W.; Chen, C.; Cai, J.; et al. Hyperspectral estimation of canopy leaf biomass phenotype per ground area using a continuous wavelet analysis in wheat. *Front. Plant Sci.* **2018**, *9*, 1360. [CrossRef] [PubMed]
88. de Almeida, C.T.; Galvão, L.S.; Aragão, L.E.d.O.C.e.; Ometto, J.P.H.B.; Jacon, A.D.; Pereira, F.R.d.S.; Sato, L.Y.; Lopes, A.P.; Graça, P.M.L.d.A.; Silva, C.V.d.J.; et al. Combining LiDAR and hyperspectral data for aboveground biomass modelling in the Brazilian Amazon using different regression algorithms. *Remote Sens. Environ.* **2019**, *232*, 111323. [CrossRef]
89. Laurin, G.V.; Chen, Q.; Lindsell, J.A.; Coomes, D.A.; Del Frate, F.; Guerriero, L.; Pirotti, F.; Valentini, R. Above ground biomass estimation in an African tropical forest with LiDAR and hyperspectral data. *ISPRS J. Photogramm. Remote Sens.* **2014**, *89*, 49–58. [CrossRef]
90. Zhang, Y.; Liu, J. Estimating forest aboveground biomass using temporal features extracted from multiple satellite data products and ensemble machine learning algorithm. *Geocarto Int.* **2023**, *38*, 2153930. [CrossRef]
91. Mascaro, J.; Asner, G.P.; Knapp, D.E.; Kennedy-Bowdoin, T.; Martin, R.E.; Anderson, C.; Higgins, M.; Chadwick, K.D. A tale of two "forests": Random forest machine learning aids tropical forest carbon mapping. *PLoS ONE* **2014**, *9*, e85993. [CrossRef]
92. Kattenborn, T.; Schiefer, F.; Frey, J.; Feilhauer, H.; Mahecha, M.D.; Dormann, C.F. Spatially autocorrelated training and validation samples inflate performance assessment of convolutional neural networks. *ISPRS Open J. Photogramm. Remote Sens.* **2022**, *5*, 100018. [CrossRef]
93. Liang, J.; Zhou, J.; Qian, Y.; Wen, L.; Bai, X.; Gao, Y. On the sampling strategy for evaluation of spectral-spatial methods in hyperspectral image classification. *IEEE Trans. Geosci. Remote Sens.* **2017**, *55*, 862–880. [CrossRef]
94. Shi, Y.; Yin, Y.; Song, X.; Cui, H.; Zhu, D.; Song, H. A nonoverlapping sampling approach with peak data utilization for hyperspectral classification. *IEEE Geosci. Remote Sens. Lett.* **2024**, *21*, 5502805. [CrossRef]
95. Zou, L.; Zhu, X.; Wu, C.; Liu, Y.; Qu, L. Spectral–spatial exploration for hyperspectral image classification via the fusion of fully convolutional networks. *IEEE J. Sel. Top. Appl. Earth Obs. Remote Sens.* **2020**, *13*, 659–674. [CrossRef]
96. López-Serrano, P.M.; Cárdenas Domínguez, J.L.; Corral-Rivas, J.J.; Jiménez, E.; López-Sánchez, C.A.; Vega-Nieva, D.J. Modeling of aboveground biomass with Landsat 8 OLI and machine learning in temperate forests. *Forests* **2020**, *11*, 11. [CrossRef]
97. Mutanga, O.; Masenyama, A.; Sibanda, M. Spectral saturation in the remote sensing of high-density vegetation traits: A systematic review of progress, challenges, and prospects. *ISPRS J. Photogramm. Remote Sens.* **2023**, *198*, 297–309. [CrossRef]
98. Kalácska, M.; Sánchez-Azofeifa, G.A.; Rivard, B.; Calvo-Alvarado, J.C.; Journet, A.R.P.; Arroyo-Mora, J.P.; Ortiz-Ortiz, D. Leaf area index measurements in a tropical moist forest: A case study from Costa Rica. *Remote Sens. Environ.* **2004**, *91*, 134–152. [CrossRef]
99. Mitchard, E.T.A.; Saatchi, S.S.; White, L.J.T.; Abernethy, K.A.; Jeffery, K.J.; Lewis, S.L.; Collins, M.; Lefsky, M.A.; Leal, M.E.; Woodhouse, I.H.; et al. Mapping tropical forest biomass with radar and spaceborne LiDAR in Lopé National Park, Gabon: Overcoming problems of high biomass and persistent cloud. *Biogeosciences* **2012**, *9*, 179–191. [CrossRef]
100. Steininger, M.K. Satellite estimation of tropical secondary forest above-ground biomass: Data from Brazil and Bolivia. *Int. J. Remote Sens.* **2000**, *21*, 1139–1157. [CrossRef]
101. Liao, Z.; Liu, X.; van Dijk, A.; Yue, C.; He, B. Continuous woody vegetation biomass estimation based on temporal modeling of Landsat data. *Int. J. Appl. Earth Obs. Geoinf.* **2022**, *110*, 102811. [CrossRef]
102. Wu, Y.; Ou, G.; Lu, T.; Huang, T.; Zhang, X.; Liu, Z.; Yu, Z.; Guo, B.; Wang, E.; Feng, Z.; et al. Improving aboveground biomass estimation in lowland tropical forests across aspect and age stratification: A case study in Xishuangbanna. *Remote Sens.* **2024**, *16*, 1276. [CrossRef]
103. Zhao, P.; Lu, D.; Wang, G.; Wu, C.; Huang, Y.; Yu, S. Examining spectral reflectance saturation in landsat imagery and corresponding solutions to improve forest aboveground biomass estimation. *Remote Sens.* **2016**, *8*, 469. [CrossRef]
104. Saatchi, S.S.; Harris, N.L.; Brown, S.; Lefsky, M.; Mitchard, E.T.A.; Salas, W.; Zutta, B.R.; Buermann, W.; Lewis, S.L.; Hagen, S.; et al. Benchmark map of forest carbon stocks in tropical regions across three continents. *Proc. Natl. Acad. Sci. USA* **2011**, *108*, 9899–9904. [CrossRef]
105. Baccini, A.; Goetz, S.J.; Walker, W.S.; Laporte, N.T.; Sun, M.; Sulla-Menashe, D.; Hackler, J.; Beck, P.S.A.; Dubayah, R.; Friedl, M.A.; et al. Estimated carbon dioxide emissions from tropical deforestation improved by carbon-density maps. *Nat. Clim. Chang.* **2012**, *2*, 182–185. [CrossRef]
106. Chazdon, R.L.; Letcher, S.G.; Van Breugel, M.; Martínez-Ramos, M.; Bongers, F.; Finegan, B. Rates of change in tree communities of secondary Neotropical forests following major disturbances. *Philos. Trans. R. Soc. B Biol. Sci.* **2007**, *362*, 273–289. [CrossRef] [PubMed]

forests

Article

Estimation of Aboveground Biomass of *Picea schrenkiana* Forests Considering Vertical Zonality and Stand Age

Guohui Zhang [1,2,†], Donghua Chen [1,2,†], Hu Li [1,3,*], Minmin Pei [4], Qihang Zhen [5], Jian Zheng [6], Haiping Zhao [1], Yingmei Hu [1] and Jingwei Fan [7]

1 College of Geography and Tourism, Anhui Normal University, Wuhu 241002, China; 2221011553@ahnu.edu.cn (G.Z.); chendonghua@chzu.edu.cn (D.C.); 2221011555@ahnu.edu.cn (H.Z.); hym1999@ahnu.edu.cn (Y.H.)
2 College of Computer and Information Engineering, Chuzhou University, Chuzhou 239000, China
3 Resources, Environment and Geographic Information Engineering Technology Research Center of Anhui Province, Wuhu 241002, China
4 College of Computer and Information, Anhui Normal University, Wuhu 241002, China; pei@ahnu.edu.cn
5 College of Computer Science and Technology, Anhui University, Hefei 230601, China; e22301247@stu.ahu.edu.cn
6 College of Geography and Tourism, Xinjiang Normal University, Urumqi 830054, China; 107622022210579@stu.xjnu.edu.cn
7 Earth Observation System and Data Center, China National Space Administration, Beijing 100101, China; fanjingwei@cpeos.org.cn
* Correspondence: lihu2881@ahnu.edu.cn
† These authors contributed equally to this work and should be considered co-first authors.

Abstract: The aboveground biomass (AGB) of forests reflects the productivity and carbon-storage capacity of the forest ecosystem. Although AGB estimation techniques have become increasingly sophisticated, the relationships between AGB, spatial distribution, and growth stages still require further exploration. In this study, the *Picea schrenkiana* (*Picea schrenkiana var. tianschanica*) forest area in the Kashi River Basin of the Ili River Valley in the western Tianshan Mountains was selected as the research area. Based on forest resources inventory data, Gaofen-1 (GF-1), Gaofen-6 (GF-6), Gaofen-3 (GF-3) Polarimetric Synthetic Aperture Radar (PolSAR), and DEM data, we classified the *Picea schrenkiana* forests in the study area into three cases: the Whole Forest without vertical zonation and stand age, Vertical Zonality Classification without considering stand age, and Stand-Age Classification without considering vertical zonality. Then, for each case, we used eXtreme Gradient Boosting (XGBoost), Back Propagation Neural Network (BPNN), and Residual Networks (ResNet), respectively, to estimate the AGB of forests in the study area. The results show that: (1) The integration of multi-source remote-sensing data and the ResNet can effectively improve the remote-sensing estimation accuracy of the AGB of *Picea schrenkiana*. (2) Furthermore, classification by vertical zonality and stand ages can reduce the problems of low-value overestimation and high-value underestimation to a certain extent.

Keywords: aboveground biomass; vertical zonality; stand age; Gaofen satellites; *Picea schrenkiana*

1. Introduction

Forest biomass stands as a pivotal indicator of the productive capacity of forest ecosystems, consistently serving as a crucial evaluation factor in assessments of forest carbon budgets [1]. The biogeochemical cycling characteristics of Xinjiang exert a profound influence on the evolution of terrestrial ecosystems in the Central Asian region, shaping regional climate patterns and impacting greenhouse gas source and sink totals [2]. At the heart of the Central Asian mountain range, the Tianshan Mountains are home to vast stands of *Picea schrenkiana* forests, which represent the most significant terrestrial ecosystems in temperate arid regions. *Picea schrenkiana*, as the dominant tree species in the mountain forests of the Tianshan Mountains, plays a vital role in water conservation, soil retention, and maintaining the ecological environment of the mountains, occupying an extremely important ecological and geographical position. By conducting research on the biomass of the mountain ecosystems in the Tianshan Mountains, with a particular focus on *Picea schrenkiana* forests, we will lay a foundation for studies on the carbon cycle of mountain forest ecosystems in Central Asia. Furthermore, this research can provide valuable insights into the evolution of terrestrial ecosystems, regional climate dynamics, and greenhouse gas emissions and sequestration in the Central Asian region, thereby possessing significant scientific importance.

Biomass is categorized into aboveground and underground components. Given the difficulties in gathering underground biomass data, researchers mainly center their studies on aboveground biomass (AGB) [3]. Traditional measurement methods, while accurate, are labor-intensive and time-consuming, making them impractical for large-scale forest biomass monitoring [4]. The advent of remote-sensing technology addresses this limitation [5]. In the realm of remote-sensing-based forest biomass estimation, scholars from both domestic and international backgrounds have extensively utilized optical remote-sensing data since the last century, achieving significant advancements [6,7]. For instance, Chen et al. pioneered the use of HJ-1 satellite data to monitor *Picea schrenkiana* forest AGB in the western Tianshan Mountains, revealing spatial heterogeneity and spatiotemporal differentiation patterns of AGB and productivity in this region [8]. However, optical remote sensing has inherent limitations, particularly its weak spectral penetrability, which restricts its ability to capture vertical vegetation information beneath the canopy [9]. To overcome these limitations, radar data, with its longer wavelengths, has been increasingly adopted. Radar can penetrate vegetation layers and provide more detailed stand structure and stand factor information, making it a valuable complement to optical data [10]. Synthetic Aperture Radar (SAR), as an advanced active remote-sensing technology, operates continuously under all weather conditions, further enhancing its utility [11]. Studies have demonstrated the effectiveness of SAR in AGB estimation. For example, Cartus et al. utilized multi-frequency radar backscatter observations to estimate tropical forest AGB, highlighting the structural discriminative capacity of SAR data [12]. Wei et al. explored the potential of GF-3 polarization decomposition components for estimating artificial forest canopy AGB, finding that multiple polarization components exhibit high sensitivity to AGB variations [13]. Multi-source remote-sensing data can fully capitalize on the complementary aspects of information derived from various data sources. By skillfully integrating remote-sensing data from diverse sensors collected at different times and with varying resolutions, the benefits of remote sensing can be maximized. Researchers such as Zhang et al. [14] and Forkuor et al. [15] have developed forest AGB estimation models using optical data and SAR data. Wang et al., in their study, utilized GF-6 and GF-3 dual-polarization data to estimate the AGB of natural forest land in Gongliu County, Xinjiang. The study revealed that the integration of optical and SAR data can remarkably enhance the accuracy of AGB estimation [16]. In their assessment of Yichun City's AGB, Liu et al. employed both optical and SAR data, concluding that AGB estimation models specifically designed for different forest types are more precise and stable compared to generalized approaches [17]. These findings underscore the importance of integrating multi-source data and considering forest-specific characteristics in AGB estimation.

As a key geographical factor, topography exerts a profound influence on forest ecosystems [18]. Variations in elevation, slope, and aspect create unique geomorphological units, driving the vertical stratification of environmental factors such as thermal conditions, precipitation patterns, and solar radiation intensity. These changes result in marked differences in the vertical distribution of climate conditions, soil properties, light intensity, and other environmental factors [19,20]. These differences, in turn, have profound effects on forest AGB. Studies have shown that the trends of AGB with elevation vary significantly across different regions and ecosystems. For example, Wang et al., using a 30-m resolution AGB dataset of the Tibetan Plateau, found that grassland AGB values exhibit a monotonically increasing trend below 4800 m [21]. Wu et al. found different biomass at different elevations by studying Qilian Mountain *Picea schrenkiana*, in which the growth rate of AGB was highest at low elevations [22]. Maza et al. focusing on the elevation gradient of AGB in the Andean-Amazonian forests, found a negative correlation between AGB and elevation [23]. These differences may stem from the interaction between elevation-induced climatic changes, such as temperature lapse rates and orographic precipitation, and differences in vegetation types. In addition to the influence of elevation, researchers have also focused on the impact of topographic factors on the accuracy of AGB estimation. For instance, Chen et al. found that the introduction of a digital elevation model (DEM) improved model accuracy by 13.5% [24], while Ye et al. demonstrated that models incorporating aspects effectively mitigate the overestimation of low values and underestimation of high values, further enhancing model precision [25]. In recent years, the application of high-resolution satellite data has further strengthened the advantages of topographic factors. Han et al., using GF-1 and Sentinel-1, found that the integration of multi-source remote-sensing data and topographic factors significantly improves AGB estimation accuracy in complex terrain regions [26]. Forest stand ages are also an important factor affecting forest AGB [27]. Huang et al., focusing on Chinese fir plantations, found that the spatial structure factors affecting biomass accumulation vary significantly with stand age and proposed corresponding management measures [28]. Lee et al. identified forest age as a key variable regulating AGB in alpine-subalpine forests, revealing that older stands exhibit higher biomass [29]. Wu et al. demonstrated that models integrating both aspect and stand age outperform other models, highlighting the importance of considering multiple factors, such as topography and stand age, in AGB estimation [30]. These findings emphasize the complexity of AGB estimation and the importance of integrating diverse variables for improved accuracy.

This study concentrates on the forest area situated within the Kashi River Basin of the Ili Valley, nestled in the western Tianshan Mountains, as its research area. The *Picea schrenkiana* (*Picea schrenkiana var. tianschanica*) in this region are categorized into three types: the Whole Forest without vertical zonation and stand age (hereinafter referred to as the whole forest), Vertical Zonality Classification without considering stand age (hereinafter referred to as vertical zonality), and Stand-Age Classification without considering vertical zonality (hereinafter referred to as stand age). Due to insufficient sample size when simultaneously considering stand age and vertical zonality, which cannot meet the basic requirements for statistical analysis, this scenario was not included in the study. For these three classification cases, the performance of three feature combinations, namely single optical data, single radar data, and opto-radar multi-source remote-sensing data, is comprehensively investigated in three models: XGBoost, BPNN, and ResNet. Moreover, a comparative analysis of the estimation accuracy is conducted. Through this multi-dimensional and multi-method integrated analysis, the study aims to (1) improve the accuracy of remote-sensing estimation for AGB of *Picea schrenkiana* forests in the western Tianshan Mountains of Xinjiang and (2) expand the application scope and depth of domestic high-resolution satellites in forest resource monitoring. The novelty of this study lies in its integration of multi-source remote-sensing data and the incorporation of key variables such as vertical zonality and stand age, proposing a more refined and accurate method for forest biomass estimation. Furthermore, the findings not only enhance the understanding of biomass distribution patterns in the forest ecosystem of the western Tianshan Mountains but also provide valuable methodological references and practical support for other regions globally with complex terrain and diverse forest structures.

2. Materials and Methods

2.1. Study Area

Nilka County (81°85′ E to 84°58′ E, 43°25′ N to 44°17′ N) is in the northwestern part of Xinjiang, China. It lies within the western hinterland of the Tianshan Mountains and within the Kashi River Basin, which is part of the Ili Valley. This area experiences a continental climate within the northern temperate zone, characterized by an average annual temperature of 6.8 °C and a total annual precipitation of 406.9 mm, with the majority of rainfall occurring from April to July. The region distinctly exhibits mountain climate characteristics. The terrain features a slope from the northeast to the southwest. The forest area has a simple composition of tree species, mainly natural *Picea schrenkiana*, a small number of *Populus* spp. and *Betula* spp., and a few species of understory vegetation. Sub-compartments, as the smallest spatial units for forest resource surveys, are divided based on differences in ecological attributes such as stand origin, age class, and site type. In this study, the sub-compartments of *Picea schrenkiana* forests in the Tianshan Mountains were used as the basic units. Pure *Picea schrenkiana* forests, i.e., sub-compartments with *Picea schrenkiana* as the tree species composition, were selected as the study area. The method of stratified sampling was adopted, and the *Picea schrenkiana* forests in the study area were divided according to two schemes: different vertical zonations and different stand ages. Finally, 540 sub-compartments were sampled from the forest resources inventory database of the Nilke Forest Farm as research samples. The average size of the sub-compartments is 18.36 hm^2. The soil in this area is rich in humus and highly fertile. The most prevalent and expansive soil type in the forest area is mountain gray-cinnamon soil, which is ideally suited for *Picea schrenkiana* growth. Figure 1 illustrates the schematic diagram of the study area.

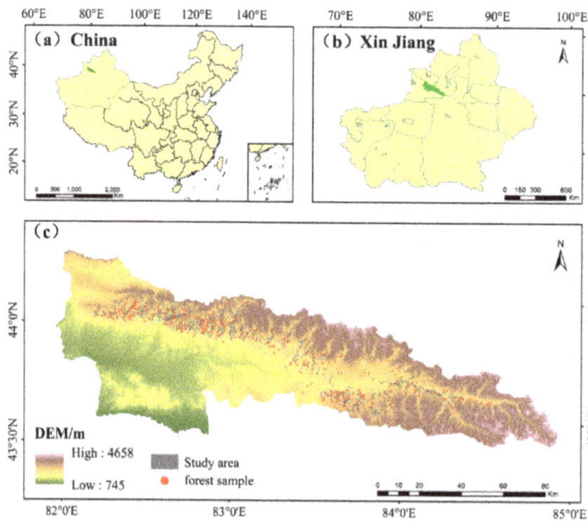

Figure 1. Geographic location map of the study area. (**a**) Position of the study area within China. (**b**) Position of the study area within Xinjiang Province. (**c**) Elevation map of the study area, along with the forest sample locations.

2.2. Data Processing

2.2.1. GF-1 PMS and GF-6 PMS Data

All the remote-sensing data used in this paper are sourced from the National Remote-Sensing Data and Application Service Platform (https://www.cpeos.org.cn/, accessed on 12 April 2024). GF-1 and GF-6 are primarily used to acquire optical remote-sensing image data of the Earth's surface. They are equipped with two distinct sensors. The high-resolution camera (PMS) is capable of capturing panchromatic black-and-white images at a resolution of 2 m and multispectral color images at a resolution of 8 m. The multispectral sensor covers four bands: blue, green, red, and near-infrared (NIR), which are utilized to obtain basic spectral information of ground objects and play a crucial role in various fields, including land resource surveying and ecological environment monitoring [31]. The 16 m multispectral medium-resolution wide-swath camera (WFV) boasts a large imaging swath width, enabling the acquisition of large-area ground images in a short period. We performed optical data preprocessing in ENVI software 5.6 (Exelis Visual Information Solutions, Inc., Boulder, CO, USA). To maintain consistency with the resolution of SAR data, no fusion operations were performed on the optical data, and only multispectral data were utilized.

2.2.2. GF-3 PolSAR Data

The GF-3 satellite, China's first independently developed C-band synthetic aperture radar (SAR) satellite, features 12 imaging modes and provides rich polarization data. The full-polarization image data can simultaneously capture the transmission and reception information of horizontal polarization (H) and vertical polarization (V), encompassing four polarization modes: horizontal transmit-horizontal receive (HH), horizontal transmit-vertical receive (HV), vertical transmit-horizontal receive (VH), and vertical transmit-vertical receive (VV). In this study, the 20 pieces of SAR data utilized are all Quad-pol stripmap (QPSI) images with a resolution of 8 m. The preprocessing of radar data encompasses radiometric calibration, multi-look processing, filtering, and geocoding [32]. After undergoing radiometric calibration, the radar data can more accurately reflect the echo characteristics of ground objects. Multi-look processing and filtering can enhance the visual quality of the image, making the geometric features of the image more akin to the actual situation on the ground while also reducing speckle noise to a certain extent [33]. Since the complex image acquired by the SAR sensor is a slant range image, geocoding is necessary to convert the SAR data from the slant range coordinate system to the geographic coordinate system [34]. The preprocessing of GF-3 data was conducted using PIE-SAR 6.3, a software developed by Piesat Information Technology Co., Ltd. in Beijing, China.

2.2.3. Auxiliary Data

Seven pieces of ASTER GDEM V3 30 m data were downloaded from the geospatial data cloud platform (https://www.gscloud.cn/, accessed on 20 April 2024). The terrain factors, including slope, aspect, and elevation, redistribute the energy of solar radiation, thereby influencing vegetation growth and the accumulation of forest AGB. Use ArcGIS 10.8 (Environmental Systems Research Institute, Inc., Redlands, CA, USA) to extract terrain factors such as elevation, slope, and aspect. Based on the classification of forest vertical zones in the Yili area by Zhang et al. [35], the forest vertical zones in the study area are categorized according to elevation. The classification criteria are outlined in Table 1. Figure 2 is the topographic feature map of the study area.

Table 1. Classification criteria for vertical zonality.

Vertical Zonality of *Picea schrenkiana* Forest	DEM
Below the middle and low mountain forest-steppe belt	Below 1500 m
Middle and low mountain forest-steppe belt	1500–1700 m
Middle mountain forest-meadow belt	1700–2250 m
Upper middle mountain forest-meadow belt	2250–2550 m
Subalpine open-forest belt	2550–2700 m
Above the subalpine open-forest belt	Above 2700 m

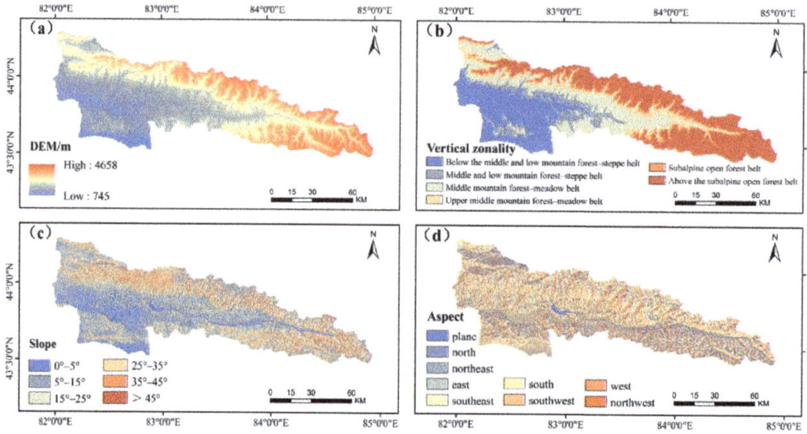

Figure 2. Topographic feature map of the study area. (**a**) altitude map of the study area. (**b**) vertical zonality division map of the study area. (**c**) slope division map of the study area. (**d**) aspect division map of the study area.

2.2.4. Resource Data

The forest resources inventory data for management encompasses fields such as sample plot number, average diameter at breast height (DBH), stand age, crown density, soil type, soil layer thickness, and standing stock volume per hectare. Projection coordinate transformation is applied to these resource data to ensure alignment with the projection coordinates of remote-sensing images. The geographic coordinate system is WGS-1984, and the projected coordinate system is Universal Transverse Mercator (UTM), with the projection zone number being UTM Zone 44N. The sub-compartments of the forest farm, categorized by different altitudes and forest ages, are delineated, and only the fields relevant to this study are retained. By referring to the regression equation of *Picea schrenkiana* forest biomass and stock volume established by Fang et al. [36], the *Picea schrenkiana* biomass is estimated using these resource data. The formula is as follows.

$$B = 0.4642V + 47.499, \tag{1}$$

Note: Biomass (B) is measured in $t{\cdot}hm^{-2}$, stem volume (V) is measured in $m^3{\cdot}hm^{-2}$.

According to the forestry industry standards of the People's Republic of China, "Regulations for age-class and age-group division of main tree species", with 20 years as the stand-age interval, Tianshan *Picea schrenkiana* forests are divided into young forest, middle-aged forest, near-mature forest, mature forest, and over-mature forest according to their different age stages. The classification criteria are presented in Table 2, and the Stand-Age Classification map of the *Picea schrenkiana* forest is shown in Figure 3. In the study area, natural forests account for the vast majority. The age class of a sample plot is determined by the average age of the trees within the plot.

Table 2. Classification criteria for stand age of *Picea schrenkiana* forests.

Stand Age of *Picea schrenkiana* Forest	Age (Unit: Year)
Young forest	Below 60
Middle-aged forest	61–100
Near-mature forest	101–120
Mature forest	121–160
Over-mature forest	Above 161

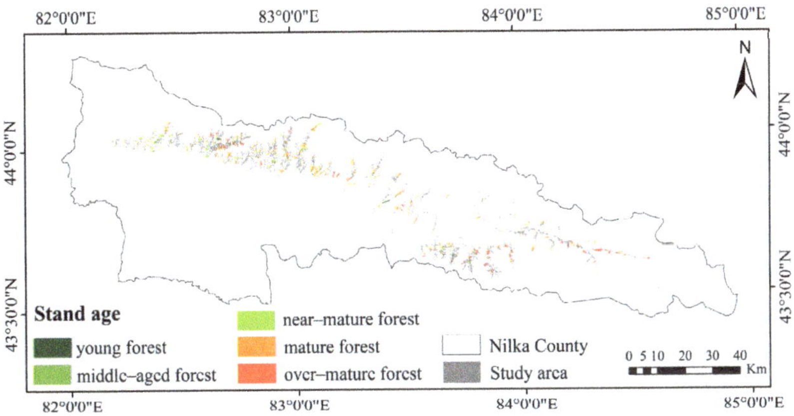

Figure 3. Classification map of stand ages of *Picea schrenkiana* forests.

Picea schrenkiana forests in the western Tianshan Mountains are mainly distributed in three key vertical zones: middle mountain forest-meadow belt, upper middle mountain forest-meadow belt, and subalpine open-forest belt. The combined conditions of climate and soil in these three vertical zones engender a highly suitable environment conducive to the growth of *Picea schrenkiana* and cultivate an ideal ecological niche tailored to it. However, the distribution of *Picea schrenkiana* forest is very scanty in the middle and low mountain forest-steppe belt and below. This is mainly because the precipitation in this area is insufficient to meet the water demand of *Picea schrenkiana* growth [37]. More importantly, human activities have caused some interference with the growth of *Picea schrenkiana*, making it difficult for *Picea schrenkiana* forests to form and develop in this area. In the area above the subalpine open-forest belt, the extreme climatic conditions exceed the ecological adaptation range of *Picea schrenkiana*, preventing *Picea schrenkiana* forest from establishing itself here. Overall, small classes of *Picea schrenkiana* in these two unsuitable areas account for only 0.05% of the total.

From the perspective of stand age, *Picea schrenkiana* occupies a large proportion in the near-mature forest, mature forest, and over-mature forest stages. Specifically, the *Picea schrenkiana* population in these stages is more stable in the ecosystem and has stronger adaptability to the environment. In contrast, the number of *Picea schrenkiana* sub-compartments in young and middle-aged forests only accounts for 8.61% of the total, which provides limited reference for this study. This is not only because the number of individuals in the whole *Picea schrenkiana* forest ecosystem is small but also because it is difficult to reflect the overall ecological characteristics and biomass distribution of *Picea schrenkiana* forest. More importantly, young and middle-aged forests are still in the dynamic stage of growth and development, with unstable ecological characteristics and large data fluctuations, which impedes the construction of accurate models and in-depth analysis and research.

Based on the previous analysis, this study centers on three main vertical zones, namely the middle mountain forest-meadow belt, the upper middle mountain forest-meadow belt, and the subalpine open-forest belt, as well as three growth stages: near-mature forest, mature forest, and over-mature forest. Through the modeling and analysis of these key areas and stages, the aim is to accurately reveal the internal relationship between the distribution of *Picea schrenkiana* forest, vertical zonality, and stand age and provide a solid theoretical basis for the ecological protection and scientific management of *Picea schrenkiana* forest in the West Tianshan Mountains.

2.3. Feature Extraction

2.3.1. Optical Image Features

(1) The Surface Reflectance

The original bands of remote-sensing images contain abundant object information and are the cornerstone of object recognition. In optical remote-sensing data, different bands correspond to different reflection characteristics of objects. The spectral information is highly correlated with vegetation parameters. The band designs of GF-1 and GF-6 are identical, although there are slight differences in the specific band ranges: the blue band (0.45~0.52 μm for both), the green band (0.52~0.59 μm for GF-1 and 0.52~0.60 μm for GF-6), the red band (0.63~0.69 μm for both), and the near-infrared band (0.77~0.89 μm for GF-1 and 0.76~0.90 μm for GF-6). Although there are slight differences, these discrepancies can be effectively mitigated through appropriate data processing. Therefore, this study combines the data from both satellites to form continuous and consistent optical satellite imagery, from which the spectral values of these four bands are extracted.

(2) Vegetation Index

Analyzing and comparing only individual bands or multiple single bands is insufficient to comprehensively understand the complexity of vegetation remote sensing. As a widely distributed object type on the Earth's surface, vegetation demonstrates complex and diverse spectral characteristics. To more effectively utilize satellite remote-sensing data to characterize vegetation status based on the spectral properties of vegetation, various linear or nonlinear combinations of satellite bands are performed, such as addition, subtraction, multiplication, and division. These operations are used to extract a total of eight vegetation indices, including the normalized difference vegetation index (NDVI), green normalized difference vegetation index (GNDVI), ratio vegetation index (RVI), enhanced vegetation index (EVI), difference vegetation index (DVI), infrared percentage vegetation index (IPVI), soil adjusted vegetation index (SAVI), and normalized difference mountain vegetation index (NVDMVI) [38,39]. The formula for calculating the vegetation index is shown in Table 3.

Table 3. Commonly used vegetation index.

Source	Type	Variable	Equations
Optical data	Vegetation Index	NDVI	$NDVI = \frac{(NIR-R)}{(NIR+R)}$
		RVI	$RVI = \frac{NIR}{R}$
		GNDVI	$GNDVI = \frac{NIR-G}{NIR+G}$
		SAVI	$SAVI = (\frac{NIR-R}{NIR+R+L}) \times (1+L)$
		DVI	$DVI = NIR - R$
		IPVI	$IPVI = \frac{NIR}{NIR+R}$

Table 3. *Cont.*

Source	Type	Variable	Equations
Optical data	Vegetation Index	EVI	$EVI = 2.5 \times \frac{(NIR-R)}{(NIR+6R-7.5B+1)}$
		NDMVI	$NDMVI = \frac{(NIR-R)+(R_{mim}-NIR_{mim})}{(NIR+R)+(R_{mim}+NIR_{mim})}$

Note: In the formula, NIR denotes the reflectance value of the near-infrared band, R denotes the reflectance value of the red band, B denotes the reflectance value of the blue wave segment, and G denotes the reflectance value of the green band. Furthermore, L is the soil adjustment coefficient, which is 0.5 in this study. In NDMVI, the minimum reflectance values of the red band and near-infrared band of the image in the study area were extracted and assigned to R_{mim} and NIR_{mim}, respectively.

(3) Texture Features

Texture features contain and reflect the spatial variation of the grayscale of the image and can better reflect the real structure of ground objects. In areas with more complex stand structures, they have a positive effect on AGB estimation [40]. Many scholars have confirmed that the inclusion of spectral texture features in the model significantly improves estimation accuracy [41]. After performing principal component analysis on the optical data in this study, it was found that the contribution rate of the first principal component is 97.5%. Based on the gray-level co-occurrence matrix (GLCM), eight texture features were extracted from six windows (3 × 3, 5 × 5, 7 × 7, 9 × 9, 11 × 11, 13 × 13) of the first principal component, including mean (MEAN), variance (VAR), homogeneity (HOM), contrast (CON), dissimilarity (DIS), entropy (ENT), second moment (ASM), and correlation (COR). The texture feature formula is shown in Table 4.

Table 4. Texture feature calculation formulas based on the gray-level co-occurrence matrix.

Source	Type	Variable	Equations
Optical data	GLCM Texture	Mean (MEAN)	$MEAN = \sum_{i,j=0}^{N-1} ip(i,j)$
		Variance (VAR)	$VAR = \sum_{i,j=0}^{N-1} p(i,j)(i-\mu_i)^2$
		Homogeneity (HOM)	$HOM = \sum_{i,j=0}^{N-1} \frac{p(i,j)}{1+(i-j)^2}$
		Contrast (CON)	$CON = \sum_{i,j=0}^{N-1} p(i,j)(i-j)^2$
		Dissimilarity (DIS)	$DIS = \sum_{i,j=0}^{N-1} p(i,j)\lvert i-j\rvert$
		Entropy (ENT)	$ENT = \sum_{i,j=0}^{N-1} p(i,j)(-\log[p(i,j)])$
		Second moment (ASM)	$ASM = \sum_{i,j=0}^{N-1} p(i,j)^2$
		Correlation (COR)	$COR = \sum_{i,j=0}^{N-1} \frac{(i-u_i)(j-u_j)}{\varphi_i\varphi_j} p(i,j)$

Note: In the formula, i and j denote the number of rows and columns of the matrix, respectively. N denotes the number of pixels. $p(i,j)$ represents the probability of the simultaneous occurrence of two gray values corresponding to row i and column j. μ_i and μ_j represent the mean values of rows and columns, respectively. φ_i and φ_j denote the variance of rows and columns.

2.3.2. Radar Image Features

(1) Backscatter Coefficient

The backscatter coefficient of radar data is a complex physical quantity, representing the result of the comprehensive influence of multiple factors within the forest stand. In the forest environment, factors such as ground roughness, vegetation coverage, and vegetation water content are intertwined and jointly determine the magnitude of the backscatter coefficient [42]. In this study, four polarized backscatter coefficients, HH, HV, VH, and VV, are extracted as the characteristic variables of the model.

(2) Polarization Decomposition

The forest represents an incoherent target and exhibits a distributed characteristic with a universal time-varying effect [43]. Based on PIE-SAR 6.3 software, this study aims to extract the four incoherent polarization decomposition parameters (the Freeman decomposition, the Pauli decomposition, the H/A/Alpha decomposition, the Yamaguchi decomposition) as well as the one coherent polarization decomposition parameter (the Krogager decomposition) in order to deeply explore the forest feature information in radar data [32]. The related parameters of polarization decomposition are shown in Table 5.

Table 5. Related parameters of polarization decomposition.

Source	Type	Variable	Description
SAR data	Polarization decomposition	Freeman decomposition	Double-bounce scattering (Dbl), Volume scattering (Vol), Surface scattering (Odd)
		Pauli decomposition	Double-bounce scattering (Dbl), Volume scattering (Vol), Surface scattering (Odd)
		H/A/Alpha decomposition	Entropy, Anisotropy, Alpha, Lambda
		Yamaguchi decomposition	Double-bounce scattering (Dbl), Volume scattering (Vol), Surface scattering (Odd), Helix scattering (Hlx)
		Krogager decomposition	Spherical scattering (KS), Dihedral scattering (KD), Helicoid angles scattering (KH)

(3) Radar Vegetation Index

The radar vegetation index is a parameter derived from eigenvector decomposition. As vegetation density increases, the radar vegetation index will change accordingly, providing important reference data for the investigation and management of forest resources [44]. The radar vegetation index, utilizing the Freeman-Durden decomposition, takes into account the proportion of the three scattering mechanism components: dihedral scattering (F_d), surface scattering (F_s), and volume scattering (F_v). The radar vegetation index incorporates this information related to vegetation scattering by employing a specific algorithm, thereby enabling it to quantitatively describe the density of vegetation. The formula is as follows.

$$Freeman\_RVI = \frac{F_v}{F_v + F_d + F_s}, \quad (2)$$

2.4. Model Introduction

The measured data and the factors, after having undergone feature optimization, under three combination forms of single optical data, single SAR data, and multi-source remote-sensing data combining optical with SAR are inputted into the eXtreme Gradient Boosting (XGBoost), Back Propagation Neural Network (BPNN), and Residual Network (ResNet) models, respectively, to estimate the AGB of *Picea schrenkiana* forests across three classification criteria: the whole forest, different vertical zonality, and different stand ages. In the model construction phase, Python 3.7 is selected as the development language, and the powerful PyCharm 3.8.3 editor is used for code writing. To ensure the reliability and generalization ability of the model, 30% of the data are randomly selected as the validation set to evaluate the performance of the model. During the model training process, through continuous attempts at different parameter combinations, a *Picea schrenkiana* forest biomass inversion model with the highest accuracy is finally established.

2.4.1. XGBoost

XGBoost is a powerful machine-learning algorithm. It demonstrates superior performance in both classification and regression tasks within the domain of weakly supervised learning in machine learning. The training process is optimized by introducing an innovative sparse-aware algorithm for sparse data processing and a weighted quantile sketch for approximate tree learning [45]. The XGBoost model aims to prevent overfitting and, at the same time, reduce computational cost by keeping predictions at optimal computational efficiency through simplification and regularization.

Suppose a dataset $\mathcal{D} = (x_i, y_i)(|\mathcal{D}| = n, x_i \in R^m, y_i \in R)$, where n is the number of samples, m is the feature dimension of each sample, and the additive model is defined as:

$$\begin{gathered} \hat{y}_i^{(0)} = 0 \\ \hat{y}_i^{(1)} = f_1(x_i) = \hat{y}_i^{(0)} + f_1(x_i) \\ \hat{y}_i^{(2)} = f_1(x_i) + f_2(x_i) = \hat{y}_i^{(1)} + f_2(x_i), \\ \cdots \\ \hat{y}_i^{(k)} = \Sigma_{k=1}^{K} f_k(x_i) = \hat{y}_i^{(t-1)} + f_t(x_i) \end{gathered} \tag{3}$$

The algorithm model of XGBoost can be expressed as:

$$\hat{y}_i = \phi(x_i) = \Sigma_{k=1}^{K} f_k(x_i), f_k \in \mathcal{F}, \tag{4}$$

Here, $\mathcal{F} = f(x) = w_{q(x)}(q : R^m \to T, w \in R^T)$ represents the sample space of regression trees (typically CART trees are used). The function q maps each sample to a leaf node index, where T denotes the number of leaf nodes in each tree and w represents the weights of the leaf nodes. Each f_k corresponds to an independent tree defined by q (tree structure) and w (leaf node weights).

2.4.2. BPNN

The BPNN is one of the currently commonly used neural networks. It calculates the error through forward propagation and realizes the training of the neural network by backpropagating the error gradient. The structure consists of three components: the input layer, the hidden layer, and the output layer [46]. Increasing the number of neurons in the hidden layer can enhance the training accuracy of the BP neural network. If the number of neurons in the hidden layer is insufficient, the network may obtain too little information to solve problems effectively; if the number is too large, not only will the training time increase, but more importantly, an overfitting problem may arise if there are too many hidden layer nodes, resulting in an increase in test error and a decrease in generalization ability. The model framework is shown in Figure 4.

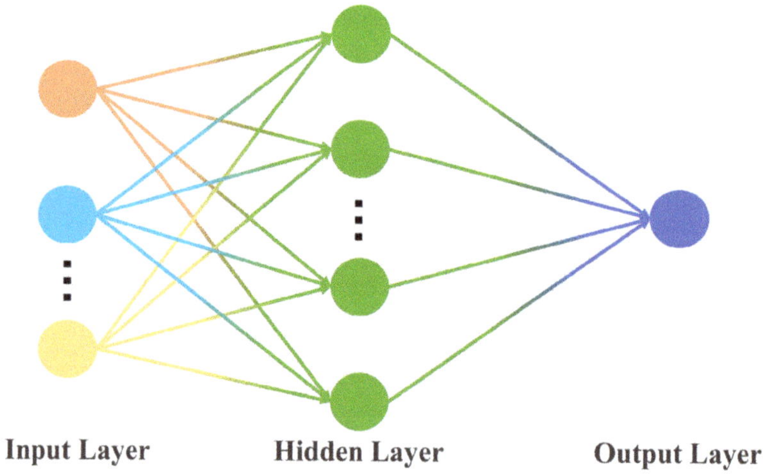

Figure 4. The framework of the Back Propagation Neural Network model.

2.4.3. ResNet

In traditional deep CNNs, as the number of network layers increases, gradient disappearance (the gradient value gradually diminishes to zero) or explosion (the gradient value skyrockets) occurs in the backpropagation process, making it difficult to train the network. Residual connections enable gradients to propagate more effectively in the network by directly passing the input signal [47]. During backpropagation, the gradient can be directly passed back through the shortcut connection without passing through all the convolutional layers, thereby reducing the risk of gradient disappearance or explosion. The model framework is shown in Figure 5.

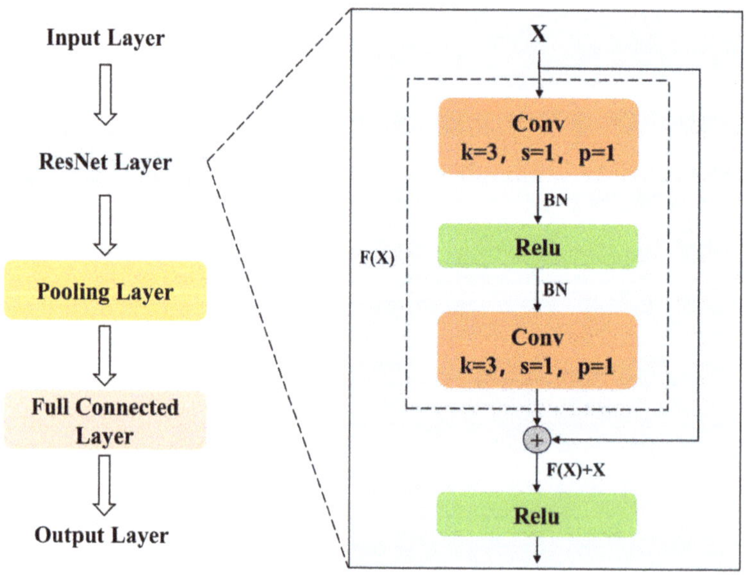

Figure 5. The framework of the Residual Network model. k represents the convolution kernel, s represents the stride, and p represents the padding.

2.5. Accuracy Verification

A total of 30% of the data are randomly selected as the test set to evaluate the model's applicability. The coefficient of determination (R^2) and the root mean square error (RMSE) are employed as evaluation metrics to assess the accuracy of each model result. R^2 is utilized to measure the goodness of fit of the model to the data and to explain the proportion of variance in the target variable. The value range is from 0 to 1. $R^2 = 1$ indicates that the model perfectly fits the data. RMSE is an index used for evaluating regression models and is used to measure the deviation between the model's predicted value and the true value.

$$R^2 = 1 - \frac{\sum\limits_{i=1}^{n} (y_i - \hat{y}_i)^2}{\sum\limits_{i=1}^{n} (y_i - \overline{y}_i)^2} \quad (5)$$

$$R_{\text{mse}} = \sqrt{\frac{\sum\limits_{i=1}^{n} (y_i - \text{y}_i)^2}{n}}, \quad (6)$$

Types (5) and (6): y_i represents the actual observed value, $\hat{y}_i$ represents the predicted value, $\overline{y}_i$ represents the mean of the actual observations, and n represents the number of samples.

3. Results

3.1. Determination of Characteristic Factors

The selection of modeling factors plays a crucial role in determining the accuracy of the model. If numerous modeling factors are introduced arbitrarily, many of them may have little or no correlation with AGB. This excessive number of factors not only increases the computational burden but also prolongs the model's training duration. To ensure the reliability of the model, prior to the modeling process, the normality of the data was first examined using Q-Q plots in the SPSS data analysis software (IBM SPSS Statistics v26, IBM Corp., Armonk, NY, USA), a widely used tool for statistical analysis in various research fields. After confirming the data's normality, the Pearson correlation coefficient was employed to examine the correlation between characteristic factors and AGB. Based on the results of this analysis, factors that were significantly associated with AGB were carefully selected. This approach helps in identifying the most relevant factors, thereby enhancing the model's accuracy and efficiency.

The correlation coefficients between different vertical zonality and characteristic factors from various data sources are presented in Table 6. When categorized by vertical zonality, Band3, DVI, HH polarization, HV polarization, Freema_Rvi, and SLOPE, all exhibit notably high correlation coefficients. In the middle mountain forest-meadow belt, MEAN_3 shows the strongest correlation with a coefficient of 0.432. Subsequently, Band3 and HV polarization have correlation coefficients of −0.372 and 0.363, respectively. The correlation coefficient between Band3 and the upper middle mountain forest-meadow belt is −0.453. In this belt, the correlations with MEAN_3 and Band2 are 0.504 and −0.473, respectively. In SAR, the highest correlation coefficients of HH polarization and HV polarization with the upper middle mountain forest-meadow belt are −0.378 and −0.344, respectively. The correlation coefficient between the vegetation index DVI and the subalpine open-forest belt is −0.374. Moreover, in the subalpine open-forest belt, the correlation of SAR data is higher than that of optical data, and the correlation coefficients of HH polarization and HV polarization are the highest, being 0.406 and 0.383, respectively.

Table 6. Correlation between factors and AGB in different vertical zonality.

	Middle Mountain Forest-Meadow Belt		Upper Middle Mountain Forest-Meadow Belt		Subalpine Open-Forest Belt	
Optical data	Band3	−0.372 **	Band2	−0.473 **	Band3	0.336 **
	Band2	−0.345 **	Band3	−0.453 **	Band4	−0.321 **
	MEAN_3	0.432 **	MEAN_3	0.504 **	Band1	0.291 *
	COR_5	0.217 **	COR_5	0.184 **	DVI	−0.374 **
	DVI	−0.251 **	DVI	−0.353 **		
			GNDVI	−0.106 **		
SAR data	HV	0.363 **	HH	−0.378 **	HH	0.406 **
	VH	0.339 **	HV	−0.344 **	HV	0.383 **
	Pauli_Vol	0.353 **	Freeman_Vol	−0.342 **	Pauli_Vol	0.351 **
	Freeman_Rvi	0.338 **	Pauli_Vol	−0.337 **		
			Freeman_Rvi	0.135 **		
Topographic Factor			SLOPE	0.327 **		

Note: * indicates significant correlation at the 0.05 level (two-tailed). ** indicates significant correlation at the 0.01 level (two-tailed). MEAN_3 represents the mean value in a 3 × 3 window. COR_5 represents the correlation in a 3 × 3 window.

The correlation coefficients of different stand ages and characteristic factors of different data sources are shown in Table 7. In near-mature forests, MEAN_3 and Band2 have the highest correlation, with correlation coefficients of 0.568 and −0.571, respectively. Second, VH polarization, HV polarization, and Pauli_Odd in SAR data have correlation coefficients of −0.424, −0.413, and −0.403, respectively. Among vegetation indices, the correlation coefficients of RVI, DVI, and NDVI are 0.346, 0.340, and 0.312, respectively. In mature forests, MEAN_5, Band3, and Band2 have the highest correlation, which is 0.515, −0.500, and −0.492, respectively. In SAR data, the correlation coefficients of HH, VH, and Freeman_Rvi are −0.431, −0.358, and 0.266, respectively. In over-mature forests, VH polarization has the highest correlation, with a correlation coefficient of −0.423. Second, Band3, DVI, and Freeman_Vol have correlation coefficients of −0.412, 0.399, and −0.390, respectively. Among topographic factors, SLOPE and DEM have high correlations with all three stand ages. The highest value of SLOPE appears in mature forests, with a correlation coefficient of 0.427.

Table 7. Correlation between factors and AGB in different stand ages.

	Near-Mature Forest		Mature Forest		Over-Mature Forest	
Optical data	Band2	−0.571 **	Band3	−0.500 **	Band3	−0.412 **
	MEAN_3	0.568 **	Band2	−0.492 **	Band2	−0.322 **
	COR_11	0.369 **	MEAN_5	0.515 **	DVI	0.399 **
	RVI	0.346 **	COR_5	0.194 **		
	DVI	0.340 **	COR_3	−0.143 **		
	NDVI	0.312 **	DVI	−0.233 **		
SAR data	VH	−0.424 **	HH	−0.431 **	VH	−0.423 **
	HV	−0.413 **	VH	−0.358 **	Freeman_Vol	−0.390 **
	Pauli_Odd	−0.403 **	Freeman_Rvi	0.266 **	Freeman_Rvi	−0.273 **
	Freeman_Vol	−0.397 **				
	Yamaguchi_Odd	−0.369 **				
Topographic Factor	SLOPE	0.325 **	SLOPE	0.427 **	DEM	0.250 **
	DEM	−0.178 **				

Note: ** indicates significant correlation at the 0.01 level (two-tailed). MEAN_3 represents the mean value in a 3 × 3 window. COR_3 represents the contrast in a 3 × 3 window. MEAN_5 represents the mean value in a 5 × 5 window. COR_5 represents the correlation in a 5 × 5 window. COR_11 represents the correlation in an 11 × 11 window.

3.2. Estimation Results of Different Vertical Zonality

Based on the in-depth correlation analysis in the early stage, this study divides the data sources into single optical data (Optical data + Topographic Factor), single radar data (SAR data + Topographic Factor), and multi-source remote-sensing data (Optical data + SAR data + Topographic Factor). The aim is to thoroughly investigate the specific impact of various data sources on the accuracy of the *Picea schrenkiana* forest biomass estimation model under different classification methods.

The accuracy of different models under different vertical zonality and different data sources is shown in Table 8. In the upper middle mountain forest-meadow belt, when only optical data are used, the R^2 of the ResNet is 0.74, which is much higher than the R^2 of the XGBoost of 0.57 and the R^2 of the BPNN of 0.66. Due to the lesser number of input values in the subalpine open-forest belt, the highest inversion accuracy combination is multi-source remote-sensing data plus ResNet, with R^2 = 0.69 and RMSE = 12.63 t·hm^{-2}. The lowest accuracy appears in the estimation using a single data source with XGBoost, where R^2 = 0.51 and RMSE = 24.56 t·hm^{-2}. It can be seen that the performance of the ResNet in combinations involving three data sources outperforms that of the XGBoost and BPNN. In addition, the performance of different data sources under the application of the same model also varies. In the middle mountain forest-meadow belt, when only optical data are input into the XGBoost, the obtained R^2 = 0.52 and RMSE = 23.40 t·hm^{-2}. Based on the SAR data source, R^2 = 0.46 and RMSE = 24.87 t·hm^{-2}. The R^2 value of *Picea schrenkiana* forest estimation utilizing multi-source data is increased to 0.62, and the RMSE value is reduced to 20.69 t·hm^{-2}, indicating that integrating various data sources can further improve the accuracy of the model. In the upper middle mountain forest-meadow belt, for the BPNN, the R^2 of the optical data source is 0.66 and RMSE = 19.65 t·hm^{-2}, while the R^2 of the SAR data source is 0.65 and RMSE = 22.21 t·hm^{-2}. When both optical and SAR data sources are used simultaneously, R^2 = 0.71 and RMSE = 19.21 t·hm^{-2}, which indicates that combining multiple data sources has a positive impact on model accuracy. The accuracy of each model using multi-source data in the case of vertical zonality is shown in Figure 6.

Table 8. The Accuracy of Each Model under Different Vertical Zonality and Different Data Sources.

		Optical Data + Topographic Factor		SAR Data + Topographic Factor		Optical Data + SAR Data + Topographic Factor	
		R^2	RMSE	R^2	RMSE	R^2	RMSE
XGBoost	Middle mountain forest-meadow belt	0.52	23.40	0.46	24.87	0.62	20.69
	Upper middle mountain forest-meadow belt	0.57	22.96	0.52	26.06	0.63	21.30
	Subalpine open-forest belt	0.51	24.56	0.54	18.66	0.57	13.40
BPNN	Middle mountain forest-meadow belt	0.67	20.24	0.67	18.02	0.72	16.87
	Upper middle mountain forest-meadow belt	0.66	19.65	0.65	22.21	0.71	19.21
	Subalpine open-forest belt	0.62	16.85	0.57	16.50	0.66	15.15
ResNet	Middle mountain forest-meadow belt	0.74	17.31	0.70	16.55	0.78	15.27
	Upper middle mountain forest-meadow belt	0.74	17.82	0.67	21.91	0.79	15.62
	Subalpine open-forest belt	0.63	22.19	0.67	12.31	0.69	12.63

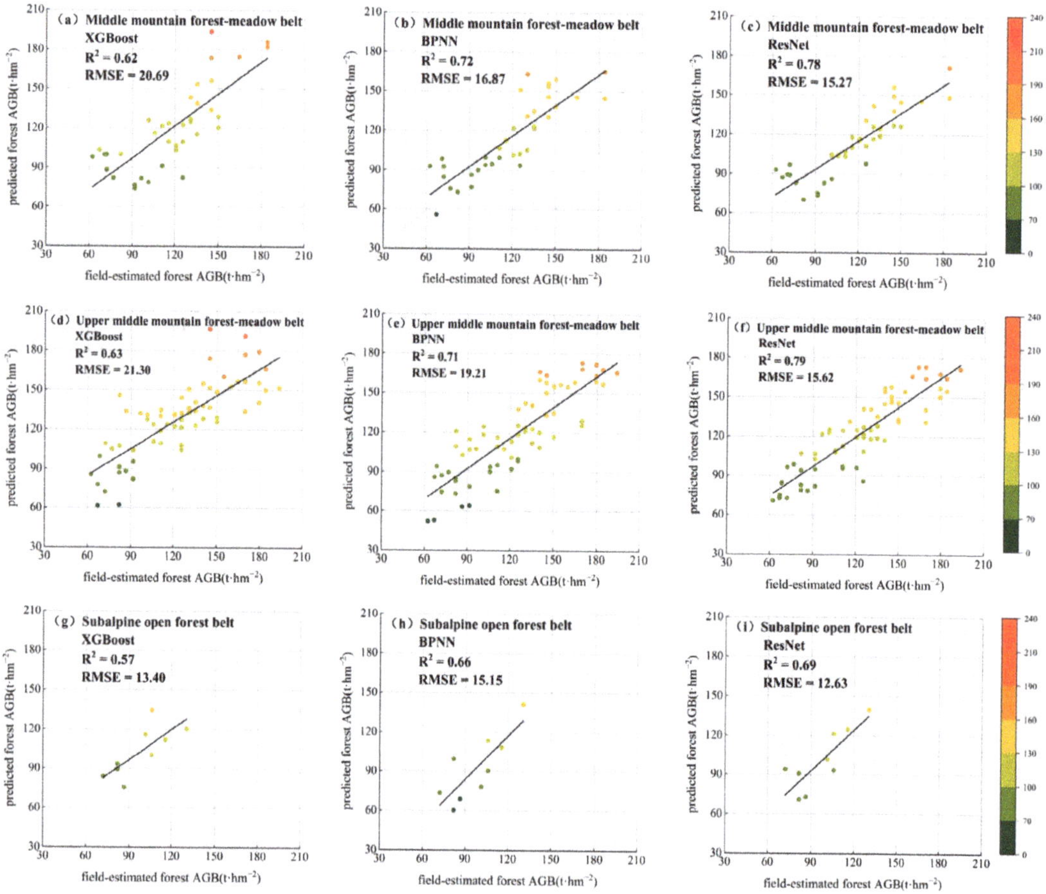

Figure 6. The accuracy of each model using multi-source data in the case of vertical zonality.

3.3. Estimation Results of Different Stand Ages

The accuracy of different models under different stand ages and different data sources is shown in Table 9. Compared to near-mature forest and mature forest, over-mature forest have a smaller area and fewer input values, resulting in lower estimation accuracy than that of near-mature forest and mature forest. In mature forest, when only optical data are used, for XGBoost, R^2 = 0.60 and RMSE = 16.47 t·hm^{-2}. For BPNN, R^2 = 0.63 and RMSE = 15.37 t·hm^{-2}. For ResNet, R^2 = 0.67 and RMSE = 14.91 t·hm^{-2}. In near-mature forest, when multi-source remote-sensing data are used, for XGBoost, R^2 = 0.60 and RMSE = 13.40 t·hm^{-2}. For BPNN, R^2 = 0.69 and RMSE = 12.60 t·hm^{-2}. For ResNet, R^2 = 0.77 and RMSE = 10.06 t·hm^{-2}. Under the same data source and different model conditions, ResNet demonstrates the highest accuracy. When the model is fixed as using ResNet, in over-mature forest, when only optical remote-sensing images are used, R^2 = 0.74 and RMSE = 21.58 t·hm^{-2}. When only SAR data are used, R^2 = 0.72 and RMSE = 22.44 t·hm^{-2}. When combining optical and SAR data, R^2 = 0.77 and RMSE = 22.68 t·hm^{-2}. This once again confirms that combining two data sources can further improve the accuracy of ResNet and enable it to achieve optimal performance. The accuracy of each model using multi-source data in the case of stand ages is shown in Figure 7.

Table 9. The Accuracy of Each Model under Different Stand Ages and Different Data Sources.

		Optical Data + Topographic Factor		SAR Data + Topographic Factor		Optical Data + SAR Data + Topographic Factor	
		R^2	RMSE	R^2	RMSE	R^2	RMSE
XGBoost	Near-mature forest	0.52	14.21	0.48	14.86	0.60	13.40
	Mature forest	0.60	16.47	0.54	17.61	0.65	15.93
	Over-mature forest	0.51	29.60	0.49	23.79	0.60	28.33
BPNN	Near-mature forest	0.65	12.87	0.64	13.05	0.69	12.60
	Mature forest	0.63	15.37	0.63	15.38	0.71	14.93
	Over-mature forest	0.64	21.78	0.60	22.85	0.67	25.59
ResNet	Near-mature forest	0.64	12.43	0.72	10.84	0.77	10.06
	Mature forest	0.67	14.91	0.68	14.64	0.83	10.62
	Over-mature forest	0.74	21.58	0.72	22.44	0.77	22.68

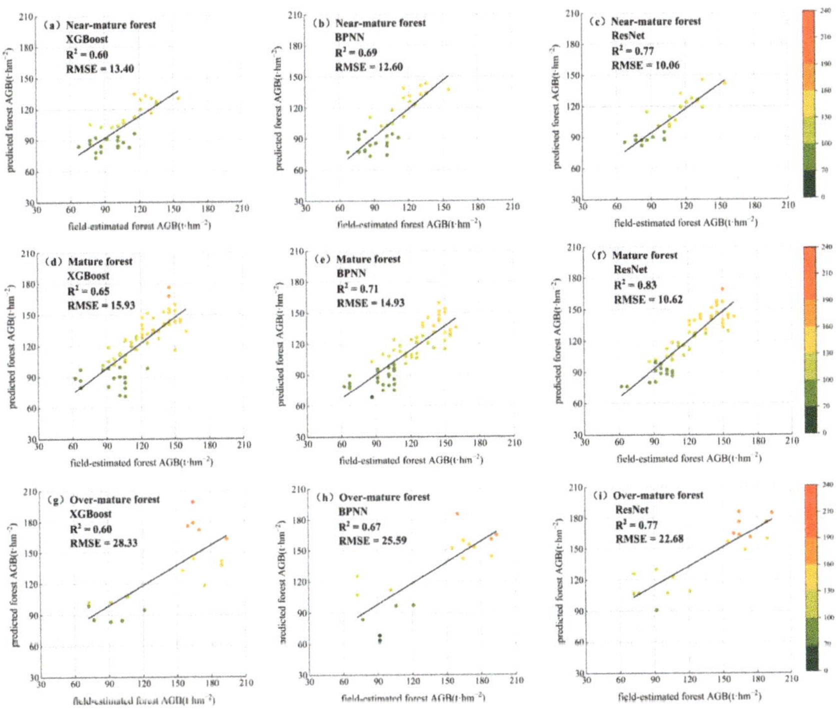

Figure 7. The accuracy of each model using multi-source data in the case of stand ages.

3.4. Estimation Results of the Whole Forest

It is easy to deduce from Tables 8 and 9 that multi-source data have higher prediction accuracy than a single data source. Therefore, multi-source data are individually incorporated into the three models, as shown in Table 10 and Figure 8, respectively. It is readily apparent that the ResNet has the highest accuracy, with R^2 = 0.71 and RMSE = 20.95 t·hm^{-2}. The XGBoost model has the lowest accuracy, with R^2 = 0.55 and RMSE = 27.71 t·hm^{-2}. To sum up, there are differences in the accuracy performance of various data sources and models under different modeling methods. Generally, in terms of data, integrating optical and SAR data sources can significantly improve the model's accuracy. The ResNet model demonstrates notably higher accuracy compared to the other two models. Among different modeling approaches, the accuracy of AGB estimation is higher for vertical zonality and stand-age scenarios than for the entire forest. Among them, the accuracy of estimation based on stand age is the highest.

Table 10. The Accuracy of different models in estimating the whole forest using multi-source data.

		XGBoost	BPNN	ResNet
Whole forest	R^2	0.55	0.66	0.71
	RMSE	27.71	23.04	20.95

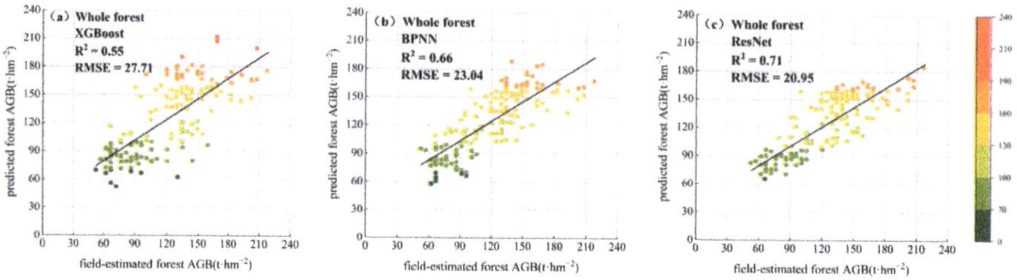

Figure 8. Accuracy of each model using multi-source data in the case of whole forest.

3.5. AGB Mapping

Through the above comparison, it can be inferred that the combination of ResNet and multi-source remote-sensing data has the highest accuracy. Using this model and data source, we draw AGB distribution maps for three scenarios: the entire forest, classification by vertical zonality, and classification by stand ages. These maps are shown in Figure 9.

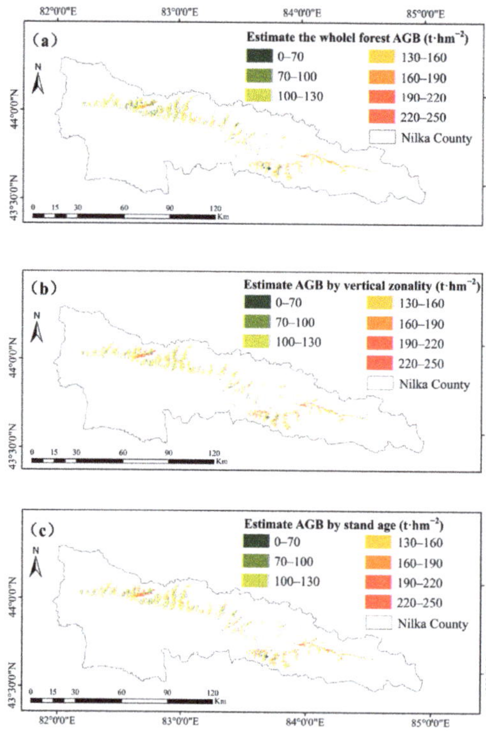

Figure 9. AGB estimation results under three different modeling methods. (**a**) shows the output map of estimated AGB for the whole forest. (**b**) based on the classification of vertical zonality, shows the output map of estimated AGB. (**c**) based on the classification of stand ages, shows the output map of estimated AGB.

4. Discussion

In the realm of AGB estimation research, the acquisition and utilization of comprehensive and precise information are of paramount significance. This study is based on the forest AGB estimation outcomes obtained from three distinct data sources: single optical data, single radar data, and integrated optical-radar data. In this study, the estimation accuracy of multi-source remote-sensing data is significantly higher than that of single-source data. This conclusion has been rigorously verified by an extensive body of research. Attarchi et al. [48] evaluated 11 distinct multiple linear regression models using optical and SAR data. Their research findings clearly show that integrating multispectral and SAR data can effectively reduce uncertainties from data limitations, thus improving the accuracy of biomass estimation. The results of our current study are highly congruent with this view. This further validates the significant advantages of multi-source remote-sensing data in biomass estimation.

Given the challenge of acquiring forest AGB products with temporal and spatial resolutions fully consistent with those of this study, we selected the AGB product with the highest resolution and the closest acquisition time (the 30 m resolution AGB product in China in 2019) for a comparative analysis with the AGB estimated in this study. As shown in Figure 9, the biomass distribution range obtained from the whole-forest estimation in this study mainly fell within the range of 70–190 $t{\cdot}hm^{-2}$, with an average biomass per unit area of 126.49 $t{\cdot}hm^{-2}$. Based on 4789 ground-measured AGB data and multi-source remote-sensing data, Yang [49] derived a 30 m resolution biomass estimation for China in 2019. After converting the research findings, the average biomass per unit area in this study area is approximately 129.34 $t{\cdot}hm^{-2}$, which is comparable to the results of this study. However, an in-depth analysis of Yang's estimation results reveals that the biomass distribution range mainly ranges from 100 to 160 $t{\cdot}hm^{-2}$. Taking the forest resources inventory data for management as the true value, the biomass in the study area is mainly distributed in the range of 70–190 $t{\cdot}hm^{-2}$. As shown in Table 11, the RMSE of the estimation based on the entire forest in this study is 22.61 $t{\cdot}hm^{-2}$, while the RMSE in Yang's study is 30.20 $t{\cdot}hm^{-2}$. From the comparison results, it can be seen that the estimated values in this study fit better with the true values across regions with different biomass levels, especially in areas with higher biomass, where Yang's study exhibited significant underestimation. In contrast, this study more accurately reflects the actual biomass conditions. This is because the spatial resolution of the dataset used in this study exceeds 30 m, and a larger-scale measured dataset has been obtained in the study area. These improvements have enhanced the reliability of biomass estimation at the extremes. The comparison of AGB estimation results between this study and Yang's study is presented in Figure 10, while the specific errors are shown in Table 11.

Table 11. The errors of the whole-forest estimation results in this study and the AGB estimation results in Yang's study when compared with the true value.

Number	True Value	Whole Forest Estimate	Error	Yang's AGB	Error
1	62.3534	93.81768	−31.4643	117.565	−55.2116
2	72.1016	84.79638	−12.6948	123.5967	−51.4951
3	81.8498	102.4973	−20.6475	117.2498	−35.4
4	86.4918	96.70109	−10.2093	109.858	−23.3662
5	96.24	110.9799	−14.7399	123.005	−26.765
6	101.3462	87.37556	13.97064	106.6862	−5.33999
7	105.9882	99.72482	6.263377	118.8634	−12.8752
8	111.0944	108.8939	2.200533	126.8149	−15.7205

Table 11. *Cont.*

Number	True Value	Whole Forest Estimate	Error	Yang's AGB	Error
9	115.7364	111.9555	3.780879	143.0097	−27.2733
10	120.8426	128.0583	−7.21566	130.8246	−9.98197
11	125.4846	114.2628	11.22175	117.4728	8.011774
12	130.5908	91.12645	39.46435	105.9736	24.61725
13	133.376	138.1766	−4.80064	135.807	−2.43097
14	136.1612	166.4629	−30.3017	146.5908	−10.4296
15	140.339	134.6607	5.67831	144.5293	−4.19033
16	144.981	131.7099	13.27107	126.5128	18.4682
17	154.7292	160.7999	−6.0707	138.5166	16.21257
18	159.8354	173.726	−13.8906	135.9558	23.87965
19	164.4774	176.8097	−12.3323	139.8075	24.66987
20	169.5836	131.8373	37.74632	145.0627	24.52095
21	183.9738	150.7507	33.22307	134.5283	49.44547
22	189.08	171.5312	17.54883	154.0613	35.01869
23	193.722	149.9356	43.78642	151.4542	42.26779
24	208.5764	162.8467	45.72974	147.4223	61.15406

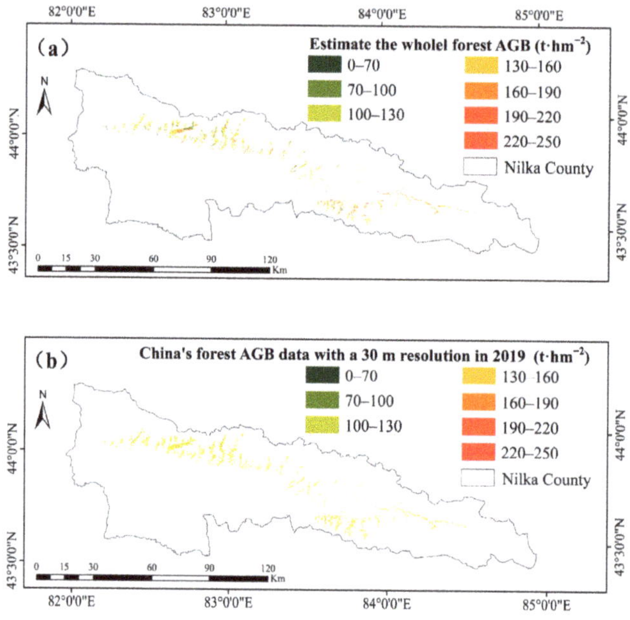

Figure 10. The comparison of AGB estimation results between this study and Yang's study. (**a**) the results of this experimental study; (**b**) The results of Yang's study.

When multi-source remote-sensing data and ResNet were used to estimate whole-forest biomass, R^2 was 0.71, and RMSE was 20.95 t·hm^{-2}. In the vertical zonality modeling method, the estimation accuracy of the subalpine open-forest belt, which has a slightly lower sample number, is lower than that of the whole forest. Conversely, the estimation accuracies of the other two vertical belts are higher than that of the whole forest. In the case of stand-age modeling, the R^2 of the model reaches up to 0.83. According to Figures 6c,f,i, 7c,f,i and 8c, when the biomass is less than 100 t·hm^{-2}, the overestimation of the whole-forest biomass is the most significant, and the deviation value significantly exceeds the estimation results of vertical zonality and stand-age modeling. This overestimation is not accidental. When the biomass reaches 170 t·hm^{-2} and above, the underestimation issue emerges again in the whole forest. Taking the biomass estimation approach integrating multi-source remote-sensing data and the ResNet model as an example, among all the estimation results, when the error between the estimated value and the actual biomass exceeds 30 t·hm^{-2}, the error proportion under different modeling methods exhibits distinct differences. When estimating the forest as a whole, the estimated values with an error exceeding 30 t·hm^{-2} account for 23.09% of the total estimated values. When the vertical zonality modeling method is applied to estimate biomass, the error ratio is significantly reduced to 5.45%. In the case of stand-age modeling, the proportion of estimates with an error greater than 30 t·hm^{-2} is the lowest, merely 4.72%. The climatic and other conditions in distinct vertical zones vary substantially, with a profound impact on vegetation growth and biomass distribution. The biomass characteristics of trees in different stand ages also differ significantly because of their disparate growth states. Dividing forests based on vertical zonation or age class allows for more precise identification of these differences. As a result, the accuracy of estimations is notably enhanced, lending support to more accurate biomass evaluations.

5. Conclusions

In the biomass estimation study of *Picea schrenkiana* forests in the West Tianshan Mountains, this study integrated GF-1, GF-6, and GF-3 PolSAR data with dem data, extracted corresponding feature factors, and applied the ResNet method to conduct the estimation work. Eventually, high accuracy in biomass estimation was achieved. It is well-established that along altitude gradients, over short distances, there are systematic alterations in temperature and precipitation. Additionally, as forests age, biomass continues to build up. Based on these principles, this study further classified *Picea schrenkiana* forests according to two methods: Vertical Zonality Differentiation without considering stand age and Stand-Age Classification without considering vertical zonality. The results showed that the model accuracy was remarkably improved.

Starting from the middle and low mountain forest-steppe belt, as the altitude continues to increase, temperature and precipitation conditions become highly conducive to AGB accumulation in *Picea schrenkiana* forests. However, if the altitude exceeds a certain critical value, the temperature will drop significantly, and this low-temperature environment will no longer be suitable for AGB accumulation in *Picea schrenkiana* forests [50]. Conversely, below the middle and low mountain forest-steppe belt, due to intensive human activities, it is also not conducive to the large-scale growth of *Picea schrenkiana* forest. This further explains why *Picea schrenkiana* forest is mainly distributed in the area 1700–2700 m above sea level.

Due to limitations in data availability, in-depth studies on the long-time-series AGB of *Picea schrenkiana* forests remain scarce. In follow-up research, remote-sensing data from the Landsat series or other sources can be integrated at 10−20-year intervals, combined with environmental factors such as precipitation and temperature, to systematically analyze the dynamic changes in *Picea schrenkiana* forest AGB. Furthermore, the influencing factors considered in the current model construction are not comprehensive enough. In future studies, additional key stand characteristic factors, such as slope position and mean DBH, can be incorporated to continuously optimize the AGB estimation model for *Picea schrenkiana* forests.

Author Contributions: Conceptualization, G.Z. and D.C.; methodology, M.P.; software, Q.Z.; investigation, J.Z.; resources, H.Z.; data curation, Y.H.; writing—original draft preparation, G.Z.; writing—review and editing, D.C. and H.L.; visualization, H.Z.; supervision, D.C.; project administration, J.F. All authors have read and agreed to the published version of the manuscript.

Funding: This research was funded by the Major Science and Technology Project of High-Resolution Earth Observation System, grant number 76-Y50G14-0038-22/23, grant number 30-Y60B01-9003-22/23; the Science Foundation for Distinguished Young Scholars of Anhui Universities grant number 2022AH020069; Anhui Provincial Special Support Plan grant number 2019.

Data Availability Statement: All data, models, or code generated or used during the study are available from the author by request (2221011553@ahnu.edu.cn).

Acknowledgments: Thanks to the data support provided by the websites of various data sources in the article. I would like to thank Donghua Chen, Hu Li et al. for their guidance on the paper, as well as their support for the projects related to this paper.

Conflicts of Interest: The authors declare no conflicts of interest.

References

1. Mo, L.; Zohner, C.M.; Reich, P.B.; Liang, J.; de Miguel, S.; Nabuurs, G.J.; Renner, S.S.; van den Hoogen, J.; Araza, A.; Herold, M.; et al. Integrated global assessment of the natural forest carbon potential. *Nature* **2023**, *624*, 92–101. [CrossRef] [PubMed]
2. Li, H.; Ci, L.; Fang, J.; Chen, D.; Liu, Y. Dynamic Monitoring of Picea schrenkiana Forest Biomass in West Tianshan Mountain Region of Xinjiang. *Sci. Silv. Sin.* **2008**, *44*, 14–19.
3. Walker, W.S.; Gorelik, S.R.; Cook-Patton, S.C.; Susan, C.; Baccini, A.; Farina, M.K.; Solvik, K.K.; Ellis, P.W.; Sanderman, J.; Houghton, R.A.; et al. The global potential for increased storage of carbon on land. *Proc. Natl. Acad. Sci. USA* **2022**, *119*, e2023803119. [CrossRef] [PubMed]
4. Liu, Q.; Yang, L.; Liu, Q.; Li, J. Review of Forest Above-Ground Biomass Inversion Methods Based on Remote Sensing Technology. *J. Remote Sens.* **2015**, *19*, 62–74.
5. Cao, G. Application of remote sensing technology in forest resources investigation. *Remote Sens.* **2022**, *11*, 46–49. [CrossRef]
6. Gou, R.; Chen, J.; Duan, G.; Yang, R.; Bu, Y.; Zhao, J.; Zhao, P. Inversion of aboveground biomass of Pinus tabuliformis plantations based on GF-2 data. *J. Appl. Ecol.* **2019**, *30*, 4031–4040.
7. Naik, P.; Dalponte, M.; Bruzzone, L. Prediction of forest aboveground biomass using multitemporal multispectral remote sensing data. *Remote Sens.* **2021**, *13*, 1282. [CrossRef]
8. Li, H.; Chen, D.; Liu, S.; Liu, Y.; Huang, W.; Zhang, N.; Yang, F.; Li, X.; Xing, F.; Liu, C.; et al. *Research on Forest Resources and Environmental Monitoring in the Western Tianshan Mountains Based on Domestic Land Satellite Data*, 1st ed.; Science Press: Beijing, China, 2022; pp. 74–145.
9. Tang, Z.; Xia, X.; Huang, Y.; Lu, Y.; Guo, Z. Estimation of National Forest Aboveground Biomass from Multi-Source Remotely Sensed Dataset with Machine Learning Algorithms in China. *Remote Sens.* **2022**, *14*, 5487. [CrossRef]
10. Li, L.; Chen, E.; Li, Z.; Feng, Q.; Zhao, L. A Review on Forest Height and Aboveground Biomass Estimation Based on Synthetic Aperture Radar. *Remote Sens. Technol. Appl.* **2016**, *31*, 625–633. [CrossRef]
11. Zhang, L.; Yin, X.; Wang, Y.; Chen, J. Aboveground Biomass Mapping in Semi-Arid Forests by Integrating Airborne LiDAR with Sentinel-1 and Sentinel-2 Time-Series Data. *Remote Sens.* **2024**, *16*, 3241. [CrossRef]
12. Cartus, O.; Santoro, M. Exploring combinations of multi-temporal and multi-frequency radar backscatter observations to estimate above-ground biomass of tropical forest. *Remote Sens. Environ.* **2019**, *232*, 111313. [CrossRef]
13. Wei, J.; Fan, W.; Yu, Y.; Mao, X. Polarimetric Decomposition Parameters for Artificial Forest Canopy Biomass Estimation Using GF-3 Fully Polarimetric SAR Data. *Sci. Silv. Sin.* **2020**, *56*, 174–183.
14. Zhang, Y.; Wang, N.; Wang, Y.; Li, M. A New Strategy for Improving the Accuracy of Forest Aboveground Biomass Estimates in an Alpine Region Based on Multi-Source Remote Sensing. *GISci. Remote Sens.* **2023**, *60*, 2163574. [CrossRef]
15. Forkuor, G.; Zoungrana, J.B.B.; Dimobe, K.; Ouattara, B.; Vadrevu, K.P.; Tondoh, J.E. Above-ground biomass mapping in West African dryland forest using Sentinel-1 and 2 datasets—A case study. *Remote Sens. Environ.* **2020**, *236*, 111496. [CrossRef]
16. Wang, P.; Zhang, H.; Tian, X.; Zhang, J.; Zhu, Y. Estimation of Forest Stem Volume of Natural Forests Based on the Optimization of Active and Passive Remote Sensing Features. *Remote Sens. Technol. Appl.* **2022**, *37*, 672–680.
17. Liu, Y.; Gong, W.; Xing, Y.; Hu, X.; Gong, J. Estimation of the Forest Stand Mean Height and Aboveground Biomass in Northeast China Using SAR Sentinel-1B, Multispectral Sentinel-2A, and DEM Imagery. *ISPRS J. Photogramm. Remote Sens.* **2019**, *151*, 277–289. [CrossRef]
18. Jucker, T.; Bongalov, B.; Burslem, D.F.R.P.; Nilus, R.; Dalponte, M.; Lewis, S.L.; Phillips, O.L.; Qie, L.; Coomes, D.A. Topography Shapes the Structure, Composition and Function of Tropical Forest Landscapes. *Ecol. Lett.* **2018**, *21*, 989–1000. [CrossRef]
19. Ni, J. Forest productivity of the Altay and Tianshan Mountains in the dryland, northwestern China. *For. Ecol. Manag.* **2004**, *202*, 13–22. [CrossRef]

20. Wu, Y.; Li, F.; Zhang, J.; Liu, Y.; Li, H.; Zhou, B.; Shen, B.; Hou, L.; Xu, D.; Ding, L.; et al. Spatial and Temporal Patterns of Above- and Below-Ground Biomass Over the Tibet Plateau Grasslands and Their Sensitivity to Climate Change. *Sci. Total Environ.* **2024**, *919*, 170900. [CrossRef]
21. Wang, Y.; Liu, Y.; Chen, P.; Song, J.; Fu, B. Interannual Precipitation Variability Dominates the Growth of Alpine Grassland Above-ground Biomass at High Elevations on the Tibetan Plateau. *Sci. Total Environ.* **2024**, *931*, 172745. [CrossRef]
22. Wu, X.; Jiao, L.; Du, D.; Xue, R.; Wei, M.; Zhang, P. Elevation Response of Above-ground Net Primary Productivity for Picea crassifolia to Climate Change in Qilian Mountains of Northwest China Based on Tree Rings. *J. Geogr. Sci.* **2024**, *34*, 146–164. [CrossRef]
23. Maza, B.; Rodes-Blanco, M.; Rojas, E. Aboveground Biomass Along an Elevation Gradient in an Evergreen Andean–Amazonian Forest in Ecuador. *Front. For. Glob. Change* **2022**, *5*, 738585. [CrossRef]
24. Chan, C.K.; Gomez, C.A.; Kothikar, A.; Baiz-Villafranca, P.M. Satellite-Based Carbon Estimation in Scotland: AGB and SOC. *Land* **2023**, *12*, 818. [CrossRef]
25. Ye, Q.; Yu, S.; Liu, J.; Zhao, Q.; Zhao, Z. Aboveground Biomass Estimation of Black Locust Planted Forests with Aspect Variable Using Machine Learning Regression Algorithms. *Ecol. Indic.* **2021**, *129*, 107948. [CrossRef]
26. Han, H.; Wan, R.; Li, B. Estimating Forest Aboveground Biomass Using Gaofen-1 Images, Sentinel-1 Images, and Machine Learning Algorithms: A Case Study of the Dabie Mountain Region, China. *Remote Sens.* **2022**, *14*, 176. [CrossRef]
27. Ali, A.; Yan, E.R.; Chen, H.Y.H.; Chang, S.X.; Zhao, Y.T.; Yang, X.D.; Xu, M.S. Stand Structural Diversity Rather Than Species Diversity Enhances Aboveground Carbon Storage in Secondary Subtropical Forests in Eastern China. *Biogeosciences* **2016**, *13*, 4627–4635. [CrossRef]
28. Huang, X.; Chen, Y.C.; Tan, H.R.; Zhang, Y.; Yu, S.H.; Chen, X.Y.; Yu, K.Y.; Liu, J. Extraction of the Spatial Structure of Chinese Fir Plantation Stands Based on Unmanned Aerial Vehicle and Its Effect on AGB. *For. Ecol. Manag.* **2024**, *558*, 121800. [CrossRef]
29. Lee, Y.J.; Park, K.E.; Lee, H.I.; Lee, C.B. Stand age-driven tree size variation and stand type regulate aboveground biomass in alpine-subalpine forests, South Korea. *Sci. Total Environ.* **2024**, *915*, 170063. [CrossRef]
30. Wu, Y.; Ou, G.; Lu, T.; Huang, T.; Zhang, X.; Liu, Z.; Yu, Z.; Guo, B.; Wang, E.; Feng, Z.; et al. Improving Aboveground Biomass Estimation in Lowland Tropical Forests across Aspect and Age Stratification: A Case Study in Xishuangbanna. *Remote Sens.* **2024**, *16*, 1276. [CrossRef]
31. Li, D.; Wang, M.; Jiang, J. China's High-Resolution Optical Remote Sensing Satellites and Their Mapping Applications. *Geo-Spat. Inf. Sci.* **2020**, *24*, 85–94. [CrossRef]
32. Zeng, P.; Zhang, W.F.; Li, Y.; Shi, J.M.; Wang, Z.H. Forest Total and Component Above-Ground Biomass (AGB) Estimation through C- and L-band Polarimetric SAR Data. *Forests* **2022**, *13*, 442. [CrossRef]
33. Lee, J.S.; Wen, J.H.; Ainsworth, T.L.; Chen, K.S.; Chen, A.J. Improved Sigma Filter for Speckle Filtering of SAR Imagery. *IEEE Trans. Geosci. Remote Sens.* **2009**, *47*, 202–213.
34. Rosenqvist, A.; Shimada, M.; Ito, N.; Watanabe, M. ALOS PALSAR: A Pathfinder Mission for Global-Scale Monitoring of the Environment. *IEEE Trans. Geosci. Remote Sens.* **2007**, *45*, 3307–3316. [CrossRef]
35. Zhang, X.; Zhang, Y.; Chen, W.; Zheng, J.; Chen, F.; Chen, K.; Mo, G. Types of clear-cut areas and their regeneration in Tianshan Snowy Mountains spruce forests. *Sci. Silvae Sin.* **1964**, *9*, 167–183.
36. Fang, J.; Liu, G.; Xu, S. Biomass and Net Production of Forest Vegetation in China. *Acta Ecol. Sin.* **1996**, *16*, 497–508.
37. Liu, J.F.; Chen, R.S.; Qin, W.W.; Yang, Y. Study on the vertical distribution of precipitation in mountainous regions using TRMM data. *Adv. Water Sci.* **2011**, *22*, 447–454.
38. Xu, D.; Wang, C.; Chen, J.; Shen, M.; Shen, B.; Yan, R.; Li, Z.; Karnieli, A.; Chen, J.; Yan, Y.; et al. The superiority of the normalized difference phenology index (NDPI) for estimating grassland aboveground fresh biomass. *Remote Sens. Environ.* **2021**, *264*, 112578. [CrossRef]
39. Chen, L.Y.; He, A.Q.; Xu, Z.H.; Li, B.; Zhang, H.F.; Li, G.T.; Guo, X.Y.; Li, Z.L. Mapping aboveground biomass of Moso bamboo (*Phyllostachys pubescens*) forests under Pantana phyllostachysae Chao-induced stress using Sentinel-2 imagery. *Ecol. Indic.* **2024**, *158*, 111564. [CrossRef]
40. Fu, B.; Wang, Y.; Campbell, A.; Li, Y.; Zhang, B.; Yin, S.; Xing, Z.; Jin, X. Comparison of object-based and pixel-based Random Forest algorithm for wetland vegetation mapping using high spatial resolution GF-1 and SAR data. *Ecol. Indic.* **2017**, *73*, 105–117. [CrossRef]
41. Bu, X.; Dong, S.; Mi, W.; Li, F. Spatial-temporal change of carbon storage and sink of wetland ecosystem in arid regions, Ningxia Plain. *Atmos. Environ.* **2019**, *204*, 89–101.
42. Li, D.; Wang, C.; Hu, Y.; Liu, S. General Review on Remote Sensing-Based Biomass Estimation. *Geom. Inf. Sci. Wuhan Univ.* **2012**, *37*, 631–635.
43. Cloude, S.; Pottier, E. A review of target decomposition theorems in radar polarimetry. *IEEE Trans. Geosci. Remote Sens.* **1996**, *34*, 498–518. [CrossRef]

44. Wang, Q.; Zeng, Q.; Liao, J. Extraction and Application of Polarimetric Characteristic Parameters Based on Polarimetric Decomposition. *Remote Sens. Nat. Resour.* **2012**, *3*, 103–110.
45. Jia, Z.; Zhang, Z.; Cheng, Y.; Buhebaoyin, B.; Borjigin, S.; Quan, Z. Grassland biomass spatiotemporal patterns and response to climate change in eastern Inner Mongolia based on XGBoost model estimates. *Ecol. Indic.* **2024**, *158*, 111554. [CrossRef]
46. Gao, Y.; Lu, D.; Li, G.; Wang, G.; Chen, Q.; Liu, L.; Li, D. Comparative Analysis of Modeling Algorithms for Forest Aboveground Biomass Estimation in a Subtropical Region. *Remote Sens.* **2018**, *10*, 627. [CrossRef]
47. Liu, T.; Yang, T.; Zhu, S.; Mou, N.; Zhang, W.; Wu, W.; Zhao, Y.; Yao, Z.; Sun, J.; Chen, C.; et al. Estimation of wheat biomass based on phenological identification and spectral response. *Comput. Electron. Agric.* **2024**, *222*, 109076. [CrossRef]
48. Attarchi, S.; Gloaguen, R. Improving the Estimation of Above Ground Biomass Using Dual Polarimetric PALSAR and ETM+ Data in the Hyrcanian Mountain Forest (Iran). *Remote Sens.* **2014**, *6*, 3693–3715. [CrossRef]
49. Yang, Q.; Niu, C.; Liu, X.; Feng, Y.; Ma, Q.; Wang, X.; Guo, Q. Mapping high-resolution forest aboveground biomass of China using multisource remote sensing data. *GISci. Remote Sens.* **2023**, *60*, 2203303. [CrossRef]
50. Tian, S.C.; Zhao, S.C.; Zheng, X.J.; Wang, Y.G.; Li, Y. Water Source of Spruce (*Picea schrenkiana*) at Different Altitudes in the Tianshan Mountains during the Growing Season. *Arid Zone Res.* **2023**, *40*, 436–444.

forests

MDPI

Article

Assessing Above-Ground Biomass Dynamics and Carbon Sequestration Potential Using Machine Learning and Spaceborne LiDAR in Hilly Conifer Forests of Mansehra District, Pakistan

Muhammad Imran [1], Guanhua Zhou [2,*], Guifei Jing [3], Chongbin Xu [4], Yumin Tan [1,3], Rana Ahmad Faraz Ishaq [2,3], Muhammad Kamran Lodhi [1,3], Maimoona Yasinzai [5], Ubaid Akbar [3] and Anwar Ali [6]

1 School of Transportation Science and Engineering, Beihang University, Beijing 100191, China; mimran@buaa.edu.cn (M.I.); tanym@buaa.edu.cn (Y.T.); kamranlodhi@buaa.edu.cn (M.K.L.)
2 School of Instrumentation and Optoelectronic Engineering, Beihang University, Beijing 100191, China; ranaahmadfarazishaq@buaa.edu.cn
3 Hangzhou International Innovation Institute, Beihang University, Hangzhou 311115, China; guifeijing@buaa.edu.cn (G.J.); ubaidakbar@buaa.edu.cn (U.A.)
4 Beijing Institute of Space Mechanics & Electricity, Beijing 100094, China; xucb_bisme@spacechina.com
5 Department of Environmental Science, International Islamic University, Islamabad 04436, Pakistan; maimoona.yasinzai@iiu.edu.pk
6 Pakistan Forest Institute, Peshawar 25130, Pakistan; anwar.ali@pfi.edu.pk
* Correspondence: zhouguanhua@buaa.edu.cn

Abstract: Consistent and accurate data on forest biomass and carbon dynamics are essential for optimizing carbon sequestration, advancing sustainable management, and developing natural climate solutions in various forest ecosystems. This study quantifies the forest biomass in designated forests based on GEDI LiDAR datasets with a unique compartment-level monitoring of unexplored hilly areas of Mansehra. The integration of multisource explanatory variables, employing machine learning models, adds further innovation to the study of reliable above ground biomass (AGB) estimation. Integrating Landsat-9 vegetation indices with ancillary datasets improved forest biomass estimation, with the random forest algorithm yielding the best performance (R^2 = 0.86, RMSE = 28.03 Mg/ha, and MAE = 19.54 Mg/ha). Validation with field data on a point-to-point basis estimated a mean above-ground biomass (AGB) of 224.61 Mg/ha, closely aligning with the mean ground measurement of 208.13 Mg/ha (R^2 = 0.71). The overall mean AGB model estimated a forest biomass of 189.42 Mg/ha in the designated moist temperate forests of the study area. A critical deficit in the carbon sequestration potential was analysed, with the estimated AGB in 2022, at 19.94 thousand tons, with a deficit of 0.83 thousand tons to nullify CO_2 emissions (20.77 thousand tons). This study proposes improved AGB estimation reliability and offers insights into the CO_2 sequestration potential, suggesting a policy shift for sustainable decision-making and climate change mitigation policies.

Keywords: temperate forest; AGB; LiDAR; random forest; CO_2; sustainable management

1. Introduction

Climate model projections indicate a temperature increase ranging from 1.92 °C to 5.2 °C by the late 21st century, depending on CO_2 and other greenhouse gases (GHGs) [1]. These alarming trends underscore the need for prompt policy interventions to mitigate the risks associated with climate change. Ecosystem services of forests are pivotal in curbing the progression of climate change, particularly by sequestering CO_2 emissions. Global CO_2

https://doi.org/10.3390/f16020330

emissions annually increase by 0.1%, reaching 35.8 Gt in 2023, further contributing to global warming [2]. This highlights the need for a holistic understanding that combines biological, ecological, and social knowledge. Such an integrated approach bridges forest ecology and management, supporting the sustainable preservation of biomass and ecosystem services. Moreover, biomass estimation is also vital to monitor progress and targets under SDG-15 (Life on Land) and the REDD+ program to ensure sustainable forest management, biodiversity preservation, and ecosystem health [3,4].

AGB is a critical parameter for assessing forest ecosystems, as it effectively encapsulates indicators, such as forest area change, net forest change, and management practices. Moreover, AGB is a vital determinant of a forest ecosystem's capacity for carbon storage. The accurate estimation of AGB is crucial for monitoring afforestation and deforestation and developing sustainable strategies to address forest management challenges under SDG-15.

Pakistan ranks 5th in climate vulnerability, according to the Global Climate Risk Index [5]. Its forests, covering just 4.51 million hectares [6], are increasingly vulnerable to climate change, necessitating advanced methodologies for accurate carbon assessment. Enhancing existing frameworks and tailoring them to local contexts is vital for developing effective mitigation strategies to control CO_2 emissions [7]. Assessing forest areas without considering AGB limits our understanding of the total carbon storage capacity and the potential effects of climate change.

Temperature and precipitation are significant climate characteristics that regulate the environmental variables affecting above-ground forest carbon stocks. Forest structure changes are determined by species distribution, composition, and density and are vulnerable to climatic-induced shifts, impacting forest productivity and functionality [8]. Additionally, Pakistan's management strategies adopted for forestry resources face multiple challenges due to climate change impacts and resource allocation among the indigenous communities living in the forest. The loss of carbon sinks, estimated at 1.1% from 2000 to 2023 by Global Forest Watch, has intensified climate change impacts, heightened susceptibility towards natural disasters, and increased habitat loss, threatening species survival and biodiversity [9]. Addressing these challenges requires integrating data fusion techniques, machine learning algorithms, and innovative approaches to improve carbon stock assessments in managed and natural forests.

Inaccurate and unreliable methods for estimating forest AGB result in substantial miscalculations of carbon storage capacities, ultimately undermining climate change mitigation and adaptation strategies [10]. Forest carbon estimates at global and regional scales face data availability challenges, estimation methods, topographical variability, and vast spatial coverage [11]. Significant data gaps and uncertainty in forest carbon sequestration and storage mainly stem from inconsistent field data collection and biomass allometric equations [12,13]. Ground-based methods for quantifying forest biomass and net primary productivity (NPP) are resource-intensive and limited in spatial and temporal coverage [14]. Therefore, a consistent methodological framework is essential to estimate AGB at national and sub-national levels.

Traditional methods of AGB estimation are statistical, requiring more resources. Allometric equations were developed using a logarithmic transformation model for biomass estimation in a sub-tropical ecoregion, using integrated cluster sampling, and using optical image segmentation to estimate carbon stocks in Himalayan temperate and sub-tropical mountain systems [15]. This ground-based methodology was supplemented with remote sensing to cover a larger area. These studies indicated the prevalent use of optical and field-based inventory data collection techniques for carbon stock estimation. Sentinel-2-derived vegetation indices and linear regression were used to estimate AGB, complemented by land cover change analysis with Landsat-7 and 8 data [16]. Similarly, temporal extent and deforestation rates were assessed in Mansehra [17]. Harmonized global maps with a spatial resolution of 300 m were developed by estimating above-ground and below-ground biomass carbon density using a rule-based decision tree method [18].

Spaceborne LiDAR is increasingly favoured for AGB estimation, because it captures biophysical vegetation parameters like plants' vertical profiles, sub-canopy topography, and biomass [19]. The cost-effectiveness and suitability of spaceborne LiDAR over large areas and inaccessible hilly terrain make it a practical choice [20]. Using different statistical probability distribution techniques, the GEDI L4A dataset was used to map Amazon forests for carbon sequestration rates concerning vegetation recovery, with regeneration and disturbance [21]. A hybrid inference model demonstrated compatibility between GEDI L4A datasets and Paraguay's national forest inventory (NFI), effectively reducing uncertainties in biomass estimation and enhancing the integration of remote sensing and field data for improved forest monitoring [22]. Similarly, the accuracy testing of GEDI L2A and ICESat-2 data using the kriging technique in tropical and sub-tropical forests in India showed superior results for GEDI [23]. However, the underestimation of GEDI (L4A and gridded L4B) footprints in tropical forests was found in comparison with Sentinel-2 estimates, indicating the need for additional explanatory variables from other datasets [24]. In regions with limited ground inventory resources, GEDI data is open, accessible geospatial information that provides a viable solution for estimating above-ground biomass. Ancillary and optical data from various sensor platforms further improved AGB estimation efficiency with GEDI L4A footprints in these studies [25–28]. The applicability of GEDI footprints and data products has been studied at various spatial (global and regional), temporal (seasonal), and species levels, highlighting the dynamic nature of carbon stock accumulation in response to slopes and aspects [29]. Despite numerous studies on reliable AGB estimation, gaps persist in assessing its local accuracy for GEDI L4A products.

GEDI L4A classifies four plant function types globally and applies an OLS model using waveform data, supporting reliability and accuracy in biomass estimation [30]. A 30 m resolution forest AGB map of China was generated using multisource remote sensing data, including meteorological and soil variables and RF regression, achieving $R^2 = 0.67$ and RMSE = 70.71 Mg/ha [25]. Similarly, in another study, optimized GEDI footprint density for regional biomass estimation using random forest was carried out. It was determined that a methodological reference for selecting GEDI footprints improve prediction accuracy, yielding an average biomass of 101.98 t/hm^2 and a total biomass of 3035.29×10^4 t/hm^2 in forest assessments [31].

Our research signifies a comprehensive approach that combines optical data with machine learning algorithms and spaceborne LiDAR data to assess AGB dynamics and the carbon sequestration potential in this specific ecological context as compared to previous studies having integrated remote sensing and machine learning for AGB estimation. The proposed study quantifies the forest biomass in a designated forest based on the integration of multisource explanatory variables, with the importance score having topographic elevation, forest canopy height, and optical green band as the prominent and major key features in biomass estimation and with a unique compartment-level assessment.

Machine learning algorithms (MLAs) are widely used in biomass estimation by inventory data, allometric equations, and remote sensing data [32]. These methods are particularly effective in handling forest heterogeneity and terrain complexity, providing robust and scalable solutions for biomass estimation [33]. Among MLAs, random forest has demonstrated superior performance in predicting AGB for plant function types, such as broadleaf, coniferous, and mixed needle-broadleaf forests [34]. The selection of random forest is due to its demonstrated high predictive accuracy with a minimal risk of overfitting, due to its ensemble-based approach and effectiveness for biomass estimation in remote sensing applications [35]. The ability of the RF algorithm to handle non-linear relationships, high-dimensional data, and complex interactions among variables makes it more suitable for AGB estimation [36]. It provides an inherent mechanism for ranking the importance of input variables, which is beneficial for understanding the contribution of predictors (e.g., spectral indices, topographic data, and GEDI data) in biomass estimation [37]. A comprehensive insight into the above discussion underscores the importance of integrating multiple diverse data sources with machine learning algorithms to obtain reliable AGB estimation and its potential for CO_2 sequestration. This integration facilitates accurate assessments of forest impact and inventory requirements for mitigating CO_2 emissions. Therefore, this study aims to explore exploratory variables using machine learning models for accurate AGB estimation and its potential to sequester CO_2 concentration. Thus, this research provides a comprehensive and efficient integrated approach consisting of exploratory variables derived from satellite and spaceborne LiDAR datasets and analytics to explore the AGB potential and requirements to tend to prevalent CO_2 emissions.

2. Materials and Methods

The major components of this study's methodology include the study area, datasets, data preparation and analytical workflow, and CO_2 emission datasets. These components are described below in detail.

2.1. Study Area

Mansehra District, located in the Khyber Pakhtunkhwa province of Pakistan, covers approximately 4579 km^2, situated between latitudes 34°14′ N to 35°11′ N and longitudes 72°49′ E to 74°08′ E (Figure 1). The temperature ranges from 2 to 36 °C, with heavy monsoon rainfall reaching 1500 mm. The elevation varies from 600 to 4500 m, ranging from low-lying plains to high mountain peaks in the Kaghan Valley of Himalayan foothills.

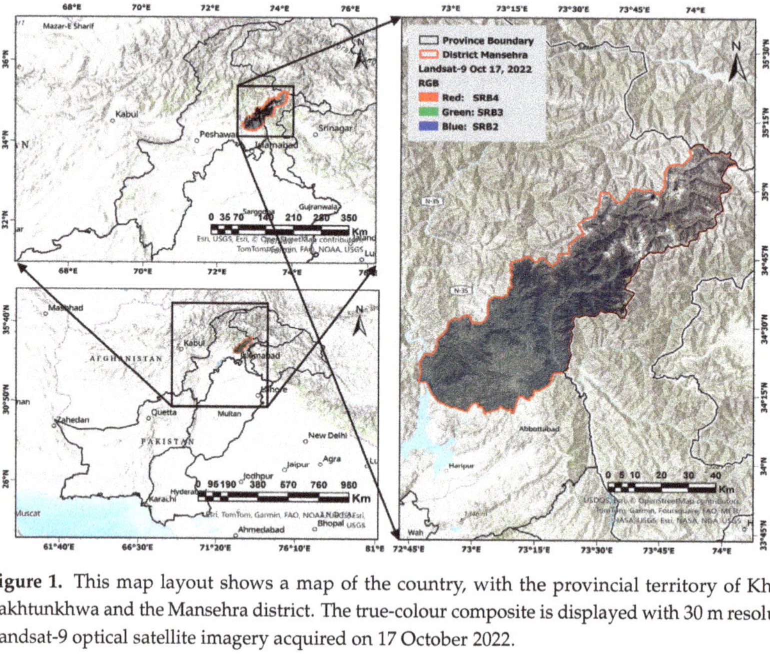

Figure 1. This map layout shows a map of the country, with the provincial territory of Khyber Pakhtunkhwa and the Mansehra district. The true-colour composite is displayed with 30 m resolution Landsat-9 optical satellite imagery acquired on 17 October 2022.

The species composition in moist temperate forests is dominated by Blue Pine (*Pinus wallichiana* A.B. Jackson), followed by Deodar (*Cedrus deodara* (Roxb. Ex Lamb.) G. Don), Fir (*Abies pindrow* Royle), and Spruce (*Picea smithiana* (Wall.) Boiss.), forming an association with broad-leaved Oak (*Quercus dilatata* Lindl. ex Royle) of high carbon storage potential. Forest covers transition to sub-alpine, moist, and dry temperate forests at higher elevations, whereas the sub-tropical chir pine dominates lower elevations. The estimated total province forest area is 1.133 million hectares, covering 70% of the temperate zone, while 30% is the sub-tropical zone [38]. This diversity highlights the region's ecological significance for biodiversity, carbon sequestration, and sustainable forest management.

2.2. Datasets

2.2.1. Forest Territorial Distribution and Compartment Data

Pakistan has 66% of state-managed forests and 34% of forests managed privately or by the community [39]. Out of the 3322.52 km^2 of forest area in Mansehra District, the total designated forest area is 1118.85 km^2. This forest territory is designated as a community locally named guzara (58.09%), reserved (30.34%), and protected (11.56%) forests. "The word "Guzara", literally meaning "subsistence" which is community-owned, either individually or collectively managed, where local residents have legally documented rights to extract wood for their domestic needs".

The Khyber Pakhtunkhwa Forest Department, under the Forest Ordinance 2002, categorizes designated forests into compartments, as in Figure 2 for geospatial monitoring, ensuring effective forest management practices and informed decision-making. Among the total 1298 compartments, community (privately owned) forests have 717, protected forests have 182, and reserved forests have 399 compartments. The distribution of designated forest categories and compartments is shown in Figure 2.

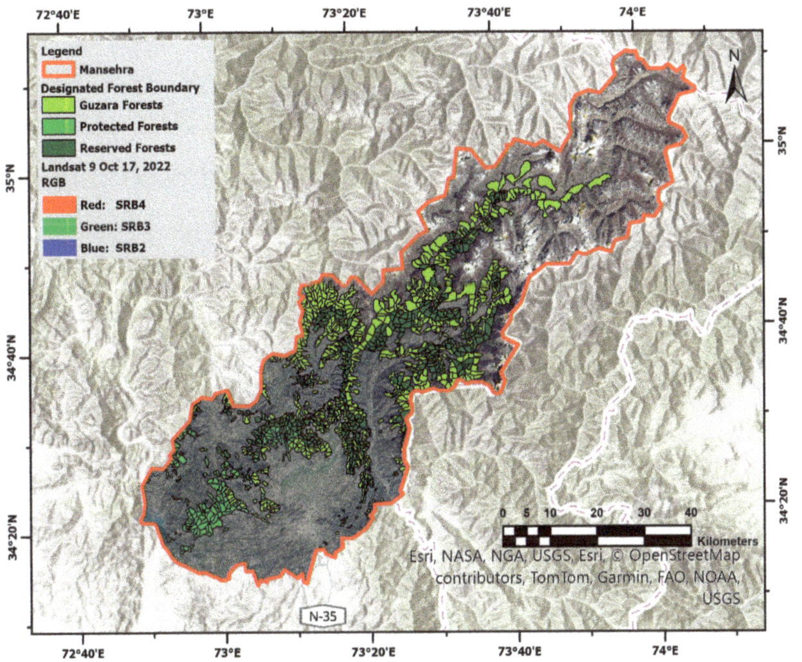

Figure 2. The territorial distribution of designated forests, showing reserved, protected, and community forest compartments obtained from the Khyber Pakhtunkhwa Forest Department.

2.2.2. Field Inventory Data

A carbon inventory survey was conducted in the Khyber Pakhtunkhwa forests using satellite data and region-specific allometric equations to estimate the carbon stocks. These equations were developed for the local major population species, with biomass expansion factors and basic wood densities. A consistent forest definition (a minimum area of 0.5 ha area, a 10% canopy cover, and 2 m in height), with a national consensus of provincial and federal departments that was adopted in 2017 for the monitoring of forests, was used to estimate the forest cover. The field inventory data from the designated forests of the Mansehra district cover geographical, environmental, and forest structural parameters. The elevation, geolocation, slope (%), aspect, crown cover (%), diameter at breast height (DBH, cm), and basal area (m^2), using allometric equations, were used to calculate the carbon stock points across dry temperate, moist temperate, and chir pine forests. The spatial distribution of these ground plot measurements is illustrated in Figure 3.

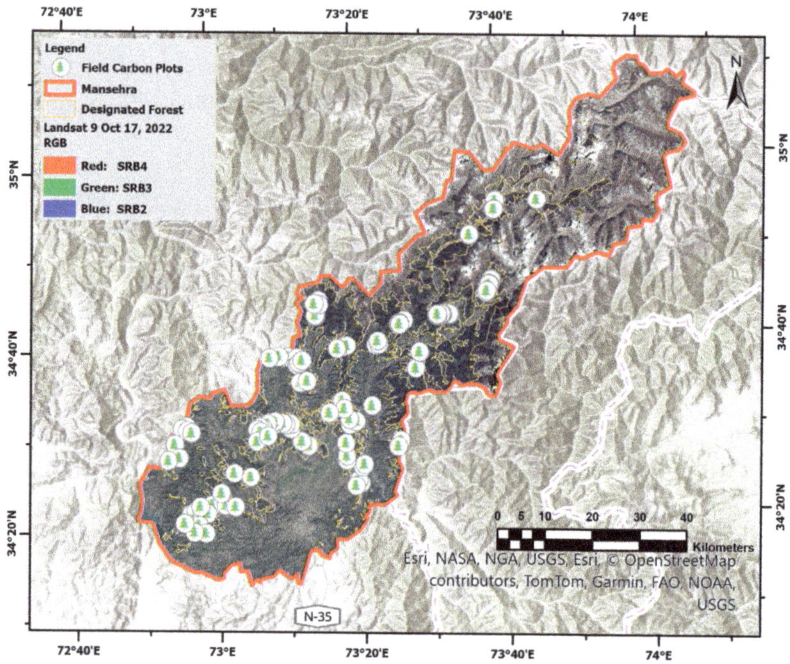

Figure 3. This nested circular plot presents the ground carbon stock points of the designed forest in the Mansehra district.

The Pakistan Forest Institute (PFI) conducted a field inventory campaign for a pilot project to develop species-specific local allometric models for Khyber Pakhtunkhwa. Among the total of 449 sample plots, 70 plots (15.59%) were designed as primary sampling units (PSUs) for accuracy assessment and validation through nested circular plots for biomass and carbon stocks. The layout and dimensions of the ground circular nested plots are shown in Figure 4. Within a nested circular plot (17.84 m radius; 1000 m^2 area), the number of trees with a diameter higher than 5 cm were enumerated. However, the diameter at breast height (DBH) for the diameter class 1–5 cm was measured from a subplot of a 5.64 m radius (area = 100 m^2). Later on, trees with a diameter of less than 1 cm (regeneration plot DBH) were counted from a 1 m radius plot within an area of 3.14 m^2. Shrub non-tree, litter, and soil biomass measurements were taken from a small plot with a radius of 0.56 m (area = 1 m^2).

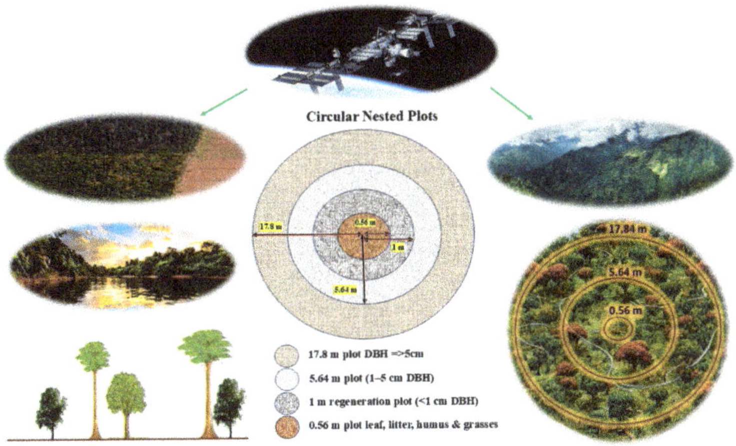

Figure 4. The circular field inventory nested plots shown in this image, with the plot size dimensions, measure tree, shrub, and below-ground carbon stock estimates.

A destructive sampling technique was employed in the coniferous forest to calculate the biomass expansion factor and basic wood density of conifer species and to develop allometric equations using regression functions, given in Table 1. Tree heights were accurately estimated by measuring new diameter-height functions developed for biomass estimation. Ground-based biomass estimates were calculated using the volume, wood density, height, and biomass expansion factor (BEF) [40]. Allometric equations given in Table 1 have four major components consisting of diameter at breast height (D), total tree height (H), regression constant (a) and regression coefficient (b). Regression constant and coefficient values depend upon geographical location and type of species.

Table 1. Allometric equations developed at local conditions for major conifer tree species.

Species	Forest Type	Allometric Equations	Model	Source
Quercus ilex L. (oak)	Dry temperate	$AGB = 0.8277(D^2H)^{0.6655}$	$M = a(D^2H)^b$	
Cedrus deodara (Roxb. Ex Lamb.) G. Don (deodar)	Dry temperate	$AGB = 0.1779(D^2H)^{0.8103}$	$M = a(D^2H)^b$	
Pinus wallichiana A.B.Jackson (kail)	Dry temperate	$AGB = 0.0631(D^2H)^{0.8798}$	$M = a(D^2H)^b$	
Cedrus deodara (Roxb. Ex Lamb.) G. Don (deodar)	Moist temperate	$AGB = 0.0491(D^2H)^{0.9167}$	$M = a(D^2H)^b$	[38]
Abies Pindrow Royle (fir)	Temperate	$AGB = 0.0452(D^2H)^{0.9029}$	$M = a(D^2H)^b$	
Picea smithiana (Wall.) Boiss (spruce)	Temperate	$AGB = 0.0821(D^2H)^{0.8363}$	$M = a(D^2H)^b$	
Pinus wallichiana A.B.Jackson (kail)	Moist temperate	$AGB = 0.0594(D^2H)^{0.881}$	$M = a(D^2H)^b$	
Pinus roxburghii Sargent (chir pine)	Sub-tropical pine	$AGB = 0.0224(D^2H)^{0.9767}$	$M = a(D^2H)^b$	

2.2.3. Satellite Datasets

Landsat-9 optical imagery offers a broad spectral resolution, covering 11 bands ranging from visible light to thermal infrared. Key bands include the red (0.64–0.67 μm) and green (0.53–0.59 μm) bands, which help distinguish foliage and canopy densities. The near-infrared band (0.85–0.88 μm) is instrumental in analysing forest health, types, and biomass volume within a tree canopy. Additionally, the two short-wave infrared bands SWIR-1

(1.57–1.65 μm) and SWIR-2 (2.11–2.29 μm) are sensitive to moisture content in soil and vegetation [41]. Open-access Landsat-9 Operational Land Imager (OLI) data of the study area, with minimum cloud (up to 10%) cover, was downloaded from USGS Earth Explorer website https://earthexplorer.usgs.gov/, (accessed on: 18 October 2024).

Digital Elevation Model

The Shuttle Radar Topography Mission (SRTM), a collaborative product of the U.S. National Geospatial-Intelligence Agency (NGA) and NASA, is widely used in geospatial applications. SRTM provides data in a standardized global WGS84 geographic coordinate system with a resolution of 1 arc second (~30 m) and 3 arc seconds (~90 m). Aspect and DEM products with a 30 m resolution and GeoTiff file format were downloaded from the USGS EROS Archive link https://lpdaac.usgs.gov/products/srtmgl1v003/ (accessed on: 20 October 2024). Several studies have observed a correlation between topographic feature, elevation, slope, and biomass prediction in forest ecosystems in steep and hilly terrains [42].

Forest Layer

The forest layer, derived from the Sentinel-1 and Sentinel-2 datasets (10 m resolution), was extracted from World Cover 2020 and 2021 products website https://viewer.esa-worldcover.org/worldcover (accessed on: 20 October 2024), developed by the United Nations' (UN) Food and Agriculture Organization (FAO) using the Land Cover Classification System (LCCS). This forest layer intersected with the GEDI-derived AGB points to ensure requisite data compatibility.

Forest Height

Tree height is a critical explanatory variable for accurately estimating biomass [43]. This study used the GEDI (RH98) L2A dataset as the primary source of forest height. Forest height coverage across the Mansehra district was ensured through the Global Forest Canopy Height (30 m raster) dataset, developed by the Global Land Analysis and Discovery (GLAD) team at the University of Maryland (UMD GLAD) as supplementary input. This dataset, available at https://glad.umd.edu/dataset/gedi/ (accessed on: 30 October 2024), allowed for seamless integration with GEDI (RH98), enabling reliable above-ground biomass (AGB) predictions for the entire study area.

Predictor Variables

Vegetation indices are essential in biomass estimation, forest cover assessment, and health monitoring. A comprehensive set of predictor variables was explored to estimate the structural parameters and biomass of forests using machine learning models. NDVI and seasonality impacts are frequently correlated, suggesting that a time series analysis improves AGB estimations, particularly during the fall [44]. The impact on biomass of combining different spectral bands and the vegetation indices NDVI [44], GNDVI [45], MSI [46], and PVI [47] were studied.

2.2.4. CO_2 Emission Dataset

CO_2 emissions were obtained from the EDGAR (Emissions Database for Global Atmospheric Research) Community GHG database, a collaborative work of the Joint Research Centre (JRC) and the International Energy Agency (IEA) [48]. These datasets were studied to observe the AGB potential and requirements to tend to CO_2 emissions.

2.3. Data Preparation and Analytical Workflow

2.3.1. Data Processing

The open-source GEDI dataset is accessible from NASA's Land Processes Distributed Active Archive Center (LPDAAC). The 200 GEDI sensor trajectory orbit tracks were downloaded from https://search.earthdata.nasa.gov (accessed on: 31 October 2024). Based on mathematical and algorithmic procedures, GEDI products are categorised into lower-level products (L1 and L2) and higher-level ones (L3 and L4). The GEDI instrument emits laser pulses with a diameter of 25 m and a wavelength of 1064 nm and a pulse rate of 242 Hz. The GEDI Level 4A version 2.1 datasets were used to estimate the AGB for tropical and temperate forests in the Mansehra district from 2019 to 2022. GEDI Level 4A data (Version 2.1) preprocessing involved several key steps to enhance accuracy and reliability. Quality filtering was applied to retain only high-quality footprints (quality_flag = 1, degrade_flag = 0). This removed footprints with low sensitivity or high uncertainty based on dataset quality flags. Strong beam footprints, which offer more reliable measurements, were prioritized over weak/coverage beams to improve data precision. Spatial alignment ensured GEDI footprints are co-registered with other remote sensing datasets, such as Landsat, Sentinel, or SRTM DEM, to prevent misalignment errors in model training. Additionally, outlier detection was performed to identify and remove erroneous, null values to ensure a rationalized, refined, and robust dataset for analysis. Derived metrics, such as RH95/RH50 ratios, were included to enhance vertical-structure characterization. Moreover, GEDI points were pre-processed to separate coverage beams and high-energy beams in complex hilly terrain areas to have only high-energy beams for GEDI L4A biomass footprints, as shown in (Figure 5) [42].

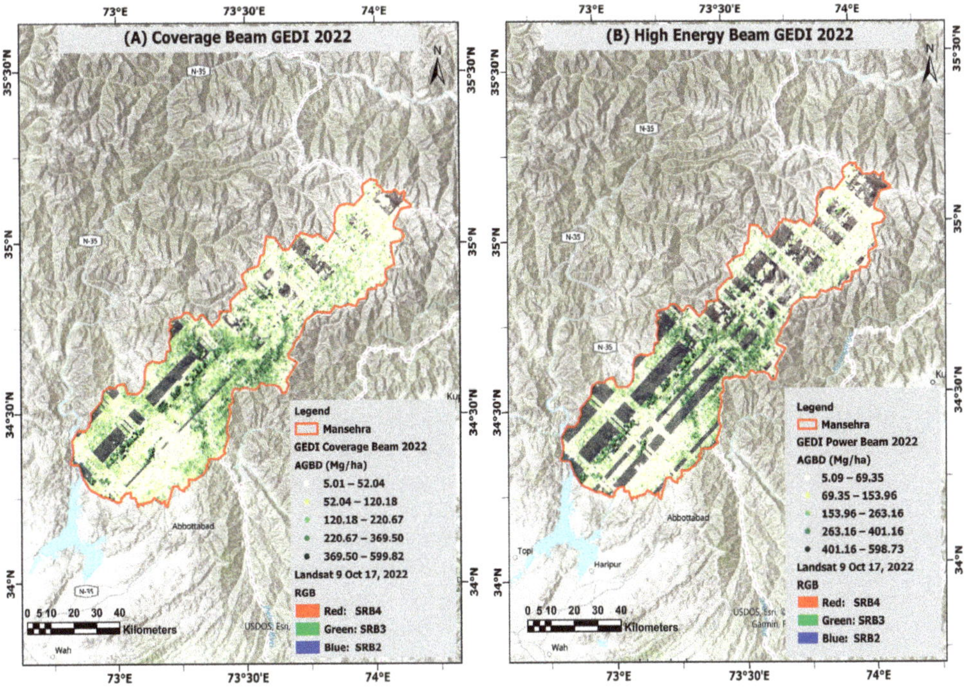

Figure 5. A spatial representation of spaceborne LiDAR GEDI L4A AGB points over the study area. In (**A**), the coverage beam is shown in the study area, while (**B**) shows the high-energy power beam shots, with the high-value-range classes shown in the legend.

The forest mask layer was intersected with GEDI power beams to obtain forest area-specific datasets, effectively removing the urban and non-forest land-use features. After preprocessing, 93,248 GEDI power beam shots were used for model training and testing within the forest mask layer. Among the total GEDI points, 21,406 points intersected with the designated forest area, distributed across 1298 compartments within the district boundary.

2.3.2. Analytical Workflow

The structural information of vegetation, such as canopy height (L2A), derived from GEDI data, was combined with spectral indices from optical datasets and other explanatory variables. These inputs were used to train and test against GEDI L4A as the dependent variable through machine learning algorithms (MLAs). An overall methodological flowchart for the proposed study to estimate forest above-ground biomass and its potential to sequester CO_2 is shown in (Figure 6).

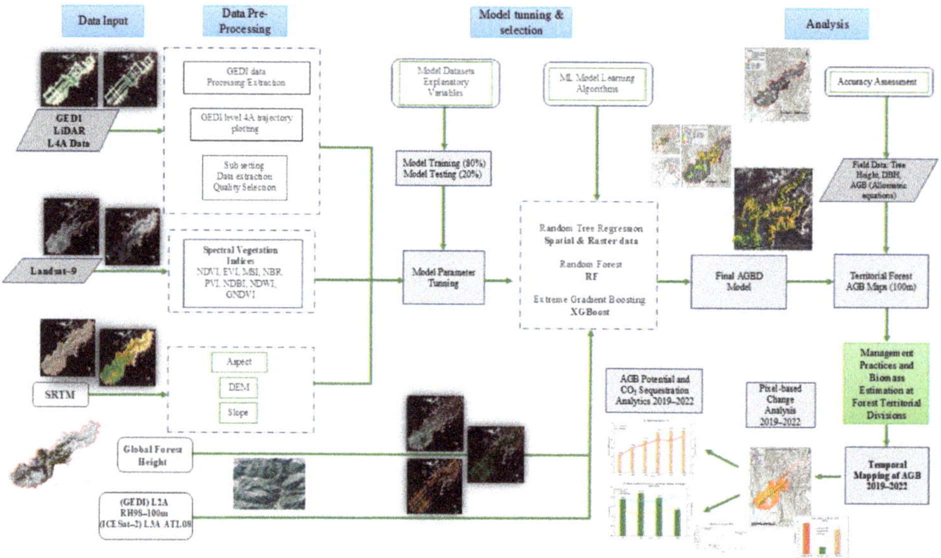

Figure 6. Methodological flowchart of forest biomass and carbon stock estimation using machine learning regression algorithms in designated forests of Mansehra District.

2.3.3. Parameter Selection

Topographic variables, including elevation and slope, were incorporated to evaluate the influence of the terrain on the forest structure and growth patterns. GEDI L4A-derived height metrics, RH98, provide critical information related to the vertical structure of a canopy height. The explanatory variables, including satellite datasets (bands and indices), were analysed using machine learning algorithms, such as random forest, XGBoost, and random tree regression, to assign importance scores to variables contributing to reliable AGB prediction. The regression models identified key variables with high importance scores, including forest height (from GEDI L2A data), the green band, DEM, and the red band, as critical factors influencing biomass estimation. Among these models, the random forest-based relationship between predictor variables and biomass is illustrated in Figure 7. Following the efficient split of 80:20%, as mentioned in the literature [49], these variables were utilized for training (80%) and testing (20%) the model, enabling the accurate prediction of above-ground biomass (AGB).

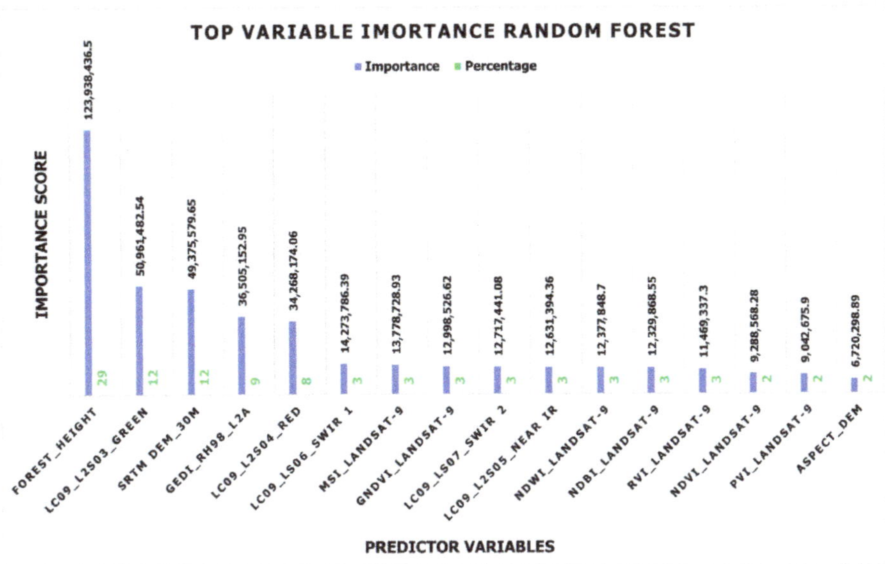

Figure 7. A descending sequence of the importance scores assigned to predictor variables using random forest.

Machine learning models were optimized using a grid search strategy combined with cross-validation. A 5-fold cross-validation was found to be suitable for optimizing model outputs. Table 2 outlines the fine-tuned hyperparameters used during the model training and testing phases for the best performance.

Table 2. Hyperparameters for training machine learning models.

Model Name	Model Parameter Characteristics	Value
Random Forest	Number of Trees	500
	Leaf Size	5
	Tree-Depth Range	36–50
	Mean Tree Depth	40
	% of Training Available per Tree	100
	Number of Randomly Sampled Variables	5
	Training and Test data %	80:20
	Model Out-of-Bag Error	805.9
Gradient Boosting	Number of Trees	500
	Leaf Size	5
	Tree-Depth Range	6–6
	Mean Tree Depth	6
	% of Training Available per Tree	100
	Number of Randomly Sampled Variables	5
	% of Training Data Excluded for Validation	20
	L2 Regularization (Lambda)	1.00
	Minimum Loss Reduction for Splits (Gamma)	0.00
	Learning Rate (Eta)	0.30
Random Tree Regression	Training Options:	
	Maximum Number of Trees	500
	Maximum Tree Depth	30
	Maximum Number of Samples	74,400
	Percent of Samples for Testing	20

Random forest inherently identifies critical features based on their ranked contribution to prediction accuracy. The Out-of-Bag (OOB) error was used to evaluate the model's predictive accuracy by providing an unbiased prediction error. Different combinations of explanatory variables, including the forest's optical, SRTM DEM, and spaceborne LiDAR structural parameters, were tested to evaluate the performance of model training that explains the variability of forest biomass and provides reliable estimates.

Model performance was evaluated based on the Root Mean Square Error (RMSE), Mean Absolute Error (MAE), and Coefficient of Determination (R^2). The optimal model demonstrated high R^2 and low RMSE and MAE values, affirming its suitability for precise and dependable AGB estimation.

3. Results

3.1. Explanatory Variable Evaluation

The variable importance matrices were studied, and 16 predictive variables, based on model training, were selected for prediction. Among the optical spectral bands and vegetation indices, B3, B4, B6, the Moisture Stress Index (MSI), and the Green Normalized Difference Vegetation Index (GNDVI) from the Landsat-9 datasets showed the highest importance score in the random forest model. These bands were particularly relevant to the ecological features of the moist and dry temperate forests. Band 3 (0.53–0.59 μm) is sensitive to vegetation health, reflecting the chlorophyll and moisture content in dense moist temperate forests and monitoring variations in canopy density. Band 4 (0.64–0.67 μm) is effective for vegetation stress detection due to its sensitivity to chlorophyll absorption, while Band 6 (1.57–1.65 μm) is sensitive to moisture content and soil–vegetation interactions, making it vital for analysing the canopy density. Similarly, in moist temperate forests, the dense canopy cover with a high moisture content was analysed by Green and SWIR-1 bands, which is effective in biomass estimation. In contrast, the red and SWIR-1 bands contribute to species health variation and moisture stress identification in the dry temperate zone for biomass estimation. Moreover, topographic and structural variables also contributed significantly. The DEM underscored the role of elevation in influencing the forest structure and biomass distribution, while GEDI RH98 provided crucial vertical-structure information at a 100 m resolution.

In contrast to the random tree regression technique, XGBoost assigned importance scores to the spectral bands B6, B4, and B3 that resemble the random forest algorithm. Forest height is the most critical predictor of AGB, followed by DEM. GEDI L2A data providing canopy cover and ground elevation estimates further enhanced our understanding of the vertical complexity and structure of the forest. The spectral bands, vegetative indices, topographic information, forest layers, and height estimation products from GEDI and the global forest canopy cover were used for enhanced biomass estimation. The random forest model achieved the highest R^2 of 0.86, demonstrating its effective predictability.

3.2. Model Selection and Accuracy Assessment

The scatter plots presented in Figure 8, corresponding to the three machine learning models, effectively depict the model's performance for the training data. Figure 8 shows the scatter plots of the training data, with 8A for random forest (R^2 = 0.97), 8B for random tree regression (R^2 = 0.97), and 8C for the XGBoost (R^2 = 0.95). The training data show a high correlation of R^2 in the range of 0.97 to 0.95.

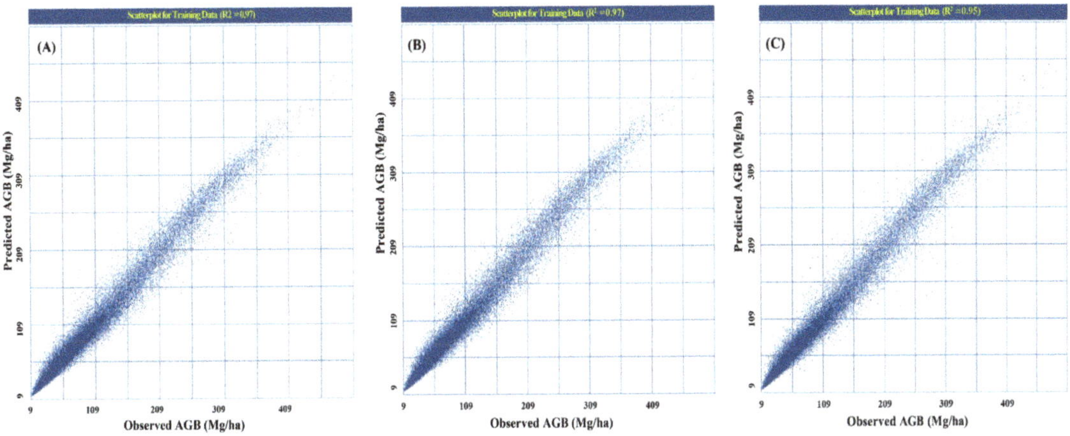

Figure 8. Scatter plots of random forest (**A**), random tree regression (**B**) and XGBoost (**C**) showing an analysis of GEDI AGB points for the training data.

Meanwhile, the test data in Figure 9 show the scatter plots with 9A for random forest (R^2 = 0.86), 9B for XGBoost (R^2 = 0.85), and 9C for random tree regression (R^2 = 0.84), underscoring the reliability and robustness of the random forest-trained model in predicting AGB based on given explanatory variables.

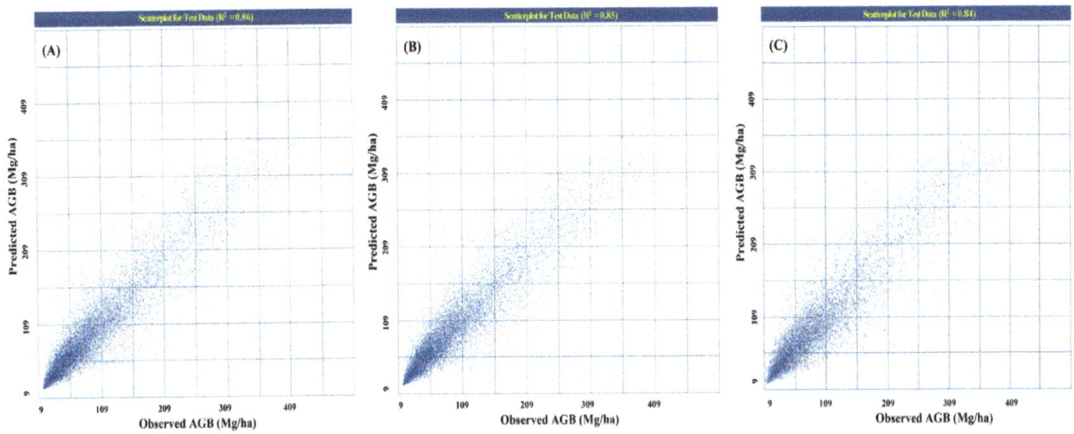

Figure 9. Scatter plots of random forest (**A**), XGBoost (**B**), and random tree regression (**C**) showing test data performed for analysing the GEDI AGB points and explanatory variables.

Table 3 presents the performance metrics of three machine learning models' random forest, random tree regression, and XGBoost for estimating the above-ground biomass (AGB) in designated forests of the Mansehra Forest. All models accurately capture the relationship between input variables and above-ground biomass (AGB), ensuring high predictive accuracy, generalizability, and robustness with the best performance by the random forest model. The performance metrics of the three models are given in the table below.

Table 3. Performance metrics of machine learning models.

Model Name	Training			Test		
	R^2	RMSE	MAE	R^2	RMSE	MAE
Random Forest	0.97	11.84	8.08	0.86	28.03	19.54
XGBoost	0.95	15.72	11.20	0.85	29.35	20.57
Random Tree Regression	0.97	14.38	10.98	0.84	31.22	21.76

A comparison of the machine learning algorithms in Figure 10 highlights the performance of the random forest, XGBoost, and random tree regression models. Among these, the random forest algorithm was selected as the best model for biomass estimation, with a high R^2 of 0.86. This model effectively utilized explanatory variables to predict the AGB variations across the designated forests in Mansehra.

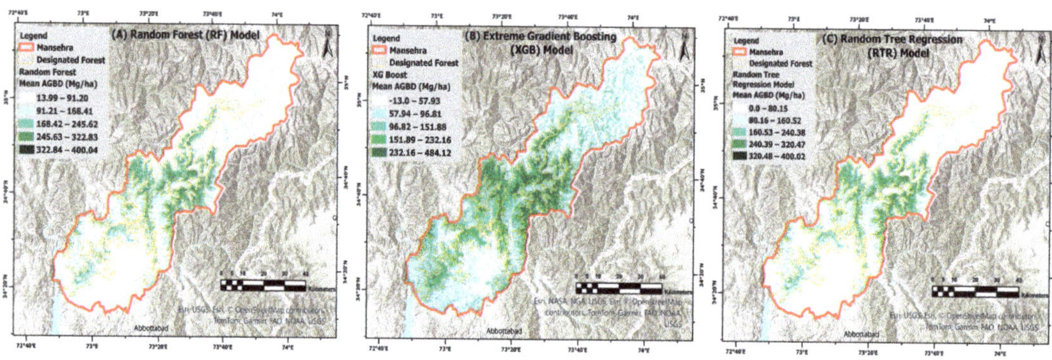

Figure 10. Biomass maps were established to compare the machine learning regression analysis of forest biomass in designated forests of Mansehra District: (**A**) XGBoost model; (**B**) random forest model; (**C**) random tree regression model.

The AGB estimates were validated using field data from various forest compartments, where allometric equations, derived through destructive sampling, correlated the tree diameter and height for ground biomass estimation. The actual AGB was calculated from ground inventory points using circular nested plots and were compared with model predictions, ensuring an accurate evaluation of the model's performance in estimating forest biomass. The predicted AGB value of 224.61 Mg/ha was 7.9% higher than the ground value of 208.13 Mg/ha, indicating a minor overestimation predicted by the proposed methodology using the GEDI L4A footprints. The validation results are encouraging, with a coefficient of determination (R^2) of 0.71 (Figure 11), indicating the reliability of the estimates and a good relation between the actual and predicted values.

The mean AGB value for the entire designated forest was 189.42 Mg/ha, closely matching the ground biomass estimate of 180.93 Mg/ha for moist temperate forests, with a difference of only 5.2%. However, the point-to-point difference was higher at 7.9%, likely due to the scale differences and the heterogeneity in the point-level data. This highlights the trained random forest model's superior, consistent, and accurate performance for generating mean-based estimates across the forest area.

Previous studies demonstrated similar overestimation tendencies in GEDI L4A data, especially for coniferous forests compared to broad-leaved forests [50]. They found that GEDI L4A AGB estimation was 8.94 times higher than ground data, primarily due to topographic variations within the footprint area distorting GEDI signals [51]. This underscores the challenges in AGB estimatation accuracy, which is influenced by the forest type and terrain complexity [52,53]. Despite these challenges, the integration of GEDI L4A and multisource data with machine learning models provides a robust approach for large-scale biomass estimation and carbon stock assessment [51].

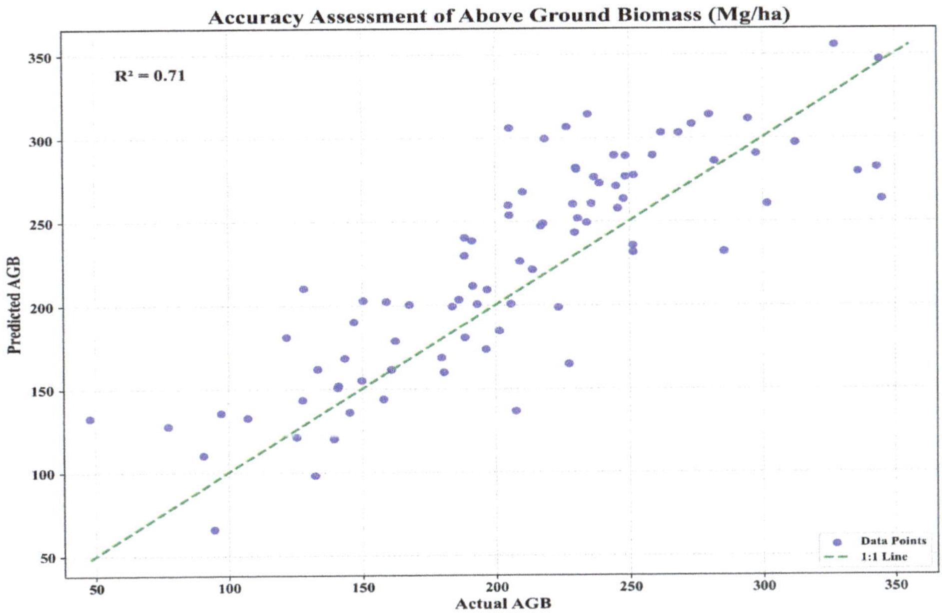

Figure 11. This scatter plot shows the actual and predicted above-ground biomass.

3.3. *Above-Ground Biomass Distribution in Designated Forests*

The distribution of AGB across protected, reserved, and community (guzara) forests provides valuable insights into carbon storage potentials. Figure 12 illustrates the carbon storage levels for protected, reserved, and guzara forests, highlighting the potential sites for future carbon storage strategies. The reserved forest exhibits the highest mean AGB of 242.19 Mg/ha, followed by the community forest at 175.23 Mg/ha. The protected forest, however, has the lowest mean AGB at 153.82 Mg/ha. These findings highlight the importance of developing biomass-specific yield strategies tailored to each forest management category's ecological and environmental conditions. This approach aligns with the single-tree selection silviculture management system, which optimizes carbon capture and storage based on site-specific characteristics [54].

The analysis focused on a compartment-wise biomass estimation managed by the forest department, revealing a mean AGB density of 189.43 Mg/ha, ranging from 23 Mg/ha to 400 Mg/ha. This range indicates the heterogeneous distribution of forest densities across the designated forests. The forest biomass in the Mansehra district shows significant spatial heterogeneity, with values ranging from a lower bound of 23 Mg/ha to an upper bound of 400.04 Mg/ha, compared to an average of 189.43 Mg/ha, as highlighted in Figure 13.

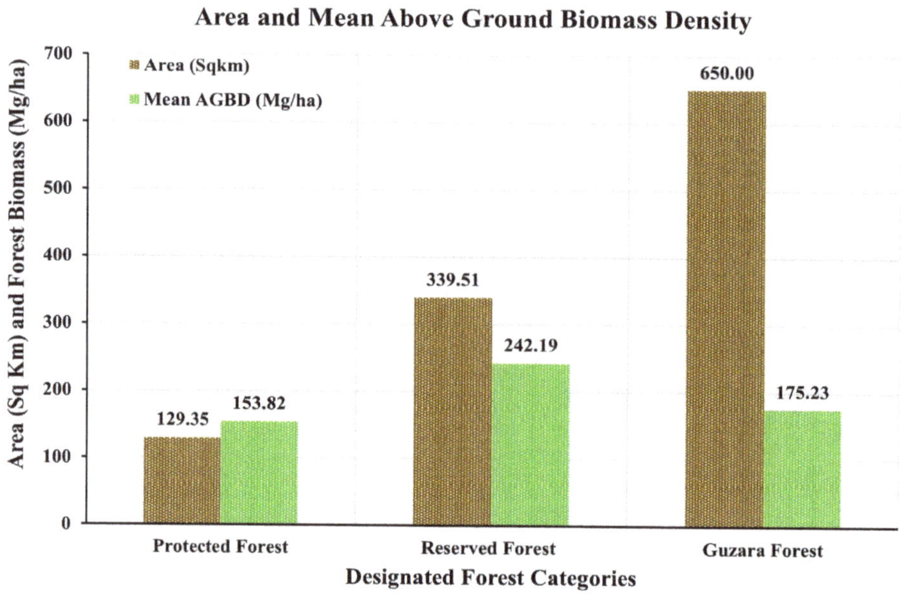

Figure 12. Category-wise area and mean AGB of the designated forests.

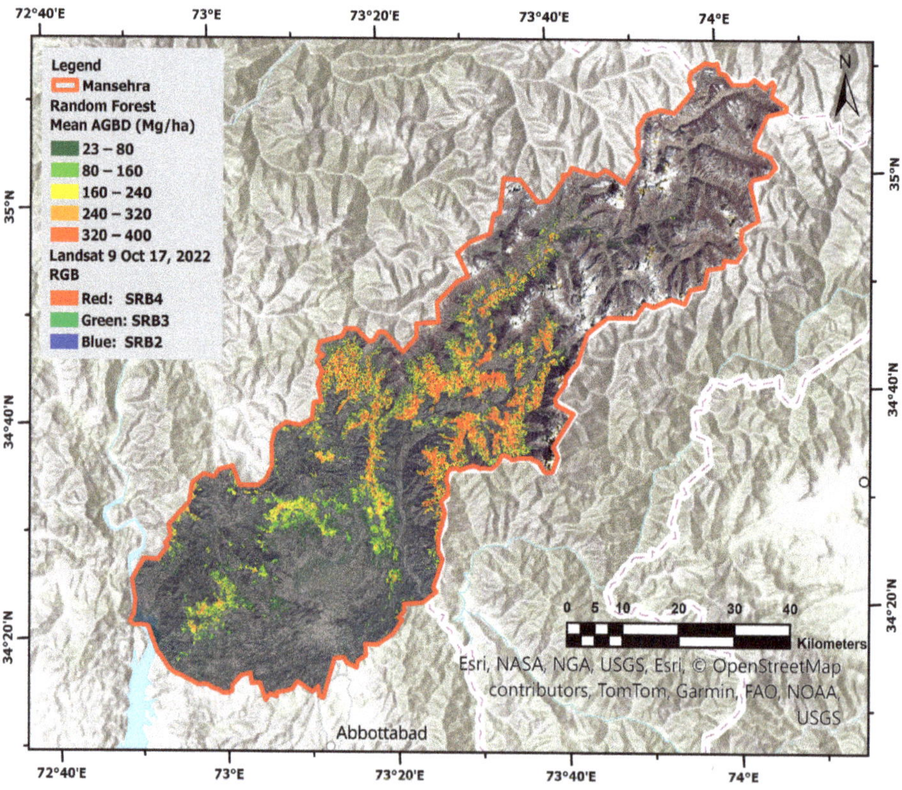

Figure 13. The spatial heterogeneity of forest biomass (Mg/ha) predicted by the random forest model in the designated forests of Mansehra District.

The compartments with high biomass values were primarily situated in the upper reserved forest region. The biomass map highlights the variability in forest carbon accumulated across compartments, with an area of high biomass in the upper region depicted in orange and red shades. The random forest algorithm demonstrated its efficiency in accurately distinguishing compartments with high and low biomass densities.

Compartments are the smallest forest management units, having an area range of 200 to 250 hectares, with the highest forest biomass accumulation illustrated in Figure 14. The highest AGB value of 270.11 Mg/ha was observed in Diwan Bela, followed by Manna at 268.52 Mg/ha. These compartments fall under the reserved forest category, excluding Batsangra and Julgran. The Batsangra and Julgran compartments belong to community forests with forest biomass values of 239.36 and 238.52 Mg/ha, respectively.

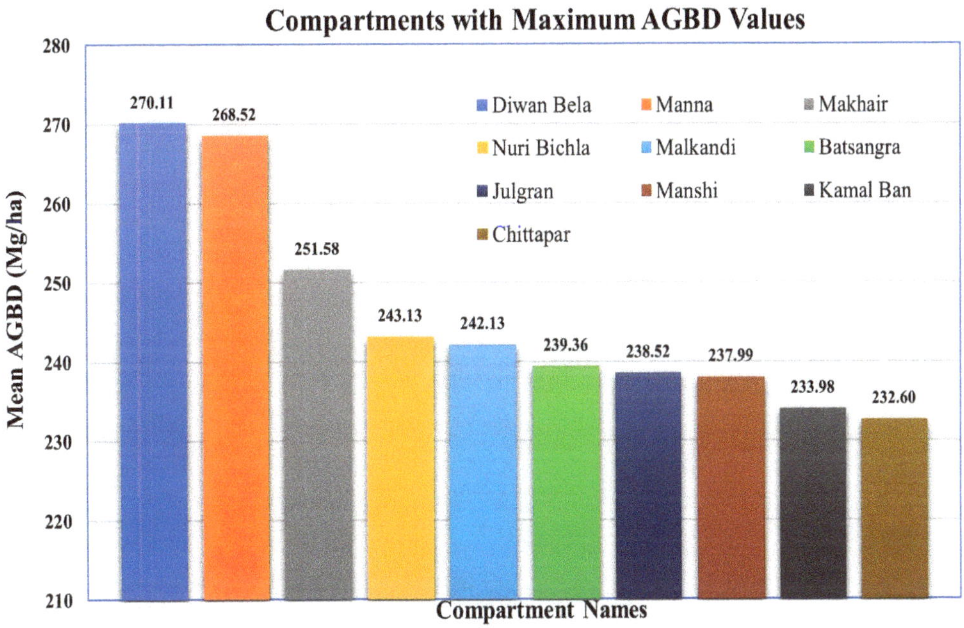

Figure 14. Compartments' order based on the highest AGB values in the designated forests of Mansehra District.

The high AGB in reserved forests is due to stringent governmental restrictions on harvesting, grazing, and local community concessions. Similarly, the high AGB in community compartments, such as Batsangra and Julgran, can be attributed to the inaccessible location. The compartment-wise AGB estimates provide actionable insights for efficient decision-making to support sustainable departmental harvesting regimes.

The methodological reliability and model performance were visually interpreted with biomass estimation across compartments. Figure 15 captures the variations in forest biomass, with the low-biomass compartments visually consistent with the area of sparse forest cover.

The geospatial insights from the biomass maps will guide critical site selection for afforestation and species regeneration campaigns, timber harvesting, fuelwood regulation, and biodiversity conservation in vulnerable areas. Figure 16 visually interprets the upper bound biomass values in compartments with a dense forest cover, offering a valuable framework for developing conservation strategies and prioritizing sustainability efforts.

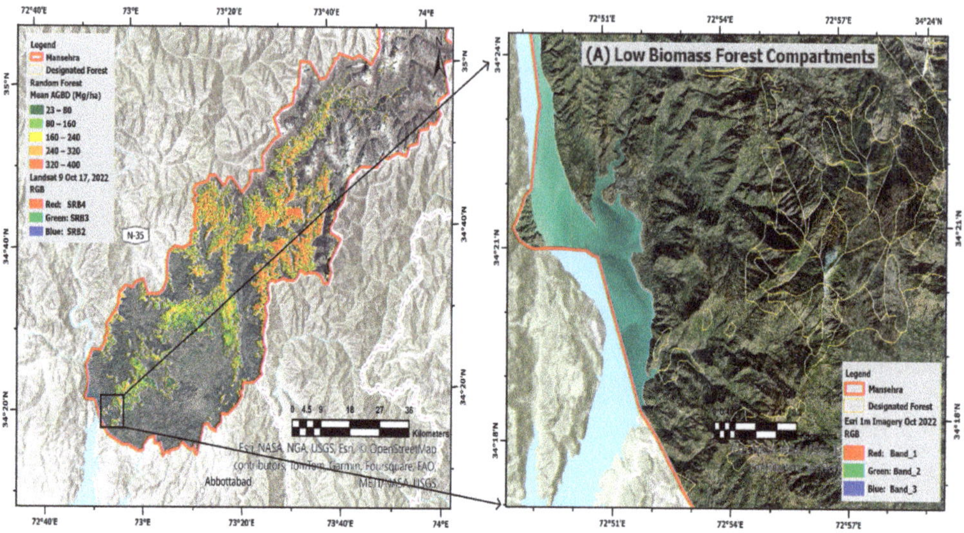

Figure 15. Potential compartments (low AGB) to demarcate new afforestation sites.

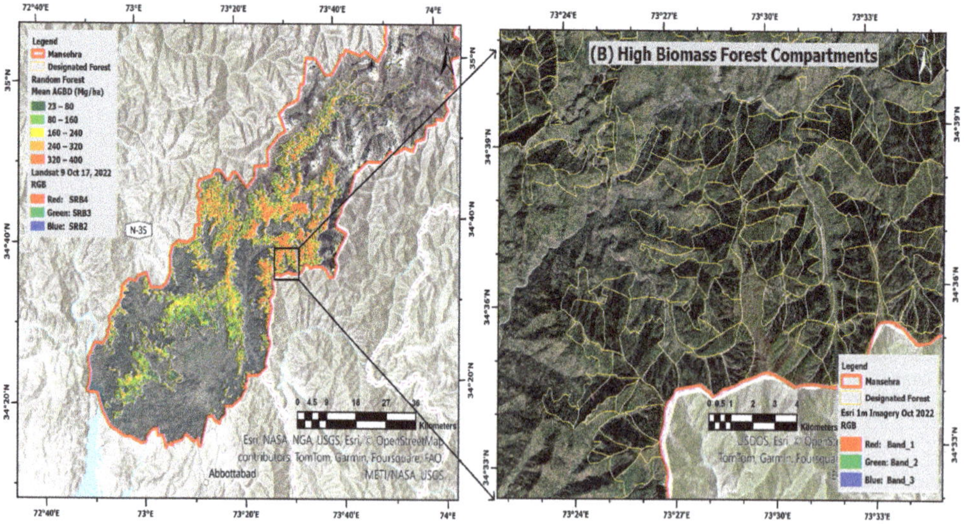

Figure 16. Qualitative analysis of the compartments, presenting the dense vegetation of mature forest stands with high AGB values (Mg/ha).

3.3.1. Reserved Forests

The state-owned reserved forests are managed under three working plan units: Kaghan, Lower Siran and Agror, and Upper Siran Reserved Forests. These units operate under "Working Plan", which are strategic documents outlining forest management practices over 5 to 10 years to estimate forest yields, restore degraded ecosystems, and ensure continuity in policies and actions. Each "Working Circle", a subdivision of the forests, follows a specific aim and silvicultural system, as outlined in the working plan.

The AGB distribution in reserved forests exhibits a histogram with a leftward skew, indicating a high mean AGB value of 242 Mg/ha. Diverse management practices within working circles contribute to variations in biomass and ecosystem conditions. The lower mean AGB values indicate reduced vegetation coverage in the lower Siran and Agror reserved working plan units (Figure 17). These observations emphasize the importance of continuous monitoring and spatial heterogeneity analysis to maintain existing carbon storage areas, conserve biodiversity, balance harvest and regrowth, restore degraded sites, and avoid land-use conversion practices.

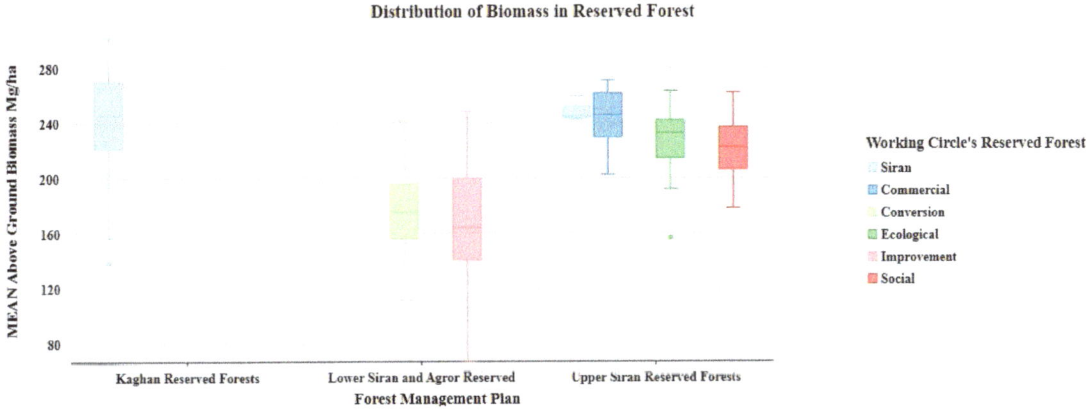

Figure 17. Box plots showing biomass distribution in reserved forest working plan management units.

High-AGB compartments are primarily located at higher altitudes, requiring robust management to mitigate erosion and landslide impacts on steep and vulnerable terrains. The histograms in Figure 18 illustrate the frequency distribution of the average AGB values across five working circles, with a normal distribution curve highlighting a high mean AGB value of 242 Mg/ha in the commercial working circle for the timber harvesting rotation patterns. In contrast, the improvement and conversion working circles have lower mean AGB values of 164 and 176 Mg/ha, respectively, reflecting the activities relevant to recovery and restoration. Thus, data-driven biomass estimation supports reliable yield-harvesting practices.

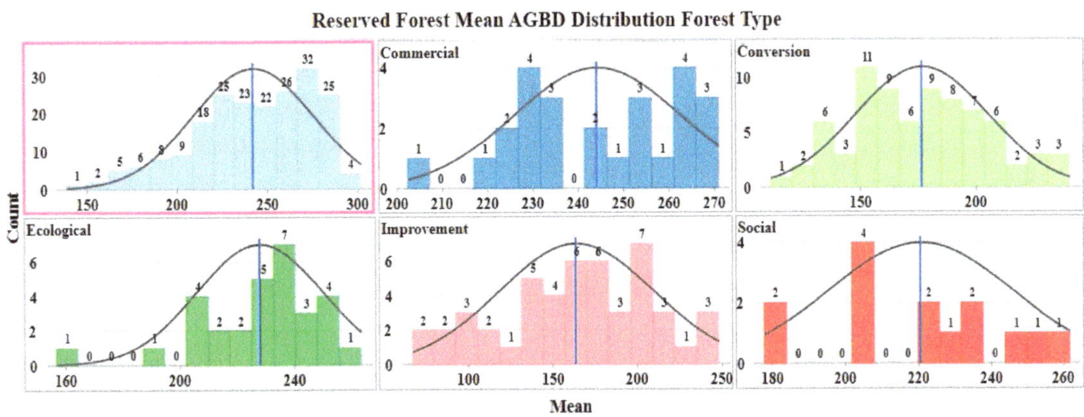

Figure 18. Mean distribution of above-ground biomass (AGB) estimates in different working circles.

The mean AGB values in reserved forest compartments, ranging from 67 Mg/ha to 300 Mg/ha (Figure 19), underscore the impact of harvesting restrictions and local community concessions on biomass levels. Compartments with high biomass, typically in mature forest stands, represent valuable sites for future management and conservation strategies.

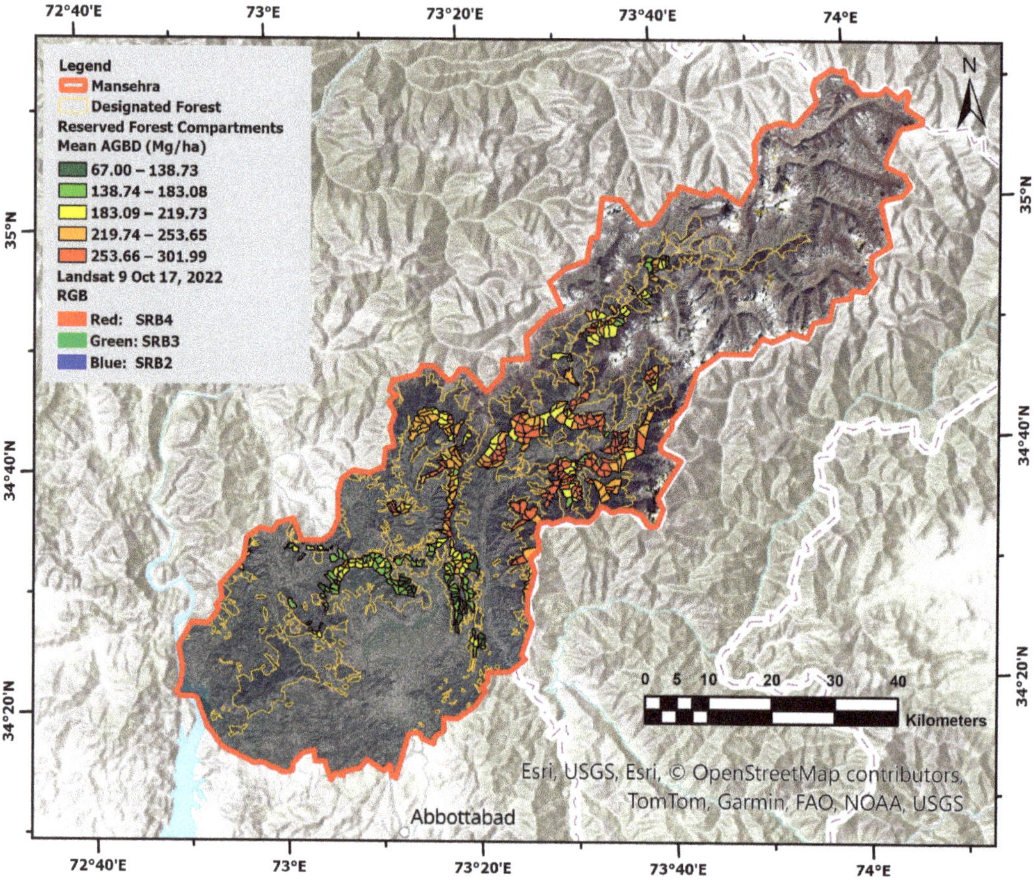

Figure 19. The spatial distribution of reserved forest compartments that shows the mean AGB values, classifying high-biomass-density compartments in a red tone.

3.3.2. Protected Forests

Protected forests, where local communities exercise government-permitted rights and concessions, exhibit a mean AGB value of 154 Mg/ha, with several compartments characterized by low biomass. These forests provide non-commercial timber, fuelwood, and fodder for local livestock. Managed under protection and social working circles, these compartments emphasize the recovery of under-stocked patches and optimized silvicultural practices.

The Gidderpur working plan management unit shows a particularly low mean AGB value of 122 Mg/ha (Figure 20). These accessible compartments face significant pressure from local compartments. Strengthening forest surveillance; fire management practices; and the promotion of alternative renewable energy sources, such as biogas and solar power, are recommended to alleviate the over-extraction of forest resources. Furthermore, controlling illegal timber harvesting and encroachments is an essential measure towards sustainable carbon storage management.

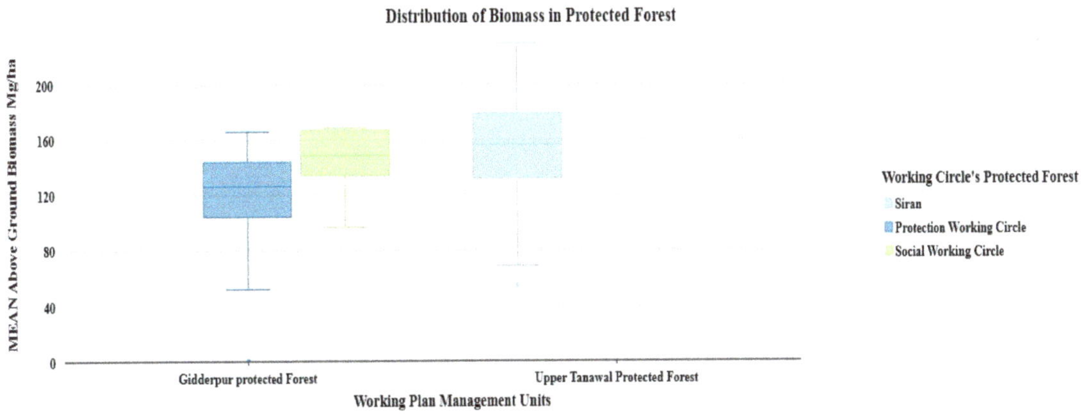

Figure 20. This box plot illustrates the distribution of mean biomass values in different working plans of protected forests.

Protected forests are managed under two working circles: protection and social. Biomass levels in the protection working circle are lower than those in the social working circle, as illustrated by the histogram in Figure 21, where high values of 144 Mg/ha are concentrated in the social working circle.

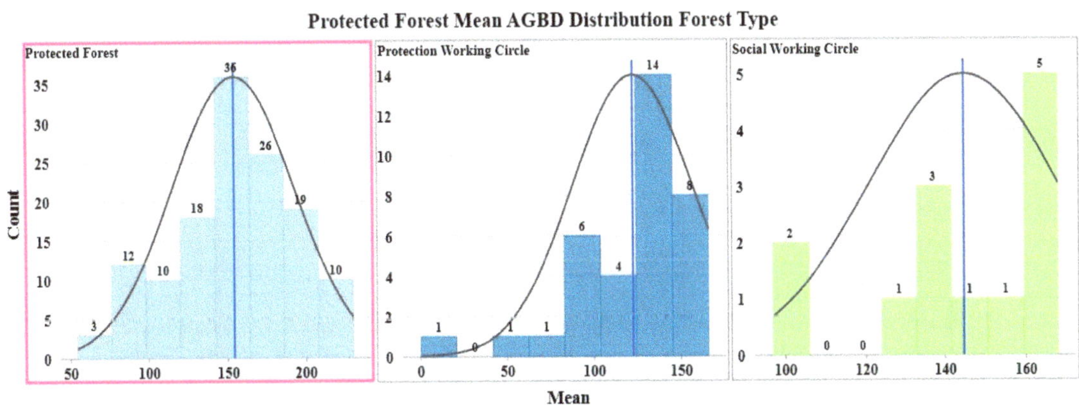

Figure 21. The histogram peaks illustrate the distributions of mean biomass values in different management units of protected forests, showing sub-mature vegetation stands.

Protected forests' relatively low AGB density highlights their suitability for future carbon sequestration projects managed under programs like REDD+. Identifying and mapping critical biodiversity hotspots in these ecosystems can align to foster a balanced approach for carbon sequestration goals with conservation priorities. The spatial distribution of AGB in the protected forest, as shown in Figure 22, ranges from 67 Mg/ha to 220 Mg/ha, highlighting the potential sites that support national and global carbon offset initiatives. These strategies can simultaneously benefit local communities and contribute to soil and water conservation efforts integral to sustainable carbon management.

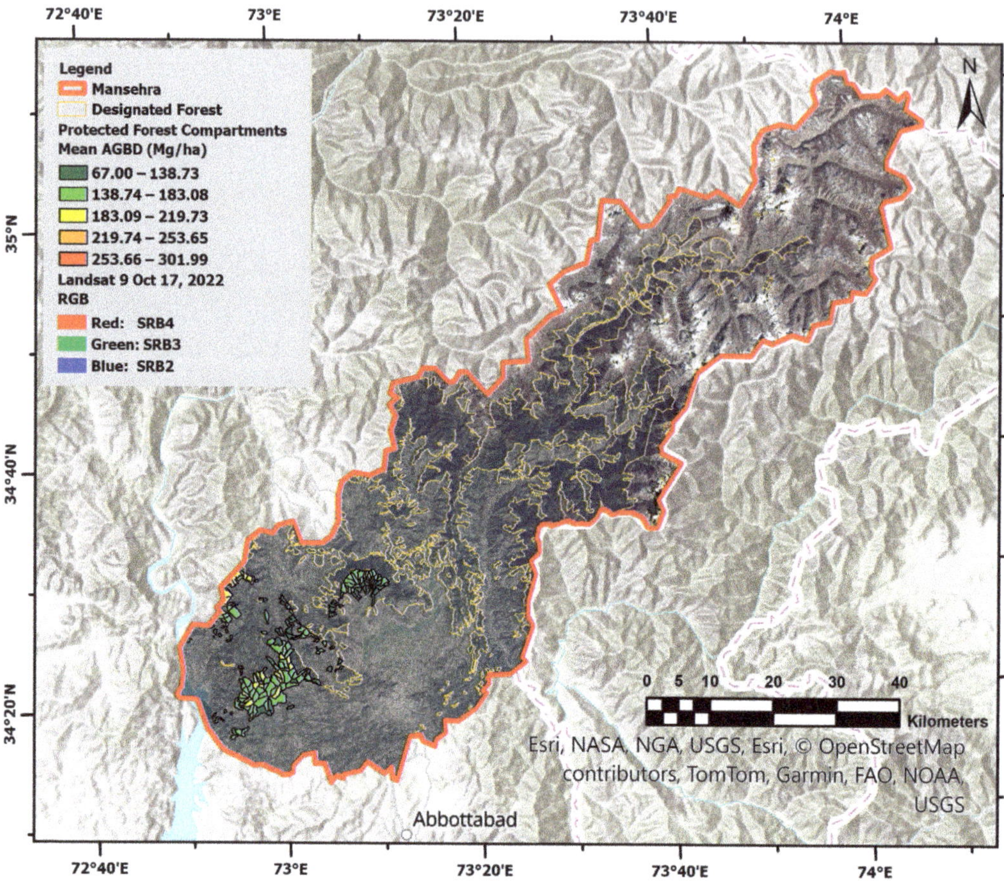

Figure 22. Mean AGB estimation value ranges in protected forest compartments are highlighted in lighter green tones, representing low biomass-value accumulation.

3.3.3. Community (Guzara) Forests

Community-owned forests account for approximately 58% of the designated forest area and are managed by the forest department. These forests exhibit diverse patterns of biomass accumulation due to variations in working circle activities. A privately-owned community forest is managed under six working plan activities, having a mean AGB value of 175 Mg/ha.

The biomass distribution in community forests (Figure 23) occupies a maximum number of compartments managed under 11 working circles, with priority given to community use, conservation, and timber production. The biomass levels exhibit significant variation, ranging from moderate to high, except in the Haripur guzara, where the biomass is 77 Mg/ha. The highest AGB values are found in the upper Siran community forest (215 Mg/ha), followed by the upper Kaghan community forest (208 Mg/ha). The Haripur guzara working plan's lower biomass values highlight the degraded forest patches. The high biomass levels in upper Siran guzara forests are due to activities such as conservation, ecotourism, biodiversity, and timber production.

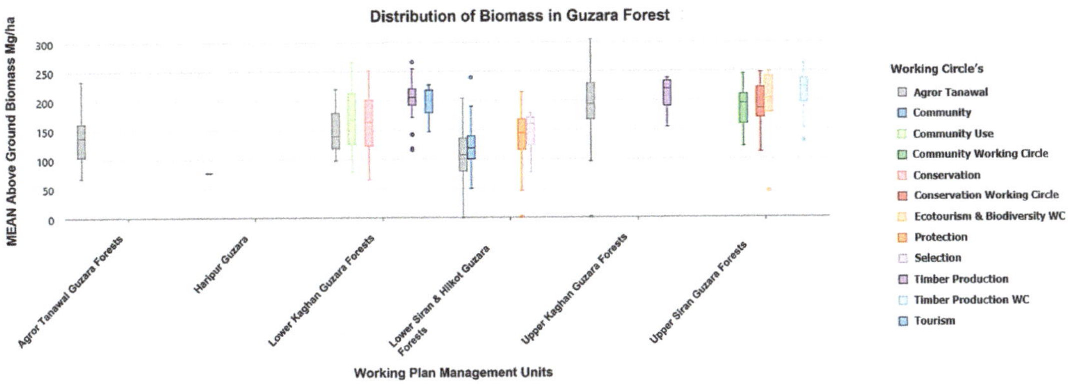

Figure 23. The biomass distribution in different working circles identifies the management practices adopted in the community-owned forests.

Community rights and concessions in these forests result in frequent disturbances like deforestation, grazing, fuelwood collection, and timber extraction, leading to AGB variations. The maximum AGB of 215 Mg/ha in timber production working circles reflects the communities' reliance on these forests for timber needs. A lower biomass value, ranging from 121 to 146 Mg/ha, was observed in community, protection, and selection working circles. Attention is required to address these disparities in need-based intense management practices (Figure 24).

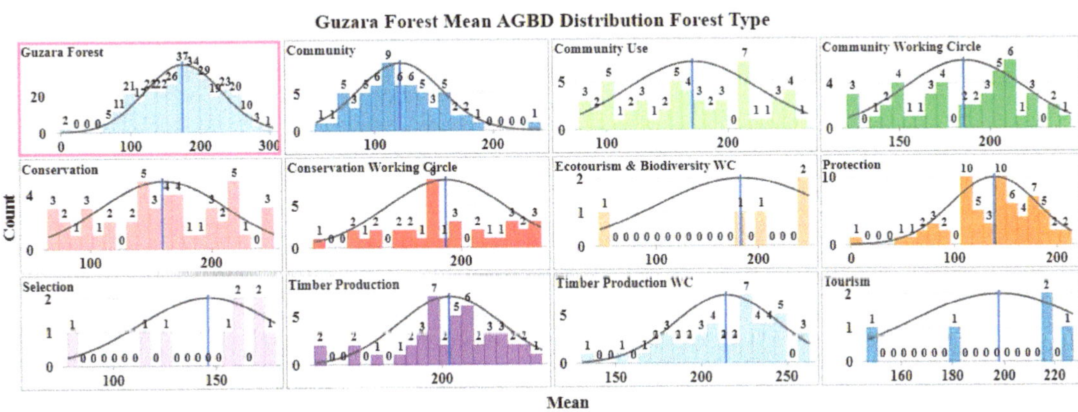

Figure 24. The biomass status in the community (Guzara) forests is represented by mean histogram values in working circles.

Extending from the low-lying areas to higher altitudes, community forests encompass a diverse range of forest cover, including moist, dry temperate, and sub-tropical chir pine forest zones. The biomass in the compartments varied from low to moderate levels, reflecting young and sub-mature forest stands. Target interventions, such as reforestation, grazing control, illegal logging prevention, agroforestry, and ecotourism initiatives, are critical for meeting and addressing community needs and conserving vulnerable Himalayan temperate forests. Certain compartments exhibit maximum biomass ranges of 250–300 Mg/ha. The carbon storage capacity in the different compartments signifies the need and demand for future carbon conservation strategies, and its spatial distribution is shown in Figure 25.

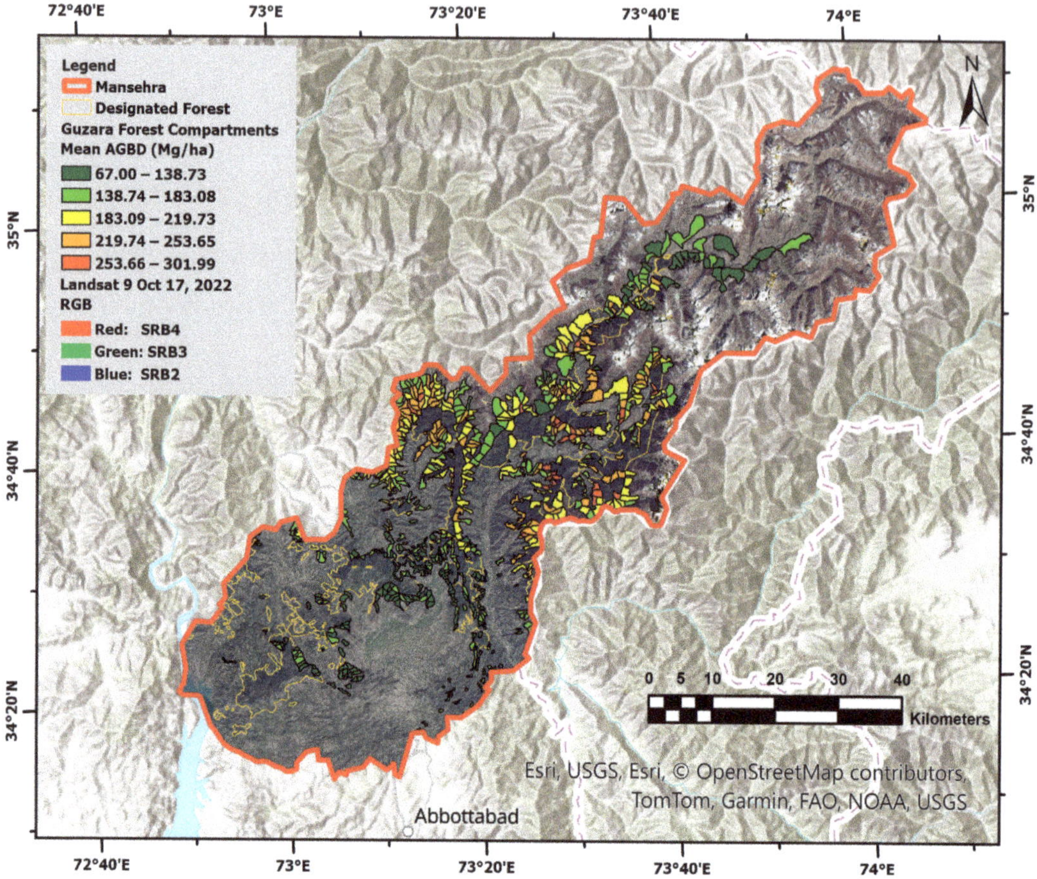

Figure 25. The extent of community forest compartments with mean AGB in all range values with different topographical locations in the district.

3.4. Ecological Analysis of Forest Cover and Biomass Dynamics in Mansehra

Mansehra District faces alarming climate change vulnerability due to increasing CO_2 emissions, escalating from 20.95 thousand tons/year in 2000 to 35.82 thousand tons/year in 2022. This trend mirrors the national increase in CO_2 emissions from 20 million tons/year in 2020 to 32 million tons/year in 2022. Although the forest cover increased in 2020–2021, AGB values declined during the same period, emphasizing the need to concentrate on AGB as a key factor for carbon sequestration rather than relying solely on the forest cover. The analytical results depicted in Figure 26 show the country and study area's CO_2 total emissions (Figure 26A) and a graphical presentation (Figure 26B) of the ecological analysis of the forest cover and biomass dynamics [55].

Forest carbon absorption rates vary by age classes and species, necessitating detailed AGB assessments for reliable CO_2 mitigation. The CO_2 mitigation potential was evaluated by converting the above-ground biomass (AGB) to above-ground carbon (AGC) and subsequently calculating the equivalent CO_2 sequestration based on IPCC guidelines [56,57]:

$$AGC = AGB \times 0.47 \tag{1}$$

$$CO_2 \text{ sequestration} = AGC \times 3.67 \tag{2}$$

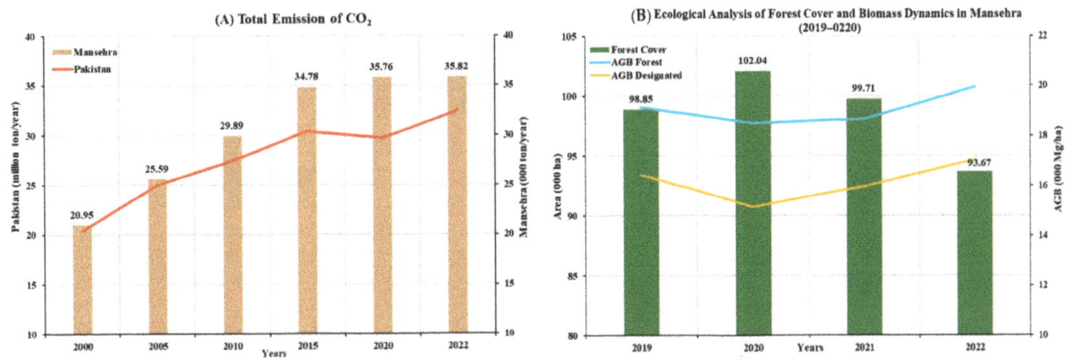

Figure 26. (**A**) Total CO_2 emissions' comparison of Mansehra District with Pakistan. (**B**) Comparison of temporal forest cover with the total sum values of above-ground biomass estimated in the designated forests and complete province.

Equation (1) indicates that 1 ton of AGB is equal to 0.47 tons of AGC, which, upon multiplication with 3.67 as per equation 2, can sequestrate 1.7249 tons of CO_2 from the atmosphere, and vice versa, 1 ton of CO_2 emission sink requirements needs 0.5798 tons of AGB. In 2022, the Mansehra district emitted 35,820 tons of CO_2 [48], requiring 20,770 tons of AGB for offsetting, compared to the available AGB of 19,940 tons, revealing a shortfall of 830 tons. Despite having 8.68% of the forest-rich KP province's area, Mansehra's AGB cannot offset CO_2 emissions. To bridge this gap, the appropriate measures required are continuous temporal monitoring to maintain minimum AGB in each compartment, mixed plantations of high-potential carbon storage, a multipurpose land-use concept of agroforestry practices, high-storage-carbon species on commercial long-term rotation periods, and awareness and community participation for long-term sustainability. Nationally, AGB requirements increased from 11.80 million tons in 2000 to 18.78 million tons in 2022 without significant changes or initiatives to increase the forest area or AGB (Table 4; Pakistan Bureau of Statistics).

Table 4. CO_2 emissions and AGB requirements in Mansehra and Pakistan.

Year	Mansehra (Values in Thousand Tons)		Pakistan (Values in Million Tons)	
	CO_2 Emissions	AGB Requirement	CO_2 Emissions	AGB Requirement
2000	20.95	12.14	20.35	11.80
2005	25.59	14.83	24.99	14.49
2010	29.89	17.33	27.43	15.90
2015	34.78	20.16	30.38	17.61
2020	35.76	20.73	29.66	17.20
2022	35.82	20.77	32.39	18.78

A temporal analysis of the AGB requirements against CO_2 emissions underscored the urgency for targeted measures. A trained model for the year 2022 was used for the prediction of AGB in 2019. Input parameters of 2019 were used in the trained random forest model to obtain an AGB prediction for 2019. A change analysis of the AGB for 2019 and 2022 was carried out by taking the difference image, as shown in (Figure 27), which reveals a net decrease in AGB across 95,000 ha compared to an increase of 22,000 ha and stability across 79,000 ha of the forest cover. Areas with significant increases and decreases in AGB are illustrated in Box 1 and Box 2, respectively. Notably, afforestation programs contributed to the rise in AGB, highlighting the potential of regeneration initiatives to counteract biomass loss.

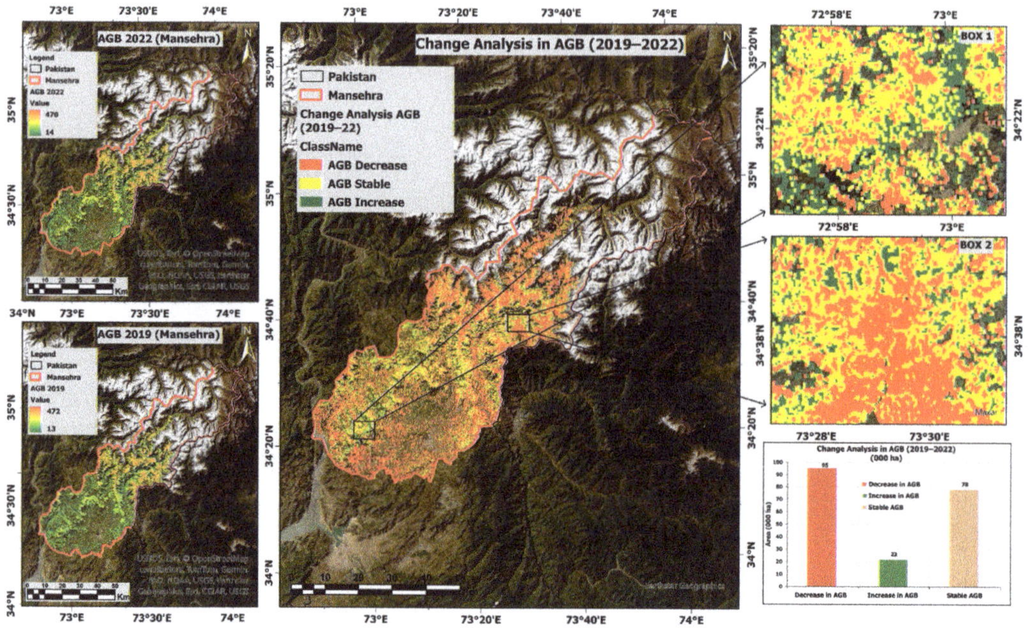

Figure 27. Carbon dynamics showing the distribution of forest biomass change patterns in the district for 2019–2022.

4. Discussion

Integrating GEDI L4A biomass density data with optical and ancillary datasets using machine learning addresses the challenges in biomass estimation in complex hilly terrains. The results provide insights into the biomass distribution and magnitude in mountainous landscapes per forest categories and demonstrate the utility of GEDI-derived data for forest biophysical parameters complemented with explanatory variables for enhanced accuracy and reliability.

4.1. Accuracy Analysis

The GEDI L4A outperforms other LiDAR systems like ICESat-1 and ICESat-2 due to its smaller footprint diameter (25 m) and higher sampling density, which are particularly advantageous for tropical and temperate forest applications [58]. Biases and underestimations in the GEDI-derived products were reduced through high-energy beam selection, improving the ground and canopy cover estimation in this South Asian region despite limited local calibration for its diverse ecosystems [59,60].

Key features contributing to AGB estimation accuracy include the canopy height, Landsat-9 green band (B3) and digital elevation, GNDVI, MSI, and GEDI L2A relative height data. These findings align with prior research [61–64]. The AGB variability patterns observed in the GEDI L4A dataset are consistent with the GEDI L4B data and other studies [62]. The model effectively predicts biomass at a detailed compartment level, capturing the Mansehra district's complex and diverse forest structures, similar to the studies by [65,66]. Recent studies show that combining the predictors related to the canopy cover, vegetation density, Landsat-9 spectral information data, and topographical variables enhances AGB estimation [67–70].

The random forest model achieved high performance, with an R^2 of 0.86, an RMSE of 28.03 Mg/ha, and an MAE of 19.54 Mg/ha on the test data. Ground validation showed satisfactory accuracy (R^2 = 0.71), demonstrating the model's robustness and generalizability. Biomass estimates ranged from around 60 to 426 Mg/ha, with R^2 ranging from 0.72 to 0.88 (Table 5). Similarly, AGB estimation using different optical and microwave datasets showed an R^2 value ranging from 0.63 to 0.77 (Table 6).

Table 5. Comparison of biomass estimation using Spaceborne LiDAR data.

Region	Data	Techniques	Mean AG (B/C)*/R^2	Ref
Himalayan moist temperate forest, Uttarakhand, India	Sentinel-1 and -2 and GEDI forest canopy height	RF[1] Algorithm	AGB 190.27 Mg ha^{-1}/0.88	[71]
NW Indian Himalayan foothills	ICESat-2 and Sentinel-1 FCH	RF model	AGB 426.41 Mg ha^{-1}/0.83	[26]
Xiaoshao, Yiliang Yunnan Province China	Sentinel-1 and -2, ALOS PALSAR-2, and GEDI L4A	RF model	AGB 59.09 Mg ha^{-1}/0.72	[51]
Biomass estimation in managed forests, Haldwani India	Forest layer, field data, and GEDI canopy height	MLR[2] models	AGB 153 Mg ha^{-1}/0.75	[11]

MLR[2] = multiple linear regression; AG (B/C)* = above-ground (biomass/carbon); RF[1] = random forest.

Table 6. Comparison of biomass estimation using optical and microwave data.

Region	Data	Techniques	Mean AG (B/C)*/R^2	Ref
Western Himalayan Indian forest	MODIS and L-band ALOS-PALSAR	RF[1] Regression	AGB 180.27 Mg ha^{-1}/0.77	[72]
Sub-tropical chir pine forest, Margalla Hill, Pakistan	DBH and height	Linear Regression	AGC 73.36 ± 32.55 Mg C ha^{-1}	[73]
Battagram KP, Pakistan	Sentinel-2 vegetation indices	Linear Regression	AGB 148.79 t ha^{-1}/0.67	[16]
Temperate and sub-tropical forests, KP, Pakistan	Spot-5 satellite (2.5 m)	Allometric Equations	AGC 85.05 ± 10.84 t ha^{-1}	[38]
Pinus roxburghii forest in Siran forest divsion, Pakistan	Landsat-8 (spectral indices)	Linear Regression	AGC 26–116 t ha^{-1}/0.63	[74]

AG (B/C)* = above-ground (biomass/carbon); RF[1] = random forest.

Limited biomass estimation research was conducted on forest compartments (basic administrative units) using LiDAR datasets, highlighting the key significance of this study. Point-based model accuracy helped the reliability and correct estimations of AGB in the compartments. This granularity is crucial for implementing target management strategies in Pakistan's diverse ecosystems, as highlighted by [75].

4.2. Comparison of Biomass Estimates

The Mansehra district stores a large percentage of carbon stock in temperate forests (83%), followed by sub-tropical pine forests (14%), sub-alpine forests (1.5%), and others (1.5%) [76]. This study predicted a mean above-ground biomass value of 189.42 Mg/ha, which differed by only 5.2% from the ground-sampled carbon stock of 180.93 Mg/ha, confirming its accuracy and efficiency. Carbon stock densities in the designated Mansehra forest range from 31 to 142 Mg/ha, aligning with values reported in the conifer-dominated forests of the western Himalayan region of India (73.30 to 245 C Mg/ha) [77]. Differences in carbon density ranges reflect variations in forest age and species distribution.

A comparison with other studies in the same area (Tables 4 and 5) validates the reliability of the AGB estimation presented in this study. Furthermore, the findings align with global AGB patterns, which rank temperate coniferous forests second to tropical forests, with an average AGB of approximately 102 Mg/ha. This study demonstrates significant improvements in AGB estimation, aligning with the ranges provided by GEDI L4B, albeit at a coarser resolution of 1 km.

4.3. AGB Potential and CO_2 Sequestration

Despite the substantial forest resources, the Mansehra district faces challenges in offsetting CO_2 emissions due to insufficient AGB. Current AGB values range from 23 to 400 Mg/ha in designated forests. Improving the forest biomass, particularly in low-AGB compartments, through efficient and sustainable forest management could enable the district to meet its emission-offset requirements.

Nationally, the gap between AGB capacity and CO_2 emissions remains significant. Pakistan currently requires at least 18.78 million tons of AGB to mitigate emissions. Projections suggest this requirement will rise to 21.58 million tons by 2030 and to 30.71 million tons by 2050, assuming a population growth of 1.7% and per capita CO_2 emissions of 0.080 tons annually. This requires a multi-faceted approach involving afforestation and reforestation by increasing the forest biomass through an increase in the forest area and AGB of existing forests by sustainable forest management, particularly in forest areas having low AGBs.

5. Conclusions

Accurate and reliable forest biomass estimation based on explanatory variables with consistent performance against all selected machine learning models with slight variations (R^2 from 0.85 to 0.86) signifies the suitability and effectiveness of explanatory variable selection. This study found the global forest canopy height, DEM, GEDI L2A canopy height data, and green and red optical bands to be efficient variables, with an RMSE of 28.03 Mg/ha, using a random forest algorithm. The average estimated AGB (189.42 Mg/ha) is 5.2% higher than the carbon inventory technique (ground) estimation of (180.93 Mg/ha), with $R^2 = 0.71$ presenting the high performance of the proposed methodology.

This study underscores the importance of monitoring AGB distributions at both the forest category and compartment scales, particularly in protected, reserved, and community forests. Detailed temporal monitoring and mapping by the forest department at the stand level or compartment scale enables informed decision-making, facilitating adjustments or shifts based on AGB threshold levels to achieve sustainable forest management. Moreover, the proposed methodological outcomes can serve as baseline information in developing the National Forestry Inventory, currently required under multiple international programs, particularly in the context of carbon credits.

Acknowledging the reliance of CO_2 sequestration on AGB capacity, this study calls for a paradigm shift in forest management strategies. Therefore, it is imperative to consider AGB as a primary metric in forest management rather than relying exclusively on forest cover areas. This necessitates a policy shift towards accentuating AGB estimation and addressing future demands. Pakistan requires 18.78 million tons of AGB to adjust its greenhouse gas budget to maintain environmental sustainability. This requirement is projected to increase to 37.23 million tons by 2030 and 52.97 million tons by 2050, respectively. Meeting these demands necessitates a multi-faceted approach, including afforestation, reforestation, and enhancing AGB in existing forests through effective management. Sustainable practices aimed at increasing AGB will be pivotal in addressing the challenges of carbon sequestration and climate change mitigation, ensuring long-term ecological and environmental stability.

Author Contributions: Conceptualization, M.I., G.Z. and R.A.F.I.; methodology, G.Z., M.I., M.K.L. and R.A.F.I.; software, C.X. and U.A.; validation, M.I., G.Z., and A.A.; formal analysis, M.I., M.K.L. and R.A.F.I.; investigation, M.I., G.Z. and R.A.F.I.; resources, G.J., Y.T. and C.X.; data curation, M.I.,

M.Y., A.A. and U.A.; writing—original draft preparation, M.I., G.Z. and R.A.F.I.; writing—review and editing, Y.T., M.Y. and G.J., visualization, M.I., G.Z. and R.A.F.I., supervision, G.Z., Y.T. and G.J.; project administration, Y.T. and C.X.; funding acquisition, G.J. and C.X. All authors have read and agreed to the published version of the manuscript.

Funding: This study was funded by the National Natural Science Foundation of China (grant no. 42471425).

Data Availability Statement: The data presented in this study will be made available upon request from the corresponding author.

Acknowledgments: We appreciate NASA/USGS for providing Landsat-9 imagery and the Khyber Pakhtunkhwa Forest Department for providing ground data to validate this research study. Moreover, Syed Rizwan Ahmad Kazmi, Aitezaz Mehfooz, Suleman Khan, and Hassan Mehmud from the Climate Change, Forestry, Environment, and Wildlife Department are specially acknowledged for their support not only in data provision but also for their assistance in the effective application of this research study.

Conflicts of Interest: All authors declared no conflicts of interest.

References

1. Sung, H.M.; Kim, J.; Shim, S.; Seo, J.B.; Kwon, S.H.; Sun, M.A.; Moon, H.; Lee, J.H.; Lim, Y.J.; Boo, K.O.; et al. Climate Change Projection in the Twenty-First Century Simulated by NIMS-KMA CMIP6 Model Based on New GHGs Concentration Pathways. *Asia Pac. J. Atmos. Sci.* **2021**, *57*, 851–862. [CrossRef]
2. Liu, Z.; Deng, Z.; Davis, S.J.; Ciais, P. Global Carbon Emissions in 2023. *Nat. Rev. Earth Environ.* **2024**, *5*, 253–254. [CrossRef]
3. Forzieri, G.; Dakos, V.; Mcdowell, N.G.; Ramdane, A.; Cescatti, A. Emerging Signals of Declining Forest Resilience under Climate Change. *Nature* **2022**, *608*, 534–539. [CrossRef]
4. Vijitharan, S.; Sasaki, N.; Tripathi, N.K.; Pramanik, M.; Tsusaka, T.W. Assessing Carbon Emission Reductions and Removals in Vavuniya District, Sri Lanka: REDD+ Project Contributions to Sustainability. *Next Sustain.* **2024**, *3*, 100035. [CrossRef]
5. Adnan, M.; Xiao, B.; Bibi, S.; Xiao, P.; Zhao, P.; Wang, H. Addressing Current Climate Issues in Pakistan: An Opportunity for a Sustainable Future. *Environ. Chall.* **2024**, *15*, 100887. [CrossRef]
6. Khan, I.A.; Khan, W.R.; Ali, A.; Nazre, M. Assessment of Above-Ground Biomass in Pakistan Forest Ecosystem's Carbon Pool: A Review. *Forests* **2021**, *12*, 586. [CrossRef]
7. Walker, W.S.; Gorelik, S.R.; Cook-Patton, S.C.; Baccini, A.; Farina, M.K.; Solvik, K.K.; Ellis, P.W.; Sanderman, J.; Houghton, R.A.; Leavitt, S.M.; et al. The Global Potential for Increased Storage of Carbon on Land. *Proc. Natl. Acad. Sci. USA* **2022**, *119*, e2111312119. [CrossRef] [PubMed]
8. Rawat, M.; Arunachalam, K.; Arunachalam, A.; Alatalo, J.M.; Kumar, U.; Simon, B.; Hufnagel, L.; Micheli, E.; Pandey, R. Relative Contribution of Plant Traits and Soil Properties to the Functioning of a Temperate Forest Ecosystem in the Indian Himalayas. *Catena* **2020**, *194*, 104671. [CrossRef]
9. Gajendiran, K.; Kandasamy, S.; Narayanan, M. Influences of Wildfire on the Forest Ecosystem and Climate Change: A Comprehensive Study. *Environ. Res.* **2024**, *240*, 117537. [CrossRef]
10. Petrokofsky, G.; Kanamaru, H.; Achard, F.; Goetz, S.J.; Joosten, H.; Holmgren, P.; Lehtonen, A.; Menton, M.C.; Pullin, A.S.; Wattenbach, M. Comparison of Methods for Measuring and Assessing Carbon Stocks and Carbon Stock Changes in Terrestrial Carbon Pools. How Do the Accuracy and Precision of Current Methods Compare? A Systematic Review Protocol. *Environ. Evid.* **2012**, *1*, 6. [CrossRef]
11. Musthafa, M.; Singh, G. Forest Above-Ground Woody Biomass Estimation Using Multi-Temporal Space-Borne LiDAR Data in a Managed Forest at Haldwani, India. *Adv. Space Res.* **2022**, *69*, 3245–3257. [CrossRef]
12. Manley, K.; Nyelele, C.; Egoh, B.N. A Review of Machine Learning and Big Data Applications in Addressing Ecosystem Service Research Gaps. *Ecosyst. Serv.* **2022**, *57*, 101478. [CrossRef]
13. Zhang, Y.; Liang, S.; Yang, L. A Review of Regional and Global Gridded Forest Biomass Datasets. *Remote Sens.* **2019**, *11*, 2744. [CrossRef]
14. Tang, G.; Beckage, B.; Smith, B.; Miller, P.A. Estimating Potential Forest NPP, Biomass and Their Climatic Sensitivity in New England Using a Dynamic Ecosystem Model. *Ecosphere* **2010**, *1*, 1–20. [CrossRef]
15. Ali, A.; Ashraf, M.I.; Gulzar, S.; Akmal, M. Development of an Allometric Model for Biomass Estimation of Pinus Roxberghii, Growing in Subtropical Pine Forests of Khyber Pakhtunkhwa, Pakistan. *Sarhad J. Agric.* **2020**, *36*, 236–244. [CrossRef]

16. Khan, K.; Iqbal, J.; Ali, A.; Khan, S.N. Assessment of Sentinel-2-Derived Vegetation Indices for the Estimation of Above-Ground Biomass/Carbon Stock, Temporal Deforestation and Carbon Emissions Estimation in the Moist Temperate Forests of Pakistan. *Appl. Ecol. Environ. Res.* **2020**, *18*, 783–815. [CrossRef]
17. Amjad, D.; Kausar, S.; Waqar, R.; Sarwar, F. Land Cover Change Analysis and Impacts of Deforestation on the Climate of District Mansehra, Pakistan. *J. Biodivers. Environ. Sci.* **2020**, *103*, 103–113. [CrossRef]
18. Spawn, S.A.; Sullivan, C.C.; Lark, T.J.; Gibbs, H.K. Harmonized Global Maps of above and Belowground Biomass Carbon Density in the Year 2010. *Sci. Data* **2020**, *7*, 112. [CrossRef] [PubMed]
19. Dubayah, R.; Blair, J.B.; Goetz, S.; Fatoyinbo, L.; Hansen, M.; Healey, S.; Hofton, M.; Hurtt, G.; Kellner, J.; Luthcke, S.; et al. The Global Ecosystem Dynamics Investigation: High-Resolution Laser Ranging of the Earth's Forests and Topography. *Sci. Remote Sens.* **2020**, *1*, 100002. [CrossRef]
20. Kumar, L.; Mutanga, O. Remote Sensing of Above-Ground Biomass. *Remote Sens.* **2017**, *9*, 935. [CrossRef]
21. Holcomb, A.; Mathis, S.V.; Coomes, D.A.; Keshav, S. Computational Tools for Assessing Forest Recovery with GEDI Shots and Forest Change Maps. *Sci. Remote Sens.* **2023**, *8*, 100106. [CrossRef]
22. Bullock, E.L.; Healey, S.P.; Yang, Z.; Acosta, R.; Villalba, H.; Insfrán, K.P.; Melo, J.B.; Wilson, S.; Duncanson, L.; Næsset, E.; et al. Estimating Aboveground Biomass Density Using Hybrid Statistical Inference with GEDI Lidar Data and Paraguay's National Forest Inventory. *Environ. Res. Lett.* **2023**, *18*, 085001. [CrossRef]
23. Musthafa, M.; Singh, G.; Kumar, P. Comparison of Forest Stand Height Interpolation of GEDI and ICESat-2 LiDAR Measurements over Tropical and Sub-Tropical Forests in India. *Environ. Monit. Assess.* **2023**, *195*, 71. [CrossRef] [PubMed]
24. Indirabai, I.; Nilsson, M. Estimation of above Ground Biomass in Tropical Heterogeneous Forests in India Using GEDI. *Ecol. Inf.* **2024**, *82*, 102712. [CrossRef]
25. Yang, Q.; Niu, C.; Liu, X.; Feng, Y.; Ma, Q.; Wang, X.; Tang, H.; Guo, Q. Mapping High-Resolution Forest Aboveground Biomass of China Using Multisource Remote Sensing Data. *GISci. Remote Sens.* **2023**, *60*, 2203303. [CrossRef]
26. Nandy, S.; Srinet, R.; Padalia, H. Mapping Forest Height and Aboveground Biomass by Integrating ICESat-2, Sentinel-1 and Sentinel-2 Data Using Random Forest Algorithm in Northwest Himalayan Foothills of India. *Geophys. Res. Lett.* **2021**, *48*, e2021GL093799. [CrossRef]
27. Forkuor, G.; Benewinde Zoungrana, J.B.; Dimobe, K.; Ouattara, B.; Vadrevu, K.P.; Tondoh, J.E. Above-Ground Biomass Mapping in West African Dryland Forest Using Sentinel-1 and 2 Datasets—A Case Study. *Remote Sens. Environ.* **2020**, *236*, 111496. [CrossRef]
28. Fayad, I.; Baghdadi, N.; Guitet, S.; Bailly, J.S.; Hérault, B.; Gond, V.; El Hajj, M.; Tong Minh, D.H. Aboveground Biomass Mapping in French Guiana by Combining Remote Sensing, Forest Inventories and Environmental Data. *Int. J. Appl. Earth Obs. Geoinf.* **2016**, *52*, 502–514. [CrossRef]
29. Zhao, X.; Hu, W.; Han, J.; Wei, W.; Xu, J. Urban Above-Ground Biomass Estimation Using GEDI Laser Data and Optical Remote Sensing Images. *Remote Sens.* **2024**, *16*, 1229. [CrossRef]
30. Duncanson, L.; Kellner, J.R.; Armston, J.; Dubayah, R.; Minor, D.M.; Hancock, S.; Healey, S.P.; Patterson, P.L. Aboveground Biomass Density Models for NASA's Global Ecosystem Dynamics Investigation (GEDI) Lidar Mission. *Remote Sens. Environ.* **2022**, *270*, 112845. [CrossRef]
31. Xu, L.; Yu, J.; Shu, Q.; Luo, S.; Zhou, W.; Duan, D. Forest Aboveground Biomass Estimation Based on Spaceborne LiDAR Combining Machine Learning Model and Geostatistical Method. *Front. Plant Sci.* **2024**, *15*, 1428268. [CrossRef]
32. Torre-Tojal, L.; Bastarrika, A.; Boyano, A.; Lopez-Guede, J.M.; Graña, M. Above-Ground Biomass Estimation from LiDAR Data Using Random Forest Algorithms. *J. Comput. Sci.* **2022**, *58*, 101517. [CrossRef]
33. Forest, M.; Wang, C.; Datcu, M.P.; Tang, Y.; Tian, S.; Tian, X.; Li, J.; Zhang, F.; Zhang, H.; Jiang, M. Forest Aboveground Biomass Estimation Using Multisource Remote Sensing Data and Deep Learning Algorithms: A Case Study over Hangzhou Area in China. *Remote Sens.* **2024**, *16*, 1074. [CrossRef]
34. Cheng, F.; Ou, G.; Wang, M.; Liu, C. Remote Sensing Estimation of Forest Carbon Stock Based on Machine Learning Algorithms. *Forests* **2024**, *15*, 681. [CrossRef]
35. Zhang, X.; Shen, H.; Huang, T.; Wu, Y.; Guo, B.; Liu, Z.; Luo, H.; Tang, J.; Zhou, H.; Wang, L.; et al. Improved Random Forest Algorithms for Increasing the Accuracy of Forest Aboveground Biomass Estimation Using Sentinel-2 Imagery. *Ecol. Indic.* **2024**, *159*, 111752. [CrossRef]
36. Wang, E.; Huang, T.; Liu, Z.; Bao, L.; Guo, B.; Yu, Z.; Feng, Z.; Luo, H.; Ou, G. Improving Forest Above-Ground Biomass Estimation Accuracy Using Multi-Source Remote Sensing and Optimized Least Absolute Shrinkage and Selection Operator Variable Selection Method. *Remote Sens.* **2024**, *16*, 4497. [CrossRef]
37. Anees, S.A.; Mehmood, K.; Khan, W.R.; Sajjad, M.; Alahmadi, T.A.; Alharbi, S.A.; Luo, M. Integration of Machine Learning and Remote Sensing for above Ground Biomass Estimation through Landsat-9 and Field Data in Temperate Forests of the Himalayan Region. *Ecol. Inform.* **2024**, *82*, 102732. [CrossRef]
38. Ali, A.; Ashraf, M.I.; Gulzar, S.; Akmal, M. Estimation of Forest Carbon Stocks in Temperate and Subtropical Mountain Systems of Pakistan: Implications for REDD+ and Climate Change Mitigation. *Environ. Monit. Assess.* **2020**, *192*, 198. [CrossRef] [PubMed]

39. Shahzad, N.; Saeed, U.; Gilani, H.; Ahmad, S.R.; Ashraf, I.; Irteza, S.M. Evaluation of State and Community/Private Forests in Punjab, Pakistan Using Geospatial Data and Related Techniques. *For. Ecosyst.* **2015**, *2*, 7. [CrossRef]
40. Nizami, S.M. The Inventory of the Carbon Stocks in Sub Tropical Forests of Pakistan for Reporting under Kyoto Protocol. *J. Res.* **2012**, *23*, 377–384. [CrossRef]
41. Masek, J.G.; Wulder, M.A.; Markham, B.; McCorkel, J.; Crawford, C.J.; Storey, J.; Jenstrom, D.T. Landsat 9: Empowering Open Science and Applications through Continuity. *Remote Sens. Environ.* **2020**, *248*, 111968. [CrossRef]
42. Lu, D.; Chen, Q.; Wang, G.; Liu, L.; Li, G.; Moran, E. A Survey of Remote Sensing-Based Aboveground Biomass Estimation Methods in Forest Ecosystems. *Int. J. Digit. Earth* **2016**, *9*, 63–105. [CrossRef]
43. Potapov, P.; Li, X.; Hernandez-Serna, A.; Tyukavina, A.; Hansen, M.C.; Kommareddy, A.; Pickens, A.; Turubanova, S.; Tang, H.; Silva, C.E.; et al. Mapping Global Forest Canopy Height through Integration of GEDI and Landsat Data. *Remote Sens. Environ.* **2021**, *253*, 112165. [CrossRef]
44. Zhu, X.; Liu, D. Improving Forest Aboveground Biomass Estimation Using Seasonal Landsat NDVI Time-Series. *ISPRS J. Photogramm. Remote Sens.* **2015**, *102*, 222–231. [CrossRef]
45. David, R.M.; Rosser, N.J.; Donoghue, D.N.M. Improving above Ground Biomass Estimates of Southern Africa Dryland Forests by Combining Sentinel-1 SAR and Sentinel-2 Multispectral Imagery. *Remote Sens. Environ.* **2022**, *282*, 113232. [CrossRef]
46. Nandy, S.; Kushwaha, S.P.S. Forest Biomass Assessment Integrating Field Inventory and Optical Remote Sensing Data: A Systematic Review. *Int. J. Plant Environ.* **2021**, *7*, 181–186. [CrossRef]
47. Alexandridis, T.; Perakis, K. Vegetation Indices: Advances Made in Biomass Estimation and Vegetation Monitoring in the Last 30 Years. *Geocarto Int.* **2006**, *21*, 21–28.
48. Centre, E.C.J.R.; Crippa, M.; Guizzardi, D.; Pagani, F.; Banja, M.; Muntean, M.; Schaaf, E.; Monforti-Ferrario, F.; Becker, W.; Quadrelli, R.; et al. *GHG Emissions of All World Countries*; Publications Office of the European Union: Luxembourg, 2024.
49. Bichri, H.; Chergui, A.; Hain, M. Investigating the Impact of Train/Test Split Ratio on the Performance of Pre-Trained Models with Custom Datasets. *Int. J. Adv. Comput. Sci. Appl.* **2024**, *15*, 331. [CrossRef]
50. Hasan, L. An Anatomy of State Failures in Forest Management in Pakistan. In *Pakistan Development Review*; Pakistan Institute of Development Economics: Islamabad, Pakistan, 2007; Volume 46.
51. Wang, C.; Zhang, W.; Ji, Y.; Marino, A.; Li, C.; Wang, L.; Zhao, H.; Wang, M. Estimation of Aboveground Biomass for Different Forest Types Using Data from Sentinel-1, Sentinel-2, ALOS PALSAR-2, and GEDI. *Forests* **2024**, *15*, 215. [CrossRef]
52. Kanmegne Tamga, D.; Latifi, H.; Ullmann, T.; Baumhauer, R.; Bayala, J.; Thiel, M. Estimation of Aboveground Biomass in Agroforestry Systems over Three Climatic Regions in West Africa Using Sentinel-1, Sentinel-2, ALOS, and GEDI Data. *Sensors* **2022**, *23*, 349. [CrossRef] [PubMed]
53. Gao, Y.; Lu, D.; Li, G.; Wang, G.; Chen, Q.; Liu, L.; Li, D. Comparative Analysis of Modeling Algorithms for Forest Aboveground Biomass Estimation in a Subtropical Region. *Remote Sens.* **2018**, *10*, 627. [CrossRef]
54. Li, Y.; Li, C.; Li, M.; Liu, Z. Influence of Variable Selection and Forest Type on Forest Aboveground Biomass Estimation Using Machine Learning Algorithms. *Forests* **2019**, *10*, 1073. [CrossRef]
55. Hoover, C.M.; Smith, J.E. Aboveground Live Tree Carbon Stock and Change in Forests of Conterminous United States: Influence of Stand Age. *Carbon Balance Manag.* **2023**, *18*, 7. [CrossRef] [PubMed]
56. IPCC. *2006 IPCC Guidelines for National Greenhouse Gas Inventories, Prepared by the National Greenhouse Gas Inventories Programme*; Eggleston, H.S., Buendia, L., Miwa, K., Ngara, T., Tanabe, K., Eds.; IGES: Hayama, Japan, 2006.
57. Bai, Y.; Ding, G. Estimation of Changes in Carbon Sequestration and Its Economic Value with Various Stand Density and Rotation Age of Pinus Massoniana Plantations in China. *Sci. Rep.* **2024**, *14*, 16852. [CrossRef] [PubMed]
58. Jia, D.; Wang, C.; Hakkenberg, C.R.; Numata, I.; Elmore, A.J.; Cochrane, M.A. Accuracy Evaluation and Effect Factor Analysis of GEDI Aboveground Biomass Product for Temperate Forests in the Conterminous United States. *GIsci. Remote Sens.* **2023**, *61*, 2292374. [CrossRef]
59. Rodda, S.R.; Nidamanuri, R.R.; Fararoda, R.; Mayamanikandan, T.; Rajashekar, G. Evaluation of Height Metrics and Above-Ground Biomass Density from GEDI and ICESat-2 Over Indian Tropical Dry Forests Using Airborne LiDAR Data. *J. Indian Soc. Remote Sens.* **2024**, *52*, 841–856. [CrossRef]
60. Liu, A.; Cheng, X.; Chen, Z. Performance Evaluation of GEDI and ICESat-2 Laser Altimeter Data for Terrain and Canopy Height Retrievals. *Remote Sens. Environ.* **2021**, *264*, 112571. [CrossRef]
61. Zhang, C.; Wang, K.; Yue, Y.; Qi, X.; Zhang, M. Assessing Regional Ecosystem Conditions Using Geospatial Techniques—A Review. *Sensors* **2023**, *23*, 4101. [CrossRef] [PubMed]
62. Dorado-Roda, I.; Pascual, A.; Godinho, S.; Silva, C.A.; Botequim, B.; Rodríguez-Gonzálvez, P.; González-Ferreiro, E.; Guerra-Hernández, J. Assessing the Accuracy of GEDI Data for Canopy Height and Aboveground Biomass Estimates in Mediterranean Forests. *Remote Sens.* **2021**, *13*, 2279. [CrossRef]

63. Rodríguez-Veiga, P.; Quegan, S.; Carreiras, J.; Persson, H.J.; Fransson, J.E.S.; Hoscilo, A.; Ziółkowski, D.; Stereńczak, K.; Lohberger, S.; Stängel, M.; et al. Forest Biomass Retrieval Approaches from Earth Observation in Different Biomes. *Int. J. Appl. Earth Obs. Geoinf.* **2019**, *77*, 53–68. [CrossRef]
64. Sainuddin, F.V.; Malek, G.; Rajwadi, A.; Nagar, P.S.; Asok, S.V.; Reddy, C.S. Estimating Above-Ground Biomass of the Regional Forest Landscape of Northern Western Ghats Using Machine Learning Algorithms and Multi-Sensor Remote Sensing Data. *J. Indian Soc. Remote Sens.* **2024**, *52*, 885–902. [CrossRef]
65. Yang, L.; Liang, S.; Zhang, Y. A New Method for Generating a Global Forest Aboveground Biomass Map from Multiple High-Level Satellite Products and Ancillary Information. *IEEE J. Sel. Top. Appl. Earth Obs. Remote Sens.* **2020**, *13*, 2587–2597. [CrossRef]
66. Hu, T.; Su, Y.; Xue, B.; Liu, J.; Zhao, X.; Fang, J.; Guo, Q. Mapping Global Forest Aboveground Biomass with Spaceborne LiDAR, Optical Imagery, and Forest Inventory Data. *Remote Sens.* **2016**, *8*, 565. [CrossRef]
67. Santoro, M.; Cartus, O.; Carvalhais, N.; Rozendaal, D.M.A.; Avitabile, V.; Araza, A.; De Bruin, S.; Herold, M.; Quegan, S.; Rodríguez-Veiga, P.; et al. The Global Forest Above-Ground Biomass Pool for 2010 Estimated from High-Resolution Satellite Observations. *Earth Syst. Sci. Data* **2021**, *13*, 3927–3950. [CrossRef]
68. Bruening, J.M.; Fischer, R.; Bohn, F.J.; Armston, J.; Armstrong, A.H.; Knapp, N.; Tang, H.; Huth, A.; Dubayah, R. Challenges to Aboveground Biomass Prediction from Waveform Lidar. *Environ. Res. Lett.* **2021**, *16*, 125013. [CrossRef]
69. Labrière, N.; Davies, S.J.; Disney, M.I.; Duncanson, L.I.; Herold, M.; Lewis, S.L.; Phillips, O.L.; Quegan, S.; Saatchi, S.S.; Schepaschenko, D.G.; et al. Toward a Forest Biomass Reference Measurement System for Remote Sensing Applications. *Glob. Chang. Biol.* **2023**, *29*, 827–840. [CrossRef] [PubMed]
70. Campbell, M.J.; Dennison, P.E.; Kerr, K.L.; Brewer, S.C.; Anderegg, W.R.L. Scaled Biomass Estimation in Woodland Ecosystems: Testing the Individual and Combined Capacities of Satellite Multispectral and Lidar Data. *Remote Sens. Environ.* **2021**, *262*, 112511. [CrossRef]
71. Bhandari, K.; Srinet, R.; Nandy, S. Forest Height and Aboveground Biomass Mapping by Synergistic Use of GEDI and Sentinel Data Using Random Forest Algorithm in the Indian Himalayan Region. *J. Indian Soc. Remote Sens.* **2024**, *52*, 857–869. [CrossRef]
72. Fararoda, R.; Reddy, R.S.; Rajashekar, G.; Chand, T.R.K.; Jha, C.S.; Dadhwal, V.K. Improving Forest above Ground Biomass Estimates over Indian Forests Using Multi Source Data Sets with Machine Learning Algorithm. *Ecol. Inf.* **2021**, *65*, 101392. [CrossRef]
73. Qasim, M.; Csaplovics, E. Comparative Study of Forest Biomass and Carbon Stocks of Margalla Hills National Park, Pakistan. *For. Sci. Technol.* **2023**, *19*, 139–154. [CrossRef]
74. Imran, A.B.; Ahmed, S. Potential of Landsat-8 Spectral Indices to Estimate Forest Biomass. *Int. J. Hum. Cap. Urban Manag.* **2018**, *3*, 303–314. [CrossRef]
75. Yusuf, M. *Forest Management in Pakistan: A Legal and Institutional Analysis*; Sustainable Development Policy Institute (SDPI): Islamabad, Pakistan, 2008.
76. Ali, A. *Forest Reference Emission Level of Khyber Pakhtunkhwa*; Pakistan Forest Institute: Peshawar, Pakistan, 2017; pp. 1–54.
77. Sharma, C.M.; Baduni, N.P.; Gairola, S.; Ghildiyal, S.K.; Suyal, S. Tree Diversity and Carbon Stocks of Some Major Forest Types of Garhwal Himalaya, India. *Ecol. Manag.* **2010**, *260*, 2170–2179. [CrossRef]

forests

MDPI

Article

Modeling Forest Regeneration Dynamics: Estimating Regeneration, Growth, and Mortality Rates in Lithuanian Forests

Robertas Damaševičius * and Rytis Maskeliūnas

Center of Excellence Forest 4.0, Real Time Computing Center, Kaunas University of Technology, 51423 Kaunas, Lithuania; rytis.maskeliunas@ktu.lt
* Correspondence: robertas.damasevicius@ktu.lt

Abstract: This study presents a novel approach to analyzing forest regeneration dynamics by integrating a Markov chain model with Multivariate Time Series (MTY) decomposition. The probabilistic tracking of age-class transitions was combined with the decomposition of regeneration rates into trend, seasonal, and irregular components, unlike traditional deterministic models, capturing the variability and uncertainties inherent in forest ecosystems, offering a more nuanced understanding of how Scots pine (*Pinus sylvestris* L.) and other tree species evolve under different management and climate scenarios. Using 20 years of empirical data from the Lithuanian National Forest Inventory, the study evaluates key growth and mortality parameters for Scots pine, Spruce (*Picea abies*), Birch (*Betula pendula*), and Aspen (*Populus tremula*). The model for Scots pine showed a 79.6% probability of advancing from the 1–10 age class to the 11–20 age class, with subsequent transitions of 82.9% and 84.1% for older age classes. The model for Birch shown a strong early growth rate, with an 84% chance of transitioning to the next age class, while the model for Aspen indicated strong slowdown after 31 years. The model indicated moderate early growth for Spruce with a high transition in later stages, highlighting its resilience in mature forest ecosystems. Sensitivity analysis revealed that while higher growth rates can prolong forest stand longevity, mortality rates above 0.33 severely compromise stand viability. The Hotelling T^2 control chart identified critical deviations in forest dynamics, particularly in years 13 and 19, suggesting periods of environmental stress. The model offers actionable insights for sustainable forest management, emphasizing the importance of species-specific strategies, adaptive interventions, and the integration of climate change resilience into long-term forest planning.

Keywords: forest regeneration dynamics; mathematical modeling; sustainable forest management

1. Introduction

Forests are integral to the health of our planet, and provide a wide array of ecological, economic, and social benefits. They act as carbon sinks, mitigating climate change by absorbing and storing significant amounts of carbon dioxide [1]. At the same time, forests contribute to maintaining the hydrological cycle, preventing soil erosion, and regulating local and global temperatures [2]. Biodiversity thrives in forest ecosystems, with countless species relying on forests for shelter, food, and breeding grounds [3]. Economically, forests are invaluable, providing timber, fuel, and non-timber forest products such as medicinal plants and edible fruits, which are essential for both global industries and local livelihoods [4]. Understanding the dynamics of forest regeneration is needed to ensure the sustainability of these benefits [5,6]. Regeneration involves establishment of new seedlings, which are the basis for the continuity of forests [7]. Growth, which includes the increase in biomass, tree height, and diameter, determines the productivity and structural complexity of forests [8]. Mortality, loss of trees due to aging, disease, competition, or external factors such as climate extremes, play a vital role in the formation of forest composition and the influence of nutrient cycling [9]. These processes drive forest dynamics, dictating how forests recover from disturbances, adapt to changing conditions, and evolve over time [10,11].

Scots pine (*Pinus sylvestris* L.) is a dominant species in Lithuanian forests, and provides an exemplary case study to understand these dynamics [12,13]. Scots pine covers a vast geographic range across Lithuania, making it one of the dominant species in the country's forest ecosystems [14]. Its adaptability to various types of soils and climatic conditions allows it to thrive in both temperate and boreal zones. Scots pine is found in a variety of age classes, from young regenerating stands to older mature forests, and is distributed throughout the lowlands and uplands of Lithuania, supporting the timber industry as a cornerstone of Lithuania's economic forest management strategies [15]. In Lithuania, Spruce (*Picea abies*), Birch (*Betula pendula*), and Aspen (*Populus tremula*) play complementary roles to Scots pine in forest ecosystems [16]. Spruce is more prevalent in younger age classes, but tends to decline in older stages, with higher mortality and vulnerability to environmental stress. Birch and Aspen, as pioneer species, dominate early successional stages, contributing to forest diversity, but their roles are more transient, compared to more resilient and dominant Scots pine. Economically, Scots pine is most valued for its timber, which is used in construction, furniture manufacturing, and paper production [17]. The species also contributes to carbon sequestration, making it a key player in climate change mitigation strategies [12].

Pine forests in Lithuania face several challenges, with the impacts of climate change, such as the increased frequency of droughts and warmer winters, playing a significant role [18]. These changes weaken trees, making them more susceptible to diseases [19] and pests [20], particularly bark beetles, which have caused widespread damage in recent years. The decline in regeneration rates is also an issue, as natural regeneration is hampered by changes in soil moisture and temperature [21]. In addition, high mortality rates [22] are observed in young pine stands due to environmental stress and pest infestations. Human activities, including intensive forest management (Lithuania is one of the largest exporters of pine materials in the northern Europe) and changes in land use, further exacerbate these issues, leading to a decrease in the resilience of pine forests.

Addressing these challenges requires a systematic and data-driven approach to quantify regeneration, growth, and mortality processes. Accurate data collection through forest inventories, remote sensing, and field studies is essential to establish baseline conditions and identify trends [12]. Mathematical models provide powerful tools to analyze these dynamics, enabling simulation of forest evolution in different scenarios [23]. These models incorporate empirical data to predict how forests might respond to management practices, environmental changes, and disturbances. By understanding the drivers of forest stand dynamics, policymakers and forest managers can develop strategies to improve forest resilience, promote biodiversity, and optimize the delivery of ecosystem services [24]. The approach is especially relevant for poorly managed forests in Lithuania [25,26]. This approach ensures that forests continue to play a vital role in the survival of life [12,13].

Previous studies such as the study by Eberhard and Hasenauer [27] utilized growth simulators such as MOSES, focusing on light competition and the regeneration dynamics of Douglas fir in Central Europe. Although these studies emphasized individual factors like light availability, they lacked the probabilistic modeling of multi-factor influences over time. Similarly, Vergarechea et al. [28] modeled climate-mediated regeneration in Mediterranean pine forests using survival analysis, which highlighted climate impacts, but did not incorporate age-specific mortality dynamics as extensively.

The key research objective in this study is the development of a mathematical model to represent the regeneration dynamics of Scots pine in Lithuania, estimating the regeneration, growth, and mortality rates for each age class. The innovative approach is based on the Markov chain and Multivariate Time Series (MTY) decomposition, incorporating 20 years of empirical data from the Lithuanian National Forest Inventory, and is evaluated through the impact of parameter variability under various scenarios.

The significance of this research lies in providing a quantitative tool to predict the outcomes of different management interventions, helping to make informed decisions that balance economic objectives with ecological sustainability, regarding the impacts of climate change on forest ecosystems.

2. Related Works

The dynamics of forest regeneration help us to understand how forests evolve over time, recover from disturbances and respond to environmental changes [29], and help us to understand the processes that drive the natural renewal of forest ecosystems [30,31]. As such, forest dynamics modeling has evolved significantly over the years, with various approaches developed to simulate complex interactions within forest ecosystems [32,33]. Early models often focused on specific aspects of forest dynamics, such as the growth or succession of stands, and utilized deterministic approaches [30]. With advances in computational power and ecological understanding, more comprehensive models have emerged that incorporate aspects such as species interactions, disturbance regimes, and climate effects [34,35]. Notable among these is the gap model, which simulates the birth, growth, and death of trees within small patches, allowing for the examination of succession and competition dynamics. The Lee–Carter model, originally developed to forecast human mortality trends, has been adapted to analyze tree mortality, providing information on how environmental factors influence long-term survival patterns [29]. A similar approach to tree mortality is illustrated by the approach of Babst et al. [36], where it was used to project future mortality rates in European forests under climate change scenarios, as the model allowed the authors to analyze how mortality is influenced by both climate variables and forest stand characteristics. Rocha et al. [37] investigated models to predict tree mortality, finding that the individual tree-level model integrating dendrometric and meteorological variables was the most efficient. Manso et al. [38] applied a model similar to the Lee–Carter model to assess how the mortality risk of tree species is influenced by stochasticity from extreme climatic events and multi-species competition, revealing effects of complementarity processes in tree mortality.

We offer an overview of related approaches in Table 1, showcasing a progression from traditional methods to more sophisticated multivariate approaches that address species-specific needs and environmental stressors. One key observation is the increasing reliance on geospatial and remote sensing technologies, as seen in the work by Ryzhkova et al. [39], which illustrates the utility of GIS in monitoring large and inaccessible forest areas. Richit et al.'s [40] study goes further by applying artificial neural networks, signaling a shift towards models that can handle nonlinear interactions and provide long-term, adaptive management solutions, particularly in ecosystems with complex hydrological dynamics such as riparian buffer strips. The use of Markov chains, Bayesian inference, and process-based models in other works highlights a growing emphasis on probabilistic approaches, reflecting the need to account for uncertainties in climate impacts and species interactions. For example, Mantero et al.'s [41] Bayesian regression model not only identifies high-priority areas for restoration, but also minimizes economic costs, showing how machine learning can enhance practical forest management. The work of Eberhard and Hasenauer [42] on light competition between Douglas firs in central Europe exemplifies how fine-scale ecological interactions are critical to regeneration success, suggesting that generalized models may overlook key factors such as canopy light availability. Additionally, Vergarechea et al.'s [28] climate-mediated modeling brings to light the intricate species-climate dynamics that affect regeneration probabilities in Mediterranean forests, reinforcing the role of predictive, climate-sensitive modeling for future forest management. The above works indicate that modern forest regeneration models must integrate multiple ecological, climatic, and spatial factors to provide actionable insights, particularly as forests face more frequent and severe disturbances from climate change and human intervention, as the trend towards integrating dynamic high-resolution models represents a shift in ensuring long-term forest resilience and sustainability in various biomes.

Table 1. Summary of related works.

Authors	Study Focus	Methodology	Key Findings/Contributions
Ryzhkova et al. [39]	Forest cover classification in southern Yenisei Siberia	Geoinformation modeling	Combined forest cover classification for regeneration dynamics monitoring
Richit et al. [40]	Riparian buffer strip regeneration	Logistic model and neural networks	Highlighted vegetation's role in improving water quality and optimizing conservation
Eberhard and Hasenauer [42]	Douglas fir regeneration in Central Europe	MOSES simulator for regeneration prediction	Light availability critical for regeneration
Vergarechea et al. [28]	Mediterranean pine regeneration under climate scenarios	Survival analysis	Identified grass cover and climate as key regeneration factors
De Frutos et al. [43]	Maritime pine regeneration after seed cutting	Field studies on summer precipitation	Regeneration driven by retained pine and broadleaf species
Mantero et al. [41]	Post-fire forest regeneration in the Italian Alps	Bayesian Additive Regression Tree model	Applied nucleation can improve forest recovery cost-effectively
Calama et al. [44]	Resin-tapped pine mortality in Spain	Spatio-temporal models	Water stress and weather extremes cause mortality, highlighting adaptive strategies
Holzer et al. [45]	Impact of ungulate browsing on tree species composition	Process-based modeling	Browsing impacts tree height development and species shifts

3. Methodology

3.1. Context Information

Lithuania, located in Northern Europe (Figure 1), has a diverse forest landscape shaped by its transitional climate and varied soil types. Lithuania experiences a transitional climate that combines maritime and continental influences, resulting in mild, moderately wet winters and relatively cool summers. The country's climate is characterized by average temperatures ranging from −5 °C in January to about 17 °C in July and significant humidity and precipitation throughout the year, with annual averages between 600 and 800 mm. Lithuanian climate supports reasonably diverse forest growth, but also predisposes forests to certain diseases and pests due to high moisture levels. Forests cover approximately 33.5% of Lithuania, with forest types shaped by both natural processes and human activities. Coniferous forests are dominated by Scots pine and Norway spruce, these forests are primarily found in sandy or podzolic soils, which are acidic and low in nutrients, formed in humid conditions. Deciduous forests are made up of Birch, Aspen, oak, and ash, located mainly on fertile soils in southern and central Lithuania. Mixed forests contain a mixture of coniferous and deciduous species and offer rich biodiversity.

Figure 1. Locations of study within Europe.

3.2. Data Collection Methodology

The methodology for data collection in national forest inventories involves a systematic approach based on field surveys with random starting points, the integration of repeated measurements in permanent maps with assessments in temporary maps and the combination of ground measurements in designated inventory plots with evaluations from satellite images and aerial photographs.

The National Forest Inventory (NFI) conducts ground measurements on forest land, but, in exceptional cases, measurements are also carried out in forest trenches as they are directly related to forest formation. Fieldwork is performed by teams assigned to both permanent and temporary inventory plots. Each team responsible for permanent plots works in a designated inventory district for five years before switching to a different district for the next five years. To evenly distribute permanent inventory plots across the country and regularly monitor transformations in other land uses and the growth of forests there, a systematic layout method with a random start is chosen. Inventory plots for ground measurement are grouped in fours, and group plots are positioned at the vertices of an equilateral triangle. Aligning with the kilometer grid of Lithuania's coordinates, permanent inventory plot groups were arranged every fourth row and every fourth kilometer column in a staggered manner every 4 km. One group of permanent inventory plots covers a territory of 16 km^2 or 400 ha per permanent inventory plot. All permanent inventory plots are measured over a 5-year period, arranged so that the tracts each year ensure the most uniform distribution throughout the country.

Data collection covers a total of 16,349 permanent observation plots across the national territory, with one-fifth of all permanent observation plots remeasured annually. Annual results are calculated using the last five years' data, ensuring continuous and overlapping data provision. Each permanent inventory plot (Figure 2) represents 400 ha of the territory:

- 500 m^2 (Area A)—for the inventory of trees and stumps with a diameter at breast height greater than 14.0 cm.

- 100 m^2 (Area B)—for the inventory of trees and stumps with a diameter at breast height greater than 6.0 cm.
- 25 m^2 (¼ of a small circle, Area C)—for the inventory of trees with a diameter at breast height greater than 2.0 cm.
- 30 m^2 (Area D)—for the inventory of undergrowth and ground vegetation.

Inventory trees in permanent plots are used to assess tree heights, while in temporary plots, they are used to evaluate tree heights, stand age, and volume growth.

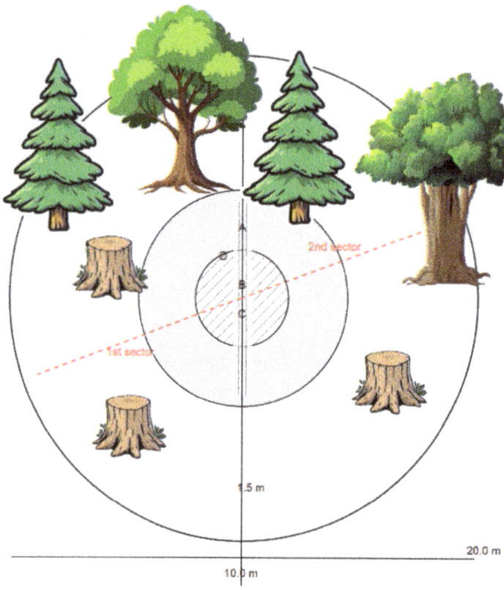

Figure 2. Schematic layout of a forest inventory plot used for systematic data collection. A, B, C, D are inventory areas.

3.3. Forest Inventory Dataset

For the purposes of this study on the dynamics of forest regeneration of Scots pine stands in Lithuania, we used a dataset compiled from the Lithuanian National Forest Inventory (NFI), which encompasses a wide range of variables collected through field surveys, spanning multiple years to capture temporal changes in forest structure and composition, including regeneration rates (RR), growth rates ($GR(a)$), and mortality rates ($MR(a)$). It provides the empirical basis for model validation and sensitivity analysis. Details for downloading the data set are provided in the Data Availability Statement.

The data set (see Table 2) includes the following key characteristics and variables, used to develop and validate the forest regeneration model.

Table 2. Summary of forest inventory data for Scots pine Stands in Lithuania.

Characteristic	Description
Spatial Coverage	Entire forested area of Lithuania
Temporal Range	2001 to 2021 (measured yearly)
Tree Species Composition	Focus on Scots pine with details on mixed species
Age Classes and Stand Structure	Distribution across different age classes, stand density, DBH, and height
Regeneration Data	Counts of seedlings and saplings, natural and assisted regeneration
Mortality and Growth Rates	Annual mortality rates by cause, DBH and height growth measurements

Table 2. Cont.

Characteristic	Description
Biomass and Carbon Stocks	Estimates of aboveground and belowground biomass
Data Collection Methods	Field surveys and remote sensing (satellite imagery and aerial photography)

Table 3 presents the distribution of forest stands in different age classes for Pine, Spruce, Birch, and Aspen in Lithuania, based on data as of 1 January 2021. The area is expressed in hectares.

Table 3. Distribution of forest stands across different age classes for Pine, Spruce, Birch, and Aspen in Lithuania, as of 1 January 2021.

Age Class (Years)	Pine (ha)	Spruce (ha)	Birch (ha)	Aspen (ha)
1–10	36,013	76,099	63,756	16,019
11–20	28,670	63,832	53,585	17,602
21–30	23,772	40,706	50,048	12,526
31–40	19,992	40,921	37,438	7812
41–50	35,580	42,434	38,726	6162
51–60	76,196	41,865	55,551	8211
61–70	115,070	36,966	71,427	11,902
71–80	96,810	31,972	50,221	9772
81–90	83,530	28,516	21,650	4394
91–100	75,054	19,623	6779	1061
>100	52,632	8309	1362	100

Figure 3 visualizes the distribution of forest area (in thousands of hectares) for four species of trees (Pine, Spruce, Birch, and Aspen) in various age classes. The age classes are categorized in 10-year intervals, starting from 1 to 10 years to greater than 100 years.

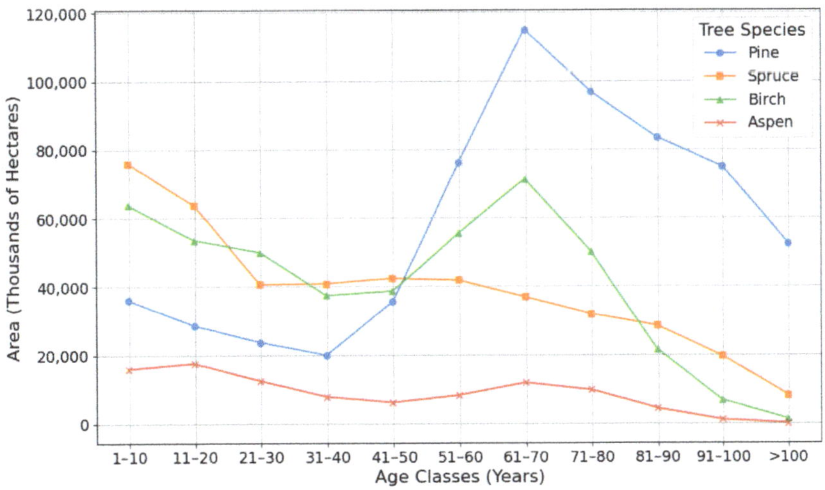

Figure 3. Forest stands distribution across tree species and age classes.

Figure 4 illustrates the distribution of forest stands in various age classes, measured in decades, from 0 to 10 years to 90–100 years.

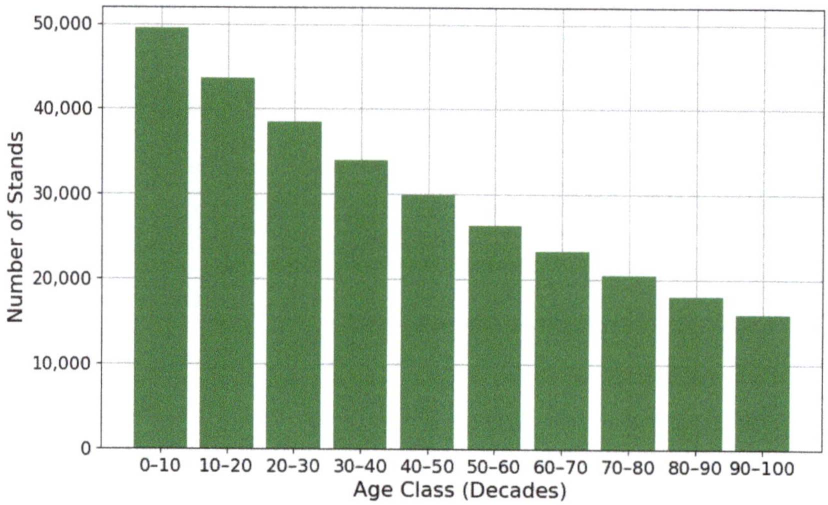

Figure 4. Total number of forest stands in age classes.

Figure 5 highlights the spatial distribution of Scots pine and other dominant tree species.

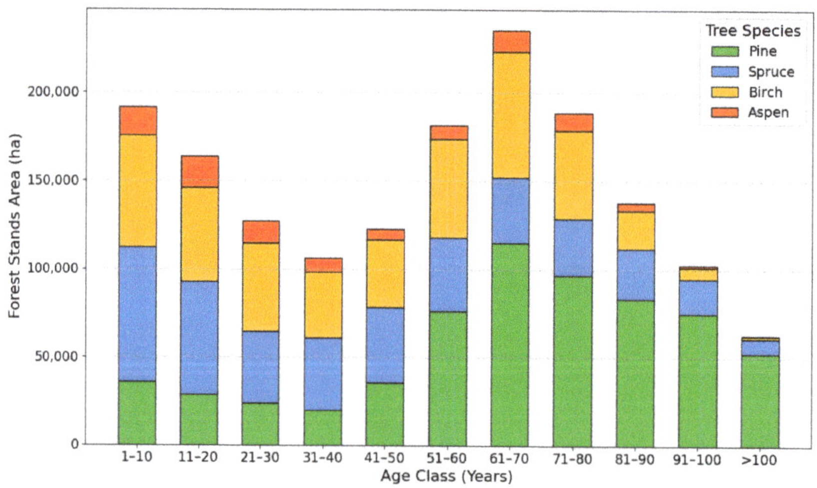

Figure 5. Forest stands distribution across different regions in Lithuania as of January 2021.

The main trends and observations from this dataset are summarized in Table 4.

Table 4. Summary of forest stand distribution trends across age classes.

Tree Species	Observation	Explanation
Pine	Dominates middle to older age classes, with the highest area in the 61–70 age class (115,070 ha).	Reflects adaptability, longevity, and possibly management practices favoring pine growth.
Spruce	Strong presence in younger age classes (1–10 and 11–20 years), diminishing significantly in older classes (>100 years, 8309 ha).	Indicates shorter lifespan or higher mortality rates in later stages.
Birch	Prominent in younger age classes (1–10 years, 63,756 ha), but sharply declines in older age classes (>100 years, 1362 ha).	Highlights its role as a pioneer species and possible succession by longer-lived species.
Aspen	Strong presence in the youngest age class, but almost no representation in the >100 age class (100 ha).	Reflects its shorter lifecycle and higher vulnerability to environmental factors.

3.4. Outline of Methodology

In this study, several mathematical methods are employed to analyze and model the dynamics of forest ecosystems, providing the quantitative backbone for understanding ecological interactions and predicting future trends based on current forest data.

To model the stochastic nature of forest growth and species succession, Markov chains [46] are employed. These provide a framework for predicting the probability of transitioning from one state to another in a discrete-time framework, namely for modeling random events in forest dynamics, such as fire outbreaks, disease spread, and the random establishment of new plant species.

Sensitivity analysis [47] is used to determine how the output of a model is affected by changes in one or more input parameters, useful for ecological modeling to assess the robustness of model predictions under uncertainty and to identify the most influential parameters driving model outcomes.

The Hotelling T^2 Control Chart [48] is used for monitoring the stability of interrelated variables that often characterize complex forest ecosystems. It helps in detecting outliers or abnormal shifts in the forest data set.

The MTY decomposition [49] is a method used to dissect the components of multivariate time series data, isolating trends, seasonal effects, and other cyclic variations, such as annual forest growth rates, seasonal pest infestations, or cyclic climatic effects on forest health. By decomposing these series, we can understand the underlying patterns and causal relationships, which may not be apparent from raw data, to obtain insights into the temporal dynamics of multiple factors influencing forest ecosystems.

3.5. Model Assumptions

Markov chain models provide a robust framework for predicting changes in forests. The assumptions for accurately interpreting the model outcomes in the forestry domain as follows:

- The forest ecosystem is segmented into discrete states or classes, typically defined by the age, size, or developmental stages of the tree, which represent groups with similar ecological characteristics. Each state encompasses a specific forest condition or age class. Time is treated in discrete intervals, with transitions assessed at these intervals, simplifying the continuous nature of forest dynamics.
- A fundamental premise of the Markov chain model is its memorylessness. The future state of the system depends solely on the current state, not on the sequence of events that preceded it. This assumption implies that the process history does not influence future state transitions.

- Transitions between states occur with constant probabilities that are assumed to remain consistent over time. Each probability P_{ij} quantifies the likelihood of transitioning from state i to state j in one time period, adhering to $\sum_j P_{ij} = 1$.
- The model assumes that transitions are independent. Changes in the state of one forest plot do not affect transitions in another, simplifying modeling by excluding spatial interactions or dependencies.
- The stationarity assumption posits that transition probabilities do not change over time, which is crucial for long-term modeling but may not always hold in real scenarios.
- It is typically assumed that all plots within a state are homogeneous. This assumption ignores within-state variability due to factors such as soil type or microclimates.

3.6. Mathematical Modeling of Forest Regeneration

In this section, we present a formal mathematical model that describes the regeneration dynamics of a forest, focusing on the regeneration rate, the growth rate, and the mortality rate of the forest stands over time. The model tracks the number of stands across different age classes in a forest, incorporating regeneration, growth, and mortality processes.

Further, we use the following notations:

- $N(t, a)$—number of stands of age class a at time t.
- RR—annual regeneration rate, representing the number of new stands established each year.
- $GR(a)$—growth rate for stands in age class a.
- $MR(a)$—mortality rate for stands in age class a.

The model is defined by the following processes:

1. Regeneration: $N(t+1, 1) = RR$
2. Growth: for each age class $1 \leq a < A$,

$$N(t+1, a+1) = N(t, a) \cdot GR(a) \tag{1}$$

3. Mortality: for each age class $1 \leq a \leq A$,

$$N(t, a) = N(t, a) \cdot (1 - MR(a)) \tag{2}$$

4. For the oldest age class A, the boundary condition is given by

$$N(t+1, A) = N(t, A-1) \cdot GR(A-1) + N(t, A) \cdot (1 - MR(A)) \tag{3}$$

The model requires initial conditions $N(0, a)$ for each age class a to simulate the forest regeneration dynamics over time.

The estimation of the model parameters was made to accurately simulate the forest regeneration dynamics determining the values of the regeneration rate (RR), growth rates ($GR(a)$), and mortality rates ($MR(a)$) for each age class a. The estimation process is based on empirical data from forest inventories or observational studies.

The regeneration rate, RR, is estimated from the number of new stands established per year. It can be directly observed or calculated from the increase in stands in the youngest age class over time,

$$RR = \frac{\Delta N(1)}{\Delta t} \tag{4}$$

where $\Delta N(1)$ is the change in the number of stands in the first age class over the time interval Δt.

The growth rate for each age class, $GR(a)$, represents the proportion of stands that transition to the next age class in a given year. It is estimated by comparing the number of stands in successive age classes,

$$GR(a) = \frac{N(t+1, a+1)}{N(t, a)} \tag{5}$$

assuming that growth is the only transition between these age classes.

The mortality rate for each age class, $MR(a)$, indicates the proportion of stands that die in a given year. It can be inferred from the reduction in the number of stands not transitioning to the next age class,

$$MR(a) = 1 - GR(a) \tag{6}$$

where $GR(a)$ is the growth rate from age class a to $a + 1$.

3.7. Analytical Solution of the Model

For certain simplified versions of the forest regeneration model, analytical solutions were derived to describe the state of the forest over time, given the initial conditions and the values of the parameters.

Consider a simplified version of the model where the growth rate ($GR(a)$) and the mortality rate ($MR(a)$) are constant across all age classes, and there is no maximum age limit. The model is represented by a linear difference equation for the number of stands in each age class,

$$N(t+1, a+1) = GR \cdot N(t, a) - MR \cdot N(t, a) \tag{7}$$

where GR and MR are constants, and the regeneration rate (RR) introduces new stands into the first age class each time period,

$$N(t+1, 1) = RR \tag{8}$$

Under these conditions, the number of stands in each age class over time can be expressed as

$$N(t, a) = RR \cdot (GR - MR)^{a-1} \tag{9}$$

assuming $GR > MR$ and the system has been running for a sufficient number of time steps to reach a steady state.

The solution to the difference equation provides a direct relationship between age class, regeneration rate, and growth and mortality rates. It shows how the number of stands decreases geometrically with age class, reflecting the cumulative effects of growth and mortality.

The analytical solution described is based on several simplifications.

- Constant rates of growth and mortality, which do not fully reflect real-world conditions where these rates vary with age, environmental factors, and density of the stand.
- Ignoring maximum age limits and other factors such as competition, disturbances, and management interventions that can affect stand dynamics.
- The assumption of a steady state may not be applicable to forests that experience significant changes or disturbances.

3.8. Model Analysis

Sensitivity analysis was conducted for model validation, aiming to measure its reliability and robustness of the model predictions by quantifying how changes in model parameters affect the model's outputs and identifying which parameters are most influential on the model's behavior, thereby guiding data collection efforts and prioritizing areas for research. Sensitivity of the model output Y with respect to a parameter x_i can be defined as

$$S_{x_i} = \frac{\partial Y}{\partial x_i} \tag{10}$$

where S_{x_i} represents the sensitivity coefficient of Y to changes in parameter x_i. Higher values of $|S_{x_i}|$ indicate that the model output is more sensitive to the parameter x_i.

The sensitivity coefficient S_{x_i} tells us how a small change in x_i (for example, a slight increase in temperature) would affect Y (for example, forest growth rate, tree mortality rate, or overall forest health). The derivative $\frac{\partial Y}{\partial x_i}$ encapsulates this responsiveness numerically. The magnitude of S_{x_i} indicates how sensitive Y is to x_i. A large absolute value $|S_{x_i}|$ suggests that Y is highly sensitive to changes in x_i; small changes in x_i could lead to significant changes in Y. The sign of S_{x_i} indicates the direction of the effect: a positive value means Y increases with an increase in x_i, while a negative value means Y decreases as x_i increases.

3.8.1. Sensitivity Analysis with Respect to Regeneration Rates

The sensitivity of the forest regeneration model to changes in the regeneration rate (RR) was carried out to understand the behavior of the model, given the direct impact of RR on the initial conditions and the subsequent dynamics of the forest stands, evaluating the influence of variations in RR on the predictions of the model.

Consider the forest regeneration model described by the discrete-time equation for the number of stands in the youngest age class,

$$N(t+1,1) = RR \tag{11}$$

The sensitivity of the model's output, specifically the total number of stands after t years, $Total(t)$, with respect to RR can be expressed as

$$S_{RR} = \frac{\partial Total(t)}{\partial RR} \tag{12}$$

Given the direct relationship between RR and $N(t+1,1)$, and subsequently $Total(t)$, we can further derive that

$$S_{RR} = \sum_{t=1}^{T} \frac{\partial N(t,1)}{\partial RR} \tag{13}$$

where T represents the total simulation time.

For the simplified model in which growth and mortality rates are assumed constant between age classes, the sensitivity S_{RR} essentially captures the cumulative impact of changing RR over time. If the model assumes that all stands regenerate directly contribute to the total stand count without loss, then

$$S_{RR} = T \tag{14}$$

indicating that the model's output is linearly sensitive to changes in the regeneration rate. In more complex models, S_{RR} would need to account for the diminished contributions of older age classes due to mortality, as well as nonlinear effects due to density-dependent growth or mortality factors.

3.8.2. Sensitivity Analysis of the Forest Growth Model with Respect to Mortality Rates

Understanding how changes in mortality rates ($MR(a)$) affect the dynamics of forest growth was based on the sensitivity analysis of a forest growth model regarding mortality rates, highlighting the interconnection of mortality and forest stand dynamics over time.

The sensitivity of the forest growth model's output, such as the total biomass or the number of mature stands at time t, to changes in mortality rates for a specific age class a, is expressed as

$$S_{MR(a)} = \frac{\partial Y(t)}{\partial MR(a)} \tag{15}$$

where $Y(t)$ represents the model output of interest at time t, and $MR(a)$ is the mortality rate for age class a. This sensitivity indicates how a small change in the mortality rate of a specific age class affects the model's output, reflecting the direct and indirect impacts of mortality on forest growth.

For a given age class a, the direct impact of an increase in $MR(a)$ reduces the number of stands that survive to the next age class. The indirect effects accumulate over time as fewer stands progress through the subsequent age classes. Assuming a simplified model where growth and transition between age classes are otherwise constant, the sensitivity can be approximated by aggregating the impacts across all affected age classes,

$$S_{MR(a)} = -\sum_{j=a}^{A} \frac{\partial N(t,j)}{\partial MR(a)} \tag{16}$$

where $N(t,j)$ is the number of stands in age class j at time t, and A is the maximum age class considered in the model.

Assuming linear relationships and no compensatory growth for loss in stands due to increased mortality, the sensitivity $S_{MR(a)}$ highlights the cumulative impact of mortality rates on the forest's ability to grow and sustain its biomass over time. A higher absolute value of $S_{MR(a)}$ indicates that forest growth and biomass are more susceptible to changes in mortality rates, underscoring the importance of understanding and managing factors contributing to tree mortality.

3.8.3. Sensitivity Analysis with Respect to Mortality Rates

The impact of mortality rates ($MR(a)$) on the forest regeneration model was analyzed to interpret the resilience and long-term sustainability of forest ecosystems. Mortality rates influence the attrition of stands in different age classes, directly affecting forest composition and stand density over time. Higher sensitivity values indicate that small changes in mortality rates could lead to significant alterations in forest composition.

Given the forest regeneration model's structure, the sensitivity of the total number of stands, $Total(t)$, with respect to changes in mortality rates for a specific age class a, $MR(a)$, can be formulated as

$$S_{MR(a)} = \frac{\partial Total(t)}{\partial MR(a)} \tag{17}$$

Considering the model's dynamics, where the number of stands in age class a at time t is $N(t,a)$, and applying the chain rule for differentiation, we obtain

$$S_{MR(a)} = \sum_{t=1}^{T} \left(\frac{\partial N(t,a)}{\partial MR(a)} + \sum_{j=a+1}^{A} \frac{\partial N(t,j)}{\partial N(t,a)} \cdot \frac{\partial N(t,a)}{\partial MR(a)} \right) \tag{18}$$

where T is the total simulation time, and A is the maximum age class.

For a simplified model where $GR(a)$ is constant and independent of $MR(a)$, the sensitivity can be approximated by considering the immediate impact of mortality rates on each age class and their downstream effects on older classes,

$$S_{MR(a)} \approx -\sum_{t=1}^{T} \left(N(t,a) + \sum_{j=a+1}^{A} N(t,j) \right) \tag{19}$$

assuming a linear response of stand numbers to changes in mortality rates. This approximation neglects potential compensatory mechanisms or density-dependent effects that could modulate the impact of increased mortality.

4. Markov Chain Model of Forest Regeneration Dynamics

The dynamics of forest regeneration were modeled using a Markov chain, where the state of a forest at any given time is determined by its state at the previous time step, with transitions between states governed by a set of probabilities. The Markov chain model for forest regeneration dynamics operates under several key assumptions:

1. The future state of the forest depends only on its current state, not on the sequence of events that preceded it (Markov property).
2. The transition probabilities are constant over time, implying stationary environmental conditions and management practices.
3. The forest is closed to external influences other than those included in the transition probabilities, such as significant disturbances or changes in the management strategy.

Let the set of states $S = \{s_1, s_2, \ldots, s_n\}$ represent the forest age classes, where s_i corresponds to the ith age class. The state s_1 represents the youngest age class, typically seedlings and saplings, while s_n represents the oldest age class within the forest.

The transition probabilities between states are represented by a matrix P, where each element p_{ij} denotes the probability of transitioning from state s_i to state s_j in one time step. For a forest regeneration model, the matrix P is structured to reflect growth (progression to the next age class), mortality (failure to progress), and regeneration processes,

$$P = \begin{bmatrix} p_{11} & p_{12} & 0 & \cdots & 0 \\ 0 & p_{22} & p_{23} & \cdots & 0 \\ \vdots & \vdots & \vdots & \ddots & \vdots \\ 0 & 0 & 0 & \cdots & p_{nn} \end{bmatrix} \tag{20}$$

where p_{ii} (for $i < n$) represents the probability of remaining in the same age class (owing to slow growth or no growth), $p_{i,i+1}$ represents the probability of progressing to the next age class, and p_{nn} represents the probability of remaining in the oldest age class.

The initial state distribution $\pi_0 = [\pi_{01}, \pi_{02}, \ldots, \pi_{0n}]$ represents the age class distribution of the forest at the beginning of the model period, where π_{0i} is the proportion of the forest in state s_i at time 0.

To effectively apply the Markov chain model for forest regeneration dynamics, we need to accurately estimate the transition probabilities between age classes. For parameter estimation, the dataset defined in Section 3.3 was used to extract information relevant to age class transitions for the primary tree species of interest, focusing on Pine, Spruce, Birch, and Aspen.

The transition probabilities p_{ij} of the Markov chain model are estimated based on the observed transitions between age classes in the dataset over a specified time interval. The formal definition for estimating these probabilities is given by

$$p_{ij} = \frac{N_{ij}}{N_i} \tag{21}$$

where p_{ij} is the probability of transition from age class i to age class j. N_{ij} is the number of stands observed to transition from the age class i to the age class j during the time interval. N_i is the total number of stands in the age class i at the beginning of the time interval.

For age classes that directly progress to the next (for example, from age class i to $i+1$), p_{ij} captures the growth probability. The probability of remaining in the same age class (p_{ii}) reflects slower growth or stagnation, and the transition to the absorbent state for the oldest age class (p_{nn}) indicates mortality or the culmination of growth.

Given potential uncertainties and variabilities in forest inventory data, a Bayesian approach was used to estimate transition probabilities, incorporating prior knowledge and observed data to generate probability distributions for each p_{ij}, rather than point estimates, as this approach improves the robustness of the model to data gaps and variations.

$$P(p_{ij}|data) \propto P(data|p_{ij}) \times P(p_{ij}) \tag{22}$$

where $P(p_{ij}|data)$ is the posterior distribution of the transition probability, $P(data|p_{ij})$ is the likelihood of the observed data given the transition probability, and $P(p_{ij})$ is the prior distribution of the transition probability.

Multivariate Time Series (MTY) Decomposition

Multivariate Time Series (MTY) decomposition is a method that we used to break down a multivariate time series into its constituent parts to better understand the underlying structure and dynamics of the data. In the context of forest stand dynamics, it involves decomposing the time series of tree ages into components such as trend, seasonal, and irregular components. MTY decomposition allows for a detailed analysis of how these components contribute to signals detected by the Hotelling T^2 control chart, which is a statistical tool used to monitor the stability of a process based on multiple variables simultaneously. For forest stand dynamics, it was used to monitor changes in the distribution of tree ages over time. When an out-of-control signal is detected, indicating a significant deviation from the expected multivariate process behavior, MTY decomposition was applied to investigate the source of this deviation.

The steps for applying MTY Decomposition are as follows:

1. Use the Hotelling T^2 control chart to identify periods in which the multivariate process; in this case, the distribution of tree ages, deviates significantly from the control limits.
2. Apply MTY Decomposition to the time series data related to the identified out-of-control signals, which involves separating the data into trend, seasonal, and irregular components for each variable, or, in this case, tree age class.
3. Analyze the decomposed components to identify patterns or anomalies. For example, a sudden change in the trend component could indicate a shift in forest regeneration

rates, while unusual patterns in the seasonal component could reflect cyclical changes in mortality rates.

5. Results

5.1. Forest Regeneration Model Rates

The Forest Regeneration Model rates were derived from Table 3 and are presented in Table 5, indicating the proportion of stands that survive and transition to the next age class, with a growth rate exceeding 100% from age class 31–40 to 41–50 due to an apparent increase in the area, which can be attributed to measurement adjustments, changes in forest management practices, or natural dynamics not captured by simple linear transitions. The RR rate represents the total area rather than an annual regeneration rate, due to the lack of explicit annual data. To derive an annual rate, additional information would be needed on the period over which this regeneration occurred. The model's mortality rates become negative from the 31–40 to the 41–50 transition onward, which is counterintuitive, as mortality rates should range between 0 and 1. These negative values likely suggest underlying issues with the data, rather than true biological phenomena. Errors in measuring or recording the forest data, such as the area covered by each age class, can lead to incorrect calculation of negative rates. For example, an overestimation of the area in a younger age class followed by an underestimation in the next age class could artificially inflate growth rates, making mortality rates appear negative when calculated as residuals. This anomaly is the limitation of our model, as we have treated that such areas can directly translate into survival and growth rates without accounting for other factors such as afforestation, reforestation, and changes in land use or measurement methodologies over time.

Table 5. Growth and mortality rates for tree species.

Age Class (Years)	Scots Pine		Spruce		Birch		Aspen	
	GR	MR	GR	MR	GR	MR	GR	MR
1–10	0.796	0.204	0.839	0.161	0.840	0.160	1.000	0.000
11–20	0.829	0.171	0.638	0.362	0.934	0.066	0.712	0.288
21–30	0.841	0.159	1.000	0.000	0.748	0.252	0.624	0.376
31–40	1.000	0.000	1.000	0.000	1.000	0.000	0.789	0.211
41–50	1.000	0.000	0.987	0.013	1.000	0.000	1.000	0.000
51–60	1.000	0.000	0.883	0.117	1.000	0.000	1.000	0.000
61–70	0.841	0.159	0.865	0.135	0.703	0.297	0.821	0.179
71–80	0.863	0.137	0.892	0.108	0.431	0.569	0.450	0.550
81–90	0.899	0.101	0.688	0.312	0.313	0.687	0.241	0.759
91–100	0.701	0.299	0.423	0.577	0.201	0.799	0.095	0.905

5.2. Markov Chain Modeling

Given the growth rates (GR) and mortality rates (MR) for Scots pine in Lithuania, the state transition matrix P for the first three age classes can be constructed, assuming that the transitions between age classes are solely dictated by the growth rates and that mortality is implicitly considered in these transitions (i.e., not surviving to the next age class is the complement of the growth rate).

$$P = \begin{pmatrix} 0.204 & 0.796 & 0 & 0 \\ 0 & 0.171 & 0.829 & 0 \\ 0 & 0 & 0.159 & 0.841 \\ 0 & 0 & 0 & 1 \end{pmatrix} \tag{23}$$

where the first row represents transitions from the 1–10 age class, with 20.4% chance of staying in the same class (mortality and non-growth) and 79.6% chance of advancing to the 11–20 age class. The second and third rows follow the same logic for transitions from the 11–20 to 21–30 age classes and from the 21–30 to 31–40 age classes, respectively. The fourth row is a simplification that represents the transition of the forest beyond the age classes considered in this model, with the possibility 100% to remain in the state, reflecting the end point of our simplified model.

Similar state transition matrices can also be calculated for other tree species. Our Markov chain model (Figure 6) showed accurate transitions between different age classes based on the growth and mortality rates estimated from the Lithuanian forest inventory dataset for Scots pine, Spruce, Birch, and Aspen.

The Markov chain models for Scots pine, Spruce, Birch, and Aspen reveal distinct growth dynamics and survival probabilities in different forest age classes, providing information on the ecological strategies and responses of each species to environmental pressures. Scots pine exhibits a higher tendency to remain in the younger age class (1–10 years), with a 20.4% probability, indicating a slower initial growth or greater challenges in early-stage survival, which suggests that Scots pine may require longer to establish or faces more significant early-life mortality risks than other species analyzed. In contrast, Spruce shows a unique pattern in which it transitions with certainty (100%) from the 21–30 to the 31+ age class, reflecting effective forest management strategies that ensure its growth beyond the mid-life stages without interruption. Birch stands out with its high transition rate (84.0%) from the 1–10 to the 11–20 age class, the highest among the species, suggesting vigorous early growth. However, it also shows a notable probability (25.2%) of remaining in the 21–30 age class, indicating possible biological or environmental limitations that affect its older populations. Aspen, on the other hand, demonstrates exceptionally dynamic early growth, with a very high probability of moving from the 1–10 to the 11–20 age class, characteristic of pioneer species known for rapid growth in youth. However, its growth slows significantly as it matures, with a transition probability of 62.4% from the 21–30 to the 31+ class, highlighting a deceleration in growth or increased mortality risks at this stage. The resulting patterns indicate that while Aspen and Birch are quick to establish and grow in their early years, they face different challenges as they mature. Scots pine and Spruce, with their higher probabilities of staying in certain age classes, adapting more effectively to longer-term environmental stresses or benefiting from conservation efforts that protect them as they age.

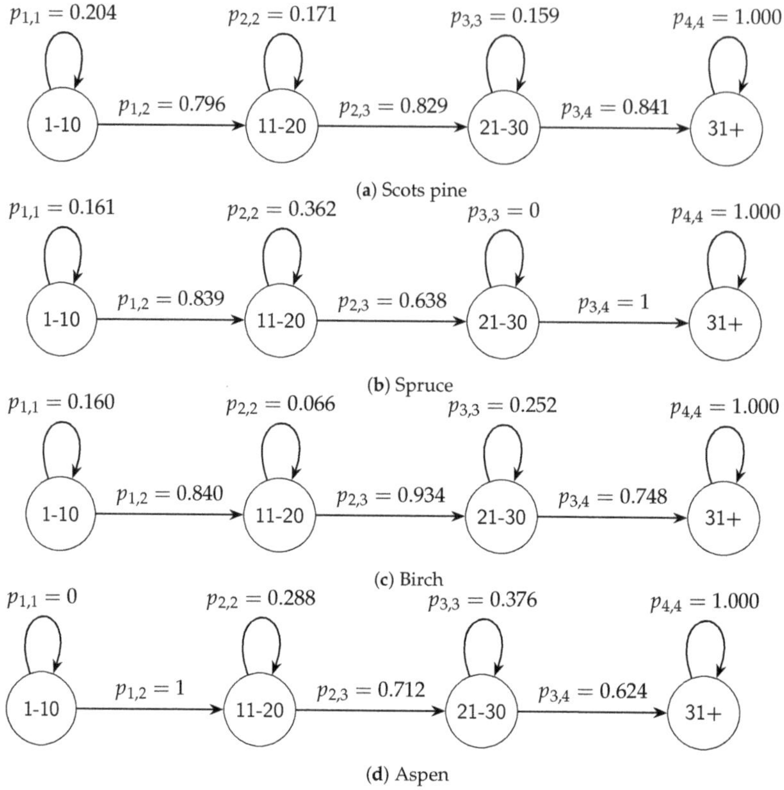

Figure 6. Markov chain models for tree species illustrating transitions between forest age classes. The probabilities indicate regeneration, growth, and mortality transitions.

5.3. Sensitivity Analysis

Figure 7 presents sensitivity analysis of the forest regeneration model. It shows the impact of variations in growth and mortality rates on the size of the forest stand over time.

The results from the sensitivity analysis provide data on how the analyzed rates influence the longevity and viability of forest stands over a century. The results show a clear trend: higher growth rates generally sustain forest stands longer, whereas higher mortality rates accelerate the decline, evident where combinations with higher GR values persist with higher stand counts far longer than those with lower GRs. Curves with higher MRs, even with a high GR, decline more rapidly than those with lower MRs, illustrating the detrimental impact of high mortality regardless of growth. Forest stands with high growth rates (GR = 0.90 and GR = 1.00) and low mortality rates (MR = 0.10) show the greatest longevity, maintaining a higher number of stands for an extended period compared to other combinations. In contrast, any scenario with MR = 0.40, regardless of the growth rate, results in a rapid decline of forest stands, where the population approaches zero in about 40 years. There is a noticeable threshold effect around a GR of 0.70. Combinations below this growth rate, even with moderate mortality rates (for example, MR = 0.18), show a steep decline in stand numbers within the first few decades. Similarly, mortality rates greater than 0.33 significantly decrease stand longevity in all growth rates, highlighting a critical limit beyond which forest recovery is not sustainable. In general, the results show the importance of improving forest growth rates through management practices such as optimal spacing, selective logging, and species selection that favor faster growing trees. Strategies to reduce mortality rates, such as pest and disease management, protection from wildfires, and mitigation of environmental stressors, remain important and are especially vital in settings where the mortality rate approaches or exceeds the identified critical threshold (MR = 0.33).

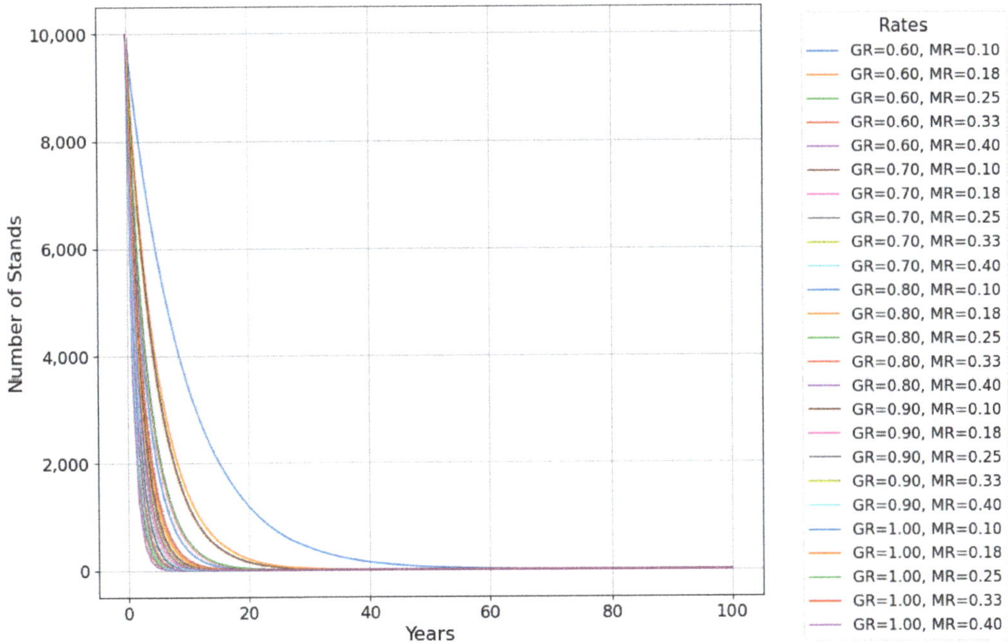

Figure 7. Sensitivity analysis of the regeneration model. Variations in growth and mortality rates significantly impact long-term forest dynamics.

5.4. Hotelling T^2 Control Chart

Figure 8 presents the Hotelling T^2 control chart monitoring multivariate forest dynamics over a series of observation years, identifying significant deviations in parameters such as regeneration, growth, and mortality rates. The Hotelling chart plots the T^2 statistic for each time point, with an upper control limit (UCL) set based on a chosen confidence level. Points exceeding the UCL, highlighted as out-of-control events, indicate potential anomalies or shifts in forest ecosystem behavior, such as unexpected mortality spikes or changes in age-class distributions. As we can see from the results, the deviations indicate that more investigation is needed to assess their causes, which could potentially include environmental stressors, management practices, or climate-related impacts, offering actionable insights for sustainable forest management.

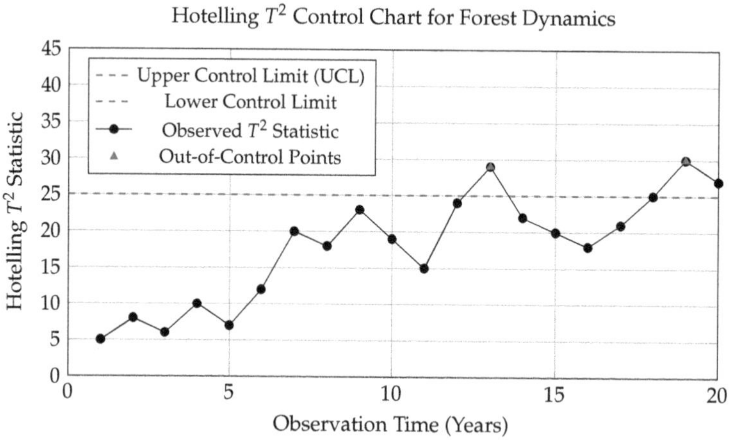

Figure 8. Hotelling T^2 control chart monitoring forest dynamics across observation years. Out-of-control points indicate significant deviations in multivariate forest characteristics.

The Hotelling T^2 control chart (Figure 8) was used for tracking various ecological indicators such as growth rates, mortality rates, and biodiversity indices, providing an overview of forest health over time. Out-of-control points, such as those observed in years 13 and 19, indicated significant deviations from expected patterns, suggesting sudden changes in forest composition potentially due to disease, pest invasions or environmental stressors (droughts in our case). Significant metric changes reflect changes in biodiversity, with implications for ecosystem functionality and health.

Table 6 presents a summary of the MTY decomposition analysis for regeneration rates between age classes. We have performed the decomposition of the regeneration rate time series data in different forest age classes to separate the observed data into trend, seasonal, and residual components. This analysis offers valuable insights into the underlying dynamics of forest regeneration within each age class: 1–10 years, 11–20 years, 21–30 years, and 31+ years. The decomposition method allowed for the identification of long-term patterns, periodic fluctuations, and unexplained anomalies in regeneration processes.

For the youngest age class, 1–10 years, the results reveal a significant degree of seasonal variability in regeneration rates, suggesting that periodic factors, such as climatic conditions or scheduled management interventions, played a role in influencing regeneration outcomes. In addition to these cyclical variations, the trend component demonstrates a steady increase, indicating a general improvement in regeneration conditions over time. The residual component shows occasional spikes, reflecting disturbances or external events that affect the youngest forest stands.

In the 11–20-year age class, the trend appears relatively stable, which indicates consistent regeneration dynamics. However, the residual component highlights notable irregularities during specific years, which point to external disturbances such as pest outbreaks, extreme weather events, or changes in forest management strategies. Unlike the youngest age class, the seasonal component is less pronounced, indicating a diminished role of cyclical influences as forests transition to mid-age stages.

The analysis of the 21–30 year age class shows a gradual increasing trend, reflecting ongoing growth and recovery within these stands. Seasonal effects are relatively minor, suggesting that the regeneration dynamics in this age class is less affected by recurring environmental or management patterns. The residual component remains low, indicating stable regeneration with fewer anomalies compared to younger age classes.

For the 31+ year age class, the trend component shows pronounced growth, indicative of forest stand maturation and the impact of sustained management practices. Seasonal variations are minimal, which is consistent with the reduced sensitivity of older forests to cyclical factors, which highlights occasional deviations, likely caused by natural disturbances or external influences that disproportionately affect mature stands.

Table 6. Summary of MTY decomposition analysis for regeneration rates across age classes.

Age Class (Years)	Trend (Mean)	Seasonal (Amplitude)	Residual (Std Dev)	Key Observations
1–10	6.8	0.8	0.6	High seasonal variability; occasional disturbances
11–20	5.8	0.5	0.9	Stable trend; irregular spikes during specific years
21–30	4.5	0.3	0.4	Gradual increase in trend; minor seasonal effects
31+	3.2	0.2	0.5	Pronounced trend growth; minimal seasonal variation

6. Discussion

The results of this study reveal trends in the regeneration dynamics, growth rates, and mortality patterns of Scots pine and other dominant tree species in Lithuanian forests. Scots pine demonstrates a robust regeneration rate and consistent dominance across middle to older age classes, with its highest concentration observed in the 61–70 age class, which highlights the adaptability and long-term resilience of Scots pine, which is further supported by its ability to thrive under varying environmental and management conditions. In contrast, spruce showed a strong presence in younger age classes, but experiences a notable decline in older age categories. We believe that the decline in the model can reflect a higher susceptibility to environmental stressors, pests, or diseases in the later stages of its lifecycle. Birch and Aspen exhibited the behavior of pioneer species, with high representation in younger age classes followed by steep declines as forest succession progresses. Even though, results highlight the relative youth of *Pinus sylvestris* (Scots pine) in Lithuanian forests versus mature *Picea abies* (Norway spruce) in older stands, which can be largely attributed to ecological dynamics and historical forest management practices. One key factor is the long-standing preference for Scots pine in forest management, particularly in Lithuania, where it has been favored for its resilience to poor soils, faster initial growth, and economic value in timber production. Scots pine is well suited to the dry, sandy soils prevalent in significant parts of Lithuania, where it thrives and has been actively promoted through management interventions such as selective thinning and reforestation. In contrast, *Picea abies*, although abundant in regeneration stages due to its tolerance to shade and its ability to survive under a closed canopy, struggles to maintain dominance in older stands, especially in environments where competition with faster-growing species like pine or birch occurs. In unmanaged or naturally regenerating forests, *Picea abies* can persist for decades in the understory due to their tolerance to shade, but their slower early growth relative to pine places them at a competitive disadvantage. In addition, traditional forest management has often prioritized Scots pine, leading to frequent thinning operations that selectively remove spruce to reduce competition and promote pine growth, further reducing the likelihood of spruce dominance in mature forests. In addition, the sensitivity of Picea abies to environmental stressors such as windthrow, fungal diseases, and drought, particularly as it matures, contributes to its scarcity in older stands; however, climate change exacerbates these vulnerabilities, with increasingly dry summers in Lithuania negatively affecting spruce, which prefers cooler, wetter conditions.

The observed dominance and resilience of Scots pine suggest that it should remain a cornerstone of forestry practices in Lithuania. The maintenance requires the implementation of adaptive management techniques that respond to both environmental changes and forest dynamics. One key approach is selective thinning, in which competing tree species such as birch and aspen are removed to reduce competition for resources such as light, water, and nutrients, ensuring that Scots pine can thrive, especially in mixed stands. In addition, assisted regeneration can be used in areas where natural regeneration rates are low, using techniques such as planting genetically resilient Scots pine varieties that are better suited to withstand drought or pest pressure. Soil management practices such as mulching or soil moisture conservation techniques can also be used in regions prone to drought, helping to maintain optimal growth conditions. Pest control strategies, such as the monitoring and targeted control of bark beetle populations, are crucial, especially in younger stands where Scots pine is more vulnerable to infestations. Finally, adaptive reforestation programs that use predictive models, such as those developed in this study, can guide planting efforts in areas where Scots pine has the highest potential for long-term survival and growth under future climate conditions.

In Lithuania, the practical application of sensitivity analysis is correlated with recent more directly informed, more nuanced, and more effective forest management decisions, particularly regarding the regeneration and mortality of Scots pine. For example, the findings are correlated with the critical impact of soil moisture on the growth of Scots pine, leading to the expansion of climate-resistant species in mixed forests. In regions like Dzūkija, which are prone to drought and characterized by sandy soils, forest managers now focus on selecting more drought-tolerant species in conjunction with Scots pine to improve forest resilience. Although Scots pine is retained for its ecological and economic importance, sensitivity analysis has shown that it performs better in mixed stands, leading to an adjustment in afforestation strategies. We believe that such an approach improves forest adaptation by addressing soil moisture sensitivity and reducing the risk of stand collapse during prolonged drought periods.

In relation to pest management, a detailed sensitivity analysis has highlighted that mortality in younger Scots pine stands is highly sensitive to pest outbreaks, particularly bark beetles. In line with this finding are the actions in regions like Aukštaitija, where forest managers have intensified both preventive and reactive pest management strategies. They have increased the frequency of aerial surveys using drones to monitor pest populations and detect early-stage infestations, allowing for more targeted interventions before pests spread widely. Furthermore, forest managers in Lithuania have expanded the use of pheromone traps specifically during peak bark beetle seasons, rather than treating large areas indiscriminately. This more focused, data-driven approach, rooted in the results of sensitivity analysis, has successfully reduced bark beetle damage, particularly in the more vulnerable young stands where mortality sensitivity is highest.

Sensitivity analysis also correlates with the importance of fine-tuning regeneration efforts. In southern Lithuania, for example, regeneration of Scots pine has been shown to be especially sensitive to competition from faster-growing species, such as Birch. Forest managers have started to adapt their thinning practices to ensure that young Scots pine stands are selectively managed to reduce competition during critical early growth phases. Such practice has been integrated into forest management plans for state-owned forests, ensuring that thinning schedules are more precisely timed and implemented in areas where

Scots pine regeneration is more sensitive to competition, as such targeted management not only improves Scots pine regeneration rates, but also ensures that it remains a dominant species in Lithuania's forestry landscape.

Our findings align with existing models of forest dynamics [50–52], in the emphasis on species-specific roles in forest ecosystems. For example, previous studies have highlighted the role of Scots pine as a long-lived dominant species in temperate forests, which is consistent with its observed trends in this study. The decline in older age classes of trees is similarly corroborated by research pointing to its vulnerability to biotic and abiotic stresses as forests mature. The behavior of Birch and Aspen was documented in the literature as pioneer species that establish quickly in disturbed areas, but are gradually replaced by more shade-tolerant species such as Pine and Spruce. However, our study extends previous work by incorporating detailed sensitivity analyses of growth and mortality rates, offering a more nuanced model to understand how variations in these parameters influence long-term forest dynamics. The inclusion of Markov chain modeling provided a more structured framework for projecting these dynamics over extended time horizons, further bridging the gap between theoretical models and practical forest management applications. For Birch and Aspen, this role as pioneer species can be exploited in post-disturbance regeneration efforts, but their rapid decline in older age classes necessitates planned transitions to longer-lived species to ensure forest sustainability. The sensitivity analysis also emphasized the importance of optimizing growth and mortality rates through management interventions to improve forest health and productivity. Our results also highlight the impacts of climate change, which still alters the dynamics of growth and mortality rates.

Naturally, this leads to the limitations of the study. First, the reliance on aggregated forest inventory data obscures finer-scale regeneration and growth patterns. Estimates for growth and mortality rates are subject to uncertainties arising from assumptions about age-class transitions and the effects of external factors like climate variability. The Markov chain model, while effective for projecting age-class transitions, simplifies complex ecological interactions and may not fully capture nonlinear or density-dependent effects. The focus on the Lithuanian scenario limits the generalizability of the findings to other regions or forest types with different ecological dynamics. Future research should aim to address these limitations by incorporating more granular data, exploring nonlinear modeling approaches, and extending the analysis to include additional forest ecosystems.

However, the findings still have implications for forest policy and sustainable management practices. Policy recommendations for promoting mixed species forests in Lithuania, particularly focused on the regeneration of Scots pine, should draw on scientific evidence that highlights the benefits of species diversity for forest resilience and ecosystem services. Studies from Scandinavian countries, such as Finland and Sweden, demonstrate that mixed species stands, which combine Scots pine with species such as Norway spruce and birch, show increased resistance to biotic stressors such as bark beetle infestations and fungal diseases, which disproportionately affect monocultures. For example, a study in Fennoscandia forests [53] showed that Scots pine mixed with birch improves overall forest productivity due to the use of complementary resources, as Birch has a shallower rooting system, reducing competition for water and nutrients with deeper-rooted Scots pine. Similarly, in Central Europe, mixed species forests have been shown to better withstand extreme weather events, such as droughts, by increasing structural and functional diversity, which buffers against environmental variability [54]. Other analyses of European forests [55] have shown that adaptive thinning in mixed forests can prioritize the growth of Scots pine by selectively removing faster-growing competitors, such as birch, in critical growth phases, thus optimizing light and resource availability for Scots pine. We believe that these findings show that policies that promote mixed species forests would not only enhance biodiversity and ecosystem functions but also make Scots pine stands more resilient to climatic and biological threats, ensuring their role as a cornerstone species in Lithuanian forests.

Limitations and Future Works

First, reliance on aggregated data from the Lithuanian National Forest Inventory (NFI), while valuable for long-term trend analysis, masks important fine-scale spatial and temporal heterogeneity in Scots pine regeneration, growth, and mortality. Given Lithuania's diverse forest ecosystems, including the dry and sandy soils of Dzūkija and the wetter and more fertile soils of Aukštaitija, aggregation obscures localized regeneration patterns, particularly in regions where Scots pine performance is strongly influenced by site-specific factors such as soil moisture, nutrient availability, and microclimatic variability. The sensitivity analysis in this study indicated that Scots pine is particularly sensitive to soil moisture conditions, especially in regions prone to drought. However, the data do not adequately capture this variability, limiting the model's capacity to provide precise guidance for region-specific management interventions.

The use of Lithuanian National Forest Inventory (NFI) data in modeling forest dynamics offers a comprehensive snapshot of forest conditions, using extensive datasets that cover various forest attributes such as species composition, age distribution, and health status. However, this approach is restricted to the variables collected in the inventory, which may limit the model's ability to capture all ecological dynamics fully. For instance, the NFI data might focus predominantly on commercially important tree species and standard forest metrics such as timber volume and tree density, potentially overlooking underrepresented species or non-timber forest values like biodiversity and ecological services. This selective data collection can introduce biases, as the model's outputs may not fully reflect the complexities of forest ecosystems, particularly those related to ecological interactions and responses to environmental stressors. Additionally, the periodic nature of the inventory may not adequately capture rapid changes or short-term ecological responses, impacting the model's sensitivity and adaptability to real-time forest dynamics. These limitations require a cautious interpretation of model predictions and underscore the importance of integrating additional data sources or conducting additional field studies to improve the robustness and ecological validity of the findings.

Second, while the Markov chain model proved efficient in modeling age-class transitions and projecting forest composition under various management scenarios, it must be clear that it inherently simplifies complex ecological processes. Nonlinear interactions such as density-dependent mortality, competition between tree species, and environmental feedback mechanisms are reduced to age-based transitions, which may not accurately reflect the dynamic nature of forest ecosystems. Scots pine's interaction with faster-growing pioneer species like birch and aspen is a critical dynamic, particularly in mixed stands where competition for light and resources plays a pivotal role in early growth phases. The sensitivity analysis highlighted the strong influence of competition on Scots pine regeneration, particularly in younger age classes, but the aggregated approach does not fully account for this spatially variable competition, especially in regions like southern Lithuania, where birch competes aggressively in early successional stages. In addition, non-linear feedback, such as the threshold effects of pest outbreaks, particularly bark beetles, is simplified. In reality, these pest dynamics are highly stochastic and often exhibit non-linear thresholds, where small increases in pest populations can lead to widespread forest mortality, a critical factor that will need to be solved in future work.

Third, the study's focus on Scots pine, although ecologically and economically important, given that it accounts for a large part of Lithuania's total forest cover, limits the broader applicability, as the forest dynamics of mixed species stands, particularly those involving spruce and birch, is not fully addressed. For example, the rapid decline of spruce in older age classes identified in the model could be related to a variety of biotic and abiotic stressors such as fungal diseases or increased susceptibility to windfall, factors that are increasingly important under climate change, but are underrepresented in the structure of this model. In some regions within Lithuania, these dynamics play a role in long-term forest stability and will be further investigated. Furthermore, the competitive behavior of birch and aspen presents a challenge to the regeneration of Scots pine, especially in unmanaged or naturally regenerating stands. The sensitivity analysis suggested that Scots pine regeneration is highly sensitive to birch competition, but the aggregated approach of the model itself does not allow a more detailed vision of how management strategies such as selective thinning or mixed species planting can mitigate these competitive pressures.

Fourth, the model's assumptions regarding climate variability also introduce limitations. Although our study touches on the potential effects of climate change, particularly drought, its approach to projecting future forest dynamics does not fully integrate the increasing unpredictability of climatic extremes, which are expected to intensify in Lithuania, particularly in southern regions prone to drought, as we do not yet have enough data on extremities to include in the model. Scots pine, while resilient, has its growth and regeneration closely tied to soil moisture availability, and future scenarios with extended dry periods could exacerbate mortality rates in ways not fully captured by the model's current sensitivity analysis.

Lastly, the focus on Lithuania's forest ecosystems limits the generalizability of the findings to other regions with different ecological and management contexts. Although Scots pine is a dominant species in northern Europe, the dynamics in mixed-species forests in Scandinavia or central Europe, where different environmental and ecological pressures exist, may differ significantly. For example, studies from Finland and Sweden show that Scots pine, when grown in mixed stands with species such as Norway spruce or birch, demonstrates greater resilience. We are planning with the Linnaeus University team, Sweden, to augment the model with additional data under the Forest 4.0 initiative.

Future research will aim to address these limitations by incorporating finer-scale, high-resolution data, particularly with respect to spatial variability in site conditions, species interactions, and climatic factors. More advanced non-linear modeling approaches, including agent-based or process-based models, could capture complex ecological interactions and stochastic events such as extreme factors due to climate change, thus improving the robustness of the projections. Furthermore, expanding the study to include mixed species forests and incorporating case studies from other regions would improve the generalizability and applicability of the findings, providing more nuanced insights for sustainable forest management in diverse ecological contexts.

7. Conclusions

The key novelty in this study lies in the use of the Markov chain model combined with Multivariate Time Series (MTY) decomposition to analyze the regeneration dynamics of Scots pine. Unlike traditional deterministic models, the Markov chain approach allowed for the probabilistic tracking of age-class transitions, enabling a more accurate representation of how Scots pine populations evolve under various management and climate scenarios. The MTY decomposition added further depth by isolating trend, seasonal, and irregular components in regeneration rates, which previous models had not integrated into their sensitivity analyzes. For example, while Ryzhkova et al. [5] focused on geoinformation modeling for large-scale forest cover classification, while our approach went further by applying statistical methods to examine the sensitivity of regeneration dynamics to parameter variability, providing actionable insights for adaptive forest management.

The results of the forest regeneration model demonstrate key findings on the growth and mortality dynamics of various tree species. Scots pine shows a 79.6% probability of advancing from the 1–10 age class to the 11–20 age class, with subsequent transition probabilities of 82.9% and 84.1% between older age classes Scots pine displays slower initial growth and a higher likelihood (20.4%) of remaining in the 1–10 age class, suggesting that it may face competition or environmental challenges early on, implying on the need for targeted management practices to support Scots pine seedlings and ensure their survival in the face of competitive pressures from faster-growing species like Birch and Aspen. In contrast, the pioneer species Birch and Aspen exhibit strong early growth, with Birch having a 84% chance of advancing from the 1–10 to the 11–20 age class and Aspen achieving a high transition rate, reflecting the competitive advantages of Birch and Aspen in disturbed or newly opened habitats, where they can rapidly colonize and dominate. However, both species show a notable slowdown in growth as they age, with Birch's transition rates declining in later age classes and Aspen's falling dramatically after 31 years, likely due to physiological limitations or increased susceptibility to environmental stressors. Spruce, on the other hand, presents a different growth trajectory, with modest early growth but a very high transition from the 21–30 to the 31+ age class, indicating its resilience and capacity for sustained growth in mature forest stages. Naturally, such a growth pattern suggests that while Spruce may not be as competitive in early succession stages, it can become dominant in later stages, particularly in mature forests.

Sensitivity analysis provide information on the interaction between growth and mortality rates, revealing that while higher growth rates can extend the lifespan of the forest stand, high mortality rates (above 0.33) drastically reduce the viability of the stand, which emphasizes the critical importance of reducing mortality, through disease management, pest control, or improved silvicultural practices. Without addressing mortality, even high growth rates cannot offset the negative impacts of stand decline, as successful forest management, must prioritize both enhancing growth and minimizing mortality, particularly in vulnerable species or age classes. The Hotelling T^2 control chart further illustrated forest dynamics, identifying significant deviations in years 13 and 19, indicating periods of environmental stress, which have impacted the growth or survival rates of certain species, showing that unforeseen stressors can disrupt even well-managed stands.

Author Contributions: Conceptualization, R.D. and R.M.; methodology, R.D.; software, R.D.; validation, R.D. and R.M.; formal analysis, R.D.; investigation, R.D.; resources, R.D.; data curation, R.D.; writing—original draft preparation, R.D.; writing—review and editing, R.D. and R.M.; visualization, R.D. and R.M.; project administration, R.M.; funding acquisition, R.D. and R.M. All authors have read and agreed to the published version of the manuscript.

Funding: This research paper has received funding from Horizon Europe Framework Programme (HORIZON), call Teaming for Excellence (HORIZON-WIDERA-2022-ACCESS-01-two-stage)—Creation of the centre of excellence in smart forestry "Forest 4.0" No. 101059985.

Data Availability Statement: The dataset used in this study is available at: https://amvmt.lrv.lt/lt/atviri-duomenys-1/misku-statistikos-leidiniai/misku-ukio-statistika/2021-m-1/ (accessed on 12 September 2024).

Conflicts of Interest: The authors declare no conflicts of interest.

References

1. Phillips, O.; Lewis, S.; Baker, T.; Chao, K.; Higuchi, N. The changing Amazon forest. *Philos. Trans. R. Soc. B Biol. Sci.* **2008**, *363*, 1819–1827. [CrossRef] [PubMed]
2. Keith, H.; Gorsel, E.; Jacobsen, K.; Cleugh, H. Dynamics of carbon exchange in a Eucalyptus forest in response to interacting disturbance factors. *Agric. For. Meteorol.* **2012**, *153*, 67–81. [CrossRef]
3. Poorter, L.; Sande, M.T.v.; Arets, E.J.M.M.; Ascarrunz, N.; Enquist, B.J.; Finegan, B.; Licona, J.C.; Martínez-Ramos, M.; Mazzei, L.; Meave, J.A.; et al. Biodiversity and climate determine the functioning of neotropical forests. *Glob. Ecol. Biogeogr.* **2017**, *26*, 1423–1434. [CrossRef]
4. Mund, M.; Schulze, E. Silviculture and Its Interactions with Biodiversity and the Carbon Balance of Forest Soils. In *Forest Diversity and Function*; Springer Series in Applied Sciences; Springer: Berlin/Heidelberg, Germany, 2005; pp. 185–208. [CrossRef]
5. Ryzhkova, V.; Danilova, I.; Mikhailova, I.; Korets, M. Multilayer forest cover map as a basis of forest regeneration dynamics estimation. In Proceedings of the 18th International Multidisciplinary Scientific GeoConference SGEM 2018, Albena, Bulgaria, 2–8 July 2018. [CrossRef]
6. Frutos Sergio, D.; Mathieu, F.; Sonia, R.G.; Ricardo, R.P.; Río Miren, D.; José Alfredo, B.F. Group selection cutting for regenerating Mediterranean Pinus pinaster plantations: Gap effects on seedling survival. *For. Ecol. Manag.* **2023**, *544*, 121219. [CrossRef]
7. Martin, M.; Girona, M.; Morin, H. Driving factors of conifer regeneration dynamics in eastern Canadian boreal old-growth forests. *PLoS ONE* **2020**, *15*, e0230221. [CrossRef]
8. Maréchaux, I.; Chave, J. An individual-based forest model to jointly simulate carbon and tree diversity in Amazonia: Description and applications. *Ecol. Monogr.* **2017**, *87*, 632–664. [CrossRef]
9. Lai, H.; Hall, J.; Turner, B.; Van Breugel, M. Liana effects on biomass dynamics strengthen during secondary forest succession. *Ecology* **2017**, *98*, 1062–1070. [CrossRef]
10. McDowell, N.; Allen, C.; Anderson-Teixeira, K.; Aukema, B.; Bond-Lamberty, B.; Chini, L.; Clark, J.S.; Dietze, M.; Grossiord, C.; Hanbury-Brown, A.; et al. Pervasive shifts in forest dynamics in a changing world. *Science* **2020**, *368*, eaaz9463. [CrossRef]
11. Miu, N.; Liu, S.; Shi, Z.; Ma, J.; Wang, H. A review of ecological effects of remnant trees in degraded forest ecosystems after severe disturbances. *Acta Ecol. Sin.* **2013**, *33*, 3889–3897. [CrossRef]
12. Brichta, J.; Šimůnek, V.; Bílek, L.; Vacek, Z.; Gallo, J.; Drozdowski, S.; Bravo-Fernández, J.A.; Mason, B.; Gomez, S.R.; Hájek, V.; et al. Effects of Climate Change on Scots Pine (*Pinus sylvestris* L.) Growth across Europe: Decrease of Tree-Ring Fluctuation and Amplification of Climate Stress. *Forests* **2024**, *15*, 91. [CrossRef]
13. Krakau, U.K.; Liesebach, M.; Aronen, T.; Lelu-Walter, M.; Schneck, V. Scots Pine (*Pinus sylvestris* L.). In *Forest Tree Breeding in Europe*; Springer: Dordrecht, The Netherlands, 2013; Volume 25, pp. 267–323. [CrossRef]
14. Linkevičius, E.; Šidlauskas, G.; Kliučius, A.; Armoška, E.; Mikalajunas, M.; Sidabriene, D.; Andriuškevičiute, P.; Augustaitis, A. The growth dynamics of East European Scots pine (*Pinus sylvestris* L.) populations—A Lithuanian field trial. *iForest-Biogeosci. For.* **2024**, *17*, 59–68. [CrossRef]
15. Šatinskas, R. Economic and Production Consequences of Current Forest Management in Mature Scots pine (*Pinus sylvestris*) forests in Lithuania. Master's Thesis, SLU, Southern Swedish Forest Research Centre, Alnarp, Sweden, 2019.
16. Kabašinskas, A.; Varnagirytė-Kabašinskienė, I. Changes of dominant tree species areas over the past century in Lithuania: A mathematical approach. *Res. Rural. Dev.* **2014**, *2*, 35.
17. Hohtola, A. Somatic Embryogenesis in Scots Pine (*Pinus sylvestris* L.). In *Somatic Embryogenesis in Woody Plants*; Springer: Dordrecht, The Netherlands, 1995; pp. 269–285. [CrossRef]
18. Linkevičius, E.; Kliučius, A.; Šidlauskas, G.; Augustaitis, A. Variability in Growth Patterns and Tree-Ring Formation of East European Scots Pine (*Pinus sylvestris* L.) Provenances to Changing Climatic Conditions in Lithuania. *Forests* **2022**, *13*, 743. [CrossRef]
19. Markovskaja, S.; Raitelaitytė, K.; Kačergius, A.; Kolmakov, P.; Vasilevich, V. Occurrence of Dothistroma needle blight in Lithuania and Belarus: The risk posed to native Scots Pine forests. *For. Pathol.* **2020**, *50*, e12626. [CrossRef]
20. Česna, V.; Gedminas, A.; Lynikienė, J.; Marčiulynienė, D. Insect Diversity in *Pinus sylvestris* Forest Stands Damaged by Lymantria monacha. *Insects* **2024**, *15*, 200. [CrossRef]
21. Tamkevičiūtė, M.; Edvardsson, J.; Pukienė, R.; Taminskas, J.; Stoffel, M.; Corona, C.; Kibirkštis, G. Scots pine (*Pinus sylvestris* L.) based reconstruction of 130 years of water table fluctuations in a peatland and its relevance for moisture variability assessments. *J. Hydrol.* **2018**, *558*, 509–519. [CrossRef]
22. Šilinskas, B.; Varnagirytė-Kabašinskienė, I.; Aleinikovas, M.; Beniušienė, L.; Aleinikovienė, J.; Škėma, M. Scots Pine and Norway Spruce Wood Properties at Sites with Different Stand Densities. *Forests* **2020**, *11*, 587. [CrossRef]
23. Jönsson, K.; Nilsson, C. Scots Pine (*Pinus sylvestris* L.) on Shingle Fields: A Dendrochronologic Reconstruction of Early Summer Precipitation in Mideast Sweden. *J. Clim.* **2009**, *22*, 4710–4722. [CrossRef]

24. Kelly, D.; Connolly, A. A Review of the Plant Communities Associated with Scots Pine (*Pinus sylvestris* L.) in Europe, and an Evaluation of Putative Indicator/Specialist Species. *For. Syst.* **2000**, *9*, 15–39. [CrossRef]
25. Beniušienė, L.; Petrauskas, E.; Aleinikovas, M.; Varnagirytė-Kabašinskienė, I.; Beniušis, R.; Šilinskas, B. Norway spruce stem parameters in sites with different stand densities in lithuanian hemiboreal forest. *Forests* **2021**, *12*, 201. [CrossRef]
26. Lekoveckaitė, A.; Jimenez, M.F.T.; Trakimas, G.; Ferenca, R.; Podėnienė, V. Tree Species Affect Beetle Diversity on the Common Deciduous Dead Wood in Lithuanian Unmanaged Forests. *Forests* **2023**, *14*, 1836. [CrossRef]
27. Eberhard, B.R.; Eckhart, T.; Hasenauer, H. Evaluating Strategies for the Management of Douglas-Fir in Central Europe. *Forests* **2021**, *12*, 1040. [CrossRef]
28. Vergarechea, M.; Calama, R.; Fortin, M.; del Río, M. Climate-mediated regeneration occurrence in Mediterranean pine forests: A modeling approach. *For. Ecol. Manag.* **2019**, *446*, 10–19. [CrossRef]
29. Carón, M.; De Frenne, P.; Brunet, J.; Chabrerie, O.; Cousins, S.; Decocq, G.; Diekmann, M.; Graae, B.; Heinken, T.; Kolb, A.; et al. Divergent regeneration responses of two closely related tree species to direct abiotic and indirect biotic effects of climate change. *For. Ecol. Manag.* **2015**, *342*, 21–29. [CrossRef]
30. Cagnacci, J.; Estravis-Barcala, M.; Lia, M.; Martínez-Meier, A.; Polo, M.G.; Arana, M.V. The impact of different natural environments on the regeneration dynamics of two Nothofagus species across elevation in the southern Andes. *For. Ecol. Manag.* **2020**, *464*, 118034. [CrossRef]
31. Piovesan, G.; Lüttge, U. Tree growth dynamics during early ontogenetic stages in closed forests. *Trees* **2018**, *32*, 671–673. [CrossRef]
32. Vodde, F.; Jõgiste, K.; Kubota, Y.; Kuuluvainen, T.; Köster, K.; Lukjanova, A.; Metslaid, M.; Yoshida, T. The influence of storm-induced microsites to tree regeneration patterns in boreal and hemiboreal forest. *J. For. Res.* **2011**, *16*, 155–167. [CrossRef]
33. Walck, J.; Hidayati, S.N.; Dixon, K.; Thompson, K.; Poschlod, P. Climate change and plant regeneration from seed. *Glob. Chang. Biol.* **2011**, *17*, 2145–2161. [CrossRef]
34. Simler-Williamson, A.B.; Metz, M.; Frangioso, K.; Meentemeyer, R.; Rizzo, D. Compound disease and wildfire disturbances alter opportunities for seedling regeneration in resprouter-dominated forests. *Ecosphere* **2019**, *10*, e02991. [CrossRef]
35. Uriarte, M.; Muscarella, R.; Zimmerman, J. Environmental heterogeneity and biotic interactions mediate climate impacts on tropical forest regeneration. *Glob. Change Biol.* **2018**, *24*, e692–e704. [CrossRef]
36. Babst, F.; Bouriaud, O.; Poulter, B.; Trouet, V.; Girardin, M.P.; Frank, D.C. Twentieth century redistribution in climatic drivers of global tree growth. *Sci. Adv.* **2019**, *5*, eaat4313. [CrossRef] [PubMed]
37. Rocha, S.J.S.S.d.; Torres, C.M.M.E.; Jacovine, L.A.G.; Leite, H.G.; Gelcer, E.M.; Neves, K.M.; Schettini, B.L.S.; Villanova, P.H.; Silva, L.F.d.; Reis, L.P.; et al. Artificial neural networks: Modeling tree survival and mortality in the Atlantic Forest biome in Brazil. *Sci. Total Environ.* **2018**, *645*, 655–661. [CrossRef] [PubMed]
38. Manso, R.; Morneau, F.; Ningre, F.; Fortin, M. Incorporating stochasticity from extreme climatic events and multi-species competition relationships into single-tree mortality models. *For. Ecol. Manag.* **2015**, *354*, 243–253. [CrossRef]
39. Ryzhkova, V.; Danilova, I.; Korets, M. Forest cover classification and geoinformation modeling of forest regeneration dynamics (Based on the example of the southern part of near-Yenisei Siberia). *Contemp. Probl. Ecol.* **2016**, *9*, 692–701. [CrossRef]
40. Richit, L.; Bonatto, C.; Carlotto, T.; da Silva, R.; Grzybowski, J. Modelling forest regeneration for performance-oriented riparian buffer strips. *Ecol. Eng.* **2017**, *106*, 308–322. [CrossRef]
41. Mantero, G.; Anselmetto, N.; Morresi, D.; Meloni, F.; Bolzon, P.; Lingua, E.; Garbarino, M.; Marzano, R. Modeling post-fire regeneration patterns under different restoration scenarios to improve forest recovery in degraded ecosystems. *For. Ecol. Manag.* **2024**, *551*, 121520. [CrossRef]
42. Eberhard, B.; Hasenauer, H. Modeling Regeneration of Douglas fir forests in Central Europe. *Austrian J. For. Sci.* **2018**, 135, 33–51.
43. De Frutos, S.; Bravo-Fernández, J.; Roig-Gómez, S.; Del Río, M.; Ruiz-Peinado, R. Natural regeneration and species diversification after seed-tree method cutting in a maritime pine reforestation. *iForest* **2022**, *15*, 500–508. [CrossRef]
44. Calama, R.; Martínez, C.; Gordo, J.; Del Río, M.; Menéndez-Miguélez, M.; Pardos, M. The impact of climate and management on recent mortality in Pinus pinaster resin-tapped forests of inland Spain. *Forestry* **2024**, *97*, 120–132. [CrossRef]
45. Holzer, D.; Bödeker, K.; Rammer, W.; Knoke, T. Evaluating dynamic tree-species-shifting and height development caused by ungulate browsing in forest regeneration using a process-based modeling approach. *Ecol. Model.* **2024**, *493*, 110741. [CrossRef]
46. McClintock, B.T.; Langrock, R.; Gimenez, O.; Cam, E.; Borchers, D.L.; Glennie, R.; Patterson, T.A. Uncovering ecological state dynamics with hidden Markov models. *Ecol. Lett.* **2020**, *23*, 1878–1903. [CrossRef] [PubMed]
47. Pianosi, F.; Beven, K.; Freer, J.; Hall, J.W.; Rougier, J.; Stephenson, D.B.; Wagener, T. Sensitivity analysis of environmental models: A systematic review with practical workflow. *Environ. Model. Softw.* **2016**, *79*, 214–232. [CrossRef]
48. Chou, Y.M.; Mason, R.L.; Young, J.C. Power comparisons for a hotelling's T2 statistic. *Commun. Stat. Part B Simul. Comput.* **1999**, *28*, 1031–1050. [CrossRef]

49. Díaz-Rojo, G.; Debón, A.; Mosquera, J. Multivariate Control Chart and Lee–Carter Models to Study Mortality Changes. *Mathematics* **2020**, *8*, 2093. [CrossRef]
50. Benson, D.L.; King, E.G.; O'Brien, J.J. Forest Dynamics Models for Conservation, Restoration, and Management of Small Forests. *Forests* **2022**, *13*, 515. [CrossRef]
51. König, L.A.; Mohren, F.; Schelhaas, M.J.; Bugmann, H.; Nabuurs, G.J. Tree regeneration in models of forest dynamics—Suitability to assess climate change impacts on European forests. *For. Ecol. Manag.* **2022**, *520*, 120390. [CrossRef]
52. Kašpar, J.; Tumajer, J.; Šamonil, P.; Vašíčková, I. Species-specific climate–growth interactions determine tree species dynamics in mixed Central European mountain forests. *Environ. Res. Lett.* **2021**, *16*, 034039. [CrossRef]
53. Huuskonen, S.; Domisch, T.; Finér, L.; Hantula, J.; Hynynen, J.; Matala, J.; Miina, J.; Neuvonen, S.; Nevalainen, S.; Niemistö, P.; et al. What is the potential for replacing monocultures with mixed-species stands to enhance ecosystem services in boreal forests in Fennoscandia? *For. Ecol. Manag.* **2021**, *479*, 118558. [CrossRef]
54. Pardos, M.; del Río, M.; Pretzsch, H.; Jactel, H.; Bielak, K.; Bravo, F.; Brazaitis, G.; Defossez, E.; Engel, M.; Godvod, K.; et al. The greater resilience of mixed forests to drought mainly depends on their composition: Analysis along a climate gradient across Europe. *For. Ecol. Manag.* **2021**, *481*, 118687. [CrossRef]
55. Coll, L.; Ameztegui, A.; Collet, C.; Löf, M.; Mason, B.; Pach, M.; Verheyen, K.; Abrudan, I.; Barbati, A.; Barreiro, S.; et al. Knowledge gaps about mixed forests: What do European forest managers want to know and what answers can science provide? *For. Ecol. Manag.* **2018**, *407*, 106–115. [CrossRef]

forests

MDPI

Article

Uncertainty Analysis of Forest Aboveground Carbon Stock Estimation Combining Sentinel-1 and Sentinel-2 Images

Bo Qiu [1,2,3], Sha Li [1,2,3], Jun Cao [1,2,3], Jialong Zhang [1,2,3,*], Kun Yang [1,2,3], Kai Luo [1,2,3], Kai Huang [4] and Xinzhou Jiang [1,2,3]

1 Key Laboratory of Forest Resources Conservation and Utilization in The Southwest Mountains of China, Ministry of Education, Southwest Forestry University, Kunming 650233, China; qiubo@swfu.edu.cn (B.Q.); lishawoyonggan@swfu.edu.cn (S.L.); caojun97525@163.com (J.C.); kunyang@swfu.edu.cn (K.Y.); luokai@swfu.edu.cn (K.L.); jxz123456@swfu.edu.cn (X.J.)

2 Key Laboratory of National Forestry and Grassland Administration on Biodiversity Conservation in Southwest China, Southwest Forestry University, Kunming 650233, China

3 Yunnan Provincial Key Laboratory for Conservation and Utilization of In-Forest Resource, Southwest Forestry University, Kunming 650233, China

4 College of Water and Soil Conservation, Southwest Forestry University, Kunming 650224, China; hk706@swfu.edu.cn

* Correspondence: jialongzhang@swfu.edu.cn; Tel.: +86-138-8802-1540

Abstract: Accurate estimation of forest aboveground carbon stock (AGC) is essential for understanding carbon accounting and climate change. In previous studies, the extracted factors, such as spectral textures, vegetation indices, and textural features, were used to estimate the AGC. However, few studies examined how different factors affect estimation accuracy in detail. Meanwhile, there are also many uncertainties in the collection and processing of the field data. To quantify the various uncertainties in the process of AGC estimation, we used the random forest (RF) to establish estimation models based on field data and Sentinel-1/2 images in Shangri-La. The models included the band information model (BIM), the vegetation index model (VIM), the texture information model (TIM), the Sentinel-2 factor model (S-2M), and the Sentinel-1/2 factor model (S-1/2M). Then, uncertainties resulting from the plot scale and estimation models were calculated using error equations. Our goal is to analyze the influence of different factors on AGC estimation and to assess the uncertainty of plot scale and estimation models quantitatively. The results showed that (1) the uncertainty of the measurement was 3.02%, while the error of the monocarbon stock model was the main uncertainty at the plot scale, which was 9.09%; (2) the BIM had the lowest accuracy (R^2 = 0.551) and the highest total uncertainty (22.29%); by gradually introducing different factors in the process of modeling, the accuracies improved significantly (VIM: R^2 = 0.688, TIM: R^2 = 0.715, S-2M: R^2 = 0.826), and the total uncertainty decreased to some extent (VIM: 14.12%, TIM: 12.56%, S-2M: 10.79%); (3) the S-1/2M with the introduction of Sentinel-1 synthetic aperture radar (SAR) data has the highest accuracy (R^2 = 0.872) and the lowest total uncertainty (8.43%). The inaccuracy of spectral features is highest, followed by vegetation indices, while textural features have the lowest inaccuracy. Uncertainty in the remote-sensing-based estimation model remains a significant source of uncertainty compared to the plot scale. Even though the uncertainty at the plot scale is relatively small, this error should not be ignored. The uncertainty in the estimation process could be further reduced by improving the precision of the measurement and the fitting of the monocarbon stock estimation model.

Keywords: carbon stock; remote sensing factors; plot scale; SAR data; uncertainty

1. Introduction

Forest ecosystems play a vital role in understanding climate change and maintaining carbon balance [1–3]. Forest aboveground carbon stock (AGC) is not only an important index of forest carbon absorption capacity but also a basis for studying forest ecosystem structure and function and evaluating forest carbon balance [4,5]. Therefore, accurate estimation of forest AGC is crucial for humans to assess and protect the forest ecosystems [6,7]. However, there are certain uncertainties in estimating AGC at both large and small regions [8]. Ignoring these uncertainties will limit the accurate estimation of forest AGC. Hence, reducing the uncertainty to improve the accuracy in the estimation process has become a significant challenge [9].

The methods for estimating AGC mainly contain the traditional plot survey and remote sensing estimation. Although the plot survey can obtain accurate data, it requires a considerable investment of human and financial resources. Whereas, remote-sensing-based methods have the characteristics of being fast, low-cost, large-scale, and less destructive. They had been widely used in the estimation of forest aboveground biomass (AGB) and AGC [10–12]. Optical remote sensing data have a great advantage in obtaining the structural parameters of the forest; the rich spectral information have been widely applied in the study of AGC estimation [13]. However, it is susceptible to the strong influence of canopy thickness, so it is difficult to obtain the vertical structural parameters of the forest, and the information it obtains tends to be saturated in areas of high biomass and carbon stock, which has a disadvantage in estimating high AGB or AGC [14,15]. Many researchers have found that using only single optical data to estimate forest AGB or AGC has high uncertainty [16–18]. Synthetic aperture radar (SAR) data have the advantages of longer electromagnetic wavelength, strong penetration ability, and sensitivity to structural attributes [19], so it can overcome the shortcomings of optical data and can obtain valuable information concerning the vertical vegetation canopy. Therefore, combining optical with SAR data to estimate forest AGB and AGC is considered a feasible method [20–22]. For instance, Fang et al. [23] combined Sentinel-1 SAR and Sentinel-2 optical data to establish a multivariate linear regression (MLR) and extreme gradient boosting (XGBoost) model for predicting forest AGB. Liu et al. [24] combined field plots and Sentinel-1 and Sentinel-2 data to map the forest stand mean height (FSMH) and AGB at a resolution of 10 m in Yichun, Northeast China. Their results showed that the AGB and AGC models generated by combining the two types of data are more robust and accurate than models derived from optical or SAR data. Given the above findings, we combined optical and SAR data to estimate forest AGC in this study.

Uncertainty is an umbrella term for concepts that include inaccuracy, ambiguity, and inconsistency [25]. It is very common in the process of carbon stock estimation. There are three primary sources of uncertainty in the whole process of AGC estimation: measurement uncertainty, sampling uncertainty, and model uncertainty [26,27]. Shettles et al. [28] regarded model uncertainty as the main source of error, accounting for about 70% of the total uncertainty. Sources of model uncertainty mainly include the uncertainty of input variables [29], improperly setting the model function form [30], the residual variability of the model [31], and the parameter error of the model [32]. Uncertainty in the input variables mainly refers to the measurement error of variables such as diameter at breast height (*DBH*) and tree height (*H*), which is primarily affected by the measurement techniques, equipment, and anthropogenic measurement methods [33]. The incorrect setting of the model form is mainly due to the lack of appropriate test data or modeling techniques [34]. For the residual uncertainty of the model, the standard deviation of the residual was used to measure it [35]. However, it can produce different results due to the differences in the study area and data. Compared to the residual uncertainty of the model, the uncertainty caused by the parameter error is relatively small and relates to the number of modeling samples. Current studies focused more on the uncertainty of the model. For example, Eduarda et al. [36] reduced the uncertainty of the biomass model in terms of modeling methods. Huang et al. [37] used the error transfer method to measure the uncertainties of parametric and nonparametric models. Cao et al. [38] combined the random forest and Monte Carlo simulation (RF-MC) to study the effects of models with different types of variables on the accuracy of carbon stock estimation.

In summary, optical and SAR data to measure uncertainties arising from estimation models have been widely used [39]. However, these studies neglected how different factors impact the accuracy and uncertainty of the model. Furthermore, few studies have combined optical and SAR data to quantitatively assess the uncertainties generated by two different scales of plot and remote sensing model. To address these research issues, the *Pinus densata* in Shangri-La was used as the research tree species, and Sentinel-1/2 data and field data were used to establish different estimation models. Then, error equations were used to calculate uncertainties of plot scale and remote sensing models. The main objectives of this study were to (1) investigate the effects of different factors and plot scale on AGC estimation; (2) analyze the primary source of uncertainty at the plot scale; and (3) explore the potential of SAR data in reducing uncertainty during the AGC estimation.

2. Materials and Methods

2.1. Study Area

Shangri-La is located in northwestern Yunnan Province in southwest China, with a total area of 11,613 km^2 (Figure 1b). It has a large undulating topography, with an elevation difference of 4042 m (the lowest elevation is 1503 m) and an average elevation of 3459 m (Figure 1d). Most rain falls from June to September, mean annual precipitation is 607 mm, and the average annual evaporation is 1643.6 mm [40]. It has four towns and seven villages with a high forest cover of 75% and is one of the world's top ten species gene pools [41]. Its main vegetation types are cold-temperate coniferous forest and rubber forest. *Pinus densata* is one of its dominant tree species (Figure 1c), which covers an area of 1848.18 km^2 and accounts for 16.18% of the area of Shangri-La [42].

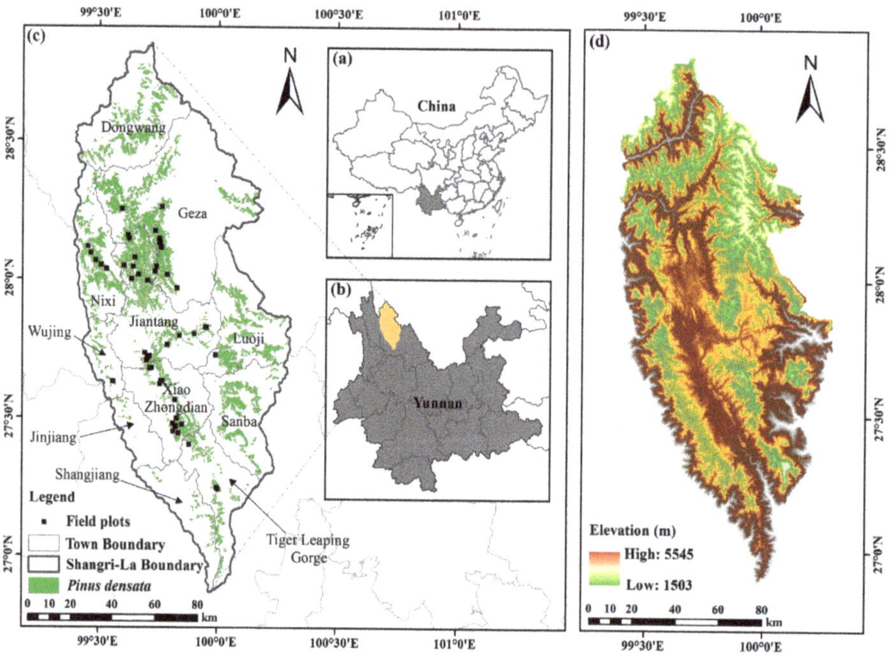

Figure 1. (**a**) Location of Yunnan Province in China; (**b**) location of Shangri-La in Yunnan Province; (**c**) distribution of *Pinus densata* and field plots; and (**d**) elevation.

The methods of this paper are divided into three stages (Figure 2). In the first stage, remote sensing images were processed, and remote sensing features were extracted; the AGC at each field plot was calculated from the field survey. AGC remote-sensing-based estimation models were established in the second stage using the RF method; measurement uncertainty and uncertainty of the monocarbon stock model at the plot scale were calculated. In the third stage, we used error equations to calculate the remote-sensing-based estimation model uncertainty and the total uncertainty at the plot scale. Then, we combined two uncertainties to obtain the total uncertainty of the AGC estimation.

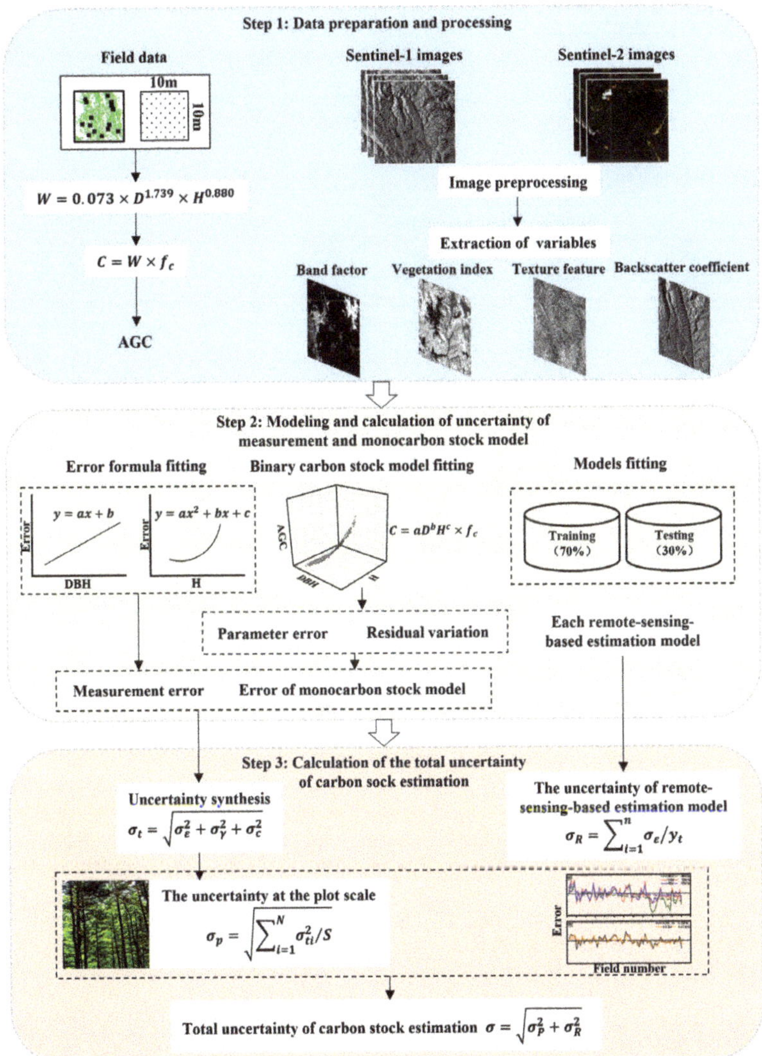

Figure 2. Overview of the methodological approach.

2.2. Data Acquisition and Processing

2.2.1. Field Survey

A total of 60 plots were surveyed in 2019 and 2021. Twenty plots were surveyed in December 2019, and the other forty were surveyed in May 2021. Plot sizes of 10 m × 10 m were considered in this study to ensure correspondence between the field measurement and pixel size in the imagery [43]. Sample points were randomly distributed in pure *Pinus densata* forest areas; each plot was spaced more than 3 km apart. The field survey mainly recorded *DBH* and *H* of pure stand of *Pinus densata* with *DBH* of 5 cm or more. The binary lumber volume table was used to calculate the capacity of individual trees in each plot [44]. The AGB of *Pinus densata* was calculated using the allometric growth equation [45]:

$$W = 0.073 \times D^{1.739} \times H^{0.880} \tag{1}$$

where W is AGB, D is the diameter at breast height, and H is the tree height. Then, the carbon stock was calculated as:

$$C = W \times f_c \tag{2}$$

where C is the AGC of *Pinus densata*, and f_c is the carbon content coefficient, which is 0.5131 [46,47]. The field survey data are shown in Table 1.

Table 1. Field survey data in Shangri-La.

Variables	Max	Min	Mean	SD
Mean DBH (cm)	29.75	8.52	15.33	5.57
Mean H (m)	19.05	4.33	9.90	3.93
AGC (t/ha)	128.34	10.49	51.05	30.54

2.2.2. DEM

The digital elevation model (DEM) used in this study was downloaded from the official website of the United States Geological Survey (USGS) (https://earthexplorer.usgs.gov (accessed on 10 July 2023)). It is the Shuttle Radar Topography Mission (SRTM) Version 3 product, with a resolution of 30 m. We resampled it to 10 m using the nearest neighbor method.

2.2.3. Remote Sensing Images and Processing

In this study, we selected two scenes of Sentinel-1 Interferometric Wide mode (IW) Ground Range Detected (GRD) images acquired in November 2021 with a resolution of 10 m (Table 2). Pre-processing operations, such as orbit correction, thermal noise removal, radiometric calibration, speckle filtering, and terrain correction, were performed in the SNAP software 10.0 provided by the European Space Agency (ESA) [48]. Owing to the significant altitude disparities in the study area, we utilized the altitude, slope, and aspect extracted from DEM to correct the image for alleviating the effect of elevation differences on the images [49]. Concerning the influence of the wave propagation path on the images, the alteration in the wave propagation path can be analyzed by extracting terrain information (altitude, slope, and aspect) from DEM; we then used SARscape software 5.6.2 to correct this impact through the alteration [50]. Finally, the processed Sentinel-1 images were exported to ENVI format, and stitching and cropping operations were performed.

Table 2. Collected images of the study area.

Sensor	ID	Acquisition Date	Cloud Cover/%
Sentinel-1	S1A_IW_GRDH_1SDV_20211104T112504_20211104T112529_040421_04CAB8_ACE9	2021/11/04	
	S1A_IW_GRDH_1SDV_20211104T112439_20211104T112504_040421_04CAB8_EC62	2021/11/04	
Sentinel-2	S2A_MSIL2A_20211108T035951_N0301_R004_T47RNK_20211108T071124	2021/11/08	1.28
	S2A_MSIL2A_20211108T035951_N0301_R004_T47RNL_20211108T071124	2021/11/08	0.16
	S2A_MSIL2A_20211108T035951_N0301_R004_T47RNM_20211108T071124	2021/11/08	0.06
	S2A_MSIL2A_20211108T035951_N0301_R004_T47RPK_20211108T071124	2021/11/08	1.79
	S2A_MSIL2A_20211108T035951_N0301_R004_T47RPL_20211108T071124	2021/11/08	0.97
	S2A_MSIL2A_20211108T035951_N0301_R004_T47RPM_20211108T071124	2021/11/08	0.29

Sentinel-2 is a multispectral imaging satellite that carries a multispectral imager (MSI) with 13 spectral bands. The image is unique in that it has three special red-edge bands, making it particularly effective in monitoring vegetation information. We selected six scenes of Sentinel-2 Level-2A (L2A) images in November 2021 (Table 2). It was atmospherically and orthographically corrected [51]. Then, all 20 m spectral bands were resampled to 10 m using the nearest neighbor method [52]. Finally, the band synthesis, splicing, and cropping were completed in the ENVI software 5.6.

2.2.4. Extraction and Selection of Remote Sensing Factors

Remote sensing factors were extracted from the Sentinel-1/2 images after pre-processing through SNAP, SARscape, and ENVI software. Studies have revealed that backscatter coefficients and texture features of SAR were crucial for AGB (AGC) estimation [53,54]. Hence, we extracted SAR backscatter coefficients (VV, VH) and SAR texture features from Sentinel-1 images. Key parameters, such as spectral textures (excluding atmospheric bands B1, B9, and B10), vegetation indices, and texture features, were extracted from Sentinel-2 images according to the relevant research [55]. The parameters extracted in this study contained 2 SAR backscatter coefficients, 10 spectral textures, 9 vegetation indices, 16 SAR texture features, and 152 optical texture features, with a total of 189 factors (Table 3). Then, we used the SPSS software 26.0 to analyze the correlation of remote sensing factors. Finally, high correlation factors were used to establish AGC estimation models. These factors mainly included 3 spectral textures, 4 vegetation indices, 5 optical texture features, and 2 SAR texture features.

Table 3. Variable information obtained from Sentinel-1 and Sentinel-2.

Sensor	Variable Type	Variable Name	Definition
Sentinel-1	Polarization	VV VH	Vertical transmit—vertical channel Vertical transmit—horizontal channel
	Textural features	Contrast (CON), Dissimilarity (DIS), Angular second moment (ASM), Entropy (ENT), Variance (VAR), Correlation (COR), Homogeneity (HOM), Mean (ME)	Grey level co-occurrence matrix
Sentinel-2	Spectral textures	B2, B3, B4, B5, B6, B7, B8, B8A, B11, B12	Blue (490 nm), Green (560 nm), Red (665 nm), Red Edge1 (705 nm), Red Edge2 (740 nm), Red Edge3 (783 nm), NIR (842 nm), Red Edge4 (865 nm), SWIR1 (1610 nm), SWIR2 (2190 nm)
	Vegetation indices	DVI RVI NDVI NDI45 GNDVI SAVI EVI S2REP MSAVI	NIR-Red NIR/Red (NIR − Red)/(NIR + Red) (RE1 − Red)/(RE1 + Red) (RE3 − Green)/(RE3 + Green) 1.5 × (NIR − Red)/8 × (NIR + Red + 0.5) 2.5 × ((NIR − Red)/(NIR + 6 × Red − 7.5 × Blue + 1)) 705 + 35 × [((RE1 + NIR)/2-RE2)/(RE3-RE2)] 2 × NIR + 1 − sqrt[(2 × NIR)^2 − 8×(NIR-Red]/2
	Textural features		Same as Sentinel-1

Note: RE is the red edge; BX is a certain single band of the image.

2.3. Modeling Method

Random forest (RF) [56] is an integrated learning model that is widely used in a variety of fields, such as classification and nonparametric regression prediction [57]. The implementation of the RF model in this study is based on the "Random Forest Regressor" algorithm provided by the "Scikit-learn" package for the Python language. In this study, different remote-sensing-based estimation models were constructed by the RF. The components of each model are BIM: spectral features, VIM: vegetation indices, TIM: optical texture features, S-2M: selected optical remote sensing factors, and S-1/2M: SAR texture features and selected optical factors (Table 4).

Table 4. Factors of different remote-sensing-based estimation models.

Model	Remote Sensing Factors
BIM: Band Information Model	B2, B3, B5
VIM: Vegetation Index Model	DVI, EVI, MSAVI2, S2REP
TIM: Texture Information Model	R5B5VAR, R5B6CON, R5B6VAR, R5B7CON, R5DVICON
S-2M: Sentinel-2 Factor Model	B5, S2REP, R5B5VAR, R5B6CON, R5B6VAR, R5B7CON, R5DVICON
S-1/2M: Sentinel-1/2 Factor Model	B5, S2REP, R5B5VAR, R5B6CON, R5B6VAR, R5B7CON, R5DVICON, R5VVME, R5VHCOR

2.4. Accuracy Evaluation

Seventy percent (42 groups) of the plots were randomly selected for model fitting, and the remaining thirty percent (18 groups) were used for validation [58]. Cross-validation was performed during the modeling. The evaluation indices of the estimation model are the coefficient of determination (R^2), root-mean-square error ($RMSE$), relative root-mean-square error ($rRMSE$), and prediction accuracy (P). To ensure that the model results were as objective as possible, each model was fitted ten times in this study to allow the mean values of evaluation indicators to be used for comparison [59]. The formulas are as follows:

$$R^2 = \frac{\sum_{i=1}^{n}(\hat{y}_i - \overline{y})^2}{\sum_{i=1}^{n}(y_i - \overline{y})^2} \tag{3}$$

$$RMSE = \sqrt{\frac{\sum_{i=1}^{n}(y_i - \hat{y}_i)^2}{n}} \tag{4}$$

$$rRMSE = \frac{RMSE}{\overline{y}} \times 100\% \tag{5}$$

$$P = \frac{1}{n}\sum_{i=1}^{n}\left(1 - \left|\frac{y_i - \hat{y}_i}{\hat{y}_i}\right|\right) \times 100\% \tag{6}$$

where y_i is the observed value, $\hat{y}_i$ is the predicted value, $\overline{y}$ is the mean of the observed values, and n represents the plot number.

2.5. The Analysis of Uncertainty at the Plot Scale

2.5.1. Calculation of the Measurement Uncertainty

The observed values of diameter at breast height and tree height were denoted as D and H, their errors from the normal distribution were denoted as ε_D, ε_H, and their standard deviations of error were σ_D, σ_H. The observed carbon stock model is $C = f(E, a)$, E is the independent variable (DBH, H), and α denotes the parameters of the model. According to Taylor's first-order expansion principle, the error of the monocarbon stock model is:

$$C_{bia} \approx f(e) - f(E) \approx f'(E)(e - E) \tag{7}$$

where $f'(E) = \frac{\partial f(E,\alpha)}{\partial E_1}$ is the partial derivative of the function $f(x)$ concerning the variable E_1. The variance matrix of the prediction error for the model can be expressed as:

$$\sigma^2_{C_{bia}} \approx G\left(f'(E)\cdot(e - E)\right)^2 = f'(E)Var_{e-E}f'(E)^T \tag{8}$$

where Var_{en-En} is the covariance matrix of $e_n - E_n$. If the error between the independent variables is uncorrelated, there is:

$$Var_n = \begin{bmatrix} Var(e_1 - E_1) & 0 & & \cdots & 0 \\ 0 & Var(e_2 - E_2) & & \cdots & 0 \\ \vdots & \vdots & \ddots & & \vdots \\ 0 & \cdots & 0 & & Var(e_n - E_n) \end{bmatrix} \quad (9)$$

For the $f(E,a)$, there are two types of models: unary and binary models. In order to maintain the consistency of the carbon stock model, the form of $f(E,a)$ used in this article was a binary model ($f(E,a) = aD^{\alpha}H^{\beta} \times f_c$), and according to the above equation:

$$\sigma^2_{C_{bia}} = f'(E)Varf(E) = \begin{pmatrix} \frac{\partial C}{\partial D} & \frac{\partial C}{\partial H} \end{pmatrix} \begin{pmatrix} \sigma^2_D & \sigma_{DH} \\ \sigma_{DH} & \sigma^2_H \end{pmatrix} \begin{pmatrix} \frac{\partial C}{\partial D} \\ \frac{\partial C}{\partial H} \end{pmatrix} \quad (10)$$

$$= C^2\left(\alpha^2 \frac{\sigma^2_D}{D^2} + \beta^2 \frac{\sigma^2_H}{H^2} + 2\alpha\beta \frac{\sigma^2_{DH}}{DH}\right) \quad (11)$$

where σ^2_D is the variance of error in *DBH*, σ^2_H is the variance of error in *H*, and σ^2_{DH} is the covariance of σ_D and σ_H. α and β are the parameters of the monocarbon stock model. The grouping method [34] was used to calculate σ^2_D: (1) the mean values of the observed *DBH* were ranked in ascending order; (2) the observed *DBH* were grouped on the basis of 10 trees by groups; (3) the mean values of *DBH* in each group as well as the standard deviations between measurements; (4) the measurement error in *DBH* was calculated by fitting a linear model between standard deviations of the measurement error and *DBH*. The formulas are as follows:

$$\overline{D_I} = \frac{1}{n}\sum\nolimits_{j=1}^{n} \overline{D_j} \quad (12)$$

$$Dif_D = D_1 - D_2 \quad (13)$$

$$\sigma_D = \frac{1}{n}\sqrt{\sum\nolimits_{j=1}^{n}\left(Dif_{D,J} - \overline{Dif_{D,j}}\right)^2} \quad (14)$$

where $\overline{D_I}$ is the mean value of *DBH* in each group, $\overline{D_j}$ is the mean value of the *j*th sample tree in each group, Dif_D is the difference between D_1 and D_2, σ_D is the standard deviation of the difference in each group of data, and the square is σ^2_D in Equation (11). $\overline{Dif_{D,j}}$ is the mean value of $Dif_{D,J}$ in each group. The linear model can be fitted by the relationship between the $\overline{D_I}$ and the corresponding σ_D in each group. The expression is given below:

$$\sigma_D = a + b\overline{D_I} \quad (15)$$

Since tree height can only be measured by the altimeter, the difference between the measured values and the true values is large in several cases. The average value of multiple measurements is still far from the true value [60]. Therefore, the absolute error between the measured value and the true value is used as σ_H, and the curve is fitted to estimate the error of the single tree height. The expression is as follows:

$$\sigma_H = aH^2 + bH + c \quad (16)$$

where σ_H is the error of tree height, *H* is measured value of tree height, and *a*, *b*, *c* are the parameters of the model. σ^2_{DH} can be calculated by σ_D and σ_H. The σ^2_{DH} can be expressed by the following equation:

$$\sigma^2_{DH} = \frac{\sum(D_i - \overline{D})(H_i - \overline{H})}{N-1} \quad (17)$$

where σ_{DH}^2 is the covariance of σ_D and σ_H, D_i is the ith measured value of DBH, $\overline{D}$ is mean value of DBH, H_i is the ith measured value of H, $\overline{H}$ is mean value of H, and N is dimensionality.

2.5.2. Calculation of the Monocarbon Stock Model Uncertainty

(1) Residual Uncertainty of the Monocarbon Stock Model

To calculate the residual uncertainty of the monocarbon stock model, we used the observed data of *Pinus densata* carbon stock to fit the monocarbon stock model. Then, the uncertainty caused by residual variation was calculated by the difference between the predicted and observed values. Let the observed value of carbon stock be C and the prediction model of carbon stock be $C' = f(E, \hat{\alpha})$, the residual ε can be expressed by the following equation:

$$\varepsilon = f\ (E, \hat{\alpha}) - C \tag{18}$$

where ε denotes the difference between the observed and predicted values, $\hat{\alpha}$ is the predicted value of the parameter in the carbon stock model, and E is the variable of the model (DBH, H).

The standard deviation of the residual can be used to measure the uncertainty caused by the variation of the model residual. It was found that the standard deviation of the residual was linearly related to the AGC [35]. Therefore, the standard deviation can be calculated by fitting a linear relationship between the standard deviation and carbon stock. The equation is as follows:

$$\sigma_\varepsilon = \beta f(E, \hat{a}) \tag{19}$$

where σ_ε is the standard deviation of residual, and β is the fitting parameter. The six-step approach [61] was used to calculate the σ_ε. The steps are as follows: (1) Rank the observed carbon stock values (y) of the plots in ascending order. (2) Calculate the residuals of model (C_ε), which are the difference between the observed and predicted values. (3) Divide the modeling data into groups of N, with a total of 10 groups; if the last group is less than N, the remaining data are counted in the previous group. (4) Calculate the mean values of the predicted carbon stock ($\overline{\hat{y}}$) and the standard deviations of residual (σ_ε) in each group. The mean value, residual, and standard deviation of the residual were calculated as follows:

$$\overline{\hat{y}} = \frac{1}{n}\sum_{j=1}^{n} \hat{y}_j \tag{20}$$

$$C_\varepsilon = y - \hat{y} \tag{21}$$

$$\sigma_\varepsilon = \frac{1}{n-1}\sqrt{\sum_{j=1}^{n}\left(C_{\varepsilon_j} - \overline{C}_{\varepsilon_j}\right)^2} \tag{22}$$

where $\hat{y}_j$ denotes the predicted value of carbon stock in the jth plot, C_{ε_j} and $\overline{C}_{\varepsilon_j}$ denote the residual and the residual mean value of the jth plot, and n denotes the number of samples.

(5) Fit the predicted mean value $\overline{\hat{y}}$ and standard deviation of residual σ_ε, the relationship can be expressed as:

$$\sigma_\varepsilon = \theta\left(\overline{\hat{y}}\right) \tag{23}$$

(6) Substitute the predicted values of carbon stock into the fitted formula. Calculate the standard deviations of the residual for each plot. Then, divide them by the sum of the observed carbon stock values to obtain the model residual's uncertainty.

(2) Parameter Uncertainty of the Monocarbon Stock Model

The Taylor series first-order expansion was used to measure the uncertainty of model parameters. The AGC model was first-order-expanded by a Taylor series as follows:

$$C' = f(E,\hat{a}) \approx f(E,a) + \frac{\partial f(E,\hat{\alpha})}{\partial_{a_j}}(\hat{\alpha} - \alpha) \tag{24}$$

where $f(E,\alpha)$ are the observed values of carbon stock, E are the independent variables, $\hat{\alpha}$ is the simulated value of parameter, α denotes the true value of parameter, $\frac{\partial f(E,\alpha)}{\partial \alpha j}$ is the partial derivative of model parameter α_j, $\frac{\partial f(E,\alpha)}{\partial \alpha j}(\hat{\alpha} - \alpha)$ is the error (σ_γ) of the model parameters. σ_γ can be approximated as:

$$\sigma_\gamma^2 \approx Z_{jk} var(a) Z_{jk}^T \tag{25}$$

where Z_{jk} denotes the matrix with Z as $j \times k$, Z_{jk}^T is the transpose matrix of Z_{jk}, and $var(\alpha)$ is the covariance matrix of estimated parameter α in the carbon stock equation.

2.5.3. Uncertainty Synthesis

If the indirectly measured quantity is a function of the individual measurements obtained from the direct measurements. Then, the uncertainty of the indirect measurement can be expressed as a synthetic uncertainty of the uncertainty of each direct measurement [62]. Therefore, the total error (M_Z) can be described as:

$$M_Z = \sqrt{M_{\mathrm{j}_1}^2 + M_{\mathrm{j}_2}^2 + M_{\mathrm{j}_3}^2 + \ldots + M_{\mathrm{j}_\mathrm{i}}^2} \tag{26}$$

where M_Z denotes the total error, and $M_{\mathrm{j}_\mathrm{i}}$ denotes the error of the ith variable. Based on this equation, the total uncertainty (σ_t) was calculated as [35]:

$$\sigma_t = \sqrt{\sigma_\varepsilon^2 + \sigma_\gamma^2 + \sigma_c^2} \tag{27}$$

where σ_ε denotes the residual uncertainty of the monocarbon stock model, σ_γ denotes the uncertainty of model parameters, and σ_c indicates the measurement uncertainty. The error transfer from the monocarbon stock model to the plot scale uncertainty (σ_p) was calculated as follows:

$$\sigma_p = \sqrt{\sum_{i=1}^{N} \sigma_{ti}^2 / S} \tag{28}$$

where N is the number of sample wood, σ_{ti} is the total uncertainty of the monocarbon stock model for the ith plot wood plant in the plot, and S is the area of the plot.

2.6. Uncertainty Analysis of Remote-Sensing-Based Estimation Models

2.6.1. The Uncertainty of Model Residual

We also used the six-step approach [61] to calculate the residual uncertainty in remote-sensing-based estimation models; the detailed steps and formulas are shown in the six-step approach Section 2.5.2, Point 1. Finally, the uncertainty of the remote sensing model (σ_R) can be expressed as:

$$\sigma_R = \sum_{i=1}^{n} \sigma_{\varepsilon'} / y_t \tag{29}$$

where $\sum_{i=1}^{n} \sigma_{\varepsilon'}$ is the sum of the standard deviation of the residuals in all plots, and y_t is the sum of the measured AGC.

2.6.2. Calculation of the Total Uncertainty in Carbon Stock Estimation

The total uncertainty (σ) of the AGC estimation in *Pinus densata* was calculated as follows:

$$\sigma = \sqrt{\sigma_p^2 + \sigma_R^2} \tag{30}$$

where σ_p is the uncertainty at the plot scale; and σ_R is the uncertainty of the remote sensing model.

3. Results and Analysis

3.1. Comparison of Accuracy for Estimation Models

Figures 3 and 4 show the scatter plots of the prediction accuracy, the distribution of R^2, and the *RMSE* values for different models. It showed that the BIM has the lowest accuracy with a R^2 of 0.551, *RMSE* of 23.049 t/ha, and *rRMSE* of 45.158% (Figure 3a). The prediction accuracies of the models were all improved after we gradually introduced different remote sensing factors during the modeling. Since the optical imagery is prone to saturation in areas with high aboveground biomass (and, therefore, AGC), it is at a disadvantage for estimating stands with high values. Therefore, after introducing Sentinel-1 SAR data based on the S-2M, the model has the highest prediction accuracy with R^2 of 0.872, *RMSE* of 10.821 t/ha, and *rRMSE* of 21.201%. Sentinel-1 SAR data can overcome the shortcomings of the optical data to a certain extent according to the results, which have an important role in improving the estimation accuracy [29]. The above results can be more intuitively shown in Figure 4. R^2 of the models gradually increases, and the *RMSE* gradually decreases with the introduction of different remote sensing factors; the model with joint Sentinel-1 SAR and Sentinel-2 optical data has the largest R^2 and the smallest *RMSE*. This provides some references for improving the accuracy of carbon stock estimation and the rational selection of variables.

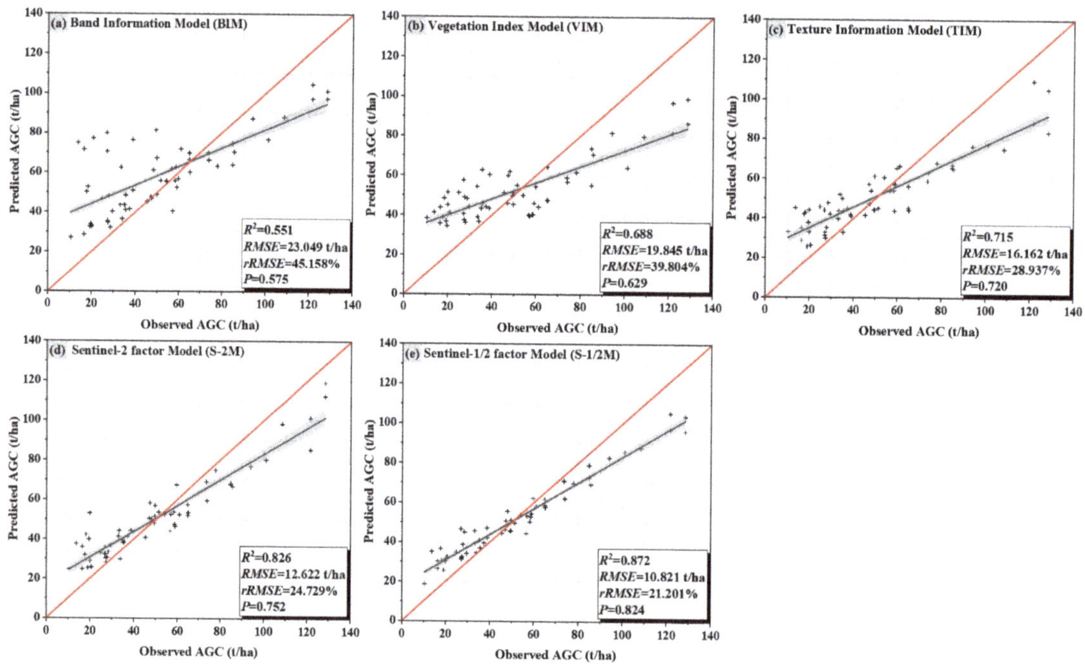

Figure 3. (**a**) Scatterplot based on the band information for modeling; (**b**) scatterplot based on the vegetation index for modeling; (**c**) scatterplot based on the texture information for modeling; (**d**) scatterplot based on the Sentinel-2 factor for modeling; and (**e**) scatterplot based on the Sentinel-1/2 factor for modeling.

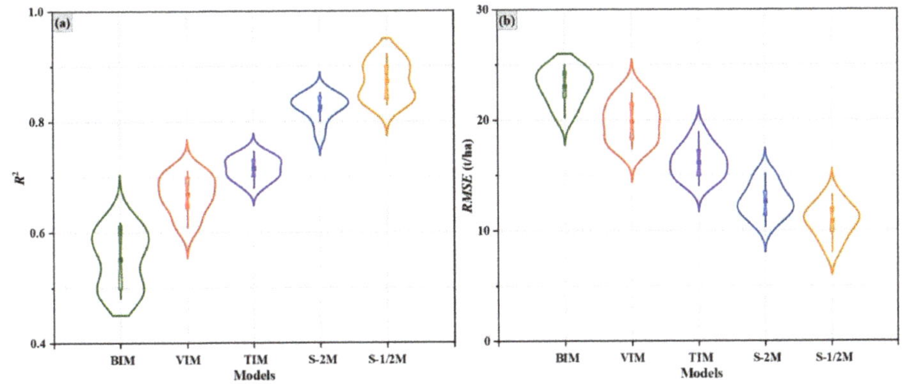

Figure 4. (**a**) The distribution of R^2 values for different models and (**b**) the distribution of *RMSE* values for different models.

3.2. Uncertainty at the Plot Scale

3.2.1. The Uncertainty of Measurement

Scatter plots of the measurement error of *DBH* can be obtained by Equations (12) and (14) (Figure 5a). It showed that the measurement error of *DBH* increases with the increase in *DBH*, which is basically a linear relationship. The error model of *DBH* was $\sigma_D = 0.1913D - 0.4964$, $R^2 = 0.665$. Then, the true values of *DBH* were substituted into the fitted model to obtain the error of *DBH*. For the measurement error of *H*, we can calculate by fitting a model through the relationship between the *H* and the measurement error of *H*. As shown in Figure 5b, similar to the measurement error of *DBH*, the error of *H* is also positively correlated with the *H*. Based on the research finding of previous scholars [60], its error form can be expressed as $\sigma_H = 0.0095H^2 - 0.075H + 1.3359$, $R^2 = 0.265$. After obtaining the error of *H*, σ^2_{DH} was calculated according to Equation (17), which is 0.70. Finally, the measurement uncertainty was calculated by Equation (11). The calculation showed that for the binary carbon stock model, the uncertainty in carbon stock estimation due to the measurement error was 3.02%.

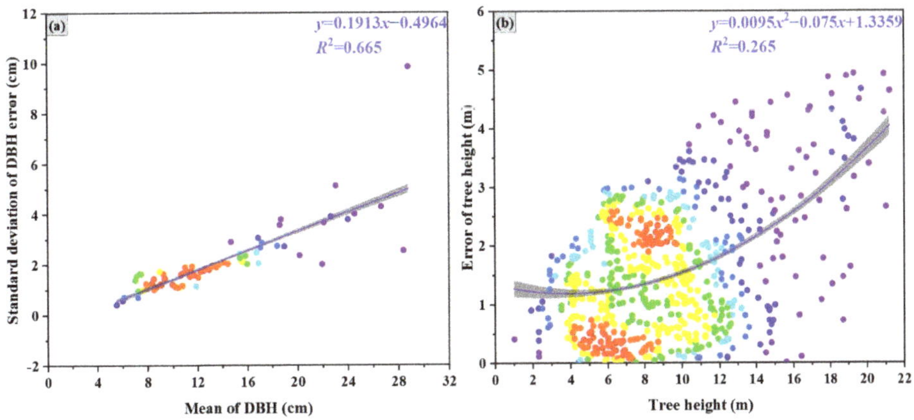

Figure 5. (**a**) Relationship between *DBH* and standard deviation of measurement error and (**b**) relationship between *H* and measurement error.

3.2.2. Uncertainty in the Monocarbon Stock Model

(1) Residual Uncertainty

Figure 6a shows the three-dimensional scatter plot of the binary carbon stock model for *Pinus densata*; since the model parameters were closely related to the number of modeling samples, different modeling samples fitted different model parameters [63]. For example, Zhao [64] established the biomass model based on 31,068 sample trees, and the model equation was $W = 0.052D^{1.988}H^{0.591}$. Qin et al. [35] established the biomass model based on 52 sample trees: the model was $W = 0.086D^{1.979}H^{0.419}$. However, the model developed in this paper based on the measured data was $C = 0.101D^{1.859}H^{0.635} \times f_c$, and the R^2 of the model was 0.984. According to the relevant study [47], the error margin of the carbon content factor for *Pinus densata* was ±1.19%. With the six-step method, we simply calculated the mean values of the predicted carbon stock and the standard deviations of the residual in each group, and then, we fitted a linear equation with the mean values as the independent variable and the standard deviations of the residual as the dependent variable. Figure 6b shows the scatter plot of the error equation for the monocarbon stock model [65], from which it can be seen that the standard deviations of residual increased with the increase in the predicted values of carbon stock. The error equation of the binary carbon stock model was $y = 0.0613x - 0.369$ and $R^2 = 0.944$, which has an excellent fitting effect. The predicted values of carbon stock were then substituted into the error equation to calculate the total error value. Finally, the residual uncertainty for the model was obtained by dividing the total error value by the total observed value of carbon stock, giving 5.96%.

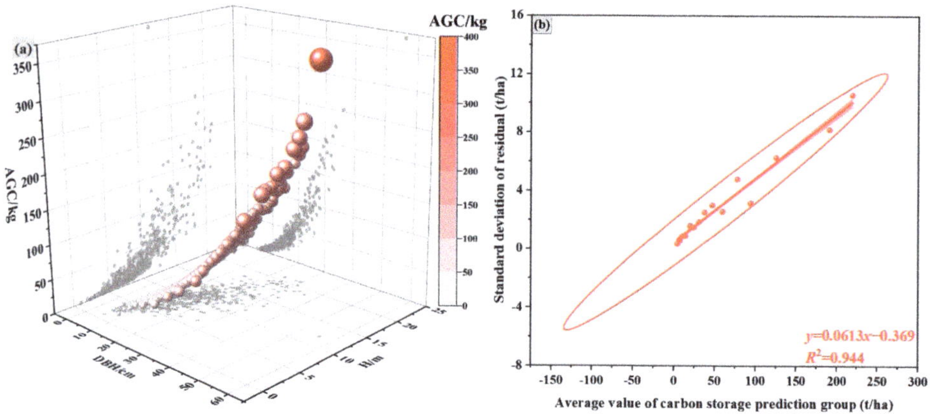

Figure 6. (**a**) Three-dimensional scatterplot of the binary carbon stock model for *Pinus densata* and (**b**) line plot of errors and accuracy for the model.

(2) Parameter Uncertainty

For the parameter uncertainty of the binary carbon stock model, we first processed the carbon stock model using Taylor's first-order expansion based on the research methods of existing scholars [35,37,65]. Then, we need to obtain the variance–covariance matrix of the model parameters ($a = 0.101$, $b = 1.859$, $c = 0.635$), and the uncertainty of the model parameters was calculated by bring it into the Equation (25). By calculating, we can know that the parameters variance–covariance matrix of the binary carbon stock model is $\begin{pmatrix} 0.00000075 & -0.00003400 & 0.00009900 \\ -0.00003400 & 0.01100000 & -0.01100000 \\ 0.00009900 & -0.01100000 & 0.04100000 \end{pmatrix}$, which substituted into Equation (25) to conclude that the value of parameter uncertainty is 6.86%. Synthesizing the two uncertainties, the total uncertainty of the binary carbon stock model was 9.09%.

3.2.3. Total Uncertainty at the Plot Scale

The total uncertainty was 9.58% by synthesizing the measurement uncertainty and the uncertainty of the monocarbon stock model through the Equation (27). When the uncertainty of the monocarbon stock model was superimposed on the plot scale, we used the Equation (28) to calculate the uncertainty of the plot scale, which was 3.71%. Table 5 shows the various sources of uncertainty in carbon stock estimation at the plot scale.

Table 5. Results of each uncertainty source at the plot scale.

Model Form	Measurement Error/%	Error of Monocarbon Stock Model/%		Total Uncertainty/%	Plot Scale Uncertainty/%
		Parameter Error/% 6.86	Residual Variation Error/% 5.96		
$C = 0.101D^{1.859}H^{0.635} \times f_c$	3.02	9.09		9.58	3.71

3.3. *The Uncertainty of Remote-Sensing-Based Estimation Models*

Figures 7–9 illustrate each model's error equations, error value of plots, and uncertainties. The uncertainties of BIM, VIM, TIM, S-2M, and S-1/2M are 21.98%, 13.63%, 12.01%, 10.14%, and 7.57% by substituting the average values of carbon stock into error equations of each model (Figure 9). Through the Figure 7, the width of the confidence ellipse for each model can reflect the magnitude of the model's R^2 to a certain extent, R^2 gradually increases as the ellipse becomes narrower. To more intuitively reflect the difference between the predicted values and the measured values for each model, we compared the observed value and the corresponding predicted value of 60 field plots (Figure 8). BIM, VIM, and TIM exhibit the phenomenon of the overestimation of low values and the underestimation of high values, and the maximum absolute errors of three models are 61.14 t/ha, 41.847 t/ha, and 36.047 t/ha, which suggests that single-factor models have large relatively errors in estimating AGC. Then, we filtered the three types of remote sensing factors to establish S-2M. As we can see, the error curve of this model is significantly lower compared to the previous three models, and its error value is also reduced (Figure 8b), as well as the absolute value of its maximum error being 28.477 t/ha. This indicates that the joint use of different types of remote sensing factors is necessary and makes up for the disadvantage of single-factor modeling, which plays an important role in reducing uncertainty [66]. However, optical data suffer from light saturation, which impacts the accurate estimation of AGC [67]. Therefore, we added SAR data to S-2M in the following experiments to further explore the potential of SAR data in reducing uncertainty. The trend of the error curve of the model after adding SAR data is further slowed down, and its error is also reduced compared to S-2M (Figure 8b); the maximum absolute value of the error is 19.808 t/ha, and most of the absolute values of the error are below 10 t/ha, which indicates that the predicted values are close to the measured values. The comparative analysis of the errors for different models shows that the single-factor model has the largest error. In order to effectively reduce errors in the estimation process, it is necessary to combine different factors for estimating AGC. We also found that SAR data play an important role in reducing errors compared to optical data.

3.4. *Total Uncertainty in Carbon Stock Estimation*

The total uncertainty of AGC estimation for *Pinus densata* is shown in Table 6. After synthesizing the uncertainties of the plot scale and estimation models by Equation (30), the total uncertainty of BIM, VIM, TIM, S-2M, and S-1/2M was 22.29%, 14.12%, 12.56%, 10.79%, and 8.43%. The BIM has the highest uncertainty, while S-1/2M with the introduction of Sentinel-1 SAR data has the lowest uncertainty compared to the S-2M. Thus, SAR data have some advantages in reducing the uncertainty of the AGC estimation.

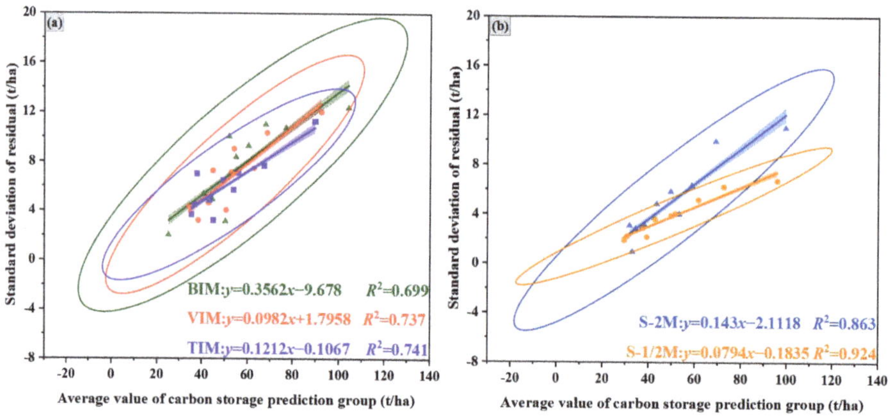

Figure 7. (**a**) Error equations for the BIM, VIM, and TIM and (**b**) error equations for the S-2M and S-1/2M.

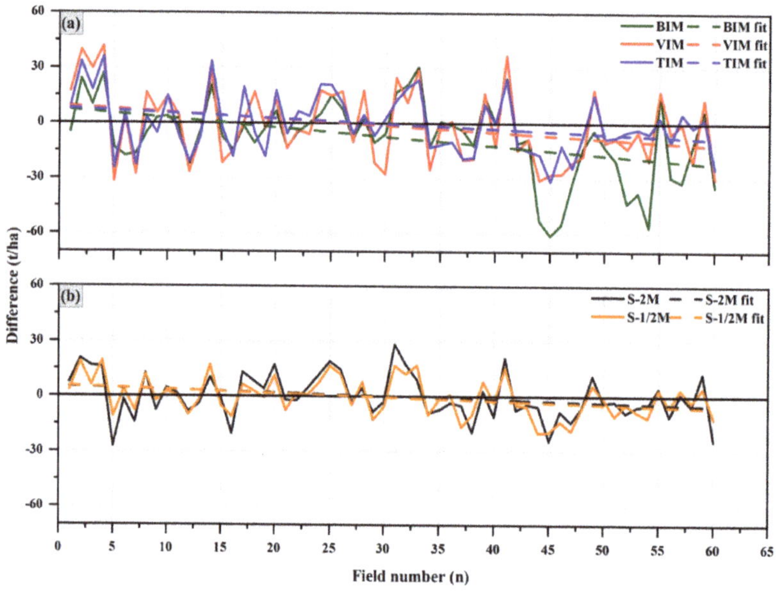

Figure 8. (**a**) Difference in each field plot for BIM, VIM, and TIM and (**b**) difference in each field plot for the S-2M and S-1/2M.

Table 6. Total uncertainty of AGC estimation of *Pinus densata* based on Sentinel-1/2 data.

Model	Uncertainty at the Plot Scale/%		Uncertainty of Remote Sensing Estimation Models/%	Total Uncertainty/%
	Measurement Error/%	Error of the MonoCarbon Stock Model/%		
	3.02	9.09		
BIM	3.71		21.98	22.29
VIM			13.63	14.12
TIM			12.01	12.56
S-2M			10.14	10.79
S-1/2M			7.57	8.43

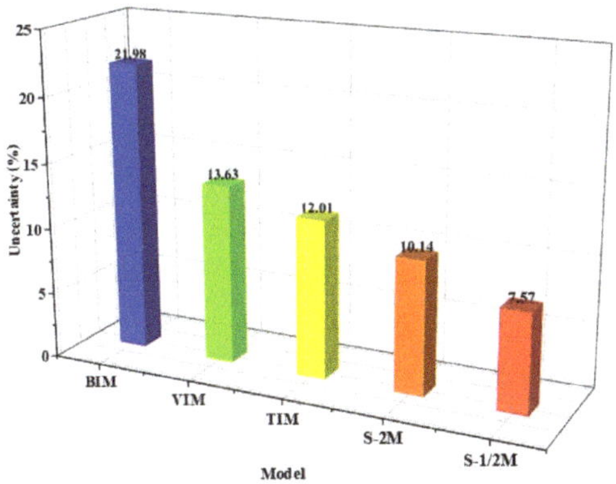

Figure 9. Uncertainty of different remote-sensing-based models.

4. Discussion

4.1. Analysis of the Uncertainty at the Plot Scale

Although many studies have been conducted on forest carbon stock estimation, there is still a great deal of uncertainty in the current estimation process. In this study, the uncertainties of measurement and residual variation and parameters error of the monocarbon stock model were calculated by error equations. The uncertainties in the measurement and the monocarbon stock model were then combined to obtain the uncertainty of the plot scale. It was found that the error of the monocarbon stock model is the most significant source of uncertainty among the uncertainties at the plot scale. Even though the measurement uncertainty is so small that its contribution to the total uncertainty is practically negligible, we identified a small systematic effect that should be considered. This error may have a greater impact if we use different personnel or equipment to collect the field data [68–70]. The error of the monocarbon stock model mainly originated from parameter variation, and the residual uncertainty was relatively low, which is consistent with the results of Huang et al. [37]. However, the parameter error of the model was higher than those of Chen et al. [71] and Wang et al. [65]. The reason is that Chen et al. [71] used 4004 plot trees for modeling, which is much higher than the number of plot trees in this study. When the number of plot trees is large enough, the uncertainty due to the model parameters can converge to zero. Wang et al. [65] used grouping combined with the Monte Carlo method to measure the errors of unitary and binary biomass models. This method can effectively reduce the variability of parameter covariance matrices. In this paper, we only calculated the parameter uncertainty and residual uncertainty of the binary model; the uncertainty of the unitary carbon stock model needs to be further investigated in the future.

4.2. Influence of Plot Size and Forest Stand Factors on AGC Estimation and Uncertainty

The plot size used in this study is 10 m × 10 m to keep up with the spatial resolution of remote sensing images. Although several studies have shown that uncertainty decreases when the plot size increases [72,73], we need to consider the available space and representative sampling, etc., during the selection of plots. Enough plots were needed to arrange in the limited space to meet the need of the modeling because of the limitation of the study area, which can ensure the representativeness and accuracy of the *Pinus densata* samples. Even though estimation accuracy and uncertainty can be affected by small-scale plots, we can effectively improve this condition by increasing the number of plots and modeling samples [74]. Secondly, representative sampling is one of the important reasons why we chose small-scale plots. The difference in vegetation density and age structure also affects the estimation of AGC due to the heterogeneity of the distribution of *Pinus densata* in the study area. Therefore, setting more small-scale plots on this basis gives a better analysis of the factors affecting the accuracy of AGC estimation, thus improving accuracy and reducing uncertainty. Canopy density and the average age of the forest stand factors are also important factors that affect the accuracy and uncertainty of AGC estimation [75]. A previous study has shown that with the gradual increase in stand age, the forest carbon stock also presents a trend of increase [76]. Still, the growth rate decreases slowly with the maturity of the forest stand and tends to balance in the later stage of development [77]. Canopy density is also an important factor affecting the change in AGC and can determine forest structure and vegetation growth to a large extent [78]. An increased canopy opening increased the potential of height growth, thereby increasing the AGC. Therefore, we should consider these two factors to analyze their specific effects on the change and uncertainty of AGC in the subsequent research.

4.3. Uncertainty of Different Remote Sensing Models

In this paper, we established different remote sensing models based on Sentinel-1/2 images. Data saturation in the optical data is a key issue limiting AGC estimation accuracy, especially in dense forests with high AGB (AGC) [79]. The reason is that optical data provide only spectral and horizontal spatial characteristics [80], limiting the effectiveness of spectral reflectance and vegetation indices for estimating high biomass or carbon stock. This is also confirmed by the high uncertainty of BIM and VIM in this study. To alleviate the effect of optical data saturation on the uncertainty of carbon stock estimation, we introduced Sentinel-1 SAR data on the basis of optical data. SAR can better obtain the vertical structure parameters of forest vegetation because of its strong penetration ability to the forest canopy and sensitivity to water content [81]. Furthermore, the combination of optical and SAR data has been proven to reduce the saturation in AGC estimation [21,82]. For example, David et al. [43] combined Sentinel-1 SAR and Sentinel-2 optical data to estimate dryland AGB, and this combination produced the best fitting effect. In addition, it was also found that the bands had different influences on the estimation effect, and the addition of SAR and optical red-edge bands (B5) significantly reduced the saturation effect. Therefore, we should try different bands and their combinations to explore their potential in reducing the saturation effects and uncertainty in the following experiments.

4.4. Limitations and Future Research

Firstly, since the study area of this paper covers only one county, and *Pinus densata* is a single layer of pure forest [83], this conclusion will be altered if compared to the different types of forest structure, tree species, etc., in other regions. Consequently, the applicability of this study's method in multilayered stands or forests of different ages with complex structures needs to be further explored. Secondly, the uncertainty in this paper is only related to the plot scale and remote-sensing-based estimation model. Still, during the total process of data collection, processing, model building, and carbon stock estimation, it inevitably generates various sources of error due to the differences in the measurement, data processing and calculation, model building methods, and methods of carbon estimation. Therefore, we need to consider the effects of climate, light saturation, topography, error transmission, and the forest carbon cycle on the estimation of carbon stock. Finally, allometric growth equation may lead to uncertainty in the estimation of carbon stock. We attempted to improve the estimation accuracy by using an allometric growth equation for each tree species in the study area. However, some uncertain factors, such as tree density, soil texture, and climatic conditions, can affect the growth of *H* and *DBH*, thereby affecting the calculation of carbon stock. In the future, researchers should consider how precipitation, soil, and climate affect the growth of *DBH* and *H* and the calculation of carbon stock. Taking these factors into account will improve the accuracy and reduce the uncertainty in the process of carbon stock estimation.

5. Conclusions

In this study, random forest was used to establish different remote-sensing-based estimation models based on Sentinel-1/2 images and field data. The uncertainties resulted from the plot scale, and different estimation models were calculated using error equations. We then analyzed the impact of uncertainty at different scales on carbon stock estimation. (1) Different remote sensing factors have certain effects on the carbon stock estimation and the uncertainty of the model. In particular, the BIM has the lowest accuracy; the introduction of vegetation and texture factors improves the accuracy of the model, while S-1/2M combining optical and SAR data has the lowest uncertainty. (2) The error of the monocarbon stock model is the main uncertainty at the plot scale, which is 9.09%. The uncertainty at the plot scale is 3.71%, which is lower than the uncertainty of all remote-sensing-based estimation models. Therefore, the uncertainty of the estimation model is the primary source of uncertainty in the process of carbon stock estimation compared to the uncertainty at the plot scale. (3) The R^2 of S-1/2M combining optical and SAR data was improved by 0.046, and the uncertainty was reduced by 2.36% compared to the S-2M. Adding SAR data to the optical data can effectively reduce the uncertainty in the estimation process. This study analyses the effect of different factors on AGC estimation and evaluates the uncertainty of plot scale quantitatively, which provides references for reducing the uncertainty in the process of carbon stock estimation.

Author Contributions: Writing—original draft, software, data curation, investigation, methodology, B.Q.; formal analysis, writing—review and editing, S.L.; methodology, writing—review and editing, J.C.; funding acquisition, project administration, supervision, writing—review and editing, J.Z.; visualization, methodology, formal analysis, writing—review and editing, K.Y.; supervision, resources, writing—review and editing, K.L.; writing—review and editing, K.H.; writing—review and editing, X.J. All authors have read and agreed to the published version of the manuscript.

Funding: This research was funded by the Forestry Innovation Programs of Southwest Forestry University (grant no: LXXK-2023Z06), "Young Top Talents" special project of the high-level talent training support program of Yunnan province, China, in 2020 (no. YNWR-QNBJ-2020-164), and the National Natural Science Foundation of China (no. 32260390).

Data Availability Statement: The Sentinel-1/2 data are available through the official website of the United States Geological Survey (USGS) (https://earthexplorer.usgs.gov (accessed on 4 and 8 November 2021)). Field data presented in this study are available on request from the corresponding author.

Acknowledgments: We would like to acknowledge all the other individuals who contributed to this paper.

Conflicts of Interest: The authors declare that they have no known competing financial interests or personal relationships that could have appeared to influence the work reported in this paper.

References

1. Ju, W.M.; Chen, J.M.; Harvey, D.; Wang, S. Future carbon balance of China's forests under climate change and increasing CO_2. *J. Environ. Manage.* **2007**, *85*, 538–562. [CrossRef] [PubMed]
2. Shanin, V.N.; Mikhailov, A.V.; Bykhovets, S.S.; Komarov, A.S. Global climate change and carbon balance in forest ecosystems of boreal zones: Simulation modeling as a forecast tool. *Biol. Bull.* **2010**, *37*, 619–629. [CrossRef]
3. Liu, K.; Wang, J.; Zeng, W.; Song, J. Comparison and evaluation of three methods for estimating forest above ground biomass using TM and GLAS data. *Remote Sens.* **2017**, *9*, 341. [CrossRef]
4. Andoh, J.; Lee, Y. National REDD+ Strategy for Climate Change Mitigation: A Review and Comparison of Developing Countries. *Sustainability* **2018**, *10*, 4781. [CrossRef]
5. Xie, Y.; Lei, X.; Shi, J. Impacts of climate change on biological rotation of Larix olgensis plantations for timber production and carbon storage in northeast China using the 3-PGmix model. *Ecol. Modell.* **2020**, *435*, 109267. [CrossRef]
6. Wang, J.; Du, H.; Li, X.; Mao, F.; Zhang, M.; Liu, E.; Ji, J.; Kang, F. Remote sensing estimation of bamboo forest aboveground biomass based on geographically weighted regression. *Remote Sens.* **2021**, *13*, 2962. [CrossRef]
7. Nandal, A.; Yadav, S.S.; Rao, A.S.; Meena, R.S.; Lal, R. Advance methodological approaches for carbon stock estimation in forest ecosystems. *Environ. Monit. Assess.* **2023**, *195*, 315. [CrossRef]
8. Cohen, R.; Kaino, J.; Okello, J.A.; Bosire, J.O.; Kairo, J.G.; Huxham, M.; Mencuccini, M. Propagating uncertainty to estimates of above-ground biomass for Kenyan mangroves: A scaling procedure from tree to landscape level. *For. Ecol. Manag.* **2013**, *310*, 968–982. [CrossRef]

9. Gregoire, T.G.; Næsset, E.; McRoberts, R.E.; Ståhl, G.; Andersen, H.E.; Gobakken, T.; Ene, L.; Nelson, R. Statistical rigor in LiDAR-assisted estimation of aboveground forest biomass. *Remote Sens. Environ.* **2016**, *173*, 98–108. [CrossRef]
10. Agata, H.; Aneta, L.; Dariusz, Z.; Krzysztof, S.; Marek, L.; Christiane, S.; Carsten, P. Forest aboveground biomass estimation using a combination of Sentinel-1 and Sentinel-2 Data. In Proceedings of the IGARSS 2018—2018 IEEE International Geoscience and Remote Sensing Symposium, Valencia, Spain, 22–27 July 2018.
11. Zharko, V.O.; Bartalev, S.A.; Sidorenkov, V.M. Forest growing stock volume estimation using optical remote sensing over snow-covered ground: A case study for Sentinel-2 data and the Russian Southern Taiga region. *Remote Sens. Lett.* **2020**, *11*, 677–686. [CrossRef]
12. Gülçin, D.; Van Den Bosch, C.C.K. Assessment of above-ground carbon storage by urban trees using LiDAR data: The case of a university campus. *Forests* **2021**, *12*, 62. [CrossRef]
13. Lu, C.; Xu, H.; Zhang, J.; Wang, A.; Wu, H.; Bao, R.; Ou, G. A Method for Estimating Forest Aboveground Biomass at the Plot Scale Combining the Horizontal Distribution Model of Biomass and Sampling Technique. *Forests* **2022**, *13*, 1612. [CrossRef]
14. Lu, D.; Chen, Q.; Wang, G.; Moran, E.; Batistella, M.; Zhang, M.; Zhang, M.; Saah, D. Aboveground-forest biomass estimation with Landsat and LiDAR data and uncertainty analysis of the estimates. *Int. J. For. Res.* **2012**, *2012*, 436537. [CrossRef]
15. Zhao, P.; Lu, D.; Wang, G.; Wu, C.; Huang, Y.; Yu, S. Examining spectral reflectance saturation in Landsat imagery and corresponding solutions to improve forest aboveground biomass estimation. *Remote Sens.* **2016**, *8*, 469. [CrossRef]
16. Cutler, M.E.J.; Boyd, D.S.; Foody, G.M.; Vetrivel, A. Estimating tropical forest biomass with a combination of SAR image texture and Landsat TM data: An assessment of predictions between regions. *ISPRS J. Photogramm. Remote Sens.* **2012**, *70*, 66–77. [CrossRef]
17. Ojoatre, S.; Zhang, C.; Hussin, Y.A.; Kloosterman, H.E.; Ismail, M.H. Assessing the uncertainty of tree height and aboveground biomass from terrestrial laser scanner and hypsometer using airborne LiDAR data in tropical rainforests. *IEEE J. Sel. Top. Appl. Earth Obs. Remote Sens.* **2019**, *12*, 4149–4159. [CrossRef]
18. Li, L.; Zhou, X.; Chen, L.; Chen, L.; Zhang, Y.; Liu, Y. Estimating urban vegetation biomass from Sentinel-2A image data. *For.* **2020**, *11*, 125. [CrossRef]
19. Yang, X.; Strahler, A.H.; Schaaf, C.B.; Jupp, D.L.; Yao, T.; Zhao, F.; Wang, Z.; Culvenor, D.S.; Newnham, G.J.; Lovell, J.L.; et al. Three-dimensional forest reconstruction and structural parameter retrievals using a terrestrial full-waveform lidar instrument (Echidna®). *Remote Sens. Environ.* **2013**, *135*, 36–51. [CrossRef]
20. Silveira, E.M.; Radeloff, V.C.; Martinuzzi, S.; Pastur, G.J.M.; Bono, J.; Politi, N.; Lizarraga, L.; Rivera, L.O.; Ciuffoli, L.; Rosas, Y.M.; et al. Nationwide native forest structure maps for Argentina based on forest inventory data, SAR Sentinel-1 and vegetation metrics from Sentinel-2 imagery. *Remote Sens. Environ.* **2023**, *285*, 113391. [CrossRef]
21. Stratoulias, D.; Nuthammachot, N.; Suepa, T.; Phoungthong, K. Assessing the spectral information of Sentinel-1 and Sentinel-2 Satellites for above-ground biomass retrieval of a tropical forest. *ISPRS Int. J. Geo-Inf.* **2022**, *11*, 199. [CrossRef]
22. Khan, M.N.; Tan, Y.; Gul, A.A.; Abbas, S.; Wang, J. Forest Aboveground Biomass Estimation and Inventory: Evaluating Remote Sensing-Based Approaches. *Forests* **2024**, *15*, 1055. [CrossRef]
23. Fang, G.; Yu, H.; Fang, L.; Zheng, X. Synergistic Use of Sentinel-1 and Sentinel-2 Based on Different Preprocessing for Predicting Forest Aboveground Biomass. *Forests* **2023**, *14*, 1615. [CrossRef]
24. Liu, Y.; Gong, W.; Xing, Y.; Hu, X.; Gong, J. Estimation of the forest stand mean height and aboveground biomass in Northeast China using SAR Sentinel-1B, multispectral Sentinel-2A, and DEM imagery. *ISPRS J. Photogramm. Remote Sens.* **2019**, *151*, 277–289. [CrossRef]
25. Shi, W. *Principles of Modeling Uncertainties in Spatial Data and Spatial Analyses*; CRC Press: Boca Raton, FL, USA, 2009.
26. Saarela, S.; Wästlund, A.; Holmström, E.; Mensah, A.A.; Holm, S.; Nilsson, M.; Fridman, J.; Ståhl, G. Mapping aboveground biomass and its prediction uncertainty using LiDAR and field data, accounting for tree-level allometric and LiDAR model errors. *For. Ecosyst.* **2020**, *7*, 43. [CrossRef]
27. Qin, L.; Meng, S.; Zhou, G.; Liu, Q.; Xu, Z. Uncertainties in above ground tree biomass estimation. *J. For. Res.* **2021**, *32*, 1989–2000. [CrossRef]
28. Shettles, M.; Hilker, T.; Temesgen, H. Examination of uncertainty in per unit area estimates of aboveground biomass using terrestrial LiDAR and ground data. *Can. J. For. Res.* **2016**, *46*, 706–715. [CrossRef]
29. Kitahara, F.; Mizoue, N.; Yoshida, S. Evaluation of data quality in Japanese national forest inventory. *Environ. Monit. Assess.* **2009**, *159*, 331–340. [CrossRef]
30. Breidenbach, J.; Antón-Fernández, C.; Petersson, H.; McRoberts, R.E.; Astrup, R. Quantifying the model-related variability of biomass stock and change estimates in the Norwegian National Forest Inventory. *For. Sci.* **2014**, *60*, 25–33. [CrossRef]
31. Lessard, V.C.; McRoberts, R.E.; Holdaway, M.R. Diameter growth models using Minnesota forest inventory and analysis data. *For. Sci.* **2001**, *47*, 301–310. [CrossRef]
32. Ståhl, G.; Holm, S.; Gregoire, T.G.; Gobakken, T.; Næsset, E.; Nelson, R. Model-based inference for biomass estimation in a LiDAR sample survey in Hedmark County, Norway. *Can. J. For. Res.* **2011**, *41*, 96–107. [CrossRef]
33. McRoberts, R.E. Estimating variation in field crew estimates of site index. *Can. J. For. Res.* **1996**, *26*, 560–565. [CrossRef]
34. Berger, A.; Gschwantner, T.; McRoberts, R.E.; Schadauer, K. Effects of measurement errors on individual tree stem volume estimates for the Austrian National Forest Inventory. *For. Sci.* **2014**, *60*, 14–24. [CrossRef]
35. Qin, L.H.; Zhang, M.Z.; Zhong, S.H.; Yu, X.H. Model uncertainty analysis in forest biomass estimation. *J. Ecol.* **2017**, *37*, 79127919.

36. Eduarda, M.O.S.; Fernando, D.E.S.; Michael, A.W.; Fausto, W.A.J.; Mônica, C.C.; Mello, C.R.; Mello, J.M.; Shimabukuro, Y.E.; Terra, M.C.N.S.; Carvalho, L.M.T.; et al. Pre-stratified modelling plus residuals kriging reduces the uncertainty of AGB estimation and spatial distribution in heterogeneous savannas and forest environments. *For. Ecol. Manag.* **2019**, *445*, 96–109.
37. Huang, Y.J.; Zhang, J.L.; Hu, Y.P.; Chen, T. Uncertainty analysis of remote sensing for aboveground biomass estimation of *Pinus densata*. *J. Zhejiang Agric. For. Univ.* **2022**, *39*, 531–539.
38. Cao, J.; Zhang, J.; Xiao, Q.; Wang, F.; Han, X.; Huang, Y. Above-ground carbon stock estimation and uncertainty analysis of *Pinus densata* based on random forest and Monte Carlo. *For. Sci. Res.* **2023**, *36*, 131–139.
39. Urbazaev, M.; Thiel, C.; Cremer, F.; Dubayah, R.; Migliavacca, M.; Reichstein, M.; Schmullius, C. Estimation of forest aboveground biomass and uncertainties by integration of field measurements, airborne LiDAR, and SAR and optical satellite data in Mexico. *Carbon Balance Manag.* **2018**, *13*, 5. [CrossRef]
40. Zhang, J.L.; Lu, C.; Xu, H.; Wang, G.X. Estimating aboveground biomass of *Pinus densata*-dominated forests using Landsat time series and permanent sample plot data. *J. For. Res.* **2019**, *30*, 1689–1706. [CrossRef]
41. Han, D.; Zhang, J.; Xu, D.; Liao, Y.; Bao, R.; Wang, S.; Chen, S. Improving *Pinus densata* Carbon Stock Estimations through Remote Sensing in Shangri-La: A Nonlinear Mixed-Effects Model Integrating Soil Thickness and Topographic Variables. *Forests* **2024**, *15*, 394. [CrossRef]
42. Chen, C.; He, Y.; Zhang, J.; Xu, D.; Han, D.; Liao, Y.; Teng, C.; Yin, T. Estimation of above-ground biomass for *Pinus densata* using multi-source time series in Shangri-La considering seasonal effects. *Forests* **2023**, *14*, 1747. [CrossRef]
43. David, R.M.; Rosser, N.J.; Donoghue, D.N. Improving above ground biomass estimates of Southern Africa dryland forests by combining Sentinel-1 SAR and Sentinel-2 multispectral imagery. *Remote Sens. Environ.* **2022**, *282*, 113232. [CrossRef]
44. Zheng, S.; Cao, C.; Dang, Y.; Xiang, H.; Zhao, J.; Zhang, Y.; Wang, X.; Guo, H. Retrieval of forest growing stock volume by two different methods using Landsat TM images. *Int. J. Remote Sens.* **2014**, *35*, 29–43. [CrossRef]
45. Sun, X.L. Research on Remote Sensing Estimation Model of Biomass of *Pinus densata* Forest in Shangri-La Based on Landsat8-OLI. Master's Thesis, Southwest Forestry University, Kunming, China, 2016.
46. Wang, J.L.; Wang, X.H.; Yue, C.R.; Cheng, F.; Xu, T.S.; Cheng, P.F.; Wang, X.M.; Gao, Y. Carbon content of four established species in Shangri-la forest, northwest Yunnan. *J. Ecol. Environ.* **2012**, *21*, 613–619. [CrossRef]
47. Wu, F.Y.; Wen, Q.; LI, Y.H.; Liu, H.; Liu, Y.Y. Analysis of carbon content in trunks of established species of major forest types in Ganzi. *Anhui Agric. Sci.* **2024**, 1–4. Available online: https://link.cnki.net/urlid/34.1076.S.20240827.1049.005 (accessed on 7 November 2024).
48. Prakash, A.J.; Behera, M.D.; Ghosh, S.M.; Das, A.; Mishra, D.R. A new synergistic approach for Sentinel-1 and PALSAR-2 in a machine learning framework to predict aboveground biomass of a dense mangrove forest. *Ecol. Inf.* **2022**, *72*, 101900. [CrossRef]
49. Huang, Z.; Tian, Y.; Zhang, Q.; Huang, Y.; Liu, R.; Huang, H.; Zhou, G.; Wang, J.; Tao, J.; Yang, Y.; et al. Estimating mangrove above-ground biomass at Maowei Sea, Beibu Gulf of China using machine learning algorithm with Sentinel-1 and Sentinel-2 data. *Geocarto Int.* **2022**, *37*, 15778–15805. [CrossRef]
50. Imperatore, P.; Azar, R.; Calo, F.; Stroppiana, D.; Brivio, P.A.; Lanari, R.; Pepe, A. Effect of the vegetation fire on backscattering: An investigation based on Sentinel-1 observations. *IEEE J. Sel. Top. Appl. Earth Obs. Remote Sens.* **2017**, *10*, 4478–4492. [CrossRef]
51. Puliti, S.; Breidenbach, J.; Schumacher, J.; Hauglin, M.; Klingenberg, T.F.; Astrup, R. Above-ground biomass change estimation using national forest inventory data with Sentinel-2 and Landsat. *Remote Sens. Environ.* **2021**, *265*, 112644. [CrossRef]
52. Naik, P.; Dalponte, M.; Bruzzone, L. Generative feature extraction from sentinel 1 and 2 data for prediction of forest aboveground biomass in the Italian Alps. *IEEE J. Sel. Top. Appl. Earth Obs. Remote Sens.* **2022**, *15*, 4755–4771. [CrossRef]
53. Forkuor, G.; Zoungrana, J.B.B.; Dimobe, K.; Ouattara, B.; Vadrevu, K.P.; Tondoh, J.E. Above-ground biomass mapping in West African dryland forest using Sentinel-1 and 2 datasets-A case study. *Remote Sens. Environ.* **2020**, *236*, 111496. [CrossRef]
54. Zhao, Y.; Mao, D.; Zhang, D.; Wang, Z.; Du, B.; Yan, H.; Qiu, Z.; Feng, K.; Wang, J.; Jia, M. Mapping phragmites Australis aboveground biomass in the momoge wetland ramsar site based on Sentinel-1/2 images. *Remote Sens.* **2022**, *14*, 694. [CrossRef]
55. Pan, L.; Sun, Y.; Wang, Y.; Chen, L.; Cao, Y. Estimation of aboveground biomass in a Chinese fir (*Cunninghamia lanceolata*) forest combining data of Sentinel-1 and Sentinel-2. *J. Nanjing For. Univ.* **2020**, *44*, 149.
56. Breiman, L. Random forests. *Mach. Learn.* **2001**, *45*, 5–32. [CrossRef]
57. Svetnik, V.; Liaw, A.; Tong, C.; Culberson, J.C.; Sheridan, R.P.; Feuston, B.P. Random forest: A classification and regression tool for compound classification and QSAR modeling. *J. Chem. Inf. Comput. Sci.* **2003**, *43*, 1947–1958. [CrossRef] [PubMed]
58. Niu, X.; Chen, B.; Sun, W.; Feng, T.; Yang, X.; Liu, Y.; Liu, W.W.; Fu, B. Estimation of Coastal Wetland Vegetation Aboveground Biomass by Integrating UAV and Satellite Remote Sensing Data. *Remote Sens.* **2024**, *16*, 2760. [CrossRef]
59. Liao, Y.; Zhang, J.; Bao, R.; Xu, D.; Han, D. Modelling the Dynamics of Carbon Storages for *Pinus densata* Using Landsat Images in Shangri-La Considering Topographic Factors. *Remote Sens.* **2022**, *14*, 6244. [CrossRef]
60. Qin, L.H. Study on the Uncertainty of Forest Carbon Stock Estimation in Zhejiang Province. Master's Thesis, Zhejiang Agriculture and Forestry University, Hangzhou, China, 2017.
61. Hosmer, D.W., Jr.; Lemeshow, S.; Sturdivant, R.X. *Applied Logistic Regression*; John Wiley & Sons: Hoboken, NJ, USA, 2013; Volume 398.
62. Zeger, S.L.; Thomas, D.; Dominici, F.; Samet, J.M.; Schwartz, J.; Dockery, D.; Cohen, A. Exposure measurement error in time-series studies of air pollution: Concepts and consequences. *Environ. Health Perspect.* **2000**, *108*, 419–426. [CrossRef]

63. Fu, Y. Estimation of forest aboveground biomass and uncertainty measure at regional scale. *Hubei For. Sci. Technol.* **2018**, *47*, 1–4+38.
64. Zhao, H. Aboveground Biomass and Uncertainty Estimation of Different Stand Classes of Major TREE species in Jiangxi Province. Ph.D. Dissertation, China Academy of Forestry Sciences, Beijing, China, 2017.
65. Wang, K.R.; Shu, Q.T.; Zhao, H.Y.; Tan, D.H.; Yuan, Z.J. Modeling uncertainty of single-timber aboveground biomass of *Pinus densata*. *J. Southwest. For. Univ.* **2021**, *41*, 100–106.
66. Wang, J.; Xiao, X.; Bajgain, R.; Starks, P.; Steiner, J.; Doughty, R.B.; Chang, Q. Estimating leaf area index and aboveground biomass of grazing pastures using Sentinel-1, Sentinel-2 and Landsat images. *ISPRS J. Photogramm. Remote Sens.* **2019**, *154*, 189–201. [CrossRef]
67. Safari, A.; Sohrabi, H.; Powell, S.; Shataee, S. A comparative assessment of multi-temporal Landsat 8 and machine learning algorithms for estimating aboveground carbon stock in coppice oak forests. *Int. J. Remote Sens.* **2017**, *38*, 6407–6432. [CrossRef]
68. Chave, J.; Condit, R.; Aguilar, S.; Hernandez, A.; Lao, S.; Perez, R. Error propagation and scaling for tropical forest biomass estimates. *Philos. Trans. R. Soc. London. Ser. B Biol. Sci.* **2004**, *359*, 409–420. [CrossRef] [PubMed]
69. Djomo, A.N.; Knohl, A.; Gravenhorst, G. Estimations of total ecosystem carbon pools distribution and carbon biomass current annual increment of a moist tropical forest. *For. Ecol. Manag.* **2011**, *261*, 1448–1459. [CrossRef]
70. Butt, N.; Slade, E.; Thompson, J.; Malhi, Y.; Riutta, T. Quantifying the sampling error in tree census measurements by volunteers and its effect on carbon stock estimates. *Ecol. Appl.* **2013**, *23*, 936–943. [CrossRef]
71. Chen, Q.; Laurin, G.V.; Valentini, R. Uncertainty of remotely sensed aboveground biomass over an African tropical forest: Propagating errors from trees to plots to pixels. *Remote Sens. Environ.* **2015**, *160*, 134–143. [CrossRef]
72. Frazer, G.W.; Magnussen, S.; Wulder, M.A.; Niemann, K.O. Simulated impact of sample plot size and co-registration error on the accuracy and uncertainty of LiDAR-derived estimates of forest stand biomass. *Remote Sens. Environ.* **2011**, *115*, 636–649. [CrossRef]
73. Mayamanikandan, T.; Reddy, S.; Fararoda, R.; Thumaty, K.C.; Praveen, M.S.S.; Rajashekar, G.; Jha, C.S.; Das, I.C.; Gummapu, J. Quantifying the influence of plot-level uncertainty in above ground biomass up scaling using remote sensing data in central Indian dry deciduous forest. *Geocarto Int.* **2022**, *37*, 3489–3503. [CrossRef]
74. Petersson, H.; Breidenbach, J.; Ellison, D.; Holm, S.; Muszta, A.; Lundblad, M.; Ståhl, G.R. Assessing uncertainty: Sample size trade-offs in the development and application of carbon stock models. *For. Sci.* **2017**, *63*, 402–412. [CrossRef]
75. Xu, L.; Shi, Y.; Fang, H.; Zhou, G.; Xu, X.; Zhou, Y.; Tao, J.; Ji, B.; Xu, J.; Li, C.; et al. Vegetation carbon stocks driven by canopy density and forest age in subtropical forest ecosystems. *Sci. Total Environ.* **2018**, *631*, 619–626. [CrossRef]
76. Mensah, S.; Salako, V.K.; Seifert, T. Structural complexity and large-sized trees explain shifting species richness and carbon relationship across vegetation types. *Funct. Ecol.* **2020**, *34*, 1731–1745. [CrossRef]
77. Yang, Y.; Luo, Y.; Finzi, A.C. Carbon and nitrogen dynamics during forest stand development: A global synthesis. *New Phytol.* **2011**, *190*, 977–989. [CrossRef] [PubMed]
78. Jucker, T.; Bouriaud, O.; Coomes, D.A. Crown plasticity enables trees to optimize canopy packing in mixed-species forests. *Funct. Ecol.* **2015**, *29*, 1078–1086. [CrossRef]
79. Mngadi, M.; Odindi, J.; Mutanga, O. The utility of sentinel-2 spectral data in quantifying above-ground carbon stock in an urban reforested landscape. *Remote Sens.* **2021**, *13*, 4281. [CrossRef]
80. Lu, D.; Chen, Q.; Wang, G.; Liu, L.; Li, G.; Moran, E. A survey of remote sensing-based aboveground biomass estimation methods in forest ecosystems. *Int. J. Digit. Earth* **2016**, *9*, 63–105. [CrossRef]
81. Baghdadi, N.; Le Maire, G.; Bailly, J.S.; Osé, K.; Nouvellon, Y.; Zribi, M.; Hakamada, R. Evaluation of ALOS/PALSAR L-band data for the estimation of Eucalyptus plantations aboveground biomass in Brazil. *IEEE J. Sel. Top. Appl. Earth Obs. Remote Sens.* **2014**, *8*, 3802–3811. [CrossRef]
82. Zhang, L.; Zhang, X.; Shao, Z.; Jiang, W.; Gao, H. Integrating Sentinel-1 and 2 with LiDAR data to estimate aboveground biomass of subtropical forests in northeast Guangdong, China. *Int. J. Digit. Earth* **2023**, *16*, 158–182. [CrossRef]
83. Wang, B.; Mao, J.F.; Gao, J.I.E.; Zhao, W.E.I.; Wang, X.R. Colonization of the Tibetan Plateau by the homoploid hybrid pine *Pinus densata*. *Mol. Ecol.* **2011**, *20*, 3796–3811. [CrossRef]

forests

MDPI

Article

Biomass Prediction Using Sentinel-2 Imagery and an Artificial Neural Network in the Amazon/Cerrado Transition Region

Luana Duarte de Faria [1,*], Eraldo Aparecido Trondoli Matricardi [1,*], Beatriz Schwantes Marimon [2], Eder Pereira Miguel [1], Ben Hur Marimon Junior [2], Edmar Almeida de Oliveira [2], Nayane Cristina Candido dos Santos Prestes [2] and Osmar Luiz Ferreira de Carvalho [3]

[1] Forestry Department, College of Technology, University of Brasília, Campus Darcy Ribeiro, Brasilia 70910-900, DF, Brazil; edermiguel@unb.br
[2] Plant Ecology Laboratory, Mato Grosso State University, Campus Nova Xavantina, P.O. Box 08, Nova Xavantina 78690-000, MT, Brazil; biamarimon@unemat.br (B.S.M.); bhmjunior@gmail.com (B.H.M.J.); edmardinei@gmail.com (E.A.d.O.); nayaneprestesnx@gmail.com (N.C.C.d.S.P.)
[3] Department of Electrical Engineering, Campus Darcy Ribeiro, Brasilia 70910-900, DF, Brazil; osmarcarvalho@ieee.org
* Correspondence: luanaduarte005@gmail.com (L.D.d.F.); ematricardi@unb.br (E.A.T.M.)

Abstract: The ecotone zone, located between the Cerrado and Amazon biomes, has been under intensive anthropogenic pressures due to the expansion of commodity agriculture and extensive cattle ranching. This has led to habitat loss, reducing biodiversity, depleting biomass, and increasing CO_2 emissions. In this study, we employed an artificial neural network, field data, and remote sensing techniques to develop a model for estimating biomass in the remaining native vegetation within an 18,864 km^2 ecotone region between the Amazon and Cerrado biomes in the state of Mato Grosso, Brazil. We utilized field data from a plant ecology laboratory and vegetation indices from Sentinel-2 satellite imagery and trained artificial neural networks to estimate aboveground biomass (AGB) in the study area. The optimal network was chosen based on graphical analysis, mean estimation errors, and correlation coefficients. We validated our chosen network using both a Student's *t*-test and the aggregated difference. Our results using an artificial neural network, in combination with vegetation indices such as AFRI (Aerosol Free Vegetation Index), EVI (Enhanced Vegetation Index), and GNDVI (Green Normalized Difference Vegetation Index), which show an accurate estimation of aboveground forest biomass (Root Mean Square Error (RMSE) of 15.92%), can bolster efforts to assess biomass and carbon stocks. Our study results can support the definition of environmental conservation priorities and help set parameters for payment for ecosystem services in environmentally sensitive tropical regions.

Keywords: biomass estimation; Amazon/Cerrado ecotone; remote sensing; artificial neural network; Google Earth Engine

1. Introduction

Brazilian biomes are recognized for their high biodiversity, with over 33,000 plant species, constituting a staggering 26.5% of all known species on Earth [1]. More specifically, the Amazonia/Cerrado ecotone is a unique transitional ecoregion covering more than 4000 km across the ecotone between the two greatest biomes of South America [2]. The region is dominated by a highly seasonal climate and a wide diversity of vegetation types. These vegetation types range from open savannas, which receive abundant solar radiation, to dense forest formations with denser canopy and higher air humidity and soil moisture levels.

Beyond its rich vegetation, this region of high ecological and biological significance harbors a large array of species. However, this biodiversity faces threats as pastures and crops expand into this ecotone, leading to massive deforestation [3,4]. The consequence is a notable decrease in the native vegetation and biomass stock [5] due to the increasing deforestation rates in the Amazon and Cerrado biomes [6], a situation often worsened by forest fires [6,7].

Forest biomass is a critical factor in assessing the carbon sequestration and carbon balance capabilities of these ecosystems [8,9]. Accurately estimating aboveground biomass (AGB) is crucial to understanding the carbon cycle and its effects on climate changes and on terrestrial ecosystems and biodiversity [8–11], especially in tropical regions where reliable data are lacking [8,9].

Biomass estimation using remote sensing data has been widely applied at global, regional, and local scales. It has substantially improved in recent years [12], replacing conventional AGB estimation approaches. It enables temporal analysis of the environment and land cover [12] and, in the case of land use changes, contributes significantly to detecting, quantifying, and understanding vegetation behavior over time [13].

Several approaches have been developed and applied to accurately estimate carbon biomass. The authors of [14] accurately estimated aboveground biomass and stand volume in Hinton, the USA, by applying a methodological approach based on the relationship of forest structure attributes acquired in the field and Landsat ETM+ imagery. The authors of [15] successfully quantified live aboveground forest biomass in the states of Arizona and Minnesota using Landsat imagery and forest inventory data. The authors of [16] assessed Landsat 8 imagery to estimate aboveground biomass in the Umgeni catchment, South Africa. The authors of [17] applied boosted regression tree models, field data, and Sentinel-2 and Synthetic Aperture Radar (SAR) combined imagery acquired on different dates and were able to estimate aboveground biomass and forest cover.

Studies carried out by [18] combined vegetation indices retrieved from a Vegetation Sensor onboard the SPOT-4 satellite and Moderate Resolution Imaging Spectroradiometer (MODIS) and climate data to estimate primary production in Harvard Forest, Petersham, MA, the USA. The study by [19] observed a strong positive correlation between vegetation indices and biomass. Another study by [20] successfully estimated forest aboveground biomass (AGB) by combining Landsat and MODIS imagery.

New technologies based on machine learning and artificial intelligence have improved even more modeling approaches to predict biomass worldwide. Empirical modeling using deep learning algorithms has achieved highly accurate results in estimating AGB based on field sampling distributions with no assumptions. For example, [21] developed Sentinel-2 imagery and a machine learning model to estimate biomass in northern Anhui, China. Similarly, ref. [22] applied radar and optical imagery and a deep learning-based approach to estimate forest biomass in Tibet, China. The authors of Ref. [23] successfully combined an Artificial Neural Network (ANN) with vegetation indices retrieved from Landsat imagery to predict aboveground biomass for a study site in the Amazon region. However, they are more difficult to interpret and require accurate field data as the model input [24].

In this study, we developed and applied a model to estimate aboveground biomass in an Amazonia/Cerrado transition zone in the state of Mato Grosso, Brazil, using field data, remote sensing, and Artificial Neural Networks (ANNs). Our goal was to accurately estimate AGB using medium spatial resolution and freely available remotely sensed data (Sentinel-2 imagery) with an ANN, a method not previously applied to this large ecotone region. These study results are significant as they can facilitate further analyses of deforestation and forest fire impacts in this tropical region, which have profoundly affected forest structure by reducing tree cover and increasing herbaceous species. These herbaceous plants are more susceptible to water stress, making the region prone to recurrent and intense fire events [25].

Our model showed promising results for estimating and monitoring aboveground biomass and can play a pivotal role in supporting the implementation of payments for ecosystem services. This represents a technological advance in environmental preservation and conservation research, particularly in transitional zones that lack information on biomass stocks. From a critical perspective, conserving biomass in this study area, which is near Brazil's largest indigenous territory (Xingu Indigenous Land), may have significant and positive impacts on the well-being and sustainable existence of traditional populations in their territories [26].

2. Materials and Methods

2.1. Regional Setting

Our study area encompassed a total of 18,863.6 Km^2 located in the Ecotone region between the Amazon and Cerrado biomes in Brazil. We selected permanent long-term measurement plots established and monitored by the Plant Ecology Laboratory of Mato Grosso State University (LABEV-UNEMAT) in the study region (Campus of Nova Xavantina, State of Mato Grosso, Brazil). The sample plots are in the municipalities of Gaúcha do Norte, Querência, and Ribeirão Cascalheira, state of Mato Grosso.

Field measurements were conducted in 12 sample plots, each measuring 100 m × 100 m and subdivided into 60 subplots of 100 m × 20 m (Figure 1). These measurements were carried out during the dry season (July to October) in 2014, 2018, 2020, and 2021. We selected this study area due to its environmental sensitivity and socioeconomic characteristics, as it is situated in the transition zone between the Cerrado and Amazonia biomes. The area is particularly notable for its proximity to indigenous lands and the significant deforestation activities reported in recent decades, especially in the region known as the "Arc of Deforestation" of the Brazilian Amazon [2].

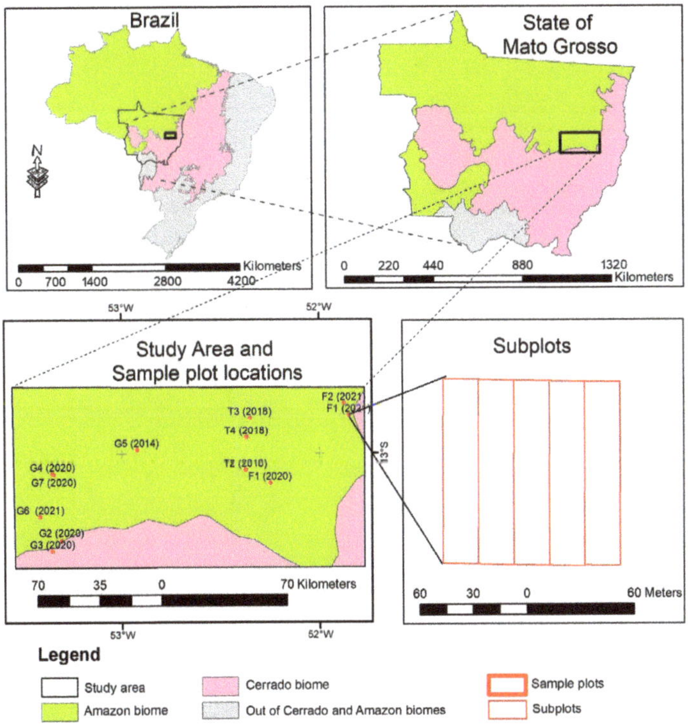

Figure 1. The study area is located within the ecotone zone of the Amazonia and Cerrado biomes in the state of Mato Grosso, Brazil. Field measurements were conducted in 12 sample plots, each measuring 10,000 m^2 and subdivided into 60 subplots of 2000 m^2 each, in the years 2014, 2018, 2020, and 2021. The year of sampling is indicated in black above each sample plot in the study area.

The study region features diverse soil types with distinct characteristics. These soils are characterized by low nutrient availability and elevated levels of aluminum toxicity. In the interfluvial areas, medium-textured red-yellow latosols predominate, creating favorable conditions for forest establishment. Additionally, these latosols feature patches of anthropogenic soils created by ancient indigenous populations, known locally as 'terra preta de índio' or Amazonian Dark Earth (ADE). ADE is rich in pyrogenic carbon, leading to a higher concentration of organic matter on the surface and increased pH in deeper layers. In floodplains, clay-textured fluvic neosols are prevalent, containing higher potassium content but facing phosphorus restriction, poor drainage, and elevated aluminum and iron levels [7,27].

The permanent plots of this study are predominantly surrounded by Seasonal Forest (Fse) and Typical Cerrado (Sd), which are characteristic of the Central-West region of Brazil [28]. According to the Köppen climate classification, the study region is characterized by an Aw climate type, which is tropical seasonal [29], with two distinct seasons: a dry season from May to October and a rainy season from November to April [30]. As described by [7], the region's topography varies from flat to gently undulating. It includes plateaus and plains in the central area, mountains to the east, and residual depressions to the south [31].

2.2. Dendrometric Variables of the Inventory

The inventories were conducted in 2014 (one plot), 2018 (three plots), 2020 (five plots), and 2021 (three plots) by collaborators from the Forest Ecology Laboratory at the State University of Mato Grosso. The objective was to monitor vegetation within permanent plots across different strata, soil types, climatic zones, and regional groups. Sampling was randomized, with 12 sampling units, each measuring 100 × 100 m. Each unit was divided into five transects, resulting in a total of 60 subsamples measuring 100 × 20 m (Figure 1). There was only one sample unit showing different dimensions, covering an area of 180 × 60 m with transects measuring 36 × 60 m. We adopted the sampling protocol proposed by [7] to ensure data reliability.

We collected detailed information on species, families, tree diameters, and heights in each plot. To estimate basic wood density, we used the ForestPlots.net database, which includes data on over 2000 neotropical species [32,33]. Aboveground biomass was calculated using Microsoft Excel 2016, incorporating data on diameter at breast height, total height, and basic wood density. All data were analyzed following RAINFOR guidelines and the methodologies outlined by these authors.

Complementarily, we conducted a statistical analysis using field-collected data to examine variations in dendrometric characteristics within our study area. Descriptive table analysis allowed us to summarize and describe inventory variables, enabling comparisons with similar areas and contributing to the scientific understanding of this field.

2.3. Forest Biomass

To effectively develop methods for assessing Aboveground Biomass (AGB), it is crucial to acquire on-site estimates of this biomass, commonly referred to as "in situ" measurements. The in-situ estimates serve as essential data for the calibration and validation of algorithms designed to calculate biomass. Additionally, field-collected data provide valuable information to estimate various tree characteristics, including basal area and the total aboveground and/or belowground biomass. In our analysis, the forest inventory data were utilized to predict the aboveground biomass within the transitional area using remotely sensed data and an artificial neural network. This prediction considers the equation proposed by [34] for our field samples located within the Amazon biome:

$$AGB = 0.0673 \times \left(Wd \times Ht \times DBH^2\right)^{0.976} \quad (1)$$

where:

AGB = Aboveground Biomass (kg);

Wd = Basic wood density for each tree species (g.cm^3);

Ht = Total height (m);

DBH = Tree diameter at 1.3 m from the ground (cm).

In addition, we calculated AGB for our field samples located within the Cerrado biome using a specific allometric equation developed for the Cerrado environment [35], as follows:

$$AGB = 0.4913 + 0.0291 \times DGH^2 \times Ht \tag{2}$$

where:

AGB = Aboveground Biomass (kg);

DGH = The diameter of trees at their base (ground), specifically for trees with a diameter equal to or greater than 5 cm;

Ht = tree height.

The biomass was estimated by applying allometric equations and utilizing tree-specific variables for each subplot within the sample plots. Subsequently, these values were normalized per unit area to calculate the results in Tons per hectare (ton·ha^{-1}).

2.4. Sentinel-2 Imagery

We utilized images acquired by the MultiSpectral Instrument (MSI) sensor aboard the Sentinel-2 satellite, which provided spectral information about vegetation. This sensor captures the red band, crucial for characterizing vegetation due to the presence of chlorophyll in plants [36]. The satellite's spatial resolution varies according to the spectral bands: 10 m for visible and near-infrared bands, 20 m for red edges and other infrared bands, and 60 m for water vapor and cirrus bands. Sentinel-2 features 13 spectral bands ranging from 0.442 μm to 2.202 μm, with a revisit frequency of every five days [37].

In this analysis, we used a total of five Sentinel-2 scenes acquired from 2016 to 2021, all during August of each year, to minimize seasonal effects on the remotely sensed products. All scenes, covering the entire study area, were level 1c orthorectified TOA (Top of Atmosphere) reflectance and were acquired in the same year as the forest inventory data for 2018, 2020, and 2021. The only exception was the image acquired in 2016, which was used to relate to field data collected in 2014 because there were no Sentinel images available for that year. Subsequently, we retrieved vegetation indices from the Sentinel-2 images using the Google Earth Engine (GEE) platform. The Sentinel-2 scenes' IDs and acquisition dates are listed in Table 1.

Table 1. Sentinel 2A sensor MSI (Multispectral Instrument) scenes acquired through Google Earth Engine (GEE) and used for retrieving the vegetation indices applied in this analysis.

ID Sentinel-2A, Sensor MSI	Data
20160807T135257_T22LBL	7 August 2016
20180802T135108_T22LCL	2 August 2018
20200801T135115_T22LBL	1 August 2020
20200803T134216_T22LCL	3 August 2020
20210813T134211_T22LDL	13 August 2021

2.5. Vegetation Indices

In this analysis, we included various vegetation indices based on different spectral band combinations to leverage their potential sensitivity in capturing diverse vegetation characteristics and enhancing the relationship between vegetation indices and forest AGB. The indices utilized were NDVI (Normalized Difference Vegetation Index), EVI (Enhanced Vegetation Index), GNDVI (Green Normalized Difference Vegetation Index), AFRI (Aerosol Free Vegetation Index), MSAVI (Modified Soil-Adjusted Vegetation Index), NDRE (Normalized Difference Red Edge Index), SAVI (Soil-Adjusted Vegetation Index), and MSAVIaf (Modified Soil-Adjusted Vegetation Index aerosol free), all described as follows.

Normalized Difference Vegetation Index (NDVI)

The NDVI, developed by [38], is one of the most widely used vegetation indices. It relies on the relationship between the difference in reflectance in the near-infrared and red spectral bands and the sum of the reflectance of these two bands. This index enables the assessment of the photosynthetic activity of vegetation, with values ranging from −1 to 1. In contrast, water surfaces or clouds typically exhibit values below 0 [39]. Its definition is as follows:

$$\mathrm{NDVI} = \frac{\rho\mathrm{NIR} - \rho\mathrm{Red}}{\rho\mathrm{NIR} + \rho\mathrm{Red}} \quad (3)$$

where ρNIR is the reflectance in the near-infrared spectral band and ρRed is the reflectance in the red spectral band.

Enhanced Vegetation Index (EVI)

The Enhanced Vegetation Index (EVI), developed by [40], aims to minimize atmospheric effects and improve NDVI sensitivity. It is notable for its sensitivity in analyses of canopy structural variations and densely forested areas [41]. Its definition is as follows:

$$\mathrm{EVI} = \mathrm{G} * \frac{(\rho\mathrm{NIR} - \rho\mathrm{Red})}{\rho\mathrm{NIR} + (\mathrm{C1} \times \rho\mathrm{Red}) - (\mathrm{C2} \times \rho\mathrm{Blue}) + \mathrm{L}} \quad (4)$$

where ρNIR is the reflectance in the near-infrared spectral band, ρRed is the reflectance in the red spectral band, ρBlue is the reflectance in the blue spectral band, G is the gain factor (default value: 2.5), L is the canopy background adjustment factor (default value: 1.0), and C1 and C2 are coefficients to correct aerosol effects.

Enhanced Vegetation Index 2 (EVI 2)

The Enhanced Vegetation Index 2 (EVI2), developed by [42], aims to achieve results similar to its original version (EVI) but using only two spectral bands (excluding the blue band). It proves particularly useful when utilizing high-quality remote sensing data with minimal atmospheric effects. Its definition is as follows:

$$\mathrm{EVI2} = \mathrm{G} * \frac{(\rho\mathrm{NIR} - \rho\mathrm{Red})}{\rho\mathrm{NIR} + 2.4 \times \rho\mathrm{Red} + 1} \quad (5)$$

where ρNIR is the reflectance in the near-infrared spectral band, ρRed is the reflectance in the red spectral band and, G is the gain factor (default value: 2.5).

GNDV (Green Normalized Difference Vegetation Index)

The Green Normalized Difference Vegetation Index (GNDVI), a modification of the NDVI developed by [43], is used to estimate chlorophyll content in vegetation. This makes it valuable for distinguishing between senescent vegetation and vegetation experiencing various degrees of water stress. GNDVI replaces the red band with the green band from NDVI, aiming to mitigate vegetation saturation effects in denser conditions [43]. Its definition is as follows:

$$\mathrm{GNDVI} = \frac{\rho\mathrm{NIR} - \rho\mathrm{Green}}{\rho\mathrm{NIR} + \rho\mathrm{Green}} \quad (6)$$

where ρNIR is the reflectance in the near-infrared spectral band and ρGreen is the reflectance in the green spectral band.

AFRI (Aerosol Free Vegetation Index)

The Aerosol Free Vegetation Index (AFRI) was developed by [44] with the aim of mitigating the effects of aerosols and atmospheric disturbances on vegetation index calculations. This index has the capability to penetrate the atmosphere more effectively, providing accurate information about vegetation and other soil characteristics, even under adverse conditions such as forest fire situations with the presence of smoke [44]. One of the main advantages of AFRI is its resilience to smoke interference in data acquisition, distinguishing it from other conventional indices [44]. Its definition is as follows:

$$\text{AFRI} = \frac{\rho\text{NIR} - 0.5\rho\text{SWIR}}{\rho\text{NIR} + 0.5\rho\text{SWIR}} \quad (7)$$

where: ρNIR is the reflectance in the near-infrared spectral band and ρSWIR is the reflectance in the shortwave infrared 1 band.

SAVI (Soil-Adjusted Vegetation Index)

The Soil-Adjusted Vegetation Index (SAVI) was developed by [45] with the aim of minimizing soil interference in canopy spectral measurements. This index allows for calibration so that variations in soil substrate are normalized in vegetation estimates [45]. Its definition is as follows:

$$\text{SAVI} = \frac{\rho\text{NIR} - \rho\text{Red}}{\rho\text{NIR} + \rho\text{Red} + \text{L}} \times (1 + \text{L}) \quad (8)$$

where ρNIR is the reflectance in the near-infrared spectral band, ρRed is the reflectance in the red spectral band, and L is the soil adjustment factor (default value = 0.5).

MSAVI (Modified Soil-Adjusted Vegetation Index)

The Modified Soil-Adjusted Vegetation Index (MSAVI), developed by [46], was designed to enhance its original version, SAVI. Both MSAVI and SAVI utilize soil adjustment factors [46]. MSAVI proves to be a more effective option in terms of time and resources, particularly in areas where vegetation density is uncertain or varies significantly [46]. Its definition is as follows:

$$\text{MSAVI} = \frac{\text{NIR} - \rho\text{Red}}{\text{NIR} + \rho\text{Red} + \text{L}} \times (1 + \text{L}) \quad (9)$$

where ρNIR is the reflectance in the near-infrared spectral band, ρRed is the reflectance in the red spectral band, and L is the soil adjustment calculated using Equation (10):

$$\text{L} = [(\rho\text{NIR} - \rho\text{Red}) \times \text{s} + 1 + \rho\text{NIR} + \rho\text{Red}]^2 - 8.0 \times \text{s} \times (\rho\text{NIR} - \rho\text{Red}) \quad (10)$$

where s = 1.2 (slope of the soil line calculated from surface reflectance at non-forested areas).

MSAVIaf (Modified Soil-Adjusted Vegetation Index aerosol free

The MSAVIaf was developed by [12] with the aim of reducing atmospheric effects on vegetation index estimations. It has been demonstrated to be more sensitive to vegetation variations than the Aerosol Free Vegetation Index under anomalous atmospheric conditions in the Amazon region [12]. Its definition is as follows:

$$\text{MSAVIaf} = \frac{\rho\text{NIR} - 0.5\rho\text{SWIR}}{\rho\text{NIR} + 0.5\rho\text{SWIR} + \text{L}} \times (1 + \text{L}) \quad (11)$$

where ρNIR is the reflectance in the near-infrared spectral band, ρSWIR is the reflectance in the shortwave infrared spectral band (central wavelength: 1.6137 μm), and L is the soil adjustment factor, calculated as previously presented (Equation (10)).

NDRE (Normalized Difference Red Edge Index)

The Normalized Difference Red Edge Index (NDRE), developed by [47], was designed to measure plant physiological parameters, particularly those associated with chlorophyll content, nitrogen concentration, and canopy structure. It can be applied in identifying and classifying crops and land covers [48]. Its definition is as follows:

$$NDRE = \frac{\rho NIR - \rho Rededge}{\rho NIR + \rho Rededge} \tag{12}$$

where ρNIR is the reflectance in the near-infrared spectral band and ρRededge is the reflectance in the red edge spectral band (central wavelength: 0.704 μm).

2.6. Correlation Analysis

The evaluation of vegetation indices for predicting biomass in our study area was performed by analyzing the correlation matrix between the nine indices retrieved from remotely sensed data and the field-measured biomass. To assess the normality of biomass and vegetation index datasets, we applied the Shapiro–Wilk test.

2.7. Modeling of the Artificial Neural Network (ANN)

In this study, we employed a Multilayer Perceptron (MLP) type of Artificial Neural Network (ANN), adjusted and trained using Statistica software (STATSOFT), version 12, to estimate forest biomass using the field-sampling data of LABEV-UNEMAT. The software utilizes the Intelligent Problem Solver (IPS) tool to optimize the network architecture, including the number of layers, neurons, and cycles to achieve more efficient results [49]. Training is conducted using the Broyden–Fletcher–Goldfarb–Shanno quasi-Newton algorithm by IPS for neural network processing, which has been shown to be highly capable of solving optimization and prediction problems, in addition to being the most popular quasi-Newton method [50–52].

In this analysis, the input layer of the neural network consisted of both categorical and numerical variables. The categorical variable pertained to the two types of strata in the study area: Perennial Seasonal Forest and typical Cerrado. The numerical variables included the vegetation indices NDVI, EVI, EVI2, GNDV, AFRI, MSAVI, NDRE, SAVI, and MSAVIaf. The hidden layer comprised 'n' neurons, while the output layer consisted of a single neuron responsible for estimating AGB.

To train the Artificial Neural Networks (ANNs), we selected 40 subsamples, representing 70% of the total 60 field-demarked subsamples during the inventories. The remaining 20 subsamples were used for result validation and testing. Multilayer Perceptron (MLP) ANNs calculate the weighted arithmetic mean of these inputs [53], and in this case, were activated by an exponential function. To assess the performance of the models developed using ANNs, we considered the parameters of the correlation coefficient (R) and root mean square error (RMSE). These coefficients have been utilized in other research involving ANNs to predict solar energy using weather data, as demonstrated by [54].

For the validation of the performance of the best ANNs, we conducted statistical analyses using Student's *t*-tests. To determine whether there was AGB underestimation or overestimation, we calculated the aggregate difference in percentage terms (AD%). The Aggregate Difference (AD%) corresponds to the difference between the sum of the observed values and the sum of the estimated values, in percentage, obtained by the following expression:

$$AD\% = \frac{\sum_{i=i}^{n} y_i - \sum_{1=1}^{n} \hat{y}_i}{\sum_{i=1}^{n} y_i} \times 100 \tag{13}$$

where AD% = Aggregate Difference; y_i = observed values; $\hat{y}_i$ = estimated values; and n = number of observations.

The statistical analyses were performed using Microsoft Excel software, Microsoft Office 365, Version 2408.

3. Results

3.1. Vegetation Inventory

The results in Table 2 show significant differences in the assessed variables, highlighting substantial variation in dendrometric characteristics between the Cerrado and the Amazon plots. Notably, trees in forest plots showed an average aboveground biomass approximately eight times higher than those in Cerrado plots. This difference can be attributed to wider trunks (37% larger in the forest compared to Cerrado) and trees that were approximately three times taller in the forest. Interestingly, the average wood density was quite similar in both formations (Amazon and Cerrado) within the study area (Table 2).

Table 2. Dendrometric variables calculated from forest inventory for the areas of the Plant Laboratory (LABEV) Mato Grosso State University (UNEMAT) plots.

Cerrado Plots					Forest Plots				
Statistics	**DBH**	**Ht**	**WD**	**AGB**	**Statistics**	**DBH**	**Ht**	**WD**	**AGB**
Minimum	10.0	4.0	0.41	14.35	Minimum	10.0	10.0	0.20	66.56
Maximum	39.0	13.0	0.84	23.49	Maximum	93.2	30.0	1.09	331.38
Mean	13.81	6.64	0.66	18.38	Mean	19.12	13.99	0.67	146.86
Variance	15.38	1.65	0.01	10.97	Variance	105.19	17.5	0.019	2572.76
Deviation	3.92	1.28	0.10	3.31	Deviation	10.25	4.18	0.14	50.72
CV (%)	28.4	19.33	15.43	18.02	CV (%)	53.64	29.9	20.4	34.54

Where DBH = diameter at breast height (cm), Ht = total height (m), WD = average wood density (g·cm^3), AGB = aboveground biomass (Ton·ha^{-1}), and CV (%) = Coefficient of Variation (%).

The biomass measurements in the Forest samples showed themselves to be statistically consistent, showing an average value of 146.84 t·ha^{-1}. When examining a forest fragment located on the southern edge of the study area, we observed biomass variability ranging from 155 to 195 t·ha^{-1}.

3.2. Correlation Analysis of Biomass and Vegetation Indices

In this study, we created a mosaic of the Sentinel-2 images acquired in August 2019 to retrieve the vegetation indices for the study area (Table 3).

Table 3. Average of the independent variables in the study area. AFRI = Aerosol Free Vegetation Index; EVI = Enhanced Vegetation Index; GNDVI = Green Normalized Difference Index; EVI2 = Enhanced Vegetation Index–2; MSAVIaf = Modified Soil-Adjusted Vegetation Index aerosol free; MSAVI = Modified Soil-Adjusted Vegetation Index; NDVI = Normalized Difference Vegetation Index; NDRE = Normalized Difference Red Edge Index; SAVI = Soil-Adjusted Vegetation Index.

Vegetation Indices	Average
AFRI	0.564
EVI	0.571
GNDVI	0.569
EVI2	0.392
MSAVIaf	0.324
MSAVI	0.545
NDRE	0.515
NDVI	0.697
SAVI	0.408

The Shapiro–Wilk test indicated non-normality of the analyzed variables (vegetation indices and biomass). We then applied the Spearman correlation matrix, recommended for non-parametric data analysis. The Spearman correlation results indicated positive and significant correlations ($\alpha < 0.05$) among aboveground biomass and all vegetation indices, as well as among the vegetation indices themselves (Table 4).

Table 4. Spearman's correlation matrix was used to analyze the relationship between aboveground biomass and vegetation indices of the study area.

	AFRI	EVI	EVI2	GNDVI	MSAVIaf	MSAVI	NDRE	NDVI	SAVI	Biomass
AFRI	1									
EVI	0.887 **	1								
EVI2	0.875 **	0.963 **	1							
GNDVI	0.897 **	0.902 **	0.951 **	1						
MSAVIaf	0.948 **	0.963 **	0.969 **	0.950 **	1					
MSAVI	0.868 **	0.975 **	0.933 **	0.866 **	0.942 **	1				
NDRE	0.954 **	0.853 **	0.882 **	0.921 **	0.922 **	0.825 **	1			
NDVI	0.972 **	0.909 **	0.902 **	0.907 **	0.943 **	0.887 **	0.971 **	1		
SAVI	0.831 **	0.853 **	0.889 **	0.863 **	0.907 **	0.850 **	0.786 **	0.820 **	1	
Biomass	0.469 *	0.443 *	0.532 **	0.621 **	0.555 **	0.404 *	0.509 **	0.466 *	0.594 **	1

** Significant at $\alpha < 0.01$; * Significant at $\alpha < 0.05$. Where: AFRI = Aerosol Free Vegetation Index; EVI = Enhanced Vegetation Index; GNDVI = Green Normalized Difference Index; MSAVIaf = Modified Soil-Adjusted Vegetation Index aerosol resistant; MSAVI = Modified Soil-Adjusted Vegetation Index; NDVI = Normalized Difference Vegetation Index; NDRE = Normalized Difference Red Edge Index; SAVI = Soil-Adjusted Vegetation Index.

Based on the results of the correlation matrix, we subsequently proceeded with a stepwise regression analysis to select our predictive variables (vegetation indices). The stepwise technique involves adding or removing independent variables from the model one at a time, based on specific criteria such as the *p*-value. This procedure is implemented automatically to identify a subset of variables that are most relevant for predicting the dependent variable (in this case, aboveground biomass).

In contrast to the correlation matrix results, this complementary stepwise regression analysis found that the AFRI, EVI, and GNDVI indices (Figure 2) were the most suitable (highest statistical significance at $\alpha < 0.05$) vegetation indices to be used as input neurons for the ANN modeling. It is likely that retrieving vegetation indices from different spectral band combinations (near-infrared, middle infrared, red, and blue bands) greatly contributed to increasing their sensitivity and capturing aboveground biomass variation in the study area.

3.3. Biomass Modeling

After training the artificial neural networks (ANNs) with the most suitable independent variables (AFRI, EVI, and GNDVI) indicated by the stepwise regression analysis, we selected the top five performing ANNs based on correlation coefficients (r) exceeding 0.90 and validation errors less than 16%. The selected ANN showed low variation between training, selection, and evaluation indices, demonstrating stability during the training process [55]. An in-depth analysis of fit and accuracy statistics revealed that Neural Network 1 showed the strongest predictive capability for aboveground biomass, as indicated by the RMSE% values in Table 5.

Additionally, the results provided by Neural Network 1 indicated a satisfactory distribution of residuals (Figure 3—B1 training, B2 testing, and B3 validation) and accurate, consistent predictions of aboveground biomass (Figure 3—A1 training, A2 testing, and A3 validation) in the study area. The model showed a good fit, which indicates that it minimized the differences between observed and predicted values without significant bias.

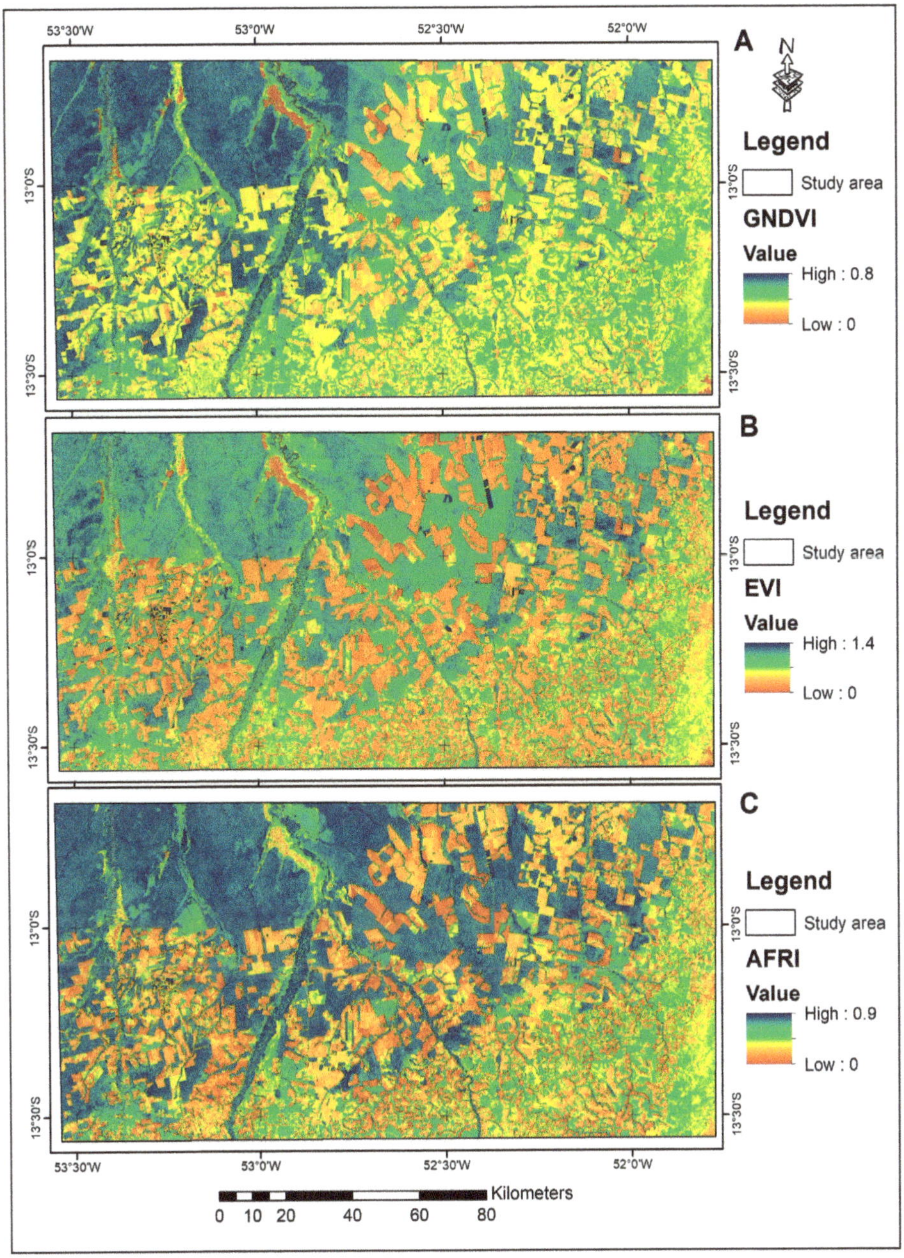

Figure 2. Vegetation indices ((**A**) = Green Normalized Vegetation Index—GNDV; (**B**) = Enhanced Vegetation Index—EVI; and (**C**) = Aerosol Free Vegetation Index—AFRI) retrieved from Sentinel-2 imagery acquired in August 2016, 2018, 2020, and 2021 covering the entire study region.

Table 5. Accuracy statistics of the selected artificial neural networks (ANNs) for prediction of aboveground biomass for the LABEV-UNEMAT plots located in the Cerrado/Amazon ecotone.

ANN	Architecture	N° of Cycles	Activation	Activation	Adjustment		Validation		Test	
			Hidden	Output	RMSE%	R	RMSE%	R	RMSE%	R
1	MLP 3-12-1	860	Tang	Tang	18.09	0.93	15.76	0.94	15.92	0.94
2	MLP 3-11-1	1630	Logistic	Exponential	19.44	0.92	16.09	0.93	16.18	0.93
3	MLP 3-8-1	910	Logistic	Identity	19.77	0.92	16.41	0.93	16.92	0.93
4	MLP 3-13-1	950	Tang	Exponential	19.53	0.92	16.62	0.93	16.91	0.93
5	MLP 3-11-1	670	Logistic	Identity	20.19	0.91	17.91	0.91	17.12	0.91

ANN	Predictor variables	Neurons per layer			Adjust			Algorithm
		Input	Hidden	Output	TI	SI	AI	
1	AFRI, EVI, GNDVI	3	12	1	0.08	0.08	0.09	BFGS
2	AFRI, EVI, GNDVI	3	9	1	0.10	0.11	0.12	BFGS
3	AFRI, EVI, GNDVI	3	5	1	0.10	0.12	0.13	BFGS
4	AFRI, EVI, GNDVI	3	13	1	0.11	0.13	0.10	BFGS
5	AFRI, EVI, GNDVI	3	7	1	0.13	0.15	0.17	BFGS

ANN = artificial neural network; MLP = Multilayer perceptron; RMSE% = Root Mean Square Error Percentage; R = correlation between observed and estimated values; TI= Training indices (network definition), SI = Selection Indices of training stop, AI = Assessment Indices (quality assessment of trained network); BFGS = Broyden–Fletcher–Goldfarb–Shannon.

The accuracy of aboveground biomass estimates is a crucial indicator of the model's effectiveness. The architecture of ANN-1 (Figure 4) comprises three layers: the input layer with three neurons representing predictor variables (EVI, AFRI, and GNDVI), a hidden layer of 12 neurons for data processing activated using a tangential function, and an output layer representing the variable of interest (AGB) activated with a logistic function.

3.4. Statistical Analysis

The Student's *t*-test is a statistical tool used to determine whether there is a significant difference between the means of two independent samples. In this test, we formulate a null hypothesis (H0) asserting that there is no difference between the means of the two samples, and an alternative hypothesis (H1) suggesting that there is a significant difference between them. Following the *t*-test, we compute a *p*-value. If the *p*-value falls below the chosen significance level (typically 0.05), it indicates statistical evidence to reject the null hypothesis in favor of the alternative hypothesis. In simpler terms, this means there is a significant difference between the means of the observed values compared to the estimated values. Conversely, if the *p*-value exceeds the significance level, there is not enough evidence to reject the null hypothesis, indicating no statistically significant difference between the observed mean values and the estimated values.

The *p*-value is a statistical measure that aids in interpreting the results of a hypothesis test in statistics. It indicates the probability of obtaining a result as extreme or more extreme than the one observed, assuming the null hypothesis is true. The null hypothesis typically states that there is no effect or difference between the compared groups, while the alternative hypothesis suggests the opposite. In short, the *p*-value provides a way to quantify how much the results support or refute the null hypothesis.

In this analysis, the application of the Student's *t*-test revealed that the calculated *p*-value for the selected neural network was greater than the established significance level ($\alpha = 0.05$), specifically $p = 0.952$. This indicates that there is insufficient statistical evidence to reject the null hypothesis, which shows no differences between the observed and predicted values by the neural network for the validation plots.

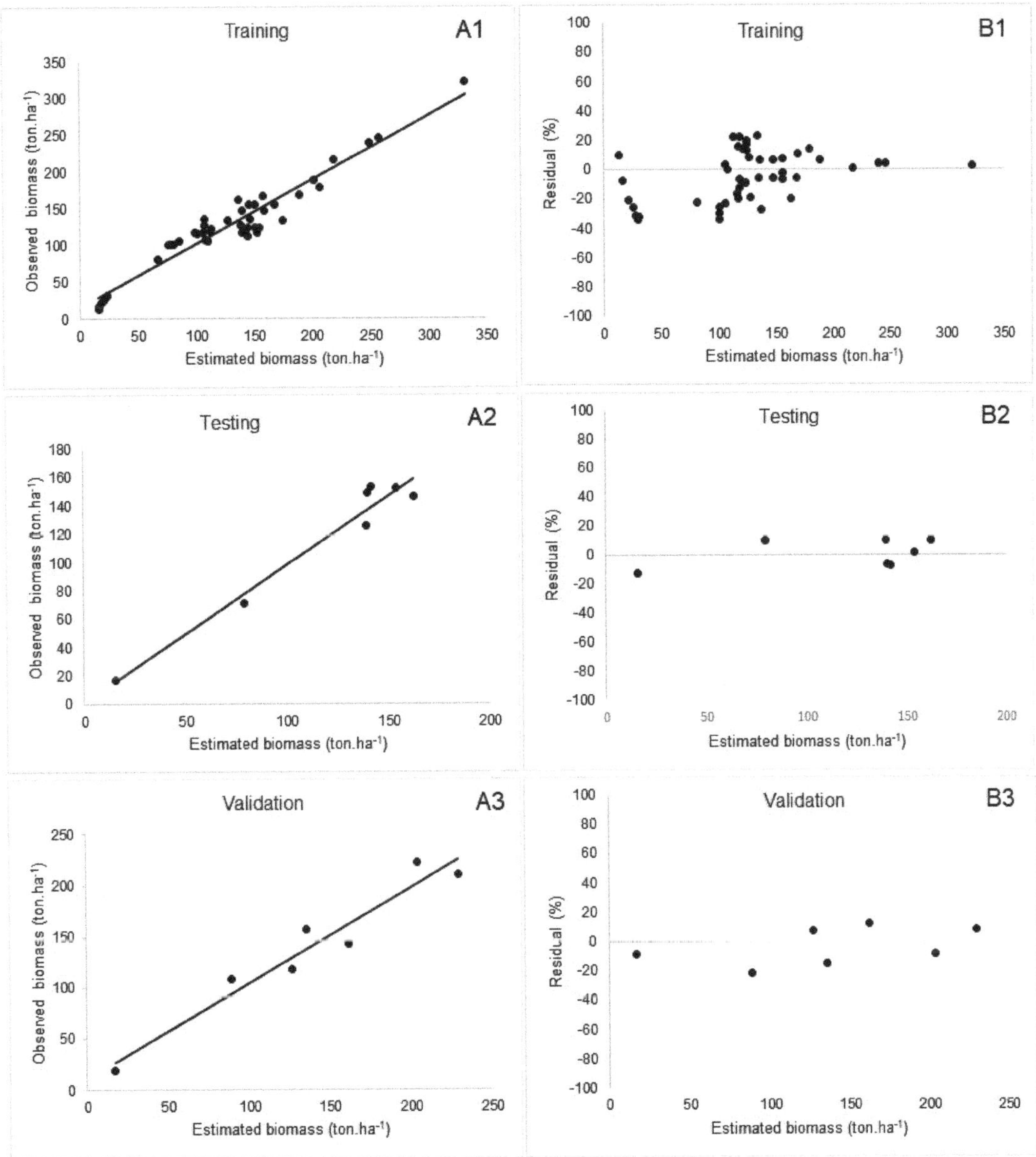

Figure 3. Observed and estimated aboveground biomass in the study area ((**A1**) = Training; (**A2**) = Testing; (**A3**) = Validation) and distribution of residuals ((**B1**) = Training; (**B2**) = Testing; (**B3**) = Validation) for Artificial Neural Network 1 (ANN-1).

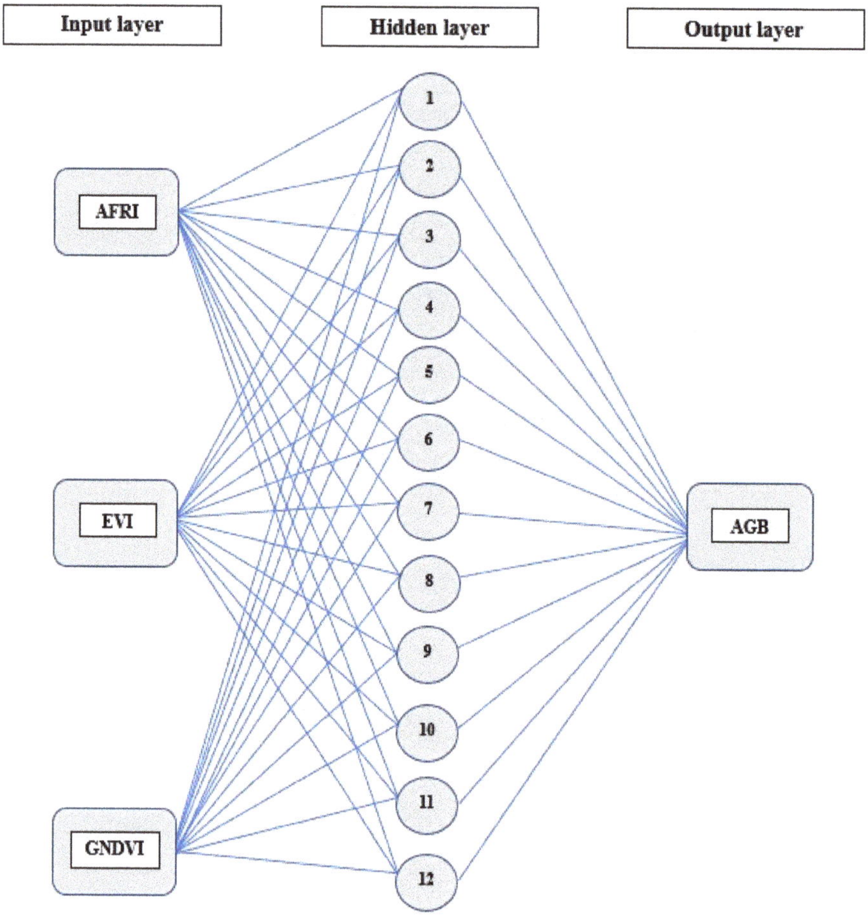

Figure 4. Architecture of ANN-1 selected for the prediction of aboveground biomass for the study area.

Additionally, the Aggregate Difference (AD) analysis indicated a slight tendency to overestimate the values predicted by the neural network, with a deviation of −0.1637%. Nevertheless, these results align with the accuracy of the information obtained during the ANN training process, confirming its proficiency in providing precise estimates for Aboveground Biomass (AGB). Consequently, these findings suggest that the ANN-generated estimates are both accurate and dependable for predicting AGB in areas of biome transition.

3.5. Analyzing the Spatial Distribution of Biomass

Based on the results obtained from the training of the neural networks, we were able to extend our estimates of AGB across the entire area covered by native vegetation in this study region. Consequently, the total biomass of the study area, considering the land use and land cover of native vegetation, was estimated at 109,118,121 tons. The most common AGB values in the study area were in the range of 0 to 50 $t \cdot ha^{-1}$, followed by the range of 100 to 150 $t \cdot ha^{-1}$ (Figure 5).

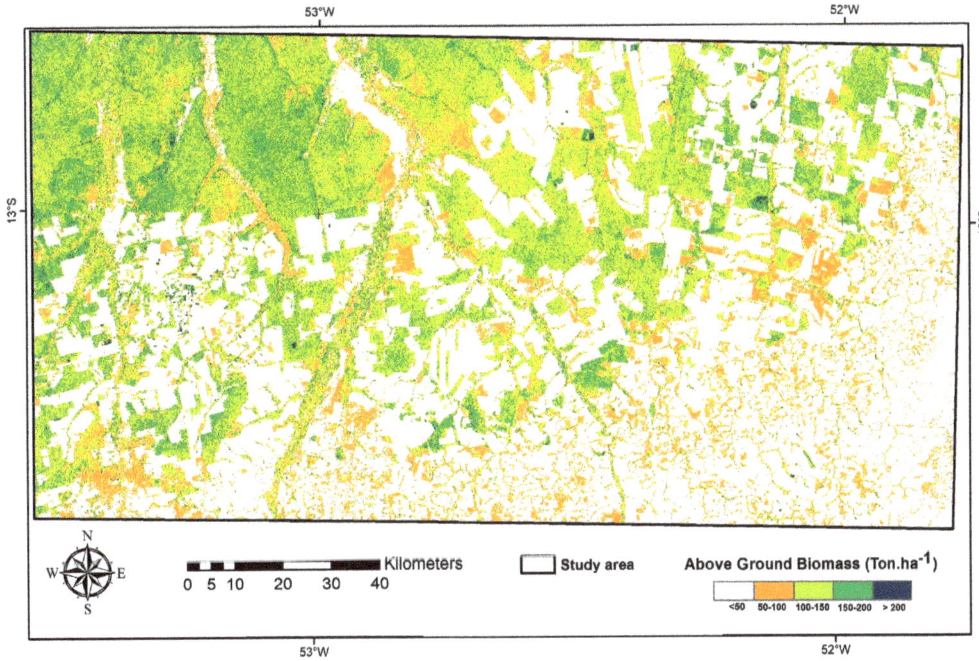

Figure 5. Spatial distribution of forest biomass is estimated for the Amazon–Cerrado ecotone zone. Darker areas indicate higher aboveground biomass, while lighter areas indicate lower biomass.

4. Discussion

4.1. Forest Biomass and Land Use and Land Cover

The amount of aboveground biomass (AGB) varies significantly within native forest formations in the study area, predominantly ranging between 100 and 150 t·ha^{-1}, followed by classes of 0–50 and 50–100 t·ha^{-1} occupied by savanna and transitional forest formations. This variation can be attributed to various factors, including climatic, geological, and soil conditions, as well as distinct previous vegetation disturbances and land use patterns in the study region [56].

The use of ANNs (Artificial Neural Networks) proved effective in estimating biomass per unit area while eliminating the basic assumptions of conventional mathematical modeling, such as normality and linearity of forest attributes [57]. These attributes often require various mathematical transformations for traditional modeling, which can result in a loss of quality and selection of models, leading to biased estimates of the variable of interest.

One hypothesis explaining this relatively low range of total AGB in the study region is the impact of anthropogenic activities, particularly agriculture, selective logging, fire, and livestock farming. These disturbances can increase edge effects and forest degradation, especially when caused by selective logging activities and forest fires [12,58]. Addressing this requires the definition and implementation of public policies to enforce sustainable land use management, conservation of natural ecosystems, environmental law enforcement, climate awareness, and fire prevention measures [59].

The increase in soybean cultivation over the last few decades has had severe impacts on natural ecosystems and the natural landscape in the study region. These impacts may directly lead to decreased rainfall, increased land surface temperatures, and soil and water contamination due to pesticides and chemical fertilizers. Additionally, pastures cover nearly 16 percent of the study area and can cause significant environmental impacts, including greenhouse gas emissions and soil and water degradation [60].

In summary, land use and land cover in the study area comprise a complex landscape mix of agricultural, livestock, and forestry activities. The potential environmental and social impacts associated with these activities add complexity to achieving a balance between economic development and the conservation of natural resources [59,61].

4.2. Selection of Independent Variables (Vegetation Indices)

The AFRI, EVI, and GNDVI indices showed the most significant correlation with aboveground biomass in our study area. The high observed correlations among vegetation indices and biomass are likely due to a combination of a broader range of spectral bands within the electromagnetic spectrum (middle- and near-infrared, red, green, and blue) required to retrieve these three vegetation indices from Sentinel-2 imagery, compared to other assessed indices in this analysis. The broader range of spectral bands increases their sensitivity to capture subtle vegetation variations and changes. Such sensitivity is crucial when using remotely sensed data, especially in ecotone regions that exhibit high vegetation variability and complexity.

The significant correlations observed between Green Reflectance (GREEN), as represented by the GNDVI (Green Normalized Difference Vegetation Index), and biomass in the study area can be attributed to variations in chlorophyll and anthocyanin content in the leaves [62]. These factors are closely related to vegetation development and maturity [62]. The Green Vegetation Index (GVI) and the Green Normalized Difference Vegetation Index (GNDVI), derived from reflectance equations, exhibit stronger correlations with nitrogen content in forest biomass leaves compared to the Ratio Vegetation Index (RVI) and the Red Normalized Difference Vegetation Index (RNDVI), indicating a greater sensitivity to variations in vegetation [63]. The combination of green and infrared bands plays an important role in aboveground biomass analysis, serving as critical descriptors in this index and providing dependable and precise information on biomass quantities at specific locations [64].

The use of the Near-Infrared (NIR) and Shortwave Spectrum (SWIR) bands in calculating the AFRI index has demonstrated efficiency in monitoring vegetation water content and dry biomass, particularly in regions with sparse vegetation [65]. Moreover, the AFRI index showed a stronger correlation with biomass in the study area located within an ecotone region between forest and savanna.

Commonly used vegetation indices such as NDVI and EVI have been applied worldwide to assess vegetation health. However, these indices are influenced by various factors, including terrain topography [66]. Our study showed that the soil adjustment factor "L" may heavily impact EVI results compared to NDVI, making EVI more sensitive to topographical conditions. This sensitivity is particularly critical in hilly terrain, where topographic effects can significantly affect vegetation indices with a simple band-ratio format, such as NDVI.

The choice of satellites for spectral data collection can influence the accuracy of biomass estimation. Nevertheless, our analysis found that Sentinel-2 satellite images were suitable for our study. The authors of [67] reported that the quality of MSI/Sentinel-2 sensor images, particularly in bands with a 10 m resolution, highlights the utility of this satellite for vegetation assessment research, especially when compared to aerial sensors with a spatial resolution of 0.13 m.

4.3. Training the Neural Networks

Our results indicate that the trained Artificial Neural Networks (ANNs) showed a satisfactory fit and high-accuracy statistics. The correlation coefficient (R) consistently equaled or exceeded 0.9, and the root mean square estimation (RMSE) errors remained below 14%. Among the five trained networks, Network 1 outperformed the others with an R^2 of 0.94 and an RMSE% of 10.76, making it a promising choice for the intended application. These findings underscore the feasibility of biomass estimation through remote sensing in natural forests.

The use of ANNs is effective in estimating biomass per unit area and does not require the basic assumptions of conventional mathematical modeling, such as normality and linearity of forest attributes [68]. These attributes often require various mathematical transformations for traditional modeling, which can result in lower model quality and selection capability, leading to biased and less accurate estimates of the variable of interest.

The authors of [68] also yielded positive results in estimating the components of total biomass, with an R^2 of 0.97 and an RMSE% of 25.04. Furthermore, the simulation of terrain elevation data along ICESat-2 and Landsat satellite profiles demonstrated significant potential for generating a forest biomass estimation product, achieving an R^2 of 0.66 [69].

These results align with the findings of our research, highlighting the robust performance of the models developed for tree biomass estimation. To assess the predictive capacity of the selected Artificial Neural Network, we examined the relationship between observed and predicted values. When analyzing the distribution of ANN errors, we observed that most errors fell within the −1.5% to −12% and 0% to 10% ranges. Additionally, errors exceeding the ±16% threshold were infrequent. Moreover, it was determined that a training dataset size of approximately 60 subplots or fewer was sufficient to achieve a good fit with the linear functional model.

5. Conclusions

Our research findings indicate that the combination of various vegetation indices integrating different spectral bands, such as EVI, AFRI, and GNDVI, with a Multilayer Perceptron Artificial Neural Network has led to more efficient and precise estimation of aboveground biomass in our study area. This approach facilitated the generation of high-resolution biomass distribution maps and provided a cost-effective and time-saving alternative to traditional forest inventories. Accurate estimates of forest biomass are crucial for understanding vegetation dynamics and ecological processes, as well as for formulating effective forest resource management policies. Additionally, our study results are valuable for forest biomass monitoring, including the assessment of environmental services and the formulation of conservation strategies for protected areas and indigenous territories. The advanced knowledge of forest biomass can also support sustainable forest management practices and enable the prediction of impacts of land use and land cover changes on forest biomass. Alternative approaches, such as deep learning and machine learning methods, could prove effective for estimating aboveground biomass in tropical regions and should be explored in future research endeavors.

Author Contributions: Conceptualization: L.D.d.F., E.A.T.M., B.H.M.J. and E.P.M.; methodology and validation: L.D.d.F., E.A.T.M., B.H.M.J., B.S.M., E.P.M. and O.L.F.d.C.; biomass data provision: B.H.M.J., B.S.M., E.A.d.O. and N.C.C.d.S.P.; formal analysis, L.D.d.F., E.A.T.M., B.S.M. and E.P.M.; investigation and data curation: L.D.d.F., E.A.T.M., B.S.M., E.P.M., O.L.F.d.C., E.A.d.O. and N.C.C.d.S.P.; writing—preparation of original draft: L.D.d.F. and E.A.T.M.; writing—review and editing: L.D.d.F., E.A.T.M., B.H.M.J., B.S.M., E.P.M. and O.L.F.d.C. All authors have read and agreed to the published version of the manuscript.

Funding: This research was funded by the National Council for Scientific and Technological Development (CNPq), Grants n. 401892/2021-2 e n. 311155/2020-0.

Data Availability Statement: The dataset will be available under direct request to the corresponding author.

Acknowledgments: This work is the result of the collaboration between the University of Brasilia (UnB) and the State University of Mato Grosso (UEMAT). The authors would like to thank these institutions for providing material and technical support for this study to be a success and Google Earth Engine for providing access to Sentinel-2 imagery and cloud processing. Our sincere thanks to the anonymous reviewers and members of the editorial team for their comments and contributions.

Conflicts of Interest: The authors declare no conflicts of interest. The funders had no role in the design of the study; in the collection, analyses, or interpretation of data; in the writing of the manuscript; or in the decision to publish the results.

References

1. Lima, S.K.R.; Coêlho, A.G.; Lucarini, M.; Durazzo, A.; Arcanjo, D.D.R. The *Platonia insignis* Mart. as the Promising Brazilian 'Amazon Gold': The State-of-the-Art and Prospects. *Agriculture* **2022**, *12*, 1827. [CrossRef]
2. Marques, E.Q.; Marimon-Junior, B.H.; Marimon, B.S.; Matricardi, E.A.T.; Mews, H.A.; Colli, G.R. Redefining the Cerrado–Amazonia transition: Implications for conservation. *Biodivers. Conserv.* **2020**, *29*, 1501–1517. [CrossRef]
3. Ratter, J.A.; Richards, P.W.; Argent, G.; Gifford, D.R. Observations on the vegetation of northeastern Mato Grosso: I. The woody vegetation types of the Xavantina-Cachimbo Expedition area. *Philos. Trans. R. Soc. Lond. Ser. B Biol. Sci.* **1973**, *266*, 449–492.
4. Marimon, B.S.; Lima, E.D.S.; Duarte, T.G.; Chieregatto, L.C.; Ratter, J.A. Observations on the vegetation of northeastern Mato Grosso, Brazil. IV. An analysis of the Cerrado-Amazonian Forest ecotone. *Edinb. J. Bot.* **2006**, *63*, 323–341. [CrossRef]
5. Balch, J.K.; Nepstad, D.C.; Curran, L.M.; Brando, P.M.; Portela, O.; Guilherme, P.; Reuning-Scherer, J.D.; de Carvalho, O. Size, species, and fire behavior predict tree and liana mortality from experimental burns in the Brazilian Amazon. *For. Ecol. Manag.* **2011**, *261*, 68–77. [CrossRef]
6. MAPBIOMAS. News: In 38 Years, Brazil Has Lost 15% of Its Natural Forests. Available online: https://brasil.mapbiomas.org/en/noticias/ (accessed on 8 March 2024).
7. Nogueira, D.S.; Marimon, B.S.; Marimon-Junior, B.H.; Oliveira, E.A.; Morandi, P.; Reis, S.M.; Elias, F.; Neves, E.C.; Feldpausch, T.R.; Lloyd, J.; et al. Impacts of Fire on Forest Biomass Dynamics at the Southern Amazon Edge. *Environ. Conserv.* **2019**, *46*, 285–292. [CrossRef]
8. Brown, S.; Sathaye, J.; Cannell, M.; Kauppi, P.E. Mitigation of carbon emissions to the atmosphere by forest management. *Commonw. For. Rev.* **1996**, *75*, 80–91.
9. Houghton, R.A.; Hall, F.; Goetz, S.J. Importance of biomass in the global carbon cycle. *J. Geophys. Res. Biogeosci.* **2009**, *114*. [CrossRef]
10. Lu, D. Aboveground biomass estimation using Landsat TM data in the Brazilian Amazon. *Int. J. Remote Sens.* **2005**, *26*, 2509–2525. [CrossRef]
11. Li, Y.; Li, M.; Li, C.; Liu, Z. Forest aboveground biomass estimation using Landsat 8 and Sentinel-1A data with machine learning algorithms. *Sci. Rep.* **2020**, *10*, 9952. [CrossRef]
12. Matricardi, E.A.T.; Skole, D.L.; Pedlowski, M.A.; Chomentowski, W.; Fernandes, L.C. Assessment of tropical forest degradation by selective logging and fire using Landsat imagery. *Remote Sens. Environ.* **2010**, *114*, 1117–1129. [CrossRef]
13. Silva, F. Sensoriamento Remoto para Detecção de Queimadas no Cerrado Maranhense: Uma Aplicação no Parque Estadual do Mirador. *Rev. Geogr. Acad.* **2019**, *13*, 90–105.
14. Hall, R.J.; Skakun, R.S.; Arsenault, E.J.; Case, B.S. Modeling forest stand structure attributes using Landsat ETM+ data: Application to mapping of aboveground biomass and stand volume. *For. Ecol. Manag.* **2006**, *225*, 378–390. [CrossRef]
15. Powell, S.L.; Cohen, W.B.; Healey, S.P.; Kennedy, R.E.; Moisen, G.G.; Pierce, K.B.; Ohmann, J.L. Quantification of live aboveground forest biomass dynamics with Landsat time-series and field inventory data: A comparison of empirical modeling approaches. *Remote Sens. Environ.* **2010**, *114*, 1053–1068. [CrossRef]
16. Dube, T.; Mutanga, O. Evaluating the utility of the medium-spatial resolution Landsat 8 multispectral sensor in quantifying aboveground biomass in uMgeni catchment, South Africa. *ISPRS J. Photogramm. Remote Sens.* **2015**, *101*, 36–46. [CrossRef]
17. Fremout, T.; De Vinatea, J.C.; Thomas, E.; Huaman-Zambrano, W.; Salazar-Villegas, M.; la Fuente, D.L.D.; Bernardino, P.N.; Atkinson, R.; Csaplovics, E.; Muys, B. Site-specific scaling of remote sensing-based estimates of woody cover and aboveground biomass for mapping long-term tropical dry forest degradation status. *Remote Sens. Environ.* **2022**, *276*, 113040. [CrossRef]
18. Xiao, X.; Zhang, Q.; Braswell, B.; Urbanski, S.; Boles, S.; Wofsy, S.; Moore, B., III; Ojima, D. Modeling gross primary production of temperate deciduous broadleaf forest using satellite images and climate data. *Remote Sens. Environ.* **2004**, *91*, 256–270. [CrossRef]
19. Patel, N.R.; Pandya, M.R.; Patel, N.K. Estimation of Biomass of Wheat Using Vegetation Indices. *Int. J. Curr. Microbiol. Appl. Sci.* **2016**, *5*, 288–296.
20. Song, X.; Li, L.; Zhuo, W.; Wu, C. Estimating forest aboveground biomass by combining Landsat and MODIS data: A case study for the Sierra National Forest, California, USA. *Remote Sens.* **2014**, *6*, 2107–2136.
21. Chen, X.; Yang, K.; Ma, J.; Jiang, K.; Gu, X.; Peng, L. Aboveground biomass inversion based on Object-Oriented Classification and Pearson-mRMR-Machine Learning Model. *Remote Sens.* **2024**, *16*, 1537. [CrossRef]
22. Lyu, G.; Wang, X.; Huang, X.; Xu, J.; Li, S.; Cui, G.; Huang, H. Toward a more robust estimation of forest biomass Carbon stock and Carbon Sink in mountainous region: A case study in Tibet, China. *Remote Sens.* **2024**, *16*, 1481. [CrossRef]
23. Costa, A.C.; Pinto, J.R.; Miguel, E.P.; Xavier, G.D.; Marimon, B.H.; Aparecido Trondoli Matricardi, E. Artificial intelligence tools and vegetation indices combined to estimate aboveground biomass in tropical forests. *J. Appl. Remote Sens.* **2023**, *17*, 024512. [CrossRef]
24. Tian, L.; Wu, X.; Tao, Y.; Li, M.; Qian, C.; Liao, L.; Fu, W. Review of remote sensing-based methods for forest aboveground biomass estimation: Progress, challenges, and prospects. *Forests* **2023**, *14*, 1086. [CrossRef]
25. Novo, E.; Ferreira, L.G.; Barbosa, C.; Carvalho, C.; Sano, E.E.; Shimabukuro, Y.E.; Miura, T. Advanced remote sensing techniques for global changes and Amazon ecosystem functioning studies. *Acta Amaz.* **2005**, *35*, 259–272. [CrossRef]
26. Bertier, F.; Silva, R.; Nora, G. Fire in the Woods, Danger for Real? Community Considerations About Using Fire in the Cerrado of Mato Grosso. *Rev. Rencima Edição Espec.* **2020**, *11*, 144–157.

27. Ivanauskas, M.M.; Ivanauskas, N.M.; Monteiro, R.; Rodrigues, R.R. Composição florística de trechos florestais na borda sul-amazônica. *Acta Amaz.* **2004**, *34*, 399–413. [CrossRef]
28. BRASIL Ministério das Minas e Energia, Secretaria Geral. *Projeto RADAMBRASIL—Levantamento dos Recursos Naturais;* Folha SB.21—Araguaia e Folha SC-22—Tocantins, geologia, geomorfologia, pedologia, vegetação e uso potencial da terra; BRASIL Ministério das Minas e Energia: Rio de Janeiro, RJ, Brazil, 1974; p. 552.
29. Peel, M.C.; Finlayson, B.L.; McMahon, T.A. Updated world map of the Köppen-Geiger climate classification. *Hydrol. Earth Syst. Sci.* **2007**, *11*, 1633–1644. [CrossRef]
30. Brasil, L.S.; Batista, J.D.; Giehl NF, D.S.; Valadão MB, X.; Santos JO, D.; Dias-Silva, K. Integridade ambiental e composição de espécies de libelinhas em riachos amazônicos na região do "arco do desmatamento", Mato Grosso, Brasil. *Acta Limnol. Bras.* **2014**, *26*, 278–287. [CrossRef]
31. IBGE—Brazilian Institute of Geography and Stastistic. Downloads—Geociências. Available online: https://www.ibge.gov.br/geociencias/downloads-geociencias.html (accessed on 13 April 2023).
32. Baker, T.R.; Phillips, O.L.; Malhi, Y.; Almeida, S.; Arroyo, L.; Di Fiore, A.; Erwin, T.; Killeen, T.J.; Laurance, S.G.; Laurance, W.F.; et al. Variation in wood density determines spatial patterns in Amazonian Forest biomass. *Glob. Change Biol.* **2004**, *10*, 545–562. [CrossRef]
33. Peacock, J.; Baker, T.R.; Lewis, S.L.; Lopez-Gonzalez, G.; Phillips, O.L. The RAINFOR database: Monitoring forest biomass and dynamics. *J. Veg. Sci.* **2007**, *18*, 535–542. Available online: https://www.jstor.org/stable/4499259 (accessed on 5 February 2024). [CrossRef]
34. Chave, J.; Muller-Landau, H.C.; Baker, T.R.; Easdale, T.A.; Ter Steege, H.; Webb, C.O. Regional and phylogenetic variation of wood density across 2456 neotropical tree species. *Ecol. Appl.* **2006**, *16*, 2356–2367. [CrossRef] [PubMed]
35. Rezende, A.; Vale, A.D.; Sanquetta, C.R.; Figueiredo Filho, A.; Felfili, J.M. Comparação de modelos matemáticos para estimativa do volume biomassa e estoque de carbono da vegetação lenhosa de um cerrado sensu stricto em Brasília, D.F. *Sci. For.* **2006**, *71*, 65 76.
36. Curran, P.J.; Dungan, J.L.; Gholz, H.L. Exploring the Relationship Between Reflectance Red Edge and Chlorophyll Content in Slash Pine. *Tree Physiol.* **1990**, *7*, 33–48. [CrossRef] [PubMed]
37. ESA—European Space Agency. Sentinel Overview. Available online: https://sentinel.esa.int/web/sentinel/missions (accessed on 3 January 2023).
38. Rouse, J.W., Jr.; Haas, R.H.; Schell, J.A.; Deering, D.W. Monitoring vegetation systems in the Great Plains with ETRS. In Proceedings of the Third Earth Resources Technology Satellite-1 Symposium., Washington, DC, USA, 10–14 December 1973; Paper A-20, pp. 309–317.
39. Jensen, J.R. *Remote Sensing of the Environment: An Earth Resource Perspective 2/e*; Pearson Education India: Bangalore, India, 2009.
40. Huete, A.; Didan, K.; Miura, T.; Rodriguez, E.P.; Gao, X.; Ferreira, L.G. Overview of the radiometric and biophysical performance of the MODIS vegetation indices. *Remote Sens. Environ.* **2002**, *83*, 195–213. [CrossRef]
41. Yan, E.; Wang, G.; Lin, H.; Xia, C.; Sun, H. Phenology-based classification of vegetation cover types in Northeast China using MODIS NDVI and EVI time series. Rev. *Int. J. Remote Sens.* **2015**, *36*, 489–512. [CrossRef]
42. Jiang, Z.; Huete, A.; Didan, K.; Miura, T. Development of a two-band enhanced vegetation index without a blue band. *Remote Sens. Environ.* **2008**, *112*, 3833–3845. [CrossRef]
43. Gitelson, A.A.; Kaufman, Y.J.; Merzlyak, M.N. Use of a green channel in remote sensing of global vegetation from EOS-MODIS. *Remote Sens. Environ.* **1996**, *58*, 289–298. [CrossRef]
44. Karnieli, A.; Bayasgalan, M.; Bayarjargal, Y.; Agam, N.; Khudulmur, S.; Tucker, C.J.; Zhang, X. Use of NDVI and land surface temperature for drought assessment: Merits and limitations. *J. Clim.* **2001**, *14*, 2833–2845. [CrossRef]
45. Huete, A.R. A Soil-Adjusted Vegetation Index (SAVI). *Remote Sens. Environ.* **1988**, *25*, 295–309. [CrossRef]
46. Qi, J.; Chehbouni, A.; Huete, A.R.; Kerr, Y.H.; Sorooshian, S. A modified soil-adjusted vegetation index. *Remote Sens. Environ.* **1994**, *48*, 119–126. [CrossRef]
47. Barnes, E.M.; Clarke, T.R.; Richards, S.E.; Colaizzi, P.D.; Haberland, J.; Kostrzewski, M.; Waller, P.; Choi, C.; Riley, E.; Thompson, T.; et al. Coincident detection of crop water stress, nitrogen status and canopy density using ground based multispectral data. In Proceedings of the Fifth International Conference on Precision Agriculture, Bloomington, MN, USA, 16–19 July 2000; Robert, P.C., Ed.; ASA: Madison, WI, USA, 2000.
48. Kang, Y.; Hu, X.; Meng, Q.; Zou, Y.; Zhang, L.; Liu, M.; Zhao, M. Land cover and crop classification based on red edge indices features of GF-6 WFV time series data. *Remote Sens.* **2021**, *13*, 4522. [CrossRef]
49. STATSOFT. Comparativo de Versões do Software Statistica. Available online: http://www.statsoft.com.br/ftp/COMP_VERS_STATISTICA.pdf (accessed on 20 March 2023).
50. Carrijo, J.V.N.; Miguel, E.; Vale, A.T.D.; Matricardi, E.; Monteiro, T.; Rezende, A.; Inkotte, J. Artificial intelligence associated with satellite data in predicting energy potential in the Brazilian savanna woodland area. *Iforest-Biogeosci. For.* **2020**, *13*, 48. [CrossRef]
51. Guerrout, E.H.; Ait-Aoudia, S.; Michelucci, D.; Mahiou, R. Hidden Markov random field model and Broyden–Fletcher–Goldfarb–Shanno algorithm for brain image segmentation. *J. Exp. Theor. Artif. Intell.* **2018**, *30*, n415–n427. [CrossRef]
52. Borsato, D.; Moreira, I.; Nobrega, M.M.; Moreira, M.B.; Dias, G.H.; Ferreira da Silva, R.S.D.S.; Bona, E. Aplicação de redes neurais artificiais na identificação de gasolinas adulteradas comercializadas na região de Londrina–Paraná. *Química Nova* **2009**, *32*, 2328–2332. [CrossRef]

53. Shiblee, M.; Chandra, B.; Kalra, P. Learning of geometric mean neuron model using resilient propagation algorithm. *Expert Syst. Appl.* **2010**, *37*, 7449–7455. [CrossRef]
54. Fischer, D.R.; Paixão, J.L.; Sausen, J.P.; Abaide, A.R. Previsão de Curto Prazo para Geração Fotovoltaica a partir de Dados Meteorológicos via RNA. In Proceedings of the Congresso Brasileiro de Automática—CBA, Porto Alegre, Brazil, 23–26 November 2020; Volume 2.
55. Binoti, M.L.M.S.; Binoti, D.H.B.; Leite, H.G. Aplicação de redes neurais artificiais para estimação da altura de povoamentos equiâneos de eucalipto. *Rev. Árvore* **2013**, *37*, 639–645. [CrossRef]
56. Bustamante, M.C.; Roitman, I.; Aide, T.M.; Alencar, A.; Anderson, L.O.; Aragão, L.; Asner, G.P.; Barlow, J.; Berenguer, E.; Chambers, J.; et al. Toward an integrated monitoring framework to assess the effects of tropical forest degradation and recovery on carbon stocks and biodiversity. *Glob. Change Biol.* **2016**, *22*, 92–109. [CrossRef]
57. Egrioglu, E.A.; Ufuk, Y.B.; Cagdas, H.A.; Eren, B. Recurrent Multiplicative Neuron Model Artificial Neural Network for Non-Linear Time Series Forecasting. *Procedia Soc. Behav. Sci.* **2014**, *109*, 1094–1100. [CrossRef]
58. Matricardi, E.A.T.; Skole, D.L.; Pedlowski, M.A.; Chomentowski, W. Assessment of forest disturbances by seletive logging and forest fires in the Brazilian Amazon using Landsat data. *Int. J. Remote Sens.* **2013**, *34*, 1057–1086. [CrossRef]
59. Santos, T. Os impactos do desmatamento e queimadas de origem antrópica sobre o clima da Amazônia brasileira: Um estudo de revisão. *Rev. Geográfica Acadêmica* **2017**, *11*, 157–181.
60. Scremin, A.P.; Kemerich, P.D.C. Impactos ambientais em propriedade rural de atividade mista. *Disc. Sci. Sér Ciências Nat. Tecnol. Santa Maria* **2010**, *11*, 126–148.
61. Silva, F.L.; Oliveira, F.D.A.; Amin, M.M.; Beltrão, N.E.S.; Sales de Andrade, V.M. Dimensões do Uso e Cobertura da Terra nas Mesorregiões do Estado do Pará. *Espacios* **2016**, *37*, 5.
62. Merzlyak, M.N.; Chivkunova, O.B.; Solovchenko, A.E.; Naqvi, K.R. Absorção de luz por antocianinas em folhas juvenis, estressadas e senescentes. *J. Exp. Bot.* **2008**, *59*, 3903–3911. [CrossRef] [PubMed]
63. Bronson, K.F.; Chua, T.T.; Booker, J.D.; Keeling, J.W.; Lascano, R.J. In-season nitrogen status sensing in irrigated cotton: II. *Leaf nitrogen and biomass. Soil Sci. Soc. Am. J.* **2003**, *67*, 1439–1448. [CrossRef]
64. Barrachina, M.; Cristóbal, J.; Tulla, A. Estimating above-ground biomass on mountain meadows and pastures through remote sensing. *Int. J. Appl. Earth Obs. Geoinf.* **2015**, *38*, 184–192. [CrossRef]
65. Huang, J.; Chen, D.; Cosh, M.H. Sub-pixel reflectance unmixing in estimating vegetation water content and dry biomass of corn and soybeans cropland using normalized difference water index (NDWI) from satellites. *Int. J. Remote Sens.* **2009**, *30*, 2075–2104. [CrossRef]
66. Matsushita, B.; Yang, W.; Chen, J.; Onda, Y.; Qiu, G. Sensitivity of the enhanced vegetation index (EVI) and normalized difference vegetation index (NDVI) to topographic effects: A case study in high-density cypress forest. *Sensors* **2007**, *7*, 2636–2651. [CrossRef]
67. Bollas, N.; Kokinou, E.; Polychronos, V. Comparison of sentinel-2 and UAV multispectral data for use in precision agriculture: An application from northern Greece. *Drones* **2021**, *5*, 35. [CrossRef]
68. Güner, Ş.T.; Diamantopoulou, M.J.; Poudel, K.P.; Çömez, A.; Özçelik, R. Employing artificial neural networks for effective biomass prediction: An alternative approach. *Comput. Electron. Agric.* **2022**, *192*, 106596. [CrossRef]
69. Narine, L.L.; Popescu, S.C.; Malambo, L. Synergy of ICESat-2 and Landsat for mapping forest aboveground biomass with deep learning. *Remote Sens.* **2019**, *11*, 1503. [CrossRef]

forests

MDPI

Article

Thinning Effects on Aboveground Biomass Increments in Both the Overstory and Understory of Masson Pine Forests

Feng Liu [1,*], Xiaolin Liu [1], Mengyuan Zeng [2], Jianjun Li [2] and Chang Tan [3]

1 Key Laboratory for Digital Dongting Lake Basin of Hunan Province, Central South University of Forestry and Technology, Changsha 410004, China; 20211100043@csuft.edu.cn
2 College of Computer Science and Mathematics, Central South University of Forestry and Technology, Changsha 410004, China; 20231200610@csuft.edu.cn (M.Z.); lijianjun_21@csuft.edu.cn (J.L.)
3 College of Economics, Central South University of Forestry and Technology, Changsha 410004, China; t20040853@csuft.edu.cn
* Correspondence: liufeng0808@csuft.edu.cn

Abstract: Masson pine (*Pinus massoniana* Lamb.) is a tree species that is widely distributed throughout southern China and holds significant economic and ecological value. The main objective of our study was to assess the effects of thinning on aboveground biomass increments and tree diversity in both the overstory and understory. Additionally, the underlying factors and mechanisms responsible for driving changes in biomass increment were analyzed. Four different thinning treatments (control, light thinning, moderate thinning, and heavy thinning) were implemented in 214 plots (~1800 tree ha^{-1}) in three Masson pine forests in Hunan Province, China. A robustly designed experiment was used with over six years of repeated measurements. The differences in biomass increment and tree diversity among the different treatments were compared using repeated measures ANOVAs. The Mantel test was used to determine environmental metrics correlated with biomass increments across tree strata. Structural equation modeling was utilized to explore the multivariate relationships among site environment, tree diversity, and post-treatment biomass increment. The results indicated that thinning overall increased biomass increment, the Shannon index, and the Gini index, while decreasing the Dominance index over time. Moderate thinning (25%–35% of trees removed) was found to promote overstory biomass increment to 9.72 $Mg \cdot ha^{-1} \cdot a^{-1}$ and understory biomass increment to 1.43 $Mg \cdot ha^{-1} \cdot a^{-1}$ six years post-thinning, which is significantly higher than that of other treatments. Environmental metrics such as light intensity, soil organic matter, and other soil physiochemical properties were positively correlated with biomass increments, and their effects on the overstory and understory differed. Structural equation modeling revealed that thinning treatments, environmental metrics, tree diversity, and their interactions could be the main drivers for biomass increments across tree strata. Specifically, thinning treatments, light intensity, and tree size diversity (Gini index) had significant effects on overstory biomass increment, while understory species richness (Shannon index) and soil organic matter affected understory biomass increment. In conclusion, moderate thinning is an effective silvicultural treatment for stimulating biomass increments of both the overstory and understory in Masson pine forests in southern China if a middle period (e.g., six years) is considered. Some factors, such as species richness, tree size diversity, and environmental metrics (e.g., light and soil), are suggested for consideration to improve the efficiency of thinning.

Keywords: thinning; biomass increment; tree strata; environmental metrics; tree diversity; Masson pine forests

1. Introduction

Masson pine (*Pinus massoniana* Lamb.) covers a total of 1.13 million hectares in China's subtropical zone, and it plays key roles in the development of the ecology and society due to its wide distribution and ability to grow and regenerate naturally [1,2]. Masson pine can form mixed conifer forests with companion species, which contributes to vegetation cover, soil and water conservation, and carbon balance [3]. Several national policies have been established to maintain the quality and stability of Masson pine forests [4]. However, most Masson pine forests at our study sites are middle-aged or nearly mature, and the protection (banning logging) strategy alone may not be sufficient for sustaining ecological service functions, biodiversity, and productivity, as well as enhancing resistance to disease and natural disturbances [5]; in such cases, thinning treatment might be warranted. Thinning is an important silvicultural activity that was initially used for commercial timber production but is now increasingly used for sustainable forest management [6]. Thinning improves tree growth and biomass productivity by regulating the growth space and microsite environment [7,8]. However, its effects in Masson pine forests are far from conclusive, particularly concerning thinning intensity, community response, and assessment methods [9].

Thinning intensity is an important factor in determining the effectiveness of thinning treatment. Some studies have reported that thinning tree cover to approximately 40%–60% can improve overstory biomass in Masson pine forests and other pine forests [2]. However, others have suggested that thinning intensities should be within 30%–40%, considering understory regeneration [10]. If thinning intensity is light, the benefits may be temporary and primarily affect the overstory rather than the understory. Conversely, excessive thinning can substantially alter environmental conditions, reduce seed sources, and suppress understory regeneration [11]. In some cases, although moderate thinning is potentially optimal, the observed effect may be weaker than expected, which can be due to various factors such as site-specific environmental conditions and follow-up treatments [12,13]. In light of these findings and the emerging situations regarding the increasing development potential of Masson pine forests, there is a need for ongoing observations and assessments of the effectiveness of various thinning intensities [14,15].

Some studies have reported that thinning reduces overstory trees, thus increasing sunlight availability and providing more water and mineral nutrients for the forest ecosystem [16,17]. These processes can promote the growth of tree height and DBH, alleviate interspecies competition, and stimulate the biomass increments of both the overstory and understory [18,19], although on occasions some authors have found that there was no such response [9,20]. For example, Liu et al. [21] reported that increased sunlight availability enhances aboveground biomass or productivity for the overstory in pine forests in southern China while simultaneously increasing underground biomass for the understory. Reports have indicated that snow disturbances significantly influence tree growth in managed forests with varying thinning intensities [22]. This influence is primarily reflected across different forest strata. While the overstory and understory are the most common strata in Masson pine forests, there is limited research on how their biomass increments relate to different site-specific environmental metrics.

Furthermore, tree species composition and forest structure are also important for post-treatment productivity or biomass increment [23,24]. Some studies have suggested that environmental metrics not only directly affect biomass increment but also indirectly influence it by shaping the diversity of tree composition and size [25]. This is a complex process, and we are still unclear about how environmental metrics, tree diversity, and their interactions affect biomass increment after thinning. The multivariate productivity–diversity hypothesis [26,27] provides us with insights, as biomass increment is a crucial component of productivity. This hypothesis has been validated at both the plot and landscape levels [28,29], but the majority of evidence comes from natural stands [30], with only a few empirical analyses of managed forests having been conducted to date. Thus, it is worthwhile to consider the effects of thinning on biomass increment within the context of this hypothesis when formulating forest management strategies.

Previous studies have utilized meta-analysis methods to assess the impact of thinning on forest biomass [6,9,16], but their findings varied due to several limitations. First, most of these meta-analyses have been conducted using data from a single research site, with little consideration given to situations across multiple sites, limiting their ability to provide a comprehensive assessment of the response patterns of post-treatment biomass change. Second, most studies directly analyze the relationship between site environment and biomass using sampled data, despite potential issues such as small sample sizes, non-normal distributions, and autocorrelation. Some studies have shown that utilizing the Mantel test with similarity matrices could improve the accuracy and interpretability of correlation analysis, avoiding result biases [28]. Third, most studies have considered the effects of factors such as thinning intensity, site environment, and species diversity on post-treatment recovery while ignoring how their interactions affect biomass increment. A simple emphasis on the effectiveness of a single observed variable may be biased, as it overlooks the causal relationships among variables, including direct and indirect effects. This approach fails to comprehensively reveal the underlying mechanisms. Therefore, it is necessary to conduct further studies on the effects of thinning on biomass increment using suitable assessment methods.

In this study, we asked the following questions: how does thinning treatment influence biomass increments of both the overstory and understory over time? What are the underlying mechanisms of these effects? Our hypotheses are detailed below. (1) The moderate thinning should have the greatest potential to promote biomass increments and tree diversity in both the overstory and understory over time. (2) The environmental metrics such as light availability and soil physiochemical properties would be correlated with biomass increments, and their effects on the overstory and understory would differ. (3) Thinning treatments, environmental metrics, tree diversity, and their interactions would be the main drivers of biomass increments, with the driving mechanisms potentially differing between the overstory and understory.

2. Materials and Methods

2.1. Site Description

This study utilized three Masson pine sites that were established in Pingjiang, Anhua, and Huitong in Hunan Province, China (Figure 1; Table 1). These sites experience a humid subtropical climate with a hot summer, and the average daily temperatures range from 4.2 °C in January to 30.5 °C in July. The mean annual precipitation is between 1300 and 1800 mm, and 60%–70% of the precipitation falls during the growing season (April to September). Average daily solar radiation in the growing season is between 14.5 and 16.5 MJ/m^2. The soils of the three sites are classified as a mountain yellow-red soil derived from granite parent material, with an average pH ranging from 4.7 to 5.9. The soil has a shallow A horizon (approximately 20 cm), but the soil profile extends from 100 cm to more than 150 cm in depth before reaching fractured granite bedrock.

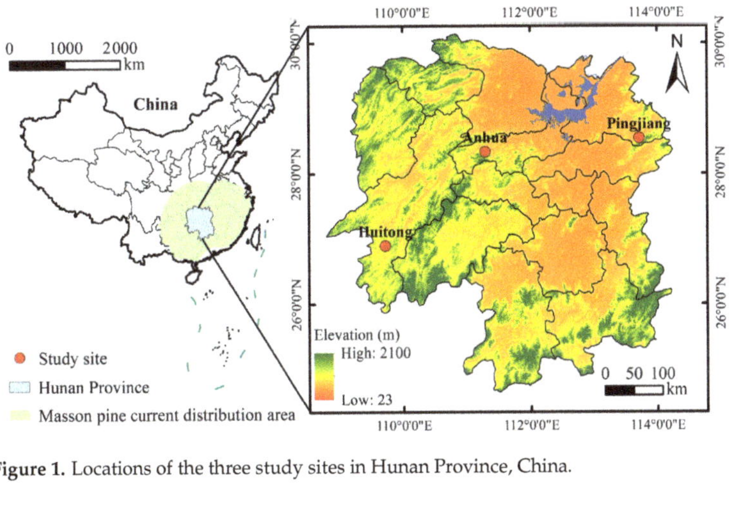

Figure 1. Locations of the three study sites in Hunan Province, China.

Table 1. Site description of the three Masson pine forests in Hunan Province, China.

Site	Pingjiang	Anhua	Huitong
Location	28°25′ N, 113°10′ E	27°44′ N, 111°58′ E	26°88′ N, 109°73′ E
Average annual temperature (°C)	16.8	16.2	17.1
Average annual precipitation (mm)	1450.8	1706.1	1361.2
Average daily solar radiation (MJ/m^2)	15.4	16.3	14.8
Soil organic matter content ($g \cdot kg^{-1}$)	21.61	24.09	23.74
Elevation (m, a.s.l.)	750	600	650
Aspect	SW	W	SW
Stand age	24	22	22
Overstory density (stems ha^{-1})	1750	1820	1860
Understory density (stems ha^{-1})	2280	2150	1975

All sites are artificially seeded Masson pine forests on timber-harvesting patches that were established in the 1990s. The forests were initially planted at a density of approximately 2300 stems ha^{-1}. Forest tending was conducted first in 2010 to improve the natural regeneration and growth of the remaining trees. The stand age ranged from 21 to 24 years (middle-aged). *P. massoniana* dominated the overstory (≥4 m tall and ≥5 cm diameter at breast height [DBH]) in the stand, and other tree species such as *Sassafras tzumu* (Hemsl.) Hemsl. and *S. superba* (*Schima superba* Gardn. et Champ.) were identified. Understory (<4 m tall) tree species mainly comprised Chinese fir (*Cunninghamia lanceolata* (Lamb.) Hook), *Cinnamomum camphora*, *Quercus glauca*, and *Castanopsis sclerophylla*. The overstory density ranged from 1750 to 1860 stems ha^{-1}, while the understory density ranged from 1975 to 2280 stems ha^{-1}. At the beginning of the experiment (2016), an initial field survey was conducted in these sites to determine homogeneity in composition, structure, and physiography.

2.2. Experimental Design

The experiment was conducted in a completely randomized block design with subsampling. Six blocks (replicates) were established adjacent to each other in reasonably uniform stand conditions in Pingjiang. Four blocks were established in Anhua and Huitong, respectively. Each block was repeatedly subdivided into four rows of rectangular subsampling units. Each subsampling unit was randomly assigned four treatment plots (20 m × 20 m): heavy thinning (HT, 35%–45% of the trees by number were removed), moderate thinning (MT, 25%–35% of the trees by number were removed), light thinning (LT, 10%–25% of the trees by number were removed), and control (CK). A total of 214 plots were established, including 93 in Pingjiang, 60 in Anhua, and 61 in Huitong. For instance, the schematic diagram of the experimental treatments in the Pingjiang field trial is shown in Figure 2.

The selective thinning strategy followed the nature-approximating management guidelines in the NFA [31], a national management publication aimed at converting even-aged pine forests into all-sized stands and enhancing forest vigor and quality. To determine which trees to cut, we first used Voronoi diagrams to partition the nearest-neighbor region of individual trees [32]; we then established the spatial relationship among trees within each plot. Trading off these structure indexes at the stand scale by marking individual trees with potential cutting requirements was an iterative process [33], in which the upper and lower limits of the residual basal area (according to the treatment assigned to that plot) were constraints [34]. In practice, priority for cutting was given to dominant trees that would be expected to damage their neighbors, suppressed trees with exceptionally poor form, trees with clumpy distributions, dead trees, or trees with minimal ecological potential. According to previous studies suggesting that the minimum residual basal area be approximately 15 to 22 m^2 ha^{-1} for pine forests [35], we determined the residual basal area for HT (15.17 $m^2 \cdot ha^{-1}$), MT (20.48 $m^2 \cdot ha^{-1}$), and LT (22.05 $m^2 \cdot ha^{-1}$). To reduce damage to understory individuals, trees were carefully felled using felling machinery so that they fell outside of the plots; the portions of the boles inside the perimeter of plots were removed manually.

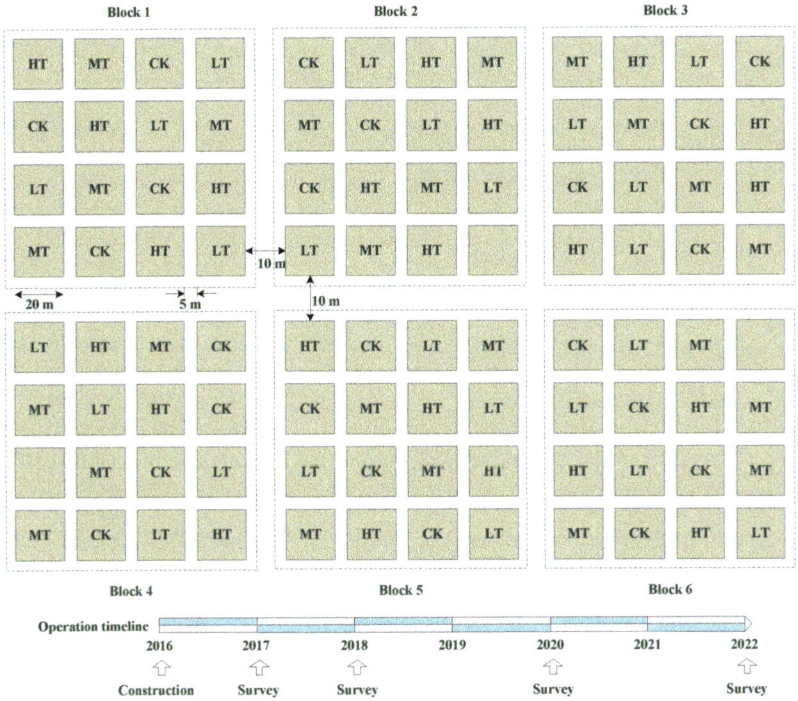

Figure 2. A schematic diagram of the experimental treatments in Pingjiang. The experiment has four types of treatments as follows: 22 heavy thinning (HT), 24 moderate thinning (MT), 24 light thinning (LT), and 23 control (CK). Unmarked plots are unsuitable for thinning. The site was established in October 2016. Subsequent surveys were made in August 2017, July 2018, July 2020, and August 2022.

2.3. Field Investigation

In 214 plots, trees were identified, and the density, diameter at breast height, and basal area were tallied. A total of 189 sampled trees were allocated as evenly as possible among diameter classes in the four treatments (HT, MT, LT, and CK). After a sample tree was felled, diameter at breast height and height were measured, and the stem, branches, and foliage were collected. Materials were dried at 70 °C for at least 72 h or until a constant dry weight was obtained; they were then added together to obtain the total aboveground biomass of each tree. Tree metrics were collected one month before and after thinning (September 2016 and November 2016, respectively) to account for the stand characteristics of pre- and post-thinning treatments (Table 2). The subsequent surveys were conducted in August 2017, July 2018, July 2020, and August 2022, corresponding to the years following the thinning process (years 1, 2, 4, and 6, respectively). *F*-tests were also used to confirm the homogeneity of stand characteristics before thinning. We calculated the aboveground biomass and annual biomass increments using the following method:

$$\mathrm{OBI} = AGB_{o(T)} - AGB_{o(T-1)} \quad (1)$$

$$\mathrm{UBI} = AGB_{u(T)} - AGB_{u(T-1)} \quad (2)$$

$$\mathrm{AGB_o} = f(dbh, h) \times D \quad (3)$$

$$AGB_u = f(d, h) \times D \quad (4)$$

where OBI and UBI are the annual biomass increments ($Mg{\cdot}ha^{-1}{\cdot}a^{-1}$) in the overstory and understory, respectively. T is the current survey year and $T - 1$ is the previous survey year. AGB_o and AGB_u are the tree aboveground biomass in the overstory and understory, respectively. f is the tree allometric growth model (Table S1) used to calculate individual tree biomass (kg), dbh is tree diameter at breast height (cm), h is tree height (m), d is ground diameter (cm), and D is stand density ($N{\cdot}ha^{-1}$).

Stand environment metrics were collected in July and August 2022 (post-thinning year 6). In each plot, the light intensity was measured using black thermopile-based pyranometers (LP02; Hukseflux, Delft, The Netherlands), and soil moisture was measured using thermistors (105T; Campbell, Logan, UT, USA). The light intensity was measured at 15 min intervals, and soil moisture was measured every 30 min, with hourly averages recorded, from 8:00 to 18:00 h under sunny conditions. After removing the upper litter and organic layer, soil samples (0–20 cm depth) were randomly collected with an auger at nine points within each plot. Soil samples were then processed through 2 mm mesh sieves, pooled as mixed samples, and stored in a refrigerator at 4 °C for each plot. Soil pH was determined in a 1:2.5 soil/water suspension. Soil organic matter was determined using the potassium dichromate volumetric method. Soil total nitrogen (TN) was measured using the Kjeldahl method, and total phosphorous (TP) and total potassium (TK) were measured using the nitrification method. Available nitrogen (AN) was extracted from 10 g of fresh soil sample using 50 mL of 2 M KCL solution by shaking at 200 rpm for 1 h; it was then quantified using colorimetric methods. Available phosphorous (AP) was extracted by 0.5 M $NaHCO_3$ at pH 8.5 (Olsen method) and then was determined by spectrophotometry. Available potassium (AK) was determined using a flame photometer (FP6430; Inesa, Shanghai, China). More detailed information on the extraction procedures for measurements of soil physicochemical characteristics is provided in previous studies [36,37]. According to our field investigation and flora records, tree strata were analyzed in two height categories: overstory (≥4 m tall and ≥5 cm diameter at breast height [DBH]) and understory (<4 m). Tree metrics and environmental metrics in both the overstory and understory were measured six years post-thinning (Table 3).

2.4. Data Analyses

2.4.1. Biomass Increment and Tree Diversity

Replicate (e.g., a thinned plot or reference area within a block) means were considered random subsamples within each block. Repeated measures ANOVA was used to test the effects of treatment intensity, survey year, and their interactions on the variables, including biomass increment, Shannon index, Dominance index, and Gini index across tree strata. The biomass increments of plots were the absolute difference of replicated biomass means between the post-thinning initial value and the value in subsequent survey years (years 1, 2, 4, and 6). Shannon–Wiener's index (hereafter referred to as the Shannon index) was used to measure species richness. The Baker–Parker dominance index (hereafter referred to as the Dominance index) was used to measure the ratio of the basal area of the most abundant species to the total basal area per hectare [38]. Tree size diversity was characterized using the Gini index, which was used to estimate the diameter distribution; it is usually conceptualized as the area between the Lorenz curve and the diagonal line of absolute equality [39]. These variables were log-transformed to meet requirements for the normalization of residuals and homogeneity of variances. Post hoc pairwise comparisons (Bonferroni-corrected) were made when group differences were detected. Simple main-effects analysis was used when a significant interaction between thinning intensity and survey year was detected. p-values < 0.05 were regarded as statistically significant. Statistical analyses were performed using R version 4.2.0 [40]. The R "nlme" package was used for ANOVAs, and the "emmeans" package [41] was used for post hoc and simple main-effects tests.

Table 2. The basic characteristics (means (standard error [se])) of the plots before and after thinning treatments in Masson pine forests in Hunan, China.

		Before Thinning					After Thinning					Thinning Amount			
	Plots (P/A/H)	Density (N·ha^{-1})	Basal Area (m^2·ha^{-1})	DBH (cm)	Height (m)	Biomass (Mg·ha^{-1})	Density (N·ha^{-1})	Basal Area (m^2·ha^{-1})	DBH (cm)	Height (m)	Biomass (Mg·ha^{-1})	Tree (N·ha^{-1})	%	Biomass (Mg·ha^{-1})	%
HT	51 (22/14/15)	1790 (32.12)	26.39 (0.67)	13.7 (0.28)	10.8 (0.24)	63.13 (1.26)	882 (15.67)	15.17 (0.25)	14.8 (0.23)	10.9 (0.19)	37.69 (0.63)	908 (13.09)	50.7	25.44 (0.38)	40.3
MT	55 (24/15/16)	1785 (35.82)	27.09 (0.64)	13.9 (0.26)	10.6 (0.23)	62.98 (1.21)	1207 (21.93)	20.48 (0.41)	14.7 (0.23)	11.1 (0.22)	43.58 (0.82)	578 (8.41)	32.4	19.4 (0.27)	30.8
LT	57 (24/16/17)	1750 (31.08)	25.05 (0.63)	13.5 (0.27)	10.4 (0.23)	61.54 (1.24)	1354 (22.40)	22.05 (0.39)	14.4 (0.22)	10.8 (0.18)	48.99 (0.83)	396 (5.88)	22.6	12.5 (0.21)	20.4
CK	51 (23/15/13)	1809 (30.24)	27.07 (0.58)	13.8 (0.25)	10.2 (0.24)	63.46 (1.23)									
	F *	0.40	0.94	1.05	0.88	0.96									

* Critical value, $F_{0.05}(3210) = 2.648$. Abbreviations: P, Pingjiang, A, Anhua, H, Huitong.

Table 3. Biomass, tree metrics of overstory and understory, and environment metrics (means (standard error [se])) in post-thinning year 6 in Masson pine forests in Hunan, China.

	HT		MT		LT		CK	
	Mean	SE	Mean	SE	Mean	SE	Mean	SE
Overstory								
Aboveground biomass (Mg·ha^{-1})	74.79	1.57	91.18	1.48	93.59	1.51	107.48	1.49
Biomass increased (Mg·ha^{-1})	37.1	0.78	47.61	0.77	44.61	0.72	44.02	0.62
Biomass increment (Mg·ha^{-1}·a^{-1})	7.79	0.16	9.73	0.16	7.71	0.12	7.32	0.11
Shannon index	0.89	0.02	1.05	0.02	0.82	0.01	0.69	0.01
Dominance index	0.58	0.01	0.51	0.01	0.49	0.01	0.62	0.01
Gini index	0.55	0.01	0.57	0.01	0.43	0.01	0.36	0.01
Understory								
Aboveground biomass (Mg·ha^{-1})	6.87	0.13	7.31	0.12	5.12	0.09	4.51	0.07
Biomass increased (Mg·ha^{-1})	4.21	0.09	4.63	0.07	2.45	0.04	1.85	0.03
Biomass increment (Mg·ha^{-1}·a^{-1})	1.22	0.02	1.41	0.02	0.43	0.01	0.32	0.00
Shannon index	1.69	0.03	1.78	0.03	1.51	0.02	0.94	0.01
Dominance index	0.28	0.01	0.21	0.00	0.26	0.00	0.45	0.01
Gini index	0.44	0.01	0.45	0.01	0.43	0.01	0.42	0.01
Environment								
Light intensity (MJ·m^{-2}·d^{-1})	8.03	0.16	6.45	0.11	4.28	0.06	3.52	0.05
Soil moisture (%)	30.5	0.62	35.43	0.56	35.25	0.57	37.56	0.54
pH	5.03	0.11	5.18	0.09	5.15	0.09	5.06	0.07
Organic matter (g·kg^{-1})	40.43	0.82	37.83	0.62	28.87	0.47	22.58	0.32
Total N (g·kg^{-1})	2.32	0.06	2.48	0.03	1.97	0.03	1.57	0.02
Total P (g·kg^{-1})	0.37	0.01	0.33	0.01	0.36	0.01	0.36	0.01
Total K (g·kg^{-1})	7.31	0.15	7.01	0.11	9.87	0.15	8.05	0.12
Available N (mg·kg^{-1})	82.56	1.74	84.77	1.35	71.23	1.16	61.09	0.87
Available P (mg·kg^{-1})	3.19	0.07	3.24	0.05	3.96	0.07	2.06	0.03
Available K (mg·kg^{-1})	40.53	0.84	43.42	0.71	41.61	0.68	57.95	0.83

2.4.2. Relationships between Biomass Increment and Environmental Metrics

To assess relationships between post-thinning biomass increment and environmental metrics, two dissimilarity matrices (i.e., plot–biomass matrix and plot–environment matrix) were prepared and examined using Mantel tests [28]. In the plot–biomass matrix, overstory biomass increment (OBI) and understory biomass increment (UBI) were used as response variables to construct row vectors for each plot: $[OBI_{1i}, OBI_{2i}, OBI_{4i}, OBI_{6i,}UBI_{1i}, UBI_{2i}, UBI_{4i}, UBI_{6i}]$, where subscripts 1, 2, 4, and 6 indicate the first, second, fourth, and sixth years after thinning, and i indicates the ith plot. Similarly, the ten environmental metrics described in Table 3 were used as explanatory variables to form a plot–environment matrix with i rows and 10 columns. All variables were standardized using z-score normalization. The significance of the normalized Mantel coefficient was calculated using a two-tailed Monte Carlo permutation test with 10,000 permutations in the R "vegan" package [42]. A significant Mantel test ($p < 0.05$) indicates a linear correlation between the biomass dissimilarity matrix and the environment dissimilarity matrix, suggesting that the differences in the environment may be an important factor influencing the differences in biomass among different plots. Correlations between environmental metrics were calculated using Pearson's correlation coefficients.

2.4.3. Multivariate Statistical Analysis

Structural equation modeling (SEM) [43] was used to estimate the multivariate relationship in post-thinning forests and reveal the relative contributions of the explanatory variables to biomass increments across tree strata. The explanatory variables included thinning treatments, Shannon index, Dominance index, and Gini index for the overstory and understory, as well as significant environmental variables according to Mantel tests.

The initial multivariate model was established based on the productivity–diversity hypothesis [25,44]. An SEM path diagram was used to characterize the complex relationships among various explanatory variables and biomass increment. The path diagram was iteratively optimized, and pathways were added according to the residual correlations, or nonsignificant pathways were eliminated unless the pathways were biologically informative. Model fitting and evaluation were carried out based on the chi-square value (χ^2, $p > 0.05$), goodness-of-fit index (GFI > 0.9), and root square mean error of approximation (RMSEA < 0.05) [45]. The maximum likelihood method was used to estimate the coefficients of each edge in the path graph. The standardized path coefficients of the SEM reflect the direct, indirect, or total effects of explanatory variables on biomass increment. The SEM tests were performed in the R "lavaan" package [46].

3. Results

3.1. Effect of Thinning on Tree Biomass and Diversity

Thinning resulted in a lower aboveground biomass (AGB) of the overstory compared to the control plots (CK), but this difference gradually diminished with years after thinning (Figure 3a). Conversely, the understory AGB exhibited the opposite trend (Figure 3b). For example, in year 6, the mean overstory AGB in thinned plots was about 71%–87% of that in the CK, while the mean understory AGB was approximately 113%–162% higher in the CK.

Furthermore, tree growth changed significantly in biomass increment, Shannon index, Dominance index, and Gini index over time (Figure 4 and Table 4). The overstory biomass increment followed a temporal dynamic reflective of regeneration development, with the maximum mean value occurring in the CK during the early years and in thinned plots during the later years (Figure 4a and Table 4). For example, the maximum mean overstory biomass increment was observed in the CK at 7.03 $Mg{\cdot}ha^{-1}{\cdot}a^{-1}$ in year 1, while it was observed under MT at 9.72 $Mg{\cdot}ha^{-1}{\cdot}a^{-1}$ in year 6. The understory biomass increment consistently remained higher than those in the CK, with this advantage becoming increasingly apparent over time (Figure 4b). The Shannon index in the two strata showed similar biomass increment patterns over time, with thinned plots gradually exceeding the CK (Figure 4c,d). Furthermore, thinning generally reduces the Dominance index for both overstory and understory (Figure 4e,f) while also having a positive effect on the Gini index for the overstory (Figure 4g).

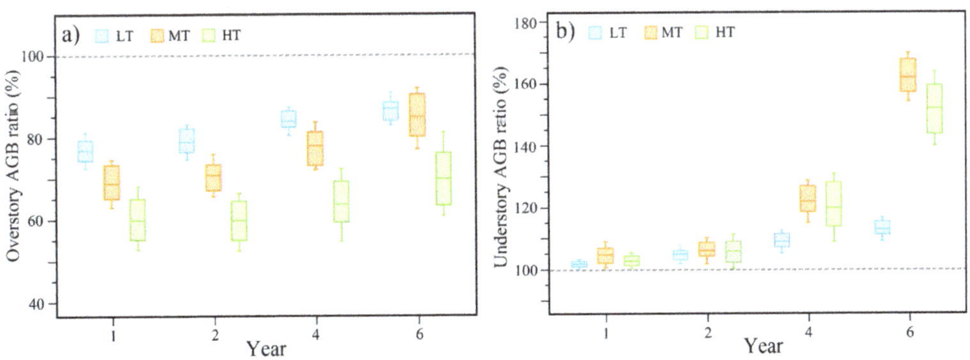

Figure 3. The relative ratios of aboveground biomass for both the (**a**) overstory and (**b**) understory during the post-thinning years compared to the CK (represented by the dashed line).

Table 4. *p*-values from full model analysis for biomass increment, Shannon index, Dominance index, and Gini index by strata class in Masson pine forests in Hunan, China. Significant values (<0.05) are in bold.

Strata Class	Effect	Biomass Increment	Shannon	Dominance	Gini
Overstory	Thinning	**<0.001**	**<0.001**	**0.002**	**<0.001**
	Year	**<0.001**	**<0.001**	**0.007**	**0.005**
	Thinning × Year	**<0.001**	**<0.001**	**<0.001**	**0.010**
Understory	Thinning	**<0.001**	**<0.001**	**<0.001**	0.320
	Year	**<0.001**	**<0.001**	**<0.001**	**<0.001**
	Thinning × Year	**<0.001**	**<0.001**	**0.003**	0.275

Because thinning and thinning × survey year were significant in most models of biomass increments and tree diversity for both the overstory and understory (Table 4), subsequent models were run by year to isolate the effects of thinning (Table 5). Thinning significantly increased biomass increments and the Shannon index for overstory and understory classes in later years (Figure 4 and Table 5). Specially, thinning initially reduced overstory biomass increment, but in later years, it exceeded that of the CK ($p \leq 0.001$ pairwise comparison). Similarly, understory biomass increment averaged 1.21 Mg·ha^{-1}·a^{-1} in HT and 1.43 Mg·ha^{-1}·a^{-1} in MT in year 6, both significantly higher than the 0.32 Mg·ha^{-1}·a^{-1} observed in the CK ($p \leq 0.001$ pairwise comparison). Thinning significantly increased the overstory Shannon index compared to the CK since year 4 ($p \leq 0.001$ pairwise comparison), peaking at a maximum mean value of 1.05 under MT in year 6, while their indices were similar in earlier years. The understory Shannon index was significantly different between various thinning treatments and the CK during post-thinning years ($p \leq 0.001$ pairwise comparison).

Thinning reduced the Dominance index for both the overstory and understory over time. For instance, the overstory Dominance index continued to decrease since the treatment, becoming significantly lower than the CK since year 4 ($p \leq 0.001$ pairwise comparison), reaching its minimum under LT (0.47) in year 6. Additionally, thinning significantly increased the Gini index for the overstory, with values notably higher than those of the CK during the post-thinning years ($p \leq 0.001$ pairwise comparison). No significant differences were observed in the understory Gini index.

Table 5. *p*-values from thinning intensity submodel analysis and overall means (standard error [se]) for biomass increment (Mg·ha^{-1}), Shannon index, Dominance index, and Gini index by survey year and stratum class in Masson pine forests in Hunan, China. Significant values (<0.05) are in bold.

Stratum Class	Year	Biomass Increment		Shannon		Dominance		Gini	
		p-Value	Mean (se)	*p*-Value	Mean (se)	*p*-Value	Mean (se)	*p*-Value	Mean (se)
Overstory	1	**0.001**	**5.46** (0.09)	0.255	0.63 (0.02)	0.424	0.68 (0.02)	**0.001**	**0.52** (0.02)
	2	**0.001**	**6.35** (0.13)	0.301	0.69 (0.01)	0.203	0.63 (0.01)	**0.001**	**0.49** (0.01)
	4	**0.001**	**7.92** (0.14)	**0.011**	**0.75** (0.02)	**0.001**	**0.57** (0.02)	**0.001**	**0.48** (0.01)
	6	**0.001**	8.09 (0.16)	**0.001**	**0.86** (0.02)	**0.001**	**0.54** (0.02)	**0.001**	**0.46** (0.01)

Table 5. *Cont.*

Stratum Class	Year	Biomass Increment		Shannon		Dominance		Gini	
		p-Value	Mean (se)	*p*-Value	Mean (se)	*p*-Value	Mean (se)	*p*-Value	Mean (se)
Understory	1	0.697	0.32 (0.01)	**0.001**	**1.05** (0.02)	0.085	0.46 (0.01)	0.834	0.33 (0.01)
	2	0.089	0.43 (0.01)	**0.001**	**1.21** (0.02)	0.001	0.36 (0.01)	0.06	0.35 (0.02)
	4	**0.001**	**0.52** (0.01)	**0.001**	**1.36** (0.03)	**0.001**	**0.32** (0.01)	0.068	0.39 (0.01)
	6	**0.001**	**0.84** (0.02)	**0.001**	**1.51** (0.03)	**0.001**	**0.29** (0.01)	0.726	0.43 (0.02)

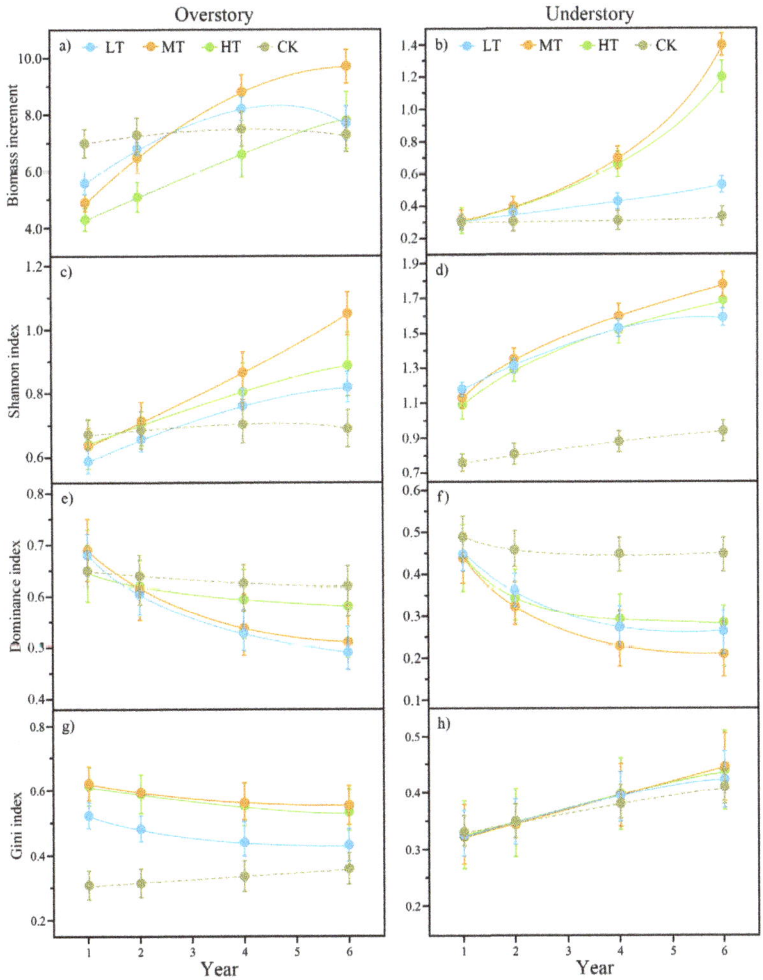

Figure 4. Mean biomass increment (**a**,**b**), Shannon index (**c**,**d**), Dominance index (**e**,**f**), and Gini index (**g**,**h**) during the post-thinning years in the overstory and understory of Masson pine forests in Hunan, China.

3.2. Correlation between Environmental Factors and Biomass Increment

We utilized the Mantel test to examine the correlations between distance-adjusted dissimilarities in biomass increments of both the overstory and understory with environmental metrics. Results showed that light intensity and soil physiochemical properties played distinct roles in driving biomass increments in the overstory and understory (Figure 5; Table 6). Specifically, light intensity (Mantel test; r = 0.502, $p < 0.05$) and soil organic matter (Mantel test; r = 0.355, $p < 0.05$) were positively correlated with overstory biomass increment. Soil moisture (Mantel test; r = −0.272, $p < 0.05$) was significantly negatively correlated with overstory biomass increment, and the correlation between soil moisture and overstory biomass increment was weaker than that between light intensity and soil organic matter. Soil organic matter (Mantel test; r = 0.424, $p < 0.05$), TN (Mantel test; r = 0.346, $p < 0.05$), and AP (Mantel test; r = 0.303, $p < 0.05$) were significantly correlated with understory biomass increment.

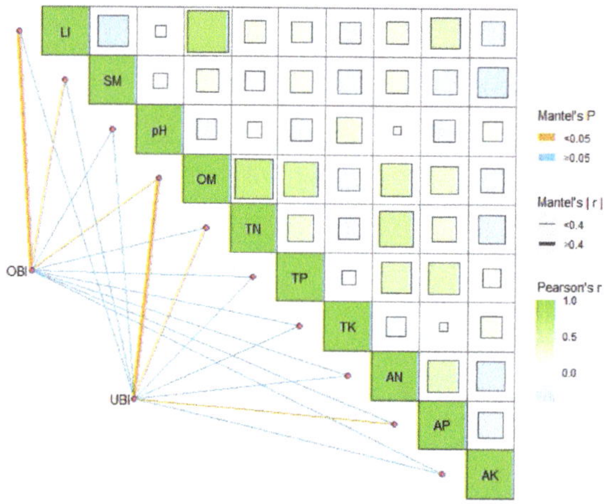

Figure 5. Biomass increments of overstory and understory were related to each factor by Mantel tests. Edge width corresponds to the Mantel's r statistic for the corresponding correlations, and edge color denotes the statistical significance based on 10,000 permutations. Pairwise comparisons of environmental factors are shown, with a color gradient denoting Pearson's correlation coefficients. Abbreviations: OBI, overstory biomass increment; UBI, understory biomass increment; LI, light intensity; SM, soil moisture; pH, soil pH; OM, soil organic matter; TN, total nitrogen; TP, total phosphorus; TK, total potassium; AN, available nitrogen; AP, available phosphorus; AK, available potassium.

Table 6. Effects of factors in the Mantel test analysis undertaken on biomass increments in the overstory and understory of Masson pine forests in Hunan, China. Significant values ($p < 0.05$) are in bold.

Factor	Overstory Biomass Increment ($Mg \cdot ha^{-1} \cdot a^{-1}$)		Factor	Understory Biomass Increment ($Mg \cdot ha^{-1} \cdot a^{-1}$)	
	p-Value	r-Value		*p*-Value	r-Value
LI	**0.001**	**0.502**	LI	0.064	0.232
SM	**0.046**	**−0.272**	SM	0.229	−0.146

Table 6. *Cont.*

Factor	Overstory Biomass Increment ($Mg{\cdot}ha^{-1}{\cdot}a^{-1}$)		Factor	Understory Biomass Increment ($Mg{\cdot}ha^{-1}{\cdot}a^{-1}$)	
	p-Value	r-Value		*p*-Value	r-Value
pH	0.169	−0.188	pH	0.612	−0.057
OM	**0.020**	**0.355**	OM	**0.001**	**0.424**
TN	0.072	0.209	TN	**0.022**	**0.346**
TP	0.053	0.243	TP	0.101	0.194
TK	0.413	−0.058	TK	0.062	−0.215
AN	0.066	0.211	AN	0.053	0.240
AP	0.153	0.189	AP	**0.041**	**0.303**
AK	0.212	−0.166	AK	0.275	−0.138

Furthermore, strong collinearity among environmental factors was observed (Figure 5). For example, decreases in soil moisture (Pearson's r = 0.37, $p < 0.05$) and increases in soil organic matter (Pearson's r = 0.73, $p < 0.05$) were accompanied by increases in light intensity. Soil moisture was negatively associated with AK (Pearson's r = 0.38, $p < 0.05$). A significant positive association was observed among soil organic matter, N, and P (Pearson's r = 0.32–0.54, $p < 0.05$).

3.3. Multivariate Statistical Analysis

We employed SEM to investigate how thinning treatments, environmental factors, tree diversity, and their interactions influence biomass increments in both the overstory and understory. The results indicated that SEM had a high level of goodness of fit for biomass increments in both the overstory (GFI = 0.932; RMSEA < 0.001) and understory (GFI = 0.978; RMSEA < 0.001), indicating a close match between the predicted and observed data. SEM accounted for 48% of the variation in overstory biomass increment (Figure 6a) and 57% of the variation in understory biomass increment (Figure 6b). Overall, the thinning treatments play an originative role in driving biomass increment via altering environmental conditions and tree diversity.

Specially, light intensity, which was directly affected by thinning treatments (standardized path coefficient, b = 0.32, $p < 0.05$), had a positive and direct effect on overstory biomass increment (b = 0.40, $p < 0.05$) (Figure 6a). Similarly, soil organic matter (b = 0.23, $p < 0.05$) and overstory Gini index (b = 0.42, $p < 0.05$), which were mainly affected by thinning, were positively correlated with overstory biomass increment. Soil moisture and overstory Shannon index had biological information for overstory biomass increment. Furthermore, soil organic matter, TN, and AP were mainly driven by thinning and positively affected (b = 0.22–0.34, $p < 0.05$) understory biomass increment (Figure 6b), which was consistent with the results of the Mantel tests (Table 6). Among tree diversity factors, the understory Shannon index (b = 0.47, $p < 0.05$) caused by thinning or environment had the strongest positive effect on understory biomass increment, followed by understory Dominance index and overstory Shannon index.

Standardized direct, indirect, and total effects (direct plus indirect effect) derived from SEM indicated that the effects of these factors on biomass increments in the overstory and understory were diverse (Figure 7); thus, the mechanisms underlying these effects might vary among tree strata. Thinning treatments (standardized total coefficient = 0.62) and the concomitant increase in light intensity (standardized total coefficient = 0.49) and overstory Gini (standardized total coefficient = 0.42) played key roles in shaping overstory biomass increment (Figure 7a). The tree diversity and environment, especially the understory Shannon and soil organic matter (standardized total coefficient = 0.47 and 0.35, respectively), induced by thinning were the main drivers of understory biomass increment (Figure 7b).

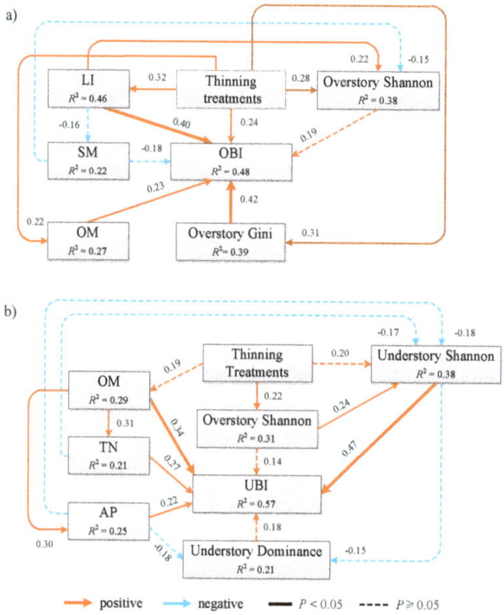

Figure 6. Structural equation model (SEM) showing the relationships among treatment, tree diversity, environment factors, and biomass increments in both the overstory (**a**) and understory (**b**). Red and blue arrows indicate positive and negative relationships, respectively. Arrow width corresponds to statistical significance. Numbers near the pathway arrow indicate the standard path coefficients. R^2 represents the proportion of variance explained for every dependent variable. Abbreviations: OBI, overstory biomass increment; UBI, understory biomass increment; LI, light intensity; SM, soil moisture; OM, soil organic matter; TN, total nitrogen; AP, available phosphorus.

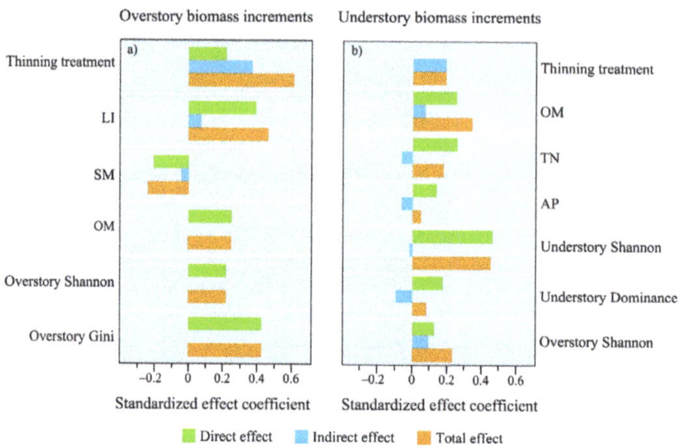

Figure 7. Standardized direct effect, indirect effect, and total effect (direct plus indirect effect) derived from SEM fitted to biomass increments in the overstory (**a**) and understory (**b**). The absolute of standardized total effect coefficient greater than 0.3 indicates that this is the key factor affecting biomass increment. Abbreviations: LI, light intensity; SM, soil moisture; OM, soil organic matter; TN, total nitrogen; AP, available phosphorus.

4. Discussion

Developing management approaches that can maintain ecosystem services and functions is crucial in the face of ongoing ecological change. Here, we tested the effect of thinning on biomass and diversity over six years in Masson pine forests in Hunan, China. The three sites exhibit similar climates, topographies, and stand conditions to ensure a stable and reliable thinning effect. In partial agreement with prediction 1, we found that MT is most effective in stimulating biomass increment and tree diversity, but this is evident in the later years. Prediction 2 was confirmed, as we found that environmental factors such as light intensity and soil physiochemical properties were not only correlated with biomass increments after thinning but also varied across tree strata. Moreover, thinning treatments, environmental factors, tree diversity, and their interactions had effects on biomass increments, and the mechanisms underlying these effects differed in the overstory and understory, which was consistent with prediction 3.

4.1. Effects of Thinning on Biomass of the Overstory and Understory

Thinning treatments can promote the growth and biomass of retained trees, but additional analysis is needed to understand their impact on the overall AGB of the stand. The short-term accumulation of retained tree biomass is not enough to make up for the biomass removed during thinning [16]. For example, in the first year, the post-treatment AGB of the overstory in the plots was noticeably lower than that of the CK, and the reduction expanded as the thinning intensity increased (Figure 3a). However, as thinning-induced biomass increment was released over time, the AGB difference between thinned plots and CK decreased. Thus, the positive effects of thinning treatments on biomass increment were evident in later years. In year 6, MT exhibited the highest average overstory biomass increment at 9.72 Mg·ha^{-1}·a^{-1}, significantly higher than both LT (7.71 Mg·ha^{-1}·a^{-1}) and HT (7.84 Mg·ha^{-1}·a^{-1}) (Figure 4a). Coupled with its moderate initial retained biomass, this resulted in the overstory AGB under MT exceeding that of other thinning treatments and approaching that of CK. Similarly, MT showed the highest average understory biomass increment at 1.43 Mg·ha^{-1}·a^{-1} in year 6, followed by HT at 1.21 Mg·ha^{-1}·a^{-1} and LT at 0.42 Mg·ha^{-1}·a^{-1} (Figure 4b). The results indicated that while thinning initially reduced AGB in the overstory, it subsequently enhanced biomass increments in both the overstory and understory. MT provided the most significant benefits in later years.

In practice, the minimum stand density or residual basal area, which affects the retention biomass, might require consideration when establishing thinning strategies. Previous studies of middle-aged Masson pine forests have suggested that stand density should be maintained between 1000 and 1200 stem ha^{-1} [47,48]. The density-dependent stand-level optimization approach proposed by Bettinger, Graetz, and Sessions [34] suggested that the minimum residual basal area in pine forests should be approximately 16.0–20.5 m^2·ha^{-1}. The range roughly coincides with the density and basal area of MT in the early years after thinning (Table 2). From this viewpoint, the MT (25%–35% tree removed) we examined could be considered as the optimal thinning intensity for the management of middle-aged Masson pine forests.

Our results indicated that overstory biomass increment from thinning treatments gradually exceeded those of the CK after year 4, suggesting that the benefits of thinning became apparent in the later years (Figure 4a). The understory biomass increment followed similar patterns over time (Figure 4b). The growth and regeneration of juvenile trees also exhibited a time lag effect in response to thinning treatments. Thus, determining the time scale at which positive responses are achieved may help explain the changes in post-processing time dynamics [9,34]. Previous studies indicated that an observation period consistent with the regeneration cycle of a forest should be adopted [23,49]. Ming [35] indicated that the post-treatment developmental pathway of a subtropical coniferous forest exhibited a unimodal pattern in which tree growth was most active for six to seven years and then gradually declined. While our study demonstrated the expected outcomes over the 6-year period, extending the observation duration remains a viable strategy for a more comprehensive analysis of forest recovery following thinning treatments.

4.2. Effects of Thinning on Diversity of the Overstory and Understory

Thinning releases growth space and increases light availability, which stimulates diverse responses by trees. Pioneer or shade-intolerant tree species exhibit stronger relative responses than other species to thinning. Wang and Liu [50] have also shown that overstory species richness increases less frequently in pine forest after cutting treatments, and emerging species are mostly saplings with a high demand for light. This also partially explains why the overstory accounted for the majority of the biomass but was not diverse in this study. Providing trees with enough space and time to grow, selectively retaining overstory species during thinning treatments, or planting trees might increase overstory species diversity [12].

Thinning had a more positive effect on understory species diversity than on overstory species diversity. Thinning can induce environmental heterogeneity and regulate understory habitat, facilitating the coexistence of different species. Some light-demanding species are likely to invade the understory after thinning, especially following MT and HT; however, such species were infrequently observed or absent in the CK. In addition, some native species do not require thinning to become established, but thinning often facilitates their establishment and expansion [11]. As shown in Figure 4d, the maximum mean Shannon index of the understory was obtained under MT within 6 years. The proportion of broadleaf and shade-tolerant species increases after thinning treatment. Although individuals of understory species are generally small, the number of species is relatively high. Furthermore, increases in understory species richness potentially induce the growth of a suite of mixed species, ranging from tree pests to disturbance-resistant species, and this can drive shifts to more stable and sustainable forest communities [21,51]. Therefore, the effective promotion of species coexistence to maintain forest resilience is a crucial consideration in implementing thinning treatments.

Tree size diversity in the stand was characterized using the Gini index, as has been conducted in several forest ecosystems [52]. Gini index values of 0, 0.5, and 1 correspond to even, uniform, and uneven forest structures, respectively [39]. In this study, MT and HT resulted in overstory Gini index values greater than 0.5; starting from a peaked reverse J, the success of natural regeneration and ingrowth can be indicated by a decreasing Gini index [39]. Under LT and the CK, the Gini index was less than 0.5, which indicates that self-thinning processes are dominant when stand development is determined by competition for light and space (Figure 4g). Tree size diversity can increase the complexity of stand structure in both the vertical and horizontal dimensions. Large trees usually occupy the canopy and are surrounded by smaller trees below, which can form a complementary growth space. A group of trees of different sizes can intercept rainfall and light according to their needs, which improves resource utilization and reduces competition among trees. In addition, large trees may provide shelter and shade for smaller trees [53], promoting their regeneration and growth. Therefore, tree size diversity should be considered when selecting MT to regulate the coexistence of trees of different sizes, reduce competition, and promote stand regeneration [23].

4.3. Correlation between Environmental Factors and Biomass Increments across Tree Strata

In this study, Mantel tests of environmental factors and biomass increment were conducted to test prediction 2, which proposes that light intensity and soil metrics were significantly correlated with biomass increments and that their effects on the overstory and understory differed. The environmental factors significantly correlated with overstory biomass in Masson pine forests were light intensity, soil organic matter, and soil moisture (Figure 5; Table 6). In a post-thinning forest, physiological regeneration niches are possessed by different species to cope with environment conditions. *P. massoniana*, which is the dominant overstory species, is the most light-demanding and thermophilic tree species, and optimum sites for this species include the upper canopy and canopy openings [21]. Under high light conditions, *P. massoniana* exhibits high photosynthetic activity and higher net CO_2 assimilation than other species over a growing period, which is consistent with the results of a previous study [54]. Carbon assimilation and xylem formation directly stimulate tree growth and regeneration, which promotes stand biomass accumulation. Furthermore, Huang et al. [55] showed that the duration of xylem formation in Masson pine forests in subtropical China was several months longer than expected due to photosynthetic activity, which indicates that the overstory might accumulate more biomass. Although the photosynthetic rate of trees increases as the amount of incident light increases, some physiological traits of trees cannot be ignored [56]. For example, under high irradiance and temperatures, native species in the understory such as *Castanopsis sclerophylla* may develop deep root systems to withstand adverse conditions or photoinhibition, and this results in the accumulation of underground biomass. In subtropical forests, intense irradiance accompanied by transpiration reduces the water potential of vegetation, leading to serious restrictions on understory trees. Thus, light has a significant positive effect on biomass increments of the overstory but not on the understory.

Mantel test results indicate that additional soil moisture over the growing season negatively affects biomass (Table 6). Most precipitation in subtropical China occurs during the growing season (April to September), which inevitably leads to increases in soil moisture. Previous studies indicate that the relationship between mean precipitation and biomass productivity in most coniferous forests is a nonlinear, concave-down function [57]. Increasing soil moisture in humid ecosystems may reduce tree biomass by reducing soil oxygen availability or increasing nutrient leaching. Therefore, Masson pine forests mostly grow well on the dry, xeric sides of mountains or ridges with high light [21,55]. This result also indicates that Masson pine forests would benefit from longer dry periods because they might result in better growth and greater biomass accumulation under continued climate warming.

Soil organic matter was strongly correlated with both overstory and understory biomass increments (Table 6), which suggests that thinning increased the content of soil organic matter and supplied more soil nutrients for tree growth [7]. In post-thinning forests, the main source of soil organic matter is litter, and this mainly stems from the remaining trees and logging residuals. Thinning enhances the abundance of understory plants (especially deciduous broadleaf species), which increases the accumulation of litterfall and enhances N storage [58]. Moreover, thinning increases solar radiation on the forest floor, soil temperature, and thus the decomposition of organic matter. The decomposition process is generally mediated by interactions between understory plants and microorganisms, which stimulate N mineralization and nitrification in forest soil [37]. The thinning-induced divergence in N demand favors an exploitative tree N-use strategy. For example, understory pioneer species had a greater demand for NO^{3-} than for NH^{4+} [59], which might promote N cycling and thus the biodiversity and structure of forests. Although the improvements to soil fertility associated with thinning are complex, organic matter and soil total N responded significantly and positively to understory biomass increments, suggesting that thinning enhances tree growth and maximizes forest production in warm regions [7].

Thinning also increased soil P availability, and this P was likely derived from organic matter, especially from logging residuals and roots [60]. As the P demand of understory plants and the number of remaining trees after thinning increased, the efficiency of P transformation from the subsoil increased, which enhanced understory biomass. However, the AP was relatively low (3.96–3.19 $mg \cdot kg^{-1}$), partly because the soil in southern China is acidic to strongly acidic, and the concentrations of free Fe^{3+} and Al^{3+} are high, which induces the precipitation of soil P [61]. In addition, thinning reduces forest canopy interception and increases surface erosion, which may increase soil eluviation and thus reduce concentrations of soil nutrients. Therefore, N and P should be supplemented to increase soil fertility during post-thinning years in Masson pine forests in southern China.

4.4. Relationships of Thinning, Environmental Factors, and Tree Diversity with Biomass Increments

We used SEM to show that thinning, tree diversity, environmental factors, and their interactions affected biomass increments (Figure 6), and the mechanisms underlying these effects differed in the overstory and understory (Figure 7); this was consistent with prediction 3. Thinning treatments, light intensity, and tree size diversity had significant effects on overstory biomass increment, and species richness and soil organic matter affected understory biomass.

Light inputs increase with thinning intensity. Liu, et al. [21] suggested that the average daily light intensity intercepted by the overstory in thinned subtropical forests is approximately 1.3 to 2.5 times higher than that of the understory. Trees with access to direct sunlight can generally respond better to thinning. In this study, dominant and codominant trees, such as *P. massoniana* and *Q. fabri*, are highly sensitive to light intensity and enhance their photosynthetic capacity under improved light environments. Previous reports indicated that thinning-induced light increase could have significant impacts on the CO_2 assimilation and nitrogen content of light-demanding trees, resulting in greater overstory biomass accumulation [35,55]. Therefore, the demand for light shapes overstory growth in a post-thinning Masson pine forest.

Although biomass generally increases exponentially with DBH, with large trees contributing most of the biomass, stands with trees of various sizes might be preferable [23]. Our results suggested that tree size diversity played an important role in driving overstory biomass increase (Figure 7a). The group selection strategy with thinning regulates the canopy tree size and stand structure and alleviates competition among neighboring trees, which may promote tree growth and biomass increments [62,63]. In this study, canopy trees of various sizes have complementary crown architectures and branch inclinations, especially under MT and HT, which might form a complex structure that intercepts resources at different points in space or at different times. But within the CK, even-sized trees invest heavily in height growth and less in branching to avoid shading from neighbors, thus inhibiting biomass increase. Jucker et al. [64] showed that competition for light and water was evident in monoculture stands, and mixing species with different sizes increased the amount of resources received and growth rates. These results suggest that both light intensity and tree size diversity could play prominent roles in mediating thinning-induced overstory biomass increase.

SEM showed that the standardized total coefficient of the understory Shannon index was larger than that of other factors, suggesting that species richness made the greatest contribution to understory biomass increment (Figure 7b). According to the diversity–productivity hypothesis, positive interactions among species improve the utilization of environmental resources when environmental conditions are favorable and different species are allowed to coexist, and this increases community biomass and productivity [65]. Complementarity and facilitation are the two primary mechanisms leading to productivity increments [66], and understory biomass gains after thinning exceeded yields in the CK stand. More diverse communities are more likely to include combinations of species that integrate resource patches by increasing niche complementarity with functionally dissimilar species [67]. Such facilitation could occur if certain species alter the environment in such a way that it enhances the fitness of other species. Seed availability is increased when the number of seed trees of different species in the overstory is higher, and this can enhance understory species richness [56]. A positive relationship between species richness and biomass increments for both the overstory and understory has also been observed in other recent studies [30,68]. Regulating the composition of species is essential for maintaining high community productivity and biomass. In practice, some native species, such as *Q. fabri* and *Castanopsis sclerophylla*, should be planted in the understory to stabilize understory tree diversity and improve productivity [35].

Although tree growth and community productivity theoretically increase with increasing soil fertility, the amplification of biomass gains in the understory post-thinning is usually pronounced in nutrient-poor soils in tropical and subtropical forests [69,70]. In this study, thinning increased soil organic matter inputs and soil N and P requirements, which can improve the fertility of soil and enhance tree growth. Our results suggest that the understory was affected to a greater degree by improvements in soil conditions compared with the overstory. When soil conditions are improved, conservative nutrient strategies might no longer be employed by some understory species, and their growth might be stimulated [36]. Therefore, understory biomass might be mainly driven by biotic interactions and improvements in soil conditions [37].

5. Conclusions and Management Implications

In conclusion, the findings of our study suggest that (1) moderate thinning (25%–35% of trees removed) was effective for biomass increment in middle-aged Masson pine forests in southern China, as well as for increasing tree diversity across tree strata; (2) diverse environmental factors were found to be correlated with biomass increment, including light intensity, soil organic matter, and other soil physiochemical properties; and (3) thinning increment, environmental factors, tree diversity, and their interactions might affect biomass increments, and the mechanisms underlying their effects might differ in the overstory and understory.

These results have implications for silvicultural practices when thinning treatments are used to regulate the regeneration and biomass of Masson pine forests. The excellent performance of moderate thinning in promoting diversity in the overstory and understory, as well as biomass increments, indicates that it could be considered the optimum treatment for maintaining Masson pine forest ecosystem services. Biomass increments are influenced by more factors than thinning increments alone, including tree diversity, light inputs, and soil physiochemical properties. Specifically, thinning increment, light intensity, tree size diversity, and their interactions had significant effects on overstory biomass increment, and species richness and soil organic matter affected understory biomass. In addition, thinning treatments should be dynamically programmed at specific intervals to improve light inputs and soil fertility, as this would enhance tree growth. Given that massive Masson pine forests have been established during the past decades in China, our findings are of significance for improving the ecosystem functions in sustainable forest management.

Supplementary Materials: The following supporting information can be downloaded at: https://www.mdpi.com/article/10.3390/f15071080/s1, Table S1: The main species and tree allometric growth model in Masson pine forests in Hunan, China.

Author Contributions: Methodology, C.T.; Software, M.Z.; Validation, X.L.; Investigation, J.L.; Writing—original draft, F.L. All authors have read and agreed to the published version of the manuscript.

Funding: This work was supported by the Natural Science Foundation of Hunan Province [grant no. 2024JJ7645; 2022JJ31000] and the Special Research Project on Education of Social Sciences Foundation of Hunan Province [grant no. JJ210525] and the Production and Education cooperation Project of Ministry of Education [grant no. 220802313140742] and the National Undergraduate Training Programs for Innovation and Entrepreneurship (S202310538023).

Data Availability Statement: Data are contained within the article and Supplementary Materials.

Acknowledgments: We thank three anonymous reviewers for their comments on an earlier version of the manuscript.

Conflicts of Interest: The authors declare they have no conflicts of interest.

References

1. Du, X.; Wang, X.; Meng, J.H. A Climate-Sensitive Transition Matrix Growth Model for Masson Pine (*Pinus massoniana* Lamb.) Natural Forests in Hunan Province, South-Central China. *Forests* **2023**, *14*, 1539. [CrossRef]

2. Deng, C.; Zhang, S.; Lu, Y.; Froese, R.; Xu, X.; Zeng, J.; Ming, A.; Liu, X.; Xie, Y.; Li, Q. Thinning effects on forest evolution in Masson pine (*Pinus massoniana* Lamb.) conversion from pure plantations into mixed forests. *For. Ecol. Manag.* **2020**, *477*, 118503. [CrossRef]
3. Bai, Y.-F.; Shen, Y.-Y.; Jin, Y.-D.; Hong, Y.; Liu, Y.-Y.; Li, Y.-Q.; Liu, R.; Zhang, Z.-W.; Jiang, C.-Q.; Wang, Y.-J. Selective thinning and initial planting density management promote biomass and carbon storage in a chronosequence of evergreen conifer plantations in Southeast China. *Glob. Ecol. Conserv.* **2020**, *24*, e01216. [CrossRef]
4. NFA. *China Forest Resources Report 2014–2018*; China Forestry Publishing House: Beijing, China, 2019. (In Chinese)
5. Ma, L.; Lian, J.; Lin, G.; Cao, H.; Huang, Z.; Guan, D. Forest dynamics and its driving forces of sub-tropical forest in South China. *Sci. Rep.* **2016**, *6*, 22561. [CrossRef] [PubMed]
6. Dieler, J.; Uhl, E.; Biber, P.; Muller, J.; Rotzer, T.; Pretzsch, H. Effect of forest stand management on species composition, structural diversity, and productivity in the temperate zone of Europe. *Eur. J. Forest Res.* **2017**, *136*, 739–766. [CrossRef]
7. Barefoot, C.R.; Willson, K.G.; Hart, J.L.; Schweitzer, C.J.; Dey, D.C. Effects of thinning and prescribed fire frequency on ground flora in mixed Pinus-hardwood stands. *For. Ecol. Manag.* **2019**, *432*, 729–740. [CrossRef]
8. Navarro-Cerrillo, R.M.; Cachinero-Vivar, A.M.; Pérez-Priego, O.; Cantón, R.A.; Begueria, S.; Camarero, J. Developing alternatives to adaptive silviculture: Thinning and tree growth resistance to drought in a *Pinus* species on an elevated gradient in Southern Spain. *For. Ecol. Manag.* **2023**, *537*, 120936. [CrossRef]
9. Zhang, H.L.; Liu, S.R.; Yu, J.Y.; Li, J.W.; Shangguan, Z.P.; Deng, L. Thinning increases forest ecosystem carbon stocks. *For. Ecol. Manag.* **2024**, *555*, 121702. [CrossRef]
10. Wang, Z.; Yang, H.; Wang, D.; Zhao, Z. Response of height growth of regenerating trees in a Pinus tabulaeformis Carr. plantation to different thinning intensities. *For. Ecol. Manag.* **2019**, *444*, 280–289. [CrossRef]
11. Abella, S.R.; Springer, J.D. Effects of tree cutting and fire on understory vegetation in mixed conifer forests. *For. Ecol. Manag.* **2015**, *335*, 281–299. [CrossRef]
12. Pretzsch, H.; Poschenrieder, W.; Uhl, E.; Brazaitis, G.; Makrickiene, E.; Calama, R. Silvicultural prescriptions for mixed-species forest stands. A European review and perspective. *Eur. J. Forest Res.* **2021**, *140*, 1267–1294. [CrossRef]
13. Oliveira, C.D.C.d.; Durigan, G.; Putz, F.E. Thinning temporarily stimulates tree regeneration in a restored tropical forest. *Ecol. Eng.* **2021**, *171*, 106390. [CrossRef]
14. Bekris, Y.; Prevéy, J.S.; Brodie, L.C.; Harrington, C.A. Effects of variable-density thinning on non-native understory plants in coniferous forests of the Pacific Northwest. *For. Ecol. Manag.* **2021**, *502*, 119699. [CrossRef]
15. Fu, L.; Lei, X.; Hu, Z.; Zeng, W.; Tang, S.; Marshall, P.; Cao, L.; Song, X.; Yu, L.; Liang, J. Integrating regional climate change into allometric equations for estimating tree aboveground biomass of Masson pine in China. *Ann. Forest Sci.* **2017**, *74*, 42. [CrossRef]
16. Bosela, M.; Štefančík, I.; Marčiš, P.; Rubio-Cuadrado, Á.; Lukac, M. Thinning decreases above-ground biomass increment in central European beech forests but does not change individual tree resistance to climate events. *Agric. For. Meteorol.* **2021**, *306*, 108441. [CrossRef]
17. Zald, H.S.J.; Callahan, C.C.; Hurteau, M.D.; Goodwin, M.J.; North, M.P. Tree growth responses to extreme drought after mechanical thinning and prescribed fire in a Sierra Nevada mixed-conifer forest, USA. *For. Ecol. Manag.* **2022**, *510*, 120107. [CrossRef]
18. Bhandari, S.K.; Veneklaas, E.J.; McCaw, L.; Mazanec, R.; Whitford, K.; Renton, M. Individual tree growth in jarrah (*Eucalyptus marginata*) forest is explained by size and distance of neighbouring trees in thinned and non-thinned plots. *For. Ecol. Manag.* **2021**, *494*, 119364. [CrossRef]
19. Cole, E.; Newton, M.; Bailey, J.D. Understory vegetation dynamics 15 years post-thinning in 50-year-old Douglas-fir and Douglas-fir/western hemlock stands in western Oregon, USA. *For. Ecol. Manag.* **2017**, *384*, 358–370. [CrossRef]
20. Aun, K.; Kukumägi, M.; Varik, M.; Becker, H.; Aosaar, J.; Uri, M.; Morozov, G.; Buht, M.; Uri, V. Short-term effect of thinning on the carbon budget of young and middle-aged Scots pine (*Pinus sylvestris* L.) stands. *For. Ecol. Manag.* **2021**, *492*, 119241. [CrossRef]
21. Liu, F.; Tan, C.; Yang, Z.; Li, J.; Xiao, H.; Tong, Y. Regeneration and growth of tree seedlings and saplings in created gaps of different sizes in a subtropical secondary forest in southern China. *For. Ecol. Manag.* **2022**, *511*, 120143. [CrossRef]
22. Bebi, P.; Kulakowski, D.; Rixen, C. Snow avalanche disturbances in forest ecosystems-State of research and implications for management. *For. Ecol. Manag.* **2009**, *257*, 1883–1892. [CrossRef]
23. Dong, L.; Jin, X.; Pukkala, T.; Li, F.; Liu, Z. How to manage mixed secondary forest in a sustainable way? *Eur. J. Forest Res.* **2019**, *138*, 789–801. [CrossRef]
24. Liang, R.T.; Xie, Y.H.; Sun, Y.J.; Wang, B.Y.; Ding, Z.D. Temporal changes in size inequality and stand growth partitioning between tree sizes under various thinning intensities in subtropica *Cunninghamia lanceolata* plantations. *For. Ecol. Manag.* **2023**, *547*, 121363. [CrossRef]
25. Lin, D.; Pang, M.; Lai, J.; Mi, X.; Ren, H.; Ma, K.; KePing, M. Multivariate relationship between tree diversity and aboveground biomass across tree strata in a subtropical evergreen broad-leaved forest. *Chin. Sci. Bull.* **2017**, *62*, 1861–1868. [CrossRef]
26. Zobel, M.; Pärtel, M. What determines the relationship between plant diversity and habitat productivity? *Glob. Ecol. Biogeogr.* **2008**, *17*, 679–684. [CrossRef]
27. Hagan, J.G.; Vanschoenwinkel, B.; Gamfeldt, L. We should not necessarily expect positive relationships between biodiversity and ecosystem functioning in observational field data. *Ecol. Lett.* **2021**, *24*, 2537–2548. [CrossRef] [PubMed]

28. Sunagawa, S.; Coelho, L.P.; Chaffron, S.; Kultima, J.R.; Labadie, K.; Salazar, G.; Djahanschiri, B.; Zeller, G.; Mende, D.R.; Alberti, A. Structure and function of the global ocean microbiome. *Science* **2015**, *348*, 1261359. [CrossRef] [PubMed]
29. Verschuyl, J.; Riffell, S.; Miller, D.; Wigley, T.B. Biodiversity response to intensive biomass production from forest thinning in North American forests—A meta-analysis. *For. Ecol. Manag.* **2011**, *261*, 221–232. [CrossRef]
30. Ali, A.; Lin, S.-L.; He, J.-K.; Kong, F.-M.; Yu, J.-H.; Jiang, H.-S. Climate and soils determine aboveground biomass indirectly via species diversity and stand structural complexity in tropical forests. *For. Ecol. Manag.* **2019**, *432*, 823–831. [CrossRef]
31. NFA. *Regulations for Forest Tending Operations*; National Forestry Administration: Beijing, China, 2014. (In Chinese)
32. Abellanas, B.; Abellanas, M.; Pommerening, A.; Lodares, D.; Cuadros, S. A forest simulation approach using weighted Voronoi diagrams. An application to Mediterranean fir Abies pinsapo Boiss stands. *Forest Syst.* **2016**, *25*, e062. [CrossRef]
33. Li, Y.; Ye, S.; Hui, G.; Hu, Y.; Zhao, Z. Spatial structure of timber harvested according to structure-based forest management. *For. Ecol. Manag.* **2014**, *322*, 106–116. [CrossRef]
34. Bettinger, P.; Graetz, D.; Sessions, J. A density-dependent stand-level optimization approach for deriving management prescriptions for interior northwest (USA) landscapes. *For. Ecol. Manag.* **2005**, *217*, 171–186. [CrossRef]
35. Ming, A. Community Structure and Carbon Dynamics during Close-to-Nature Transformation in South Subtropical Conifer Plantation. Doctor Thesis, Chinese Academy of Forestry, Beijing, China, 2017.
36. Lei, L.; Xiao, W.; Zeng, L.; Frey, B.; Huang, Z.; Zhu, J.; Cheng, R.; Li, M.-H. Effects of thinning intensity and understory removal on soil microbial community in Pinus massoniana plantations of subtropical China. *Appl. Soil. Ecol.* **2021**, *167*, 104055. [CrossRef]
37. Zhou, T.; Wang, C.; Zhou, Z. Thinning promotes the nitrogen and phosphorous cycling in forest soils. *Agr. Forest Meteorol.* **2021**, *311*, 108665. [CrossRef]
38. Berger, W.H.; Parker, F.L. Diversity of Planktonic Foraminifera in Deep-Sea Sediments. *Science* **1970**, *168*, 1345–1347. [CrossRef] [PubMed]
39. Valbuena, R.; Packalén, P.; Martı'n-Fernández, S.; Maltamo, M. Diversity and equitability ordering profiles applied to study forest structure. *For. Ecol. Manag.* **2012**, *276*, 185–195. [CrossRef]
40. R Core Team. *R: A Language and Environment for Statistical Computing*; R Foundation for Statistical Computing: Vienna, Austria, 2022; Available online: https://www.R-project.org/ (accessed on 21 September 2023).
41. Russell, V.L. Emmeans: Estimated Marginal Means, aka Least-Squares Means. R Package Version, 1.5.3. 2020. Available online: https://rvlenth.github.io/emmeans/ (accessed on 16 January 2023).
42. Oksanen, J. Vegan: Community Ecology Package. R Package Version, 2.6.2. 2022. Available online: https://github.com/vegandevs/vegan/ (accessed on 11 January 2023).
43. Hoyle, R.; St, C. *Handbook of Structural Equation Modeling*; Guilford Press: New York, NY, USA, 2022.
44. Xu, W.; Zhou, P.; González-Rodríguez, M.Á.; Tan, Z.; Li, Z.; Yan, P. Changes in Relationship between Forest Biomass Productivity and Biodiversity of Different Type Subtropical Forests in Southern China. *Forests* **2024**, *15*, 410. [CrossRef]
45. Wu, L.; Zhang, Y.; Guo, X.; Ning, D.; Zhou, X.; Feng, J.; Yuan, M.M.; Liu, S.; Guo, J.; Gao, Z.; et al. Reduction of microbial diversity in grassland soil is driven by long-term climate warming. *Nat. Microbiol.* **2022**, *7*, 1054–1062. [CrossRef]
46. Rosseel, Y. Lavaan: Latent Variable Analysis. R Package Version 0.6-12. 2022. Available online: https://lavaan.ugent.be/ (accessed on 9 March 2023).
47. Cheng, Z.; Zeng, S. *Management Model and Management Number Table of P. massoniana Conservation Forest (in Chinese)*; China Forestry Publishing House: Beijing, China, 2003.
48. Meng, X.; He, B.; Ma, Z.; Hou, Y.; Li, Y. Current Situation of Masson Pine Forest Management and Its Practice of Close to nature Silviculture in China. *World For. Res.* **2018**, *31*, 63–67, (In Chinese with English Abstract). [CrossRef]
49. Hu, J.; Herbohn, J.; Chazdon, R.L.; Baynes, J.; Vanclay, J.K. Above-ground biomass recovery following logging and thinning over 46 years in an Australian tropical forest. *Sci. Total Environ.* **2020**, *734*, 139098. [CrossRef]
50. Wang, G.; Liu, F. The influence of gap creation on the regeneration of Pinus tabuliformis planted forest and its role in the near-natural cultivation strategy for planted forest management. *For. Ecol. Manag.* **2011**, *262*, 413–423. [CrossRef]
51. Metlen, K.L.; Fiedler, C.E. Restoration treatment effects on the understory of ponderosa pine/Douglas-fir forests in western Montana, USA. *For. Ecol. Manag.* **2006**, *222*, 355–369. [CrossRef]
52. Hui, G.; Zhang, G.; Zhao, Z.; Yang, A. Methods of Forest Structure Research: A Review. *Curr. For. Rep.* **2019**, *5*, 152–154. [CrossRef]
53. Liu, F.; Yang, Z.-g.; Zhang, G. Canopy gap characteristics and spatial patterns in a subtropical forest of South China after ice storm damage. *J. Mt. Sci.* **2020**, *17*, 1942–1958. [CrossRef]
54. Mayoral, C.; Calama, R.; Sánchez-González, M.; Pardos, M. Modelling the influence of light, water and temperature on photosynthesis in young trees of mixed Mediterranean forests. *New Forests* **2015**, *46*, 485–506. [CrossRef]
55. Huang, J.; Guo, X.; Rossi, S.; Zhai, L.; Yu, B.; Zhang, S.; Zhang, M. Intra-annual wood formation of subtropical Chinese red pine shows better growth in dry season than wet season. *Tree Physiol.* **2018**, *38*, 1225–1236. [CrossRef] [PubMed]
56. Oguchi, R.; Hiura, T.; Hikosaka, K. The effect of interspecific variation in photosynthetic plasticity on 4-year growth rate and 8-year survival of understorey tree seedlings in response to gap formations in a cool-temperate deciduous forest. *Tree Physiol.* **2017**, *37*, 1113–1127. [CrossRef]
57. Hsu, J.S.; Powell, J.; Adler, P.B. Sensitivity of mean annual primary production to precipitation. *Glob. Chang. Biol.* **2012**, *18*, 2246–2255. [CrossRef]

58. Lagomarsino, A.; Mazza, G.; Agnelli, A.E.; Lorenzetti, R.; Bartoli, C.; Viti, C.; Colombo, C.; Pastorelli, R. Litter fractions and dynamics in a degraded pine forest after thinning treatments. *Eur. J. For. Res.* **2020**, *139*, 295–310. [CrossRef]
59. Tilman, D. Nitrogen-Limited Growth in Plants from Different Successional Stages. *Ecology* **1986**, *67*, 555–563. [CrossRef]
60. Rocha, J.H.T.; Menegale, M.L.C.; Rodrigues, M.; Gonçalves, J.L.d.M.; Pavinato, P.S.; Foltran, E.C.; Harrison, R.; James, J.N. Impacts of timber harvest intensity and P fertilizer application on soil P fractions. *For. Ecol. Manag.* **2019**, *437*, 295–303. [CrossRef]
61. Hall, S.J.; Huang, W. Iron reduction: A mechanism for dynamic cycling of occluded cations in tropical forest soils? *Biogeochemistry* **2017**, *136*, 91–102. [CrossRef]
62. Bontemps, J.; Bouriaud, O. Predictive approaches to forest site productivity: Recent trends, challenges and future perspectives. *Forestry* **2014**, *87*, 109–128. [CrossRef]
63. Dănescu, A.; Albrecht, A.; Bauhus, J. Structural diversity promotes productivity of mixed, uneven-aged forests in southwestern Germany. *Oecologia* **2016**, *182*, 319–333. [CrossRef]
64. Jucker, T.; Bouriaud, O.; Daniel, A.; Danila, I.; Duduman, G.; Valladares, F.; Coomes, D. Competition for light and water play contrasting roles in driving diversity-productivity relationships in Iberian forests. *J. Ecol.* **2014**, *102*, 1202–1213. [CrossRef]
65. Fraser, L.H.; Pither, J.; Jentsch, A.; Sternberg, M.; Zobel, M.; Askarizadeh, D.; Bartha, S.; Beierkuhnlein, C.; Bennett, J.A.; Bittel, A.; et al. Worldwide evidence of a unimodal relationship between productivity and plant species richness. *Science* **2015**, *349*, 302–305. [CrossRef]
66. Hooper, D.U.; Chapin, F.S., III; Ewel, J.J.; Hector, A.; Inchausti, P.; Lavorel, S.; Lawton, J.H.; Lodge, D.; Loreau, M.; Naeem, S. Effects of biodiversity on ecosystem functioning: A consensus of current knowledge. *Ecol. Monogr.* **2005**, *75*, 3–35. [CrossRef]
67. Finegan, B.; Peña-Claros, M.; de Oliveira, A.; Ascarrunz, N.; Bret-Harte, M.S.; Carreño-Rocabado, G.; Casanoves, F.; Díaz, S.; Eguiguren Velepucha, P.; Fernandez, F.; et al. Does functional trait diversity predict above-ground biomass and productivity of tropical forests? Testing three alternative hypotheses. *J. Ecol.* **2015**, *103*, 191–201. [CrossRef]
68. Liang, J.; Crowther, T.W.; Picard, N.; Wiser, S.; Zhou, M.; Alberti, G.; Schulze, E.-D.; McGuire, A.D.; Bozzato, F.; Pretzsch, H.; et al. Positive biodiversity-productivity relationship predominant in global forests. *Science* **2016**, *354*, aaf8957. [CrossRef]
69. Prado-Junior, J.A.; Schiavini, I.; Vale, V.S.; Arantes, C.S.; van der Sande, M.T.; Lohbeck, M.; Poorter, L. Conservative species drive biomass productivity in tropical dry forests. *J. Ecol.* **2016**, *104*, 817–827. [CrossRef]
70. Ali, A.; Yan, E.-R. The forest strata-dependent relationship between biodiversity and aboveground biomass within a subtropical forest. *For. Ecol. Manag.* **2017**, *401*, 125–134. [CrossRef]

forests MDPI

Article

Construction of Additive Allometric Biomass Models for Young Trees of Two Dominate Species in Beijing, China

Shan Wang [1], Zhongke Feng [1,2,*], Zhichao Wang [3,*], Lili Hu [1], Tiantian Ma [1], Xuanhan Yang [1], Hening Fu [1] and Jinshan Li [4]

1 Precision Forestry Key Laboratory of Beijing, Beijing Forestry University, Beijing 100083, China; wangshan@bjfu.edu.cn (S.W.); lizihu666@bjfu.edu.cn (L.H.); matiantian2019@bjfu.edu.cn (T.M.); xuanhanyang@bjfu.edu.cn (X.Y.); fuhening@bjfu.edu.cn (H.F.)
2 Key Laboratory of Genetics and Germplasm Innovation of Tropical Special Forest Trees and Ornamental Plants, Ministry of Education, Hainan University, Haikou 570228, China
3 Surveying and 3S Engineering Research Center, Beijing Forestry University, Beijing 100083, China
4 College of Science, Beijing Forestry University, Beijing 100083, China; lijinshan@bjfu.edu.cn
* Correspondence: zhongkefeng@bjfu.edu.cn (Z.F.); zhichao@bjfu.edu.cn (Z.W.)

Abstract: The traditional volume-derived biomass method is limited because it does not fully consider the carbon sink of young trees, which leads to the underestimation of the carbon sink capacity of a forest ecosystem. Therefore, there is an urgent need to establish an allometric biomass model of young trees to provide a quantitative basis for accurately estimating the carbon storage and carbon sink of young trees. The destructive data that were used in this study included the biomass of the young trees of the two dominant species (*Betula pendula* subsp. *mandshurica* (Regel) Ashburner & McAll and *Populus* × *tomentosa* Carrière) in China, which was composed of the aboveground biomass (B_a), belowground biomass (B_b), and total biomass (B_t). Univariate and bivariate dimensions were selected and five candidate biomass models were independently tested. Two additive allometric biomass model systems of young trees were established using the proportional function control method and algebraic sum control method, respectively. We found that the logistic function was the most suitable for explaining the allometric growth relationship between the B_a, B_t, and diameter at breast height (D) of young trees; the power function was the most suitable for explaining the allometric growth relationship between the B_b and D of young trees. When compared with the independent fitting model, the two additive allometric biomass model systems provide additive biomass prediction which reflects the conditions in reality. The accuracy of the B_t models and B_a models was higher, while the accuracy of the B_b models was lower. In terms of the two dimensions—univariate and bivariate, we found that the bivariate additive allometric biomass model system was more accurate. In the univariate dimension, the proportional function control method was superior to the algebraic sum control method. In the bivariate dimension, the algebraic sum control method was superior to the proportional function control method. The additive allometric biomass models provide a reliable basis for estimating the biomass of young trees and realizing the additivity of the biomass components, which has broad application prospects, such as the monitoring of carbon stocks and carbon sink evaluation.

Keywords: young tree; forest carbon sink; allometric growth; additive model

1. Introduction

The assessment of the carbon sink capacity must be based on an accurate biomass, which is then converted into the carbon content and carbon dioxide equivalent. The volume-derived biomass method is used for the evaluation of forest carbon sinks and considers trees with a diameter at breast height >5 cm. However, the volume-derived biomass method has not been able to assess the carbon sink of young trees, which leads to the underestimation of the carbon sink capacity of forest ecosystems [1]. The assessment of the carbon sink capacity of forest ecosystems has received extensive global attention [2–4]. To address the limitations of the volume-derived biomass method, it is necessary to evaluate the carbon sink of young trees.

The lack of allometric biomass models of young trees affects the accuracy of assessing the available forest biomass, forest fuel load, and carbon sink [5]. Due to the small size of young trees, not calculating the volume of a few young trees will not have a significant impact on the estimation of the carbon stock. However, young trees contribute significantly to the carbon sink because they grow faster than large-diameter trees [6,7]. In addition, reliable biomass models of young trees are particularly important in fire-prone forest ecosystems. For example, in the *Pinus brutia* Ten. forests in Turkey, nearly 15% of the forest area is dominated by young trees (D ranges from 0.1 to 8) [1].

There are differences in the definition of a young tree in different regions. In Turkey, trees with a diameter at breast height of <8 cm are considered to be young trees and are not measured in conventional forest inventory applications such as industrial round-wood production [1]. In China, trees with a diameter at breast height of <5 cm are considered to be young trees and are not measured in forest resource inventories [6]. The biomass estimation of young trees in Turkey mainly targeted the crown biomass component and was based on a small sample size [8]. Due to the difficulty of obtaining biomass samples, the development of an allometric biomass model of young trees in China has been limited to a few studies.

The main methods for estimating the forest biomass include the model and remote sensing inversion methods. The most reliable way to determine the forest biomass would be to cut and weigh all the trees in the forest. However, this would be destructive, time-consuming, costly, and could only be conducted on a small scale [9]. The model method can be used to estimate the forest biomass non-destructively. It estimates the forest biomass using readily measurable tree factors [9,10]. In the model method, the biomass can be estimated either by tree volume and biomass expansion factor or by the allometric biomass model. Biomass estimation on a large spatial scale can be realized using the remote sensing inversion method but atmospheric interference can affect the estimation accuracy of satellite data [11]. Therefore, using allometric biomass models is often the best choice for estimating the forest biomass if there is information on individual trees.

The allometric relationship of young trees is different from that of old trees [12,13]. Bond-Lamberty et al. (2002) found that when using data samples with a large diameter at breast height, the allometric biomass models were significantly biased in estimating the biomass of small-diameter trees [14]. Small-diameter trees play an important role in estimating forest biomass because they account for a large number of the individual trees that make up the biomass [12]. Therefore, it is necessary to separately develop an allometric biomass model of young trees. However, only a few studies have modeled the biomass of young trees [12,15,16].

The selection of the predictor is particularly important when developing an allometric biomass model. Many allometric biomass models were established between tree biomass and easily measured tree variables, such as the diameter at breast height, tree height, crown width, and wood density [17–19]. For these developed models, the diameter at breast height is the most commonly used and reliable predictor [20,21]. It has also been suggested that adding tree height as a predictor to allometric biomass models can significantly improve model performance [22,23].

Model form selection is an important uncertainty in estimating tree biomass. The power function is the most commonly used to model allometric biomass [24,25]. The exponential growth of biomass based on individual size is described in a power function form [26,27]. However, due to resource competition, the continuous acceleration and infinite growth of individual tree biomass in forest ecosystems is not valid. The logistic model is a classical method for predicting population size. The logistic model has similar rapid growth to the power function, which then gradually flattens out and finally approaches the asymptotic value [28]. The logistic model and power function have the same statistical validity, but the logistic model has better ecological significance and can better estimate shrub biomass [29].

For the modeling of tree biomass, the additivity of the biomass components should be ensured, that is, the total biomass of the trees should be equal to the sum of the biomass of each component. The total biomass of the trees is usually divided into different components based on their physiological function, such as the trunk, branch, leaf, and root biomass. When more than two tree components are involved, if the biomass model of each component is fitted separately, the intrinsic correlation between the tree components is not considered. In some studies, mathematical models were selected for the different tree components, parameter fitting was carried out independently, and allometric biomass models of each component were developed. When these models were used for prediction, there was a non-additivity problem between the predicted total biomass of the trees and the predicted biomass of each component [14,30–32].

To solve the additivity problem, different models and estimation methods have been proposed, such as the generalized moment method (GMM) [33], error-in-variable simultaneous equations method (EIV) [34], proportional function control method, and algebraic sum control method [35,36]. Among these methods, there is no unified conclusion on the best method. Zheng et al. (2022) showed that the prediction accuracy of the proportional function control method was higher [37]. Moreover, Xiong et al. (2023) showed that the GMM method had a better fitting performance [25]. Fu et al. showed that the EIV method has more advantages and potential [38].

Considering that the growth of young trees is different from that of old trees, it needs to be confirmed that the conclusions made in previous literature based on the allometric biomass model are applicable to young trees. In this study, based on the measured destructive data of young trees of *Betula pendula* subsp. *mandshurica* (Regel) Ashburner & McAll and *Populus* × *tomentosa* Carrière, the additive allometric biomass model system was established with the diameter at breast height and tree height as the predictors to ensure the additive relationship between the total biomass, aboveground biomass, and belowground biomass. We compared two additive methods, namely the proportional function control method and the algebra sum control method, to determine which method was better. We hypothesized that (1) the bivariate additive allometric biomass model system is more accurate; (2) when compared with the power function, the logistic model can better estimate the allometry of young trees; and (3) among the two additive methods, the proportional function control method is superior to the algebra sum control method.

2. Materials and Methods

2.1. Study Site and Data

2.1.1. Study Site

Beijing is located at the junction of the Inner Mongolia Plateau and the North China Plain. The elevation is ≤100 m and the elevation of most areas ranges between 30 and 50 m. The climate is a warm temperate semi-humid continental monsoon climate with four distinct seasons, a hot and rainy summer and a cold and dry winter. The average annual temperature is about 11.5 °C and the frost-free period is 5 to 6 months annually. The annual average precipitation is 585 mm, with the summer precipitation accounting for about 74% of the annual precipitation. According to zonal vegetation types, Beijing belongs to the warm temperate deciduous broad-leaved forest area [39].

2.1.2. Data Collection

We obtained data during the peak annual biomass accumulation period from September to October 2021. A total of 44 plantation plots of 30 m × 30 m were investigated, and all the young trees with diameters below 5 cm and heights above 130 cm were measured (Table S1).

Table 1 shows the descriptive statistics of the data. The data was collected from 167 young trees: 104 *Betula pendula* subsp. *mandshurica* (Regel) Ashburner & McAll trees and 63 *Populus* × *tomentosa* Carrière trees. The factors that were measured for each tree included the diameter at breast height, tree height, aboveground biomass, belowground biomass, and total biomass. For each tree, the fresh weight of the trunk, branches, and leaves were weighed and samples were taken. The sample was dried in the oven at 105 °C to obtain the dry mass. According to the proportion of the fresh mass and dry mass of the sample, the dry mass of each component was calculated, and then the parts of the tree were added together to obtain the aboveground biomass. The belowground biomass was determined using the full excavation method. The whole root system was dug out manually, the soil on the root was cleared, and then the total fresh weight of the rhizome (≥5 mm), coarse roots (2–5 mm), and fine roots (<2 mm) were weighed. The sample was dried in the oven at 105 °C to obtain the dry mass. According to the proportion of the fresh mass and dry mass of the sample, the dry mass of each component was calculated, and then the parts of the tree were added together to obtain the belowground biomass. The total biomass of the tree was obtained by adding the aboveground and belowground biomass.

Table 1. Statistics of the tree characteristics (N, D, and H) and biomass components (B_a, B_b, and B_t) of two tree species (*Betula pendula* subsp. *mandshurica* (Regel) Ashburner & McAll and *Populus* × *tomentosa* Carrière).

Tree Species	N	D (Mean ± S.D.)	H (Mean ± S.D.)	B_a (Mean ± S.D.)	B_b (Mean ± S.D.)	B_t (Mean ± S.D.)
Betula pendula subsp. *mandshurica* (Regel) Ashburner & McAll	104	3.0 ± 1.0	4.4 ± 1.4	2.095 ± 1.425	0.631 ± 0.540	2.727 ± 1.778
Populus × *tomentosa* Carrière	63	3.1 ± 1.0	4.5 ± 1.4	1.650 ± 1.184	0.445 ± 0.389	2.095 ± 1.513

Note: S.D.—Standard deviation, N—number of samples, D—diameter at breast height (cm), H—tree height (m), B_a—aboveground biomass (kg), B_b—belowground biomass (kg), B_t—total biomass (kg).

2.2. Statistical Analysis

2.2.1. Independent Fitting Model

Many biomass models have been widely used to assess the carbon sink of global forest ecosystems [29,32,40,41]. In this study, five kinds of biomass models commonly used in the past were tested. Univariate and bivariate combinations were considered: (1) diameter at breast height (D); and (2) D and tree height (H). Among them, the three model forms of logistics function (Model 1), quadratic polynomial function (Model 2), and power function (Model 3) only include D.

Model 1: $B = a_0/\left(1 + e^{a_1 + a_2 \cdot D}\right)$

Model 2: $B = a_0 + a_1 D + a_2 D^2$

Model 3: $B = a_0 D^{a_1}$

Model 4: $B = a_0 D^{a_1} H^{a_2}$

Model 5: $B = \exp\left[a_0 + a_1 \cdot \ln\left(H \times D^2\right)\right]$

Model 5: The Akaike information criterion (AIC) statistics were used to assess the model complexity and its goodness of fit, with preference being given to the model with a smaller AIC value. Using the AIC minimization criterion, the optimal model form for the aboveground biomass, belowground biomass, and total biomass in terms of the univariate and bivariate combinations was selected.

2.2.2. Proportional Function Control Method

The basic principle of the proportional function control method is to directly fit the total biomass model and then assign the total biomass to the aboveground biomass and the belowground biomass. The method is specified below.

Steps: based on the optimal model form for the total biomass (B_t) in Section 2.2.1, $B_t = f_1(D)$ and $B_t = f_2(D, H)$ were developed to obtain the estimated value of the total biomass under two dimensions. Then, the scale function under two dimensions was set to: $g_1(D) = b_1 D^{c_1}$ and $g_1(D, H) = d_1 D^{e_1} H^{f_1}$. With the estimated total biomass as the control, the biomasses of the two components were combined into a simultaneous equations system, and the parameters of the system were estimated by nonlinear seemingly unrelated regression. The univariate and bivariate additive allometric biomass model systems were expressed as follows:

$$\begin{cases} B_a = \frac{1}{1+g_1(D)} \times f_1(D) + \varepsilon_1 \\ B_b = \frac{g_1(D)}{1+g_1(D)} \times f_1(D) + \varepsilon_2 \end{cases}$$

$$\begin{cases} B_a = \frac{1}{1+g_1(D,H)} \times f_2(D,H) + \varepsilon_1 \\ B_b = \frac{g_1(D,H)}{1+g_1(D,H)} \times f_2(D,H) + \varepsilon_2 \end{cases}$$

2.2.3. Algebraic Sum Control Method

The basic principle of the algebraic sum control method is that the aboveground biomass, belowground biomass, and total biomass are combined into equations, and the total biomass model is obtained by adding the two-component models. The regression model of each component contains its own independent variables. The method is specified below.

Steps: based on the optimal model form from Section 2.2.1, the optimal model form of the aboveground biomass (B_a) in two dimensions was determined as follows: $B_a = m_1(D)$ and $B_a = m_2(D,H)$, and the optimal model form of the belowground biomass (B_b) under the two dimensions was calculated as follows: $B_b = n_1(D)$ and $B_b = n_2(D,H)$. The two biomass components and the total biomass were combined into a set of equations, and the parameters of the equations were estimated by nonlinear seemingly uncorrelated regression. The univariate and bivariate additive allometric biomass model systems were expressed as follows:

$$\begin{cases} B_a = m_1(D) + \varepsilon_1 \\ B_b = n_1(D) + \varepsilon_2 \\ B_t = m_1(D) + n_1(D) + \varepsilon_3 \end{cases}$$

$$\begin{cases} B_a = m_2(D,H) + \varepsilon_1 \\ B_b = n_2(D,H) + \varepsilon_2 \\ B_t = m_2(D,H) + n_2(D,H) + \varepsilon_3 \end{cases}$$

2.2.4. Model Evaluation

The coefficient of determination (R^2) represents the ratio of the proportion of the variance that is explained by the independent variable to the variance of the dependent variable. When R^2 is close to 1, it indicates that the model can explain the change in the dependent variable well. The root mean square error (*RMSE*) measures the average deviation between the observed and predicted values. The smaller the *RMSE*, the better the predictive ability of the model. The formulae for the R^2 and *RMSE* are specified below:

$$RMSE = \sqrt{\frac{1}{n}\sum_{i=1}^{n}(M_i - \hat{M}_i)^2}$$

$$R^2 = 1 - \frac{\sum_{i=1}^{n}(M_i - \hat{M}_i)^2}{\sum_{i=1}^{n}(M_i - \overline{M})^2}$$

where, M_i is the measured value (%), $\hat{M}_i$ is the predicted value (%), $\overline{M}$ is the average measured value (%), and n is the sample number.

Figure 1 shows the data collection and analysis process. All the statistical calculations were performed using R 4.3.1 [42]. The systemfit package was used to estimate the parameters of the simultaneous equations [43]. The ggplot2 package (version 3.4.4) was used to display the data [44].

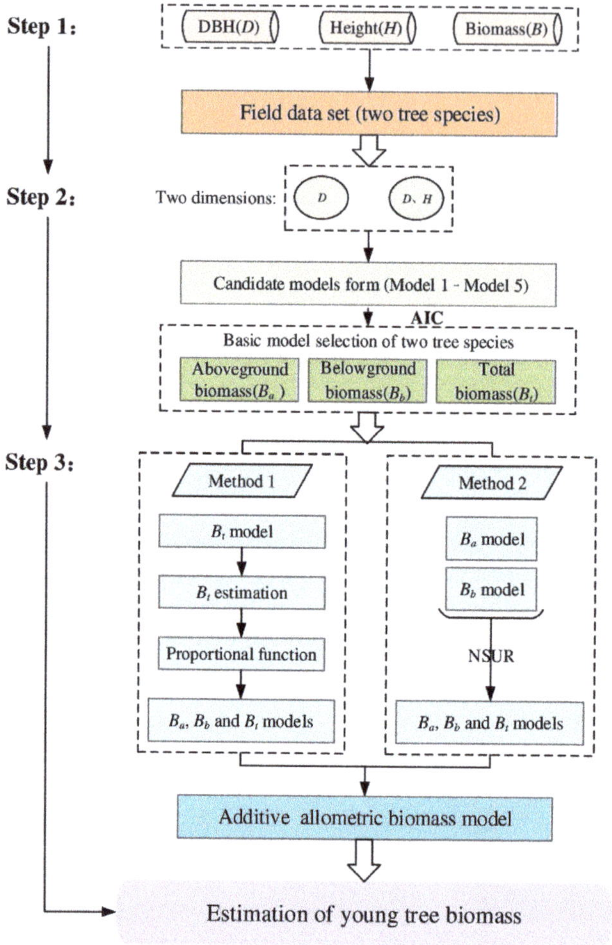

Figure 1. Flowchart of the data collection and analysis.

3. Results

3.1. Correlation Analysis of Variables

The correlation analysis results are shown in Figure 2. Both D and H were positively correlated with B_a, B_b, and B_t. The correlation coefficient of *Betula pendula* subsp. *mandshurica* (Regel) Ashburner & McAll ranged from 0.3 to 0.97. The correlation coefficient of *Populus* × *tomentosa* Carrière ranged from 0.52 to 0.99.

The stacked kernel density of B_a, B_b, and B_t is shown in Figure 3. Skewness is a measure of the asymmetry degree in data distribution. The skewness of *Betula pendula* subsp. *mandshurica* (Regel) Ashburner & McAll ranged from 0.4973 to 2.0447, and that of *Populus* × *tomentosa* Carrière ranged from 0.7338 to 2.0037. The asymmetry degree of B_b is higher, and the asymmetry degree of B_a and B_t is lower.

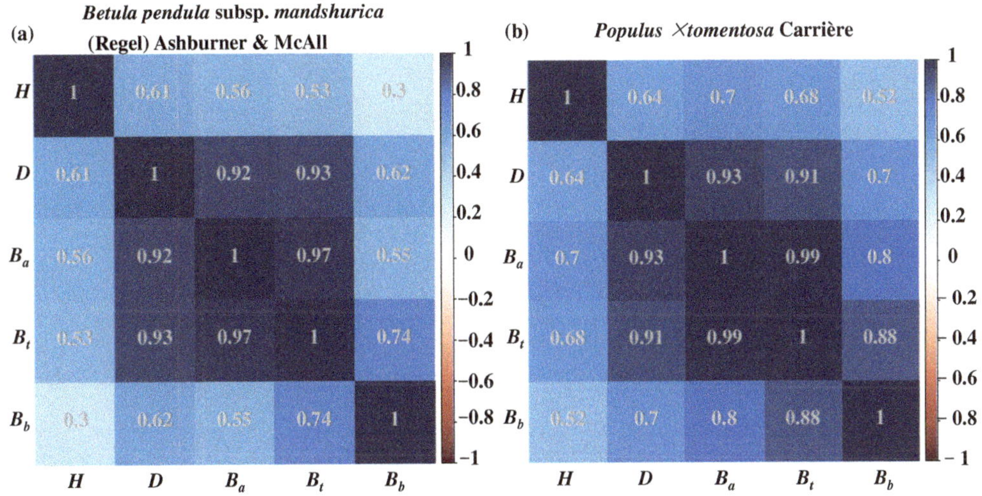

Figure 2. Correlation heat map of five variables (diameter at breast height [D], tree height [H], aboveground biomass [B_a], belowground biomass [B_b], and total biomass [B_t]). Blue indicates positive correlation. Red indicates negative correlation. (**a**) *Betula pendula* subsp. *mandshurica* (Regel) Ashburner & McAll. (**b**) *Populus* × *tomentosa* Carrière.

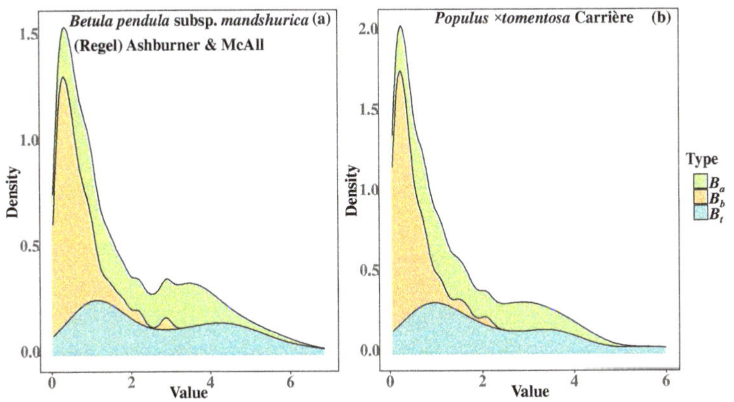

Figure 3. Stacked kernel density plot of three biomass components (aboveground biomass [B_a], belowground biomass [B_b], and total biomass [B_t]). (**a**) *Betula pendula* subsp. *mandshurica* (Regel) Ashburner & McAll. (**b**) *Populus* × *tomentosa* Carrière.

3.2. Analysis of the Independent Fitting Model

Based on the AIC minimization principle, the optimal model form was selected from the five candidate models. In the univariate dimension, the optimal model form for the aboveground biomass of the two species was Model 1, the optimal model form for the belowground biomass was Model 3, and the optimal model form for the total biomass was Model 1 (Figure 4, Table 2). In the bivariate dimension, the optimal model form for the aboveground biomass, belowground biomass, and total biomass of the two species was Model 4 (Table 3).

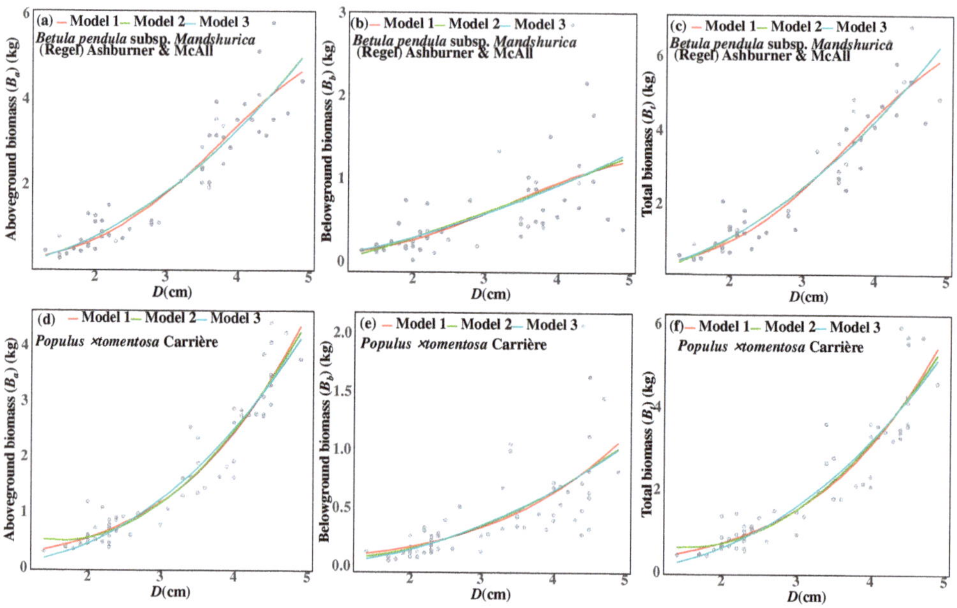

Figure 4. Comparative analysis of three univariate candidate models (Model 1, Model 2, and Model 3) with two tree species and three biomass components (aboveground biomass [B_a], belowground biomass [B_b], and total biomass [B_t]). **(a–c)** is the result of *Betula pendula* subsp. *mandshurica* (Regel) Ashburner & McAll. **(d–f)** is the result of *Populus* × *tomentosa* Carrière.

Table 2. Parameter estimation (a0, a1, and a2) and Akaike information criterion (AIC) results for three univariate candidate models (Model 1, Model 2, and Model 3) with two tree species (*Betula pendula* subsp. *mandshurica* (Regel) Ashburner & McAll and *Populus* × *tomentosa* Carrière) and three biomass components (aboveground biomass [B_a], belowground biomass [B_b], and total biomass [B_t]).

Tree Species	Component	Model	a0	a1	a2	AIC
Betula pendula subsp. *mandshurica* (Regel) Ashburner & McAll	B_a	(1)	6.0309	4.1417	−1.1056	160.28
	B_a	(2)	0.0385	−0.034	0.215	166.39
	B_a	(3)	0.2085	2.0017	NA	164.41
	B_b	(1)	1.4627	3.5013	−1.0489	123.81
	B_b	(2)	−0.2264	0.2456	0.0122	125.17
	B_b	(3)	0.107	1.5734	NA	123.23
	B_t	(1)	7.4355	3.9978	−1.0944	202.02
	B_t	(2)	−0.1882	0.212	0.2272	210.81
	B_t	(3)	0.3099	1.8962	NA	208.64
Populus × *tomentosa* Carrière	B_a	(1)	16.5001	4.9433	−0.8015	54.30
	B_a	(2)	1.4302	−1.1264	0.3487	55.26
	B_a	(3)	0.0877	2.4293	NA	56.36
	B_b	(1)	4.6766	4.5959	−0.6928	24.74
	B_b	(2)	0.0914	−0.0682	0.053	24.78
	B_b	(3)	0.038	2.0698	NA	22.81
	B_t	(1)	22.3301	4.9061	−0.7718	114.68
	B_t	(2)	1.5216	−1.1946	0.4017	115.44
	B_t	(3)	0.124	2.3484	NA	114.84

Note: NA indicates no parameter.

Table 3. Parameter estimation (a0, a1, and a2) and Akaike information criterion (AIC) results of two bivariate candidate models (Model 4 and Model 5) with two tree species (*Betula pendula* subsp. *mandshurica* (Regel) Ashburner & McAll and *Populus* × *tomentosa* Carrière) and three biomass components (aboveground biomass [B_a], belowground biomass [B_b], and total biomass [B_t]).

Tree Species	Component	Model	a0	a1	a2	AIC
Betula pendula subsp. *mandshurica* (Regel) Ashburner & McAll	B_a	(4)	0.2157	2.0291	−0.0442	166.14
	B_a	(5)	−1.6713	0.6432	NA	220.91
	B_b	(4)	0.1879	2.0841	−0.7946	117.52
	B_b	(5)	−2.299	0.4976	NA	135.52
	B_t	(4)	0.3538	2.0019	−0.1724	206.67
	B_t	(5)	−1.2791	0.6106	NA	273.25
Populus × *tomentosa* Carrière	B_a	(4)	0.0649	2.2219	0.3585	41.19
	B_a	(5)	−2.6711	0.8104	NA	67.90
	B_b	(4)	0.0268	1.8741	0.3782	22.78
	B_b	(5)	−3.6567	0.7321	NA	22.82
	B_t	(4)	0.0905	2.1431	0.3649	106.15
	B_t	(5)	−2.3654	0.7943	NA	120.52

Note: NA indicates no parameter.

3.3. Analysis of the Two Additive Allometric Biomass Models

According to the estimation results of the optimal total biomass that was selected in Tables 2 and 3, the proportional function was set and the equations were combined into simultaneous equations. The parameter estimation of the proportional function control method is shown in Table 4. According to the optimal model forms for the aboveground and belowground biomass that were selected in Tables 2 and 3, the equations were combined into simultaneous equations. The parameter estimation using the algebraic sum control methods is shown in Table 5.

Table 4. Parameter results of the total biomass model and proportional function for two tree species (*Betula pendula* subsp. *mandshurica* (Regel) Ashburner & McAll and *Populus* × *tomentosa* Carrière) using the univariate and bivariate proportional function control method.

Species	Dimension	Model	Total Biomass			Proportional Function		
			a0	a1	a2	b0	b1	b2
Betula pendula subsp. *mandshurica* (Regel) Ashburner & McAll	Univariate	1	7.4355	3.9978	−1.0944	0.5107	−0.4223	/
	Bivariate	4	0.3538	2.0019	−0.1724	0.9139	−0.0397	−0.6976
Populus × *tomentosa* Carrière	Univariate	1	22.3301	1.9061	0.7718	0.3929	−0.2906	/
	Bivariate	4	0.0905	2.1431	0.3649	0.3879	−0.3167	0.0305

Table 5. Parametric results of the aboveground biomass and belowground biomass model for two tree species (*Betula pendula* subsp. *mandshurica* (Regel) Ashburner & McAll and *Populus* × *tomentosa* Carrière) using the univariate and bivariate algebraic sum control method.

Species	Dimension	Model	Aboveground Biomass			Model	Belowground Biomass		
			b0	b1	b2		c0	c1	c2
Betula pendula subsp. *mandshurica* (Regel) Ashburner & McAll	Univariate	1	5.9573	4.1662	−1.1197	3	0.1086	1.5628	/
	Bivariate	4	0.2153	2.0213	−0.0366	4	0.1867	2.0909	−0.7964
Populus × *tomentosa* Carrière	Univariate	1	12.2232	4.7389	−0.8437	3	0.0374	2.0816	/
	Bivariate	4	0.0642	2.2329	0.3555	4	0.0247	1.9306	0.3798

Figure 5 shows the logistic function results in Table 4. Both coefficients of the logistic function have ecological significance; a0 refers to the equilibrium biomass and −a2 is the growth rate relative to the equilibrium biomass. A larger −a2 value indicates that individual trees will rapidly increase in biomass at a younger stage, which is known as the equilibrium growth rate.

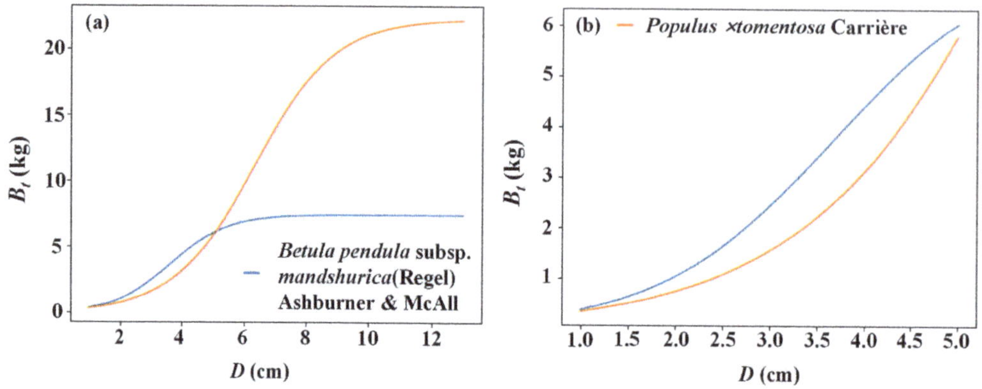

Figure 5. Visualizations of logistic function in Table 4. (**a**) Comparative analysis of the equilibrium biomass of two tree species (*Betula pendula* subsp. *mandshurica* (Regel) Ashburner & McAll and *Populus* × *tomentosa* Carrière). (**b**) Comparative analysis of the equilibrium growth rate of two tree species (*Betula pendula* subsp. *mandshurica* (Regel) Ashburner & McAll and *Populus* × *tomentosa* Carrière).

The results showed that the equilibrium biomass of B_t and B_a of *Populus* × *tomentosa* Carrière was higher than that of *Betula pendula* subsp. *mandshurica* (Regel) Ashburner & McAll. The equilibrium growth rate of B_t and B_a of *Betula pendula* subsp. *mandshurica* (Regel) Ashburner & McAll is higher than that of *Populus* × *tomentosa* Carrière (Tables 4 and 5).

The parameter estimation processes of the two additive allometric biomass models were different but the accuracy performance of the models was similar. For the proportional function control method, the R^2 of the total biomass model and aboveground biomass model was higher (0.861–0.9292) when compared with the R^2 of the belowground biomass model (0.3899–0.5101). For the algebraic sum control methods, the R^2 of the total biomass model and aboveground biomass model was high (0.8604–0.9293), while the R^2 of the belowground biomass model was low (0.3795–0.5100; Table 6).

Table 6. Precision index (R^2 and *RMSE*) results of the proportional function control and algebraic sum control methods in the univariate and bivariate dimensions with two tree species (*Betula pendula* subsp. *mandshurica* (Regel) Ashburner & McAll and *Populus* × *tomentosa* Carrière) and three biomass components (aboveground biomass [B_a], belowground biomass [B_b], and total biomass [B_t]).

Species	Dimension	Additive Method	Total Biomass		Aboveground Biomass		Belowground Biomass	
			R^2	*RMSE*	R^2	*RMSE*	R^2	*RMSE*
Betula pendula subsp. *mandshurica* (Regel) Ashburner & McAll	Univariate	1	0.8756	0.6272	0.8683	0.5247	0.3899	0.4257
	Univariate	2	0.8749	0.6289	0.8681	0.5252	0.3795	0.4293
	Bivariate	1	0.8795	0.6174	0.8748	0.5091	0.4221	0.4164
	Bivariate	2	0.8804	0.6150	0.8753	0.5106	0.4239	0.4157
Populus × *tomentosa* Carrière	Univariate	1	0.8610	0.5643	0.9128	0.3552	0.4943	0.2809
	Univariate	2	0.8604	0.5655	0.9127	0.3584	0.4941	0.281
	Bivariate	1	0.8786	0.5273	0.9292	0.3229	0.5101	0.2788
	Bivariate	2	0.8786	0.5272	0.9293	0.3227	0.5100	0.2789

Combining the prediction accuracy of the three biomasses, the two dimensions were compared. The bivariate additive allometric biomass model system was the most accurate (Table 6). Then, the two additive methods were compared. In the univariate dimension, the proportional function control method was superior to the algebraic sum control method. In the bivariate dimension, the algebraic sum control method was superior to the proportional function control method (Table 6).

For *Betula pendula* subsp. *mandshurica* (Regel) Ashburner & McAll, the model performance was optimal when the algebraic sum control methods were used in the bivariate dimension (total biomass model: $R^2 = 0.8804$, aboveground biomass model: $R^2 = 0.8753$, belowground biomass model: $R^2 = 0.4239$). For *Populus* × *tomentosa* Carrière, the model performance was optimal when the algebraic sum control methods were used in the bivariate dimension (total biomass model: $R^2 = 0.8786$, aboveground biomass model: $R^2 = 0.9293$, belowground biomass model: $R^2 = 0.5100$; Figure 6).

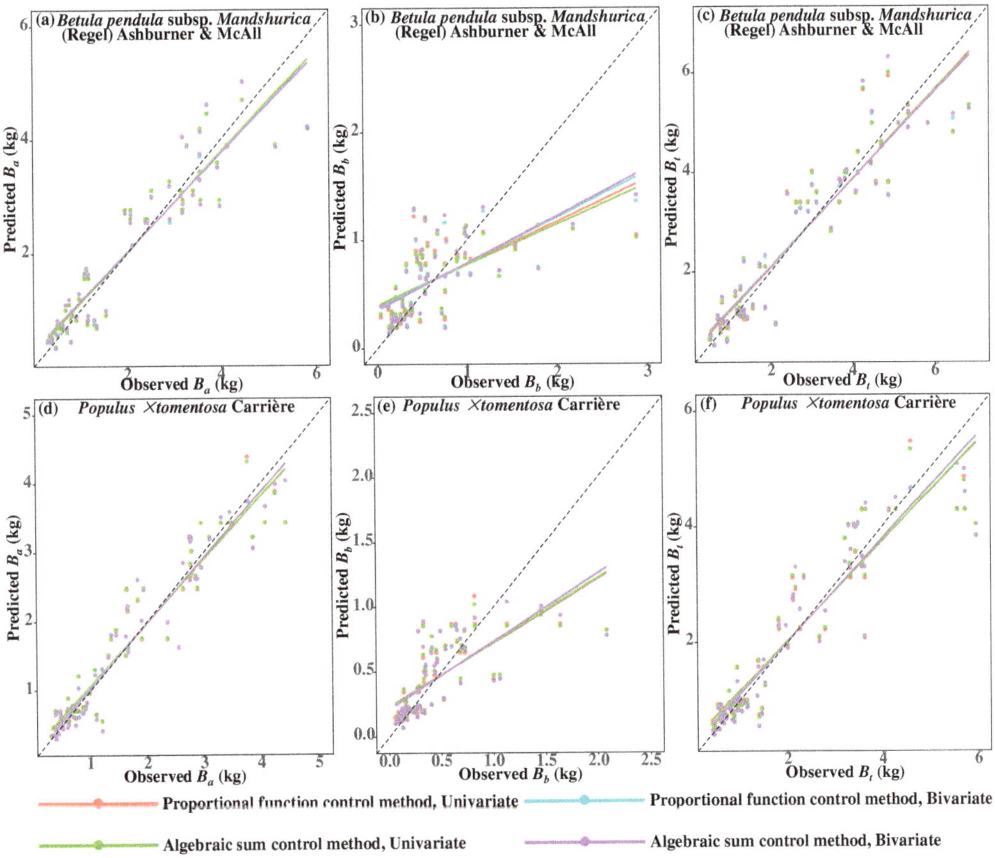

Figure 6. Regression results of the observed values and the predicted values of the proportional function control and algebraic sum control methods in the univariate and bivariate dimensions with two tree species and three biomass components (aboveground biomass [B_a], belowground biomass [B_b], and total biomass [B_t]). **(a–c)** is the result of *Betula pendula* subsp. *mandshurica* (Regel) Ashburner & McAll. **(d–f)** is the result of *Populus* × *tomentosa* Carrière.

In addition, we conducted validation and found that the two additive allometric biomass models were additive and met the needs of practical applications, and the independent regression models were not additive (Figure 7).

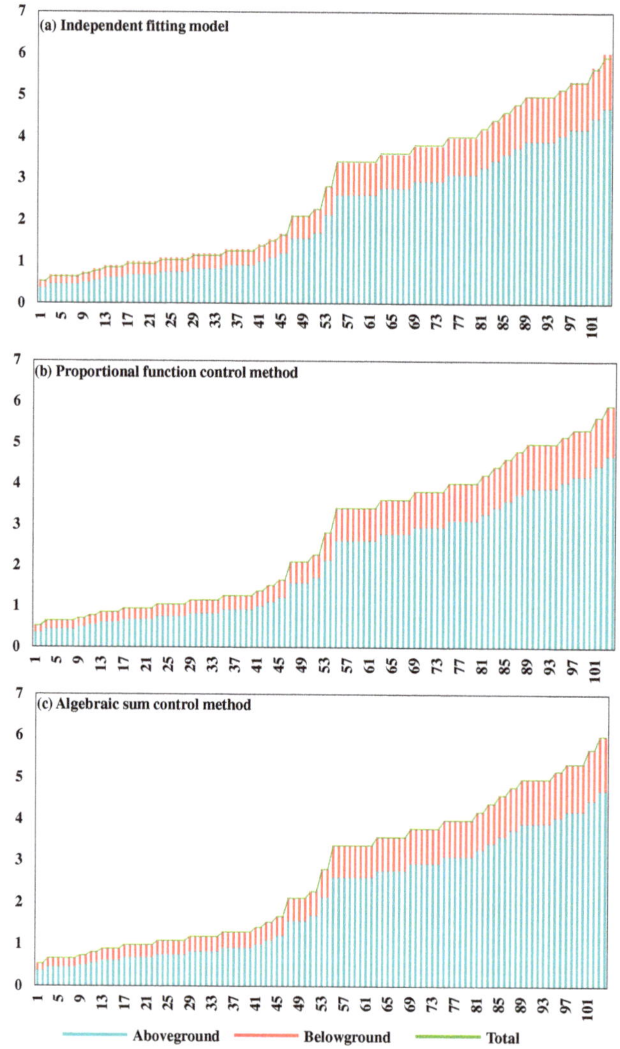

Figure 7. Additivity verification of the independent fitting model and two additive allometric biomass models (proportional function control method and algebraic sum control method). (**a**) Independent fitting model. (**b**) Proportional function control method. (**c**) Algebraic sum control method.

4. Discussion

A robust allometric biomass model should be built from a large number of data samples. When the sample size of the biomass data is relatively small, the accuracy of the model may be reduced. Consequently, this study included 167 young trees, which was sufficient to conduct robust biomass modeling for two tree species. Wang (2006) established independent biomass models with only 10 trees per species using biomass data from *Pinus koraiensis* and *Larix gmelinii* [45]. Additionally, Zheng et al. (2022) used the biomass data from 137 young trees on the Qinghai–Tibet Plateau to establish independent biomass models with the ground diameter instead of the diameter at breast height as a predictor [37]. Wang et al. used destructive biomass data from 501 trees in three provinces of young trees in northeast China to establish a biomass model [13]. Furthermore, Dong et al. (2014) established an additive allometric biomass model system with sample sizes of 41 Pinus koraiensis and 122 *Larix gmelinii* [46]. Then, Cui et al. (2020) harvested 45 *Robinia pseudoacacia* L. in the Loess Plateau of Shaanxi Province and established an additive allometric biomass model system [22]. This study did not collect samples from different ecological regions, so this is a potential limitation. Therefore, it is suggested that young trees of *Betula pendula* subsp. *mandshurica* (Regel) Ashburner & McAll and *Populus × tomentosa* Carrière should be sampled in different ecological zones in the future.

We found that the logistic function was the optimal model form for the aboveground biomass and total biomass, and the power function was more suitable for fitting the belowground biomass. Whether the traditional allometric biomass model (that is, the power function model) can fit all the observed biomass data well has been investigated by ecologists [24,47,48]. Although the power function has been verified statistically in previous biomass studies, it has been challenged theoretically [26,29]. Consistent with our study, Ma et al. (2021) found that the logistic function was superior to the power function for estimating the allometry relationship of shrub biomass [29]. In addition, Zhou et al. (2021) proposed the concept of a dynamic allometric scaling relationship between the trunk biomass and aboveground biomass, which was fitted to an asymptotic allometric model, and it was verified that it could fit biomass data better than a power function [26].

As hypothesized, we found that the prediction accuracy of the model that included tree height as a predictor was significantly improved. This is consistent with many other studies [22,49,50]. In contrast, Zhang et al. (2016) discovered that the addition of tree height to the biomass model did not improve the model performance as expected, especially for the branch biomass and leaf biomass [51]. Tree height is often overlooked in forest models because it is difficult to accurately measure tree height in closed-canopy forests, and there has been substantial debate on whether to use tree height as a predictor for biomass models [52]. For young trees, it is easy to measure the tree height. Therefore, in practical applications, it is more appropriate to use the bivariate additive allometric biomass model that was developed in this study.

We have verified that the sum of the predicted values of each biomass component model was different from the predicted values of the total biomass model when using the independent fitting model. The disadvantage of the independent fitting model is that additivity is not satisfied. In contrast, the two additive allometric biomass models that were developed have clear advantages. The models of the total biomass, aboveground biomass, and belowground biomass were fitted using simultaneous equations to explain the intrinsic correlation between the biomass components of the same tree. Therefore, it is crucial to emphasize the benefit of using the additive allometric biomass model in practical applications.

There are many additive modeling methods. However, we found that the proportional function control method was superior to the algebraic sum control method in the univariate dimension, and the algebraic sum control method was superior to the proportional function control method in the bivariate dimension. Many studies have used algebraic sum and proportional function control methods to construct additive allometric biomass model systems. For instance, Liu et al. (2023) conducted destructive sampling of trees on Hainan Island and established an additive allometric biomass model using the algebraic sum control method, which satisfied the additivity of the aboveground biomass, branch biomass, and leaf biomass [19]. Furthermore, Wang et al. (2018) established an additive allometric biomass model based on diameter at breast height and height in a young forest of *Betula pendula* subsp. *mandshurica* (Regel) Ashburner & McAll in northeast China using the algebraic sum control method [13]. Moreover, Fu et al. (2016) established an additive allometric biomass model with *Pinus massoniana* Lamb. in southern China using the algebraic sum control method [38]. Then, Zhang et al. (2016) established one-, two-, and three-variable additive allometric biomass models for *Populus × tomentosa* Carrière in the Jiangsu Province, China using the proportional function control method [51]. Zeng et al. (2017) realized the additivity between the aboveground biomass and four biomass components, the trunk, bark, branches, and leaves [53]. The proportional function control method is first fitted to the whole tree biomass, and then the proportional function is used to allocate the tree biomass to each biomass component. The algebraic sum control method is used to directly model the biomass component, and then the total biomass is obtained by adding the biomasses of each component. In the practice of forestry production, the goal is to obtain the whole tree biomass or the aboveground biomass, so the additive model that is developed using the proportional function control method is more practical.

Whether the sample data need to be divided into modeling data and testing data is still a controversial issue. Some studies suggest that the applicability of evaluating the predictive ability of the model by calculating the evaluation index of the modeling data must be tested [54]. However, Kozak and Kozak (2003) concluded that grouping samples for suitability tests would result in the loss of part of the modeling information and would not provide additional information for model evaluation [55]. To make full use of the sample information, this study did not distinguish between modeling samples and test samples, and all the sample data were used to build the biomass models.

5. Conclusions

In this study, two additive allometric biomass model systems of young trees of *Betula pendula* subsp. *mandshurica* (Regel) Ashburner & McAll and *Populus* × *tomentosa* Carrière were established, these provide a theoretical reference and technical support for estimating the biomass of young trees at a single tree scale. The two yield table is given for the application of the model (Tables S2 and S3). Our research results will provide a quantitative basis for the monitoring of carbon stocks and carbon sink evaluation of young trees in China. We found that the logistic function was more suitable for explaining the allometric growth relationship between the aboveground biomass, total biomass, and diameter at breast height of young trees; the power function was more suitable for explaining the allometric growth relationship between the belowground biomass and diameter at breast height of young trees. In the actual modeling process, an appropriate model form should be selected for the different biomass components since the biomass results of independent fitting models are not additive. The bivariate additive allometric model system has higher accuracy. Thus, in practical applications, we recommend the bivariate additive allometric model as the first choice. There was no consensus on which of the two additive methods was better. In the univariate dimension, the proportional function control method was superior to the algebraic sum control method. In the bivariate dimension, the algebraic sum control method was superior to the proportional function control method. In the actual modeling process, it is necessary to compare the methods and choose the best additive method.

The biomass of young trees is influenced by a variety of abiotic and biological factors, including climate, stand structure, and site conditions. Thus, it is suggested that future studies should consider including these factors as additional predictors. Mixed effect models have been shown to have advantages in improving the accuracy of model estimation. Therefore, the biomass prediction could be improved by combining the mixed effect model with the additive model.

Supplementary Materials: The following supporting information can be downloaded at: https://www.mdpi.com/article/10.3390/f15060991/s1, Table S1: Location and basic stand factors of 50 plantations plots. Table S2: Yield table of *Betula pendula* subsp. *mandshurica* (Regel) Ashburner & McAll. Table S3: Yield table of *Populus* × *tomentosa* Carrière.

Author Contributions: S.W.: Conceptualization, Formal analysis, Writing—Original draft preparation; Z.F.: Conceptualization, Formal analysis, Writing—Reviewing and Editing; Z.W.: Conceptualization, Formal analysis, Writing—Reviewing and Editing; L.H.: Formal analysis, Writing—Reviewing and Editing; T.M.: Investigation, Writing—Reviewing and Editing; X.Y.: Investigation, Writing—Reviewing and Editing; H.F.: Investigation, Writing—Reviewing and Editing; J.L.: Investigation, Writing—Reviewing and Editing. All authors have read and agreed to the published version of the manuscript.

Funding: This study was supported by 5·5 Engineering Research & Innovation Team Project of Beijing Forestry University (BLRC2023A03), the Natural Science Foundation of Beijing (8232038, 8234065), and the Key Research and Development Projects of Ningxia Hui Autonomous Region (2023BEG02050).

Data Availability Statement: The data used to support the findings of this study are available from the corresponding author upon request.

Acknowledgments: The authors would like to thank all the reviewers who participated in the review.

Conflicts of Interest: The authors declare no conflicts of interest.

References

1. Eker, M.; Poudel, K.P.; Özçelik, R. Aboveground Biomass Equations for Small Trees of Brutian Pine in Turkey to Facilitate Harvesting and Management. *Forests* **2017**, *8*, 477. [CrossRef]
2. Pan, Y.; Birdsey, R.A.; Fang, J.; Houghton, R.; Kauppi, P.E.; Kurz, W.A.; Phillips, O.L.; Shvidenko, A.; Lewis, S.L.; Canadell, J.G. A Large and Persistent Carbon Sink in the World's Forests. *Science* **2011**, *333*, 988–993. [CrossRef]
3. Gómez-García, E. Estimating the Changes in Tree Carbon Stocks in Galician Forests (NW Spain) between 1972 and 2009. *For. Ecol. Manag.* **2020**, *467*, 118157. [CrossRef]
4. Dixon, R.K.; Solomon, A.M.; Brown, S.; Houghton, R.A.; Trexier, M.C.; Wisniewski, J. Carbon Pools and Flux of Global Forest Ecosystems. *Science* **1994**, *263*, 185–190. [CrossRef]
5. Wang, S.; Zhang, H.; Feng, Z.; Wang, Y.; Su, J.; Gao, K.; Li, J. Dispersal Limitation Dominates the Spatial Distribution of Forest Fuel Loads in Chongqing, China. *Ecosyst. Health Sustain.* **2023**, *9*, 0079. [CrossRef]
6. Zhang, H.; Feng, Z.; Shen, C.; Li, Y.; Feng, Z.; Zeng, W.; Huang, G. Relationship between the Geographical Environment and the Forest Carbon Sink Capacity in China Based on an Individual-Tree Growth-Rate Model. *Ecol. Indic.* **2022**, *138*, 108814. [CrossRef]
7. Zhang, H.; Feng, Z.; Chen, P.; Chen, X. Development of a Tree Growth Difference Equation and Its Application in Forecasting the Biomass Carbon Stocks of Chinese Forests in 2050. *Forests* **2019**, *10*, 582. [CrossRef]
8. Bilgili, E.; Kucuk, O. Estimating Above-Ground Fuel Biomass in Young Calabrian Pine (*Pinus brutia* Ten.). *Energy Fuels* **2009**, *23*, 1797–1800.
9. Yuen, J.Q.; Fung, T.; Ziegler, A.D. Review of Allometric Equations for Major Land Covers in SE Asia: Uncertainty and Implications for above-and below-Ground Carbon Estimates. *For. Ecol. Manag.* **2016**, *360*, 323–340. [CrossRef]
10. Luo, Y.; Wang, X.; Ouyang, Z.; Lu, F.; Feng, L.; Tao, J. A Review of Biomass Equations for China's Tree Species. *Earth Syst. Sci. Data* **2020**, *12*, 21–40. [CrossRef]
11. Huang, H.; Liu, C.; Wang, X.; Zhou, X.; Gong, P. Integration of Multi-Resource Remotely Sensed Data and Allometric Models for Forest Aboveground Biomass Estimation in China. *Remote Sens. Environ.* **2019**, *221*, 225–234. [CrossRef]
12. Chaturvedi, R.K.; Raghubanshi, A.S. Aboveground Biomass Estimation of Small Diameter Woody Species of Tropical Dry Forest. *New For.* **2013**, *44*, 509–519. [CrossRef]
13. Wang, X.; Zhao, D.; Liu, G.; Yang, C.; Teskey, R.O. Additive Tree Biomass Equations for *Betula Platyphylla* Suk. Plantations in Northeast China. *Ann. For. Sci.* **2018**, *75*, 60. [CrossRef]
14. Bond-Lamberty, B.; Wang, C.; Gower, S.T. Aboveground and Belowground Biomass and Sapwood Area Allometric Equations for Six Boreal Tree Species of Northern Manitoba. *Can. J. For. Res.* **2002**, *32*, 1441–1450. [CrossRef]
15. Daryaei, A.; Sohrabi, H. Additive Biomass Equations for Small Diameter Trees of Temperate Mixed Deciduous Forests. *Scand. J. For. Res.* **2016**, *31*, 394–398. [CrossRef]
16. Nelson, A.S.; Weiskittel, A.R.; Wagner, R.G.; Saunders, M.R. Development and Evaluation of Aboveground Small Tree Biomass Models for Naturally Regenerated and Planted Species in Eastern Maine, USA. *Biomass Bioenergy* **2014**, *68*, 215–227. [CrossRef]
17. Alvarez, E.; Duque, A.; Saldarriaga, J.; Cabrera, K.; de Las Salas, G.; del Valle, I.; Lema, A.; Moreno, F.; Orrego, S.; Rodríguez, L. Tree Above-Ground Biomass Allometries for Carbon Stocks Estimation in the Natural Forests of Colombia. *For. Ecol. Manag.* **2012**, *267*, 297–308. [CrossRef]
18. Zeng, W.; Tang, S. Modeling Compatible Single-Tree Aboveground Biomass Equations for Masson Pine (*Pinus Massoniana*) in Southern China. *J. For. Res.* **2012**, *23*, 593–598. [CrossRef]
19. Liu, B.; Bu, W.; Zang, R. Improved Allometric Models to Estimate the Aboveground Biomass of Younger Secondary Tropical Forests. *Glob. Ecol. Conserv.* **2023**, *41*, e02359. [CrossRef]
20. Cole, T.G.; Ewel, J.J. Allometric Equations for Four Valuable Tropical Tree Species. *For. Ecol. Manag.* **2006**, *229*, 351–360. [CrossRef]
21. Zhou, X.; Brandle, J.R.; Schoeneberger, M.M.; Awada, T. Developing Above-Ground Woody Biomass Equations for Open-Grown, Multiple-Stemmed Tree Species: Shelterbelt-Grown Russian-Olive. *Ecol. Model.* **2007**, *202*, 311–323. [CrossRef]
22. Cui, Y.; Bi, H.; Liu, S.; Hou, G.; Wang, N.; Ma, X.; Zhao, D.; Wang, S.; Yun, H. Developing Additive Systems of Biomass Equations for *Robinia pseudoacacia* L. in the Region of Loess Plateau of Western Shanxi Province, China. *Forests* **2020**, *11*, 1332. [CrossRef]
23. Rutishauser, E.; Noor'an, F.; Laumonier, Y.; Halperin, J.; Hergoualc'h, K.; Verchot, L. Generic Allometric Models Including Height Best Estimate Forest Biomass and Carbon Stocks in Indonesia. *For. Ecol. Manag.* **2013**, *307*, 219–225. [CrossRef]

24. Picard, N.; Rutishauser, E.; Ploton, P.; Ngomanda, A.; Henry, M. Should Tree Biomass Allometry Be Restricted to Power Models? *For. Ecol. Manag.* **2015**, *353*, 156–163. [CrossRef]
25. Xiong, N.; Qiao, Y.; Ren, H.; Zhang, L.; Chen, R.; Wang, J. Comparison of Parameter Estimation Methods Based on Two Additive Biomass Models with Small Samples. *Forests* **2023**, *14*, 1655. [CrossRef]
26. Zhou, X.; Yang, M.; Liu, Z.; Li, P.; Xie, B.; Peng, C. Dynamic Allometric Scaling of Tree Biomass and Size. *Nat. Plants* **2021**, *7*, 42–49. [CrossRef]
27. Zheng, X.-J.; Wang, Y.-G.; Wu, X.; Ren, W.; Wu, Y.; Li, Y.; Cao, X.; Ma, J.; Zhou, H. An Expanded Allometric Model for Crowns of Four Co-Existing Desert Shrubs. *Trees* **2019**, *33*, 1423–1433. [CrossRef]
28. Bertsimas, D.; King, A. Logistic Regression: From Art to Science. *Stat. Sci.* **2017**, *32*, 367–384. [CrossRef]
29. Ma, J.; Yuan, C.; Zhou, J.; Li, Y.; Gao, G.; Fu, B. Logistic Model Outperforms Allometric Regression to Estimate Biomass of Xerophytic Shrubs. *Ecol. Indic.* **2021**, *132*, 108278. [CrossRef]
30. Jenkins, J.C.; Birdsey, R.A.; Pan, Y. Biomass and NPP Estimation for the Mid-Atlantic Region (USA) Using Plot-level Forest Inventory Data. *Ecol. Appl.* **2001**, *11*, 1174–1193. [CrossRef]
31. Xiao, C.-W.; Ceulemans, R. Allometric Relationships for Below-and Aboveground Biomass of Young Scots Pines. *For. Ecol. Manag.* **2004**, *203*, 177–186. [CrossRef]
32. Mugasha, W.A.; Eid, T.; Bollandsås, O.M.; Malimbwi, R.E.; Chamshama, S.A.O.; Zahabu, E.; Katani, J.Z. Allometric Models for Prediction of Above-and Belowground Biomass of Trees in the Miombo Woodlands of Tanzania. *For. Ecol. Manag.* **2013**, *310*, 87–101. [CrossRef]
33. Greene, W.H. *Econometric Analysis*; Pearson Education: Delhi, India, 2003; ISBN 81-7758-684-X.
34. Tang, S.; Wang, Y. A Parameter Estimation Program for the Error-in-Variable Model. *Ecol. Model.* **2002**, *156*, 225–236. [CrossRef]
35. Zeng, W.; Tang, S. *Using Measurement Error Modeling Method to Establish Compatible Single-Tree Biomass Equations System*; Forest Research: Beijing, China, 2010; Volume 23, pp. 797–803.
36. Liu, Q.; Peng, D.; Huang, G.; Zeng, W.; Wang, X. Compatible standing tree volume and above-ground biomass equations for spruce (*Picea asperata*) in northeastern China. *J. Beijing For. Univ.* **2015**, *37*, 8–15. (In Chinese)
37. Zheng, X.; Yi, L.; Li, Q. Developing biomass estimation models of young trees in typical plantation on the Qinghai-Tibet Plateau, China. *Chin. J. Appl. Ecol.* **2022**, *33*, 2923–2935. (In Chinese)
38. Fu, L.; Lei, Y.; Wang, G.; Bi, H.; Tang, S.; Song, X. Comparison of Seemingly Unrelated Regressions with Error-in-Variable Models for Developing a System of Nonlinear Additive Biomass Equations. *Trees* **2016**, *30*, 839–857. [CrossRef]
39. Fang, J.; Yoda, K. Climate and Vegetation in China II. Distribution of Main Vegetation Types and Thermal Climate. *Ecol. Res.* **1989**, *4*, 71–83. [CrossRef]
40. Zianis, D.; Muukkonen, P.; Mäkipää, R.; Mencuccini, M. *Biomass and Stem Volume Equations for Tree Species in Europe*; FI: Helsinki, Finland, 2005; ISBN 951-40-1983-0.
41. Henry, M.; Picard, N.; Trotta, C.; Manlay, R.; Valentini, R.; Bernoux, M.; Saint André, L. Estimating Tree Biomass of Sub-Saharan African Forests: A Review of Available Allometric Equations. *Silva Fenn.* **2011**, *45*, 477–569. [CrossRef]
42. R Core Team. *R: A Language and Environment for Statistical Computing*; R Foundation for Statistical Computing: Vienna, Austria, 2013.
43. Henningsen, A.; Hamann, J.D. Systemfit: A Package for Estimating Systems of Simultaneous Equations in R. *J. Stat. Softw.* **2008**, *23*, 1–40. [CrossRef]
44. Wickham, H. Ggplot2. *Wiley Interdiscip. Rev. Comput. Stat.* **2011**, *3*, 180–185. [CrossRef]
45. Wang, C. Biomass Allometric Equations for 10 Co-Occurring Tree Species in Chinese Temperate Forests. *For. Ecol. Manag.* **2006**, *222*, 9–16. [CrossRef]
46. Dong, L.; Zhang, L.; Li, F. A Compatible System of Biomass Equations for Three Conifer Species in Northeast, China. *For. Ecol. Manag.* **2014**, *329*, 306–317. [CrossRef]
47. Poorter, H.; Jagodzinski, A.M.; Ruiz-Peinado, R.; Kuyah, S.; Luo, Y.; Oleksyn, J.; Usoltsev, V.A.; Buckley, T.N.; Reich, P.B.; Sack, L. How Does Biomass Distribution Change with Size and Differ among Species? An Analysis for 1200 Plant Species from Five Continents. *New Phytol.* **2015**, *208*, 736–749. [CrossRef]
48. Muller-Landau, H.C.; Condit, R.S.; Chave, J.; Thomas, S.C.; Bohlman, S.A.; Bunyavejchewin, S.; Davies, S.; Foster, R.; Gunatilleke, S.; Gunatilleke, N. Testing Metabolic Ecology Theory for Allometric Scaling of Tree Size, Growth and Mortality in Tropical Forests. *Ecol. Lett.* **2006**, *9*, 575–588. [CrossRef]
49. Dong, L.; Zhang, L.; Li, F. Developing Two Additive Biomass Equations for Three Coniferous Plantation Species in Northeast China. *Forests* **2016**, *7*, 136. [CrossRef]
50. Wang, X.; Fang, J.; Tang, Z.; Zhu, B. Climatic Control of Primary Forest Structure and DBH–Height Allometry in Northeast China. *For. Ecol. Manag.* **2006**, *234*, 264–274. [CrossRef]
51. Zhang, C.; Peng, D.-L.; Huang, G.-S.; Zeng, W.-S. Developing Aboveground Biomass Equations Both Compatible with Tree Volume Equations and Additive Systems for Single-Trees in Poplar Plantations in Jiangsu Province, China. *Forests* **2016**, *7*, 32. [CrossRef]
52. Chave, J.; Réjou-Méchain, M.; Búrquez, A.; Chidumayo, E.; Colgan, M.S.; Delitti, W.B.; Duque, A.; Eid, T.; Fearnside, P.M.; Goodman, R.C. Improved Allometric Models to Estimate the Aboveground Biomass of Tropical Trees. *Glob. Change Biol.* **2014**, *20*, 3177–3190. [CrossRef]

53. Zeng, W.; Zhang, L.; Chen, X.; Cheng, Z.; Ma, K.; Li, Z. Construction of Compatible and Additive Individual-Tree Biomass Models for Pinus Tabulaeformis in China. *Can. J. For. Res.* **2017**, *47*, 467–475. [CrossRef]
54. Shao, J. Linear Model Selection by Cross-Validation. *J. Am. Stat. Assoc.* **1993**, *88*, 486–494. [CrossRef]
55. Kozak, A.; Kozak, R. Does Cross Validation Provide Additional Information in the Evaluation of Regression Models? *Can. J. For. Res.* **2003**, *33*, 976–987. [CrossRef]

forests

MDPI

Article

Driving Factors and Spatial Distribution of Aboveground Biomass in the Managed Forest in the Terai Region of Nepal

Yam Bahadur KC [1,2], Qijing Liu [1,*], Pradip Saud [3], Chang Xu [1], Damodar Gaire [2] and Hari Adhikari [4,5,*]

1 School of Forestry, Beijing Forestry University, Haidian District, Beijing 100107, China
2 Institute of Forestry, Tribhuvan University, Hetauda 44107, Nepal
3 College of Forestry, Agricultural and Natural Resources, University of Arkanas at Monticello, Monticello, AR 71656, USA
4 Department of Geosciences and Geography, University of Helsinki, P.O. Box 64, FI-00014 Helsinki, Finland
5 Forest Nepal, Amar Marg 88, C3534, Butwal 32907, Nepal
* Correspondence: liuqijing@bjfu.edu.cn (Q.L.); hari.adhikari@helsinki.fi (H.A.)

Abstract: Above-ground biomass (AGB) is affected by numerous factors, including topography, climate, land use, or tree/forest attributes. Investigating the distribution and driving factors of AGB within the managed forests in Nepal is crucial for developing effective strategies for climate change mitigation, and sustainable forest management and conservation. A total of 110 field plots (circular 0.02 ha plots with a 9 m radius), and airborne laser scanning (ALS)-light detection and ranging (LiDAR) data were collected in 2021. The random forest (RF) model was employed to predict the AGB at a 30 m $\times$ 30 m resolution based on 32 LiDAR metrics derived from ALS returns. The study assessed the relationships between the AGB distribution and nine independent variables using statistical techniques like the random forest model and partial dependence plots. Results showed that the mean value of the estimated AGB was 120 tons/ha, ranging from 0 to 446.42 tons/ha. AGB showed higher values in the northeast and southeast regions, gradually decreasing towards the northwest. Land use land cover, mean annual temperature, and mean annual precipitation were identified as the primary factors influencing the variability in AGB distribution, accounting for 64% of the variability. Elevation, slope, and distance from rivers were positively correlated with AGB, while proximity to roads had a negative correlation. The increase in precipitation and temperature contributed to the initial rise in AGB, but beyond a certain lag, these variables led to a decline in AGB. This study showed the efficiency of the random forest model and partial dependence plots in examining the relationship between the AGB and its driving factors within managed forests. The study highlights the importance of understanding the AGB driving factors and utilizing LiDAR data for informed decisions regarding the region's sustainable forest management and climate change mitigation efforts.

Keywords: LiDAR; forest biomass; pattern; random forest; mean annual temperature; national forest; carbon; Nepal

1. Introduction

Forests play a crucial role in absorbing atmospheric carbon dioxide, acting as a reservoir that helps counterbalance human-caused greenhouse gas emissions to mitigate climate change impacts [1–3]. Carbon storage in forests represents the largest portion, accounting for 82.5% of the total carbon stored in terrestrial vegetation. This significant carbon reservoir plays a vital role in acting as the primary component of the vegetation carbon sink [4,5]. Tropical forests store about 55% of the total carbon in forests and contribute to 70% of the global forest carbon sink [3,6]. Deforestation and forest degradation can lead to carbon emissions entering the atmosphere, affecting global climate and environmental change [7–10]. Despite the critical role of forests in mitigating climate change through carbon sequestration, there is a significant challenge in accurately estimating the forest biomass and understanding the factors influencing its dynamics. The current concerns about global change and the functioning of ecosystems require accurate forest biomass estimates and an examination of its dynamics [11].

In terrestrial forest ecosystems, the above-ground biomass (AGB) of trees serves as the most crucial and prominent carbon reserve [12,13]. Though field measurements offer precise data on AGB estimation, the sampling process can be constrained by challenging terrain or limited resources. In recent years, remote sensing (RS) technology has emerged as the most preferred method, enabling researchers to obtain a broad-scale, real-time overview of vegetation conditions. This advancement has provided a valuable tool for studying and monitoring vegetation on a large scale [14,15]. Integrating remote sensing data with forest inventory data has evolved into a potent technique for accurately estimating AGB in forest stands [16,17]. Based on remote sensors' information and allometric equations, the predicted AGB has been calibrated and validated with ground truth to develop biomass estimation models [18]. Remote sensing data, such as light detection and ranging (LiDAR) data, proves advantageous in assessing forest characteristics like tree height, which directly correlates with forest biomass [17,19]. Over the past few years, airborne laser scanning (ALS), alternatively referred to as light detection and ranging (LiDAR), has emerged as the prevailing technology for acquiring precise topographic information, and it has been extensively applied in vegetation mapping and forest inventory, respectively [17,20,21]. ALS data captures the horizontal and vertical distribution of the forest canopies and does not saturate the spectral response of dense canopies, in contrast to multispectral imagery or aerial photography [22]. This advancement of RS technology, integrated with intensive site-based inventory methods, has also played a crucial role in monitoring and managing forests, particularly in initiatives like REDD+ (reducing emissions from deforestation and forest degradation) [23].

In tropical and subtropical forests, carbon stocks are declining at a rate of 1–2 billion tons per year [24] and are primarily affected by different drivers, such as the forest management regime and natural disturbance [25–28], the species composition of forests and forest type [29], and stand age structure [30,31]. The accumulation of AGB and its distribution in forested ecosystems are also significantly influenced by climate [32,33], as well as soil characteristics and topography [34,35]. Climatic data plays a significant role in understanding how temperature and precipitation influence tree growth [36], resulting in variation in AGB accumulation [37]. Moreover, the variation in AGB of forest stands is triggered by changes in land use and land cover because of human-induced activities [38]. Variations in soil properties and nutrient availability to trees also offer valuable insights into AGB dynamics [39]. AGB of trees is also influenced by variations in water availability, tree cover [40], and altitude [41–43]. In a broader context, the ALS-generated AGB maps can be combined with various geospatial data, including climate data, soil attributes, vegetation types, and land use patterns, to investigate the relationships between these factors and the AGB distribution. In the present research, we used the random forest (RF) model to analyze and describe the spatial distribution of AGB in managed forests in Nepal. The RF model is a machine learning algorithm capable of handling complex datasets and identifying important predictors of AGB distribution [44].

The forest of Nepal is categorized based on its own protected compasses, "private forest" and "national forest", with the latter further classified into five types: government-managed forest, community forest, leasehold forest, religious forest, and protection forest. Managed forests, such as community, leasehold, and religious forests, are crucial in promoting sustainable resource utilization and supporting local livelihoods. Protected forests contribute significantly to biodiversity conservation and are crucial ecological habitats [45]. Nepal covers about 23.39% of its land area as protected areas, aiming to conserve biodiversity and maintain terrestrial carbon stocks. Forests, which cover approximately 45.3% of Nepal's total land area [45], serve a significant amount of AGB and store about 1055 million tons of atmospheric carbon [45]. Nepal has over 22,000 community forest groups (CFs), representing 3 million households nationwide. These groups manage over 2.4 million hectares of forests, equivalent to about one-third of Nepal's forest cover (https://mofe.gov.np/, accessed on 9 September 2022). These forests play a crucial role in sequestering carbon and mitigating potential greenhouse gas emissions in the region through their biomass.

While ALS has been increasingly used for estimating and mapping AGB in Nepal [46–48] to support the REDD+ implementation, there is limited information about the spatial distribution of AGB across different forest types and management regimes. The underlying factors that influence AGB, particularly in managed forests, are not well understood. LiDAR technology has the capability to capture detailed vegetation structure and topography at high resolutions [49] to provide reliable estimates of AGB and forest carbon stock at the landscape level [50–52]. Combined with ancillary data sources, LiDAR can offer valuable insights into the spatial variation of AGB estimates and understand the factors that control it [53]. Therefore, the study aimed to estimate aboveground biomass (AGB) and map its spatial pattern in the managed forest of Nepal, specifically focusing on the Sagarnath Forest Development Project. The study also sought to investigate the influence of climatic and topographic variables on AGB spatial distribution and identify the main driving factors. The study focuses on the following questions: (1) What are the distribution patterns of forest AGB within the study area? (2) What are the determinants of forest AGB in the study area? How do topography, climate, and soil factors influence AGB levels in the forests? Understanding the determinants of forest AGB in study sites is crucial for improving forest carbon management practices and accurately estimating carbon storage. By establishing relationships between AGB and environmental factors, such as topography, climate, and soil characteristics, the study enhances our understanding of how these factors impact AGB dynamics in forest ecosystems.

2. Materials and Methods

2.1. Study Area

The study area is situated within the Sagarnath Forest Development Project (SFDP) in the Central Terai region of Nepal (Figure 1), and it is located between 85°67′49″ east longitude and 26°99′74″ north latitude [54]. The government of Nepal manages the SFDP, established in 1985 on previously owned forest land. It covers a total area of 13,512 ha across two districts, namely Sarlahi and Mahottarai districts, in the lowland (Terai region) of Nepal. The total area consists of various land categories, including plantations (11,796 ha), natural forests (395 ha), protected forests (707 ha), and water bodies (615 ha). A large amount of Eucalyptus (*Eucalyptus camaldulensis*) and Teak (*Tectona grandis*) have been planted in the project area since its inception. The native forest type is characterized by mixed hardwood tropical forests, with Sal (*Shorea robusta*) being the dominant species, accounting for approximately 90% of the forest composition. The altitude in the Terai region ranges from 60 to 330 m above mean sea level. The climate in this region is characterized by hot summers, with temperatures ranging from 35 °C to 45 °C in April and May, and dry winters, with temperatures ranging from 10 °C to 15 °C in January. The region receives annual precipitation ranging from 1130 mm to 2680 mm [55]. The region consists of a piedmont plain formed by recent and post-Pleistocene alluvial deposits [45].

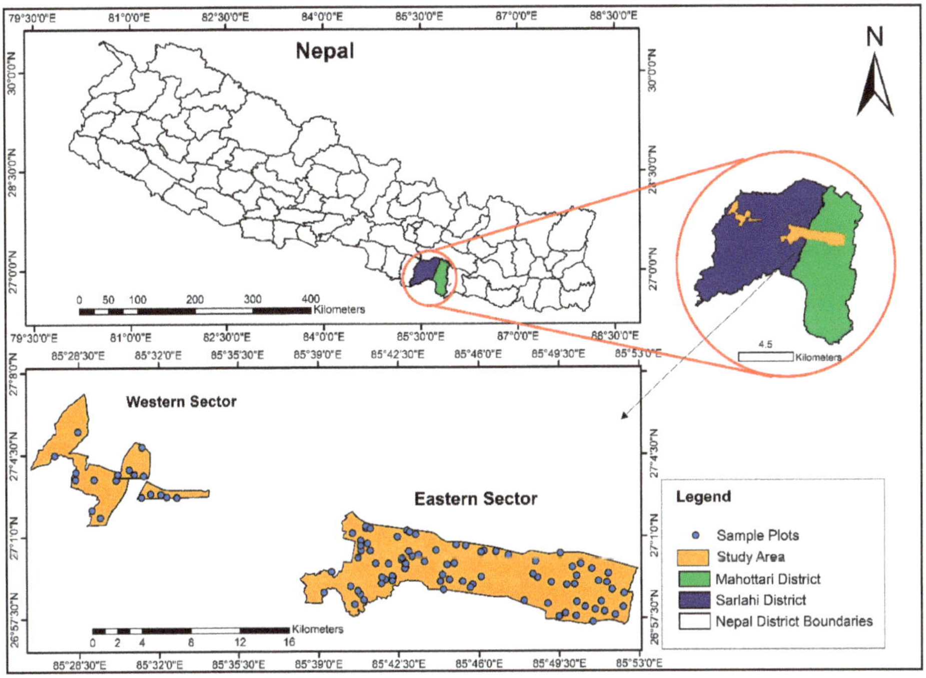

Figure 1. Study area location, and the distribution of the sampling plots.

2.2. Field Measurements and AGB Estimates

Field data were collected from 110 circular inventory plots randomly distributed in the forest, each covering an area of 0.02 ha with a radius of 9 m. Tree attributes, including diameter at breast height (DBH), and tree height (H), were measured for every individual tree in each plot. Tree height was recorded using a Vertex III hypsometer, while diameters were measured using diameter tapes. The data collection was conducted in January 2021, and the GPS coordinates of the plot centers were also recorded. Out of the initial sampling design, 7 plots were excluded because they were located either on roads or inside riverbeds, and additionally, 13 plots visited in the field had no trees with a diameter of at least 5 cm for considering measurements. In the remaining sample plots, a total of 1138 trees with a DBH greater than or equal to 5 cm were measured. The total above-ground tree biomass (DBH > 5 cm) was obtained by summing up the stem biomass, branch biomass, and foliage biomass. Stem biomass was estimated by multiplying stem volume with the wood density of the species. The stem volume is determined using the equation developed by Sharma and Pukkala [56] for Nepalese tree species, which was used to compute stem volume. The stem volume equation for calculating the volume of trees is:

$$\ln(v) = a + b \times \ln(DBH) + c \times \ln(H) \quad (1)$$

Here,

"v" is the volume per hectare (m^3/ha);
"ln" is the natural logarithm with base 2.71828;
"DBH" is the diameter of trees at breast height (cm);
"H" is the height of trees (m).
Additionally, the coefficients a, b, and c are species-dependent.

The species wood density values for Nepalese tree species were obtained from Jackson [57]. Species-specific branch-to-stem biomass and foliage-to-stem biomass ratios were utilized to calculate branch and foliage biomasses from stem biomass [56]. Based on the corresponding plot area, the total AGB for each plot was then scaled to a per hectare (ton/ha) (Table 1).

Table 1. Summary of plot-level inventory plots.

Attributes	Mean ± Standard Deviation	Range (Minimum to Maximum)
Density (trees/ha)	462 ± 343	39–2122
DBH (cm)	24 ± 14	6–101
Height (m)	17 ± 7	2–28
Basal area (m^2)	12 ± 10	0.2–47
Volume (m^3/ha)	108 ± 112	0.6–519
AGB (ton/ha)	131 ± 137	1–640

2.3. LiDAR Data

The ALS LiDAR data were acquired by Geo3dModeling, a local vendor, using a helicopter in January 2021. The recorded LiDAR data were provided by Nepal Ban Nigam Limited, a governmental organization in Nepal. The LiDAR provided has a point density of at least 15 points per square meter. Using the LiDAR package version 4.0.3 in R 4.3.0 software, the LiDAR data were processed [58]. LiDAR data were normalized with a digital terrain model (DTM) of 1 m^2 resolution to remove ground elevation from the height of returns. Subsequently, the point cloud data were clipped to the size of the field inventory sampling plots, ensuring that only relevant portions of the LiDAR data were retained for further analysis. Canopy density, which represents the ratio of vegetation to ground as observed from above, and canopy height, which measures the vertical distance between the top of the canopy and the ground, were calculated using the normalized point cloud and the clipped plots. These canopy height and canopy density metrics, along with the field inventory data from the plots, were combined for modeling purposes. The LiDAR metrics were computed at a resolution of 1 m^2 and used as the predictor variables [54] (Table 2).

Table 2. Predictor variables extracted from ALS-LiDAR metrics (height, density, and canopy) for modeling the AGB.

ALS- LiDAR Metrics	Predictor Variables	Characteristics
Height metrics	Percentiles height (zq5 to zq95)	Percentiles of the ALS height distributions, where the "z" typically stands for height and "q" stands for quantile or percentile (including 5th, 10th, 15th, 20th, 25th, 30th, 35th, 40th, 45th, 50th, 55th, 60th, 65th, 70th, 75th, 80th, 85th, 90th, 95th) for all points above 2 m
	Maximum heights (zmax)	Maximum heights above 2 m for all points
	Mean heights (zmean)	Mean heights above 2 m for all points
	Coefficient of variation of height (zcv)	Coefficient of variation of heights for all points above 2 m
	Standard deviation (zsd)	Standard deviation of heights for all points above 2 m
	Skewness (zskew)	Skewness of heights for all points above 2 m
	Kurtosis (zkurt)	Kurtosis of the heights for all points above 2 m
	Entropy (zentropy)	Entropy of the height distribution

Table 2. *Cont.*

ALS- LiDAR Metrics	Predictor Variables	Characteristics
Density metrics	pzabove2	Percentages of first returns above 2 m
	pzabovezmean	Percentage of returns greater than the mean returns height
	zpcum1	Cumulative percentage of first returns in the lower 10% of maximum elevation
	zpcum2	Cumulative percentage of first returns in the lower 20% of maximum elevation
	zpcum3	Cumulative percentage of first returns in the lower 30% of maximum elevation
Relative shape of the canopy	Canopy relief ratio (CRR)	Calculated as (height mean-height min)/(height max-height min), which represents the relative shape of the canopy

2.4. *Above-Ground Biomass Mapping*

Statistical techniques, such as random forest (RF) were used to establish a correlation between LiDAR point cloud data metrics and the above-ground biomass (AGB). The LiDAR metrics were considered independent variables, while AGB (ton/ha), which was determined at the plot level using field data, was the dependent variable.

RF is a powerful non-parametric machine learning algorithm that can be applied for both regression and classification [59]. The RF regression yields an arbitrary number of simple trees, which are a subset of independent variables–point cloud-derived metrics when estimating the dependent variable (AGB). The RF regression models are powerful for capturing complex, non-linear relationships between predictor variables (such as LiDAR metrics) and response variables (such as forest AGB). Unlike traditional linear regression models, the assumption of normality in the data is not necessary for RF regression [44].

We fitted the RF model using the ModelMap package in R [60]. This package utilizes the RF (random forest) function, a machine learning tool, to accurately capture the intricate and non-linear connections between LiDAR metrics and the AGB. This approach also allows for the determination of variable importance. RF utilizes bootstrap aggregation to create models that exhibit enhanced predictive abilities for estimation [61]. The estimation of AGB using the RF algorithm was carried out by considering two parameters: Mtry, which represents the number of predictor variables, and Ntree, which represents the number of decision trees. The function automatically optimizes Mtry parameter, denoting the number of randomly chosen variables at each node. For this specific case, the Ntree parameter was set to 500, indicating the quantity of trees grown in the model. The RF method was applied to estimate AGB using 32 point-derived metrics extracted from ALS LiDAR.

To assess the accuracy of AGB estimations, we split the inventory plots into two sets: a training dataset and a validation dataset. The data were randomly split at a ratio of 70:30, employing the createDataPartion function of the "caret" package [62]. The RF method was used in the R studio for modeling and accuracy evaluation [63]. The coefficient of determination (R^2), root mean square error (RMSE), and MAE were applied to compare the performance of the RF algorithm [64,65]. The equation is as follows:

$$R^2 = 1 - \frac{\sum\left(Y_{obs,i} - \hat{Y}_{mod,i}\right)^2}{\sum\left(Y_{obs,i} - \overline{Y}_{obs}\right)^2} \quad (2)$$

$$RMSE = \sqrt{\frac{1}{n}\sum_{i=1}^{n}\left(Y_{obs,i} - \hat{Y}_{mod,i}\right)^2} \quad (3)$$

$$MAE = \frac{1}{N}\sum_{i=1}^{N}\left|Y_{obs,i} - \hat{Y}_{mod,i}\right| \quad (4)$$

Here,

R^2 denotes the coefficient of determination;
$Y_{obs,i}$ denotes the measured value;
$\hat{Y}_{mod,i}$ denotes the model predicted value;
$\overline{Y}_{obs}$ denotes the average value;
n denotes the total number of samples;
$RMSE$ denotes the root mean square error;
and MAE denotes the mean absolute error.

The "raster" package [66] in R was used to predict the spatial AGB in the study site. The "predict ()" function was employed, taking the raster dataset and the final model as inputs. The resulting AGB raster was utilized for the subsequent analysis process. Spatial grids of ALS metrics were generated for the study site at a resolution of 30 × 30 m. Using R 4.3.0 software, an AGB map was created with a spatial resolution of 30 × 30 m, utilizing LiDAR-derived variables obtained from ALS returns.

2.5. Climatic and Topographic Data

To assess the influence of environmental factors on AGB variability, climatic, topographic, soil, and land use land cover data were randomly collected for the 600 samples within the study area. Explanatory variables, including elevation, slope, aspect, land use land cover, and climate data such as mean annual temperature (MAT), and mean annual precipitation (MAP), were derived from geospatial datasets. Airborne LiDAR data were utilized to obtain high-resolution terrain information for the Earth's surface with a resolution of 10 m (Table 3). For this process, a digital elevation model (DEM) was developed to obtain a digital representation of ground surface topography or terrain. Terrain variables were extracted from LiDAR ground points with a resolution of 10 m, as indicated in Table 3. The climatic variables, namely MAT (deg C) and MAP (mm) were obtained for the study sites from the Department of Hydrology and Meteorology (DHM) of Nepal (https://www.dhm.gov.np/, accessed on 5 September 2023), respectively. We created a 10 m resolution grid of mean annual precipitation (MAP) and mean annual temperature (MAT) data, monthly rainfall records, and temperature records of 11 ground stations in the study sites from 1981 to 2019 and interpolated using the ArcGIS 10.1 package. The land use land cover (LULC) types for the study area, with a resolution of 10 m, were acquired from ArcGIS online (https://livingatlas.arcgis.com/landcover/, accessed on 5 September, 2023). The soil type was extracted from the ICIMOD (International Centre for Integrated Mountain Development) in Nepal (https://rds.icimod.org/, accessed on 5 September 2023). Finally, both the AGB map and the explanatory variables were prepared into a 30 m × 30 m grid cell.

Table 3. Description of explanatory variables related to environmental factors.

Variable Type	Description	Spatial Resolution	Data Source
Climatic variables	Mean annual temperature (deg C) from 1981 to 2021	10 m × 10 m	DHM (http://www.dhm.gov.np/, accessed on 5 September 2023)
	Mean annual precipitation (mm) from 1981 to 2021	10 m × 10 m	
Topographic and soil variables	Elevation (m a.s.l.) based on DEM	10 m × 10 m	DEM-LiDAR
	Slope (deg) based on DEM	10 m × 10 m	DEM-LiDAR
	Aspect (deg) based on DEM	10 m × 10 m	DEM-LiDAR

Table 3. Cont.

Variable Type	Description	Spatial Resolution	Data Source
	Soil type	10 m × 10 m	ICIMOD (https://rds.icimod.org/home/datadetail?metadataid=1889, accessed on 5 September 2023)
	Road distance	10 m × 10 m	ICIMOD (https://rds.icimod.org/home/datadetail?metadataid=1889, accessed on 5 September 2023)
	River distance	10 m × 10 m	ICIMOD (https://rds.icimod.org/home/datadetail?metadataid=1889, accessed on 5 September 2023)
Land use land cover	Sentinel-2: Land Use/Land Cover 2021	10 m × 10 m	ArcGIS online (https://livingatlas.arcgis.com/landcover/, accessed on 5 September 2023)

2.6. Statistical Model and Analysis

We used AGB as the dependent variable, while climatic, topographic, and soil variables were treated as independent variables for the statistical modeling. We employed the RF model to examine the relationship between AGB and the explanatory variables. We employed the random forest model (RF) in the R 4.3.0 software. The RF model, which utilizes machine learning algorithms based on decision trees, was utilized to assess the impact of various anthropogenic and environmental factors on AGB variability in managed forests [67]. The RF model is suitable for analyzing large datasets with numerous variables, accommodating both continuous and categorical variables, and demonstrating robustness against the multicollinearity problem [18]. We calculated the relative importance of potential predictor variables on AGB, calculating variable importance values using the RF algorithm [68,69]. The higher the percentage increase in mean square error (%IncMSE) and increase in nodePurity (IncNodePurity), the stronger the importance of these predictor variables.

In addition, the relative importance of variables was estimated using the mean decrease accuracy (MDA) metric used in the RF model. The MDA metric calculates the change in model accuracy on a test set by randomly shuffling the values of a feature, where a greater decrease in accuracy indicates a higher feature importance. We used the generated partial dependence plots to visualize the marginal effects of predictor variables on the response variable within the model. The partial plot function under the :randomForest" package version 4.7.1.1 in the R 4.3.0 software was used, following the methodology proposed by [70] Friedman (2001). Partial dependence plots are commonly employed to examine the linearity, non-linearity, or other intricate relationships between predictors and response variables [71].

These plots aid our analysis to assess the relationship between individual predictors and the response variable. To calculate the partial dependence function, we utilized the "pdp" R package version 0.8.1. The utilization of the partial dependence analysis results contributes to ascertaining the impact of individual variables on the response, while excluding the influence of other variables.

3. Results

3.1. Aboveground Biomass—ALS Based Map

Independent variables in the RF model were derived from a total of 32 LiDAR-based metrics, which included zmax, zmean, zsd, zcv, zskew, zkurt, zentropy, pzabovemean, pzabove2, zq5, zq10, zq15, zq20, zq25, zq30, zq35, zq40, zq45, zq50, zq55, zq60, zq65, zq70, zq75, zq80, zq85, zq90, zq95, zpcum1, zpcum2, zpcum3, and CRR, respectively. The RF model calculated and plotted the variable importance, showing the top variables for AGB estimation (Figure 2).

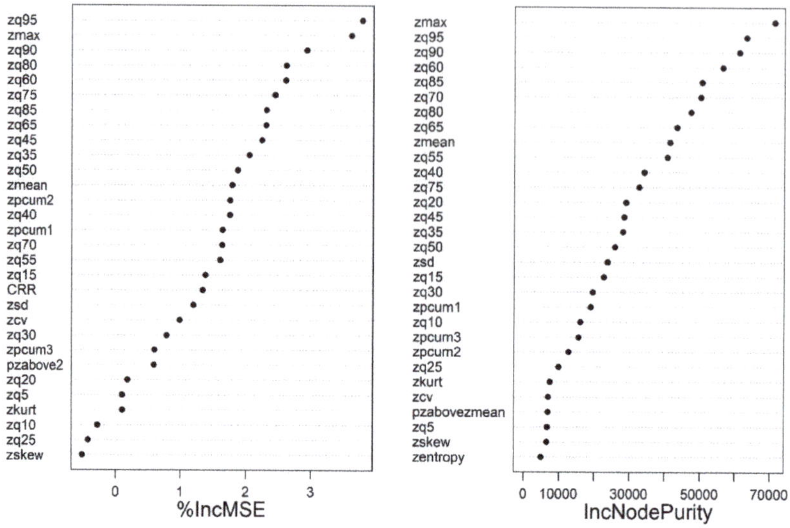

Figure 2. Variable importance ranking for the AGB estimation RF model.

However, among them, height-related metrics such as zmax, zmean, zq75, zq80, zq90, zq95, and density-based metrics, such as zpcum1, and zpcum2, exhibited relatively higher values for %IncMSE and IncNodepurity. It was found that zq95 and zmax were the most influential LiDAR metrics. Based on the training set, the model with the independent variables zmax, zmean, zq75, zq80, zq90, zq95, zpcum1, and zpcum2 achieved the best accuracy, with R^2 of 0.93, RMSE of 38.45 ton/ha, and MAE of 25.06 ton/ha (Figure 3a). The model performance of the test data resulted in an accuracy of R^2 of 0.85, RMSE of 60.9 ton/ha, and MAE of 39.7 ton/ha (Figure 3b). A visual representation of the relationship between predicted and observed values using a scatter plot is presented in Figure 3. This plot provides a visual comparison, allowing us to evaluate the models' predictive capabilities for the training set and the test set using a random forest model.

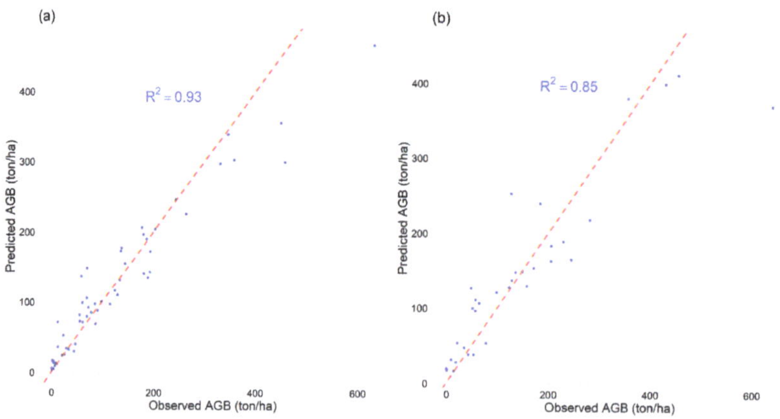

Figure 3. Scatterplot displaying correlation between observed and predicted AGB values for the training set (**a**) and the test set (**b**), using the best selected RF model.

Figure 4 illustrates the AGB map produced using the random forest model with a resolution of 30 × 30 m. The predicted AGB values in the study area varied from 0 to 446.42 ton/ha, with a mean value of 120 ton/ha. There is a noticeable variation in the spatial distribution of AGB within the study area. This distribution exhibited a distinct pattern, with AGB levels increasing from the east towards the center, and then decreasing further, highlighting the gradient of AGB levels across the study area (Figure 4). Parts of the eastern and western regions were characterized as low-value areas, with AGB levels recorded below 75.20 ton/ha. Parts of the southwestern and southeastern regions exhibited moderate AGB values, ranging between 75.20 and 211.63 ton/ha. Furthermore, most parts of the northcentral and northeastern regions displayed the highest AGB values, with values larger than 211.63 ton/ha. The spatial pattern of AGB within the study area demonstrated significant heterogeneity, with distinct variations observed across different regions.

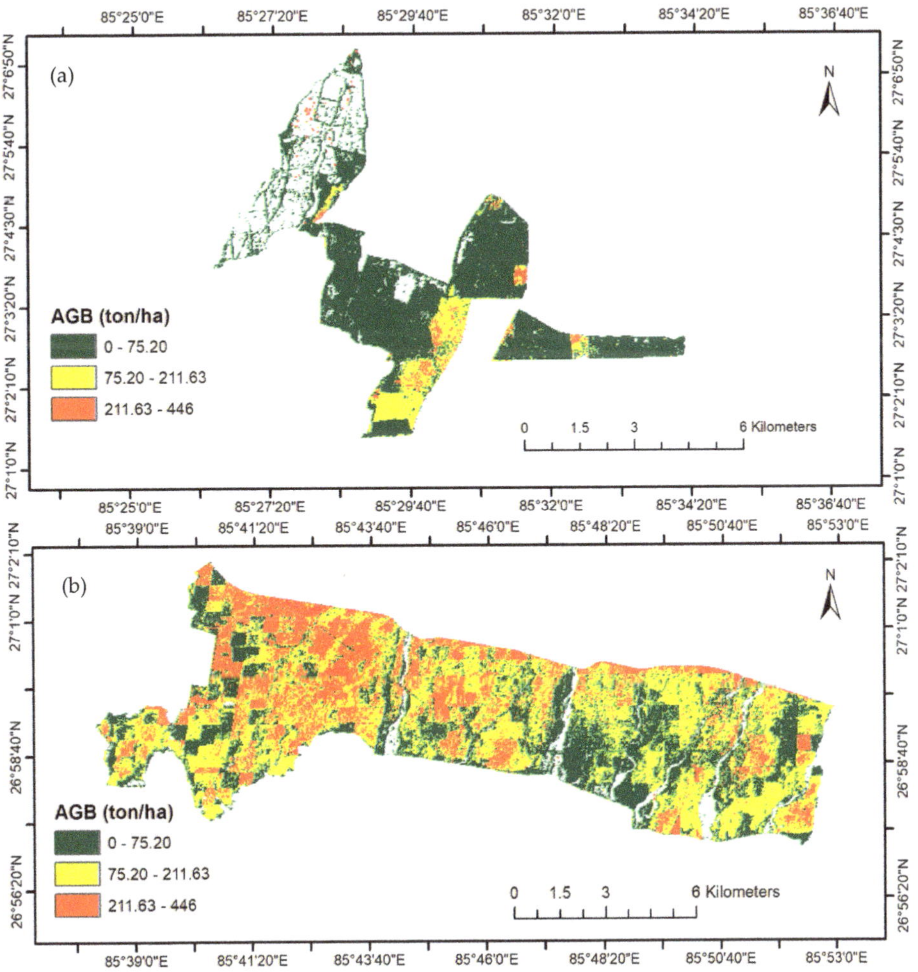

Figure 4. ALS AGB map based on the RF model: (**a**) Western sector and (**b**) Eastern sector.

3.2. *Driving Factors of Aboveground Biomass*

3.2.1. Variables Used in the RF Model

Figure 5 provides a visual representation of the explanatory variables used in our analysis. By examining these variables in relation to AGB, we aimed to gain a deeper understanding of the factors influencing the distribution of biomass in the study area.

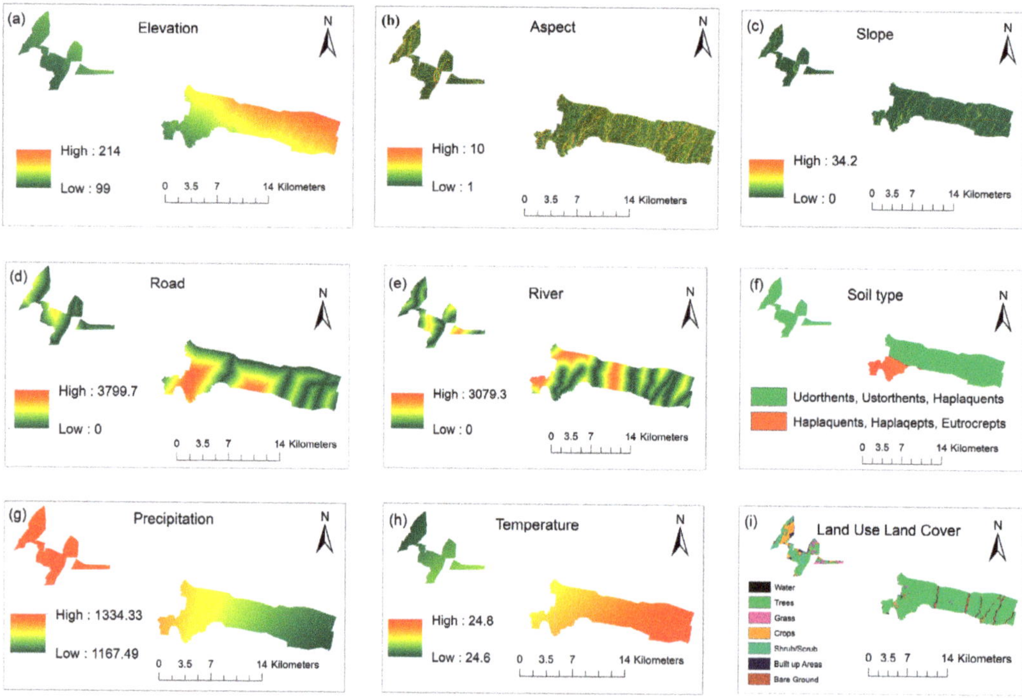

Figure 5. Environmental variables map for input determinant variables: (**a**–**i**) explanatory variables at 30 × 30 m resolution: (**a**) elevation, (**b**) aspect, (**c**) slope, (**d**) road, (**e**) river, (**f**) soil type, (**g**) average annual precipitation, (**h**) average annual temperature, and (**i**) land use land cover.

In this study, the explanatory variables of the study area were in terms of climatic, topographic, soil, and land use land cover. The variables related to climate were mean annual precipitation (MAP) and mean annual temperature (MAT). MAP was mainly from 1167 mm to 1334 mm across the study area. MAT was between 24.6 and 24.8 degrees Celsius for the study area. Topographic variables included elevation, slope, and aspect. Elevations ranged from 99 m to 214 m. Slope ranging from 0 degrees to 34.2 degrees. Aspect refers to the direction in which slope faces, categorized into 10 ranges (0 = flat, 2 = north, 3 = northeast, 4 = east, 5 = southeast, 6 = south, 7 = southwest, 8 = west, 9 = northwest, 10 = north), respectively. Soil included soil type 2 (Udorthents, Ustorthents, and Haplaquents) and soil type 4 (Haplaquents, Haplaqepts, and Eutrocrepts). Anthropogenic variables included road distance and river distance. Road distance ranges from 0 to 3799.7 m. River distance ranging from 0 to 3079.3 m. LULC included water, trees, grass, crops, shrubs, built-up area, and bare ground, respectively.

3.2.2. Relative Variables Importance in the RF Model

The selected nine environmental variables for explaining the spatial distribution of AGB, respectively, showed different relative importance values in the RF model (Figure 6). Predictor variables included: land use land cover (LULC), average annual precipitation (precip), average annual temperature (temp), elevation, river, soil, road, aspect, and slope, respectively (Figure 6). Among the variables, LULC, precipitation, and temperature emerged as the most influential factors, with relative importance percentages of 26.6%, 19%, and 18%, respectively. Elevation also played a significant role, with a percentage of 17.35%. Other variables (soil, river, road, slope, aspect) had lower relative importance percentages, ranging from 0.94% to 10.43%.

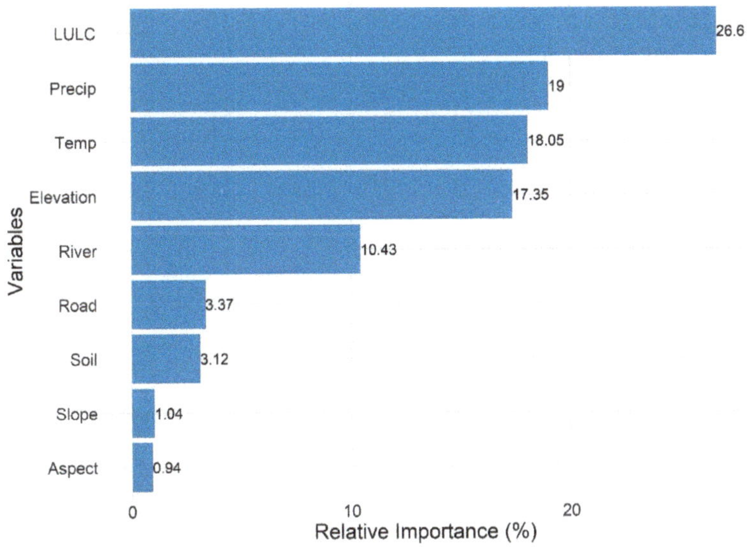

Figure 6. Relative importance of variables, percentage, for AGB distribution using the RF model.

3.2.3. Partial Dependence Plots (Response Plots)

The factors used in the RF model contributed differently to the AGB in the study area, and their partial dependencies reflected their relationship to the AGB.

A single-variable partial dependence plot along with smoothed response curves for the explanatory variables is shown in Figure 7. The y-axis displays the fitted function for the response variable (AGB), and the model used is the random forest model. An increase in the distance to the road from the forests up to 2000 m contributed to the decrease in AGB, while an increase in AGB was found for longer distances. In contrast, river proximity up to 2000 m contributed to an increase in AGB, and afterward, it contributed to a decrease in AGB. An increase in precipitation up to 1250 mm contributed to the higher AGB, and a higher precipitation amount decreased the AGB. Similarly, an increase in temperature up to 24.80 degrees Celsius contributed to the increase in AGB, and after that, the variable decreased AGB. An increase in elevation and slope further increased AGB. The amount of AGB increased with aspects between 2.5 and 6, and then the amount of AGB stayed stable, while there was an increase in AGB between aspects 7.5 and 10. Soil type 2 (Udorthents, Ustorthents, and Haplaquents) contributed more to AGB than soil type 4 (Haplaquents, Haplaqepts, and Eutrocrepts). Lastly, the comparison of land use land cover types (water, tree, shrub, grass, crops, built-up area, and bare ground) revealed that trees contributed more to AGB, and bare ground contributed less to AGB.

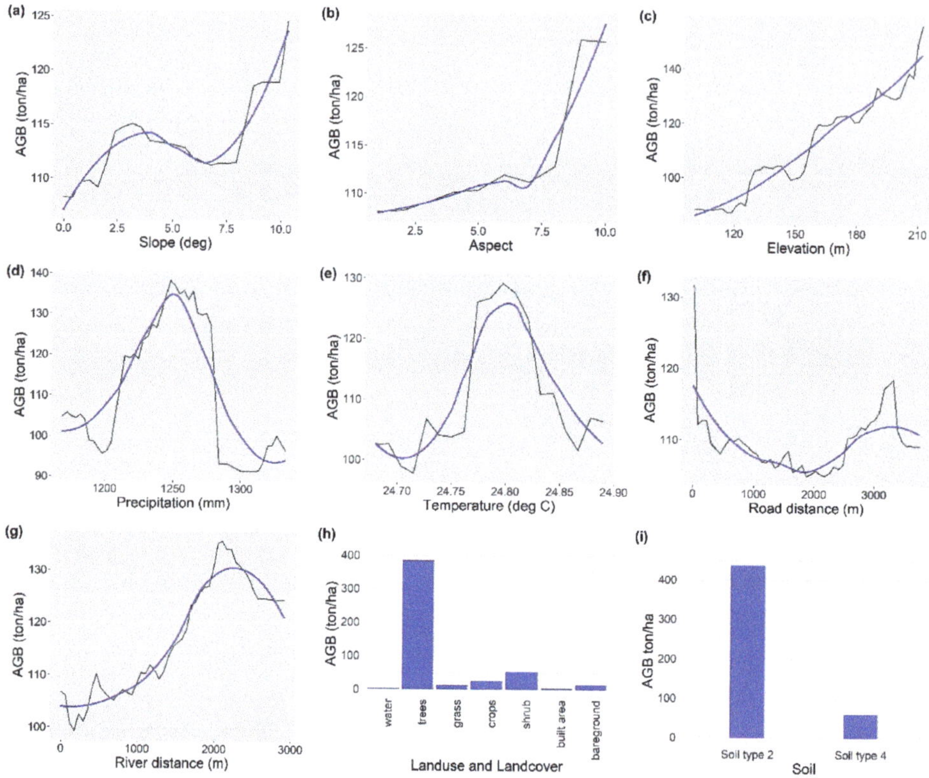

Figure 7. The partial dependence plot of the RF model, for each explanatory variable: (**a**) AGB and slope, (**b**) AGB and aspect, (**c**) AGB and elevation, (**d**) AGB and precipitation, (**e**) AGB and temperature, (**f**) AGB and road distance, (**g**) AGB and river distance, (**h**) AGB and land use land cover, and (**i**) AGB and soil. In (**a**–**g**), the black line represents the partial dependence plot based on the random forest predictions, and the blue line represents the LOESS smoothed line.

4. Discussion

In our study, the random forest (RF) model was used to estimate and understand the variability and spatial distribution of AGB in the managed forest. Powell et al. [41] highlighted the RF model's effectiveness, surpassing the performance of multiple linear regression. The application of the RF model not only provided estimates for predictor variables but also allowed for an assessment of their relative importance and the visualization of non-linear relationships through partial dependence plots (Figure 7). The RF model is capable of modeling non-linear relationships without requiring explicit assumptions about the functional form of the relationship and has been widely employed in forest AGB estimation [18]. The predicted AGB in the study varied from 0 to 446 ton/ha with a mean of 120 ton/ha, which closely aligned with the mean AGB of the field plots (Figure 4). However, the average AGB (120 ton/ha) of trees was lower than the AGB (190 ton/ha) estimated in the forest of the Terai region of Nepal [45]. This difference in estimates could be because the samples cover the entire Terai region and possibly a more mature forest with a more diverse species composition compared to our study site. Moreover, this study explained the spatial distribution of AGB using the AGB map and all the explanatory variables (Figures 4 and 5). The spatial distribution of AGB values in the study area showed higher values in the northeast and southwest regions, gradually decreasing towards the northwest. The study found that the factors influencing the spatial pattern of AGB were not uniform throughout the entire study area. The variables such as land use land cover (LULC), precipitation, temperature, and elevation were identified as having higher relative importance percentages in explaining AGB patterns. Conversely, variables like slope and aspect had a lesser influence on AGB variation (Figure 6). The main factors influencing the variability in AGB distribution were found to be land use land cover, MAP, and MAT, collectively explaining 64% of the variability in AGB patterns (refer to Figure 6). The vegetation density, water availability, and temperature conditions emerge as essential factors significantly influencing AGB levels across our study area.

Past studies have highlighted the influence of various factors such as topography, species composition, climate, elevation, and soil fertility on the spatial distribution of aboveground biomass (AGB) at the regional scale [72–76]. In our study area, while considering land use land cover, the AGB increased with a higher percentage of land use land cover in managed forests, especially with trees. The increase in the number of trees is a result of reforestation efforts, such as planting trees in the harvested area (logging) and sustainable forest management practices, including selective logging (thinning), proper harvesting methods, and ensuring natural regeneration. These practices have led to the growth of new trees and promoted the growth and sustainability of forests, resulting in higher AGB. With regard to climatic variables, precipitation, and temperature explained non-linear effects on AGB in the study site, respectively (Figure 7). Bowman et al. [77,78] study in Australian temperate and subtropical eucalyptus forests found that plants require temperatures that encourage growth while minimizing transpiration or autotrophic respiration. This indicates the importance of maintaining optimal temperature conditions for plants to maximize their growth potential. Lewis et al. [79] found an increase in AGB in African tropical forests with precipitation during the driest nine months of the year and a decrease during the wettest three months of the year. Malla et al. [71] reported a positive effect on AGB of the precipitation of the driest month and the maximum temperature of the warmest month in the forests throughout Nepal. The positive effect of precipitation during the driest month suggests that ensuring water availability during periods of rainfall can contribute to increased growth in the growing season [36], resulting in higher AGB. Similarly, the positive influence of maximum temperature during the warmest months indicates the importance of favorable temperature conditions for promoting forest growth and forest biomass accumulation. The different climatic conditions can affect the dynamics of AGB throughout the year. Previous studies, together with our results, show that precipitation and temperature can have both positive and negative effects on the AGB distribution in forests. However, other factors, such as soil characteristics, nutrient availability, disturbance regimes, and species composition, also interact with temperature and precipitation to influence AGB patterns.

When considering slope, Du et al. [80] indicated that vegetation on higher slopes tends to experience less human disturbance, allowing these areas to be better preserved, fostering abundant forest growth, and promoting biomass accumulation. In terms of aspect, studies conducted by Fan et al. [81,82] have demonstrated that the south-, southwest-, west-, and northwest-facing slopes are often referred to as sunny slopes. These aspects receive a greater amount of sunlight, leading to increased rates of photosynthesis and greater vegetation productivity. As a result, the amount of AGB in these aspects tends to be higher compared to other aspects. Regarding elevation, higher elevations are often associated with cooler temperatures and increased moisture availability [42]. These favorable conditions create an environment conducive to plant growth and the accumulation of biomass. Furthermore, elevated regions may exhibit distinct soil characteristics, nutrient availability, and vegetation compositions, which can contribute to increased AGB levels.

In our study area, the AGB was most abundant at the higher altitudes, particularly in areas dominated by soil type 2 (comprising Udorthents, Usotorthents, and Haplaquents). These regions are less conducive to agricultural activities and have limited accessibility via road networks. Previous studies have also indicated a positive relationship between altitude and AGB in similar areas [34,83]. Similarly, Nepal et al. [84] reported increasing AGB of trees with increasing elevation in the subtropical forest of Nepal. The elevation gradient is associated with changes in temperature, precipitation, and forest-type succession [85]. The elevation of our research site, typically ranging from 99 to 214 m above sea level, suggests that a significant climate change is unlikely to occur. Contrary to the findings of many studies [86–90] that indicate a decline in AGB with increasing elevation, we observe an opposing trend. This discrepancy could be attributed to the relatively narrow range of elevation (99 m to 214 m) encompassing the forested areas within our study site.

Regarding the road feature, the presence of a road has a negative impact on AGB up to a certain distance, potentially due to factors such as increased human disturbance and land conversion near roads. However, beyond a specific threshold distance, the negative effects diminish, or other factors such as reduced human activity or improved environmental conditions lead to an increase in AGB. The contribution of distance to the nearest road is consistent with [91], who observed lower AGB in the distance from the forests to the road up to 2000 m, while higher AGB was found for longer distances. AGB distribution is likely to be higher in areas with less human disturbance [92,93].

Regarding rivers, the initial increase in AGB with proximity to rivers could be attributed to factors such as increased water availability, moisture gradient, nutrient deposition, or favorable soil conditions near riverbeds. These factors can promote plant growth and result in higher AGB. However, beyond the threshold, the decrease in AGB with increasing river distance suggests that other factors may come into play. These could include factors such as reduced water availability, increased competition for resources, or changes in soil properties farther away from the river. These conditions may lead to decreased vegetation growth and, consequently, lower AGB.

Soil properties play a significant role in influencing the AGB of tropical forests [39,79,94,95]. Various soil properties, such as pH, organic matter, total nitrogen, total phosphorus, and others, are analyzed to assess their impact. Within our study area, soil type 2 contributed more to AGB than soil type 4 (consisting of Haplaquents, Haplaqepts, and Eutrocrepts). The soil type 2 exhibits higher organic matter content, enhanced water-holding capacity, and improved nutrient availability [96], thereby fostering greater plant growth and biomass accumulation. Moreover, these soil types possess superior drainage and aeration properties, which facilitate root development and nutrient uptake. Conversely, soil type 4 exhibits lower organic matter content, diminished water retention capacity, and limited nutrient availability. These characteristics can impede plant growth and biomass production within these soil types. Our findings regarding the impact of soil on AGB align with previous studies. However, it is important to note that soil type alone may not be the sole determinant of AGB. Other factors, such as climate, topography, land use, and vegetation composition can also interact with soil type to influence AGB patterns. The complex interplay of these factors should be considered when understanding the dynamics of AGB in forest ecosystems.

It is crucial to understand the limitations of our study. Firstly, our investigation exclusively focused on managed forests in the Terai region of Nepal, which may limit the generalization of the findings to other forest types or areas. Additionally, we solely examined AGB and did not consider below-ground forest biomass. The study did not consider the influence of biotic factors such as forest types or stand age, which could also affect AGB in forests. While our results provide valuable insights, it is crucial to interpret them within the context of these limitations. Future studies should address these limitations to obtain a more comprehensive understanding of the subject matter.

5. Conclusions

The study examined the spatial patterns and influencing factors of forest aboveground biomass (AGB) in a managed forest in the Terai region of Nepal using geospatial and statistical techniques. The mean forest AGB in the study area was 120 ton/ha, with a range from 0 to 446 ton/ha in the 30 m resolution. AGB exhibited a higher distribution in the northeast and southeast regions, gradually decreasing towards the northwest. AGB positively correlated with elevation, slope, and distance from rivers, while it negatively correlated with proximity to roads. The increase in precipitation and temperature contributed to the initial rise in AGB, but beyond a certain lag, these variables led to a decline in AGB. Land use land cover, precipitation, and temperature predominantly contributed to the spatial distribution of AGB variation, accounting for 64% of the variability. The aspect had the least effect on AGB distribution. This study showed the influence of climate, land cover land use, and topography on the AGB pattern in the forest. With the help of the ALS-based AGB maps and various explanatory variables, it was possible to better understand the spatial pattern of AGB and the factors influencing AGB distribution across the managed forest. The results obtained from our study hold significant importance for making decisions about managing forests sustainably and mitigating climate change in the Terai region of Nepal. Understanding the factors that drive AGB variation such as climate, soil characteristics, species composition, and disturbance regimes, allows us to develop more accurate AGB, and predictions of forest productivity. The accuracy of the model can be improved further using larger forest biomass datasets and other explanatory variables.

Author Contributions: Y.B.K. was responsible for the research design, data collection, analysis, and manuscript writing. The conceptualization and supervision were conducted by Q.L. and H.A. The data visualization was conducted by C.X., P.S. and H.A. Each author made contributions to the data analysis, review, and editing. D.G. assisted with proofreading. All authors have read and agreed to the published version of the manuscript.

Funding: This research project was funded by the China Scholarship Council (CSC 2020SLJ017262). Open access funding was arranged by Forest Nepal.

Data Availability Statement: The data are not publicly available because they are intended to be protected before official publications and used in other ongoing research.

Acknowledgments: We would like to thank Nepal Ban Nigam Limited, Ministry of Forests and Environment, Government of Nepal, for providing us with the important data. We also thank the kind support of Arbonaut Ltd., Finland, for providing us with a copy of this data. We are grateful to Tribhuvan University, Institute of Forestry, Hetauda, Nepal. We also acknowledge the Key Laboratory for Silviculture and Conservation of the Ministry of Education, Beijing Forestry University, and International College of Beijing Forestry University, China, for providing us with optimal research conditions. Likewise, we thank to the University of Arkansas System Division of Agriculture, the University of Arkansas at Monticello, USA and the University of Helsinki, Finland for their support. We would like to thank Bikram Singh Thakuri, Subash Singh, and Animesh Poudel for their help.

Conflicts of Interest: The authors declare no conflict of interest.

References

1. Goodale, C.L.; Apps, M.J.; Birdsey, R.A.; Field, C.B.; Heath, L.S.; Houghton, R.A.; Jenkins, J.C.; Kohlmaier, G.H.; Kurz, W.; Liu, S. Forest carbon sinks in the northern hemisphere. *Ecol. Appl.* **2002**, *12*, 891–899. [CrossRef]
2. Woodbury, P.B.; Smith, J.E.; Heath, L.S. Carbon sequestration in the U.S. forest sector from 1990 to 2010. *For. Ecol. Manag.* **2010**, *241*, 14–27. [CrossRef]
3. Pan, Y.; Birdsey, R.A.; Fang, J.; Houghton, R.; Kauppi, P.E.; Kurz, W.A.; Phillips, O.L.; Shvidenko, A.; Lewis, S.L.; Canadell, J.G.; et al. A large and persistent carbon sink in the world's forests. *Science* **2011**, *333*, 988–993. [CrossRef] [PubMed]
4. Cusack, D.F.; Axsen, J.; Shwom, R.; Hartzell-Nichols, L.; White, S.; Mackey, K.R.M. An interdisciplinary assessment of climate engineering strategies. *Front. Ecol. Environ.* **2014**, *12*, 280–287. [CrossRef] [PubMed]
5. Kauranne, T.; Joshi, A.; Gautam, B.; Manandhar, U.; Nepal, S.; Peuhkurinen, J. LiDAR-assisted multi-source program (LAMP) for measuring above ground biomass and forest carbon. *Remote Sens.* **2017**, *9*, 154. [CrossRef]
6. Urbazaev, M.; Thiel, C.; Cremer, F.; Dubayah, R.; Migliavacca, M.; Reichstein, M.; Schmullius, C. Estimation of forest aboveground biomass and uncertainties by integration of field measurements, airborne LiDAR, and SAR and optical satellite data in Mexico. *Carbon Balance Manag.* **2018**, *13*, 1–20. [CrossRef] [PubMed]
7. Achard, F.; Eva, H.D.; Mayaux, P.; Stibig, H.J.; Belward, A. Improved Estimates of Net Carbon Emissions from Land Cover Change in the Tropics for the 1990s. *Glob. Biogeochem. Cycles* **2004**, *18*, 1–11. [CrossRef]

8. Hese, S.; Lucht, W.; Schmullius, C.; Barnsley, M.; Dubayah, R.; Knorr, D.; Neumann, K.; Riedel, T.; Schröter, K. Global Biomass Mapping for an Improved Understanding of the CO_2 Balance-the Earth Observation Mission Carbon-3D. *Remote Sens. Environ.* **2005**, *94*, 94–104. [CrossRef]
9. Houghton, R.A. Aboveground Forest Biomass and the Global Carbon Balance. *Glob. Chang. Biol.* **2005**, *11*, 945–958. [CrossRef]
10. Frolking, S.; Palace, M.W.; Clark, D.B.; Chambers, J.Q.; Shugart, H.H.; Hurtt, G.C. Forest Disturbance and Recovery: A General Review in the Context of Spaceborne Remote Sensing of Impacts on Aboveground Biomass and Canopy Structure. *J. Geophys. Res. Biogeosciences* **2009**, *114*, G00E02. [CrossRef]
11. LeToan, T.S.; Quegan, M.; Davidson, W.J.; Balzter, H.; Paillou, P.; Papathanassiou, K.; Plummer, S. The BIOMASS Mission: Mapping Global Forest Biomass to Better Understand the Terrestrial Carbon Cycle. *Remote Sens. Environ.* **2011**, *115*, 2850–2860. [CrossRef]
12. Lu, D. The potential and challenge of remote sensing-based biomass estimation. *Int. J. Remote Sens.* **2006**, *27*, 1297–1328. [CrossRef]
13. Vashum, K.T.; Jayakumar, S. Methods to Estimate Above-Ground Biomass and Carbon Stock in Natural Forests—A Review. *Ecosyst. Ecography* **2012**, *2*, 1–7. [CrossRef]
14. Du, L.; Zhou, T.; Zou, Z.; Zhao, X.; Huang, K.; Wu, H. Mapping forest biomass using remote sensing and national forest inventory in China. *Forests* **2014**, *5*, 1267–1283. [CrossRef]
15. Tang, X.; Fehrmann, L.; Guan, F.; Forrester, D.; Guisasola, R.; Kleinn, C. Inventory based estimation of forest biomass in Shitai County, China: A comparison of five methods. *Ann. For. Res.* **2016**, *59*, 269–280. [CrossRef]
16. Dang, A.T.N.; Nandy, S.; Srinet, R.; Luong, N.V.; Ghosh, S.; Senthil Kumar, A. Forest aboveground biomass estimation using machine learning regression algorithm in Yok Don National Park, Vietnam. *Ecol. Inform.* **2019**, *50*, 24–32. [CrossRef]
17. Mura, M.; McRoberts, R.E.; Chirici, G.; Marchetti, M. Estimating and mapping forest structural diversity using airborne laser scanning data. *Remote Sens. Environ.* **2015**, *170*, 133–142. [CrossRef]
18. Lu, D.; Chen, Q.; Wang, G.; Liu, L.; Li, G.; Moran, E. A survey of remote sensing-based aboveground biomass estimation methods in forest ecosystems. *Int. J. Digit. Earth* **2014**, *9*, 63–105. [CrossRef]
19. Sačkov, I.; Santopuoli, G.; Bucha, T.; Lasserre, B.; Marchetti, M. Forest inventory attribute prediction using lightweight aerial scanner data in a selected type of multilayered deciduous forest. *Forests* **2016**, *7*, 12. [CrossRef]
20. Lim, K.S.; Treitz, P.M. Estimation of above ground forest biomass from airborne discrete return laser scanner data using canopy-based quantile estimators. *Scand. J. For. Res.* **2004**, *19*, 558–570. [CrossRef]
21. Hyyppä, J.; Hyyppä, H.; Xiaowei, Y.; Kaartinen, H.; Kukko, A.; Holopainen, M. *Topographic Laser Ranging and Scanning: Principles and Processing*; CRC Press Taylor & Francis Group: Boca Raton, FL, USA, 2009; pp. 335–370.
22. Zhao, K.; Popescu, S. Lidar-based mapping of leaf area index and its use for validating GLOBCARBON satellite LAI product in a temperate forest of the southern USA. *Remote Sens. Environ.* **2009**, *113*, 1628–1645. [CrossRef]
23. Birdsey, R.; Angeles-Perez, G.; Kurz, W.A.; Lister, A.; Olguin, M.; Pan, Y.; Wayson, C.; Wilson, B.; Johnson, K. Approaches to monitoring changes in carbon stocks for REDD+. *Carbon Manag.* **2013**, *4*, 519–537. [CrossRef]
24. Subedi, M.; Matthews, R.; Pogson, M.; Abegaz, A.; Balana, B.; Oyesiku-blakemore, J.; Smith, J. ScienceDirect Can biogas digesters help to reduce deforestation in Africa ? *Biomass Bioenergy* **2014**, *70*, 87–98. [CrossRef]
25. Law, B.E.; Turner, D.; Campbell, J.; Sun, O.J.; Van Tuyl, S.; Ritts, W.D.; Cohen, W.B. Disturbance and climate effects on carbon stocks and fluxes across Western Oregon USA. *Glob. Chang. Biol.* **2004**, *10*, 1429–1444. [CrossRef]
26. Gough, C.M.; Vogel, C.S.; Harrold, K.H.; George, K.; Curtis, P.S. The legacy of harvest and fire on ecosystem carbon storage in a north temperate forest. *Glob. Chang. Biol.* **2007**, *13*, 1935–1949. [CrossRef]
27. Hudiburg, T.; Law, B.; Turner, D.P.; Campbell, J.; Donato, D.; Duane, M. Carbon dynamics of Oregon and Northern California forests and potential land-based carbon storage. *Ecol. Appl.* **2009**, *19*, 163–180. [CrossRef] [PubMed]
28. Hanberry, B.B.; He, H.S. Effects of historical and current disturbance on forest biomass in Minnesota. *Landsc. Ecol.* **2015**, *30*, 1473–1482. [CrossRef]
29. Zhang, Y.; Gu, F.; Liu, S.; Liu, Y.; Li, C. Forest Ecology and Management Variations of carbon stock with forest types in subalpine region of southwestern China. *For. Ecol. Manag.* **2013**, *300*, 88–95. [CrossRef]
30. Clark, K.L.; Gholz, H.L.; Castro, M.S. Carbon dynamics along a chronosequence of slash pine plantations in North Florida. *Ecol. Appl.* **2004**, *14*, 1154–1171. [CrossRef]
31. Orihuela-Belmonte, D.E.; de Jong, B.H.J.; Mendoza-Vega, J.; van der Wal, J.; Paz-Pellat, F.; Soto-Pinto, L.; Flamenco-Sandoval, A. Carbon stocks and accumulation rates in tropical secondary forests at the scale of community, landscape and forest type. *Agric. Ecosyst. Environ.* **2013**, *171*, 72–84. [CrossRef]
32. Yang, Y.; Watanabe, M.; Li, F.; Zhang, J.; Zhang, W.; Zhai, J. Factors affecting forest growth and possible effects of climate change in the Taihang Mountains, Northern China. *Forestry* **2006**, *79*, 135–147. [CrossRef]
33. Ajaz Ahmed, M.A.; Abd-Elrahman, A.; Escobedo, F.J.; Cropper, W.P., Jr.; Martin, T.A.; Timilsina, N. Spatially-explicit modeling of multi-scale drivers of aboveground forest biomass and water yield in watersheds of the Southeastern United States. *J. Environ. Manag.* **2017**, *199*, 158–171. [CrossRef] [PubMed]
34. Alves, L.F.; Vieira, S.A.; Scaranello, M.A.; Camargo, P.B.; Santos, F.A.M.; Joly, C.A.; Martinelli, L.A. Forest Ecology and Management Forest structure and live aboveground biomass variation along an elevational gradient of tropical Atlantic moist forest (Brazil). *For. Ecol. Manag.* **2010**, *260*, 679–691. [CrossRef]

35. Asner, G.P.; Flint Hughes, R.; Varga, T.A.; Knapp, D.E.; Kennedy-Bowdoin, T. Environmental and biotic controls over aboveground biomass throughout a tropical rain forest. *Ecosystems* **2009**, *12*, 261–278. [CrossRef]
36. Saud, J.; Lynch, P.; Cram, T.; Guldin, D. An Annual basal area growth model with multiplicative climate modifier fitted to longitudi-nal data for shortleaf pine. *Forestry* **2019**, *92*, 538–553. [CrossRef]
37. Yan, Y.; Wu, F.; Wang, B. Estimating spatiotemporal patterns of aboveground biomass using Landsat TM and MODIS images in the Mu Us Sandy Land, China. *Agric. For. Meteorol.* **2015**, *200*, 119–128. [CrossRef]
38. Tadese, S.; Soromessa, T.; Aneseye, A.B.; Gebeyehu, G. The impact of land cover change on the carbon stock of moist afromontane forests in the Majang Forest Biosphere Reserve. *Carbon Balance Manag.* **2023**, *18*, 24. [CrossRef] [PubMed]
39. Hofhansl, F.; Chacón-Madrigal, E.; Fuchslueger, L.; Jenking, D.; Morera-Beita, A.; Plutzar, C. Climatic and edaphic controls over tropical forest diversity and vegetation carbon storage. *Sci. Rep.* **2020**, *10*, 5066. [CrossRef]
40. RequenaSuarez, D.; Rozendaal, D.M.A.; De Sy, V.; Gibbs, D.A.; Harris, N.L.; Sexton, J.O. Variation in aboveground biomass in forests and woodlands in Tanzania along gradients in environmental conditions and human use. *Environ. Res. Lett.* **2021**, *16*, 044014. [CrossRef]
41. Powell, S.L.; Cohen, W.B.; Healey, S.P.; Kennedy, R.E.; Moisen, G.G.; Pierce, K.B. Quantification of live aboveground forest biomass dynamics with Landsat time-series and field inventory data: A comparison of empirical modeling approaches. *Remote Sens. Environ.* **2010**, *114*, 1053–1068. [CrossRef]
42. VanderLaan, C.; Verweij, P.A.; Quiñones, M.J.; Faaij, A.P.C. Analysis of biophysical and anthropogenic variables and their relation to the regional spatial variation of aboveground biomass illustrated for North and East Kalimantan, Borneo. *Carbon Bal. Manag.* **2014**, *9*, 8. [CrossRef] [PubMed]
43. Rajput, B.S.; Bhardwaj, D.R.; Pala, N.A. Factors influencing biomass and carbon storage potential of different land use systems along an elevational gradient in temperate northwestern Himalaya. *Agrofor. Syst.* **2017**, *91*, 479–486. [CrossRef]
44. Belgiu, M.; Csillik, O. Sentinel-2 cropland mapping using pixel-based and object-based time-weighted dynamic time warping analysis. *Remote Sens. Environ.* **2018**, *204*, 509–523. [CrossRef]
45. DFRS. *State of Nepal's Forests*; Department of Forest Research and Survey: Kathmandu, Nepal, 2015; ISBN 9789937889636.
46. Kandel, P.N. Estimation of Above Ground Forest Biomass and Carbon Stock by Integrating Lidar, Satellite Image and Field Measurement in Nepal. *J. Nat. Hist. Mus.* **2015**, *28*, 160–170. [CrossRef]
47. Murthy, M.S.R.; Wesselmann, S.; Hammad, G. Multi-Scale Forest Biomass Assessment and Monitoring in the Hindu Kush Himalayan Region: A Geospatial Perspective. *Icimod* **2008**, *322*, 202.
48. Rana, P.; Popescu, S.; Tolvanen, A.; Gautam, B.; Srinivasan, S.; Tokola, T. Estimation of tropical forest aboveground biomass in Nepal using multiple remotely sensed data and deep learning. *Int. J. Remote Sens.* **2023**, *44*, 5147–5171. [CrossRef]
49. Estornell, J.; Ruiz, L.A.; Velázquez-Martí, B.; Fernández-Sarría, A. Estimation of shrub biomass by airborne LiDAR data in small forest stands. *Ecol. Manag.* **2011**, *262*, 1697–1703. [CrossRef]
50. Lefsky, M.A.; Cohen, W.B.; Harding, D.J.; Parker, G.G.; Acker, S.A.; Gower, S.T.; Service, F.; Way, S.W.J.; Goddard, N.; Flight, S. Lidar remote sensing of above-ground biomass in three biomes. *Glob. Ecol. Biogeogr.* **2002**, *11*, 393–399. [CrossRef]
51. Li, Y.; Andersen, H.; Mcgaughey, R. A Comparison of Statistical Methods for Estimating Forest Biomass from Light Detection and Ranging Data. *J. Appl. For.* **2008**, *23*, 223–231. [CrossRef]
52. Asner, G.P.; Mascaro, J. Mapping tropical forest carbon: Calibrating plot estimates to a simple LiDAR metric. *Remote Sens. Environ.* **2014**, *140*, 614–624. [CrossRef]
53. Asner, G.P.; Powell, G.V.N.; Mascaro, J.; Knapp, D.E.; Clark, J.K.; Jacobson, J.K.; Bowdoin, T.; Balaji, A.; Paez-Acosta, G.; Victoria, E.; et al. High-resolution forest carbon stocks and emissions in the Amazon. *Proc. Natl. Acad. Sci. USA* **2010**, *107*, 16738–16742. [CrossRef] [PubMed]
54. Kc, Y.B.; Liu, Q.; Saud, P.; Gaire, D.; Adhikari, H. Estimation of Above-Ground Forest Biomass in Nepal by the Use of Airborne LiDAR, and Forest Inventory Data. *Land* **2024**, *13*, 213. [CrossRef]
55. FRA/DFRS. *Forest Resource Assessment Nepal Project/Department of Forest Research and Survey*; FRA/DFRS: Babarmahal, Kathmandu, 2014.
56. Sharma, E.R.; Pukkala, T. *Volume Equations and Biomass Prediction of Forest Trees in Nepal*; ResearchGate: Berlin, Germany, 1990.
57. Jackson, J.K. *Afforestation, Manual of Forest, in Nepal*, 2nd ed.; Research and Survey Center: Kathmandu, Nepal, 1994; Volume I.
58. Roussel, J.R.; Auty, D.; Coops, N.C.; Tompalski, P.; Goodbody, T.R.H.; Meador, A.S.; Bourdon, J.F.; de Boissieu, F.; Achim, A. lidR: An R package for analysis of Airborne Laser Scanning (ALS) data. *Remote Sens. Environ.* **2020**, *251*, 112061. [CrossRef]
59. Fawagreh, K.; Gaber, M.M.; Elyan, E. Systems Science & Control Engineering: An Open Access Random forests: From early developments to recent advancements. *Syst. Sci. Control. Eng. Open Access J.* **2014**, *2583*, 602–609. [CrossRef]
60. Freeman, A.E.; Frescino, T.; Moisen, G.G. *ModelMap: An R Package for Model Creation and Map Production*; R Package Version 4; R Foundation for Statistical Computing: Vienna, Austria, 2023; pp. 6–12.
61. Pandit, S.; Tsuyuki, S.; Dube, T. Estimating above-ground biomass in sub-tropical buffer zone community forests, Nepal, using Sentinel 2 data. *Remote Sens.* **2018**, *10*, 601. [CrossRef]
62. Kuhn, M. Building Predictive Models in R Using the caret Package. *J. Stat. Softw.* **2008**, *28*, 1–26. [CrossRef]
63. R Core Team R. A Language and Environment for Statistical Computing. R Foundation for Statistical Computing, Vienna. Available online: www.R-project.org (accessed on 5 September 2023).

64. Vafaei, S.; Soosani, J.; Adeli, K.; Fadaei, H.; Naghavi, H.; Pham, T.D.; Bui, D.T. Improving accuracy estimation of Forest Aboveground Biomass based on incorporation of ALOS-2 PALSAR-2 and Sentinel-2A imagery and machine learning: A case study of the Hyrcanian forest area (Iran). *Remote Sens.* **2018**, *10*, 172. [CrossRef]
65. Jiang, X.; Li, G.; Lu, D.; Chen, E.; Wei, X. Stratification-based forest aboveground biomass estimation in a subtropical region using airborne lidar data. *Remote Sens.* **2020**, *12*, 1101. [CrossRef]
66. Van Etten, J.; Sumner, M.; Cheng, J.; Baston, D.; Bevan, A.; Bivand, R.; Busetto, L.; Canty, M.; Fasoli, B.; Forrest, D.; et al. Package 'raster' R topics documented. *R Package* **2023**, *734*, 473.
67. Jin, Z.; Shang, J.; Zhu, Q.; Ling, C.; Xie, W.; Qiang, B. RFRSF: Employee Turnover Prediction Based on Random Forests and Survival Analysis. In Proceedings of the Lecture Notes in Computer Science (Including Subseries Lecture Notes in Artificial Intelligence and Lecture Notes in Bioinformatics), Fisciano, Italy, 29 June–3 July 2020.
68. Breiman, L. Random Forests. *Mach. Learn.* **2001**, *45*, 5–32. [CrossRef]
69. Liaw, A.; Wiener, M. Classification and Regression by randomForest. *R News* **2002**, *2*, 18–22.
70. Friedman, J.H. Greedy function approximation: A gradient boosting machine. *Ann. Stat.* **2001**, *29*, 1189–1232. [CrossRef]
71. Malla, R.; Neupane, P.R.; Köhl, M. Assessment of above ground biomass and soil organic carbon in the forests of Nepal under climate change scenario. *Front. For. Glob. Change* **2023**, *6*, 1209232. [CrossRef]
72. Ali, A.; Lin, S.L.; He, J.K.; Kong, F.M.; Yu, J.H.; Jiang, H.S. Climate and soils determine aboveground biomass indirectly via species diversity and stand structural complexity in tropical forests. *For. Ecol. Manag.* **2019**, *432*, 823–831. [CrossRef]
73. Yuan, S.; Tang, T.; Wang, M.; Chen, H.; Zhang, A.; Yu, J. Regional Scale Determinants of Nutrient Content of Soil in a Cold-Temperate Forest. *Forests* **2018**, *9*, 177. [CrossRef]
74. Slik, J.W.F.; Paoli, G.; Mcguire, K.; Amaral, I.; Barroso, J.; Bastian, M.; Blanc, L.; Bongers, F.; Boundja, P.; Clark, C.; et al. Large trees drive forest aboveground biomass variation in moist lowland forests across the tropics. *Glob. Ecol. Biogeogr.* **2013**, *22*, 1261–1271. [CrossRef]
75. Liu, L.; Lim, S.; Shen, X.; Yebra, M. Assessment of generalized allometric models for aboveground biomass estimation: A case study in Australia. *Comput. Electron. Agric.* **2020**, *175*, 105610. [CrossRef]
76. Laurance, W.F.; Fearnside, P.M.; Laurance, S.G.; Lovejoy, T.E.; Merona, J.M.R.; Jeffrey, Q.; Gascon, C. Relationship between soils and Amazon forest biomass: A landscape-scale study. *For. Ecol. Manag.* **1999**, *118*, 127–138. [CrossRef]
77. Bowman, D.; Williamson, K.; Prior, L. A warmer world will reduce tree growth in evergreen broadleaf forests: Evidence from Australian temperate and subtropical eucalypt forests. *Glob. Ecol. Biogeogr.* **2014**, *23*, 925–934. [CrossRef]
78. Medlyn, B.; Zeppel, M.; Brouwers, N.; Howard, K.; Gara, E.; Hardy, G.; Lyons, T.; Li, L.; Evans, B. *An Assessment of the Vulnerability of Australian Forests to the Impacts of Climate Change*; Griffith University: Brisbane, Australian, 2011.
79. Lewis, S.L.; Sonké, B.; Sunderland, T.; Begne, S.K.; Lopez-Gonzalez, G.; van der Heijden, G.M.F.; Phillips, O.L.; Affum-Baffoe, K.; Baker, T.R.; Banin, L.; et al. Above-ground biomass and structure of 260 African tropical forests. *Philos. Trans. R. Soc. B Biol. Sci.* **2013**, *368*, 295. [CrossRef]
80. Du, Q.; Xu, J.; Wang, J.; Zhang, F.; Ji, B. Correlation between forest carbon distribution and terrain elements of altitude and slope. *J. Zhejiang A F Univ.* **2013**, *30*, 330–335.
81. Fan, Y.; Zhou, G.; Shi, Y.; Du, H.; Zhou, Y.; Xu, X. Effects of terrain on stand structure and vegetation carbon storage of phyllostachys edulis forest. *Sci. Silvae Sin.* **2013**, *49*, 177–182.
82. Li, P.; Wei, X.; Tang, M. Forest site classification based on nfi and dem in zhejiang province. *J. Southwest For. Univ.* **2018**, *38*, 137–144.
83. De Castilho, C.V.; Magnusson, W.E.; de Araújo, R.N.O.; Luizão, R.C.C.; Luizão, F.J.; Lima, A.P.; Higuchi, N. Variation in aboveground tree live biomass in a central Amazonian Forest: Effects of soil and topography. *For. Ecol. Manag.* **2006**, *234*, 85–96. [CrossRef]
84. Nepal, S.; Kc, M.; Pudasaini, N.; Adhikari, H. Divergent Effects of Topography on Soil Properties and Above-Ground Biomass in Nepal's Mid-Hill Forests. *Resources* **2023**, *12*, 136. [CrossRef]
85. Sanaei, A.; Ali, M.; Chahouki, Z.; Ali, A.; Jafari, M.; Azarnivand, H. Science of the Total Environment Abiotic and biotic drivers of aboveground biomass in semi-steppe rangelands. *Sci. Total Environ.* **2018**, *615*, 895–905. [CrossRef] [PubMed]
86. Raich, J.W.; Russell, A.E.; Vitousek, P.M. Primary productivity and ecosystem development along an elevational gradient on Mauna Loa, Hawaii. *Ecology* **1997**, *78*, 707–721.
87. Waide, R.B.; Zimmerman, J.K.; Scatena, F.N. Controls of primary productivity: Lessons from the Luquillo Mountains in Puerto Rico. *Ecology* **1998**, *79*, 31–37. [CrossRef]
88. Aiba, S.; Kitayama, K. Structure, composition and species diversity in an altitude-substrate matrix of rain forest tree communities on Mount Kinabalu, Borneo. *Plant Ecol.* **1999**, *140*, 139–157. [CrossRef]
89. Kitayma, K.; Aiba, S. Ecosystem structure and productivity of tropical rain forests along altitudinal gradients with contrasting soil phosphorus pools on Mount Kinabalu, Borneo. *J. Ecol.* **2002**, *90*, 37–51. [CrossRef]
90. Leuschner, C.; Moser, G.; Bertsch, C.; Röderstein, M.; Hertel, D. Large altitudinal increase in tree root/shoot ratio in tropical mountain forests of Ecuador. *Basic Appl. Ecol.* **2007**, *8*, 219–230. [CrossRef]
91. Broich, M.; Hansen, M.; Stolle, F.; Potapov, P.; Margono, B.A.; Adusei, B. Remotely sensed forest cover loss shows high spatial and temporal variation across Sumatera and Kalimantan, Indonesia 2000–2008. *Environ. Res. Lett.* **2011**, *6*, 014010. [CrossRef]

92. Mehta, V.K.; Sullivan, P.J.; Walter, M.T.; Krishnaswamy, J.; Degloria, S.D. Impacts of disturbance on soil properties in a dry tropical forest in Southern India. *Ecohydrology* **2008**, *175*, 161–175. [CrossRef]
93. Rad, J.E.; Valadi, G.; Salehzadeh, O.; Maroofi, H. Effects of anthropogenic disturbance on plant composition, plant diversity and soil properties in oak forests, Iran. *J. For. Sci.* **2018**, *2018*, 358–370.
94. Ma, L.; Li, W.; Shi, N.; Fu, S.; Lian, J.; Ye, W. Temporal and spatial patterns of aboveground biomass and its driving forces in a subtropical forest: A case study. *Pol. J. Ecol.* **2019**, *67*, 95–104. [CrossRef]
95. Oberleitner, F.; Egger, C.; Oberdorfer, S.; Dullinger, S.; Wanek, W.; Hietz, P. Forest Ecology and Management Recovery of aboveground biomass, species richness and composition in tropical secondary forests in SW Costa Rica. *For. Ecol. Manag.* **2021**, *479*, 118580. [CrossRef]
96. Ojha, R.B.; Panday, D. (Eds.) *The Soils of Nepal*; Springer International Publishing: Berlin/Heidelberg, Germany, 2021.

forests

MDPI

Article

Tree Biomass Modeling Based on the Exploration of Regression and Artificial Neural Networks Approaches

Şerife Kalkanlı Genç [1], Maria J. Diamantopoulou [2] and Ramazan Özçelik [3,*]

[1] Graduate Education Institute, Isparta University of Applied Sciences, East Campus, 32260 Isparta, Türkiye; serifekalkanli9@gmail.com

[2] Faculty of Agriculture, Forestry and Natural Environment, School of Forestry and Natural Environment, Aristotle University of Thessaloniki, 54124 Thessaloniki, Greece; mdiamant@for.auth.gr

[3] Faculty of Forestry, Isparta University of Applied Sciences, East Campus, 32260 Isparta, Türkiye

* Correspondence: ramazanozcelik@isparta.edu.tr; Tel.: +90-246-214-6546

Abstract: Understanding the dynamics of tree biomass is a significant factor in forest ecosystems, and accurate quantitative knowledge of its development provides support for the optimization of forest management. This work aimed to employ innovative practices in tree biomass modeling, artificial neural network approaches along with the least-squares regression methodology, in order to construct reliable and accurate estimation and prediction models that contribute to solving the emerging problems in the field of sustainable forest management. Based on this aim, different modeling strategies were developed and explored. The nonlinear seemingly unrelated regression (NSUR) methodology, the generalized regression (GRNN), the resilient propagation (RPNN) and the Bayesian regularization (BRNN) artificial neural network algorithms were utilized for the construction of reliable biomass models to attain the most accurate and reliable tree biomass components and total tree biomass estimations. The work showed that GRNN models provided a significantly better performance compared with the other modeling methodologies tested. Considering the non-parametric nature of the GRNN neural network algorithm, the fact that it was designed for nonlinear regression-type problems capable of dealing with small datasets, this modeling approach warrants consideration as an effective alternative to nonlinear regression or to other neural network approaches to the field of tree biomass modeling.

Keywords: aboveground biomass; modeling strategies; artificial neural network; cedar

1. Introduction

Both the role of forests in the global carbon cycle and the emergence of forest biomass as a source of energy require accurate and reliable estimates of the amount of carbon and vegetative mass stored in forest ecosystems. An accurate and reliable estimation of biomass is essential for sustainable management and contributes to, inter alia, the planning of forest resources, biomass energy, carbon stock and climate change studies, forest health, forest productivity and nutrient cycling [1,2].

Nowadays, traditional forest inventory studies mostly focus on determining timber stocks and its increments with time. However, volume functions and the tree volume tables used for estimating growth are not useful for biomass estimations. Therefore, it is necessary to develop statistical functions or specific tables that provide biomass quantities for the whole tree and tree components. Biomass is defined as the total mass (weight) of a tree, comprising the foliage, stem, branches, bark, and roots. Biomass is divided into two parts, aboveground and belowground. Aboveground biomass refers to the whole visible living mass, including the stem (to the root collar), branches, bark, fruit/seeds, and leaves, while belowground biomass consists of both the structural and fine root systems. Xiao et al. [3] reported that the amount of belowground biomass in an old-growth Scots pine forest is 14% of the aboveground biomass; Czapowskyj et al. [4] stated that 80% of the total biomass is retained in the aboveground components and 20% in the belowground components. Since most of the carbon stored in forest ecosystems is sequestered in the aboveground vegetative mass, an estimation of the aboveground vegetative mass is much more important for estimating the amount of carbon stored in forest areas and monitoring the temporal change than knowing the total biomass present.

Aboveground biomass is generally divided into three main components, stem, bark and crown (branches and leaves) [5,6]. Estimating the biomass of these components is of importance both for determining the intra-tree variability of biomass and for the fact that these components can be utilized for different purposes. Stem biomass is relevant for wood production planning, crown biomass for fuel content and assessments of the fire spread rate, and biomass in small branches and foliage for bioenergy production [6]. Previous reports indicated that the amount of biomass in tree components varies from species to species and from region to region [7]. He et al. [8] reported that approximately 72% of the aboveground biomass of a tree is in the stem, while the amounts of biomass in branches, foliage and fruit are 11%, 13% and 4%, respectively. De-Miguel et al. [9] reported that in brutian pine stands that are 20, 40 and 60 years old in Syria, 79.8%, 80.5% and 80.6% of the aboveground biomass was in tree stems, while 20.2%, 19.5% and 19.4% was in the crown, respectively. These variations between species in the proportions of biomass in different components indicate that it is necessary to develop species-based component models.

In addition, the amount of biomass of a tree and the distribution of this biomass to tree components can vary greatly according to numerous factors, such as growing environment conditions, stand density, soil properties and competition between trees within the stand. Environmental factors and genetic variability lead to variations in tree stem form, thus limiting the utilization of biomass equations developed for one region in other areas or leading to large estimation errors. Therefore, biomass equations should also take into account regional differences [9].

In recent years, everchanging market conditions and the increasing adoption of biomass or weight as a measure of forest productivity have required accurate estimates of total tree and component biomass in Türkiye [10]. However, the current information on tree biomass estimates is not sufficient for the preparation of management plans for complex forest ecosystems in Türkiye. In this country, aboveground biomass estimation equations for the whole tree and its components have been developed for some tree species at the regional level [10–19]. Except for Özçelik et al. [10] and Güner et al. [19], the estimations generally utilized linear or nonlinear traditional regression equations with one or more independent variables. However, when separate biomass equations are developed for all components of a tree (stem, branches, bark, etc.) with traditional equations, the correlation between the biomass quantities of different components is not taken into account, and as a result, the sum of the estimates obtained for the components may be more or less than the biomass estimate obtained for the whole tree. In recent years, systems of equations such as seemingly unrelated regression (SUR or NSUR) and the generalized method of moments (GMM) have gained more popularity for parameter estimation in biomass models in order to overcome this problem and similar drawbacks and to provide more accurate and reliable estimates [1,5].

Weiskittel et al. [20] stated that there are limitations in the development of tree biomass models such as the cost of biomass data collection and the employment of different methods for this purpose, the lack of data and models for belowground biomass, and the utilization of simple model forms and explanatory variables. It is necessary, therefore, to develop new models and methods to increase the accuracy of tree biomass estimates. In this context, due to their ability to overcome fundamental regression analysis assumptions (independency, normality etc.), the most widely used modeling methodology, data mining and artificial intelligence methods, may be beneficial. It is well known that tree biomass is nonlinear in nature. Traditional regression modeling needs much effort to be spent on the regression assumptions examination along with the selection of the optimal form of a function. Previous studies [10,19] have shown that artificial neural networks (ANNs), part of the scientific area of machine learning, are worth more exploration since these systems have shown their potential to overcome the aforementioned difficulties. As powerful non-parametric machine learning techniques included in the artificial intelligence methods, the structure of ANNs has been thoroughly described and discussed [21–24]. In forest research, ANNs have shown the potential to successfully learn from noisy and nonlinear data in data from nature, such as primary data collected from the field. In order for the efficiency of the different learning algorithms embedded in ANNs to be assessed, different ANN modeling approaches are tested by the research forest community. For example, Diamantopoulou [25] used the cascade correlation algorithm in the feedforward ANNs for an estimation of tree stem diameters, whereas Özçelik et al. [10] applied the Levenberg–Marquardt algorithm for tree biomass prediction, and Vieira et al. [26] estimated tree growth and height using the Levenberg–Marquardt algorithm. Ercanlı [27] used deep learning for modeling the relationship between tree height and diameter at breast height. The increasing research interest, raised by the need to construct the most reliable and accurate models of tree and forest attributes based on innovative and advanced modeling methodologies, is safely driving the optimal forest management decisions. Testing and evaluating the potential algorithms which incorporate innovative modeling perspectives, along with modeling capability, is therefore more than a necessity for the best forestry practices to be applied.

Natural cedar (*Cedrus libani* A. Rich) forests are extremely valuable for Türkiye, both ecologically and economically. Due to unplanned production, overgrazing and fires in Syria and Lebanon, where the species is also naturally distributed, it has almost become extinct, and the distribution area has become restricted to Türkiye [28]. Therefore, natural cedar forests are a natural treasure and indispensable to the cultural heritage of Türkiye and the world. Although natural cedar forests have their most important distribution in the Mediterranean region, their total distribution area in Türkiye is approximately 465,000 ha and the yield from these areas is approximately 27.4 million cubic meters per annum. Due to the valuable and important properties of cedar wood, it is amongst the most important tree species for the forest products industry in Türkiye. In addition to their economic value in Türkiye, cedar forests play a key role in major environmental issues such as the conservation of soil and water resources, mitigating and adapting to the negative impact of climate change, and protecting biodiversity [29]. As a natural consequence of their wide distribution in the Mediterranean region, cedar forests can exhibit significant differences in growth and development characteristics depending on factors such as climate, growing environment conditions and origin. Therefore, in order to make accurate and reliable biomass estimates, it is necessary to develop separate biomass estimation models for different regions where natural cedar forests occur.

In this context, the aim of the work described here was to test the reliability and accuracy of possible modeling methodologies which incorporate innovative perspectives in the field of forest tree biomass modeling procedures. For this purpose, an evaluation of the performances of modern modeling approaches, utilized in recent years by the forest scientific community for estimates of the aboveground biomass estimation of trees, was conducted. The nonlinear seemingly unrelated regression modeling method (NSUR), the generalized regression (GRNN), the resilient propagation (RPNN) and the Bayesian regularization (BRNN) artificial neural network algorithms were utilized to construct reliable biomass models. These modeling alternatives were applied and evaluated to enhance the sustainable management of natural cedar stands in the northwestern Mediterranean region by providing effective tools for the decision-making processes of forest managers.

2. Materials and Methods

2.1. Field and Laboratory Studies

A total of fifty-five sample trees of different diameter and height classes were selected randomly in natural cedar stands in the Isparta Regional Forest District to represent different stand structures (Figure 1). The diameter at breast height (D) was measured and the trees were cut at the stump height ($D_{0.30}$). The total height (H) and merchantable height (the height on the stem at which the diameter drops to 8 cm) of the cut trees were measured, and the stem heights corresponding to 1/3 and 2/3 of the merchantable height were also calculated. In order to be utilized in volume predictions for the chosen trees, in addition to over-bark diameter at breast height (D), over-bark stem diameters were measured at 2 m intervals starting from a height of 2.30 m to the top of the tree. Diameter measurements were conducted with digital calipers with an accuracy of 0.1 cm, and height (length) measurements of the tree sections were made with a tape measure with an accuracy of 0.01 m. The bark thickness of the sample trees at all stem heights where diameter measurements were obtained was also measured with a precision of 1 mm. Using this method, the double bark thickness was calculated. The volume of the sample trees with and without bark were estimated by summing the tree section volumes obtained via Smalian's formula [30], including the top section volume which was calculated as a cone. The bark volume values of the sample trees were obtained from the difference between the outside volume and the inside volume.

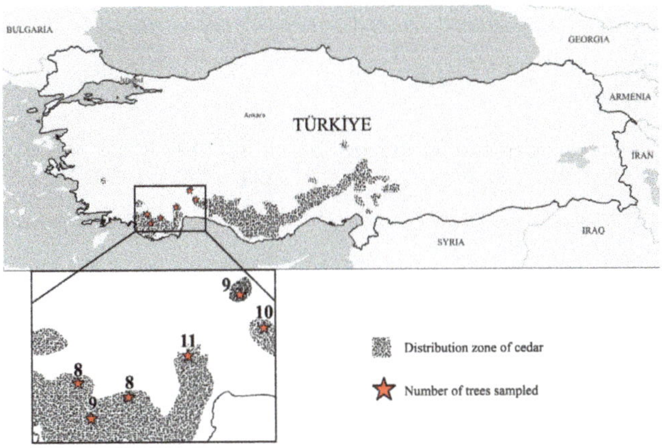

Figure 1. Location of sample trees in distribution zone of cedar.

The methods proposed by Alemdag [31,32] were utilized to determine the kiln-dried weights of the stem wood and bark of the sample trees. Dry weights of the branch and needle samples were obtained using the methods of Porté et al. [33]. In order to estimate the biomass of stem wood and bark, a total of 4 discs of 5–7 cm thickness were cut at breast height of each tree (1.30 m), from the 1/3 and 2/3 heights of the merchantable stem section and from the point at which the stem diameter dropped to 8 cm. In order to determine branch and needle biomass, branch length was measured, along with the diameter at the point where the branch joined the stem. All branches were cut and clustered, and the average branch diameter and the average branch length were calculated for each sample tree. A branch sample with average values matching this description was obtained. The needles of each branch sample were extracted. In this way, branch and needle samples were obtained.

Furthermore, the four discs and the extracted branch, along with the needle sample from each tree, were returned to the laboratory in polyethylene bags to determine the kiln-dried weights of the whole tree and the biomass components (stem, bark, branch and needles). To obtain the kiln-dried weights of the stem wood, the bark was peeled from the 4 discs taken from each sample tree. The un-barked discs and the bark, branch and needle samples were dried in a drying oven at 105 ± 3 °C for 72 h, and the dry weights were determined on a precision balance. Full details of the methods for estimating the kiln-dried stem wood and bark biomass of sample trees are given in Alemdag [31,32] and Sakıcı et al. [18]. Details for determining the total twig and needle weight were those of Porté et al. [33].

The problems of convergence and high multicollinearity in the simultaneous adjustment of biomass components, branches and leaves, were accounted for by combining the data in a single component named "crown", which resulted in an increased accuracy of estimations [5]. This modification corresponded with the three components (stem, bark, crown) into which aboveground biomass is usually divided [34].

The total aboveground biomass of the sample trees was calculated by summing the kiln-dried weights obtained for the tree components.

$$dw_{total} = dw_{stem} + dw_{bark} + dw_{crown} \tag{1}$$

Descriptive statistics of kiln-dried whole tree and tree components for sample trees from natural cedar stands are presented in Table 1.

Table 1. Summary statistics of the sample of 55 trees used in estimation of total and separate components of biomass.

Variables	n	Min	Max	Mean	Std. Dev.
Diameter at breast height (D, cm)	55	10.00	58.70	30.09	13.72
Total height (H, m)	55	7.88	27.10	17.22	5.01
Dry aboveground biomass (dw_{total}, kg)	55	36.32	1750.76	554.00	492.80
Dry stem biomass without bark (dw_{stem}, kg)	55	10.97	966.89	294.79	270.41
Dry crown biomass (dw_{crown}, kg)	55	10.46	844.91	210.56	199.70
Dry bark biomass (dw_{bark}, kg)	55	2.40	150.50	48.65	38.29

2.2. Method

2.2.1. Seemingly Unrelated Regression Model (SUR)

Wang and Xing [35] stated that a good biomass equation should strike a balance between accuracy, simplicity and practical feasibility. In the development of tree biomass equations, only the diameter at breast height (D) or sometimes tree height (H) can be included as independent variables. In developing biomass models with these independent variables, the ordinary least-squares method (OLS) is often employed. However, when the components of trees are measured, such as the stem, branches or bark, and separate equations are developed for each component, then these models cannot take into account the inherent correlation between the biomasses of tree components measured on the same tree, resulting in a violation of the additivity behavior of the models. Therefore, many of the biomass equations developed provide inaccurate estimates and the principle of additivity between the results of the tree component equations and the total tree biomass remain incomplete. Due to the crucial involvement of the estimated tree biomass quantities in the estimation of the carbon content sequestered by trees, the need for reliable and, at the same time, accurate biomass modeling systems is of vital importance. As stated by Parresol [34], the carbon sequestration in each component cannot exceed the amount of carbon sequestration of the whole tree.

The utilization of biomass equation systems has been proposed to overcome this problem and to ensure the aggregability of biomass components [5,34]. Different approaches (SUR, NSUR, GMM) can be employed for estimations of model parameters. Among these approaches, NSUR has become most popular, because it has a more general and flexible structure, allows each component model to have its own independent variable and its own weight function to deal with the problem of different variance in each component, and allows a total tree biomass model to be obtained with smaller variance [1,36]. In this work, therefore, the NSUR approach was selected for developing the biomass equation system, which can estimate simultaneously both the biomass of the whole tree and different tree components. For this purpose, a total of thirty-three linear and nonlinear models obtained from different sources were adapted independently for the estimation of the biomass of different tree components through the ordinary least-squares method (OLS). The most successful model for each tree component was chosen for further analysis based on three different evaluation criteria: the coefficient of determination (R^2), the root means square error (RMSE), and the mean absolute error (MAB) (results not displayed here). Two important problems encountered in the development of biomass equations were the problems of heteroscedasticity and multicollinearity. To overcome heteroscedasticity, weighted regression was employed, with each observation weighted by the inverse of its variance. The approach proposed by Park [37] was utilized to determine which independent variable is more correlated with the residual values obtained for the components, so that the appropriate weight function can be determined for each tree component. The weighting factor for heteroscedasticity $1/(x_i)^k$ was included in the NSUR fit of the SAS/ETS statistical package. In the final stage, all component equations were solved simultaneously in order to enable a system of equations to estimate both total tree and component biomass. The set of equations was fitted simultaneously by NSURs implemented in the PROC MODEL procedure of SAS/ETS [38].

The presence or absence of multicollinearity is analyzed by the condition number (CN). According to Belsley [39], a value of CN between 1000–3000 indicates severe multicollinearity, while for a CN value less than 10, the possibility of the existence of multicollinearity can safely be ignored. A CN value between the above indicates the presence of this problem, and it needs to be properly handled.

2.2.2. Artificial Neural Network Modeling

Due to their ability to learn and successfully imitate the behavior of real-life systems such as the attributes of both trees and forests, artificial neural networks are an effective modeling solution that can produce valuable results. Their capacity to model nonlinear systems that are affected by many factors can be boosted by the optimal algorithm used for each case.

Generalized regression neural networks (GRNNs), which are often known as regression (Bayesian) networks, were first introduced and described by Speckt [40]. This type of network is a kernel-based approximation, single-layer feedforward neural network, which is scaled by a smoothing parameter (σ) that controls the network complexity. Gaussian kernel functions are located at each training case [41]. Due to their ability to successfully approximate any nonlinear mapping between continuous variables used as input and output vectors directly from the training data, they have been utilized in different problems. A detailed description of the algorithm is available in the literature [40,42,43]. Indicatively, the Bayesian techniques that the GRNN algorithm uses to estimate the expected mean value ($E[y/x]$) of the output (y) of an input case (x) lead to the single-bandwidth (smoothing factor) GRNN fundamental expression:

$$E[y/x] = \hat{y}(x) = \left(\sum_{i=1}^{n} y_i \cdot exp\left(-\frac{\sum_{r=1}^{k}(x_r - x_{ir})^T \cdot (x_r - x_{ir})}{2 \cdot \sigma^2}\right)\right) \Big/ \left(\sum_{i=1}^{n} exp\left(-\frac{\sum_{r=1}^{k}(x_r - x_{ir})^T \cdot (x_r - x_{ir})}{2 \cdot \sigma^2}\right)\right) \quad (2)$$

where, $\hat{y}(x)$ is the estimated output value based on x (vector variable with k number of elements), n is the number of training patterns, x_i is the training sample, y_i is the output of the input sample x_i, $\sum_{r=1}^{k}(x_r - x_{ir})^T \cdot (x_r - x_{ir}) = d_i^2$ is the square Euclidean distance between the training sample and the point of prediction, σ is the width of the Gaussian kernel function (smoothing factor) and superscript (^{T}) indicates the transposed action.

As can be seen (Equation (2)), the accuracy and the generalization ability of the network training estimation is totally dependent on the smoothing factor (σ); therefore, its value has to be carefully specified. If the smoothing factor value is too small, then a high estimation variance would be produced by the system, while if the value selected is too large, then the system would be led to a high estimate bias. In this work, the optimum value of the smoothing factor was determined using the exhaustive grid-search methodology [44] for values included in the range of [0, 10] by 0.001.

The structure of the GRNN consists of four layers, where the information movement is feedforward, with direction from the first to the fourth layer. The first layer is the input layer where the variables are introduced as input information to the system. This layer is followed by a pattern layer which includes the same number of nodes as the input data cases. The information of this layer is used for the square Euclidean distance calculation, and the Gaussian radial kernel function can be calculated for each node. This results in the information included in the third layer, which is the summation layer with two nodes which are the values of the nominator and the denominator of the Equation (2). The final layer is the output layer where the expected mean value ($E[y/x]$) of the output (y) of an input case (x) is derived.

Due to its efficiency in overcoming problems of the traditional backpropagation algorithm, which can be slow at converging, require effort at parameter tuning, and get stuck in local minima, the resilient back-propagation artificial neural network (RPNN) supervised learning algorithm is considered as a powerful algorithm with desired properties [45–47]. As has been introduced and described by Riedmiller and Braun [45], the innovation of this algorithm that boosts its learning strength in aiming to overcome local minima is that it performs a direct adaptation of weight step based on local gradient information. That is, an individual update value (Δ_{ij}) is calculated for each weight of the system in order for the partial derivative of the corresponding weight (w_{ij}) to change its sign, meaning that the updated weight value (w_{ij}^{t+1}) of the previous weight value (w_{ij}^{t}) between the i and j nodes in two consecutive layers can be achieved as

$$w_{ij}^{t+1} = w_{ij}^{t} + \Delta w_{ij}^{t} \tag{3}$$

where the (Δw_{ij}^{t}) is calculated following the update rule [45]:

$$\Delta_{wij}^{(t)} = \begin{cases} -\Delta_{ij}^{(t)}, if \dfrac{\partial E^{(t)}}{\partial w_{ij}} > 0 \\ +\Delta_{ij}^{(t)}, if \dfrac{\partial E^{(t)}}{\partial w_{ij}} < 0 \\ 0, else \end{cases} \tag{4}$$

where the individual update value for the interaction (t) can be calculated using the equation [45]

$$\Delta_{ij}^{(t)} = \begin{cases} \eta^{+} \times \Delta_{ij}^{(t-1)}, & if \frac{\partial E^{(t-1)}}{\partial w_{ij}} \times \frac{\partial E^{(t)}}{\partial w_{ij}} > 0 \\ \eta^{-} \times \Delta_{ij}^{(t-1)}, & if \frac{\partial E^{(t-1)}}{\partial w_{ij}} \times \frac{\partial E^{(t)}}{\partial w_{ij}} < 0 \\ \Delta_{ij}^{(t-1)}, & else \end{cases} \tag{5}$$

where η is the increasing or decreasing factor of the system with $0 < \eta^{-} < 1 < \eta^{+}$.

The initial values of η^{-}, η^{+} following the logical order have been described in previous research [45,46] and set to 0.5 and 1.2, respectively. According to the choice of the initial value of Δ_0, this was set to its default value equal to 0.07 [48]. Finally, the structure of the RPNN used consisted of three layers (input–hidden–output).

Bayesian regularization neural networks (BRNNs) have become popular due to their robustness as compared to the multilayer perceptron back-propagation nets, and they are able to minimize the need for lengthy cross-validation [49]. In order for the variance of the network system to be avoided, thus aiming for the best regularization behavior of the system, Bayesian regularization was embedded, so that the parameters of the loss function of the net could be optimized. The Bayesian approach, which is reliant on the probability distribution of the network weights, involves the Bayesian theorem, resulting to the probability distribution of the network predictions. In the training process, the mean square network error included the Bayesian regularization term is minimized [50]:

$$F = b_0 \cdot E_{IO}(IO|w, net) + b_1 \cdot E_w(w|net) \tag{6}$$

where, b_0 and b_1 are the system's hyperparameters, E_{IO} is the mean square of the network error, *IO* is the input–output pairs of the training data, *net* is the network specific architecture that is the trained BRNN, and E_w is the mean sum of the square weights.

Bayesian regularization takes place within the Levenberg–Marquardt algorithm, meaning that the Jacobian matrix that contains the first derivatives of the network errors with respect to the weights and biases is computed. Finally, the structure of BRNN consisted of three layers (input–hidden–output).

The structure of the above artificial neural network structures is shown in Figure 2.

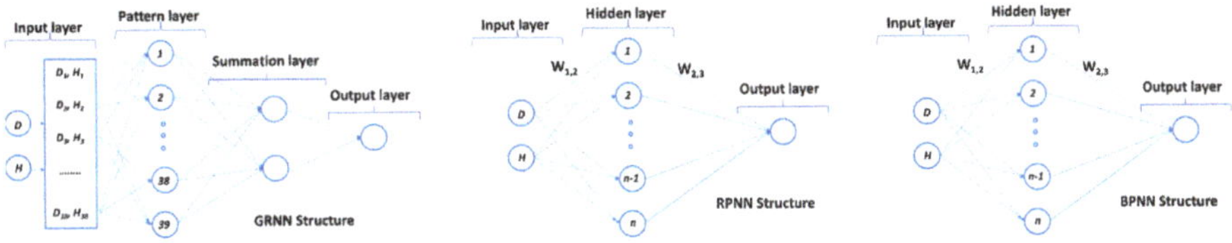

Figure 2. Artificial neural network modeling structures.

In order for the generalization ability of the neural network models to be achieved, so as to assess the stability and consistency of these models across different datasets, the available dataset was randomly divided into fitting data, which constitutes 70% of the total dataset, and test data, which consists of the remaining 30% data sets. The first dataset was used for the choice of the "best" model, while the latter was used for the exploration of the predictive ability of the constructed model. This way, the reliability of the ANN-constructed model was revealed. Further, the methodology of the k-fold cross validation [51] was used for the fitting dataset which was further divided into training and validation datasets ten consecutive times, with k = 10, in order for all the available information of the fitting dataset to be included in the training process of the models.

The learning of generalized regression neural network (GRNN) modeling, resilient propagation artificial neural network (RPNN) modeling and Bayesian regularization neural network (BRNN) modeling were performed using the MATLAB R2022a [48] programming language.

2.2.3. Statistical Evaluation Criteria

The following evaluation criteria were utilized to assess the model performances, namely, bias (*BIAS*%); root mean square error (*RMSE*); coefficient of variation (*CV*%); coefficient of determination (R^2); the mean absolute bias (*MAB*); and the second-order Akaike's information criterion (*AICc*) including the correction for small sample sizes [52,53]:

$$BIAS\,\% = 100 \times \frac{\left(\sum_{i=1}^{i=n}(y_i - \hat{y}_i)/n\right)}{\overline{y}}\% \tag{7}$$

$$RMSE = \sqrt{\frac{\sum_{i=1}^{i=n}(y_i - \hat{y}_i)^2}{n}} \tag{8}$$

$$CV\% = 100 \times \frac{RMSE}{\overline{y}}\% \tag{9}$$

$$R^2 = 1 - \left[\frac{\sum_{i=1}^{i=n}(y_i - \hat{y}_i)^2}{\sum_{i=1}^{n}(y_i - \overline{y})^2}\right] \tag{10}$$

$$MAB = \frac{\sum_{i=1}^{i=n}|y_i - \hat{y}_i|}{n} \tag{11}$$

$$AICc = nlog\left(\sum_{i=1}^{i=n} (y_i - \hat{y}_i)^2/n\right) + 2p + \left(\frac{2p(p+1)}{n-p-1}\right) \tag{12}$$

where, y_i and $\hat{y}_i$ are the observed and predicted values for the ith observation, respectively, $\overline{y}$ is the mean of the y_i, and n is the number of observations and p is the number of independent variables plus the intercept used in each model.

3. Results

As a result of the graphical evaluation of the relationships between the dependent variables (whole tree and tree components biomass) and the independent variables (*D* and *H*) utilized in the study, it was observed that there was a nonlinear relationship between the variables as expected (Figure 3).

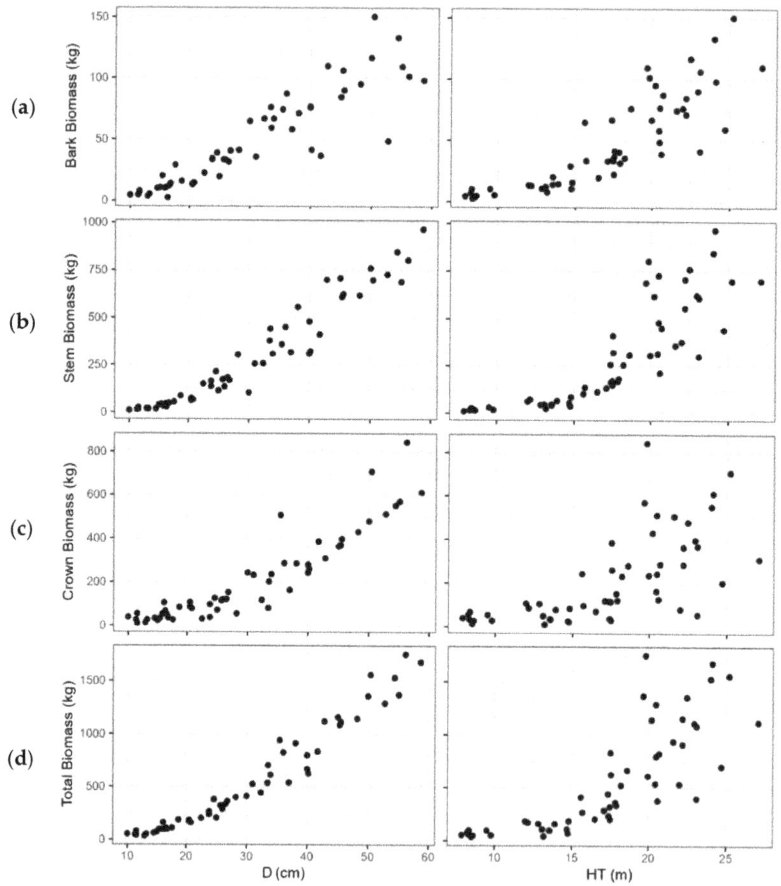

Figure 3. Relationship between *D* and *H* with (**a**) bark, (**b**) stem, (**c**) crown, and (**d**) whole tree biomass.

In general, kiln-dried biomass estimates obtained for both the whole tree and its components displayed higher variation for tree height than for tree diameter (Figure 3). In terms of tree components, the variation obtained for crown (needle and branch) biomass was relatively higher than that obtained for stem wood biomass. Due to the variability of the crown (foliage and branch) structure, the number of branches, and variation in wood density along with branches, the crown (foliage and branch) biomass variance was greater, in relative terms, than that obtained in the estimation of wood biomass. Bark biomass also demonstrated greater variability, especially in the thicker diameter classes. All wood components exhibited greater variability with increasing height.

Under the same reasoning, different modeling systems, i.e., the NSUR, GRNN, RPNN and BRNN modeling approaches, were employed for biomass estimations of the whole tree and the different tree components, and the relative results are provided below. Separate models were first developed for each biomass component (stem, crown, and bark) before a simultaneous solution was implemented utilizing the different modeling approaches to ensure the aggregability of the biomass for the tree components.

According to the NSUR approach, each biomass component was first weighted considering the weighting factors adopted when developing the separate models for the components. The estimated values of the parameters, the weighting factors and the condition numbers obtained from the simultaneous solution of the three sets of biomass equations are presented in Table 2. When the weight factors for the tree components were analyzed, the weighting factors for all components were similar and within a relatively narrow range. As can be seen (Table 2), the constructed models for all tree components were described by different allometric forms. The parameter estimates for all models forming the system of equations were significant at the 0.05 level except for one parameter (c_0) of the model developed for bark.

Table 2. Parameter estimates and standard errors in parentheses (SE) for the biomass equations of each component (crown (dw_{crown}), stem (dw_{stem}), and bark (dw_{bark})) and total tree biomass (dw_{total}) obtained from simultaneous NSUR fit.

Model	Parameter	Estimate (SE)	Approx Pr. > |t|	Weight Factors
$dw_{crown} = a_0 + a_1 D^2 + a_2 H$	a_0	41.2232 (7.6996)	<0.0001	$1/D^{0.1150}$
	a_1	0.2378 (0.0069)	<0.0001	
	a_2	−5.6033 (0.8017)	<0.0001	
$dw_{stem} = b_0 D^{b_1} H^{b_2}$	b_0	0.0322 (0.0069)	<0.0001	$1/D^{0.09507}$
	b_1	1.5266 (0.0469)	<0.0001	
	b_2	1.2929 (0.0686)	<0.0001	
$dw_{bark} = c_0 D H^{c_1}$	c_0	0.0137 (0.0084)	0.1110	$1/D^{0.1038}$
	c_1	1.6064 (0.1999)	<0.0001	
$dw_{total} = \left(a_0 + a_1 D^2 + a_2 H\right) + \left(b_0 D^{b_1} H^{b_2}\right) + \left(c_0 D H^{c_1}\right)$		CN:160		$1/D^{0.07860}$

w_i : dry weight of components i (kg), a_i, b_i, and c_i: regression parameters for the crown, stem wood, and bark, respectively, D: diameter at breast height (cm), H: total height (m), and CN: condition number.

ANNs are free from regression-type restrictions and assumptions. For this reason, they were selected to be tested as possible alternatives. However, there are hyperparameters, different in each ANN algorithm, that require optimization via tuning in order for accurate and reliable ANN models to be produced. The number of hidden nodes in the hidden layer of each model is included in Table 3.

The optimal values of the training elements of the constructed neural network models were assessed through trial-and-error methodologies, taking into account the estimation and prediction mean square errors of both the fitting and test datasets. According to the GRNN-constructed models, the smoothing factor values (σ_i) were tuned for 4950 fits, using the exhaustive grid search methodology. The optimal (σ) values that led to the best biomass components models were equal to 1.879, 1.359 and 1.000 for the stem, bark and crown biomass estimations, respectively. The optimal weight values for the RPNN-constructed models were attained after 303, 83 and 36 epochs for the stem, bark, and crown biomass estimations, respectively, while the respective epochs for the BRNN models were 7, 5 and 5 for the stem, bark, and crown biomass estimations. The generalization ability along with the reliability of each neural network-constructed model was attained through the test dataset. As can be seen (Table 4), all ANN models produced both reliable estimations and predictions for the biomass components, supporting the reliability of the models. All constructed models showed an ability to generalize prediction errors and correlation coefficient values for the test datasets more or less similar to those derived from the model estimations using the fitting dataset (Table 4). Furthermore, according to the error histograms derived via the three networks for the available dataset, these modeling approaches can be considered as healthy networks, with symmetric curves with a peak around zero (Figure 4).

Table 3. Number of nodes in each layer of the "best" artificial neural network estimation models for each biomass component.

Model	Biomass Component											
GRNN	dw_{stem}				dw_{bark}				dw_{crown}			
	number of nodes											
	I	P	S	O	I	P	S	O	I	P	S	O
	* 2 (38)	39	2	1	2 (38)	39	2	1	2 (38)	39	2	1
RPNN	dw_{stem}				dw_{bark}				dw_{crown}			
	number of nodes											
	I	H	O		I	H	O		I	H	O	
	2	4	1		2	3	1		2	8	1	
BRNN	dw_{stem}				dw_{bark}				dw_{crown}			
	number of nodes											
	I	H	O		I	H	O		I	H	O	
	2	3	1		2	4	1		2	4	1	

I: input layer, P: pattern layer, S: summation layer, O: output layer, H: hidden layer, * variables introduced to the input layer: 2: *D*, *H* with 38 rows (70% of the total dataset).

Table 4. Evaluation criteria for the fitting and the test datasets for the constructed ANN models.

ANN Model	Output	Dataset	CV%	Correlation Coefficient, r	45-Degree Line Test Slope
GRNN	dw_{stem}	fitting	8.85	0.9962	45.34
		test	10.03	0.9899	43.78
	dw_{bark}	fitting	10.84	0.9928	44.91
		test	11.15	0.9831	43.99
	dw_{crown}	fitting	10.08	0.9948	45.16
		test	11.96	0.9878	43.69
RPNN	dw_{stem}	fitting	10.30	0.9935	44.90
		test	15.59	0.9824	44.90
	dw_{bark}	fitting	26.18	0.9408	42.33
		test	26.38	0.9402	39.61
	dw_{crown}	fitting	31.00	0.9535	42.50
		test	31.46	0.9145	40.11
BRNN	dw_{stem}	fitting	11.47	0.9921	44.41
		test	15.43	0.9824	44.37
	dw_{bark}	fitting	26.15	0.8934	43.41
		test	28.46	0.8387	41.21
	dw_{crown}	fitting	28.55	0.9249	44.89
		test	34.51	0.8492	41.13

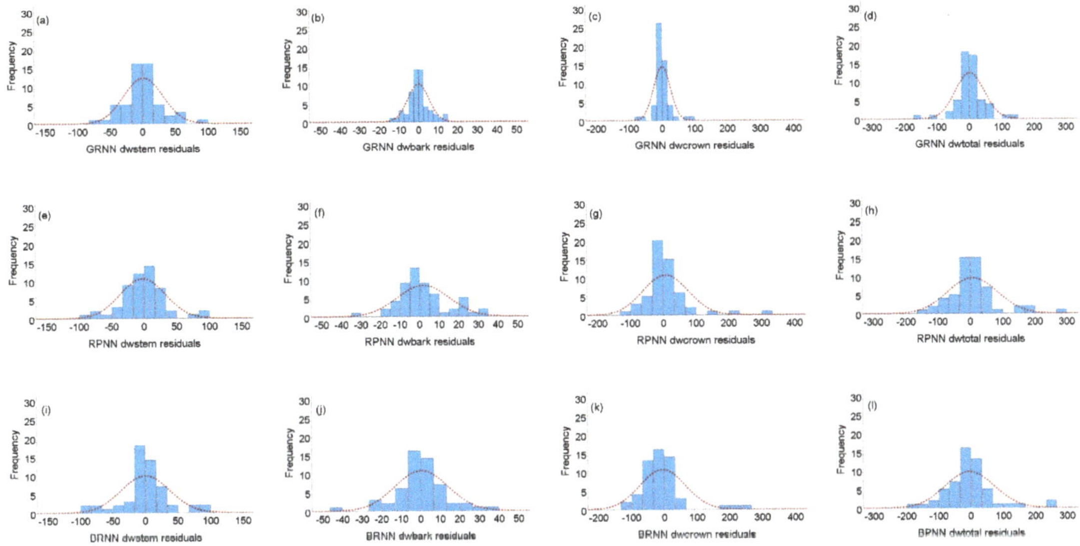

Figure 4. ANN modeling approaches residual histograms with normal curve for the biomass components (**a**,**e**,**i**) for stem, (**b**,**f**,**j**) for bark, (**c**,**g**,**k**) for crown and (**d**,**h**,**l**) for the total tree biomass.

Both the NSUR (Table 2) and the ANN-constructed models (Table 3) were used for the estimation of the biomass components and the total tree biomass. The criterion values obtained by all different modeling approaches for the available dataset, for both tree biomass components and the total biomass, are presented in Table 5. According to the NSUR approach, the most successful predictions were obtained with the equations developed for stem and whole tree. RMSE values were 83.77, 43.84, 70.45 and 13.55 kg/tree for the whole tree, stem, crown, and bark biomass, respectively.

Table 5. Evaluation statistics for all tested modeling approaches for biomass components and for the total tree biomass (n = 55).

Model	Biomass	R^2	BIAS%	RMSE	CV%	MAB	AICc
NSUR	dw_{crown}	0.8823	2.67	70.45	33.46	45.80	210
GRNN		0.9845	−0.05	25.14	11.94	14.01	161
RPNN		0.8866	3.02	67.73	32.17	40.25	208
BRNN		0.8842	−2.62	68.20	32.39	44.07	208
NSUR	dw_{stem}	0.9751	−2.61	43.84	14.87	28.94	187
GRNN		0.9881	0.35	29.65	10.06	19.74	168
RPNN		0.9842	−0.82	34.09	11.56	24.34	175
BRNN		0.9819	−0.04	36.61	12.42	24.27	178
NSUR	dw_{bark}	0.8793	0.21	13.55	27.86	9.53	131
GRNN		0.9802	−0.26	5.40	11.09	3.79	90
RPNN		0.8877	3.54	13.21	27.14	9.70	129
BRNN		0.8761	0.59	13.49	27.75	9.49	131
NSUR	dw_{total}	0.9753	−0.35	83.77	15.12	51.02	194
GRNN		0.9920	0.14	44.07	7.95	28.74	187
RPNN		0.9884	1.02	75.67	13.66	50.87	213
BRNN		0.9883	−0.97	75.32	13.60	50.90	213

All models included diameter at breast height (*D*) and tree height (*H*) as independent variables. The coefficient of determination values ranged from approximately 0.88 to 0.99 for all models.

The models developed for stem and whole tree were able to explain approximately 97% to 99%, depending on the modeling approach, of the total variability in the corresponding biomasses, while the 88% to 98% of the crown and bark biomass variability was reached by the different modeling approaches (Table 5). Considering the results in Table 5, all neural network-constructed models outperformed the NSUR-developed models and, at the same time, the most reliable results among the neural network techniques used were derived by the GRNN models. Specifically, according to the evaluation criteria used, GRNN-constructed models gave the most accurate results for all tree biomass components and for the total tree biomass. The root mean square error values were 2.80, 1.48 and 2.51 times smaller than the values derived from the NSUR model for the dry crown, stem, and bark biomass, respectively, meaning that the mean estimation error values were 45.31 kg for the dry crown biomass, 14.19 kg for the dry stem biomass and 8.15 kg for the dry bark biomass. These are more accurate than the mean estimation error values derived from the NSUR model. Finally, according to the total dry tree biomass, the root mean square error values were 1.900, 1.112 and 1.107 times smaller for the GRNN, RPNN and BRNN models, respectively, than the corresponding values derived from the NSUR model. In terms of the performance evaluation of all models for the tree components, the models developed for the crown biomass produced poorer results for all criteria values as compared to their performances for stem wood.

The dry crown biomass, with variations that ranged from 11.94% to 33.46%, was found the most difficult factor to be estimated accurately, followed by the dry bark biomass which produced variations ranging from 11.09% to 27.86%. A higher accuracy was obtained for the dry stem biomass, with variation ranging from 10.06% to 14.87% for all modeling techniques (Figure 5). As noted by Poudel et al. [54], crown biomass can vary greatly between species and even between members of the same species.

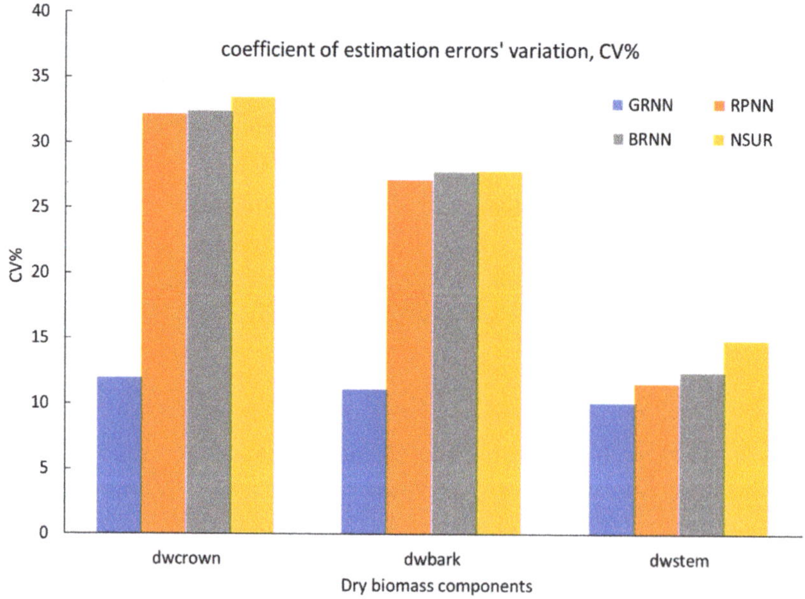

Figure 5. Variations in coefficient of estimation errors (CV%) for all biomass components.

The coefficient of the variation values obtained for the whole tree dry biomass ranged from 7.95% for the GRNN model to 15.12% for the NSUR model, and the relative mean absolute error values ranged from 28.74 to 51.02 kg/tree, respectively.

4. Discussion

Due to the importance of tree biomass for the sustainable management of forests, much effort has been made in forest science in order to develop accurate and reliable biomass models [1,2,4,6,19,36,55]. Over the years, many different modeling strategies have been developed, explored, and proposed in order to achieve the best biomass estimations, with the most widely spread focus on the least-squares regression approach. Much effort has been spent on overcoming ground-truth data heteroscedasticity by transformations and weighted procedures. Finally, the optimal form of the regression model that could reliably be adapted to the data in hand was one of the main difficulties confronted in the modeling procedure. Nowadays, novel non-parametric modeling methodologies based on the principals of artificial intelligence and machine learning are being developed and explored in order to adopt new, reliable modeling solutions [56].

In this context, the work described in this paper focused on the exploration of modeling behavior of three different artificial neural algorithms and structures for achieving the best possible fit, namely the generalized regression, the resilient propagation, and the Bayesian regularization artificial neural networks. These are different techniques within the realm of machine learning, each one of them having both advantages and drawbacks. Specifically, the generalized neural network algorithm [40–43] encompasses traditional feedforward neural networks and shows flexibility for nonlinear regression-type problems to be modeled. However, if the algorithm is not properly treated, it may be trapped into local minima or can be overfitted. The resilient backpropagation algorithm [45–47] can be considered as a variant of the traditional backpropagation algorithm. It is robust in the training phase of the network, and its efficiency to overcome problems of the traditional backpropagation algorithm, such as being slow at converging, taking effort at parameter tuning, and getting stuck in local minima, is considered significant. Finally, the Bayesian regression algorithm [49,50] which belongs to a probabilistic framework for modeling uncertainty, is combined with the principles of Bayesian statistics with neural networks. Due to its nature, it is able to produce not only a single estimation, but a probability distribution over prediction. Considering the available information from the literature [10,19,21–27,40–47,49–51,57], we chose to use these specific approaches because (a) they have the potential to address the tree biomass estimation problem comprehensively, from different methodological perspectives, (b) each one of them has shown its potential to model forest attributes, (c) the number of hyperparameters that must be tuned is low for each one of them making their application more or less simple, and (d) we felt that the usage of all three algorithms for modeling the same attribute, which is the tree biomass, can produce significant results and conclusions regarding which algorithm could most scientifically serve the problem of estimating standing tree biomass. Finally, a pathway for their effective application is described as well. For the development of a stable basis for the evaluation of the tested ANN models, due to its flexibility regarding the biomass estimation problems, the NSUR approach was also tested.

Among the many available algorithms that can be embedded in neural network building, the ability of the algorithms generally to cope with regression-type problems under the constraint of the relatively small dataset available primarily drove our selection. GRNN modeling was rapid and simple, as it required one main parameter to be tuned, the smoothing parameter (σ) that determines the influence of the data points on predictions and the overall complexity of the network. The optimal values selection of the smoothing parameter, adjusted by a smoothing factor of 0.5, led the constructed GRNN models to global minima of the kernel functions used so as the generalization ability of the prediction models for all different biomass cases was obvious (Table 4). As for the resilient propagation-constructed models, their training was established by selecting the optimum number of hidden nodes, while the size of the weight change along with the initial value of Δ_0 were determined initially, and then the algorithm automatically adjusted the Δ_0 value for each weight change. The main advantage of this algorithm is robustness which arises because the direction of the gradient, rather than the magnitude, is used, with the aim of overcoming local minima and being resistant to extreme or outlier values. This generalization ability was found adequate (Table 4), while its performance was the second best when compared with the other modeling approaches (Table 5 and Figure 3). The Bayesian regularization modeling technique was found to be rapid and was able to reduce overfitting by introducing probability distributions to the network weights. The optimal combination of errors and weights was found by determining the optimal number of hidden nodes following the trial-and-error procedure and by initially determining the Levenberg–Marquardt adjustment parameter as 0.005 along with its decreasing and increasing steps to 0.1 and 10, respectively. Both performance and generalization abilities proved adequate for all different cases of biomass estimation and prediction (Tables 4 and 5 and Figure 3). The NSUR modeling approach was used to account for the inherent correlation among biomass components measured on the same tree and to address the heteroscedasticity problem. NSUR allowed each component model to have its own independent variable and its own weight function to deal with the problem of different variances in each component and allowed the total tree biomass model to be obtained with smaller variance. This process accorded with the results of previous studies [2,5], that fitting tree and tree component biomass equations by NSUR results in efficient parameter estimates with low standard errors. The performance of NSUR to predict the total tree biomass and its components were generally acceptable and adequate.

Considering the evaluation criteria of the different modeling techniques used for accurate biomass estimation, all approaches were efficient and able to estimate and predict tree biomass. Advantages and disadvantages of each modeling methodology can be a guide in the selection or rejection of each of them when applied to specific problems. Although nonlinear regression modeling is a well-known and understandable method, it has serious drawbacks, such as assumptions that should be followed (normality and homogeneity), the predefinition of the form of the fitting function by the modeler, and the prerequired good initial values for accurate parameter estimations of the nonlinear models [10]. In general, the NSUR approach can be used for whole tree biomass and tree component biomass predictions. As indicated in several publications [1,2], this approach provided more accurate biomass predictions than the traditional approach of separately fitting whole tree and its component biomass equations using least-squares regression. As they are non-parametric processes, the artificial neural network approaches tested do not rely on assumptions, while the model form does not have to be specified in advance. However, there are hyperparameters that need to be tuned, while the final/trained model does not have a conventional form. Therefore, computational skills are required for its use. The selection of the proper model should be based on the specific problem being solved, the desired accuracy and the available means.

5. Conclusions

This work examined the adaptation of different modeling approaches to develop a flexible, simple, and fast system of tree component biomass along with total tree biomass estimation. For this purpose, NSUR, GRNN, RPNN and BRNN modeling techniques were applied for the biomass estimation of cedar trees in natural stands. All different modeling approaches appeared to provide reliable biomass estimations using data from only two variables that have to be measured in the field, diameter at breast height and total tree height, meaning that field effort was minimized.

The overall results suggested that the artificial neural network algorithms produced models with a higher performance when compared with the NSUR relative models.

The generalized regression neural network models outperformed the others, in terms of all evaluation criteria used, providing more reliable and accurate estimations for all different parts of tree biomass. Finally, the high predictive ability of the GRNN models for the "unseen" data strongly indicates that this modeling approach is one of the most useful methods for modeling forest biomass and is worthy of consideration as an alternative approach to tree biomass modeling.

Author Contributions: Conceptualization R.Ö., M.J.D. and Ş.K.G.; methodology, M.J.D. and R.Ö.; software, M.J.D. and R.Ö.; validation, M.J.D., R.Ö. and Ş.K.G.; formal analysis, M.J.D., R.Ö. and Ş.K.G.; investigation, Ş.K.G., M.J.D. and R.Ö.; data curation, Ş.K.G., R.Ö. and M.J.D.; writing—original draft preparation, Ş.K.G., M.J.D. and R.Ö.; and writing—review and editing, M.J.D., R.Ö. and Ş.K.G. All authors have read and agreed to the published version of the manuscript.

Funding: This study was conducted as part of the project titled "Development of growth models for natural cedar (*Cedrus libani* A. Rich.) stands in Lakes Region (BAP 2023-D3-0217)" that was funded by The Scientific Research Projects Coordination Unit of the Isparta University of Applied Sciences.

Data Availability Statement: The data that support the findings of this study are available from the corresponding author upon reasonable request.

Acknowledgments: We thank the Turkish General Directorate of Forestry for its contribution to field work. We also thank Steve Woodward from University of Aberdeen for his valuable comments and suggestions for revising the English grammar of the text.

Conflicts of Interest: The authors declare no conflict of interest.

References

1. Dong, L.; Zhang, L.; Li, F. A compatible system of biomass equations for three conifer species in Northeast, China. *For. Ecol. Manag.* **2014**, *329*, 306–317. [CrossRef]
2. Zhao, D.; Kane, M.; Markewitz, D.; Teskey, R.; Clutter, M. Additive tree biomass equations for midrotation loblolly pine plantations. *For. Sci.* **2015**, *61*, 613–623. [CrossRef]
3. Xiao, C.-W.; Yuste, J.C.; Janssens, I.; Roskams, P.; Nachtergale, L.; Carrara, A.; Sanchez, B.; Ceulemans, R. Above-and belowground biomass and net primary production in a 73-year-old Scots pine forest. *Tree Physiol.* **2003**, *23*, 505–516. [CrossRef] [PubMed]
4. Czapowskyj, M.M.; Robison, D.J.; Briggs, R.D.; White, E.H. *Component Biomass Equations for Black Spruce in Maine*; Research Paper NE-564; US Department of Agriculture, Forest Service, Northeastern Forest Experiment Station: Broomall, PA, USA, 1985; Volume 564.
5. Parresol, B.R. Additivity of nonlinear biomass equations. *Can. J. For. Res.* **2001**, *31*, 865–878. [CrossRef]
6. Poudel, K.; Temesgen, H. Methods for estimating aboveground biomass and its components for Douglas-fir and lodgepole pine trees. *Can. J. For. Res.* **2016**, *46*, 77–87. [CrossRef]
7. Luo, Y.; Zhang, X.; Wang, X.; Lu, F. Biomass and its allocation of Chinese forest ecosystems: Ecological Archives E095-177. *Ecology* **2014**, *95*, 2026. [CrossRef]
8. He, Q.; Chen, E.; An, R.; Li, Y. Above-ground biomass and biomass components estimation using LiDAR data in a coniferous forest. *Forests* **2013**, *4*, 984–1002. [CrossRef]
9. De-Miguel, S.; Pukkala, T.; Assaf, N.; Shater, Z. Intra-specific differences in allometric equations for aboveground biomass of eastern Mediterranean Pinus brutia. *Ann. For. Sci.* **2014**, *71*, 101–112. [CrossRef]
10. Özçelık, R.; Diamantopoulou, M.J.; Eker, M.; Gürlevık, N. Artificial neural network models: An alternative approach for reliable aboveground pine tree biomass prediction. *For. Sci.* **2017**, *63*, 291–302.
11. Uğurlu, S.; Araslı, B.; Sun, O. *Stepe Geçiş Yörelerindeki Sarıçam Meşcerelerinde Biyolojik Kütlenin Saptanması*; Ormancılık Araştırma Enstitüsü Yayınları: Ankara, Türkiye, 1976.
12. Sun, O.; Ugurlu, S.; Ozer, E. *Kizilçam (P. brutia Ten.) Türüne ait Biyolojik Kütlenin Saptanması*; Technical Bulletin No: 104; Türkiye Foresty Research Institute: Ankara, Türkiye, 1980; 32p.
13. Saraçoğlu, N. Biomass tables of beech (Fagus orientalis Lipsky). *Turk. J. Agric. For.* **1998**, *22*, 93–100.
14. Durkaya, B. *Zonguldak Orman Bölge Müdürlüğü Meşe Meşcerelerinin Biyokütle Tablolarının Düzenlenmesi*; Yüksek Lisans Tezi, Zonguldak Karaelmas Üniversitesi: Zonguldak, Türkiye, 1998.
15. İkinci, O. *Zonguldak Orman Bölge Müdürlüğü kestane meşcerelerinin biyokütle tablolarının düzenlenmesi*; Basılmamış Yüksek Lisans Tezi, Zonguldak Karaelmas Üniversitesi: Zonguldak, Türkiye, 2000.
16. Ülküdür, M. *Antalya Orman Bölge Müdürlüğü Sedir Meşcerelerinin Biyokütle Tablolarının Düzenlenmesi*; Yüksek Lisans Tezi, Bartın Üniversitesi: Bartın, Türkiye, 2010.
17. Aydın, A.C. Toros Sediri (Cedrus libani A. Rich.)'nde Biyokütle Araştırmaları. Ph.D. Thesis, Suleyman Demirel University, Isparta, Turkey, 2016.
18. Sakici, O.E.; Seki, M.; Saglam, F. Above-ground biomass and carbon stock equations for crimean pine stands in Kastamonu region of Turkey. *Fresenius Environ. Bull.* **2018**, *27*, 7079–7089.

19. Güner, Ş.T.; Diamantopoulou, M.J.; Poudel, K.P.; Çömez, A.; Özçelik, R. Employing artificial neural network for effective biomass prediction: An alternative approach. *Comput. Electron. Agric.* **2022**, *192*, 106596. [CrossRef]
20. Weiskittel, A.R.; MacFarlane, D.W.; Radtke, P.J.; Affleck, D.L.; Temesgen, H.; Woodall, C.W.; Westfall, J.A.; Coulston, J.W. A call to improve methods for estimating tree biomass for regional and national assessments. *J. For.* **2015**, *113*, 414–424. [CrossRef]
21. Patterson, D.W. *Artificial Neural Networks: Theory and Applications*; Prentice Hall Singapore: Singapore, 1996.
22. Aggarwal, C.C. *Neural Networks and Deep Learning*; Springer: Berlin/Heidelberg, Germany, 2018; Volume 10, p. 3.
23. Russell, S.J.; Norvig, P. *Artificial Intelligence a Modern Approach*; Prentice Hall: London, UK, 2010.
24. Gurney, K. *An Introduction to Neural Networks*; CRC Press: Boca Raton, FL, USA, 2018.
25. Diamantopoulou, M.J. Predicting fir trees stem diameters using Artificial Neural Network models. *S. Afr. For. J.* **2005**, *205*, 39–44. [CrossRef]
26. Vieira, G.C.; de Mendonça, A.R.; da Silva, G.F.; Zanetti, S.S.; da Silva, M.M.; Dos Santos, A.R. Prognoses of diameter and height of trees of eucalyptus using artificial intelligence. *Sci. Total Environ.* **2018**, *619*, 1473–1481. [CrossRef] [PubMed]
27. Ercanlı, İ. Innovative deep learning artificial intelligence applications for predicting relationships between individual tree height and diameter at breast height. *For. Ecosyst.* **2020**, *7*, 12. [CrossRef]
28. Boydak, M. Regeneration of Lebanon cedar (*Cedrus libani* A. Rich.) on karstic lands in Turkey. *For. Ecol. Manag.* **2003**, *178*, 231–243. [CrossRef]
29. Fischer, R.; Lorenz, M.; Kohl, M.; Becher, G.; Granke, O.; Christou, A. *The Conditions of Forests in Europe: 2008 Executive Report*; United Nations Economic Commission for Europe, Convention on Long-Range Trans Boundary Air Pollution, International Co-operative Programme on Assessment and Monitoring of Air Pollution Effects on Forests; ICP Forests: Eberswalde, Germany, 2008; p. 23.
30. Li, R.; Weiskittel, A.R. Comparison of model forms for estimating stem taper and volume in the primary conifer species of the North American Acadian Region. *Ann. For. Sci.* **2010**, *67*, 302. [CrossRef]
31. Alemdag, I. *Manual of Data Collection and Processing for the Development of Forest Biomass Relationships*; Environment Canada, Canadian Forestry Service, Petawawa National Forestry Institute: Chalk River, ON, Canada, 1980.
32. Alemdag, I. *Aboveground-Mass Equations for Six Hardwood Species from Natural Stands of the Research Forest at Petawawa*; Environment Canada, Canadian Forestry Service, Petawawa National Forestry Institute: Chalk River, ON, Canada, 1981.
33. Porte, A.; Trichet, P.; Bert, D.; Loustau, D. Allometric relationships for branch and tree woody biomass of Maritime pine (*Pinus pinaster* Aıt.). *For. Ecol. Manag.* **2002**, *158*, 71–83. [CrossRef]
34. Parresol, B.R. Assessing tree and stand biomass: A review with examples and critical comparisons. *For. Sci.* **1999**, *45*, 573–593.
35. Wang, L.-H.; Xing, Y.-Q. Remote sensing estimation of natural forest biomass based on an artificial neural network. *Ying Yong Sheng Tai Xue Bao = J. Appl. Ecol.* **2008**, *19*, 261–266.
36. Canga, E.; Diéguez-Aranda, U.; Elias, A.; Cámara, A. Above-ground biomass equations for Pinus radiata D. Don in Asturias. *For. Syst.* **2013**, *22*, 408–415. [CrossRef]
37. Park, R.E. Estimation with heteroscedastic error terms. *Econom. (Pre-1986)* **1966**, *34*, 888. [CrossRef]
38. SAS Institute Inc. *SAS/SHARE®9.4: User's Guide*, 2nd ed.; SAS Institute Inc.: Cary, NC, USA, 2016.
39. Belsley, D.A. A guide to using the collinearity diagnostics. *Comput. Sci. Econ. Manag.* **1991**, *4*, 33–50. [CrossRef]
40. Specht, D.F. A general regression neural network. *IEEE Trans. Neural Netw.* **1991**, *2*, 568–576. [CrossRef] [PubMed]
41. Diamantopoulou, M.J. Assessing a reliable modeling approach of features of trees through neural network models for sustainable forests. *Sustain. Comput. Inform. Syst.* **2012**, *2*, 190–197. [CrossRef]
42. Dreyfus, G. *Neural Networks: Methodology and Applications*; Springer Science & Business Media: Berlin, Germany, 2005.
43. de Bragança Pereira, B.; Rao, C.R.; de Oliveira, F.B. *Statistical Learning Using Neural Networks: A Guide for Statisticians and Data Scientists with Python*; CRC Press: Boca Raton, FL, USA, 2020.
44. Belete, D.M.; Huchaiah, M.D. Grid search in hyperparameter optimization of machine learning models for prediction of HIV/AIDS test results. *Int. J. Comput. Appl.* **2022**, *44*, 875–886. [CrossRef]
45. Riedmiller, M.; Braun, H. A direct adaptive method for faster backpropagation learning: The RPROP algorithm. In Proceedings of the IEEE International Conference on Neural Networks, San Francisco, CA, USA, 28 March–1 April 1993; pp. 586–591.
46. Florescu, C.; Igel, C. Resilient backpropagation (RPROP) for batch-learning in tensorflow. In Proceedings of the 6th International Conference on Learning Representations, Vancouver, BC, Canada, 30 April–3 May 2018; pp. 1–5.
47. Karatepe, Y.; Diamantopoulou, M.J.; Özçelik, R.; Sürücü, Z. Total tree height predictions via parametric and artificial neural network modeling approaches. *Iforest-Biogeosci. For.* **2022**, *15*, 95. [CrossRef]
48. *Matlab*, Version R2022a; The MathWorks Inc.: Natick, MA, USA, 2022.
49. Burden, F.; Winkler, D. Bayesian regularization of neural networks. In *Artificial Neural Networks*; Methods in Molecular Biology Book Series; Springer: Berlin/Heidelberg, Germany, 2009; pp. 23–42.
50. Kayri, M. Predictive abilities of Bayesian regularization and Levenberg–Marquardt algorithms in artificial neural networks: A comparative empirical study on social data. *Math. Comput. Appl.* **2016**, *21*, 20. [CrossRef]
51. Olson, D.L.; Delen, D. *Advanced Data Mining Techniques*; Springer Science & Business Media: Berlin, Germany, 2008.
52. Hurvich, C.M.; Tsai, C.-L. Regression and time series model selection in small samples. *Biometrika* **1989**, *76*, 297–307. [CrossRef]
53. Burnham, K.P.; Anderson, D.R. Multimodel inference: Understanding AIC and BIC in model selection. *Sociol. Methods Res.* **2004**, *33*, 261–304. [CrossRef]

54. Poudel, K.P.; Temesgen, H.; Gray, A.N. Evaluation of sampling strategies to estimate crown biomass. *For. Ecosyst.* **2015**, *2*, 1. [CrossRef]
55. Zhao, Y.; Ma, Y.; Quackenbush, L.J.; Zhen, Z. Estimation of Individual Tree Biomass in Natural Secondary Forests Based on ALS Data and WorldView-3 Imagery. *Remote Sens.* **2022**, *14*, 271. [CrossRef]
56. Özçelik, R.; Diamantopoulou, M.J.; Trincado, G. Evaluation of potential modeling approaches for Scots pine stem diameter prediction in north-eastern Turkey. *Comput. Electron. Agric.* **2019**, *162*, 773–782. [CrossRef]
57. Thanh, T.N.; Tien, T.D.; Shen, H.L. Height-diameter relationship for Pinus koraiensis in Mengjiagang Forest Farm of Northeast China using nonlinear regressions and artificial neural network models. *J. For. Sci.* **2019**, *65*, 134–143.

forests

MDPI

Article

Thinning Combined with Prescribed Burn Created Spatially Heterogeneous Overstory Structures in Contemporary Dry Forests: A Comparison Using LiDAR (2016) and Field Inventory (1934) Data

Sushil Nepal [1,*], Bianca N. I. Eskelson [1,*], Martin W. Ritchie [2] and Sarah E. Gergel [3]

[1] Department of Forest Resources Management, The University of British Columbia, 2424 Main Mall, Vancouver, BC V6T 1Z4, Canada

[2] USDA, Forest Service Pacific Southwest Research Station, 3644 Avtech Parkway, Redding, CA 96002, USA; martin.ritchie@usda.gov

[3] Department of Forest and Conservation Sciences, The University of British Columbia, 2424 Main Mall, Vancouver, BC V6T 1Z4, Canada; sarah.gergel@ubc.ca

* Correspondence: snepal1@student.ubc.ca (S.N.); bianca.eskelson@ubc.ca (B.N.I.E.); Tel.: +1-6048270629 (B.N.I.E.)

Abstract: Restoring current ponderosa pine (*Pinus ponderosa* Dougl. Ex P. and C. Laws)-dominated forests (also known as "dry forests") to spatially resilient stand structures requires an adequate understanding of the overstory spatial variation of forests least impacted by Euro-American settlers (also known as "reference conditions") and how much contemporary forests (2016) deviate from reference conditions. Because of increased tree density, dry forests are more spatially homogeneous in contemporary conditions compared to reference conditions, forests minimally impacted by Euro-American settlers. Little information is available that can be used by managers to accurately depict the spatial variation of reference conditions and the differences between reference and contemporary conditions. Especially, forest managers need this information as they are continuously designing management treatments to promote contemporary dry forest resiliency against fire, disease, and insects. To fill this knowledge gap, our study utilized field inventory data from reference conditions (1934) along with light detection and ranging and ground-truthing data from contemporary conditions (2016) associated with various research units of Blacks Mountain Experimental Forest, California, USA. Our results showed that in reference conditions, above-ground biomass—a component of overstory stand structure—was more spatially heterogeneous compared to contemporary forests. Based on semivariogram analyses, the 1934 conditions exhibited spatial variation at a spatial scale < 50 m and showed spatial autocorrelation at shorter ranges (150–200 m) compared to those observed in contemporary conditions (>250 m). In contemporary conditions, prescribed burn with high structural diversity treatment enhanced spatial heterogeneity as indicated by a greater number of peaks in the correlograms compared to the low structural diversity treatment. High structural diversity treatment units exhibited small patches of above-ground biomass at shorter ranges (~120 to 440 m) compared to the low structural diversity treatment units (~165 to 599 m). Understanding how spatial variation in contemporary conditions deviates from reference conditions and identifying specific management treatments that can be used to restore spatial variation observed in reference conditions will help managers to promote spatial variation in stand structure that has been resilient to wildfire, insects, and disease.

Keywords: Blacks Mountain Experimental Forest; LiDAR; overstory spatial variation; above-ground biomass; semivariogram; Moran's I correlogram

1. Introduction

Overstory stand structure of ponderosa pine-dominated forests—hereafter "dry forests" [1]—has undergone substantive changes since the Euro-American settlement of California, USA. Such changes have included shifts in species composition, an increase in the density of small trees [2], and a decline in the density of large trees [3–5]. An increase in densities of small trees and shifts in species composition are attributed to a wide range of factors, including fire suppression, logging, grazing, and climate change [2,3].

In California, tree-ring reconstructions indicate that spatial variation in the overstory of dry forests impacted by indigenous land use but prior to harvesting activities following Euro-American settlement (hereafter termed "reference conditions") consisted of a mosaic of individual trees, tree groups, and gaps at small scales (<0.4 ha or 40–70 m). Such spatial variation in overstory stand structure resulted in open forests with sparse, large individuals of fire-resistant species [6,7]. Spatial variations in stand structure are the result of interactions among prior processes such as fire, regeneration, competition, and mortality [8,9]. However, spatial variations in stand structure such as tree density, basal-area, and above-ground biomass (AGB) have substantially changed following Euro-American settlement [10,11].

Within the dry forests of California, following Euro-American settlement, spatial variation in overstory stand structure has shifted from fire resilient to fire prone forests due to increased tree density of shade-tolerant species such as white fir (*Abies concolor (Grod. & Glend)*) and incense-cedar (*Calocedrus decurrens (Torr.)*) [10–12]. Frequent fires with return intervals of about 25 years are among the most important drivers of spatial variation in dry forests [13,14]. However, it is unclear how overstory stand structures may have been altered spatially due to the exceptionally long fire-free period after Euro-American settlement [3,15]. Therefore, quantitative descriptions of spatial changes in overstory stand structures are crucial for land managers as they can be used to assess the potential of wildfire due to increased fuel loads in the forest overstory [16,17].

The spatial variations in overstory stand structure over time have rarely been studied, which is potentially a result of both a general lack of spatially-explicit data collected prior to active management [3] and the fact that such data collection is extremely labor intensive and expensive. Hence, it is practically impossible to obtain census data over large areas [18]. Remote sensing technology, especially light detection and ranging (LiDAR), provides the capacity to obtain spatially explicit data over large areas in a timely and cost-effective manner [18]. Although LiDAR data are being extensively used in enhanced forest inventory, ground data are still required [19]. LiDAR-derived variables such as height metrics can be utilized with ground-based observations such as basal area (m^2/ha), volume (m^3/ha), and AGB (Mg/ha) to predict forest overstory stand structure at different times [20]. Thus, LiDAR data complement and can be used in conjunction with ground-based inventories to identify spatial changes in the forest overstory structure [21].

Furthermore, many studies examining the spatial variation of forest structure in California, USA, have been restricted to particular elevation ranges [2,22], management units [23,24], certain functional types, and small study areas [3,25,26]. Numerous studies have provided a general description of dry forests prior to active management following Euro-American settlement [27,28]. However, a description of the spatial variation of overstory stand structure over time is generally lacking. Many studies have investigated spatial variation in tree density and tree size (e.g., [9,29]), and at different scales based on averages (e.g., [30,31]). However, they have failed to capture the spatial variation of overstory over a larger landscape utilizing different metrics such as AGB as a measure of overstory stand structure. AGB is closely related to forest productivity and can be more accurately predicted and modeled from ground-measured biomass and LiDAR height metrics compared to trees per hectare or basal area per hectare [20]. Metrics such as trees per hectare and basal area per hectare are sensitive to the inability of LiDAR to capture small and understory trees very accurately [31].

This study was conducted in the dry forests of Blacks Mountain Experimental Forest (BMEF) in northern California, USA. BMEF remained untouched by selective logging operations from the late 1800s through 1940s [32], but may have been impacted by indigenous land use for hunting mule deer [33]. Within BMEF, our study focused on the section defined as the Blacks Mountain Ecological Research Project (BMERP), initiated in 1991. Within BMERP, two structural diversity thinning treatments with or without prescribed burn were implemented [32]. A low structural diversity treatment (LOD) was designed to produce a single canopy layer by removing dominant and large-sized trees [32]. A high structural diversity treatment (HID) was designed to leave all the dominant trees, abundant snags, and multiple canopy and forest openings [32]. To quantify the spatial variation of AGB, we utilized three types of data collected for the BMERP project area: ground inventory data from 1934 as reference data, as well as contemporary 2015 LiDAR data, and 2016 ground verification data. The specific objectives of our study were to:

1. compare the spatial variation of overstory AGB between contemporary forests and reference conditions using 2015 LiDAR data and 1934 census data;
2. compare the spatial variation of overstory AGB among various structural diversity treatments in contemporary conditions.

The variogram analyses implemented in this study, provide information on the inherent patch size and spatial heterogeneity for overstory AGB in both contemporary forests and reference conditions. Understanding the spatial differences in overstory AGB at two points in time across a landscape has various applications in forest management policies such as fuel classification, fire spread prediction, and post-disturbance vegetation changes [34–36]. Such information can improve our understanding of how trees and forests respond and will continue to respond towards changes in disturbance regimes [37] and help silviculturists design restoration treatments that move forests towards more resilient conditions similar to reference conditions.

2. Materials and Methods

2.1. Study Area

The BMEF, managed by the USDA Forest Service Pacific Southwest Research Station, is located in northeastern California (Figure 1) (40°40′ N, 10 121°10′ W), northeast of Lassen Volcanic National Park. The elevation of BMEF ranges between 1700 and 2100 m [32]. Slopes rarely exceed 30 percent [32]. Aspects are primarily west- and south-facing. At lower elevations, stands are dominated by ponderosa pine (*Pinus ponderosa* Dougl. Ex P. and C. Laws) with occasional occurrence of some Jeffrey pine (*Pinus jeffreyi* (Grev. And Balf.) [32]. At higher elevations, white fir (*Abies concolor* (Gord. And Glend.) Lindl.) and incense-cedar (*Calocedrus decurrens* (Torr.) Florin) dominate the stands. Classified as an interior ponderosa pine forest type [38], the 4358 ha forest has a wide range of stand conditions as a result of past research and management activities, as well as disturbance events [39].

For this study, we focused on ten of the twelve research units in the BMERP and four research natural areas (RNA, Figure 1C). BMERP was initiated as an interdisciplinary large-scale, long-term ecological research project at BMEF in 1991 [32]. The goals of BMERP were to: (a) understand the effects of forest structural complexity on the health and vigor of ponderosa pine ecosystems, (b) quantify the ecosystem's resilience to natural and human-caused disturbances, and (c) determine how these ecosystems can be managed for sustained resource values [32]. The forests in the ten BMERP research units were subjected to two different types of treatments (Figure 1C, for details about treatments see Appendix A, Table A1). The first treatment consisted of three stand structures: low structural diversity (LOD), high structural diversity (HID), and research natural areas (RNAs) (Figure 1C; [32]). LOD and HID treatments had been randomly assigned to the ten BMERP research units ranging in size from 77 to 144 ha (Figure 1C). Each research unit was then split in half with one randomly assigned half receiving prescribed burn treatments (hereafter "burned"), whereas the other half did not receive the prescribed burn treatment (hereafter "unburned")

(Figure 1C). Collectively, the twelve units consisted of a total of twenty-four stands in our study: four RNAs, ten LOD stands, and ten HID stands (Figure 1C and Table A1). LOD stands were thinned to a uniformly spaced density of ~40 trees ha^{-1} retaining a single canopy layer of intermediate trees with height ranging from 12 to 30 m and a crown ratio > 50% [32]. In contrast, thinning in HID stands was conducted to retain all canopy layers that represented an overstory stand structure of a forest with multiple age classes and varying crown structures [32]. All large old trees were maintained with one smaller tree retained within the larger tree's crown circumference [32]. As a part of the prescription, within the HID units, caches of high-density and small-diameter conifers were left [32,38].

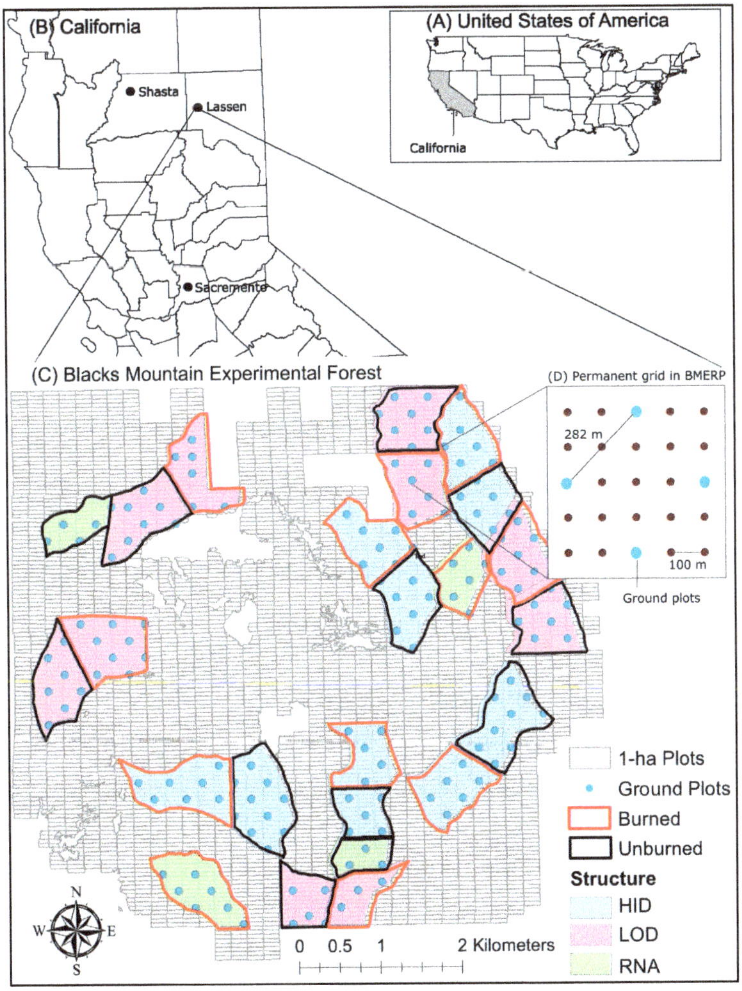

Figure 1. Study area map. Panel (**A**) represents the United States of America with California being highlighted in grey. California with its county boundaries is shown in Panel (**B**). Blacks Mountain Experimental Forest is represented in Panel (**C**) with the 1 ha plots used for the 1934 census survey. Panel (**C**) also includes the polygons for the Blacks Mountain Ecological Research project (BMERP). Inside the BMERP polygons, the blue dots represent the permanent grid system within BMEF as shown in panel (**D**). The ground-truthing data were collected using a staggered pattern in 2016, as shown in Panel (**D**).

The four RNAs (~40 ha each; Figure 1C) were set aside to serve as unmanaged, qualitative controls representative of the interior ponderosa pine type [32]. These RNAs have never received mechanical treatments, but fire exclusion has greatly increased their understory tree densities [32]. Two of the four RNA stands (RNA-B and RNA-C) received one application of prescribed burn in the late 1990s [32].

2.2. Data

2.2.1. 1934 Survey Data

During the fall of 1934, BMEF was divided into a total of 4074 rectangular plots of 1 ha (hereafter referred to as "1 ha plots") in size to conduct a census survey ([40], Figure 1C). Within each 1 ha plot, all live overstory trees > 8.9 cm (3.5 inches) were tallied by species group and diameter class [40]. Diameter classes were 5.08 cm (2 inches) wide and labeled by even inches (i.e., 4, 6, 8, 10, etc.). Tree species were recorded as pine (Jeffrey or ponderosa pine), white fir, and incense-cedar [40].

2.2.2. 2015 LiDAR Data Acquisition and Processing

An airborne Light Detection and Ranging (LiDAR) dataset was acquired during the summer of 2015 using a Leica ALS50 PHASE II laser system (near-infrared) discrete return sensor mounted on a fixed-wing aircraft [41]. The aircraft was flown at an altitude of 900 m using an opposing-flight line with a side lap of at least 50% [41]. The scanning angle of the sensor was $\pm 14^{\circ}$ with an average return of 6.9 points per m^2 and a standard deviation of 5.9 points per m^2 (see [41]). LiDAR point cloud was processed and LiDAR metrics were calculated using the *'lidR'* package in R ([42], see Appendix B for a full description of the process).

2.2.3. 2016 Field Data

The ten research units and four RNAs each have a permanent 100 m lattice grid (Figure 1D; [32]). The grid serves as the center points for most of the plot-level research conducted in BMEF [32]. In the summer of 2016, at every other grid point in all diagonal directions (282 m spacing, Figure 1D), 16 m radius plots (804 m^2, hereafter referred to as "circular plots") were measured within each treatment unit [43]. Standing live and dead trees $\geq$ 9 cm diameter at breast height (DBH) were stem mapped from the plot center and measured for total height and DBH [43]. These ground-truthing data were collected in a total of 154 circular plots: 65 LOD, 69 HID, and 20 RNA plots (Figure 1C; blue dots).

2.2.4. Overstory Above-Ground Biomass for 1935 and 2016

Using the 1934 survey data, I calculated biomass (Mg) for foliage, branch, and bole of individual trees > 9 cm DBH using species-dependent equations that were developed locally at BMEF [44]. Then, the above-ground biomass (AGB, Mg) for each tree was calculated by summing the individual biomass from foliage, bole, and branch. The height values used in the equations were estimated from local height–diameter equations developed by Dolph et al. [45]. For white fir and incense-cedar overstory AGB, we used equations and parameters suggested by Jenkins et al. [46]. The total plot overstory AGB was calculated by adding the overstory AGB of each species. We then converted plot AGB to AGB per hectare (Mg/ha) based on the given plot sizes.

For the 2016 field data, we calculated the AGB for individual trees using the same species equation parameters that were used for the 1934 biomass calculations. The total overstory AGB for each circular plot was calculated by taking the sum of the AGB calculated for individual trees of each species and converted into per ha values.

2.2.5. Biomass Model to Link LiDAR Metrics to 1 ha Plots for 2016

The distribution of the response variable—overstory above-ground biomass (AGB, Mg/ha)—was skewed to the right with values > 0 (Figure A1). Therefore, we fit generalized linear mixed effect models (glm) with a *'gamma'* distribution and a *'log link'* function to ensure that the expected value of AGB is always positive [47]. Modeling was performed in R using the '*lme4*' package ([48]; see Appendix C for full details on the model building process and sumary results).

We divided the study area within BMERP into cells of size 32 × 32 m to match the resolution of the ground-truthing plots (Figure A4). LiDAR metrics were extracted at the cell level following the method described in Mauro et al. [43]. There was a total of 12,647 cells. The selected biomass model was then applied to the cells to predict overstory AGB. To calculate the overstory AGB for 1 ha plots in 2016, first, the predicted values of overstory AGB at cell level were created as a map (Figure A4). Then, the map was overlaid with the 1 ha plot map with the BMERP units. The intersect function in ArcMap 10.4.1 was used to extract the cells that fell within 1 ha plots [49]. If a cell straddled multiple 1 ha plots, overstory AGB was weighted based on the area of the cell, and area weighted values of cells that fell within the plots were summed to calculate the overstory AGB (Mg/ha) for 1 ha plots.

2.3. Data Analysis

We computed semivariograms at the scale of each BMERP unit and Moran's I correlograms as a measure of spatial variation to evaluate our research objectives.

2.3.1. Comparing Semivariogram Components and Moran's Correlogram between 1934 and 2016

Semivariograms—To meet our first research objective, we used semivariogram models following the methods of Rossi et al. [50] with the assumption of stationarity, i.e., that the variance in above-ground biomass (AGB) is the function of separation distance only [51]. The semivariance was calculated for a pair of observations of overstory AGB as a function of the separation distance (hereafter "lag distance") between the sampled locations [51]. Using the '*gstat*' spatial package in R version 4.1.1 [52], semivariogram models were built for all fourteen units using a 1 ha plot-level overstory AGB for 1934 and 2016. For the 2016 study units, we did not differentiate between the burned and unburned halves; hence, variograms represent the pooled variogram for each unit. Following the method of Fry and Stephens [53], we fit three semivariogram models—exponential, Gaussian, and spherical—for each unit in 1934 and 2016. We also checked the assumption of stationarity in our exploratory analysis using directional variograms and found that ranges were not different; hence, semivariance was only distance dependent and not direction dependent [53]. Furthermore, to allow for comparisons at a common scale, all variograms were standardized by dividing the semivariance by the overall sample variance [50]. For both 1934 and 2016, the best semivariogram models were selected based on the minimized root mean squared error (RMSE, [53]). Following the method suggested by Fry and Stephens [53], we used the selected semivariograms from both points in time and compared the values of range, nugget, and sill for all fourteen units using dot plots. The range describes the distance up to which overstory AGB values exhibited spatial autocorrelation and provides information on the inherent patch size and spatial heterogeneity for overstory AGB [54]. The sill values were compared to understand whether the amount of spatially dependent variance within a given range in overstory AGB differed between 1934 and 2016 [53,55]. Nugget values were compared to understand if there was spatial variation at a scale smaller than 50 m (hereafter referred as "fine-scale spatial variation"), which was the shortest distance between adjacent 1 ha plots in overstory AGB [55].

Moran's I correlogram—For a more local measure of spatial autocorrelation, we followed the method of Jaquette et al. [56] and calculated Moran's I over the range of 20 lags at an interval of 50 m between lags, which was the shortest possible distance between 1 ha plot centers. From our exploratory analysis, we found that Moran's I could be calculated up to a distance of 1000 m for all units except RNA-D because the number of observations was <5% of total observations for the given unit and the spatial variation could not be interpreted easily with so few observations [57]. RNA-D was an exception and only allowed 800 m for the Moran's I calculations. We also tested if Moran's I at each lag was significantly different from 0 (alpha = 0.05) using Monte Carlo simulations with 1000 permutations [56]. Using the results from the 1000th permutation, all directional Moran's I correlograms were constructed with lag distance (m) on the x-axis and Moran's I value on the y-axis [57,58] for all units. We used the Moran's I correlograms for 1934 and 2016 to compare spatial variation in overstory AGB in terms of the differences in:

(a) *fine-scale spatial variation*—We evaluated whether the magnitude of Moran's I at the first lag was significantly different from 0 ($p < 0.05$) for each unit in both years. A Moran's I value at the first lag that is significantly different from 0 indicates a lack of fine-scale spatial variation within study units, i.e., patches of overstory AGB < 50 m do not exist [57]. If Moran's I was not significantly different from 0, patches of AGB < 50 m exist in the study units.

(b) *periodicity in Moran's I correlogram*—Moran's I values that are significantly different from 0 at different lag distances result in peaks (positive Moran's I) and troughs (negative Moran's I) at different lag intervals creating a periodic correlogram for overstory AGB [57,58]. A greater number of peaks and troughs in the correlogram indicates greater spatial variation, whereas fewer peaks in the correlogram suggest less spatial variation in AGB [57,58]. We visually compared if the number of peaks and troughs combined (collectively referred to as "peaks") in the correlograms for the units were different between years as an indicator of greater or less spatial variation in AGB [57,58].

2.3.2. Effect of Management Treatments on Spatial Variation of Above-Ground Biomass in the Contemporary Forests

To compare the effect of management treatments on spatial variation of overstory AGB, we used semivariogram models built for each of the burned and unburned halves of the HID and LOD treatment units (Table A1). A total of 20 semivariograms—10 each for the burned and unburned halves of HID and LOD treatment units—were selected based on low RMSE values and used to compare the range, nugget, and sill. We also used Moran's I correlogram constructed for both burned and unburned halves of HID and LOD treatment units to compare the fine-scale spatial variation and periodicity in spatial variation in overstory AGB as described in Section 2.3.1. From our exploratory analysis, we found that maximum distance for which we could construct Moran's I correlograms was 1000 m for all the burned and unburned halves of the units.

3. Results

3.1. Spatial Variation between 1934 and 2016

3.1.1. Spatial Autocorrelation in Above-Ground Biomass Exhibited at Larger Ranges in 2016

Within research natural areas (RNAs), Gaussian and spherical models for various units exhibited low RMSE; thus, they were selected for comparison of spatial variation in overstory above-ground biomass (AGB) between 1934 and 2016 (Table 1, Figure A5). The models that did not converge for either year are not presented in the results. Within RNAs, the values of range did not differ substantially between RNA-A and RAN-B for both years (Figures 2 and A5). However, within RNA-C and RNA-D, we observed larger ranges of ~400 m and 250 m, respectively, in 2016 compared to 1934 (~243 m for RNA-C and 167 m for RNA-D, Figures 2 and A5). RNAs exhibited larger nugget values in 1934 compared to extremely small values in 2016 indicating the presence of fine-scale spatial variation in 1934 compared to 2016 (Figure 3 and Table 1). In 2016, the sill values were generally similar to those observed in 1934. We only observed higher sill values in RNA-D in 2016 compared to 1934, without much difference in other RNAs (Table 1).

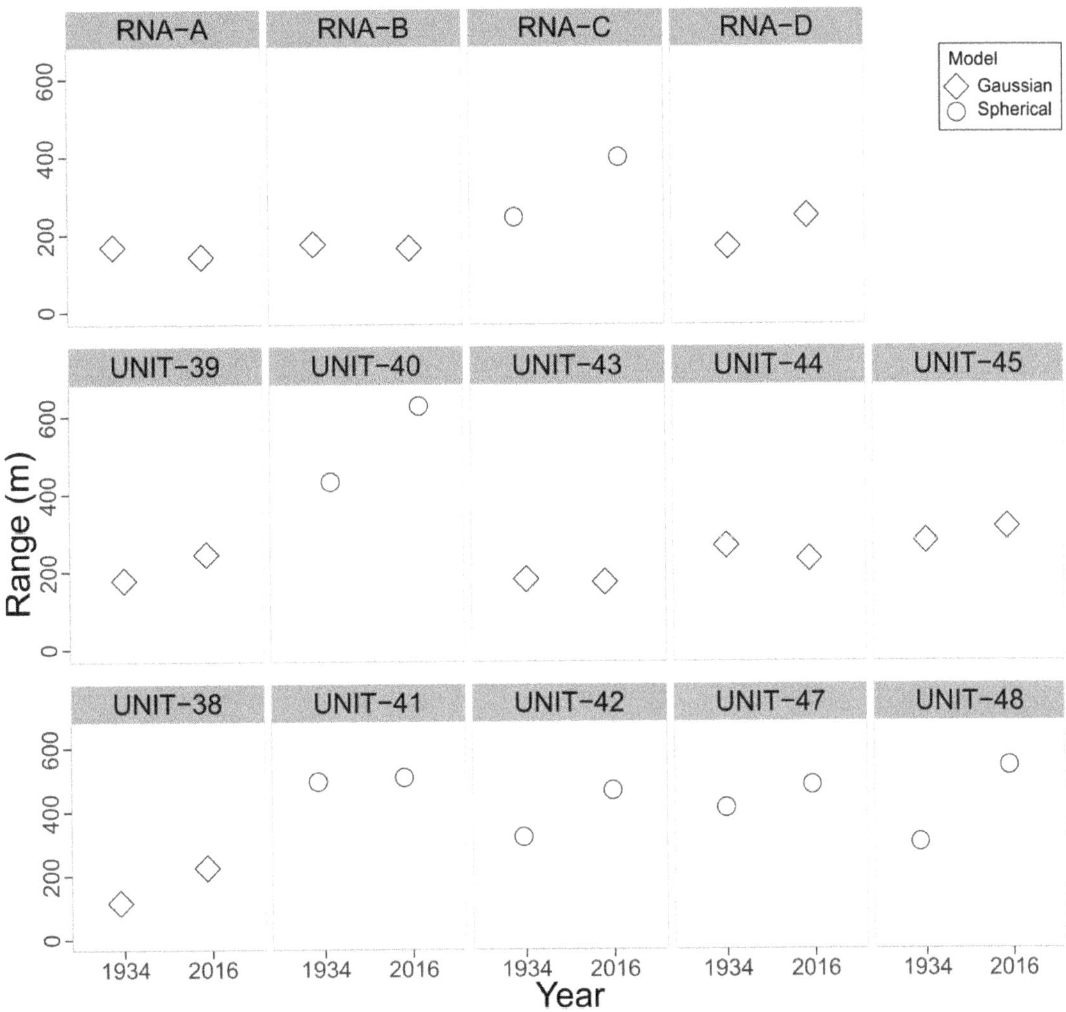

Figure 2. Range values for above-ground biomass for the selected variogram models between 1934 vs. 2016. The top panel shows the range for research natural areas (RNA), the middle panel shows the range for the low structural diversity (LOD) units, and the bottom panel shows the range for the high structural diversity (HID) units in Blacks Mountain Ecological Research Project.

Within units other than RNAs, spherical and Gaussian models exhibited low RMSE values and were selected (Table 1 and Figure A6). All units except 41 and 44 exhibited short ranges in 1934 compared to longer ranges in 2016 (Figures 2, A6 and A7). There was a very small difference in range values between both years in units 41, 43, 44, and 45 (Figure 2). Nugget values observed in 1934 were larger than those observed in 2016 within 14 units of the study, which indicated the presence of fine-scale spatial variation (Figure 3). The amount of spatial autocorrelation indicated by the sill values was greater in 1934 compared to 2016 in most of the units (Table 1 and Figures A6 and A7).

Table 1. Summary of the root mean square error (RMSE), and nugget values for the models that converged. The selected variogram models for each unit are highlighted with bold font.

Units	Models	RMSE		Sill	
Research natural areas (RNA)		**1934**	**2016**	**1934**	**2016**
RNA-A	Spherical	0.81	0.85	1.15	1.09
	Exponential	0.82	0.84	1.91	1.75
	Gaussian	**0.74**	**0.80**	**1.01**	**0.99**
RNA-B	Spherical	0.83	0.96	1.21	1.28
	Exponential	0.82	0.95	2.69	3.84
	Gaussian	**0.79**	**0.94**	**1.09**	**0.99**
RNA-C	**Spherical**	**0.63**	**0.80**	**0.93**	**1.11**
	Exponential	0.72	0.82	1.01	1.49
RNA-D	Gaussian	0.50	0.65	1.01	1.56
Low structural diversity (LOD)					
UNIT-39	Spherical	0.52	0.74	0.99	1.06
	Exponential	0.57	0.74	1.94	1.92
	Gaussian	**0.49**	**0.70**	**0.95**	**0.98**
UNIT-40	**Spherical**	**0.76**	**0.73**	**1.04**	**1.11**
	Exponential	0.75	0.75	1.92	1.94
UNIT-43	Spherical	0.65	0.70	1.03	0.91
	Exponential	0.69	0.71	1.16	1.06
	Gaussian	**0.63**	**0.67**	**0.98**	**0.87**
UNIT-44	Spherical	0.30	0.51	1.42	0.96
	Exponential	0.31	0.53	2.62	1.47
	Gaussian	**0.28**	**0.48**	**0.80**	**0.76**
UNIT-45	Spherical	0.69	0.80	2.50	1.12
	Gaussian	**0.64**	**0.80**	**1.10**	**1.27**
High structural diversity (HID)					
UNIT-38	Spherical	0.48	0.67	0.81	0.95
	Exponential	0.52	0.69	0.85	1.07
	Gaussian	**0.47**	**0.64**	**0.79**	**0.89**
UNIT-41	**Spherical**	**0.72**	**0.71**	**1.03**	**0.94**
	Exponential	0.75	0.71	1.20	1.35
UNIT-42	Spherical	0.63	0.71	0.98	0.95
	Exponential	**0.86**	**0.84**	**1.54**	**2.52**
UNIT-47	Spherical	0.85	0.84	1.14	1.18
	Exponential	0.84	0.86	0.92	1.55
UNIT-48	**Spherical**	**0.64**	**0.75**	**0.83**	**1.04**
	Exponential	0.66	0.75	0.00	0.00

3.1.2. Moran's I Correlogram Exhibited Differences in Fine-Scale Spatial Variation and Periodicity between Two Years

Moran's I correlogram suggested that fine-scale spatial variation was more pronounced in 1934 conditions compared to 2016, as indicated by the Moran's I values—not significantly different from 0—at the first lag in most of the units (Table 2). For example, in 1934, nine out of fourteen units exhibited a Moran's I value at the first lag that was not significantly different from 0, but in 2016, ten out of fourteen units had Moran's I values at the first lag that were significantly different from 0 (Table 2). This was in agreement with all the higher nugget values found in 1934 as compared to low nugget values in 2016 (Figure 3). Thus, only four out of fourteen units exhibited fine-scale spatial variation in 2016 (Table 2).

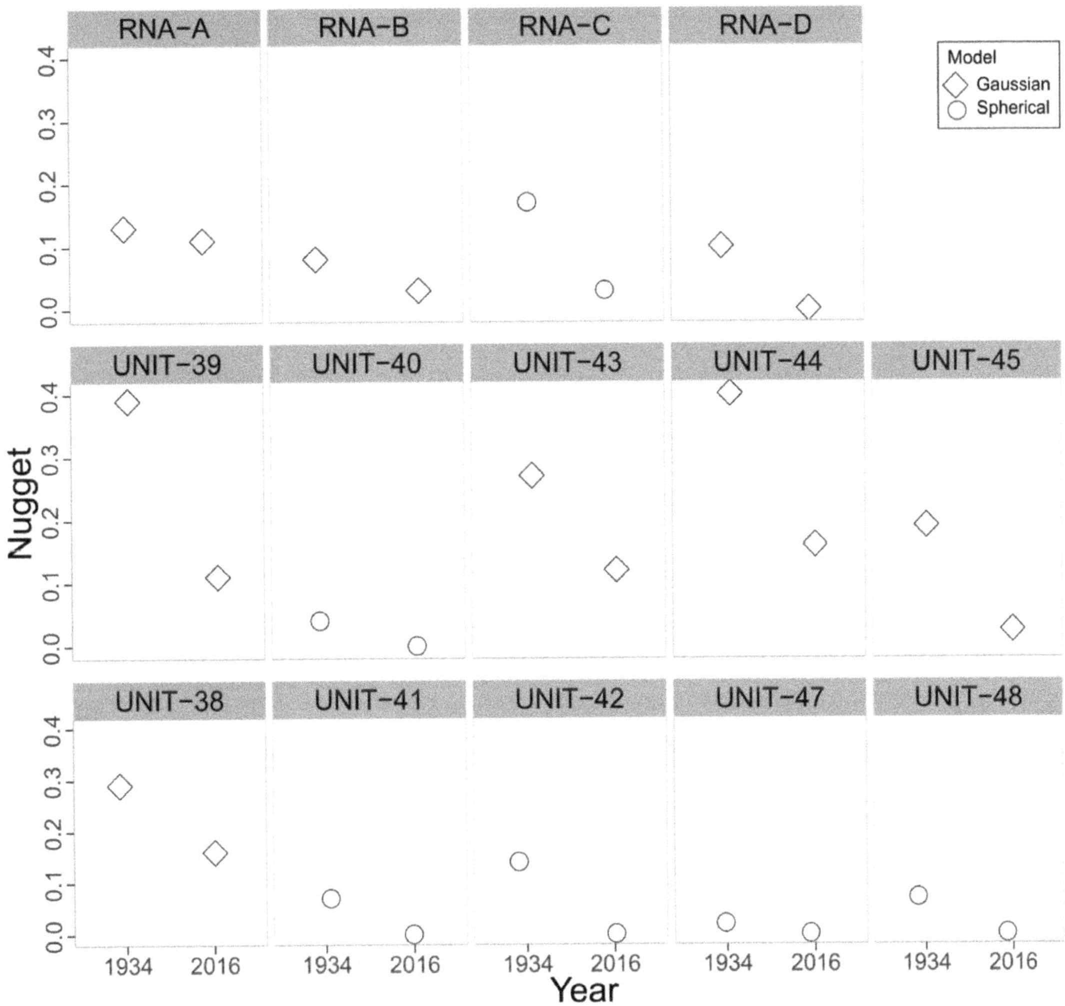

Figure 3. Nugget values for above-ground biomass for the selected variogram models for 1934 and 2016. The top panel shows the nuggets for research natural areas (RNA), the middle panel shows the nuggets for the low structural diversity (LOD) units, and the bottom panel shows the nuggets for the high structural diversity (HID) units in Blacks Mountain Ecological Research Project.

In general, periodicity did not vary substantially between 2016 and 1934, as indicated by similar numbers of peaks between both years (Table 2, Figure A8). However, the presence of periodicity in the Moran's I correlograms in both years indicated that overstory AGB occurred in heterogeneous patches (Figure A8). Exceptions were RNA-A and RNA-C, where the spatial variation in overstory AGB was more pronounced in 2016, as indicated by a larger number of peaks in 2016 compared to 1934 (Table 2 and Figure 4). The periodicity in the correlogram occurred at larger lag intervals (>250 m) for units 39, 43, and 48 in 2016, which is an indication of the presence of bigger patches of overstory AGB (Figure A8).

Table 2. Summary of the number of peaks and troughs of the Moran's I correlograms and p-values for the Moran's I at the first lag for research natural areas (RNAs) and other units in 1934 and 2016.

Unit			First Lag	
	1934	2016	1934	2016
	# Peaks	# Peaks		
Research natural area (RNA)				
RNA-A	5	3	$p = 0.009$ *	$p = 0.009$ *
RNA-B	3	3	$p = 0.23$ ^{ns}	$p = 0.35$ ^{ns}
RNA-C	3	5	$p = 0.13$ ^{ns}	$p = 0.06$ *
RNA-D	1	3	$p = 0.16$ ^{ns}	$p = 0.47$ ^{ns}
Low structural diversity (LOD)				
UNIT-39	1	1	$p = 0.009$ *	$p = 0.009$ *
UNIT-40	2	2	$p = 0.06$ ^{ns}	$p = 0.02$ *
UNIT-43	2	4	$p = 0.13$ ^{ns}	$p = 0.009$ *
UNIT-44	0	2	$p = 0.16$ ^{ns}	$p = 0.03$ *
UNIT-45	1	1	$p = 0.009$ *	$p = 0.009$ *
High Structural diversity (HID)				
UNIT-38	2	2	$p = 0.009$ *	$p = 0.009$ *
UNIT-41	2	4	$p = 0.06$ ^{ns}	$p = 0.17$ ^{ns}
UNIT-42	0	2	$p = 0.72$ ^{ns}	$p = 0.93$ ^{ns}
UNIT-47	1	1	$p = 0.75$ ^{ns}	$p = 0.05$ *
UNIT-48	2	2	$p = 0.009$ *	$p = 0.009$ *

* indicates significant at alpha = 0.05; ^{ns} = non-significant; # = number.

3.2. 2016 Spatial Variation in Treatment Units

3.2.1. HID Burned Halves Exhibited Spatial Autocorrelation at Short Ranges

Variogram models with the lowest RMSE for both burned and unburned halves of HID and LOD treatments were selected for comparing range, nugget, and sill (Table A5). Irrespective of the burned and unburned halves, all the HID treatment units exhibited spatial autocorrelation for overstory AGB at shorter ranges (~120 to 440 m) compared to the LOD treatment units (~165 to 599 m, Figures 5, A9 and A10). All the burned halves of HID showed larger nugget values compared to unburned halves and most of the LOD treatments, indicating the presence of fine-scale spatial variation in overstory AGB within burned halves (Figure 6).

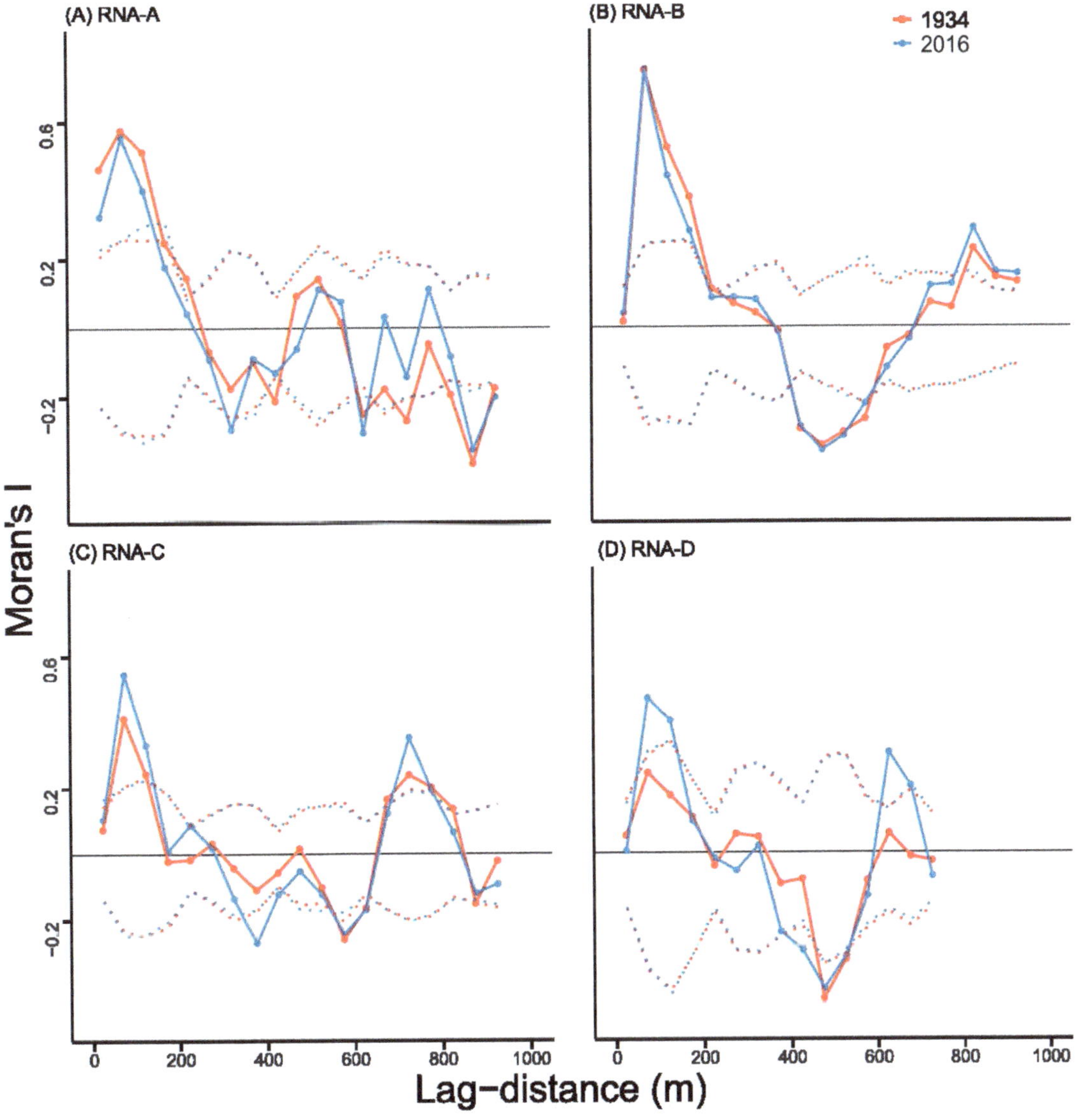

Figure 4. Moran's I correlogram for 1934 vs. 2016 within the four research natural areas (RNAs) in Blacks Mountain Ecological Research Project. RNA-B and RNA-C received prescribed burn treatments in 1997 and 1998, respectively. Dotted lines represent the lower and upper limit of the non-significant spatial autocorrelation using 95% confidence envelopes for 1934 (red) and 2016 (blue) from Monte Carlo simulations [56]. Points connected with solid lines indicate Moran's I at a given lag distance (m). Points above the dotted lines in the upper part of the envelope indicate a positive Moran's I that is significantly different from 0, whereas points below the dotted lines in the lower part of the envelope show a negative Moran's I that is significantly different from 0. Points within the dotted envelope show Moran's I values that are not significantly different from 0.

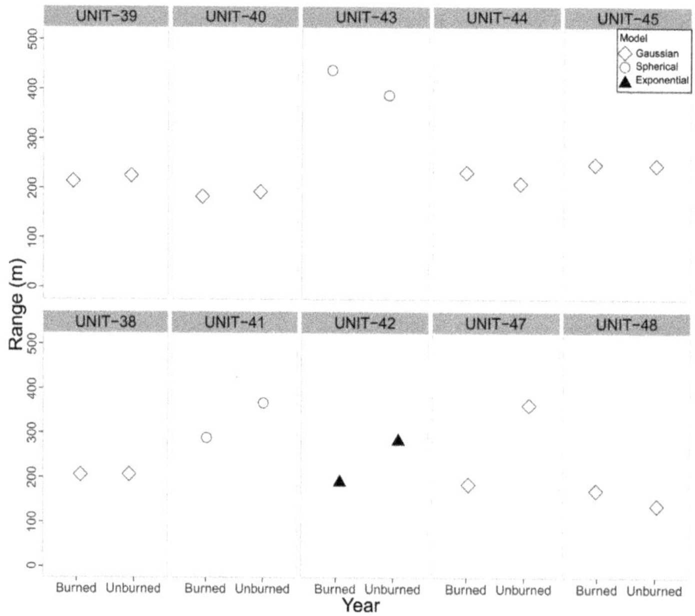

Figure 5. Differences in range values for above-ground biomass for the selected variogram models in burned and unburned halves. The top panel shows the range values for low structural diversity (LOD) units, whereas the bottom panel shows the range values for high structural diversity (HID) units in the Blacks Mountain Ecological Research Project.

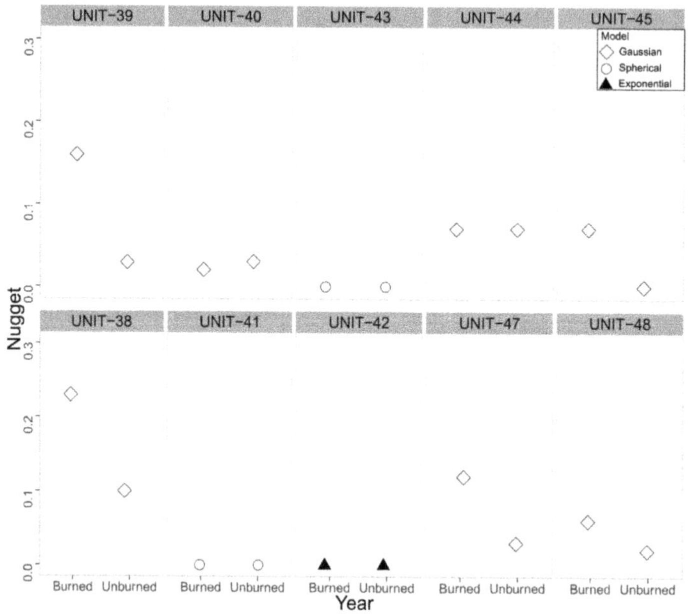

Figure 6. Differences in sill values for above-ground biomass for the selected variogram models in burned and unburned halves. The top panel shows the sill values for low structural diversity (LOD) units, whereas the bottom panel shows the sill values for high structural diversity (HID) units in the Blacks Mountain Ecological Research Project.

Within LOD treatment units, most of the burned halves exhibited spatial autocorrelation of overstory AGB at a smaller range compared to unburned halves, but the difference was very small (Figure 5). Exceptions were units 43 and 44, where spatial autocorrelation in overstory AGB was exhibited at shorter ranges in unburned halves compared to burned halves (Figure 5). Within HID treatment units, all the unburned halves exhibited spatial autocorrelation in overstory AGB at larger ranges than the burned halves, except for units 38 and 48, where the differences in range between burned and unburned halves was very small (Figures 5 and A10). The presence of fine-scale spatial variation in overstory AGB was indicated by larger nugget values in burned halves compared to unburned halves, except for units 41 and 42, which exhibited no nuggets (Figure 6).

3.2.2. HID Burned Halves Exhibited Greater Spatial Variation Indicated by Periodicity at Shorter Lag Distances

Irrespective of treatments, most of the burned and unburned halves exhibited Moran's I values at the first lag that were significantly different from 0, which indicated the absence of spatial variation at distances below 50 m (Table 3, Figure A11). We found a greater number of peaks that were significantly different from 0 at shorter lag distances within burned halves of HID treatments than within unburned halves of HID and LOD treatments (Figure A11). For example, the burned half of unit 38, showed eight peaks at the interval of 100–150 m lag distances compared to only two peaks in the unburned half of unit 39, and three peaks in the burned half of unit 39, all of which occurred at larger lag distances between 300 and 400 m (Table 3, Figure A11A–F).

Table 3. Summary of the number of peaks and troughs of Moran's I correlogram and p-values for Moran's I at first lag for burned and unburned halves of low structural diversity treatment (LOD) and high structural diversity treatment (HID) units.

Unit			**First Lag**	
	Burned	**Unburned**	**Burned**	**Unburned**
	# Peak	**# Peaks**		
Low structural diversity				
UNIT-39	3	2	$p = 0.009$ *	$p = 0.009$ *
UNIT-40	5	4	$p = 0.11$ ^{ns}	$p = 0.009$ *
UNIT-43	5	2	$p = 0.009$ *	$p = 0.009$ *
UNIT-44	3	2	$p = 0.005$ *	$p = 0.009$ *
UNIT-45	6	5	$p = 0.009$ *	$p = 0.009$ *
High structural diversity				
UNIT-38	8	3	$p = 0.009$ *	$p = 0.002$ *
UNIT-41	4	3	$p = 0.007$ *	$p = 0.27$ ^{ns}
UNIT-42	4	4	$p = 0.009$ *	$p = 0.009$ *
UNIT-47	5	3	$p = 0.009$ *	$p = 0.009$ *
UNIT-48	5	3	$p = 0.009$ *	$p = 0.009$ *

* indicates significant at alpha = 0.05; ^{ns} = non-significant; # = number.

Correlograms for LOD treatments were more uniform with few significant peaks ($p = 0.0009$) of Moran's I at longer lag distances compared to HID treatments (Figure A11, LOD vs. HID). However, between burned and unburned halves of LOD treatment units, we observed a greater number of significant ($p = 0.0009$) negative and positive Moran's I values at short lag distances for the burned halves (Table 3, Figure A11, LOD). In addition, between unburned halves of HID and LOD, HID unburned halves for units 41, 42, 47, and 48 exhibited a greater number of peaks in Moran's I values significantly different from 0 at shorter lag distances (Figure A11). Hence, both HID burned and unburned halves exhibited more spatial variation in AGB compared to LOD treatments (Figure A11, LOD vs. HID).

4. Discussion

Results showed that ranges, fine-scale variation, and periodicity in spatial variation of overstory above-ground biomass (AGB) were different among units in BMEF based on management and the point in time. Forests of 1934 were heterogeneous without marked human-induced management. In contrast, by 2016 these forests had been subjected to some form of thinning, burning, or a combination of both at various points in time [32,59]. Hence, spatial variation in overstory AGB for 2016 was likely influenced by these treatments. Our results showed that spatial variation in 2016 was more pronounced in prescribed burns.

4.1. The 1934 Forest Was Spatially Heterogeneous Particularly at Fine Scales

Most forest units had greater spatial variation in overstory AGB biomass in 1934 compared to 2016, as indicated by the short value of ranges (<200 m) from semivariogram, periodicity of Moran's I correlogram and Moran's I value at first lag not significantly different from 0 in RNAs [57,58]. The spatial variation in overstory AGB in BMEF is consistent with several other studies describing small and frequent patch size distributions (ranging from 60 to 150 m) of the overstory in old growth ponderosa pine forests in northern California [9,60] and Washington [1].

Further, our results identifying fine-scale variation in most of the units were consistent with other studies, which attributed the presence of fine-scale variation to frequent fire [61] and fine-scale variation in growing environmental conditions [62]. Exceptions occurred in units such as RNA-A and units 45 and 48, which lacked fine-scale (<50 m) spatial variation. The absence of fine-scale spatial variation is likely due to the absence of frequent fire after around 1880s at BMEF (unpublished data from Carl Skinner). In the absence of frequent fire, stand density possibly increased due to the infilling of gaps with shade-tolerant species such as incense-cedar and white fir [9] in units such as RNA-A and units 45 and 48, which occurred at higher elevations with abundant shade-tolerant species.

4.2. Spatial Autocorrelation at Long Ranges and Less Spatial Varaitons in 2016 except When Burned

The long ranges (>250 m) of the variograms suggested that overstory AGB in most units in 2016 consisted of small patch size and spatial variations, possibly due to increases in tree densities within 1934 forest gaps [3,63]. With the long-term (century-long) absence of frequent fire, heterogeneity at small scales (<50 m) could have decreased via a loss of fine-scale patches along with expansion of existing patches into gaps [3]. The loss of fine-scale patchiness in BMEF was evidenced by the decrease in nugget values and significant Moran's I at first lag in 2016 compared to 1934, consistent with [61]. On the other hand, no difference in periodicity between 1934 and 2016 within prescribed burn RNA units indicates that at localized scales, prescribed burns likely emulated much of the 1934 spatial structure by killing trees in patches [64].

4.3. Prescribed Burns Enhanced Spatial Variation in Both LOD and HID Treatments

The high structural diversity (HID) treatment for BMEF was designed to approximately emulate a heterogeneous overstory stand structure, with numerous small openings and patches of large old trees [59]. Therefore, our results regarding spatial variation in overstory AGB—presence of fine-scale spatial variation, periodicity in patchiness at short lags, and short ranges—for HID treatments suggest that treatments were effective in creating greater spatial variation of overstory stand structure [58]. Furthermore, when prescribed burns were coupled with the HID treatment, spatial variation in overstory AGB was further enhanced as evidenced by greater periodicity in overstory AGB as compared to the unburned half of the HID units.

Prescribed burns can be patchy and localized due to a slow rate of spread and thus can kill small trees in groups and create openings [64,65]. In addition, second-order post-fire mortality of trees can also remove patches of trees [65,66]. For example, low-severity prescribed burns can leave fire-injured conifers that are receptive hosts for bark beetles [66].

The subsequent mortality of weakened trees—especially large old ponderosa pine—due to beetle attacks can produce openings and gaps within stands [66,67], therefore creating a heterogeneous overstory similar to our HID burned halves. Our results in HID burned units are consistent with Dodson and Peterson [68], who found that thinning increased spatial aggregation of residual trees at fine scales (50–150 m) and that prescribed fire of different burning intensity further promoted a mosaic of gaps with burned and unburned trees followed by beetle-related mortality.

The LOD treatment was designed to create open, even-aged stand conditions with a single-layer canopy consisting of evenly spaced trees [59]. The largest and smallest trees were removed from these stands for a unimodal diameter distribution only leaving intermediate-sized trees [32]. Especially within the unburned halves of the treatments, the long ranges from the semivariograms and the uniform correlograms with few peaks at greater lag distances suggested that LOD unburned halves consist of a more spatially homogeneous overstory AGB compared to HID and LOD burned units. Our results from unburned halves of the LOD units are consistent with [69], who found that after uniform removal of trees, mixed-conifer stands showed little spatial variation at broad scales. Similarly little spatial variation in spruce-fir forests was found by Kuehne et al. [70] when using thinning treatments involving the removal of small and large dominant trees. Irrespective of both LOD and HID treatments, burned halves consistently showed more periodicity in overstory AGB, indicating that fire is a key component in enhancing spatial heterogeneity in overstory AGB.

4.4. Management Implications

Our findings about enhanced spatial variation after post-treatment prescribed burns are similar to what other studies have reported for dry forests across California (e.g., [7,71]). Our comparison of spatial variation between reference and contemporary forests provides a multi-faceted, quantitative approach for evaluating forests over different time periods with a variety of potential implications. First, the spatial variation of overstory AGB that we detected in the 1934 reference forests helps portray the types of variation associated with very few forest management activities (i.e., in the absence of harvest or prescribed burning) and thus can serve as a useful point of reference for managers. Then, in utilizing the values of ranges from the semivariograms across time, managers can understand the distance or scale over which spatial variation in the overstory in contemporary forests have potentially departed from that of reference conditions. Secondly, it is important to remember that these reference conditions represent the accumulated overstory stand structures of dry forests that have been influenced by multiple past disturbances, rather than a condition at a single point in time. Nonetheless, when examined over time, changes in spatial heterogeneity can be used to understand and disentangle the fundamental environmental factors driving forest overstory variation. We were unable to quantify changes in species composition, because our data from 1934 were not spatially explicit at the individual tree level. However, in future work the evaluation of species composition changes over time may reveal different spatial variation than we have detected here in both reference and contemporary dry forests.

In addition, our comparison of reference and contemporary overstory spatial variation can help managers to explore the impact of fire exclusion on driving overstory spatial variation in dry forests [56]. Furthermore, our deeper comparison between reference conditions and contemporary forests that subsequently received different management treatments provides information on which treatments are useful in dry conifer forests such as BMEF for emulating overstory spatial variation in reference conditions. For example, in managing contemporary forests, treatments similar to HID with prescribed burns that preserve and/or create patchy spatial variation similar to reference conditions, may be warranted. Similarly, LOD with prescribed burn may be warranted whenever the goal of management is to reduce canopy fuel to promote resiliency against fire. In addition, comparing spatial variation among various management treatments in contemporary forests will allow managers to understand the effectiveness of restoration treatments such as HID with prescribed burns in creating desirable spatial variation for contemporary dry forests.

5. Conclusions

This study provides a unique opportunity to examine the spatial variation of overstory stand structure in forest reference conditions using field-collected data as opposed to using tree size and density variables derived from dendro-chronological reconstructions. Furthermore, we were able to fill a gap in the literature related to understanding the spatial variation of overstory above-ground biomass between contemporary and reference forests.

The spatial variation of above-ground biomass in reference conditions described in this study comes from forests that have minimum human impact following Euro-American settlement and hence represent a relatively intact dry forest ecosystem. Therefore, knowledge about spatial variation in such intact forests in reference conditions provides insights into stand development, tree interactions with each other, regeneration, and mortality. Such information can help guide sustainable forest management in the face of growing natural environmental disturbances. Our results further indicate that low-severity fire seems to be key for emulating the mosaic of alternating patches of biomass at regular intervals throughout these dry forests. Therefore, managers seeking to enhance ecological resilience are advised to use prescribed burning alone or in combination with treatments that include some degree of thinning.

Author Contributions: Conceptualization, S.N., B.N.I.E. and M.W.R.; Data curation, S.N. and M.W.R.; Formal analysis, S.N.; Investigation, S.N., B.N.I.E. and M.W.R.; Methodology, S.N.; Project administration, B.N.I.E.; Resources, B.N.I.E. and M.W.R.; Supervision, B.N.I.E.; Visualization, S.N.; Writing—original draft, S.N.; Writing—review & editing, B.N.I.E., S.E.G. and M.W.R. All authors have read and agreed to the published version of the manuscript.

Funding: This research was funded by the USDA Forest Service, Pacific Southwest Research Station (grant number: 15-IJ-11272139-016) and UBC four-year fellowship (4YF) program.

Data Availability Statement: The 1934 data have been submitted to U.S. Forest Service Research Data Archive and will be publicly available there.

Acknowledgments: We thank Lassen National Forest and Pacific Southwest Research Station for providing the data for this study. Special thanks go to Ethan Hammett and Brian Wing for providing the LiDAR and GIS data layers and support on any related questions and Carl Skinner for the unpublished fire data. We would also like to thank Paul Hacker and Francisco Mauro for valuable insights during LiDAR data processing.

Conflicts of Interest: The authors declare no conflict of interest.

Appendix A. Data Summary

Table A1. Summary of the applied combination of structural diversity treatments and prescribed burn in various units of BMERP.

Unit	Structural Treatments *	Treatment Year	Prescribed Burn	Burn Year	# of 1 ha Plots
RNA-A	No treatment	-	Unburned	-	55
RNA-B	No treatment	-	Burned	1997	63
RNA-C	No treatment	-	Burned	1997	76
RNA-D	No treatment	-	Unburned	-	35
UNIT-39	LOD	1996	Burned	1997	89
UNIT-39	LOD	1996	Unburned	-	85
UNIT-40	LOD	1998	Burned	2000	87
UNIT40	LOD	1998	Unburned	-	79

Table A1. *Cont.*

Unit	Structural Treatments *	Treatment Year	Prescribed Burn	Burn Year	# of 1 ha Plots
UNIT-43	LOD	1996	Burned	1997	68
UNIT-43	LOD	1996	Unburned	-	90
UNIT-44	LOD	1997	Burned	1999	56
UNIT-44	LOD	1997	Unburned	-	49
UNIT-45	LOD	1997	Burned	1999	57
UNIT-45	LOD	1997	Unburned	-	75
UNIT-38	HID	1996	Burned	1997	87
UNIT-38	HID	1996	Unburned	-	93
UNIT-41	HID	1996	Burned	1997	82
UNIT-41	HID	1996	Unburned	-	79
UNIT-42	HID	1997	Burned	1999	83
UNIT-42	HID	1997	Unburned	-	101
UNIT-47	HID	1997	Burned	1999	59
UNIT-47	HID	1997	Unburned	-	48
UNIT-48	HID	1998	Burned	2000	81
UNIT-48	HID	1998	Unburned	-	76
Total					1720

* HID: high structural diversity treatment; LOD: low structural diversity treatment; RNA: research natural areas; # = number.

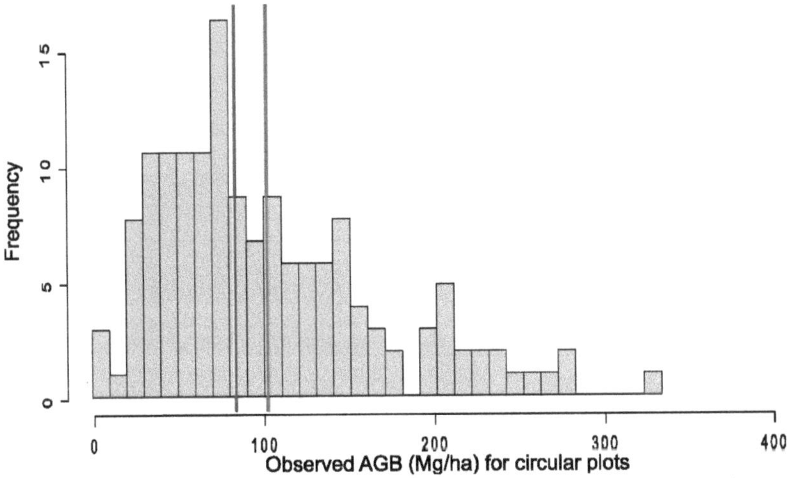

Figure A1. Histogram for above-ground biomass (Mg/ha) for 2016 ground data. The red and blue lines indicate the mean and median, respectively.

Appendix B. LiDAR Point Cloud Processing and Model Building Process

The LiDAR point cloud was processed using the *'lidR'* package in R [42]. We filtered duplicates for the overlapping region of the point clouds and then classified the ground returns [42]. All the ground returns were used to obtain a digital terrain model of 1 × 1 m grid cell size [42]. The point cloud was normalized by subtracting the digital terrain model from all returns to remove the influence of terrain on above-ground returns [42]. From the normalized point cloud, we used the area-based approach [42] to calculate the LiDAR metrics (Table A2)—hereafter referred to as auxiliary variables—using the *'cloudmetrics'* function related to the 154 circular ground plots. We also extracted average elevation (Table A2) for each ground plot in 2016 from a digital elevation model at 1 m resolution provided by the Pacific Southwest Research Station, Redding, USA, using the zonal statistics function in ArcMap 10.4.4. [72].

Table A2. LiDAR-derived and topographic auxiliary variables were used for biomass modeling.

Groups	LiDAR Variables	Description
Group A		
	zmean	Mean elevation for all first returns above 2 m
	zq5	Elevation for first return in 5th percentile
	zq10	Elevation for first return in 10th percentile
	zq15	Elevation for first return in 15th percentile
	zq20	Elevation for first return in 20th percentile
	zq25	Elevation for first return in 25th percentile
Group B		
	zq30	Elevation for first return in 30th percentile
	zq35	Elevation for first return in 35th percentile
	zq40	Elevation for first return in 40th percentile
	zq45	Elevation for first return in 45th percentile
	zq50	Elevation for first return in 50th percentile
Group C		
	zq55	Elevation for first return in 55th percentile
	zq60	Elevation for first return in 60th percentile
	zq65	Elevation for first return in 65th percentile
	zq70	Elevation for first return in 70th percentile
	zq75	Elevation for first return in 75th percentile
Group D		
	zq80	Elevation for first return in 80th percentile
	zq85	Elevation for first return in 85th percentile
	zq90	Elevation for first return in 90th percentile
	zq95	Elevation for first return in 95th percentile
	pzmean	Percentage of first return above mean
	Elev (m)	Elevation from digital elevation model @1 m
	Treatment × prescribed burn	

Appendix C. Model Building, Selection Process, and Biomass Prediction Summary

To avoid over fitting of the model and to have about 10–15 observations per auxiliary variable, we divided the auxiliary variables into four groups (Table A2, [43,73]). Within each variable group, following the top-down model-building strategy for glm models described by Zuur et al. [47], the LiDAR-derived variables and the six treatments—three structural diversity treatments crossed with two prescribed burn treatments—were used as fixed effects. A random unit effect was also included in the model [43]. The variables that were not statistically significant (p-value > 0.05) and had a variance inflation factor (VIF) of 10 or greater were dropped sequentially [47,74]. The variables that were retained from each auxiliary variable group were combined into a single model and were retained if they were statistically significant ($p < 0.05$) and had VIF < 10 [47,74]. Variables that were not statistically significant during group-wise selection were brought back into the model to check if the performance of the combined model improved. The model goodness-of-fit at each model building step was assessed using a graph showing observed vs. predicted values (Figure A2) and graphs of the residual deviance [47]. We selected the biomass model with the lowest AIC and lowest residual deviance (Table A3) as our final model. Our final model consisted of the mean height for all first returns above 2 m (zmean, $p = 1.4 \times 10^{-7}$), the height for the first return in the 5th percentile (zq5, $p = 0.05$), crossed treatments as fixed effects ($p = 0.05$), and unit level random effects (Table A3).

The range of predicted values of overstory AGB for the cells was within the range of the observed values for the circular ground plots (Table A4, Figure A3). The mean and median predicted values were very close to the mean and median observed values (Table A4, Figure A3). Overstory AGB predicted within the low structural diversity (LOD) units was low and consistent with observed overstory AGB (Figure A4). Predicted overstory

AGB in high structural diversity (HID) units and research natural areas (RNAs) was high compared to LOD but within the range of observed overstory AGB for HID and RNA units (Figure A4).

Table A3. Summary of the best-selected models from each auxiliary variable group. Highlighted in bold is the final model selected for above-ground biomass (Mg/ha) prediction.

Variable Group	Model	AIC	Residual Deviance	*p*-Value
Group A	Fixed effects = zmean + zq5 + Treatment × prescribed burn Random effect = units	1577.9	1557.9	zmean ($p < 0.0001$) zq5 ($p = 0.00087$)
Group B	Fixed effects = zq50+ Treatment × prescribed burn Random effect = units	1590.01	1572.0	zq50 ($p = 0.00034$)
Group C	Fixed effects = zq75+ Treatment × prescribed burn Random effect = units	1582.9	1564.1	zq75 ($p < 0.0001$)
Group D	Fixed effects = zq95+ Treatment × prescribed burn Random effect = units	1581.9	1561.9	zq95 ($p < 0.0001$)
Final	**Fixed effects = zmean + zq5 + Elev Random effects = Treatments × prescribed fire**	**15,916.6**	**1577.6**	**Zmean (<0.001)** **Zq5 (<0.001)** **Elev (<0.05)**

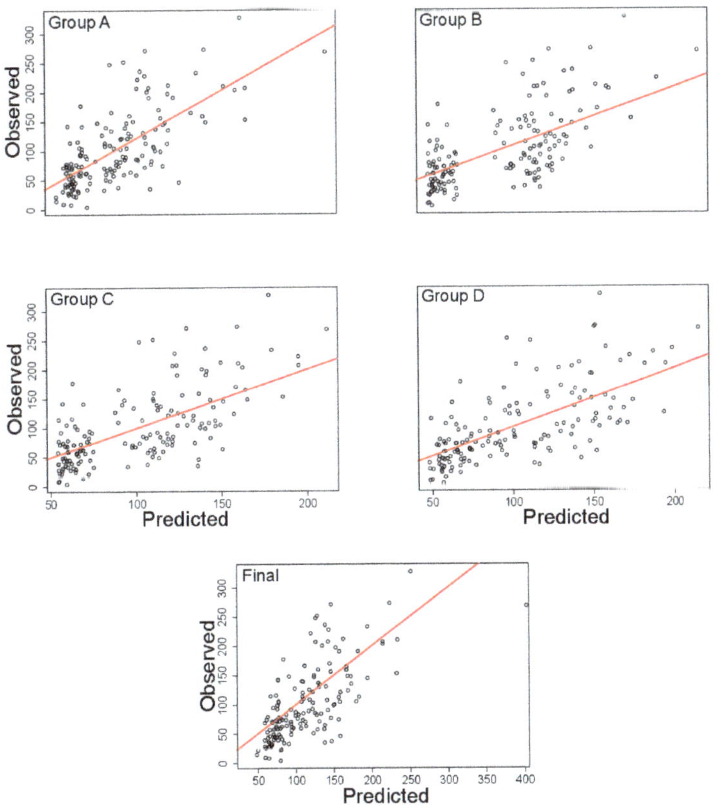

Figure A2. Observed vs. predicted above-ground biomass (Mg/ha). The models shown above represent the best model from each of the variable groups along with the final model. The red line is the best fitted line.

Table A4. Summary statistics of the observed and predicted overstory above-ground biomass (Mg/ha) values for circular plots (n = 153) and cells (n = 12,647).

Above-Ground Biomass (Mg/ha)	Min	Max	Mean	Median
Observed (Circular plots)	4.33	327.53	101.71	83.48
Predicted (32 × 32 m cells)	10.33	381.65	101.02	89.03

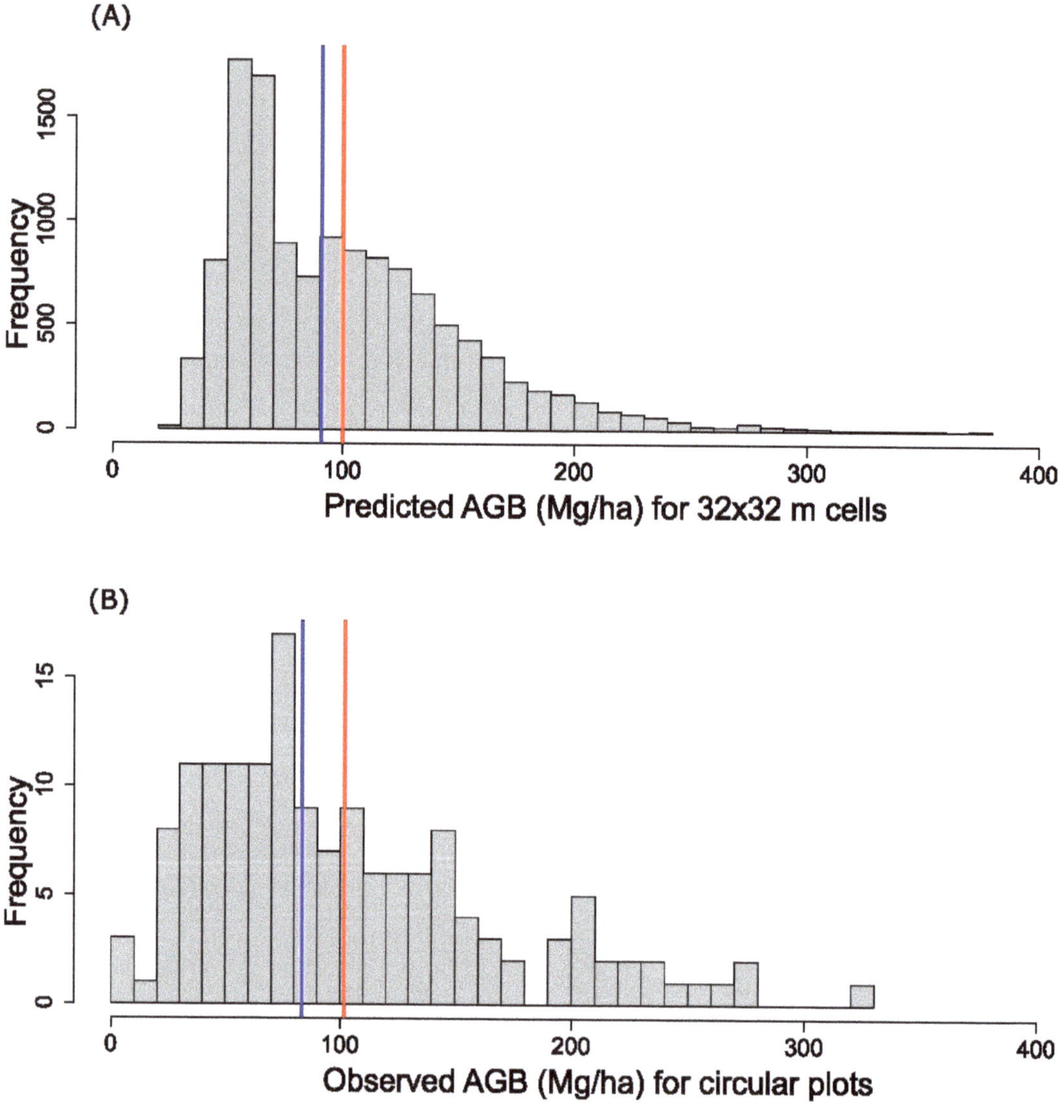

Figure A3. Predicted above-ground biomass (AGB, Mg/ha). The predictions were made at the cell level for overstory AGB and compared with the overstory AGB from the circular ground-truthing plots. The blue and red lines represent the median and mean of overstory AGB, respectively.

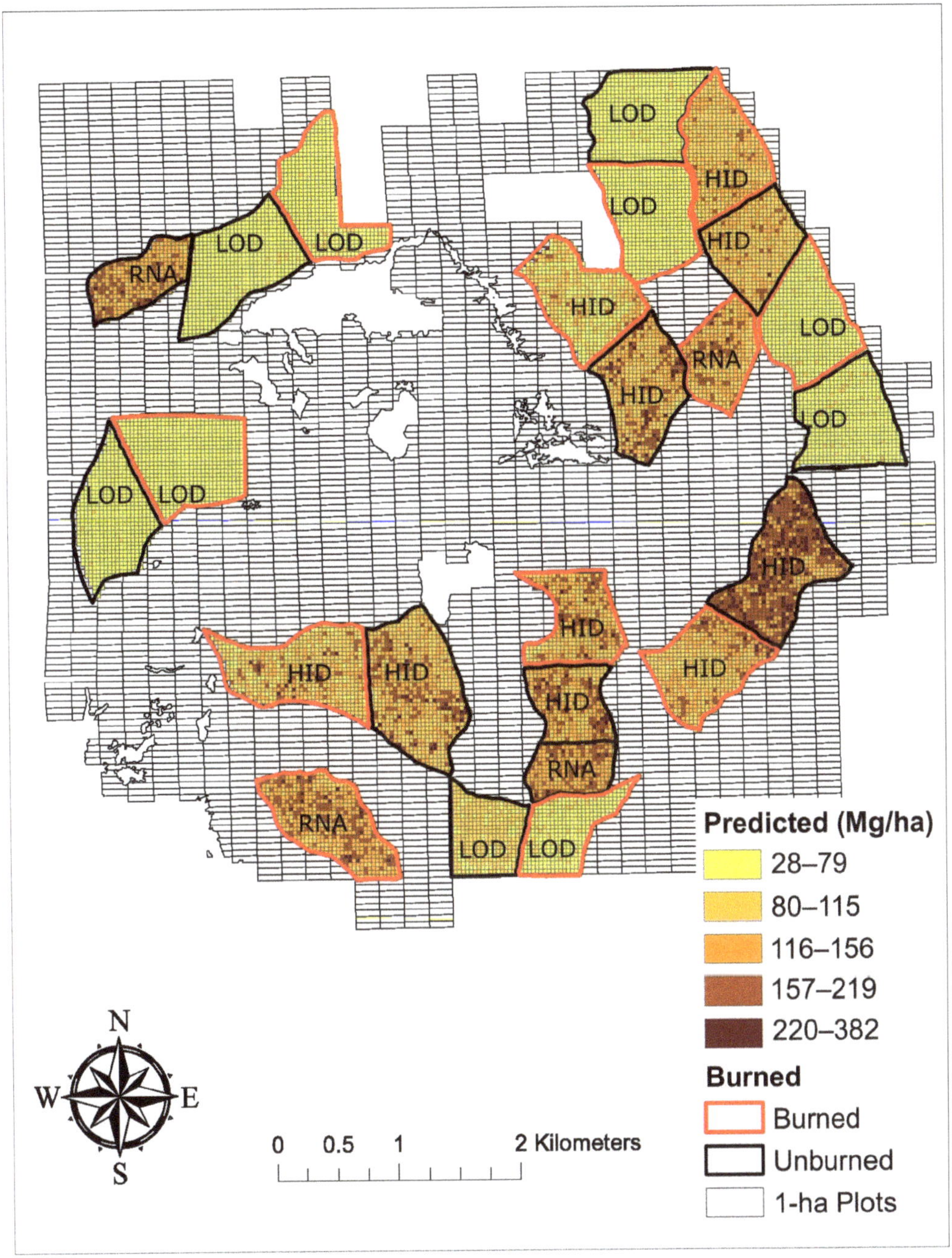

Figure A4. Predicted above-ground biomass (Mg/ha). The predictions were made using the final model and LiDAR derived metrics in 2016 at 32 m × 32 m pixel level for high structural diversity treatments (HID), low structural diversity treatments (LOD), and research natural areas (RNA) within Blacks Mountain Experimental Forest (BMEF).

Appendix D. Additional Table and Figures for the Results

Table A5. Summary of root mean squared error (RMSE) and values for the spherical, exponential, and Gaussian models selected for burned and unburned halves of HID and LOD units.

Unit	Fire	Model	RMSE	Sill
Low structural Diversity (LOD)				
UNIT-39	Burned	Gaussian	0.54	0.86
UNIT-39	Unburned	Gaussian	0.71	1.04
UNIT-40	Burned	Gaussian	0.72	0.93
UNIT-40	Unburned	Gaussian	0.73	1.05
UNIT-43	Burned	Spherical	0.75	1.03
UNIT-43	Unburned	Spherical	0.74	1.00
UNIT-44	Burned	Gaussian	0.64	1.15
UNIT-44	Unburned	Gaussian	0.49	0.92
UNIT-45	Burned	Gaussian	0.58	1.14
UNIT-45	Unburned	Gaussian	0.65	1.07
High structural diversity (HID)				
UNIT-38	Burned	Gaussian	0.65	0.92
UNIT-38	Unburned	Gaussian	0.59	0.87
UNIT-41	Burned	Spherical	0.74	0.84
UNIT-41	Unburned	Spherical	0.76	0.98
UNIT-42	Burned	Exponential	0.74	1.13
UNIT-42	Unburned	Exponential	0.73	1.32
UNIT-47	Burned	Gaussian	0.63	0.90
UNIT-47	Unburned	Gaussian	0.68	2.81
UNIT-48	Burned	Gaussian	0.70	0.92
UNIT-48	Unburned	Gaussian	0.74	0.88

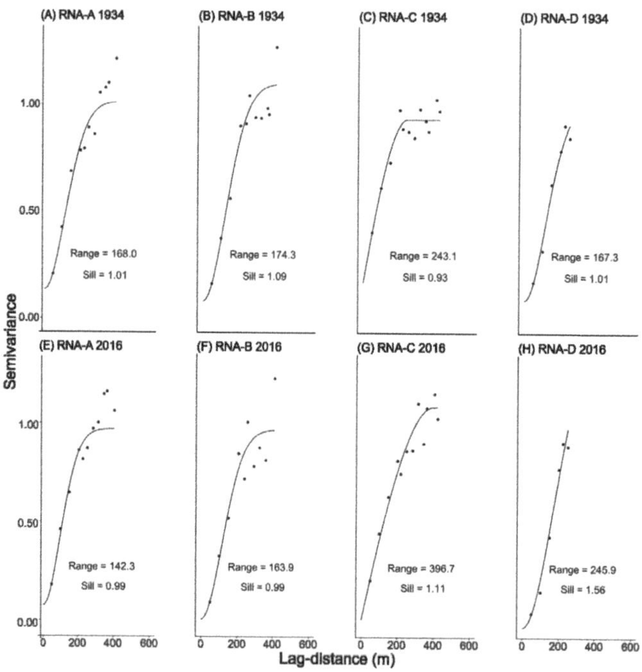

Figure A5. Variogram models for research natural areas (RNA) in 1934 and 2016.

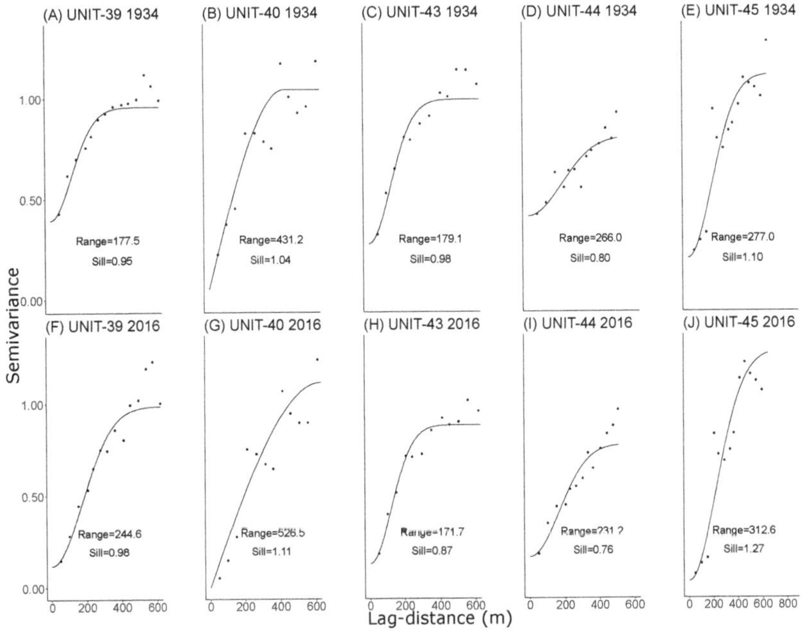

Figure A6. Variogram models for low structural diversity units (LOD) in 1934 and 2016.

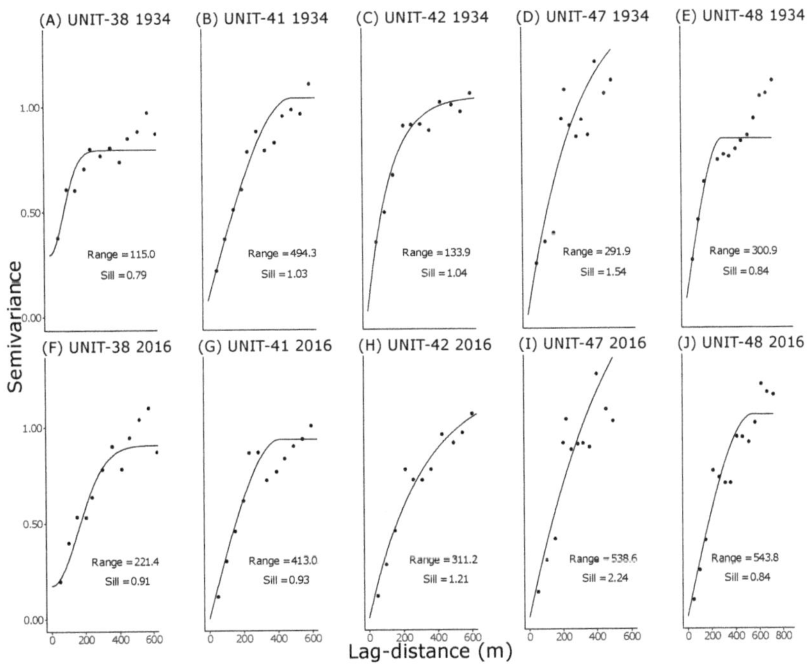

Figure A7. Variogram models for high structural diversity units (HID) in 1934 and 2016.

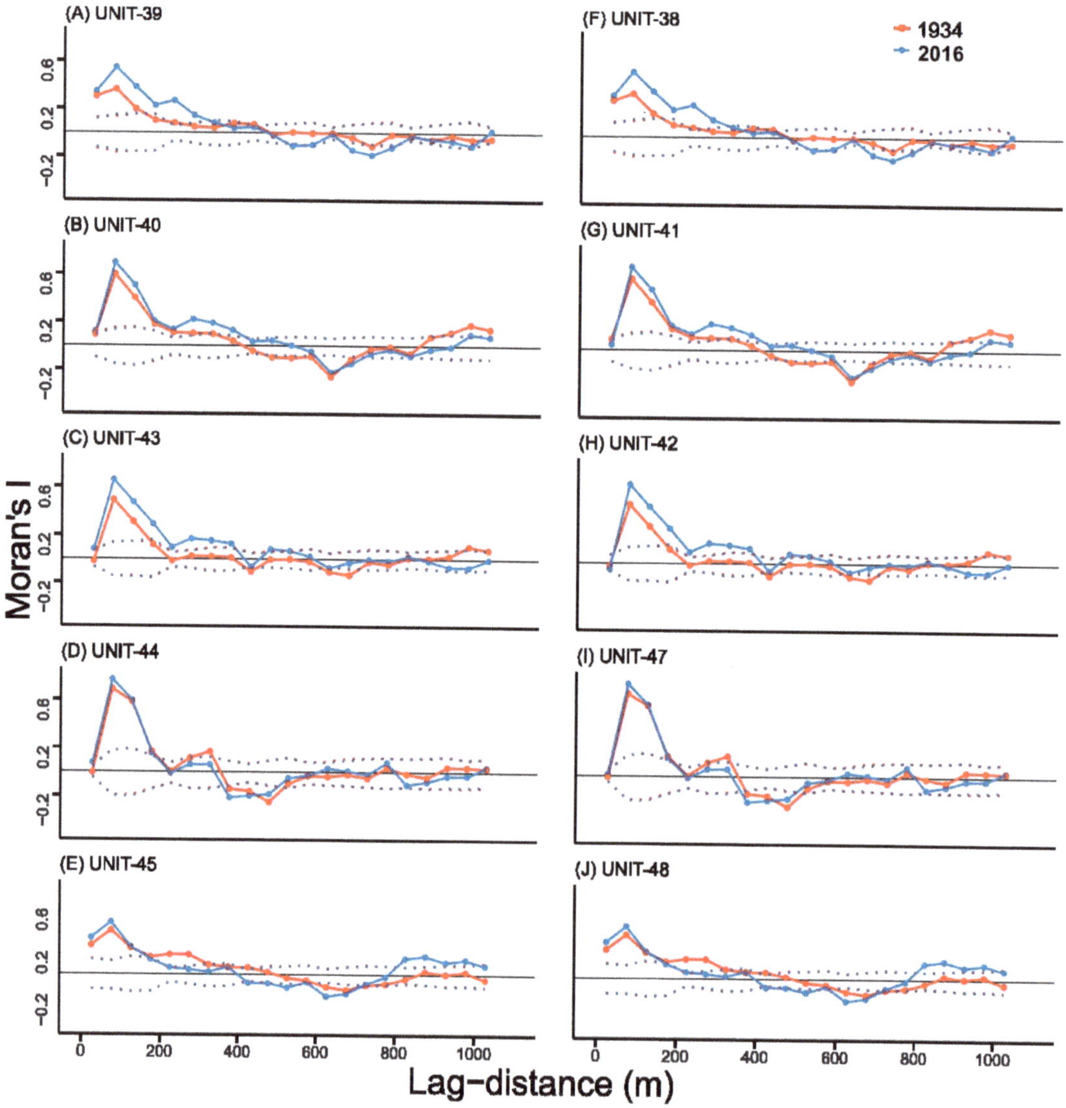

Figure A8. Moran's I correlogram for 1934 vs. 2016 within different units under study in Blacks Mountain Experimental Forest. Dotted lines represent the lower and upper limit of the non-significant spatial autocorrelation using 95% confidence envelopes for 1934 (red) and 2016 (blue) from Monte Carlo simulations [56]. Points connected with solid lines indicate Moran's I at a given lag distance (m). Points above the dotted lines in the upper part of the envelope indicate a positive Moran's I that is significantly different from 0, whereas points below the dotted lines in the lower part of the envelope show a negative Moran's I that is significantly different from 0. Points within the dotted envelope show Moran's I values that are not significantly different from 0.

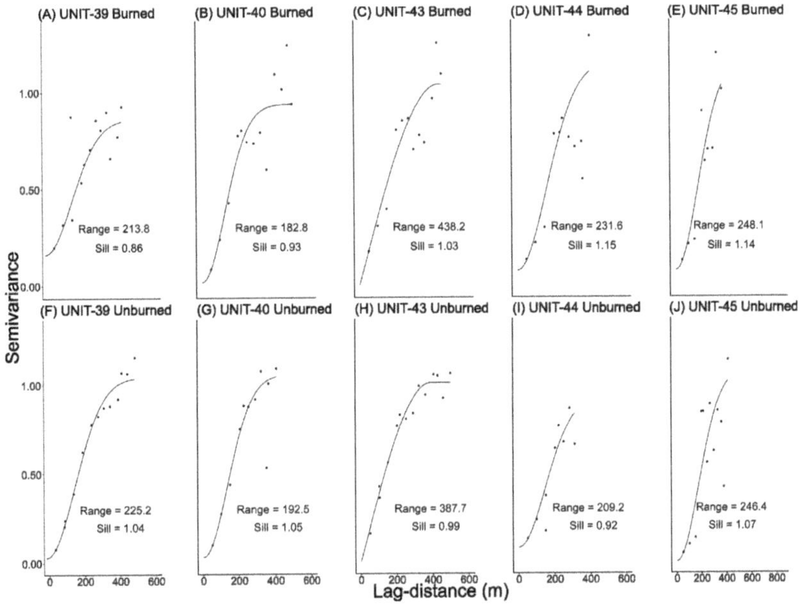

Figure A9. Variogram models for burned and unburned halves of low structural diversity units (LOD) in 2016.

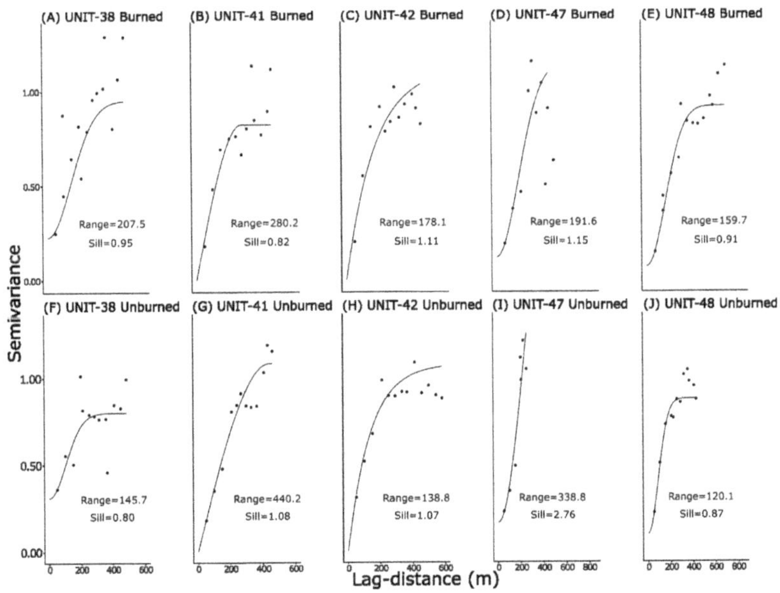

Figure A10. Variogram models for burned and unburned halves of high structural diversity units (HID) in 2016.

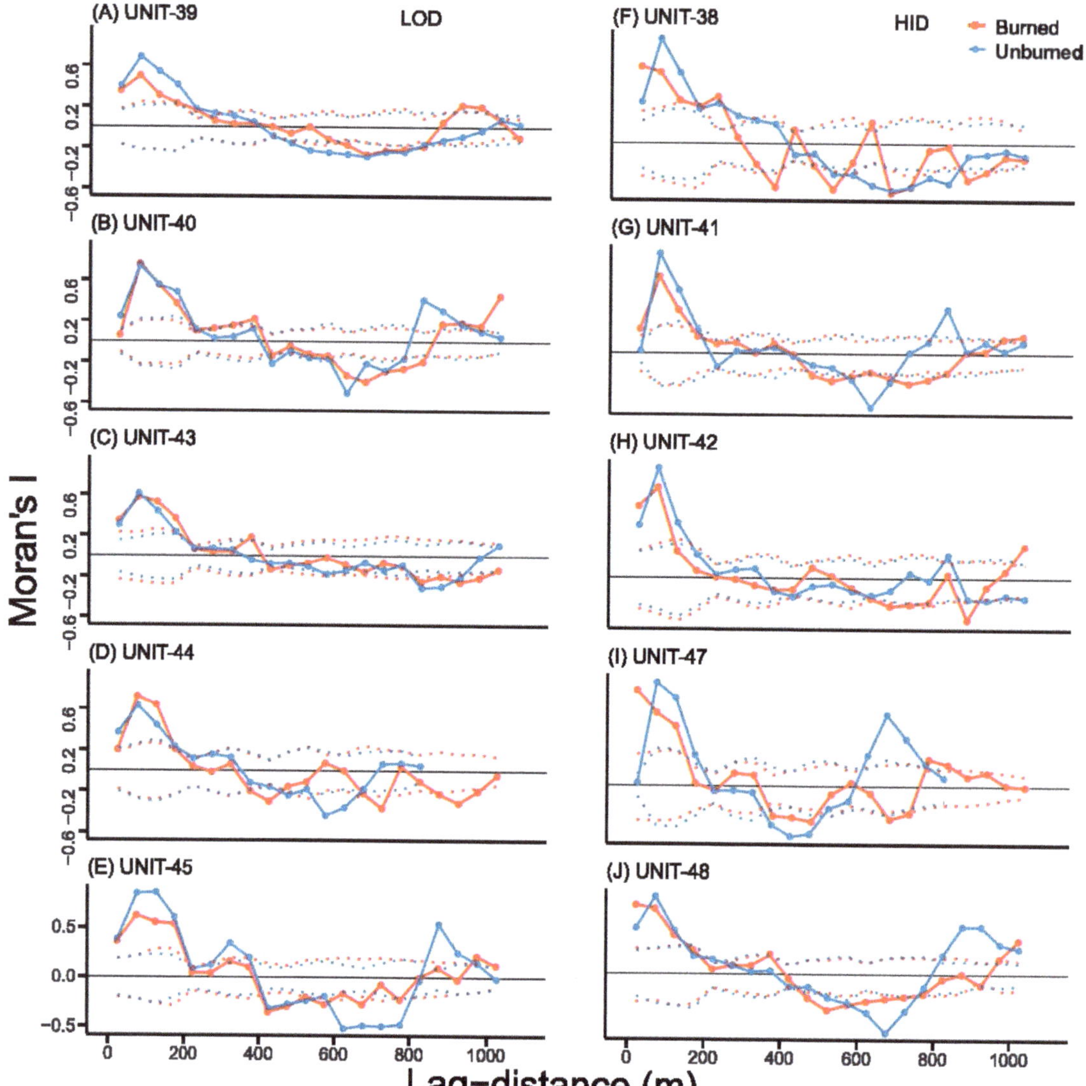

Figure A11. Moran's I correlograms for burned and unburned halves within different HID and LOD units in Blacks Mountain Experimental Forest. Dotted lines represent the lower and upper limit of the non-significant spatial autocorrelation using 95% confidence envelopes for Burned (red) and Unburned (blue) from Monte Carlo simulations [56]. Points connected with solid lines indicate Moran's I at a given lag distance (m). Points above the dotted lines in the upper part of the envelope indicate a positive Moran's I that is significantly different from 0, whereas points below the dotted lines in the lower part of the envelope show a negative Moran's I that is significantly different from 0. Points within the dotted envelope show Moran's I values that are not significantly different from 0.

References

1. Harrod, R.J.; Gaines, W.L.; Hartl, W.E.; Camp, A. *Estimating Historical Snag Density in Dry Forests East of the Cascade Range*; U.S. Department of Agriculture, Forest Service, Pacific Northwest Research Station: Portland, OR, USA, 1998; p. 116.
2. Dolanc, C.R.; Safford, H.D.; Thorne, J.H.; Dobrowski, S.Z. Changing Forest Structure Across the Landscape of the Sierra Nevada, CA, USA, since the 1930s. *Ecosphere* **2014**, *5*, 1–26. [CrossRef]
3. Lydersen, J.M.; North, M.P.; Knapp, E.E.; Collins, B.M. Quantifying Spatial Patterns of Tree Groups and Gaps in Mixed-Conifer Forests: Reference Conditions and Long-Term Changes Following Fire Suppression and Logging. *For. Ecol. Manag.* **2013**, *304*, 370–382. [CrossRef]
4. North, M.; Stine, P.; O'Hara, K.; Zielinski, W.; Stephens, S. *An Ecosystem Management Strategy for Sierran Mixed-Conifer Forests*; U.S. Department of Agriculture, Forest Service, Pacific Southwest Research Station: Albany, CA, USA, 2009.
5. van Mantgem, P.J.; Stephenson, N.L. Apparent Climatically Induced Increase of Tree Mortality Rates in a Temperate Forest. *Ecol. Lett.* **2007**, *10*, 909–916. [CrossRef] [PubMed]
6. Abella, S.R.; Denton, C.W. Spatial Variation in Reference Conditions: Historical Tree Density and Pattern on a Pinus Ponderosa Landscape. *Can. J. For. Res.* **2009**, *39*, 2391–2403. [CrossRef]
7. Churchill, D.J.; Larson, A.J.; Dahlgreen, M.C.; Franklin, J.F.; Hessburg, P.F.; Lutz, J.A. Restoring Forest Resilience: From Reference Spatial Patterns to Silvicultural Prescriptions and Monitoring. *For. Ecol. Manag.* **2013**, *291*, 442–457. [CrossRef]
8. Moore, D.A.; Carpenter, T.E. Spatial Analytical Methods and Geographic Information Systems: Use in Health Research and Epidemiology. *Epidemiol. Rev.* **1999**, *21*, 143–161. [CrossRef] [PubMed]
9. Youngblood, A.; Max, T.; Coe, K. Stand Structure in Eastside Old-Growth Ponderosa Pine Forests of Oregon and Northern California. *For. Ecol. Manag.* **2004**, *199*, 191–217. [CrossRef]
10. Clyatt, K.A.; Keyes, C.R.; Hood, S.M. Long-Term Effects of Fuel Treatments on Aboveground Biomass Accumulation in Ponderosa Pine Forests of the Northern Rocky Mountains. *For. Ecol. Manag.* **2017**, *400*, 587–599. [CrossRef]
11. Collins, B.M.; Fry, D.L.; Lydersen, J.M.; Everett, R.; Stephens, S.L. Impacts of Different Land Management Histories on Forest Change. *Ecol. Appl.* **2017**, *27*, 2475–2486. [CrossRef]
12. Oswalt, S.N.; Smith, W.B.; Miles, P.D.; Pugh, S.A. *Forest Resources of the United States, 2012: A Technical Document Supporting the Forest Service Update of the 2010 RPA Assessment*; U.S. Department of Agriculture, Forest Service, Washington Office: Washington, DC, USA, 2014; 218p.
13. Kilgore, B.M. The Ecological Role of Fire in Sierran Conifer Forests. Its Application to National Park Management. *Quat. Res.* **1973**, *3*, 496–513. [CrossRef]
14. Agee, J.K.; Skinner, C.N. Basic Principles of Forest Fuel Reduction Treatments. *For. Ecol. Manag.* **2005**, *211*, 83–96. [CrossRef]
15. Taylor, A.H. Fire Disturbance and Forest Structure in an Old-Growth Pinus Ponderosa Forest, Southern Cascades, USA. *J. Veg. Sci.* **2010**, *21*, 561–572. [CrossRef]
16. Chen, J.; Song, B.; Rudnicki, M.; Moeur, M.; Bible, K.; North, M.; Shaw, D.C.; Franklin, J.F.; Braun, D.M. Spatial Relationship of Biomass and Species Distribution in an Old-Growth. *For. Sci.* **2004**, *50*, 364–375.
17. Kashian, D.M.; Romme, W.H.; Tinker, D.B.; Turner, M.G.; Ryan, M.G. Carbon Storage on Landscapes with Stand-Replacing Fires. *Bioscience* **2006**, *56*, 598–606. [CrossRef]
18. Hall, S.A.; Burke, I.C.; Box, D.O.; Kaufmann, M.R.; Stoker, J.M. Estimating Stand Structure Using Discrete-Return Lidar: An Example from Low Density, Fire Prone Ponderosa Pine Forests. *For. Ecol. Manag.* **2005**, *208*, 189–209. [CrossRef]
19. McRoberts, R.E.; Tomppo, E.O.; Næsset, E. Advances and Emerging Issues in National Forest Inventories. *Scand. J. For. Res.* **2010**, *25*, 368–381. [CrossRef]
20. Lefsky, M.A.; Cohen, W.B.; Acker, S.A.; Parker, G.G.; Spies, T.A.; Harding, D. Lidar Remote Sensing of the Canopy Structure and Biophysical Properties of Douglas-Fir Western Hemlock Forests. *Remote Sens. Environ.* **1999**, *70*, 339–361. [CrossRef]
21. Skowronski, N.S.; Lister, A.J. *The Utility of Lidar for Large Area Forest Inventory Applications*; U.S. Department of Agriculture, Forest Service, Northern Research Station: Newtown Square, PA, USA, 2012.
22. Millar, C.I.; Stephenson, N.L.; Stephens, S.L. Climate Change and Forests of the Future: Managing in the Face of Uncertainity. *Ecol. Appl.* **2007**, *17*, 2145–2151. [CrossRef]
23. Vankat, J.L.; Major, J. Vegetation Changes in Sequoia National Park, California. *J. Biogeogr.* **1978**, *5*, 377–402. [CrossRef]
24. Beaty, R.M.; Taylor, A.H. Fire History and the Structure and Dynamics of a Mixed Conifer Forest Landscape in the Northern Sierra Nevada, Lake Tahoe Basin, California, USA. *For. Ecol. Manag.* **2008**, *255*, 707–719. [CrossRef]
25. Ansley, J.S.; Battles, J.J. Forest Composition, Structure, and Change in an Old-Growth Mixed Confer Forest in the Northern Sierra Nevada. *J. Torrey Bot. Soc.* **1998**, *125*, 297–308. [CrossRef]
26. Smith, T.F.; Rizzo, D.M.; North, M.P. Patterns of Mortality in an Old-Growth Mixed-Conifer Forest of the Southern Sierra Nevada, Californi. *For. Sci.* **2005**, *51*, 266–275.
27. Knight, C.A.; Cogbill, C.V.; Potts, M.D.; Wanket, J.A.; Battles, J.J. Settlement-Era Forest Structure and Composition in the Klamath Mountains: Reconstructing a Historical Baseline. *Ecosphere* **2020**, *11*, e03250. [CrossRef]
28. Fry, D.L.; Stephens, S.L.; Collins, B.M.; North, M.P.; Franco-Vizcaíno, E.; Gill, S.J. Contrasting Spatial Patterns in Active-Fire and Fire-Suppressed Mediterranean Climate Old-Growth Mixed Conifer Forests. *PLoS ONE* **2014**, *9*, e88985. [CrossRef] [PubMed]
29. Sanchez Meador, A.J.; Parysow, P.F.; Moore, M.M. Historical Stem-Mapped Permanent Plots Increase Precision of Reconstructed Reference Data in Ponderosa Pine Forests of Northern Arizona. *Restor. Ecol.* **2010**, *18*, 224–234. [CrossRef]

30. Sheridan, R.D.; Popescu, S.C.; Gatziolis, D.; Morgan, C.L.S.; Ku, N.W. Modeling Forest Aboveground Biomass and Volume Using Airborne LiDAR Metrics and Forest Inventory and Analysis Data in the Pacific Northwest. *Remote Sens.* **2015**, *7*, 229–255. [CrossRef]
31. Richardson, J.J.; Moskal, L.M. Strengths and Limitations of Assessing Forest Density and Spatial Configuration with Aerial LiDAR. *Remote Sens. Environ.* **2011**, *115*, 2640–2651. [CrossRef]
32. Oliver, W. *Ecological Research at the Blacks Mountain Experimental Forest in Northeastern California*; PSW-GTR-179; Pacific Southwest Research Station, Forest Service, U.S. Department of Agriculture: Albany, CA, USA, 2000; 66p.
33. Gordon, D.T. *History of the Blacks Mountain Experimental Forest, 1933 through 1981*; U.S. Department of Agriculture, Forest Service, Pacific Southwest Forest and Range Experiment Station: Berkeley, CA, USA, 1981; pp. 1–209.
34. Jia, G.J.; Burke, I.C.; Goetz, A.F.H.; Kaufmann, M.R.; Kindel, B.C. Assessing Spatial Patterns of Forest Fuel Using AVIRIS Data. *Remote Sens. Environ.* **2006**, *102*, 318–327. [CrossRef]
35. Keane, R.E.; Nurgan, R.E.; Wagtendonk, J.W.V. Mapping Wildland Fuels for Fire Management across Multiple Scales: Integrating Remote Sensing, GIS, and Biophysical. *Int. J. Wild. Fire* **2001**, *10*, 301–319. [CrossRef]
36. Rollins, M.G.; Keane, R.E.; Parson, R.A. Mapping Fuels and Fire Regimes Using Remote Sensing, Ecosystem Simulation, and Gradient Modeling. *Ecol. Appl.* **2004**, *14*, 75–95. [CrossRef]
37. Swetnam, T.W. Fire History and Climate Chage in Giant Sequoia Groves. *Science* **1993**, *262*, 885–889. [CrossRef] [PubMed]
38. Eyre, F.H. *Forest Cover Types of the United States and Canada*; U.S. Depratment of Agriculture, Forest Service, Washington Office: Washington, DC, USA, 1980.
39. Ritchie, M.W. Multi-Scale Reference Conditions in an Interior Pine-Dominated Landscape in Northeastern California. *For. Ecol. Manag.* **2016**, *378*, 233–243. [CrossRef]
40. Hasel, A.A. *Instruction for Type Map and Inventory of Experimental Forest*; Pacific Southwest Research Station: Berkeley, CA, USA, 1935; 9p.
41. Wing, B.M.; Ritchie, M.W.; Boston, K.; Cohen, W.B.; Gitelman, A.; Olsen, M.J. Prediction of Understory Vegetation Cover with Airborne Lidar in an Interior Ponderosa Pine Forest. *Remote Sens. Environ.* **2012**, *124*, 730–741. [CrossRef]
42. Roussel, J.R.; Auty, D.; Coops, N.C.; Tompalski, P.; Goodbody, T.R.H.; Meador, A.S.; Bourdon, J.F.; de Boissieu, F.; Achim, A. LidR: An R Package for Analysis of Airborne Laser Scanning (ALS) Data. *Remote Sens. Environ.* **2020**, *251*, 112061. [CrossRef]
43. Mauro, F.; Ritchie, M.; Wing, B.; Frank, B.; Monleon, V.; Temesgen, H.; Hudak, A. Estimation of Changes of Forest Structural Attributes at Three Di Ff Erent Spatial Aggregation Levels in Northern California Using Multitemporal LiDAR. *Remote Sens.* **2019**, *11*, 923. [CrossRef]
44. Ritchie, M.W.; Zhang, J.; Hamilton, T.A. Aboveground Tree Biomass for Pinus Ponderosa in Northeastern California. *Forests* **2013**, *4*, 179–196. [CrossRef]
45. Leroy Dolph, K.; Mori, S.R.; Oliver, W.W. *Height-Diameter Relationship for Conifer Species on the Blacks Mountain Experimental Forest*; Research Paper; U.S. Department of Agriculture, Forest Service: Washington, DC, USA, 1995; p. 5.
46. Jenkins, J.C.; Chojnacky, D.C.; Heath, L.S.; Birdsey, R.A. *Comprehensive Database of Diameter-Based Biomass Resgressions for North American Tree Species*; U.S. Department of Agriculture, Forest Service, Northeastern Research Station: Newtown Square, PA, USA, 2003.
47. Zuur, A.F.; Ieno, E.N.; Walker, N.J.; Saveliev, A.A.; Smith, G.M. *Mixed Effects Models and Extensions in Ecology with R*; Springer: New York, NY, USA, 2009; p. 579.
48. Bates, D.; Mächler, M.; Bolker, B.; Walker, S. Fitting Linear Mixed-Effects Models Using Lme4. *J. Stat. Softw.* **2015**, *67*, 1–48. [CrossRef]
49. Reed, T.W.; Gulland, E.; West, G.; Mcmeekin, D.A.; Moncrieff, S. Geographic Metadata Searching with Semantic and Spatial Filtering Methods. In Proceedings of the GEOProcessing 2016: The Eighth International Conference on Advanced Geographic Information Systems, Applications, and Services, Venice, Italy, 24–28 April 2016.
50. Rossi, R.E.; Mulla, D.J.; Journel, A.G.; Franz, E.H. Geostatistical Tools for Modeling and Interpreting Ecological Spatial Dependence. *Ecol. Monogr.* **1992**, *62*, 277–314. [CrossRef]
51. Isaaks, E.; Srivastava, R.M. *An Introduction to Applied Geostatistics*, 1st ed.; Oxford University Press: New York, NY, USA, 1989; Volume 17.
52. Pebesma, E.J. Multivariable Geostatistics in S: The Gstat Package. *Comput. Geosci.* **2004**, *30*, 683–691. [CrossRef]
53. Fry, D.L.; Stephens, S.L. Stand-Level Spatial Dependence in an Old-Growth Jeffrey Pine-Mixed Conifer Forest, Sierra San Pedro Mártir, Mexico. *Can. J. For. Res.* **2010**, *40*, 1803–1814. [CrossRef]
54. Keane, R.E.; Gray, K.; Bacciu, V.; Leirfallom, S. Spatial Scaling of Wildland Fuels for Six Forest and Rangeland Ecosystems of the Northern Rocky Mountains, USA. *Landsc. Ecol.* **2012**, *27*, 1213–1234. [CrossRef]
55. Zawadzki, J.; Cieszewski, C.J.; Zasada, M.; Lowe, R.C. Applying Geostatistics for Investigations of Forest Ecosystems Using Remote Sensing Imagery. *Silva Fenn. Monogr.* **2005**, *39*, 599–617. [CrossRef]
56. Jaquette, M.; Sánchez Meador, A.J.; Huffman, D.W.; Bowker, M.A. Mid-Scale Drivers of Variability in Dry Mixed-Conifer Forests of the Mogollon Rim, Arizona. *Forests* **2021**, *12*, 622. [CrossRef]
57. Legendre, P.; Fortin, M.-J. Spatial Pattern and Ecological Analysis. *Vegetatio* **1989**, *80*, 107–138. [CrossRef]
58. Radeloff, V.C.; Miller, T.F.; He, H.S.; Mladenoff, D.J. Periodicity in Spatial Data and Geostatistical Models: Autocorrelation between Patches. *Ecography* **2000**, *23*, 81–91. [CrossRef]

59. Crotteau, J.S.; Ritchie, M.W. Long-Term Stand Growth of Interior Ponderosa Pine Stands in Response to Structural Modifications and Burning Treatments in Northeastern California. *J. For.* **2014**, *112*, 412–423. [CrossRef]
60. Arthur, G.; Janet, F. Second-Order Neighborhood Analysis of Mapped Point Patterns. *Ecology* **1987**, *68*, 473–477. [CrossRef]
61. Freeman, E.A.; Moisen, G.G. Evaluating Kriging as a Tool to Improve Moderate Resolution Maps of Forest Biomass. *Environ. Monit. Assess.* **2007**, *128*, 395–410. [CrossRef]
62. Ziegler, J.P.; Hoffman, C.M.; Fornwalt, P.J.; Sieg, C.H.; Battaglia, M.A.; Chambers, M.E.; Iniguez, J.M. Tree Regeneration Spatial Patterns in Ponderosa Pine Forests Following Stand-Replacing Fire: Influence of Topography and Neighbors. *Forests* **2017**, *8*, 391. [CrossRef]
63. North, M.P.; Tompkins, R.E.; Bernal, A.A.; Collins, B.M.; Stephens, S.L.; York, R.A. Forest Ecology and Management Operational Resilience in Western US Frequent-Fire Forests. *For. Ecol. Manag.* **2022**, *507*, 120004. [CrossRef]
64. Kerns, B.K.; Thies, W.G.; Niwa, C.G. Season and Severity of Prescribed Burn in Ponderosa Pine Forests: Implications for Understory Native and Exotic Plants. *Ecoscience* **2006**, *13*, 44–55. [CrossRef]
65. Sackett, S.S.; Haase, S.M.; Harrington, M.G. Prescribed Burning in Southwestern Ponderosa Pine. *Eff. Fire Madrean Prov. Ecosyst. A Symp. Proc.* **1996**, *289*, 178–186.
66. Hood, S.M.; Smith, S.L.; Cluck, D.R. Predicting Mortality for Five California Conifers Following Wildfire. *For. Ecol. Manag.* **2010**, *260*, 750–762. [CrossRef]
67. Davis, R.S.; Hood, S.; Bentz, B.J. Fire-Injured Ponderosa Pine Provide a Pulsed Resource for Bark Beetles. *Can. J. For. Res.* **2012**, *42*, 2022–2036. [CrossRef]
68. Dodson, E.K.; Peterson, D.W. Dry Coniferous Forest Restoration and Understory Plant Diversity: The Importance of Community Heterogeneity and the Scale of Observation. *For. Ecol. Manag.* **2010**, *260*, 1702–1707. [CrossRef]
69. Larson, A.J.; Stover, K.C.; Keyes, C.R. Effects of Restoration Thinning on Spatial Heterogeneity in Mixed-Conifer Forest. *Can. J. For. Res.* **2012**, *42*, 1505–1517. [CrossRef]
70. Kuehne, C.; Weiskittel, A.; Pommerening, A.; Wagner, R.G. Evaluation of 10-Year Temporal and Spatial Variability in Structure and Growth across Contrasting Commercial Thinning Treatments in Spruce-Fir Forests of Northern Maine, USA. *Ann. For. Sci.* **2018**, *75*, 20. [CrossRef]
71. Knapp, E.E.; Lydersen, J.M.; North, M.P.; Collins, B.M. Efficacy of Variable Density Thinning and Prescribed Fire for Restoring Forest Heterogeneity to Mixed-Conifer Forest in the Central Sierra Nevada, CA. *For. Ecol. Manag.* **2017**, *406*, 228–241. [CrossRef]
72. Wilson, J.P. GIScience Research at the Thirty-Second Annual Esri International User Conference. *Trans. GIS* **2012**, *16*, 267–269. [CrossRef]
73. Harrell, F.E.J.; Lee, K.L.; Califf, R.M.; Pryor, D.B.; Rosati, R.A. Regression Modelling Strategies for Improved Prognostic Prediction. *Stat. Med.* **1984**, *3*, 143–152. [CrossRef]
74. Sheskin, D.J. *Handbook of Parametric and Nonparametric Statistical Procedures*, 5th ed.; Chapman & Hall: NewYork, NY, USA, 2000; p. 1928. [CrossRef]

forests

MDPI

Article

Formulating Equations for Estimating Forest Stand Carbon Stock for Various Tree Species Groups in Northern Thailand

Khwanchai Duangsathaporn *, Narapong Sangram *, Yenemurwon Omule, Patsi Prasomsin, Kritsadapan Palakit and Pichit Lumyai

Department of Forest Management, Faculty of Forestry, Kasetsart University, Bangkok 10900, Thailand; ayomule@gmail.com (Y.O.); fforpsp@ku.ac.th (P.P.); fforkpp@ku.ac.th (K.P.); fforpcl@ku.ac.th (P.L.)
* Correspondence: fforkcd@ku.ac.th (K.D.); narapong.sa@ku.th (N.S.)

Abstract: Through this study, we established equations for estimating the standing tree carbon stock based on 24 tree species in multiple size classes in a case study at the Ngao Demonstration Forest (NDF) in northern Thailand. Four hundred thirty-nine wood samples from trees in mixed deciduous forest (MDF), dry dipterocarp forest (DDF), and dry evergreen forest (DEF) were collected using non-destructive methods to estimate aboveground carbon equations through statistical regression. The equations were established based on four criteria: (1) the coefficient of determination (R^2), (2) standard error of estimate (SE), (3) F-value, and (4) significant value (p-value, $\alpha \leq 0.05$). The aboveground carbon stock (C) equations for standing trees in the MDF was $C = 0.0199DBH^{2.1887}H^{0.5825}$, for DDF was $C = 0.0145DBH^{2.1435}H^{0.748}$, for DEF was $C = 0.0167DBH^{2.1423}H^{0.7070}$, and the general equation for all species/wood density groups was $C = 0.017543DBH^{2.1625}H^{0.6614}$, where DBH is tree diameter at breast height, and H is tree total height. The aboveground carbon stock in the DDF, MDF, and DEF was 142, 53.02, and 12 tons/ha, respectively, and the estimated aboveground carbon stock in the Mae Huad sector at the NDF was 61 tons/ha.

Keywords: carbon stock; standing-tree carbon equation; Ngao Demonstration Forest

1. Introduction

Trees can potentially trap atmospheric carbon through the photosynthesis process [1], which involves the conversion of carbon from carbon dioxide (CO_2) to carbohydrates, glucose, and starch that are stored in the leaves, stems, branches, and roots, and contribute to a plant's growth [2]. As such, plants store carbon as living biomass, which becomes a part of the food chain and enters the soil as soil carbon [3]. It is estimated that forests contain 77% of the carbon stored in land vegetation, out of which approximately 60% of carbon is stored in tropical forests, 17% in temperate forests, and 23% in boreal forests [4].

Normally, the carbon stored in trees is estimated as the product of the volume of biomass and the carbon fraction (generally assumed as 0.47 [5]) based on field data collection methods and estimations of different complexity levels [6–8]. Tree biomass can be estimated using either direct or indirect methods. The direct method involves the felling of trees and weighing various tree components [9], while the indirect method involves the use of allometric equations for estimating the tree sample biomass [10].

The biomass or tree volume equations to estimate the tree carbon storage specific to Thailand are inaccurate as the commonly used allometric equations are biased (i.e., they tend to over or under-estimate the tree volume) [11]. Additionally, the existing equations do not cover the major tree species frequently found in forests, such as *Tectona grandis*, teak [12], or various dipterocarp species [13]. This is primarily due to the fact that the estimations are based on equations constructed using the destructive sampling of a relatively small number of trees. Some volume equations use only the diameter at breast height (DBH) as the independent variable and do not include tree height [14,15]. Moreover, some equations were constructed only to estimate the traded logged volume and did not include the smaller trees [15]. Therefore, a novel approach that addresses these weaknesses is proposed to estimate the standing tree carbon content as a function of tree attributes in a natural forest with different sample tree size classes. This approach would also avoid the felling of trees and would use combustion methods to estimate the real carbon fraction.

This study aims to formulate the standing tree carbon equations to estimate the carbon stocks in three forest types: a mixed deciduous forest (MDF), a dry dipterocarp forest (DDF), and a dry evergreen forest (DEF) at the Mae Huad sector, Ngao Demonstration Forest (NDF) in northern Thailand. The Mae Huad sector has a vast forest cover in the NDF, with several tree species, and is one of the five most important biosphere reserve areas in Thailand [16]. The equations determined in this research to estimate the carbon stock were constructed using specific carbon fractions of tree species without the need to calculate the biomass to estimate the tree carbon stock. The non-destructive method used to establish the equations for many tree species sampled from the MDF, DDF, and DEF can also be used to estimate the carbon stored in other sites in Thailand.

2. Materials and Methods

The methodology consists of 3 steps, i.e., forest inventory and sample collection, sample preparation and carbon fraction analysis, data analysis including carbon storage in the wood sample, the calculation of standing tree carbon stock, constructing the standing tree carbon equation, and estimating stand carbon stock. These steps are described in detail in Figure 1.

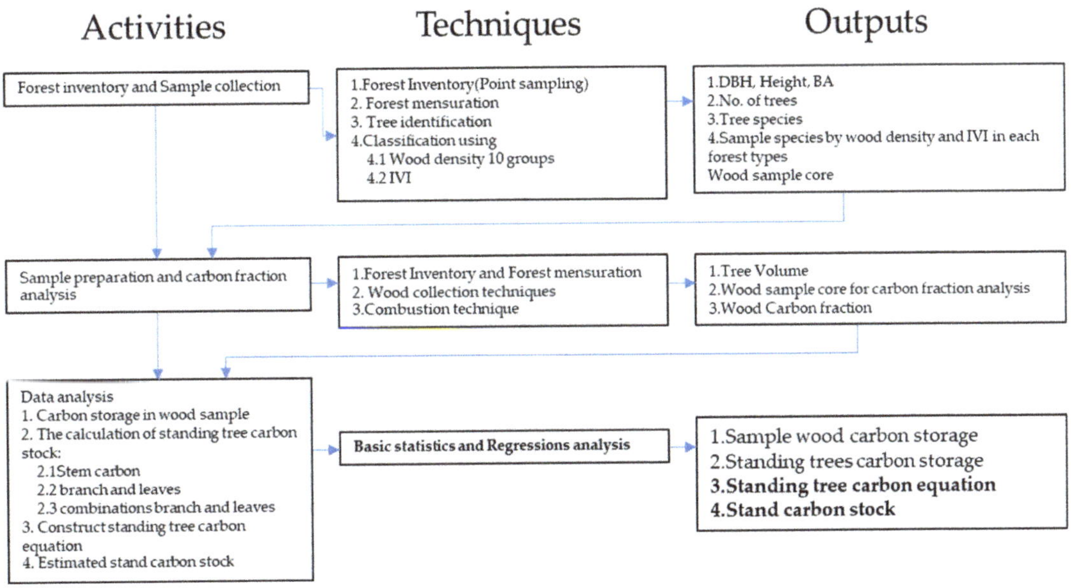

Figure 1. Schematic diagram of the study methodology.

2.1. Study Area

The Mae Huad Sector was chosen as the study site (Figure 2) and is one of the four designated sectors in the NDF. The NDF consists of four sectors, Mae Heang, Mae Huat, Mae Ngao, and Mae Teeb, and covers an area of approximately 43,431.75 hectares, including several forest types. It is located in the north-western part of the Lampang Province in northern Thailand between 18°30′ and 18°54′ north latitude and 99°50′ and 100° east. The NDF was established in 1961 and is the only demonstration forest in Thailand; and has a long history of functioning as a base for the introduction, testing, and adaption of new forest management techniques [15]. Most of the land in the Mae Huad sector is under forest cover, i.e., 38,557.50 hectares or 84.246% of the total area. Most of the tree cover is part of the Ngao Demonstration Forest, while a total of 6526.80 hectares is classified as agricultural land, or 14.261%, and is located in the national reserve forest by law. The forest area of the Mae Huad sector includes mixed deciduous forest, MDF (67.26%), dry dipterocarp forest, DDF (20.87%), dry evergreen forest, DEF (3.59%), and teak plantation (8.27%). The topography of the Mae Huad sector consists of hill ridges. The elevations vary from 200 m to 1400 m above mean sea level. The geography of this study area showed that recent alluvial terraces are characterized by alluvial deposits that were transported through the river and streams. Soil textures in this area vary from sand to clay. The climate of the year is divided into 3 seasons, i.e., the hot season from February to May, the rally season from June to September, and the cool season from October to January. The average annual rainfall is about 1117.3 cm.

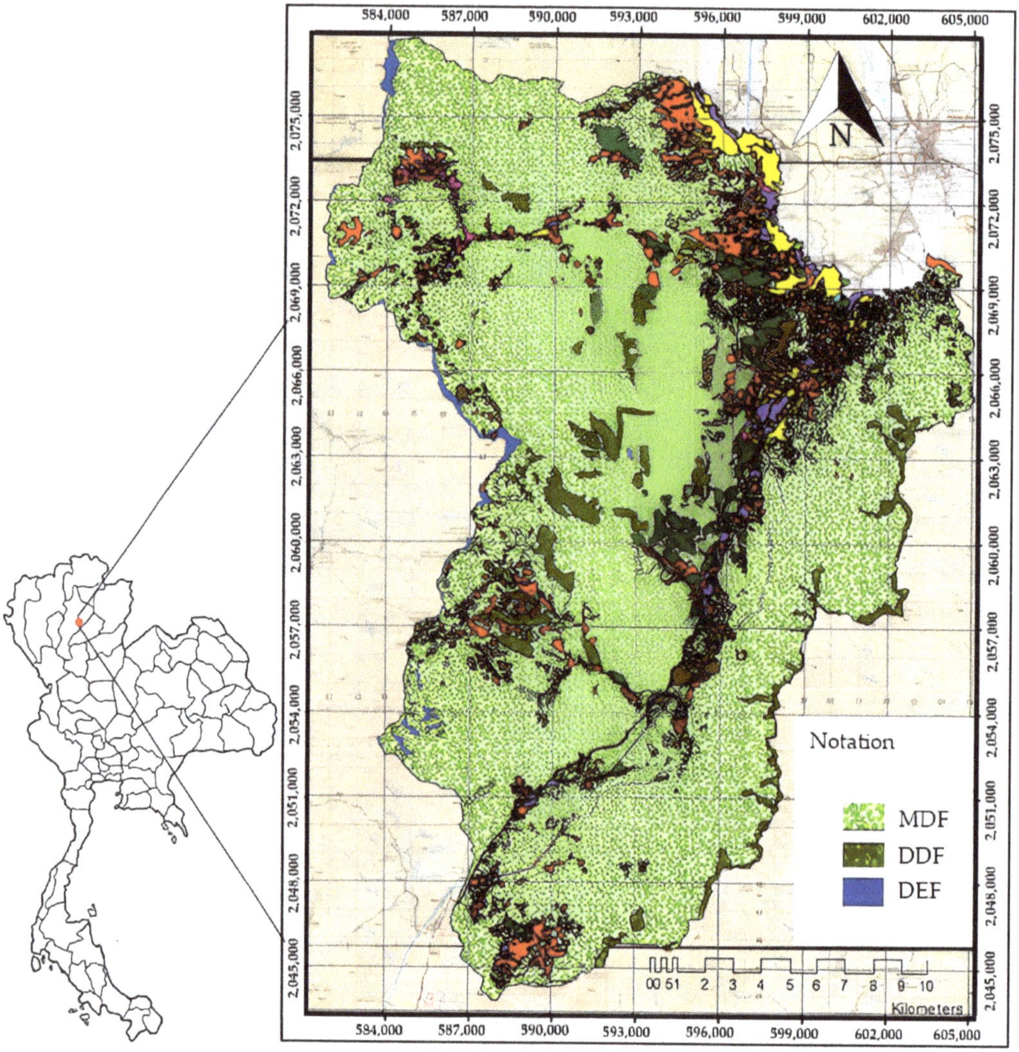

Figure 2. The study area of the Mae Huad sector, NDF, in northern Thailand.

2.2. Forest Inventory and Sample Collection

Trees from plotless inventory data are used for the collection of tree samples, wood samples, and calculated stand carbon stock. The distribution of trees in the Mae Huad sector NDF, Northern Thailand, was determined using stratified sampling [17,18] and a uniform fixed grid of 3 × 3 km systematic arrangement that covered the whole of the Mae Huad sector. The point sampling technique [19–21] was used to collect tree data which included diameter at breast height (DBH), total height (H), tree species, and forest type at each sample point. This grid and point sampling were part of the APFNET project [15]. The point sampling data were used to calculate the importance value index (IVI), which is the quantitative value for measured dominance of tree species [22] that was used to select the sample trees by diameter classes. The suitable sample size (i.e., the number of sampling points) was calculated using Equation (1) [23]

$$n = \frac{t^2(cv)^2}{AE^2} \tag{1}$$

where, n is the target number of sample points, t is the *t*-value at the 95% probability level, cv is the coefficient of variation in DBH, AE is the allowable sampling error in DBH at point sampling (this research used 10%).

In each forest type, all the selected tree species were grouped into 10 groups based on their wood density. The species with the highest IVI in each group was selected as a representative of the group for tree data and wood sample collection. Each selected species was further classified into one of three diameter classes (small, medium, and large) (15 tree samples in each species, 12 tree samples for establishing the equation process, and tree samples for the validation process. The total was 450 sample trees, 360 sample trees for establishing the equation process and 90 sample trees for the validation process).

The bole of each sample tree was measured for the stem diameter by 2 m sections from the base to the first major branch to calculate the tree bole volume. The wood samples of the selected species with the highest IVI, as described above, were collected in the sample tree bole in the north and east directions using an increment borer or a handsaw at 1.3 m height (2 wood samples in each tree for a total of 900 wood samples) to determine the carbon fraction. The wood samples were collected only at 1.3 m height as the literature indicated that the carbon fraction did not vary significantly along the stems [24].

2.3. Sample Preparation and Carbon Fraction Analysis

Wood sample preparation: This process was for estimating the wood carbon fraction in sample trees. The wood wet volume of the collected sample wood was calculated using Newton's formula Equation (2) [21,25]:

$$V_t = \sum_{i=1}^{n} \frac{L}{6}(Ab_i + 4Am_i + Au_i) \tag{2}$$

where, V_t is the tree wet volume, Ab_i is the cross-sectional area at the base of stem segment i, Am_i is the cross-sectional area at the middle of stem segment i, Au_i is the cross-sectional area at the upper of stem segment i, and L is the length of stem segment i (m).

The wet volumes of the wood samples were calculated. The wood samples were weighed and dried in an air-dry oven at 80 °C for 24–48 h until their weights became constant to determine the final dry weights. Two dry samples from the same tree were then pulverized together using a crushing machine to obtain a 100 g dry-weight sample.

Carbon fraction analysis: A 100 g pulverized sample was analyzed for carbon fraction using combustion methods via a carbon analyzer (e.g., PerkinElmer 2400 series II CHNS/O Elemental Analyzer), recommended by Kraenzel et al. and Wulzler et al. [26,27].

2.4. Data Analysis

(1) Carbon storage in the wood samples: This process was calculated using the relationships between carbon fraction and wood sample dry weight.

The carbon proportion (carbon fraction) was obtained as a percentage of dry weight using the method described by Duangsathaporn et al. [14] and Khantawan et al. [28] to convert the carbon fraction to carbon weight in a wood sample Equation (3):

$$C_c = C_w \times W_d \tag{3}$$

where, C_c is the weight of carbon in a wood sample core (kg), W_d is the dry weight of a wood sample core (kg), C_w is the carbon fraction in a sample core (%).

Furthermore, the carbon wood sample and carbon fraction in each species was used to estimate the carbon stored in the standing tree using Equation (4):

$$C_t = \frac{C_c}{V_w} \times V_t \tag{4}$$

where, C_t is the weight of carbon in a standing sample tree bole (kg), C_c is the weight of carbon in a wood sample core (kg), V_w is the wet volume of the wood sample core, and V_t is the wet volume of the standing tree bole.

(2) The calculation of standing tree carbon stock: This process calculated the standing tree carbon storage in tree samples to estimate the carbon equation. The aboveground standing tree carbon was determined through three steps.

In the first step, a piece of sample tree in tree bole was used to estimate the bole volume and carbon. The wet bole volume (V) of every sample from a total of 362 sample trees was calculated using Smalian's formula Equation (5) [21,25], and the carbon stock in each wood sample core was then estimated using the dry weight carbon in the wood sample core multiplied by the carbon fraction in each wood sample core [14]. The whole-bole carbon stock of each sample tree was then calculated using the proportion of dry weight carbon in a wood sample core and the wet volume of the wood sample core multiplied by the wet volume of the standing tree bole Equation (4).

$$V_t = \sum_{i=1}^{n} \frac{L}{2}(Ab_i + Au_i) \tag{5}$$

where, Ab_i is the cross-sectional area at the base of the stem segment i, Au_i is the cross-sectional area at the upper of the stem segment i, and L is the length of the stem segment I (m).

In the second step, the branch and leaf carbon stock were estimated using the leaf and branch biomass of the tree, estimated using the standard equation multiplied by the carbon fraction. The equation recommended by Tsutsumi et al. was used to estimate the branch and leaf biomass for trees from the DEF [29], and the equation recommended by Ogawa et al. was used to estimate the branch and leaf biomass for trees from the MDF and DDF [30]. These equations for estimating carbon stock in leaves and branches in each tree are shown in Table 1.

In the third step, the aboveground carbon stock in each sample tree was obtained by combining stem, branch, and leaf carbon stock. This was then used to develop the tree carbon storage equations.

(3) The construction of standing tree carbon equations: The equations to estimate the aboveground standing tree carbon were constructed using the model $C = aDBH^bH^c$, where C is the standing tree carbon stock, DBH is the diameter at breast height, H is the total height, and a, b and c are model parameters to be estimated using Minitab statistics program [31]. The model parameters were estimated using log transformation and linear multiple regression.

Table 1. The equation for estimating carbon storage in leaves and branches in individual trees.

Forest Type	Equation	Location	Source
Dry evergreen forest	$W_b = 0.00893(DBH^2H)^{0.977}$ $W_l = 0.0140(DBH^2H)^{0.669}$	Phitsanulok Thailand	Tsutsumi et al., 1983 [29]
Dry deciduous forest	$W_s = 0.0396(DBH^2H)^{0.9326}$ $W_b = 0.003487(DBH^2H)^{1.0270}$ $W_l = (28.0/W_{sb} + 0.025)^{-1}$	Nakhon Ratchasima Thailand	Ogawa et al., 1965 [30]
Mixed deciduous forest	$W_s = 0.0396(DBH^2H)^{0.9326}$ $W_b = 0.003487(DBH^2H)^{1.0270}$ $W_l = (28.0/W_{sb} + 0.025)^{-1}$	Nakhon Ratchasima Thailand	Ogawa et al., 1965 [30]

Remark: W_s is the biomass of the stem (kg/tree), W_b is the biomass of the branches (kg/tree), W_l biomass of leaves (kg/tree), W_{sb} is the biomass of the stem + biomass of branches (kg/tree), DBH is the diameter at breath height, and H is the height of the tree.

Standing trees data were divided into 2 groups, 80% for established standing trees equations and 20% for validation of the study equations using a *t*-test statistical analysis. The equations were fitted for each forest type. In order to select the optimal tree carbon equations, statistics which included the coefficient of determination (R^2), standard error of estimate (SE), F-value, and significance value (p value, $\alpha \leq 0.05$), were evaluated. The normality of the model residuals was also examined using a basic program of statistics. The validation technique [32] was used to verify the accuracy of the equation by calculating the carbon storage in 20% of the collected samples. The methodology used to calculate the carbon stock of standing trees was also applied as described in the subsection on the calculation of standing tree carbon stock within the data analysis section. The carbon storage in each method was compared with the carbon from the established equation using the *t*-test statistical analysis. The equations of the three forest types were compared with the general equation for all species/wood density groups. This was done by calculating the relative differences and statistics between the mean of the equations of the three forest types and the optimal forest type equations. Data from 30 randomly selected sample trees were used to test the differences between the optimal equation and forest-type equations and compared the previous equation and present equation using the *t*-test analysis.

(4) Estimated stand carbon stock: All trees in the point sampling inventory from Section 2.1 were used for calculating the stand carbon storage. The carbon stock per hectare (ha) at each sampling point was estimated by summing the estimated carbon content of the sample tree and expressing it on a per unit area basis for the major forest types in the study area, using the Equations (6)–(9) adapted from van Laar and Akça [20].

$$C_p = BAF \times \sum_{i=1}^{n} \frac{C_i}{\mathbf{BA}_i} \tag{6}$$

where, C_p is the carbon stock at the sampling point (kg/ha), BAF is the basal area factor, C_i is the carbon storage in tree i of point sampling, and $\mathbf{BA}_i$ is the basal area in tree i of point sampling.

$$C_a = A_t \times \bar{C} \tag{7}$$

where, C_a is the mean carbon stock in forest area, A_t is the forest area in the study, and $\bar{C}$ is the average carbon stock in all sampling points.

$$C_t = C_a \pm t \times SE_{C_a} \tag{8}$$

and

$$SE_{C_a} = A_t \times SE_{\bar{c}} \tag{9}$$

where, C_t is the carbon stock of the forest area, SE_{c_a} is the standard error in the stand carbon stock of the forest area, and $SE_{\bar{c}}$ is the standard error of the mean carbon stock in the forest area.

3. Results

3.1. Forest Inventory for Building a Species List, Sample Trees Selection, and Wood Sample Extraction

A 54-sample fixed grid of size 3 × 3 km was established in the Mae Huad sector. Forty-four sampling points fell in the forested area and were classified under either of the three forest types, while the remaining 10 sampling points were in the agriculture field. Seventy-six tree species were found in the Mae Huad sector, with 46 tree species in the MDF, 18 in the DDF, and 31 in the DEF. The IVI was calculated and used to classify and select the sample trees. The highest species IVI in the MDF were *Xylia xlocarpa, Tectona grandis,* and *Prerocapus macrocapus*. In the DDF, they were *Shorea siamensis, Shorea obtusa,* and *P. macrocarpus*, and in the DEF, they were *Mallorus macrostachyus, Hopea odorata,* and *Duabanga grandiflora*. The *X. xylocarpa, Dalbergia oliveri, P. macrocarpus, Terminalia corticosa, Terminalia. alata,* and *Quercus kerri* were found in all three forest types. Within the three forest types and 10 species groups for each forest type, the sample trees were grouped into wood density classes for a total of 30 groups. In each group, the selected species had the highest value of IVI for the sample tree species. The 10 sample tree species per forest type were classified into three DBH classes (small, medium, and large) from inventory data covering a DBH range from 4.50 to 147.00 cm. The wood density range and representative tree species are shown in Table 2.

Table 2. Number of sample trees, carbon content, and carbon stock in the sample trees.

Forest Type	Density Class	Wood Density Range * (kg/m^3)	Representative Species (Scientific Name)	DBH Range (cm)	No. Sample trees	%Carbon	Carbon Stock in Sample Trees (Stem + Branch + Leaf) (kg)		
							min	max	Average
Mixed deciduous forest	1	283–385	*Cananga latifolia.*	4.50–43.00	15	47.75	23.90	454.29	163.37
	2	386–488	*Litsea glutinosa*	4.50–62.40	15	46.86	38.65	1297.63	505.81
	3	489–591	*Lannea coromandelica*	4.50–58.00	16	45.75	11.19	1252.27	407.75
	4	592–694	*Tectona grandis*	4.50–71.00	16	49.66	8.18	1385.72	589.75
	5	695–797	*Albizia odoratissima*	4.50–42.50	15	46.84	12.17	502.36	186.04
	6	798–900	*Terminalia nigrovenulosa*	4.50–61.29	16	47.13	38.10	1161.93	402.95
	7	901–1003	*Pterocarpus macrocarpus*	4.50–61.50	15	48.41	20.22	1489.53	445.37
	8	1004–1106	*Xylia xylocarpa*	4.50–66.80	15	48.03	29.40	1340.78	489.37
	9	1107–1209	*Dalbergia oliveri*	4.50–42.80	17	47.13	14.89	724.67	264.32
	10	1210–1312	*Terminalia corticosa*	4.50–66.30	15	48.55	22.87	2006.99	590.11
Dry dipterocarp forest	1	401–485	*Mitragyna brunonis*	4.50–41.00	15	47.57	16.05	496.35	189.90
	2	486–570	*Bridelia pierrei*	4.50–25.80	12	47.16	6.12	186.67	70.35
	3	571–655	*Gardenia sootepensis*	4.50–32.40	15	46.06	23.53	680.13	175.37
	4	656–740	*Haldina cordifolia*	4.50–41.9	15	48.26	8.86	604.76	177.12
	5	741–825	*Dipterocarpus obtusifolius*	4.50–42.50	15	47.62	9.77	505.84	145.02
	6	826–910	NA (not applicable)						
	7	911–995	*Pterocarpus macrocarpus*	4.50–61.50	15	48.41	20.22	1489.53	445.37
	8	996–1080	*Shorea siamensis*	4.50–58.20	15	46.76	11.99	1148.05	438.29
	9	1081–1165	*Dalbergia oliveri*	4.50–42.80	17	47.13	14.89	724.67	264.33
	10	1166–1250	*Terminalia corticosa*	4.50–66.30	15	48.55	23.87	2006.99	590.11
Dry evergreen forest	1	388–474	*Duabanga grandiflora*	4.50–147.00	15	46.92	59.58	8673.15	2572.99
	2	475–561	*Croton roxburghii*	4.50–42.00	15	47.77	16.81	353.85	130.37
	3	562–648	*Careya sphaerica*	4.50–38.30	15	47.47	12.97	256.03	117.36
	4	649–735	*Artocarpus lakoocha*	4.50–47.30	15	48.31	13.12	915.60	269.66
	5	736–822	*Cratoxylum formosum*	4.50–22.60	15	46.83	8.45	119.54	42.31
	6	823–909	*Anogeissus acuminata*	4.50–71.70	15	46.81	56.61	2365.23	761.73
	7	910–996	*Pterocarpus macrocarpus*	4.50–61.50	15	48.41	20.22	1489.53	445.37
	8	997–1083	*Terminalia alata*	4.50–50.00	15	45.75	25.75	1271.14	410.04
	9	1084–1170	*Xylia xylocarpa*	4.50–66.80	15	48.03	29.40	1340.78	489.37
	10	1171–1257	*Quercus kerrii*	4.50–43.7	15	45.43	11.78	499.12	181.19

Source: * Forest Research and Development Bureau (2007; 2010) [33,34].

3.2. Wood Carbon Fraction Analysis

The carbon fraction of trees in the NDF analyzed using combustion techniques from the PerkinElmer 2400 series II CHNS/O Elemental Analyzer in the laboratory was between 45.75% and 49.66%, with an average of 47.43%. The carbon fraction of MDF for 10 species and 155 samples ranged from 45.75% to 49.66%, with an average of 47.61%. The third highest carbon fraction in each MDF sample species was *Tectona grandis*, 49.66%; *Terminalia Corticosa*, 48.55%; and (3) *Lannea coromandelica*, 45.75%, respectively. The carbon fraction of DDF for 9 species and 134 samples ranged from 46.06% to 48.55% with an average of 47.50%, and each third highest species carbon fraction was *T. corticosa*, 48.55%, *Pterocarpus macrocarpus*, 48.41%, and *Haldina cordifolia*, 48.26%, respectively. The carbon fraction of DEF for 10 species and 150 samples ranged from 45.43% to 48.41% with an average of 47.17%, and each third highest species carbon fraction was *P. macrocarpus*, 48.41%, *Artocarpus lakoocha*, 48.31%, and *Xylia xylocarpa*, 48.03% respectively. The carbon fraction of sample trees in the Mae Huad sector, NDF, are listed in Table 2.

3.3. Carbon Storage

The standing trees' carbon stock in each species was calculated using Equations (3)–(5), and the branch and leaf carbon was calculated using the equations in Table 1. Aboveground carbon stock in sample trees of NDF ranged between 6.12 and 8673.15 kg. In MDF, the aboveground carbon stock from 155 sample trees ranged from 8.18 to 2006.99 kg. The aboveground carbon stock in DDF from 134 sample trees ranged from 6.12 to 2006.99 kg, and the aboveground carbon stock in DEF from 150 sample trees ranged from 8.45 to 8673.15 kg. The carbon stock by tree component and the aboveground carbon stock per cubic meter are shown in Table 2. All aboveground carbon stock sample tree data were used to develop the standing tree carbon stock equations using regression analysis (Section 3.4).

3.4. Standing Tree Aboveground Carbon Equations

The aboveground carbon stock sample data were used to establish standing tree carbon equations for MDF, DDF, and DEF and a general equation for all the species/wood density groups. Eighty percent of sample standing trees data were used to estimate equations. Multiple regression analysis was used, where the dependent variable was carbon stock (C), and the independent variables included DBH and H. The two variables, DBH and H, both showed high relationships to C more than only DBH or only H (Table 3).

Table 3. The regression equations tested to estimate the standing tree carbon stock.

Forest Type	Variables	Statistic Criterion Value				Remark
		R^2(%)	SE	F-Value	*p*-Value	
MDF	DBH	0.9604	0.11	1708.54	<0.001	
	H	0.7361	0.29	426.8	<0.001	
	DBH, H	0.9699	0.10	1963.05	<0.001	* Best variables
DDF	DBH	0.9259	0.16	1649.54	<0.001	
	TH	0.7303	0.30	357.5	<0.001	
	DBH, H	0.9405	0.14	846.14	<0.001	* Best variables
DEF	DBH	0.9633	0.13	3888.38	<0.001	
	TH	0.7039	0.36	351.89	<0.001	
	DBH, H	0.9770	0.10	2482.67	<0.001	* Best variables
NDF	DBH	0.9526	0.13	4779.48	<0.001	
	TH	0.7171	0.32	1107.98	<0.001	
	DBH, H	0.9611	0.12	3544.38	<0.001	* Best variables

* Shown the best variable for constructed the equation.

The equations for the MDF, DDF, and DEF were estimated from 10, 9, and 10 species, respectively, and the general equation was estimated from 24 species. The DBH range of the trees used in the construction of equations for MDF, DDF, DEF, as well as the general equation, was between 8.70 and 71.00 cm, 10.00 and 66.80 cm, 9.70 and 147.00 cm, and 8.70 and 147.00 cm, respectively. The suitable equations are shown in Table 4.

Table 4. Carbon stock equations, DBH range, and statistical goodness of fit values of the constructed general equation.

Forest Type	Equation	DBH Range (cm)	R^2 (%)	SE	F-Value	*p*-Value
MDF	$C_{MDF} = 0.0194DBH^{2.2152}H^{0.5580}$	8.70–71.00	0.9699	0.10	1963.05	<0.01
DDF	$C_{DDF} = 0.0132DBH^{2.1570}H^{0.7630}$	10.00–66.80	0.9405	0.14	846.148	<0.01
DEF	$C_{DEF} = 0.0185DBH^{2.1371}H^{0.6804}$	9.70–147.00	0.9770	0.10	2482.67	<0.01
NDF	$C_{NDF} = 0.017754DBH^{2.1899}H^{0.6260}$	8.70–147.00	0.9611	0.12	3544.38	<0.01

Remark C_{NDF}, C_{MDF}, C_{DDF}, and C_{DEF} indicate the aboveground standing tree carbon stock in the general equation for all species/wood density groups in the NDF, MDF, DDF, and DEF, respectively (kg/tree), while DBH is the diameter at breast height of the tree (cm), H is the total height of the tree (m).

The coefficient of determination (R^2), standard error of estimate (SE), F-value, and significant value (*p*-value, $\alpha \leq 0.05$) to determine the best fit equations were determined for each forest type. The R^2 values for the equations constructed for MDF, DDF, DEF, and NDF were 0.9678, 0.9412, 0.9770, and 0.9642, while the SE was 0.101, 0.139, 0.100, and 0.114, respectively. The F-value was 2281.89, 1048.28, 2127.52, and 5870.00, respectively, while the *p*-value for all the equations was less than 0.01, which was highly significant. All the related statistical values for each forest type are shown in Table 4.

The residuals between the actual and estimated carbon stock for the various values of carbon stock are shown in Figure 3. Residuals for the overall model can be seen to be unbiased, as were for all species in the MDF, DDF, DEF, and all species in the NDF. In other words, the errors are distributed uniformly with no apparent dependence on any of the potential predictors.

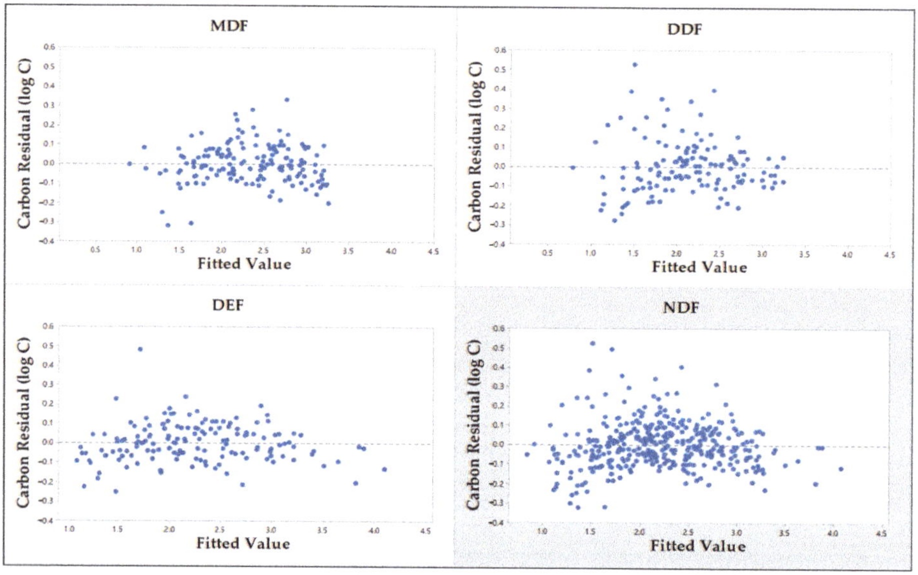

Figure 3. Residuals or the difference between observed and predicted aboveground carbon content of the selected trees: MDF, DDF, DEF, and Mae Huad sector NDF.

Sample trees were used to estimate the tree carbon stock for each forest type using tree DBH and H. The carbon storage of tree samples was estimated using the equations constructed for the MDF, DDF, DEF, and the optimal equation of this project. The equations to estimate the carbon content in the MDF, DDF, and DEF were similar to the optimal equation. The relative difference between the two carbon equations was between 0.088 and 2.416%, 0.050 and 2.545%, and 1.076 and 2.191%, respectively. The validity of the constructed equations was confirmed by employing a *t*-test statistical analysis to compare the carbon storage values of 30 trees, as estimated by the constructed equations and the carbon estimations explained in Section 3.3 (Figure 4). The results of the *t*-test revealed that there was no significant difference in carbon storage between these two groups (Table 5). The comparison of the mean between the equations of the three forest types and the optimal equation was not a significant difference.

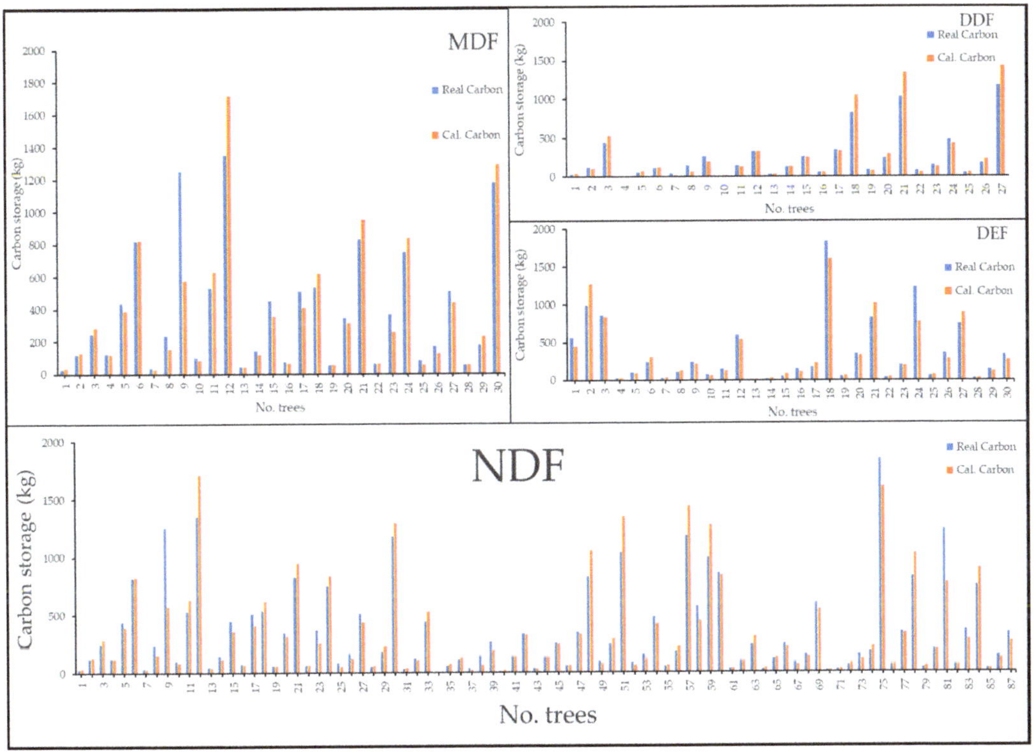

Figure 4. The comparison of the standing tree carbon storage. Real Carbon is actual carbon as estimated in Section 3.3, and Cal. Carbon is carbon storage estimated with the constructed equations.

3.5. Forest Stand Carbon Stock in the NDF

The standing tree carbon stock was used to calculate the carbon stock in the NDF forest stand using the equation from van Laar and Akça [20]. The carbon stock of the 44 sampling points ranged from 6.15 to 175.64 tons/ha, with an average per point of 61,837.96 kg/ha (Table 6). Carbon stock per hectare by forest type in the DDF, MDF, and DEF was 142 tons/ha, 53.02 tons/ha, and 12 tons/ha, respectively. The carbon stock in the MDF was approximately between 0.932 and 1.4 million tons (1.20 mean million tons), and that in the DDF was approximately between 0.289 and 0.454 million tons (0.371 mean million tons), and that in the DEF was approximately between 0.049 and 0.078 million tons (0.063 mean million tons). The carbon storage in the Mae Huad sector forest was approximately between 1.27 and 1.99 million tons (average of 1.632 million tons).

Table 5. Value of *t*-test between the verification and the validation value.

Forest Type	Statistic	Variable 1	Variable 2
MDF	Mean	388.49	376.33
	Observations	30.00	30.00
	$P(T \leq t)$ two-tail	0.67	
DDF	Mean	254.50	278.85
	Observations	27.00	27.00
	$P(T \leq t)$ two-tail	0.18	
DEF	Mean	464.87	529.91
	Observations	30.00	30.00
	$P(T \leq t)$ two-tail	0.43	
NDF	Mean	373.25	399.04
	Observations	87.00	87.00
	$P(T \leq t)$ two-tail	0.39	

Table 6. Carbon stock (CS) per sample point in the Mae Huad sector.

Point NO.	CS (kg/ha)	Forest Type	Point NO.	CS (kg/ha)	Forest Type	Point NO.	CS (kg/ha)	Forest Type
1	88,287.97	MDF	16	126,052.64	DDF	31	9129.03	DEF
2	17,097.92	DEF	17	20,736.35	MDF	32	23,084.19	MDF
3	69,643.47	MDF	18	42,646.39	MDF	33	64,055.07	MDF
4	7201.58	DEF	19	47,857.28	MDF	34	22,489.32	DEF
5	128,574.47	DDF	20	165,600.93	DDF	35	106,388.19	MDF
6	100,360.65	DDF	21	38,493.44	MDF	36	67,442.07	MDF
7	58,061.08	MDF	22	11,156.50	MDF	37	148,058.31	DDF
8	6152.98	DEF	23	59,036.21	MDF	38	43,768.32	MDF
9	27,286.41	MDF	24	162,671.46	DDF	39	79,015.26	MDF
10	63,391.82	MDF	25	38,514.85	MDF	40	70,904.44	MDF
11	59,217.74	MDF	26	42,606.07	MDF	41	133,507.34	DDF
12	46,099.49	MDF	27	63,438.04	MDF	42	57,309.07	MDF
13	28,610.93	MDF	28	63,581.88	MDF	43	46,216.42	MDF
14	8623.92	DEF	29	9828.38	DEF	44	11,595.44	DEF
15	61,435.68	MDF	30	175,641.25	DDF	Average	61,837.96 kg/ha	

4. Discussion

4.1. Carbon Fraction

Normally, the carbon fraction is assumed to be 50% of a tree's total biomass [6,35,36]. The carbon fraction in this study ranged from 45.75% to 49.66%, with an average of 47.43%. This is less than the normally assumed value but more than the Intergovernmental Panel on Climate Change (IPCC) carbon fraction value of 47% of tree biomass [5]. However, much research has explained that the variations in carbon fraction estimates might result from the methods used for different species, the components of a tree or a stand used (stem, roots, and leaves), and the age of the stand [6,37]. For example, the study by Thomas and Martin, which reports on the difference in carbon fraction in parts of trees, shows 37%, 76%, 48%, 81%, and 63%, respectively, of the variation in bark, branch, twig, coarse root, and fine root carbon fraction values [6]. IPCC reports confirmed the difference in carbon fractions. The amounts of components of wood tissues such as cellulose, hemicellulose, lignin, and a variety of nonstructural chemicals resulted in different amounts of carbon by mass [38]. The carbon fraction of trees growing in plantations in Thailand was reported by Diloksumpun and Staporn, who estimated the carbon stock through combustion techniques. They found that the carbon fraction for *eucalyptus* spp. was 48.36% [39], while Duangsathaporn et al., who estimated the sequestered carbon in standing teak trees in the Thong Phaphum teak plantation through combustion techniques, reported a carbon fraction of 46.58% [14].

We investigated the relationship between average carbon per cubic meter and wood density; higher-density wood had a higher carbon content per cubic meter (Table 7). The relationship between average carbon weight per wood volume (kg/m^3) and wood density class was analyzed using a linear relationship. This linear relationship was not significant (Figure 5), but there was a trend showing variation in the wood samples due to different wood elements (e.g., lignin, cellulose, and hemicellulose) in a unit of tree sample volume. Thus, the carbon stock per volume will be different, similar to the study of Campbell and Sederoff, who found differences in lignin in different tree species in sample trees [40]. A study by Navarro et al. also found that indirect indicators of wood density and carbon fraction affected carbon storage, as high wood density in some species of tropical forests was shown to have high carbon content [41]. Other studies have also not found such a relationship between carbon storage and wood density. For example, Weber et al. studied the variations between tree growth, density, and carbon concentration and did not find any significant relation between wood density and carbon concentration [42].

Table 7. The average carbon per cubic meter in sample trees and wood density.

Density Class	Carbon in a Cubic Meter (kg) in MDF				Carbon in a Cubic Meter (kg) in DDF				Carbon in a Cubic Meter (kg) in DEF			
	Stem	**Branch**	**Leaf**	**Total**	**Stem**	**Branch**	**Leaf**	**Total**	**Stem**	**Branch**	**Leaf**	**Total**
1	220.34	60.06	17.76	298.15	289.33	73.00	27.95	390.27	227.50	167.51	9.03	404.03
2	281.49	78.52	22.89	382.90	284.83	84.54	33.00	402.37	260.01	164.63	10.81	435.45
3	221.62	48.75	14.48	284.85	365.20	89.50	34.70	489.40	257.70	187.24	12.10	457.04
4	293.32	94.68	27.66	415.66	301.62	105.00	39.93	446.55	314.15	187.81	11.52	513.47
5	319.23	68.76	20.35	408.33	317.04	79.18	30.63	426.85	314.15	223.06	15.37	552.57
6	354.41	108.68	31.72	494.81	NA (not applicable)				307.47	195.46	10.48	513.40
7	385.07	98.06	28.83	511.96	385.07	98.06	28.83	511.96	385.07	98.06	28.83	511.96
8	345.14	84.59	24.77	454.51	350.46	79.55	29.77	459.77	348.71	162.78	9.69	521.17
9	386.94	68.10	20.10	475.13	386.94	68.10	20.10	475.13	345.14	84.59	24.77	454.51
10	314.15	84.83	24.92	423.91	314.15	84.83	24.92	423.91	342.86	128.51	9.03	480.40

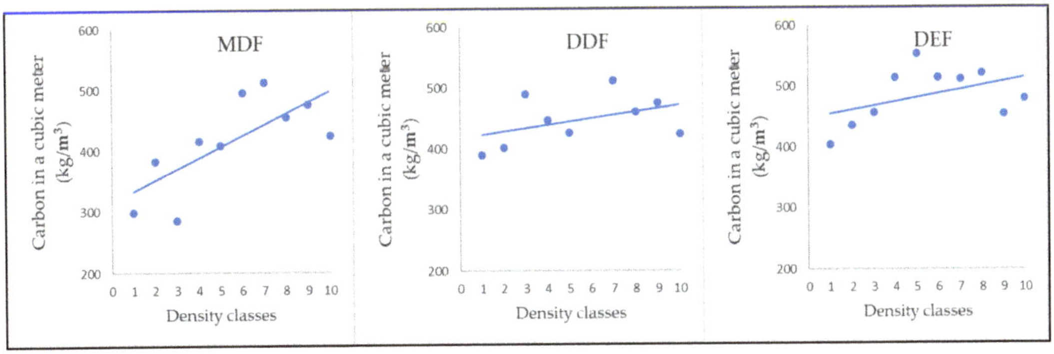

Figure 5. The relationships shown between stored carbon per cubic meter and wood density class.

4.2. *Aboveground Carbon Equation*

Generally, equations for estimating carbon storage use indirect methods, such as the product of tree biomass and carbon fraction, to evaluate the carbon stored in a standing tree. In Thailand, to estimate carbon storage, Viriyabuncha used an aggregate of six equations in a mixed-species forest [12], Yuan et al. used 11 equations in a mixed-species forest [43], and the Department of Environmental Quality Promotion used six equations from trees in a mixed deciduous, dry dipterocarp, dry evergreen, pine, and mangrove forest which included mixed species [44]. All of these studies conducted in Thailand used destructive sampling methods [43]. Destructive methods involve the cutting down of all the trees in the sampling area and measuring the weight of the different components, such as the tree trunk, leaves, and branches, and measuring the oven-dried weight of these components [45,46]. The carbon storage from the existing equation was similar to the new equations.

In this research, the equations for estimating carbon storage were constructed by combining the non-destructive method of Montès et al. [47] and the collection of the wood samples as proposed by Duongsathaporn et al. [14] and Khantawan et al. [28]. The regression technique was used to estimate the tree carbon storage in only the mixed deciduous, dry dipterocarp, and dry evergreen forest types. In addition, these equations can only be used for estimating the carbon stored in the standing trees with a DBH from 8.70 to 147.00 cm in the three tropical forest types. Thus, similar studies need to be done in other forest types in Thailand and with trees of a wider range of DBH. The advantage of the non-destructive sampling method is that, in Thailand, the destructive sampling method cannot be used as there has been an ongoing logging ban in natural forests since 1989 [48].

The most frequently used equations for estimating tree biomass in Thailand are those proposed by Ogawa et al. These equations were based on 90 standing sample trees in MDF and DDF (the coefficient of determination (R^2) = 0.9326) [30]. Another equation widely used is that of Tsutsumi et al., which used six standing sample trees in a DEF (R^2 = 0.97) [29]. All these equations are suitable for estimating tree biomass in the respective forest types, but the estimation of standing tree carbon is arduous as it still requires the estimation of the carbon fraction. Thus, the equations developed in this study are more suitable for directly estimating the carbon stored in standing trees in the MDF, DDF, and DEF forest types. The carbon equations were not developed by species as this would be too costly. There are many species in each forest type (46 tree species in the MDF, 18 in the DDF, and 31 in the DEF). Instead, the equations were developed using representative species in the various wood density classes.

5. Conclusions

The optimal aboveground carbon equations were formulated from a large sample of trees (155, 134, and 150 trees samples in MDF, DDF, and DEF, respectively) of various sizes and tree species (24 tree species in 3 forest types). We conclude that such equations can be used to estimate the carbon stocks in Thailand and in the assessment of carbon stock. However, the present carbon estimation did not cover other species in other forest types, such as mangrove forests. These are endeavors of future study.

6. Patents

This research was supported by the Asia-Pacific Network for Sustainable Forest Management (APFNet).

Author Contributions: Validation, Y.O. and P.P.; Data curation, K.P. and P.L.; Writing—original draft, N.S.; Writing—review & editing, K.D.; Supervision, K.D. All authors have read and agreed to the published version of the manuscript.

Funding: This research was funded by the Asia-Pacific Network for Sustainable Forest Management (APFNet) grant number [2015P6-THA-PD].

Data Availability Statement: Not applicable.

Conflicts of Interest: The authors declare no conflict of interest.

References

1. Lukac, M.; Calfapietra, C.; Lagomarsino, A.; Loreto, F. Global climate change and tree nutrition: Effects of elevated CO_2 and temperature. *Tree Physio.* **2010**, *30*, 1202–1220. [CrossRef]
2. Duca, M. *Plant Physiology*; Spriger: Berlin/Heidelberg, Germany; New York, NY, USA, 2015.
3. Gao, Y.; Cheng, J.; Ma, Z.; Zhao, Y.; Su, J. Carbon storage in biomass, litter, and soil of different plantations in a semiarid temperate region of northwest China. *Ann. For. Sci.* **2014**, *71*, 427–435. [CrossRef]
4. Griffiths, H.; Javis, G.P. *The Carbon Balance of Forest Biomes*; Taylor & Francis: Oxon, UK, 2005.
5. IPCC. Guidelines for National Greenhouse Gas Inventories—Volume 4: Agriculture, Land Use and Forestry (GL-AFOLU). Available online: http://www.ipcc-nggip.iges.or.jp/public/2006gl/vol4.htm (accessed on 15 December 2022).
6. Thomas, C.S.; Martin, R.A. Carbon Content of Tree Tissues: A Synthesis. *Forests* **2012**, *3*, 332–352. [CrossRef]
7. Mensah, S.; Veldtman, R.; du Toit, B.; Glèlè Kakaï, R.; Seifert, T. Aboveground Biomass and Carbon in a South African Mistbelt Forest and the Relationships with Tree Species Diversity and Forest Structures. *Forests* **2016**, *7*, 79. [CrossRef]
8. Bartholomée, O.; Grigulis, K.; Colace, M.P.; Arnoldi, C.; Lavorel, S. Methodological Uncertainties in Estimating Carbon Storage in Temperate Forests and Grasslands. *Ecol. Indic.* **2018**, *95*, 331–342. [CrossRef]
9. West, P.W. *Tree and Forest Measurement*; Springer International Publishing: Berlin/Heidelberg, Germany, 2015.
10. Njana, M.A. Indirect methods of tree biomass estimation and their uncertainties. *South For. A J. For. Sci.* **2017**, *79*, 41–49. [CrossRef]
11. Losi, J.C.; Siccama, G.T.; Condit, R.; Morales, E.J. Analysis of alternative methods for estimating carbon stock in young tropical plantations. *For. Ecol. Manag.* **2003**, *184*, 355–368. [CrossRef]
12. Viriyabuncha, C.; Chittachumnonk, P.; Sutthisrisinn, C.; Samran, S.; Peawsa-ad, K. Adjusting equation to estimate the above-ground biomass of teak plantation in Thailand. In Proceedings of the 7th Silvicultural Seminar, Bangkok, Thailand, 12–14 December 2002.
13. Wongsing, Y.; Poungparn, S.; Patanaponpaiboon, P. Allometric relationship for estimating above- and below-ground biomass of Dipterocarpaceous seedlings. *Thai J. Bot.* **2012**, *4*, 37–46.
14. Duangsathaporn, K.; Sagunthum, P.; Prasomsin, P. *Carbon Sequestration of Timber Product in Teak Plantation*; Kasetsart University: Bangkok, Thailand, 2011.
15. Kasetsart University. Asia-Pacific Network for Sustainable Forest Management and Rehabilitation. In *Technical Report NO.1: Development of Standing—Tree Carbon Equation in to Demonstrate the Development and Application of Standing—Tree Carbon Equations to Improve the Accuracy of Forest-Cover Carbon Stock Estimates in Thailand*; Kasetsart University: Bangkok, Thailand, 2018.
16. UNESCO. Biosphere Reserves in Asia and Pacific. Available online: http://en.unesco.org/biosphere/aspac (accessed on 3 May 2023).
17. Tongco, M.D.C. Purposive sampling as a tool for informant selection. *Ethnobot. Res. Appl.* **2007**, *5*, 147–158. [CrossRef]
18. Palinkas, L.A.; Horwitz, S.M.; Green, C.A.; Wisdom, J.P.; Duan, N.; Hoagwood, K. Purposeful Sampling for Qualitative Data Collection and Analysis in Mixed Method Implementation Research. *Adm. Policy Ment. Health Ment. Health Serv. Res.* **2015**, *42*, 533–544. [CrossRef] [PubMed]
19. Pieter, G.V. *Sampling Theory for Forest Inventory*, 1st ed.; Springer: Berlin/Heidelberg, Germany, 1986.
20. Van Laar, A.; Akça, A. *Forest Mensuration*; Springer: Dordrecht, The Netherlands, 2007.
21. Kershaw, J.A.; Ducey, M.J.; Beers, T.W.; Husch, B. *Forest Mensuration*, 5th ed.; John Wiley & Sons: Chichester, UK, 2017.
22. Ismail, M.H.; Zaki, P.H.; Fuad, M.F.A.; Jemali, N.J.N. Analysis of importance value index of unlogged and logged peat swamp forest in Nenasi Forest Reserve, Peninsular Malaysia. *Int. J. Bonorowo Wetl.* **2017**, *7*, 74–78. [CrossRef]
23. Shiver, B.D.; Borders, B.E. *Sampling Techniques for Forest Resource Inventory*, 1st ed.; Wiley: Hoboken, NJ, USA, 1996.
24. Castaño-Santamaría, J.; Bravo, F. Variation in carbon concentration and basic density along stems of sessile oak (Quercus petraea (Matt.) Liebl.) and Pyrenean oak (Quercus pyrenaica Willd.) in the Cantabrian Range (NW Spain). *Ann. For. Sci.* **2012**, *69*, 663–672. [CrossRef]
25. Prasomsin, p.; Duangsathaporn, K. *Handbook of Field Forest Mensuration I*; Kasetsart University, Forest Management Department, Faculty of Forestry: Bangkok, Thailand, 2005.
26. Kraenzel, M.; Castillo, A.; Moore, T.; Potvin, C. Carbon storage of harvest-age teak (*Tectona grandis*) plantations, Panama. *For. Ecol. Manag.* **2003**, *173*, 213–225. [CrossRef]
27. Wutzler, T.; Köstner, B.; Bernhofer, C. Spatially explicit assessment of carbon stocks of a managed forest area in eastern Germany. *Eur. J. For. Res.* **2007**, *126*, 371–383. [CrossRef]
28. Khantawan, C.; Duangsathaporn, K.; Prasomsin, P. Relationship between Carbon Content and Growth of Teak in Natural Forest and Plantation, Lampang Province, Thailand. *Agric. Nat. Resour.* **2019**, *53*, 267–273.
29. Tsutsumi, T.; Yoda, K.; Shahunalu, P.; Dhamamnoda, P.; Prachaiyo, B. Chapter 3: Forest: Felling, Burning and Regeneration. In *Shifting Cultivation: An Experiment at NamPhrom, Northeast ThailBnd, and its Implications for Upland Farming in the Monsoon Tropics*; Kyuma, K., Pairintra, C., Eds.; Kyoto University: Kyoto, Japan, 1983; pp. 13–62.
30. Ogawa, H.; Yoda, K.; Ogino, K.; Kira, T. Comparative ecological studies on three main types of forest vegetation in Thailand. II. Plant biomass. *Nat. Life South East Asia* **1965**, *4*, 49–80.
31. *Minitab version 19 Statistical Software*; Minitab: State College, PA, USA, 2020.
32. Suwanborirak, N. *Local Merchantable Volume Table of Teak (*Tectona grandis *Linn. f.) in Smallholder Farmer's Plantations at Chiang Klang District, Nan Province*; Kasetsart University: Bangkok, Thailand, 2020.

33. Forest_Research_and_Development_Bureau. *The Thai Hardwoods*; Royal Forest Department: Bangkok, Thailand, 2007.
34. Royal Forest Department. *General Characteristics of Thai Timbers*; Royal Forest Department: Bangkok, Thailand, 2010.
35. Martin, A.R.; Domke, G.M.; Doraisami, M.; Thomas, S.C. Carbon fractions in the world's dead wood. *Nat. Commun.* **2021** *12*, 889. [CrossRef]
36. Mbah, M.F.; Shingruf, A.; Molthan-Hill, P. Policies and practices of climate change education in South Asia: Towards a support framework for an impactful climate change adaptation. *Clim. Action* **2022**, *1*, 28. [CrossRef]
37. IPCC. *Good Practice Guidance for Land Use, Land-Use Change and Forestry*; Penman, J., Gytarsky, M., Hiraishi, T., Krug, T., Kruger, D., Pipatti, R., Buendia, L., Miwa, K., Ngara, T., Tanabe, K., et al., Eds.; IGES: Kanagawa, Japan, 2003.
38. Lamlom, S.H.; Savidge, R.A. Carbon content variation in boles of mature sugar maple and giant sequoia. *Tree Physiol.* **2006**, *26*, 459–468. [CrossRef]
39. Diloksumpun, S.; Staporn, D. Carbon Storage of Eucalypts Planted on Paddy Bunds in Chachoengsao Province. *Thai J. For.* **2009**, *28*, 72–84.
40. Campbell, M.M.; Sederoff, R.R. Variation in lignin content and composition (mechanisms of control and implications for the genetic improvement of plants). *Plant Physiol.* **1996**, *110*, 3. [CrossRef]
41. Navarro, M.; Moya, R.; Chazdon, R.; Ortiz, E.; Vilchez, B. Successional variation in carbon content and wood specific gravity of four tropical tree species. *Bosque* **2013**, *34*, 33–43. [CrossRef]
42. Weber, J.C.; Sotelo Montes, C.; Abasse, T.; Sanquetta, C.R.; Silva, D.A.; Mayer, S.; Muñiz, G.I.B.; Garcia, R.A. Variation in growth, wood density and carbon concentration in five tree and shrub species in Niger. *New For.* **2018**, *49*, 35–51. [CrossRef]
43. Yuen, J.Q.; Fung, T.; Ziegler, A.D. Review of allometric equations for major land covers in SE Asia: Uncertainty and implications for above- and below-ground carbon estimates. *For. Ecol. Manag.* **2016**, *360*, 323–340. [CrossRef]
44. Department of Environmental Quality Promotion. *The Developing Method for Assessing Carbon Sequestration and Carbon Exchange Processes of Trees and Forest under the Tool/Methods Development of Carbon Sequestration Assessments*; Environmental Research and Training Center, Department of Environmental Quality Promotion: Bangkok, Thailand, 2018.
45. Ravindranath, N.H.; Ostwald, M. Methods for Estimating Above-Ground Biomass. In *Carbon Inventory Methods Handbook for Greenhouse Gas Inventory, Carbon Mitigation and Roundwood Production Projects*; Ravindranath, N.H., Ostwald, M., Eds.; Springer: Dordrecht, The Netherlands, 2008.
46. Supriya Devi, L.; Yadava, P.S. Aboveground biomass and net primary production of semi-evergreen tropical forest of Manipur, north-eastern India. *J. For. Res.* **2009**, *20*, 151–155. [CrossRef]
47. Montès, N.; Gauquelin, T.; Badri, W.; Bertaudière, V.; Zaoui, E.H. A non-destructive method for estimating above-ground forest biomass in threatened woodlands. *For. Ecol. Manag.* **2000**, *130*, 37–46. [CrossRef]
48. Subcommittee for Drafting National Forest Policy and Draft National Forest Development Master Plan. *National Forest Policy. The National Forest Policy Committee*; Royal Forest Department: Bangkok, Thailand, 2019.

MDPI AG
Grosspeteranlage 5
4052 Basel
Switzerland
Tel.: +41 61 683 77 34

Forests Editorial Office
E-mail: forests@mdpi.com
www.mdpi.com/journal/forests

www.ingramcontent.com/pod-product-compliance
Lightning Source LLC
Chambersburg PA
CBHW061822210926
51850CB00006B/777
* 9 7 8 3 7 2 5 8 6 1 3 7 8 *